ADMINISTRATIVE JUSTICE
IN THE
UNITED STATES

ADMINISTRATIVE JUSTICE IN THE UNITED STATES

SECOND EDITION

Peter L. Strauss
BETTS PROFESSOR OF LAW
COLUMBIA UNIVERSITY, NEW YORK

CAROLINA ACADEMIC PRESS
Durham, North Carolina

ISBN 0-89089-042-0
LCCN 2002103137

CAROLINA ACADEMIC PRESS
700 Kent Street
Durham, NC 27701
Telephone (919) 489-7486
Fax (919) 493-5668
www.cap-press.com

Printed in the United States of America

CONTENTS

TABLE OF CASES	xi
TABLE OF STATUTES	xix
TABLE OF TEXT AND PERIODICAL CITATIONS	xxiii
REPORTS OF COMMISSIONS AND COMMITTEES	xxxvii
PREFACE	xxxix

I. INTRODUCTION	3
II. CONSTITUTIONAL BACKGROUND	9
A. General character of the Constitution	9
B. Stability and change	12
C. The separation of powers	17
1. The agencies Congress has created are not ones of separated powers	20
2. Although Congress is given "all legislative power," executive agencies (and the courts) are often authorized to adopt regulations that, if valid, have the force of statutes	26
D. Fundamental rights	36
1. Speech/consumer protection	41
2. Inspection/unreasonable search	42
3. Information/incrimination	46
4. "Due process of law" as procedure	48
a. Introductory	48
b. Goldberg v. Kelly	53
c. Threshold issues	56
d. The procedures due	59
5. "Due process of law" as substance: the expropriation problem	65
III. THE MACHINERY OF GOVERNMENT	69
A. The actors the Constitution names— Congress, President and Court	70
1. Congress	70
a. Legislation and appropriations	72

b. Committee oversight of agency functioning   82
c. Congressional agencies—Congressional Budget Office
    and the General Accounting Office   85
2. President   87
    a. Political and administrative authority   90
    b. Appointments and removals   94
    c. "Opinion, in writing"   101
    d. The White House staff   109
3. Federal Judiciary   112
    a. The Supreme Court   121
    b. The Circuit Courts of Appeal   123
    c. The District Courts   126
    d. Special courts   126

B. The political leadership of administration   127
1. Cabinet departments   128
    a. Departmental bureaus   130
2. Independent executive agencies   131
3. Independent regulatory commissions   133

C. The civil service and senior executive service   135
1. Administrative adjudicators and the corps controversy   137

D. State and local government   139

E. Enforcement officials   143

IV. THE SCOPE OF ADMINISTRATIVE LAW   147

A. Governmental powers generally   147

B. Contexts for regulation   152
1. Economic regulation   152
    a. Economic concentration   153
    b. Common carrier and public utility regulation   154
    c. Regulation of the professions   157
    d. Regulation of the economic conditions of labor   158
    e. Consumer protection   159
    f. Allocation of artificial or public goods   161
2. Health and safety regulation   162
3. Private land   168
4. Social security, health and welfare   169
5. Taxes and excises   172
6. Public services   173
7. Custodial institutions   176
8. Immigration, deportation   179
9. International commerce   180

10. Public land and other state goods   181
11. Government contracting   182
12. State employment   183
13. State enterprises   184
14. Other matters   185

V. THE PROCEDURAL FORMS OF ADMINISTRATIVE ACTION   187

A. The sources of structure for federal administrative procedure   188
   1. Constitution   188
   2. The Administrative Procedure Act   191
   3. Other statutes   194
   4. Presidential (and other political) controls   196
   5. The courts   197
   6. The agencies   199

B. Adjudication   199
   1. Formal agency adjudications   199
      a. Model on-the-record adjudication   201
      b. License applications   207
      c. License sanctions   210
   2. Informal agency adjudications   210
   3. Participation claims of the protected public   212
      a. Private actions requiring initiation of proceedings 213
      b. Compulsory private intervention in agency proceedings 215
   4. Alternative dispute resolution   218

C. Rulemaking   219
   1. The APA models   220
      a. Notice and comment rulemaking   220
      b. Publication rulemaking   222
      c. Formal rulemaking   225
   2. The transformation of rulemaking   226
      a. Bureaucratic structures of rulemaking, the rulemaking
         "record," and rulemaking decision   230
      b. The uncertainties of "legislative" judgment and
         disputes about general fact   232
      c. The impact of open government legislation   233
      d. The "paper hearing"   234
      e. The siren call of the model of judicial trial   238
      f. The impact of increasing political oversight   244
   3. Negotiated rulemaking   252
   4. Forcing the agency's hand in rulemaking   254

D. Choice between rulemaking and adjudication   258

E. Investigation   263
   1. Inspections   263
   2. Required forms and reports   265
   3. Compulsory process   266
F. State administrative law   268

VI. CONTROLS OF ADMINISTRATIVE ACTION OTHER THAN JUDICIAL   271

A. Political intervention or oversight   271
   1. In on-the-record proceedings   273
   2. Extraneous factors   275
B. "Open government" regulations   276
   1. Freedom of Information Act   276
   2. Electronic FOIA   282
   3. Government in the Sunshine Act   285
   4. Federal Privacy Act   287
   5. Federal Advisory Committee Act   289
C. Ombudsmen and watchdog agencies   290
D. Informal policy oversight: the general and trade press   292
E. "Public Interest" model, and actors   294

VII. OBTAINING JUDICIAL REVIEW   297

A. Jurisdictional bases for review   298
   1. Statutory and non-statutory review of administrative action   298
   2. The presumption of reviewability   303
   3. Statutory preclusion of review   305
      a. Explicit preclusion   305
      b. Implicit preclusion   308
   4. Matters committed to agency discretion by law 310
B. Preliminary issues on judicial review   312
   1. Standing   314
   2. Special rules of timing and place   322
      a. Finality   322
      b. Exhaustion   326
      c. Ripeness   328
      d. Primary jurisdiction   331
   3. Preliminary relief   332
C. Available judicial remedies   332

VIII. Scope of Judicial Review   335

A. In general   335
1. Constitutional issues   337
2. The APA framework   340

B. Questions of fact   341
1. Substantial evidence   343
2. "Arbitrary, capricious"   348

C. Questions of law   349
1. The American practice of statutory interpretation   349
2. Statutory interpretation at the agency level   360
3. Agency or court?   365

D. Judgment and the exercise of discretion   375
1. Citizens to Preserve Overton Park v. Volpe   376
a. The elements of review   376
b. The problems of record, findings, and reasons   378
c. Inquiry into mental processes   380
2. Consistency   381
3. Hard look review   384

IX. Liability of Public Authorities and Their Agents   387

A. Relief against the sovereign   388

B. Tort actions as a form of review   391
1. Against governmental units   391
2. Against government officials   394
a. Theories of liability   394
b. Defenses to liability   396
c. Integration with tort action against government   398
3. The implied cause of action   398

C. Liability in contract   400

Index   403

TABLE OF CASES

A.L.A. Schechter Poultry Corp. v. United States 31, 97

Abbott Laboratories v. Gardner, 227, 303, 304, 308, 324, 328, 329, 333

Abbs v. Sullivan, 330

Action for Children's Television v. FCC, 241

Adamo Wrecking Co. v. United States, 308

Adams v. Richardson, 311

Adamson v. California, 38, 39

Addison v. Holly Hill Fruit Products, Inc., 363

Alden v. Maine, 387

Alexander v. Sandoval, 117, 175, 373, 400

Allen v. Grand Central Aircraft Co., 327

Allen v. Wright, 320

Allentown Mack Sales & Service, Inc. v. NLRB, 261, 346-348, 357

Allison v. Block, 255, 261

Amalgamated Meatcutters & Butcher Workmen v. Connally, 186

American Ass'n of Councils of Medical Staffs of Private Hospitals, Inc. v. Califano, 307

American Automobile Mfrs. Assn v. Mass. Dept. Environmental Protection, 331

American Telephone and Telegraph Co., 210

Ameron, Inc. v. United States Army Corps of Engineers, 86

Anastasoff v. United States, 124, 223

Appalachian Power Co. v. EPA, 257, 258, 325

Arieff v. U.S. Department of the Navy, 279

Arizona v. Evans, 43

Arnette v. Kennedy 57, 136

Arthur Andersen & Co. v. Internal Revenue Service, 280

Associated Fisheries of Maine, Inc. v. Daley, 250

Associated Industries of New York State v. Ickes, 300

Association of Administrative Law Judges v. Heckler, 138

Association of American Physicians and Surgeons v. Clinton, 290

Association of Data Processing Service Organizations v. Camp, 318

Association of Data Processing Service Organizations, Inc. v. Board of Governors of the Federal Reserve System, 349

Atchison, Topeka & Santa Fe Ry. Co. v. Wichita Bd. of Trade, 382

Atlantic Richfield Co. v. U.S. Department of Energy, 266

Atlas Roofing Co. v. Occupational Safety and Health Review Comm'n, 119

Automotive Parts & Accessories v. Boyd, 235

Baltimore Dep't Social Services v. Bouknight, 48

Barlow v. Collins, 318

Bates v. State Bar of Arizona, 158

Bellis v. United States, 47

Bennett v. Spear, 318

Berkovitz v. United States, 393

Bi-Metallic Investment Co. v. State Bd. of Equalization of Colorado 50, 189, 190, 227

Bivens v. Six Unknown Named Agents of the Federal Bureau of Narcotics, 116, 396

Block v. Community Nutrition Institute 157, 217, 309

Board of Governors, Federal Reserve System v. Dimension Financial Corp., 370

Board of Regents of State Colleges v. Roth, 56

Boddie v. Connecticut, 55

Bolling v. Sharpe, 36

Booth v. Churner, 327

Bose Corp. v. Consumers Union of U.S., Inc., 339

Bowen v. Georgetown University Hospital, 259, 333

Bowen v. Massachusetts, 299, 390

Bowen v. Michigan Academy of Family Physicians, 307, 309

Bowers v. Hardwick, 16

Bowles v. Seminole Rock & Sand Co., 374

Bowles v. Willingham, 186

Bowsher v. Synar, 19, 24, 77, 90, 98

Boyd v. United States, 45

Bradley v. Fisher, 397

Branti v. Finkel, 136

Braswell v. United States, 47

Brock v. Roadway Express, 62

Brogan v. United States, 48

Brown v. Board of Education, 15

Buckley v. Valeo, 19, 81, 96, 99

Bureau of National Affairs v. United States Department of Justice, 278

Bush v. Lucas, 399

Bush-Quayle '92 Primary Committee v. Federal Election Commission, 382

Butz v. Economou, 397

Cafeteria Workers v. McElroy, 52

California ex rel Water Resources Board v. FERC, 83

Calvert Cliffs' Coordinating Comm. v. USAEC, 249

Camara v. Municipal Court, 43

Cammarano v. United States, 365

Camp v. Pitts, 348, 379

Carlson v. Green, 398

Carter v. Carter Coal Co., 31, 97

Central Bank of Denver v. First Interstate Bank of Denver, 358

Central Hudson Gas & Elec. Corp. v. Public Service Comm'n, 41

Cervase v. Office of the Federal Register, 302

Chamber of Commerce v. Reich, 108

Chamber of Commerce v. United States Dep't of Labor, 165, 183

Checkosky v. SEC, 334

Chemical Waste Management, Inc. v. EPA, 200

Chevron U.S.A., Inc., v. National Resources Defense Council, Inc., 32, 93, 164, 217, 218, 247, 272, 357, 368-374, 377, 384

Chisholm v. Georgia, 389

Chrysler Corp. v. Brown, 107, 183, 220, 281, 401

Citizens to Preserve Overton Park v. Volpe, 91, 130, 141, 151, 174, 235, 240, 243, 272, 341, 343, 354, 376-381

City of Monterey v. Del Monte Dunes at Monterey, Ltd., 66

Clark v. Securities Industry Association, 309

Clark-Cowlitz Joint Operating Agency v. Federal Energy Regulatory Comm'n, 261

Cleveland Board of Education v. Loudermill, 15, 57, 136

Clinton v. City of New York, 20, 77

CNI v. Young, 168

Coca-Cola Co. v. Federal Trade Commission, 323

Cohen v. Beneficial Loan Corp., 323

Commodity Futures Trading Commission v. Schor, 19, 24, 120

Common Cause v. Nuclear Regulatory Commission, 285

Compare Board of Curators of the University of Missouri v. Horowitz, 264

Consumer Energy Council of America v. FERC, 35

Cooley v. Board of Wardens, 116

Copper & Brass Fabricators Council, Inc. v. Department of the Treasury, 318

County of Sacramento v. Lewis, 40

Crawford-El v. Britton, 397

Critical Mass Energy Project v. Nuclear Regulatory Comm'n, 281

Crowell v. Benson, 19, 50, 118, 119, 339

Curry v. Block, 261

D.C. Federation of Civic Associations v. Volpe, 246, 275

Dalehite v. United States, 393

Dalton v. Specter, 77, 324

Darby v. Cisneros, 324, 328, 330

Davis v. Bandemer, 70

Davis v. Commissioner, 382

Department of Defense v. Federal Labor Relations Authority, 288

Department of Interior v. Klamath Water Users Protective Ass'n, 280

Department of the Air Force v. Rose, 279

Dickenson v. Zurko, 344, 355

Dickerson v. United States, 14, 47, 117

Director, Office of Workers' Compensation Programs v. Greenwich Collieries, 201, 202, 342, 355

Doe v. United States, 47

Dolan v. City of Tigard, 67

Donovan v. Dewey, 43

Duke Power Co. v. Carolina Environmental Study Group, 38

Duncan v. Louisiana, 38

Dunlop v. Bachowski, 159, 213

D'Oench, Duhme & Co v. FDIC, 117

Eastern Enterprises v. Apfel, 67, 259

Edelman v. Jordan, 395

Ellis v. Blum, 302

Elrod v. Burns, 136

Envirocare of Utah v. Nuclear Regulatory Commission 155, 218, 314

Environmental Defense Fund v. Hardin, 326

Environmental Defense Fund v. Ruckelshaus, 326

Environmental Defense Fund v. Thomas 105, 256

Erie R. R. Co. v. Tompkins 113, 116

Ethyl Corp. v. EPA, 242

Ex Parte McCardle, 306

Ex parte Young, 388

Fahey v. Mallonee, 51

Farmworker Justice Fund, Inc. v. Brock, 256

FCC v. ITT World Communications, 286

FCC v. WNCN Listener's Guild, 262

FDA v. Brown & Williamson Tobacco Corp., 357

FEC v. Akins, 319

Federal Crop Ins. Corp. v. Merrill, 383, 401

Federal Power Commission v. Texaco, Inc., 262

Federal Trade Commission v. Standard Oil Company of California, 325

Ferguson v. Skrupa, 38

Fiallo v. Bell, 179

First English Evangelical Lutheran Church of Glendale v. County of Los Angeles, California, 66

First Nat'l Bank of Boston v. Bellotti, 81

Ford Motor Co. v. FTC, 261

Forsham v. Harris, 278

Franklin v. Massachusetts, 70

Freytag v. Commissioner, 20, 24, 90, 95

Friedman v. Rogers, 158

Friends of the Earth v. Laidlaw, 213, 317, 321

FTC Line of Business Report Litigation, 265

FTC v. Ruberoid Co., 188

Gardner v. Broderick, 47

Gibson v. Berryhill, 158

Gideon v. Wainwright, 39

Gildea v. Ellershaw, 394

Glickman v. Wileman Brothers & Elliott, Inc., 42

Goldberg v. Kelly 14, 53-57, 59-61, 64, 119, 120, 211, 338

Golden State Transit Corp. v. Los Angeles, 395
Goldfarb v. Virginia State Bar, 158
Gomillon v. Lightfoot, 70
Gonzalez v. Freeman, 305, 402
Goss v. Lopez, 14, 58, 63
Gray Panthers v. Schweiker, 62, 63, 170
Greene v. McElroy, 52
Gregoire v. Biddle, 397
Grove City College v. Bell, 175
Gulf Oil Corp. v. United States Department of Energ,y, 323, 326
Hale v. Henkel, 47
Hannah v. Larche, 52
Hans v. Louisiana, 387
Harlow v. Fitzgerald, 397
Harmon v. Brucker, 305
Hart v. Massanari, 124
Hazardous Waste Treatment Council v. EPA, 83
Heckler v. Campbell, 64, 170, 262
Heckler v. Chaney, 214, 255, 257, 303, 310, 311, 385
Home Box Office, Inc. v. FCC, 239, 241, 243-245, 273, 285, 379
Hotel & Restaurant Employees Union v. Attorney General, 179
Hudson v. Palmer, 395
Humphrey's Executor v. United States, 19, 99
Hunt v. Cromartie, 70
ICC v. Louisville & Nashville R. Co., 225
Idaho v. Coeur d'Alene Tribe of Idaho, 388, 390
Immigration & Naturalization Service v. Chadha, 20, 35, 76
In the Matter of Edlow International Co., 180
Independent U.S. Tanker Owners Committee v. Lewis, 380
Indian Towing Co. v. United States, 393
Industrial Union Department, AFL-CIO v. American Petroleum Institute, 167

Industrial Union Department, AFL-CIO v. Hodgson, 347
Ingraham v. Wright, 58
INS v. Cardoza-Fonseca, 370
INS v. St. Cyr, 180, 301, 305
Jimenez Fuentes v. Gaztambide, 136
Johnson v. Robison, 119, 120, 305
Joint Anti-Fascist Refugee Committee v. McGrath, 53
Kalaris v. Donovan, 137, 204
Kendall v. United States, 91, 388
Kennecott Copper Corp. v. EPA, 237
Keystone Bituminous Coal Ass'n v. De Benedictis, 67
Kissinger v. Reporters Committee for Freedom of the Press, 278
Kyllo v. United States, 45
Lampf, Pleva, Lipkind, Prupis & Petigrow v. Gilbertson, 117
Langevin v. Chenango Court, Inc., 176
Leedom v. Kyne, 309, 327
Lichter v. United States, 186, 223, 224
Lincoln v. Vigil, 310
Lochner v. New York, 37, 38, 65, 66
Londoner v. Denver, 13, 50, 189, 190
Loving v. United States, 30
Lucas v. South Carolina Coastal Council, 66
Lujan v. Defenders of Wildlife, 213, 217, 315-317, 319-321
Lujan v. G & G Fire Sprinklers, Inc., 58, 402
Lujan v. National Wildlife Federation, 330
Mapother v. U.S. Dept. of Justice, 279
Marbury v. Madison, 10, 21, 91, 99, 302, 306, 366, 396
Marcello v. Bonds, 51, 137, 200
Marchetti v. United States, 265
Mariani v. United States, 81
Marquez v. Screen Actors Guild, 331
Marshall v. Barlow's Inc., 43
Mathews v. Diaz, 179
Mathews v. Eldridge, 59-64, 201
McCarthy v. Madigan, 327
McGee v. United States, 328

MCI Telecommunications Corp. v. American Tel. & Tel. Co., 357

McKart v. United States, 328

McNary v. Haitian Refugee Center, 305

Meachum v. Fano, 177

Metropolitan Washington Airports Authority v. Citizens for the Abatement of Airport Noise, 20, 96

Middlesex County Sewerage Authority v. National Sea Clammers Association, 399

Minnesota State Board for Community Colleges v. Knight, 189

Minnesota v. Carter, 42

Miranda v. Arizona, 47

Mistretta v. United States, 31

Mobil Oil Exploration & Producing Southeast Inc. v. United States, 402

Monroe v. Pape, 395

Morgan v. United States (Morgan I), 13

Morgan v. United States (Morgan II), 13

Morrison v. Olson, 90, 100

Morrissey v. Brauer, 177

Morton v. Ruiz, 261

Motor Vehicle Manufacturers Assn. v. State Farm Mutual Ins. Co., 244, 255, 377

Myers v. Bethlehem Shipbuilding Corp., 327

Myers v. United States, 98, 99

N.Y. Employees' Retirement System v. SEC, 215

NAACP v. Smith, 175

Nash v. Bowen, 138

National Ass'n of Mfrs. v. Department of the Interior, 328

National Automatic Laundry and Cleaning Council v. Shultz, 325

National Board of YMCA v. United States, 389

National Cable Television Ass'n, Inc. v. FCC, 34, 80

National Credit Union Administration v. First Nat'l Bank & Trust, 318, 319

National Federation of Federal Employees, Local 1309 v. Department of the Interior, 384

National Organization for Women, Washington D.C. Chapter v. Social Security Administration, 282

National Parks and Conservation Assn. v. Morton, 281

National Petroleum Refiners Assn. v. Federal Trade Comm., 221

National Welfare Rights Organization v. Finch, 141, 216, 295

Neal v. United States, 117, 358

Nebbia v. New York, 37

New York Times Co. v. Sullivan, 41

New York v. Burger, 43

New York v. United States, 11, 184

Ng Fung Ho v. White, 339

NLRB v. Bell Aerospace Co., 261

NLRB v. Hearst Publications, Inc., 366, 367, 369

NLRB v. International Medication Systems, Ltd., 266

NLRB v. Sears, Roebuck & Co., 233, 279

Nollan v. California Coastal Commission, 67

North American Cold Storage Co. v. Chicago, 51, 394

Northern Pipeline Construction Co. v. Marathon Pipe Line Co., 16, 20, 119, 120

Norwegian Nitrogen Prod. Co. v. United States, 363

O'Bannon v. Town Court Nursing Center, 57, 176

Office of Communication of the United Church of Christ v. FCC, 216

Office of Personnel Management v. Richmond, 383

Ohio Bell Telephone Co. v. Public Utilities Commission of Ohio, 13

Ohio Forestry Ass'n, Inc. v. Sierra Club, 330

Ohio Valley Water Company v. Ben Avon Borough, 339

Oklahoma Press Publishing Co. v. Walling, 267

Open America v. Watergate Special Prosecution Force, 277

Pacific Gas & Electric Co. v. Federal Power Comm., 223

Pacific States Box & Basket Co. v. White, 227, 376

Packard Motor Car Co. v. NLRB, 367

Palko v. Connecticut, 38

Panama Refining Co. v. Ryan, 31

Paralyzed Veterans of America v. D.C. Arena L.P., 375

Parham v. J.R., 176

Paul v. Davis, 58

Pembaur v. Cincinnati, 395

Penn. Central Transp. Co v. City of New York, 66

Pennhurst State School & Hospital v. Halderman, 178

Pension Benefit Guaranty Corp. v. LTV Corp., 198

People v. Keta, 43

People v. Porpora, 264

Pepsico, Inc. v. Federal Trade Commission, 323

Pergram v. Hedrich, 116

Perry v. Sindermann, 56

Phillips v. Commissioner, 51

Phillips v. Washington Legal Foundation, 67

Pickens v. United States Board of Parole, 177

Pillsbury Co. v. FTC, 274

Planned Parenthood of Southeastern Pennsylvania v. Casey, 15

Plaut v. Spendthrift Farm, 20

Portland Audubon Society v. The Endangered Species Committee, 93, 101, 205, 273, 276

Portland Cement Assn v. Ruckleshaus, 237

Portmann v. United States, 401

Printz v. United States, 11

Process Gas Consumers Group v. Consumer Energy Council of America, 35

Professional Air Traffic Controllers Organization v. Federal Labor Relations Authority 101, 205, 274

Public Citizen Health Research Group v. FDA, 281

Public Citizen v. Department of Justice, 17, 290, 319

Reeves, Inc. v. Stake, 184

Regents of University of Michigan v. Ewing, 264

Regions Hospital v. Shalala, 259

Reno v. Catholic Social Services, Inc., 330

Reno v. Condon, 11

Reynolds v. Martin, 359

Reynolds v. Sims, 70

Richardson v. Perales, 64

Robertson v. Methow Valley Citizens' Council, 249

Rochin v. California, 38

Roe v. Wade, 15, 16, 40

Rosebush v. United States, 393

Rosenthal & Co. v. Bagley, 327

Saco River Cellular v. FCC, 266

San Luis Obispo Mothers for Peace v. NRC, 285

Sandin v. Conner, 59, 178

Scenic Hudson Preservation Conference v. FPC, 296

Scheuer v. Rhodes, 397

Seacoast Anti-Pollution League v. Costle, 200, 203, 208, 210

SEC v. Chenery Corp (I), 260

SEC v. Chenery Corp. (II), 260, 381

SEC v. Collier, 364

See v. City of Seattle, 43, 46

Seminole Tribe of Florida v. Florida, 388

Seven-Up Co. v. Federal Trade Commission, 323

Shalala v. Illinois Council on Long Term Care, Inc., 308

Shaughnessy v. Pedreiro, 305

Shaw v. Hunt, 70
Shaw v. Reno, 70
Sierra Club v. Costle, 20, 83, 92, 94, 101, 132, 238, 244, 245, 247, 249, 273, 275, 385
Simon v. Eastern Kentucky Welfare Rights Organization, 320
Sims v. Apfel, 328
Skidmore v. Swift & Co., 223, 363, 367, 371-373, 375
Smiertka v. United States Dept. of Treasury, 288
Socop-Gonzales v. INS, 311
South Dakota v. U.S. Department of the Interior, 34
Southern Pacific Co. v. Jensen, 113
Spectrum Leasing Corp. v. United States, 390
St. Joseph Stock Yards Co. v. United States, 339
St. Louis Fuel and Supply v. FERC, 200
Steel Co. v. Citizens for a Better Environment, 213
Stinson v. United States, 374
Strycker's Bay Neighborhood Council v. Karlen, 174
Stump v. Sparkman, 397
Switchmen's Union v. National Mediation Board, 309
Telecommunications Research and Action Center v. FCC, 332
Tennessee Valley Authority v. Hill, 174, 369
Terry v. Ohio, 42
Texas & Pacific R. Co. v. Abilene Cotton Oil Co., 331
Thomas Jefferson University v. Shalala, 375
Thomas v. Union Carbide Agricultural Products Co., 119, 120, 338
Ticor Title Ins. Co. v. FTC, 322
Toilet Goods Association v. Gardner, 330
Touche Ross & Co. v. Securities and Exchange Commission, 327
Transco Security, Inc. v. Freeman, 402

Troxel v. Granville, 40
U.S. ex rel Parco v. Morris, 275
Udall v. Tallman, 374
United States Lines, Inc. v. Federal Maritime Commission, 273
United States v. Winstar Corp., 402
United States v. American Trucking Associations, 361, 362, 366, 370
United States v. Carolene Products Co., 40
United States v. Doe, 45, 47, 48
United States v. Florida East Coast Railway Co., 225
United States v. Gaubert, 393
United States v. Grimaud, 29
United States v. Haggar Apparel Corp., 180
United States v. Karo, 42
United States v. Lanier, 397
United States v. Lopez, 12, 38
United States v. Mead Corp., 118, 180, 223, 224, 258, 349, 357, 363, 371-373, 375
United States v. Mendoza, 383
United States v. Midwest Oil Co., 107
United States v. Morgan, 381
United States v. Morrison, 12, 38
United States v. Morton Salt Co., 45
United States v. Nova Scotia Food Products Corp., 238
United States v. Perkins, 95
United States v. Playboy Entertainment Group, Inc., 41
United States v. S.A. Empresa De Viacao Aerea Rio Grandense (Varig Airlines), 392
United States v. United Foods, 42
United States v. US Department of Labor, 44
United States v. Western Pacific Railroad Co., 331
United Steelworkers of America, AFL-CIO-CLC v. Marshall, 151
Universal Camera Corp. v. National Labor Relations Board, 272, 345, 347, 354

Valentine v. Christensen, 41

Van Harken v. City of Chicago, 62

Vaughn v. Rosen, 280

Vermont Yankee Nuclear Power Corp. v. Natural Resources Defense Council, Inc., 189, 192, 198, 229, 242-244, 262, 379, 386

Vernonia School District 47J v. Acton, 264

Virginia Petroleum Jobbers Ass'n v. FPC, 332

Walpole v. Hill, 177

Walters v. National Association of Radiation Survivors, 59, 63, 120, 305, 338

Warth v. Seldin, 315

Washington Research Project, Inc. v. Department of Health, Education and Welfare, 281

Washington v. Glucksberg, 40

Watkins v. United States, 52

Wayman v. Southard, 28

Webster v. Doe, 310

Weinberger v. Romero-Barcelo, 333

West Coast Hotel Co. v. Parrish, 37

West Virginia University Hospitals, Inc. v. Casey, 295, 359

Westfall v. Erwin, 395

Whitman v. American Trucking Assn, 29, 31, 248, 273, 306, 356, 357, 370

Wilderness Society v. Thomas, 330

Wirtz v. Baldor Electric Co., 203

Wisconsin v. Constantineau, 58

Withrow v. Larkin, 22, 26

Wong Yang Sung v. McGrath, 51, 192, 200, 229, 354

Work v. Rives, 302

Wright v. City of Roanoke Redevelopment and Housing Authority, 176, 395

Wyman v. James, 44, 264

Yakus v. United States 186, 306

Youngstown Sheet and Tube Co. v. Sawyer, 30, 108

Zurcher v. The Stanford Daily, 46

TABLE OF STATUTES

UNITED STATES CONSTITUTION

Article		Amendment	
I	11	1	41, 42, 81, 136
I, §8	11, 27	4	42-46, 188
I, §8, cl. 18	21, 88	5	13, 36, 45-47, 65, 188
I, §9, ¶3	301	6	39
I, §9, cl. 7	77	11	387, 389
II	11, 87, 118	13	9
II §3	255	14	9, 13, 36, 38, 39, 48, 50, 343
III	11, 25, 112, 118, 120, 121, 123, 269, 306, 312, 317	15	9
		17	9, 71
IV.	11, 269, 270	19	9
		22	9
		25	87

UNITED STATES CODE

2 U.S.C. - The Congress			
Sec.	Pg.		
431 et seq.	81		
1501 et seq.	11, 102, 251		
1601 et seq.	82		

5 U.S.C. - Government Organization and Employees

Administrative Procedure Act

Sec.	Pg.	Sec.	Pg.
551	192	552(a)(2)	220
551(1)	147, 277	553	192, 220, 240, 256
551(6)	199	553(b)	222, 229
551(7)	199	553(b)(A)	222
551(11)(c)	147	553(c)	221, 225
551(13)	147, 304, 326	553(e)	224
552	192, 193, 220, 277	554	192, 199
552(a)	186	554(d)	205
552(a)(1)	222	554(d)(A)	209
		555	192
		555(b)	202
		555(c)	263
		555(e)	210
		556	192, 199
		556(d)	208
		556(e)	203
		557	199
		557(b)(1)	209
		557(c)(A)	203

Sec.	Pg.
557(d)	205, 206
558	192
558(c)	210
559	192
701	192
701(a)	304
701(a)(2)	92
702	192, 194, 299, 318
703	192, 194, 298, 299, 303
704	192, 299, 302, 303, 322, 323
705	192, 217, 332
706	19, 50, 118, 119, 192, 339
706(1)	326
706(2)	56
706(2)(a)	92
706(2)(A)	311
706(2)(B)	397
706(2)(C)	136
706(2)(D)	47
706(2)(E)	339
706(2)(F)	62

Freedom of Information Act

552(a)(4)(A)	277
552(a)(4)(B)	277
552(a)(4)(C)	277
552(a)(4)(E)	277
552(a)(4)(F)	277
552(a)(6)	277
552(b)	234, 278
552(b)(7)(E)	263

Privacy Act

552a	194, 287

Government in the Sunshine Act

552b	194

Negotiated Rulemaking

561	194
570	253

Alternative Dispute Resolution

571.	194, 218
572	219

Sec.	Pg.
573	219
574	219

Regulatory Flexibility Act

601	250
601-612	102
801(b)	35
802(g)	35
1305	193
3105	193
3344	193
5372	193
7521.	193
App.	291
App. I.	289

18 U.S.C. - Crimes and Criminal Procedure

2386	82

21 U.S.C. - Food and Drugs

348(c)(3)(A)	166

28 U.S.C. - Judiciary and Judicial Procedure

1292(b)	323
1331	299, 300
1337	300
1339	300
1346	390
1346(b)	391
1361	301
1491	390
1651	332
2201	300
2202	300
2679(b)(1)	395
2680(a)	392
2764	391

29 U.S.C. - Labor

655(b)(5)	166

31 U.S.C. - Money and Finance

1400.	79

42 U.S.C. - The Public Health and Welfare

Sec.	Pg.
902	132
1983	58, 388, 395
1997e(a)	327
4331	101
4332	101

Sec.	Pg.
4333	101
4334	101, 174
4335	101

44 U.S.C. - Public Printing and Documents

Sec.	Pg.
3501-3520	265
3507(c)	102

EXECUTIVE ORDERS

Exec. Or.	Pg.	Exec. Or.	Pg.
12,600	282	12,875	11
12,778	219	12,988	219
12,866	102, 104, 105, 108, 110, 112, 248-250, 256, 273	13,132	11

REGULATIONS
CODE OF FEDERAL REGULATIONS

Title	Pg.	Title	Pg.
1, §305.77-3	241	48, Pts. 1-53	401

FEDERAL REGISTER

Vol.	Pg.	Vol.	Pg.
52 , p. 23,781	282	58, p. 51735	104

STATE STATUTES
Revised Model State Administrative Procedure Act

Sec.	Pg.	Sec.	Pg.
1-102(1)	147	3-201 to -204	269
1-102(2)	147	4-101(a)	270
1-102(2)(iii)	148	4-102(b)	270
3-102.	269	4-201 to -221	270
3-103(3)	269	4-301	270
3-104.	269	4-401 to -403	270
3-105	269	4-501	270
3-107	269	4-502 to -506	270
3-112	269		

TABLE OF TEXT AND PERIODICAL CITATIONS

Aberbach, J.
Keeping a Watchful Eye: The Politics of Congressional Oversight (Brookings 1990), 28
Ackerman, B.
Beyond Carolene Products, 98 Harv. L. Rev. 713 (1985), 40
Reconstructing American Law (Harvard University 1984), 8, 386
We The People (Belknap Press 1991), 16
Ackerman, B. and Hassler, W.
Clean Coal, Dirty Air (Yale 1981), 7, 92, 132, 244, 386
Beyond the New Deal: Coal and the Clean Air Act, 89 Yale L. J. 1466 (1980), 244
Ackerman, B. and Stewart, R.
Reforming Environmental Law, 37 Stan. L. Rev. 1333 (1985), 182
Alder, A. and Halperin, M.
Litigation Under the Federal FOIA and Privacy Act (9th ed. Center for National Security Studies 1984), 288
Aleinikoff, A. and Shaw, T.
The Costs of Incoherence: A Comment on Plain Meaning, *West Virginia Hospitals, Inc. v. Casey*, and Due Process of Statutory Interpretation, 45 Vand. L. Rev. 687 (1992), 359
Aman, A.
Administrative Law in a Global Era (Cornell Univ. Press 1992), 6
Aman, A. and Mayton, W.
Administrative Law (2d ed. West 2001), 6

Anthony, R.
"Interpretive" Rules, "Legislative" Rules and "Spurious" Rules: Lifting the Smog, 8 Admin. L. J. Am. U. 1 (1994), 371
Arnold, R.D.
Congress and the Bureaucracy: A Theory of Influence (1979), 28
Asimow, M.
Symposium: Speed Bumps on the Road to Administrative Law Reform in California and Pennsylvania, 8 Widener J. Pub. L. 9 (1999), 268
Asimow, M., Bonfield, A. and Levin, R.
State and Federal Administrative Law (2d ed. 1998), 7

Baker, L.
Conditional Federal Spending and States Rights, 574 Annals 104 (2001), 175
Baker, T. and McFarland, D.
The Need for a New National Court, 100 Harv. L. Rev. 1400, 1405-06 (1987), 122
Bardach, E. and Kagan, R.
Going by the Book: The Problem of Regulatory Unreasonableness (Temple University Press 1982), 44, 143
Berg, R. and Klitzman, S.
An Interpretive Guide to the Government in the Sunshine Act (G.P.O 1978), 285
Berman, L.
The Office of Management and Budget and the Presidency, 1921-1979 (Princeton University 1979), 112

Bermann, G.
La Responsabilité Civile des Function-
naires au Niveau Fédéral aux États-
Unis: Vers la Solution d'une Crise,
1983 Revue Internationale de Droit
Comparé No. 2, p. 319 (1983), 391
Federal Tort Claims at the Agency
Level: The FTCA Administrative
Process, 35 Case W. Res. L. Rev. 509
(1985), 391
Bhagwat, A.
Three-Branch Monte, 72 Notre Dame
L. Rev. 157 (1996), 215
Bickel, A.
The Least Dangerous Branch (Bobbs
Merrill 1962), 15, 312
Bittker, B. and Denning, B.
Bittker on the Regulation of Interstate
and Foreign Commerce (Aspen Law
& Business 1999), 180
Black, C.
The Working Balance of the American
Political Departments, 1 Hast. Con.
L. Q. 13 (1974), 89
The People and the Court (1960), 13
Blanch, J.
Citizen Suits and Qui Tam Actions: Pri-
vate Enforcement of Public Policy
(National Legal Center for the Pub-
lic Interest 1996), 213
Blasi, V.
The Checking Value in First Amend-
ment Theory, 1977 Am. B.F. Res. J.
521, 41
Bonfield, A.E.
State Law in Teaching of Administrative
Law: A Critical Analysis of the Sta-
tus Quo, 61 Tex. L. Rev. 95
(1982), 7
Brakel, S.
The Mentally Disabled and the Law
(Am. Bar. Found., 3d ed. 1985), 176
Breger, M.
Regulatory Flexibility and the Adminis-
trative State 32 Tulsa L. J. 325
(1996), 102

Brennan Jr., W.J.
Reason, Passion and "The Progress of
the Law," 10 Cardozo L. Rev. 3
(1988), 61
Brest, P.
The Misconceived Quest for the Origi-
nal Understanding, 60 B.U. L. Rev.
204 (1980), 15
Breyer, S.
Breaking the Vicious Circle: Toward Ef-
fective Risk Regulation (Harvard
University 1992), 8, 165
Regulation and its Reform (Harvard
University Press 1982), 8, 153
Breyer, S., Stewart, R., Sunstein, C.
and Spitzer, M.
Administrative Law and Regulatory
Policy (4th ed. Aspen Law & Busi-
ness 1999), 7
Brown R.
Separated Powers and Ordered Liberty,
139 U. Pa. L. Rev. 1513 (1991), 11,
18
Bruff, H.
Presidential Management of Agency
Rulemaking, 57 Geo. Wash. L. Rev.
533 (1989), 104
Presidential Power and Administrative
Rulemaking, 88 Yale L. J. 451 (1979),
100
Specialized Courts in Administrative
Law, 43 Admin. L. Rev. 329, 352-53
(1991), 120
Bruff, H. and Shane, P.
Separation of Powers Law: Cases and
Materials (Carolina Academic Press
1996), 17
Burke, J.
The Institutional Presidency (1992),
109
Burt, R.
Forcing Protection on Children and
Their Parents: The Impact of
Wyman v. James, 69 Mich. L. Rev.
1259 (1971), 264

Buzbee, W. and Schapiro, R.
Legislative Record Review, 54 Stan. L.
Rev. 87 (2001), 12, 38
Bybee, J.
Advising the President: Separation of
Powers and the Federal Advisory
Committee Act, 104 Yale L. J. 51
(1994), 290
Byse, C.
Vermont Yankee and the Evolution of
Administrative Procedure: A Some-
what Different View, 91 Harv. L.
Rev. 1823 (1978), 244
Byse, C. and Fiocca, J.
Section 1361 of the Mandamus and
Venue Act of 1962 and "Nonstatu-
tory" Judicial Review of Federal Ad-
ministrative Action, 81 Harv. L. Rev.
308 (1967), 302

Calabresi, G.
A Common Law for the Age of Statutes
(1982), 115
Calabresi, S. and Prakash, S.
The President's Power to Execute the
Laws, 104 Yale L. J. 541 (1994), 21,
90
Caminker, E.
State Sovereignty and Subordinacy:
May Congress Commandeer State
Officers to Implement Federal
Laws?, 95 Colum. L. Rev. 1001
(1995), 11
Cary, W.
Politics and the Regulatory Agencies
(McGraw-Hill1967), 101, 271
Cass, R.
Damage Suits Against Public Officers,
129 U. Pa. L. Rev. 1110 (1981),
391
Chayes, A.
The Role of the Judge in Public Law
Litigation, 89 Harv. L. Rev. 1281
(1976), 178
Chemerinsky, E.
Federal Jurisdiction (2d ed. 1994), 395

Choper, J.
Federalism and Judicial Review: An
Update, 21 Hastings Const. L. Q.
577 (1994), 12
Cibinic Jr., J. and Nash, R.
Administration of Government Con-
tracts (George Washington Univer-
sity 1995), 400
Retroactive Legislation and Regulations
and Federal Government Contracts,
in Symposium, 51 Ala. L. Rev. 963
(2000), 402
Cohen, M.
Regulatory Reform, Assessing the Cali-
fornia Plan, 1983 Duke L. J. 231, 270
Cole, D.
"Machiavelli's Rules of Civil Procedure,"
Legal Times, Nov. 3, 1997 p. 23, 396
Cooper, F.
State Administrative Law (1965), 7
Corr, C. and Zissis, K.
Convergence and Opportunity: The
WTO Government Procurement
Agreement and U.S. Procurement
Reform, 18 N.Y. L. Sch. J. Int'l &
Comp. L. 303 (1999), 400
Corwin, E.
The President: Office and Powers 80-81
(4th rev. ed. 1957), 90
Costle, D.
Brave New Chemical: The Future Regu-
latory History of Phlogiston, 33
Admin. L. Rev. 195 (1981), 238
Croley, S.
Theories of Regulation, Incorporating
the Administrative Process, 98
Colum. L. Rev. 1 (1998), 7
Croley, S. and Funk, W.
The Federal Advisory Committee Act
and Good Government, 14 Yale J.
Reg. 452 (1997), 289
Currie, D. and Goodman, F.
Judicial Review of Federal Administra-
tive Action: The Quest for the Opti-
mum Forum, 75 Colum. L. Rev. 1
(1975), 298

Dam, K.
The American Fiscal Constitution, 44
U. Chi. L. Rev. 271 (1977), 92
Davis, K.C. 1 Administrative Law Treatise 207-08 (2d ed. 1978), 186
5 Administrative Law Treatise 332
(2d ed. K.C. Davis Pub. Co. 1984),
336
Davis, K.C. and Gellhorn, W.
Present at the Creation: Regulatory Reform Before 1946, 38 Admin. L.
Rev. 507 (1986), 191, 220
Davis, K.C. and Pierce Jr., R.J.
Administrative Law Treatise (3d ed.
Aspen Law & Business 1994), 6
DeMuth, C. and Ginsburg, D.
White House Review Of Agency Rulemaking, 99 Harv. L. Review 1075
(1986), 109
Derthick, M. and Quirk, P.
Why the Regulators Chose to Deregulate, as in R. Noll, ed., Regulatory
Policy and the Social Sciences 215
(University of California 1986), 207
Duffy, J.
Administrative Common Law in Judicial Review, 77 Texas L. Rev. 113
(1998), 301, 330
Durant, R.
The Administrative Presidency Revisited: Public Lands, the BLM, and
the Reagan Revolution (State University of New York 1992), 182

Elliott, E.D. TQM-ing OMB: Or Why
Regulatory Review Under Executive
Order 12,291Works Poorly and
What President Clinton Should Do
About It, 57 L. & Contemp. Prob.
167 (1994), 104
Reinventing Rulemaking, 41 Duke L. J.
1480, 1492 (1993), 252
Ely, J.
Democracy and Distrust, A Theory of
Judicial Review (Harvard University
1980), 15, 40

The Wages of Crying Wolf: A Comment on Roe v. Wade, 82 Yale L. J.
920 (1973), 40
Emerson, T.
The System of Freedom of Expression
(1970), 41
Epstein, R.
Substantive Due Process by Any Other
Name: The Abortion Cases, 1973
Sup. Ct. Rev. 159, 40

Fallon, R.
As-Applied and Facial Challenges and
Third-Party Standing, 113 Harv. L.
Review 1321 (2000), 314
Claims Court at the Crossroads, 40
Cath. U. L. Rev. 517 (1991), 390
Fallon, R., Meltzer, D. and Shapiro, D.
Hart & Wechsler's The Federal Courts
and the Federal System (4th ed. Foundation Press 1996), 306, 312, 395
Farber, D. and Frickey, P.
Law and Public Choice: A Critical Introduction, p. 17 ff. (University of
Chicago Press 1991), 8, 28
Farina, C.
Conceiving Due Process, 3 Yale J.L. &
Feminism 189 (1991), 48, 175
Keeping Faith: Government ethics and
Government Ethics Regulation, 45
Admin. L. Rev. 287 (1993), 293
On Misusing "Revolution" and "Reform": Procedural Due Process and
the New Welfare Act, 50 Admin. L.
Rev. 591 (1998), 48, 57, 178
The Consent of the Governed: Against
Simple Rules for a Complex World,
72 Chi-Kent L. Rev. 987 (1997), 90
Fiss, O.
Reason in All Its Splendor, 56 Brooklyn
L. Rev. 789, 801 (1990), 61
Against Settlement, 93 Yale L. J. 1073
(1984), 219
Flaherty, M.
The Most Dangerous Branch, 105 Yale
L. J. 1725 (1996), 90

Fletcher, W.
The Structure of Standing, 98 Yale.L. J. 221 (1988), 314

Flynn, J.
The Costs and Benefits of "Hiding the Ball:" NLRB Policy-making and the Failure of Judicial Review, 75 B. U. L. Rev. 387 (1995), 346

Friendly, H.
Some Kind of Hearing, 123 U. Pa. L. Rev. 1267, 1279 et seq. (1975), 64, 109
Federal Jurisdiction: A General View (Columbia University1973), 298

Fuller, L.
The Forms and Limits of Adjudication, 92 Harv. L. Rev. 353, 394-405 (1978), 209

Funk, W.
When Smoke Gets in Your Eyes: Regulatory Negotiation and the Public Interest – EPA's Woodstove Standards, 18 Envtl. L. 55 (1987), 254

Funk W., Lubbers J. & Pou, C.
Federal Administrative Procedure Sourcebook (3d ed. ABA 2000), 7

Gellhorn, E. and Robinson, G.
Perspectives in Administrative Law, 75 Colum. L. Rev., 771, 780-781 (1975), 335
Rulemaking "Due Process": An Inconclusive Dialogue, 48 U. Chi. L. Rev. 201 (1981), 241

Gellhorn, W.
When Americans Complain (Harvard 1966), 290
Ombudsmen and Others: Citizens' Protectors in Nine Countries (Harvard 1966), 290
The Abuse of Occupational Licensing, 44 U. Chi. L. Rev. 6 (1976), 157, 158

Gifford, D.
The Morgan Cases: A Retrospective View, 30 Admin. L. Rev. 237 (1978), 381

Gordon, C. and Mailman, S.
Immigration Law and Procedure (M. Bender & Co. 1988), 179

Greenawalt, K.
Reflections on Holding and Dictum, 39 J.Leg.Ed. 431 (1989), 115

Gunther, G.
Congressional Power to Curtail Federal Court Jurisdiction: An Opinionated Guide to the Ongoing Debate, 36 Stan. L. Rev. 895 (1984), 120, 306
Foreword: In Search of an Evolving Doctrine on a Changing Court: A Model for a Newer Equal Protection, 86 Harv. L. Rev. 1 (1972), 38

Hage, W.
Storm over Rangelands: Private Rights in Federal Lands (Free Enterprise Press 1989), 182

Hahn, R.
Assessing Regulatory Impact Analyses: The Failure of Agencies to Comply with Executive Order 12,866, 23 Harv.J.L. & Pub. Pol. 859, 878-79 and n. 51 (2000), 106
Empirical Analysis: Assessing Regulatory Impact Analyses: The Failure of Agencies to Comply with Executive Order 12,866, 23 Harv. J. L. & Pub. Pol'y 859 (2000), 249
Reviving Regulatory Reform: A Global Perspective (2000), 249

Hamilton, R.
Procedures for the Adoption of Rules of General Applicability: The Need for Procedural Innovation in Administrative Rulemaking, 60 Calif. L. Rev. 1276 (1972), 225

Hanus, J. and Relyea, H.
A Policy Assessment of the Privacy Act of 1974, 25 Amer. U. L. Rev. 555 (1976), 288

Hart, H.
The Power of Congress to Limit the Jurisdiction of Federal Courts: An Exercise in Dialectic, 66 Harv. L. Rev. 1362 (1953), 120

Hart, H. and Sacks, A.
The Legal Process 1124 (W. Eskridge & P. Frickey eds. Foundation Press1994), 352

Hartnett, E.
Questioning Certiorari: Some Reflections Seventy-five Years after the Judges' Bill,100 Colum. L. Rev. 1643 (2000) 60-64, 115, 313

Heclo, H.
A Government of Strangers, Executive Politics in Washington (Brookings Institute 1977), 95, 112, 136

Hodges, A.
Dispute Resolution Under the Americans with Disabilities Act: A Report to the Administrative Conference of the United States, 9 Admin. L. J. Am. U. 1007 (1996), 219

Jaffe, L.
Judicial Control of Administrative Action, Chapter 4 (Little Brown 1965), 7, 119, 310, 331, 335, 386
The Illusion of the Ideal Administration, 86 Harv. L. Rev. 1183 (1973), 293

Jones, H.
The Rule of Law and the Welfare State, 58 Colum. L. Rev. 143 (1958), 54

Kaden, L.
Politics, Money, and State Sovereignty: The Judicial Role, 79 Colum. L. Rev. 847 (1979), 71

Kagan, E.
Presidential Administration, 114 Harv. L. Rev. 2245 (2001), 17, 90, 249

Kagan, R.
Regulatory Justice: Implementing a Wage-Price Freeze (Russell Sage 1978), 186

Katzmann, R.
Institutional Disability: The Saga of Transportation Policy for the Disabled (Brookings Institute 1986), 175

Kaufman, H.
The Administrative Behavior of Federal Bureau Chiefs (Brookings 1981), 8, 130
The Forest Ranger (Resources for the Future 1960), 181

Kelman, S.
Regulating America, Regulating Sweden: A Comparative Study of Occupational Safety and Health Regulations (MIT Press 1981), 44, 143

Kessler, D.
A Question of Intent : A Great American Battle with a Deadly Industry (Public Affairs 2001), 7, 94

Keyes, W.
Government Contracts Under the Federal Acquisition Regulation (2d ed., West 1996), 400

Koch, C.
Administrative Law and Practice (2d ed. West 1997), 6
Administrative Presiding Officials Today, 46 Admin. L. Rev. 271 (1994), 137
Judicial Review of Administrative Discretion, 54 Geo. Wash. L. Rev. 469 (1986), 385

Kramer, L.
Foreword: We the Court, 115 Harv. L. Rev. 4 (2001), 38

Krent, H. Preserving Discretion without Sacrificing Deterrence: Federal Governmental Liability in Tort, 38 U.C.L.A. L. Rev. 871 (1991), 391, 393
Reviewing Agency Actions for Inconsistency with Prior Rules & Regulations, 72 Chi-Kent L. Rev. 1187 (1987), 382

Kuran, T. and Sunstein, C.
Availability Cascades and Risk Regulation, 51 Stan. L. Rev. 683 (1999), 165

Laitala, L.
BLM Advisory Boards Past, Present, and Future (BLM 1975), 182
Landis, J.
The Administrative Process (Yale University 1938), 7
Lash, W.
U.S. International Trade Regulation: a Primer (A.E.I. Press 1998), 180
Lawson, G.
The Rise and Rise of the Administrative State, 107 Harv. L. Rev. 1231 (1994), 17, 69
Lessig, L.
Fidelity and Constraint, 65 Fordham L. Rev.1365 (1997), 13
Lessig, L. and Sunstein, C.
The Presidency and the Administration, 94 Colum. L. Rev. 1 (1994), 17, 21, 90, 129
Levi, E.
An Introduction to Legal Reasoning (194), 115
Levin, R.
The Anatomy of Chevron: Step Two Reconsidered, 72 Chi-Kent L. Rev. 1253 (1997), 374
Scope of Review Doctrine Restated: An Administrative Law Section Report, 38 Admin. L. Rev. 239 (1986), 335
Understanding Unreviewability in Administrative Law, 74 Minn. L. Rev. 689 (1990), 306, 310, 358
Libecap, G.
Locking up the Range 81 (Ballinger 1981), 182
Liebman, G.
Delegation to Private Parties in American Constitutional Law, 50 Ind. L. J. 650 (1975), 158

Linde, H.
Due Process of Lawmaking, 55 Neb. L. Rev. 197 (1976), 189
Linzer, P.
The Carolene Products Footnote and The Preferred Position of Individual Rights: Louis Lusky and John Hart Ely vs. Harlan Fiske Stone, 12 Const. Comm. 277 (1995), 40
Low, P. and Jeffries, J.
Federal Courts and the Law of Federal-State Relations (3d ed. 1994), 395
Lowi, T.
The Personal Presidency (1985), 89
Lubbers, J.
A Guide to Federal Agency Rulemaking (3d ed., American Bar Association 1998), 7
Developments in Administrative Law and Regulatory Practice 1999-2000 (ABA 2000), 6
Developments in Administrative Law and Regulatory Practice 1999-2000 105 (ABA 2001), 308
Luneberg, W.
Retroactivity and Administrative Rulemaking, 1991 Duke L. J. 106, 109-110, 159
The Lobbying Manual: A Compliance Guide for Lawyers and Lobbyists (2d ed. 1998), 82
Lusky, L. Footnote Redux, A Carolene Products Reminiscence, 82 Colum. L. Rev. 1093 (1982), 40

Magill, E.
The Real Separation in Separation of Powers Law, 86 Va. L. Rev. 1127 (2000), 17, 26, 90
Manning, J.
Constitutional Structure and Judicial Deference to Agency Interpretation of Agency Rules, 96 Colum. L. Rev. 612 (1996), 375

Mashaw, J.
Bureaucratic Justice: Managing Social
    Security Disability Claims (Yale Uni-
    versity 1983), 7, 131
Due Process in the Administrative State
    (Yale University 1985), 7, 48, 50
Greed, Chaos & Governance: Using
    Public Choice to Improve Public
    Law (Yale 1997), 8, 28
Prodelegation: Why Administrators
    Should Make Political Decisions, 5 J.
    L. Econ. & Org. 81 (1985), 93
Social Security Hearings and Appeals
    (1978), 84
Mashaw, J. and Harfst, D.
Regulation and Legal Culture: The Case
    of Motor Vehicle Safety, 4 Yale J.
    Reg. 257 (1987), 235, 238
The Struggle for Auto Safety (Harvard
    1990), 7, 166, 235, 304
Mason, A.
Implied-in-Fact Contracts under the
    Federal Acquisitions Regulation, 41
    Wm & Mary L. Rev. 709 (2000), 31
Massengale, E.
Fundamentals of Federal Contract Law
    (Quorum Books1991), 375
McGarity, T.
Some Thoughts on "Deossifying" the
    Rulemaking Process, 41 Duke L. J.
    1385 (1992), 304
The Courts and the Ossification of
    Rulemaking: A Response to Profes-
    sor Seidenfeld, 75 Tex. L. Rev. 525
    (1997), 252
McGarity, T. and Shapiro, S. Workers
    at Risk: The Failed Promise of the
    Occupational Safety and Health Ad-
    ministration (Praeger 1993), 164,
    242
McGraw, T.
Prophets of Regulation (Belknap Press
    1984), 7
McKennan, J.
The Constitutional Protection of Pri-
    vate Papers: The Role of a Hierar-

chical Fourth Amendment, 53 Ind.
    L. J. 55 (1977), 45
Melnick, R.S.
Between the Lines (Brookings 1994), 7
Regulation and the Courts: The Case of
    the Clean Air Act (Brookings Insti-
    tute 1983), 308, 335, 384
Mendeloff, J.
The Dilemma of Toxic Substances Reg-
    ulation: How Overregulation Causes
    Underregulation at OSHA (MIT
    Press 1988), 164
Merrill, T.
High Level, "Tenured" Lawyers, 61 Law
    & Contemp. Prob. 83 (1998), 136
Textualism and the Future of the
    Chevron Doctrine, 72 Wash. U. L. Q.
    351, 354, 372-73 (1994), 357, 359
Merrill, T. and Hickman, K.
Chevron's Domain, 89 Georgetown L.
    J. 833 (2001), 368
Merry, H.
Five Branch Government: The Full
    Measure of Constitutional Checks
    and Balances (University of Illinois
    Press 1980), 136
Miller, G.
Independent Agencies, 1986 Sup. Ct.
    Rev. 41 (1987), 100, 105
Miller, J.
Environmental Law Institute: Private
    Enforcement of Federal Pollution
    Control Laws (Wiley 1987), 213
Moghen, F.
The GAO: The Quest for Accountabil-
    ity in American Government
    (1979), 86
Monaghan, H.
Constitutional Fact Review, 85 Colum.
    L. Rev. 229 (1985), 340
Federal Statutory Review Under Section
    1983 and the APA, 91 Colum. L.
    Rev. 233 (1991), 395
Marbury v. Madison and the Adminis-
    trative State, 83 Colum. L. Rev. 1
    (1983), 21, 50, 91, 302

State Law Wrongs, State Law Remedies, and the Fourteenth Amendment, 86 Colum. L. Rev. 979 (1986), 177
The Protective Power of the Presidency, 93 Colum. L. Rev. 1 (1993), 108, 307

Morrison, A.
OMB Interference With Agency Rulemaking: The Wrong Way To Write A Regulation, 99 Harv. L. Rev. 1059 (1986), 109

Mosher, F.
A Tale of Two Agencies : A Comparative Analysis of the General Accounting Office and the Office of Management and Budget (1984), 86, 112

Moss, R.
Executive Branch Legal Interpretation: A Perspective from the Office of Legal Counsel 52 Admin. L. Rev. 303 (2000), 144

Neuman, G.
Federal Courts Issues in Immigration Law, 78 Texas L. Rev. 1661 (2000), 180
Habeas Corpus, Executive Detention, and the Removal of Aliens, 98 Colum. L. Rev. 961 (1998), 301
Strangers to the Constitution: Immigrants, Borders, and Fundamental Law (Princeton University 1996), 179

Nichol, G., Jr.
Rethinking Standing, 72 Calif. L. Rev. 68 (1984), 314

Noah, L.
Sham Petitioning as a Threat to the Integrity of the Regulatory Process, 74 N.C. L. Rev. 1 (1995), 213

Note
Government Tort Liability, 111 Calif. L. Rev. 2009 (1998), 391
Looking It Up: Dictionaries and Statutory Interpretation, 107 Harv. L. Rev. 1437, 1454 (1994), 354

The Argument for Agency Self-Enforcement of Discovery Orders, 83 Colum. L. Rev. 215 (1983), 46
The Federal Tort Claims Act: A Proposal for Institutional Reform, 100 Colum. L. Rev. 1538 (2000), 393

O'Reilly, J.
Federal Information Disclosure (3d ed., West 2000), 7

Pedersen, W.
Formal Records and Informal Rulemaking, 85 Yale L. J. 38 (1975), 231, 238

Perry, M.
Abortion, the Public Morals, and the Police Power: The Ethical Function of Substantive Due Process, 23 U.C.L.A. L. Rev. 689 (1976), 40

Pierce, R. Jr.
Is Standing Law or Politics? 77 N.C. L. Rev. 1741 (1999), 314
Seven Ways to Deossify Agency Rulemaking, 47 Admin. L. Rev. 59 (1995), 252, 304
The Due Process Counter-revolution of the 1990s?, 96 Colum. L. Rev. 1973 (1996), 48, 178
Two Problems in Administrative Law: Political Polarity on the District of Columbia Circuit and Judicial Deterrence of Agency Rulemaking, 1988 Duke L. J. 300, 308-09, 259

Pierce, R., Shapiro, S. and Verkuil, P.
Administrative Law and Process (2d ed. Foundation Press 1992), 397

Pildes, R. and Sunstein, C.
Reinventing the Regulatory State, 62 U. Chi. L. Rev. 1 (1995), 381

Plater, Z.
Statutory Violations and Equitable Discretion, 70 Calif. L. Rev. 524 (1982), 333

Posner, R.
The Federal Courts: Crisis and Reform 69 (1985), 123

Post, R.
The Constitutional Status of Commercial Speech, 48 U.C.L.A. L. Rev. 1 (2000), 42
Pound, R.
Common Law and Legislation, 21 Harv. L. Rev. 383 (1908), 116
Project
Government Information and the Rights of Citizens, 73 Mich. L. Rev. 1323 (1975), 288
Prosser, W. and Keeton, P.
Prosser and Keeton on the Law of Torts 1044-45 (West 1984), 389
Purcell, E.
Brandeis and the Progressive Constitution: Erie, the Judicial Power, and the Politics of the Federal Courts in Twentieth-Century America (2000), 115, 116

Quarles, J.
Cleaning up America (1976), 92, 132
Quayle, D.
"Standing Firm: Personal Reflections on being Vice President," in T. Walch, Ed., At the President's Side—The Vice Presidency in the Twentieth Century 169, 175 (1997), 109

Rabin, R.
Federal Regulation in Historical Perspective, 38 Stan. L. Rev. 1189 (1986), 7, 192
Rakoff, T.
Brock v. Roadway Express, Inc. and the New Law of Regulatory Due Process, 1987 Sup. Ct. Rev. 157, 48
The Shape of Law in the American Administrative State, 11 Tel Aviv U. Studies in Law 9 (1992), 22, 26
Reed, P.
The Role of Federal Courts in U.S. Customs and International Trade Law (Oceania Publications 1997), 180

Reich, C.
The New Property, 73 Yale L. J. 733 (1964), 14, 54
Richards, D.
A Theory of Free Speech, 34 U.C.L.A. L. Rev. 1837 (1987), 41
Rosenthal, A.
Conditional Federal Spending and the Constitution, 39 Stan. L. Rev. 1103 (1987), 142, 175
Rothman, D. and S.
Special Project: The Remedial Process in Institutional Reform Litigation, 78 Colum. L. Rev. 788 (1978), 178
The Willowbrook Wars (Harper & Row 1984), 178

Scalia, A.
Vermont Yankee: The APA, the D.C. Circuit, and the Supreme Court, 1978 Sup. Ct. Rev. 345, 126, 244
Schick, A.
The Federal Budget: Politics, Policy, Process (1995), 85
The First Five Years of Congressional Budgeting, in R. Penner, The Congressional Budget Process After Five Years 3 (1981), 85
Schoenbrod, D.
Power Without Responsibility (1993), 30
The Phoenix Rises Again: The Nondelegation Doctrine from Constitutional and Policy Perspective, 20 Cardozo L. Rev. 731 (1999), 30
Schuck, P.
Suing Government (Yale University 1983), 391
Schwartz, J.
Liability for Sovereign Acts: Congruence and Exceptionalism in Public Contract Law, 64 Geo. Wash. L. Rev. 633 (1993), 402
The Irresistible Force Meets the Immoveable Object: Estoppel Remedies for an Agency's Violations of its own

Regulations or Other Misconduct, 44 Admin. L. Rev. 653 (1992), 383

Seidenfeld, M.

Demystifying Deossification, 75 Tex. L. Rev. 483 (1997), 252

Rulemaking Table, 27 Fla. St. L. Rev. 533 (2000), 195, 252

Shane, P.

Independent Policymaking and Presidential Power: A Constitutional Analysis, 57 Geo. Wash. L. Rev. 596, 603-606 (1989), 100

Political Accountability in a System of Checks and Balances: The Case of Presidential Review of Rulemaking, 48 Ark. L. Rev. 161 (1995), 104, 109, 249

Shapiro, D.

Abstention and Primary Jurisdiction: Two Chips Off the Same Block? – A Comparative Analysis, 60 Corn. L. Rev. 75 (1974), 331

Some Thoughts on Intervention Before Courts, Agencies, and Arbitrators, 81 Harv. L. Rev. 721 (1968), 215

The Choice of Rulemaking and Adjudication in the Development of Administrative Policy, 78 Harv. L. Rev. 921 (1965), 259

Shapiro, M.

Administrative Discretion: The Next Stage, 92 Yale L. J. 1487, 1507 (1983), 386

APA: Past, Present, Future, 72 Va. L. Rev. 447 (1986), 192

Shapiro, S.

Political Oversight and the Deterioration of Regulatory Policy, 46 Admin. L. Rev. 1 (1994), 249

Siegel, J.

Suing the President: Nonstatutory Review Revisited, 97 Colum. L. Rev. 1612 (1997), 303

Textualism and Contextualism in Administrative Law, 78 B. U. L. Rev. 1023 (1998), 360

Skowronek, S.

Building a New American State: The Expansion of National Administrative Capacities, 1877-1920 (Cambridge University Press 1982), 136

Sofaer, A.

The Change-of-Status Adjudication: A Case Study of the Informal Agency Process. 1 J. Leg. Stud. 349 (1972), 84

Special Project: The Remedial Process in Institutional Reform Litigation, 78 Colum. L. Rev. 788 (1978), 84

Stevenson, R.

Protecting Business Secrets Under the Freedom of Information Act: Managing Exemption 4, 34 Admin. L. Rev. 207 (1982), 282

Stewart, R.

The Development of Administrative and Quasi-Constitutional Law in Judicial Review of Environmental Decisionmaking: Lessons from the Clean Air Act, 62 Iowa L. Rev. 713 (1977), 238

The Discontents of Legalism: Interest Group Relations in Administrative Regulation, 1985 Wisc. L. Rev. 655, (1985), 292

The Reformation of American Administrative Law, 88 Harv. L. Rev. 1669, 1756 (1975), 215, 217

Vermont Yankee and the Evolution of Administrative Procedure, 91 Harv. L. Rev. 1805 (1978), 244

Stewart, R. and Sunstein, C.

Public Programs and Private Rights, 95 Harv. L. Rev. 1195 (1982), 214

Stone, H.F.

The Common Law in the United States, 50 Harv. L. Rev. 4 (1936), 116

Strauss, D.

The Solicitor General and the Interests of the United States, #1 at 165, 144

Strauss, P.

Changing Times; The APA at Fifty, 63 U. Chi. L. Rev. 1389 (1996), 221, 354

Disqualification of Decisional Officials in Rulemaking, 80 Colum. L. Rev. 990 (1980), 293

Formal and Functional Approaches to Separation of Powers Questions – A Foolish Inconsistency? 72 Cornell L. J. 488 (1987), 24, 26, 98

From Expertise to Politics: The Transformation of American Rulemaking, 31 Wake Forest L. Rev. 745 (1996), 195, 221

Legislative Theory and the Rule of Law: Some Comments on Rubin, 89 Colum. L. Rev. 427 (1989), 32, 312

On Resegregating the Worlds of Statute and the Common Law, 1994 Sup. Ct. Rev. 427, 202

One Hundred Fifty Cases Per Year: Some Implications Of The Supreme Court's Limited Resources For Judicial Review of Agency Action, 87 Colum. L. Rev. 1093 (1987), 123, 172, 313, 362, 368

Presidential Rulemaking, 72 Chi-Kent L. Rev. 965 (1997), 90, 94

Publication Rules in the Rulemaking Spectrum: Assuring Proper Respect for an Essential Element, 53 Admin. L. Rev. 803 (2001), 222, 257, 365, 368

Resegregating the Worlds of Statute and Common Law, 1994 Sup. Ct. Rev. 427, 355

Revisiting Overton Park: Political and Judicial Controls Over Administrative Actions Affecting the Community, 39 U.C.L.A. L. Rev. 1251 (1992), 151, 235, 296

Rules, Adjudications, and Other Sources of Law in an Executive Department: Reflections on the Interior Department's Administration of the Mining Law, 74 Colum. L. Rev. 1231 (1974), 259

The Internal Relations of Government: Cautionary Tales from Inside the Black Box, #2 at 155, 144

The Place of Agencies in Government: Separation of Powers and the Fourth Branch, 84 Colum. L. Rev. 573 (1984), 8, 17, 19, 21, 23, 90, 100

The Rulemaking Continuum, 41 Duke L. J. 1463 (1992), 222

When The Judge is not the Primary Official With Responsibility to Read: Agency Interpretation and the Problem of Legislative History 66 Chi.-Kent L. Rev. 321 (1992), 360

Strauss, P. and Cohen, D.

Congressional Review of Agency Regulations, 49 Admin. L. Rev. 95 (1997), 35

Strauss, P., Rakoff, T., Schotland, R. and Farina, C. Gellhorn & Byse's Administrative Law: Cases and Comments (9th ed. Foundation Press 1995), 7, 30, 138, 142, 172, 268, 336, 340, 382

Strauss, P. and Sunstein, C.

The Role of the President and OMB in Informal Rulemaking, 38 Admin .L. Rev. 181 (1986), 105, 108

Sunstein, C.

After the Rights Revolution: Reconceiving the Regulatory State (Harvard 1990), 8

Cognition and Cost-Benefit Analysis, 29 J. Leg. Stud. 1059 (2000), 165

Cost-Benefit Analysis and the Separation of Powers, 23 Ariz.L. Rev. 1267 (1981), 108

Section 1983 and the Private Enforcement of Federal Law, 49 U. Chi. L. Rev. 394 (1982), 399

Standing and the Privatization of Public Law, 88 Colum. L. Rev. 1432 (1988), 330

What's Standing after *Lujan*? Of Citizen Suits, "Injuries," and Article III, 91 Mich. L. Rev. 163 (1992), 314, 315

Sunstein, C. and Lessig, L.
The President and the Administration, 94 Colum. L. Rev. 1 (1994), 17

Survey
The Paths of Civil Litigation: VI. ADR, the Judiciary and Justice: Coming to Terms with the Alternatives, 113 Harv. L. Rev. 1851 (2000), 219

Symposium
Fifty Years of the BLM, 32 Land & Water Review 339 ff. (1997), 182

Government Lawyering, 61 Law & Contemp. Prob. Nos. 1 and 2 (1998), 144

Recent Developments: Electronic Freedom of Information Act, 50 Admin. L. Rev. 339 (1998), 283

Recent Developments: Regulatory Reform & the 104th Congress. 49 Admin. L. Rev. 111 ff (1997), 195

The Administrative Procedure Act, A Fortieth Anniversary Symposium, 72 Va. L. Rev. 215 (1986), 191

Taylor, S.
Making Bureaucracies Think: The Environmental Impact Statement Strategy of Administrative Reform (Stanford University 1984), 102, 249

Thach, C.
The Creation of the Presidency 1775-1789 (1923), 87

Thomas, R.
Prosecutorial Discretion and Agency Self-Regulation, *CNI v. Young* and the Aflatoxin Dance, 44 Admin. L. Rev. 131 (1992), 168

Tribe, L.
American Constitutional Law (3d ed. Foundation Press 1999), 16, 41, 312

Tushnet, M.
Constitutional Law (Dartmouth 1992), 16

Taking the Constitution Away From the Courts (Princeton University1999), 16

Unah, I.
The Courts of International Trade: Judicial Specialization, Expertise, and Bureaucratic Policy-making (University of Michigan 1998), 180

Verkuil, P.
A Critical Guide to the Regulatory Flexibility Act, 1982 Duke L. J. 213, 102

A Study of Informal Adjudication Procedures, 43 U. Chi. L. Rev. 739 (1976), 55

Rulemaking Ossification – A Modest Proposal, 47 Admin. L. Rev. 453 (1995), 252

Vermeule, A.
The Cycles of Statutory Interpretation,68 U. Chi. L. Rev. 149 (2001), 336, 351, 353

Walch, T., ed.
At the President's Side – The Vice Presidency in the Twentieth Century (1997), 87, 109

Wald, P.
Regulation at Risk: Are Courts Part of the Solution or Most of the Problem? 67 S. Cal. L. Rev. 621 (1994), 334

Wander, W., Hebert, F. and Copeland, G.
Congressional Budgeting: Politics, Process and Power (1984), 85

Wechsler, H.
The Political Safeguards of Federalism: The Role of the States in the Composition and Selection of the National Government, 54 Colum. L. Rev. 543 (1954), 12

Weko, T.
The Politicizing Presidency: The White House Personnel Office (1995), 95

Welborn, D., Lyon, W. and Thomas, L.
Implementation and Effects of the Federal Government in the Sunshine Act (1984), 286
West, W.
Administrative Rulemaking: Politics and Processes (Greenwood 1985), 242
White, L.
The Federalists: A Study in Administrative History (Macmillan 1948), 129, 172

Wildavsky, A.
The New Politics of the Budgetary Process (2d ed. 1992), 85
Wilson, J.Q.
Bureaucracy: What Government Agencies Do and Why They Do It (Basic Books 1989), 8

Zillman, D.
Protecting Discretion: Judicial Interpretation of the Discretionary Function Exception to the [FTCA], 47 Me. L. Rev. 366 (1995), 393

Reports of Commissions and Committees

ABA, Commission on Law and the Economy, Federal Regulation: Roads to Reform (1979), 292

ABA, Comm'n On Law And The Economy, Federal Regulation: Roads to Reform 70, 156-61 (1979), 279, 280, 292

Administrative Office of the U.S.Courts, Judicial Business:2000 138-140, 395

Annual Report of the Directors of the Administrative Office of the United States Courts 133 (1984), 170

Attorney General's Committee on Administrative Procedure, Final Report: Administrative Procedure in Government Agencies, Sen. Doc. 186, 76th Cong., 3d Sess. (1940) and Sen. Doc. 8, 77th Cong. 1st Sess. (1941), 187, 192

Boyer, Report on the Trade Regulation Rulemaking Procedures of the Federal Trade Commission 1980 ACUS Ann.Rep. 33, 262

Boyer, Report on the Trade Regulation Rulemaking Procedures of the Federal Trade Commission, 1979 ACUS Ann.Rep. 41, 325

Funk, W., Governmental Management, a report as part of the ABA's Administrative Law and Regulatory Practice Section APA Project, p. 7 n. 7, 251

GAO, Environmental Protection: Collaborative EPA-State Effort Needed to Improve New Performance Partnership System (GAO/RCED 99-171), 142

GAO, Occupational Safety and Health: Changes Needed in the Combined Federal-State Approach (Chapter Report, 02/28/94, GAO/HEHS-94-10), 142

GAO, Status of Open Recommendations 72 (1999), 142

General Accounting Office, Federal Rulemaking: Agencies' Use of Information Technology to Facilitate Public Participation, B-284527 (June 30, 2000), 197

OMB, Agency Compliance with Title II of the Unfunded Mandates Reform Act of 1995, 4th Annual Report to Congress (1999), 102

OMB Circular No. A-19, 103

OMB, Fourth Annual Report to Congress, Agency Compliance with Title II of the Unfunded Mandates Reform Act of 1995 (1999), 251

Practicing Law Institute, Coping with U.S. Export Controls (1986), 180

Report of the Attorney General's Committee on Administrative Procedure, S. Doc. 8, 77th Cong., 1st Sess. (1941), 7

Report of the Privacy Protection Study Commission, Personal Privacy in an Information Society (1977), 288

Report of the Secretary of Health, Education and Welfare's Advisory Committee Records, Computers, and the Rights of Citizens 41 (1973), 287

Rosenblum, V., The Administrative Law Judge in the Administrative Process, in Subcommittee on Social Security, House Committee on Ways and Means, 94th Cong., 1st Sess., Report on Recent Studies Relevant to Disability Hearings and Appeals Crisis 171-245 (Comm.Print 1975), 50

Senate Committee on the Judiciary, Judicial Review of Agency Action, Sen.Rep. No 94-996 on S. 800, 94th Cong., 2d Sess. 11-12 (1976), 390

Special Committee to Review the Government in the Sunshine Act, Report and Recommendation, 49 Admin. L. Rev. 421 (1997), 287

Staff of Subcomm. on Administrative Practice and Procedure to the Senate Comm. on the Judiciary, 86th Cong., Report on Regulatory Agencies to the President-Elect 71 (1960) (written by James M. Landis), 316

The Attorney General's Manual on the Administrative Procedure Act (1947), 7

U.Va. Center for Law and National Security, Technology Control, Competition, and National Security: Conflict and Consensus (1987), 180

PREFACE

This book had its origin in a project under the editorship of the late Professor Aldo Piras of the University of Rome, to create a collection of essays describing the system of administrative justice in the United States and seven European democracies.[1] His hope was that exposing the governmental law of our countries to professionals trained under other legal systems would both enrich understanding in an increasingly interdependent world, and provide helpful information about alternatives to jurisdictions considering changes in their public law. Professor Piras died before the project could reach completion, but the collection has been published by the Guiffre Press. The first edition of this monograph was also published separately in the United States, by Carolina Academic Press.

The years following have confirmed the usefulness of this undertaking. In Asia, Europe and South America, this book has proved helpful to lawyers and law students seeking a basic introduction to American public law and, in particular, administrative law. It has been useful inside the United States as well, for law students and others seeking an overview of our administrative justice system or a jumping-off place into the voluminous literature on the subject. The current edition was developed with both audiences in mind, after experiences teaching with it on four continents. It reflects significant changes that have occurred in American administrative law and government, as well as substantial elements of continuity.

Thanks are owing to many in any project like this. My late mentor Walter Gellhorn, introduced me to Professor Piras, only one of many acts of kindness and support, and he comes first in place. My casebook colleagues Clark Byse, Cynthia Farina, Todd Rakoff, and Roy Schotland, along with Richard Pierce and John Manning here at Columbia, and my many friends in the American Bar Association's Section of Administrative Law and Regulatory Practice, have read and responded helpfully to my work, and added immea-

---

1. Administrative Law: The Problem of Justice in the Western Democracies, (1991). This monograph appeared in Volume I, alongside essays by William Wade (U.K.) and Hans Ragnemalm (Sweden).

surably to my knowledge of the subject and ability to see its many facets. The faculties of the University of Leiden, the University of Buenos Aires, Ludwig Maximillians University of Munich, Tokyo University, and the European University Institute have been gracious and supportive hosts for weeks of visits that deepened my appreciation of alternative approaches to both the difficult business of securing fair, effective, and efficient government relationships with citizens and their businesses, and the strangenesses that many will find in American approaches. My students, at Columbia and abroad, have through occasional research and the work of our classes together equally helped me to understand what is not so obvious about American administrative law. Belinda Smith, now a lecturer on public law at Sydney University in Australia, has been particularly helpful in this regard, and in helping me to keep my diction straightforward and clear. Casandra Perez energetically and thoughtfully prepared the table of authorities and the index. Kristie Hart, my extraordinary assistant, cheerfully saw the text through countless revisions and authorial grumbles. Keith Sipe at Carolina Academic Press has been as supportive a publisher as one could wish. And none of this, nor much else that is satisfying in my life, could have happened without the patience and love of my wife Joanna.

The demerits of this book are wholly my own. I hope only that, given the vast landscape to be sketched, the occasional splotch or want of definition can be forgiven.

Peter L. Strauss
Lenox, MA 2001

ADMINISTRATIVE JUSTICE
IN THE
UNITED STATES

I

INTRODUCTION

The subject matter of administrative law is, first and foremost, government and its operation. In the United States, its concerns reach any governmental action touching citizen interests that is not a matter of criminal law and its enforcement, the enactment of ordinary legislation, or the resolution of private civil disputes unconnected to administrative regimes. Understanding and assessing administrative justice thus entails an engagement with the institutions of government, their operation and their interaction. Particularly for the reader from abroad, but also for Americans wishing to understand the special character of their institutions, it is useful to focus at the outset on some unique and possibly surprising features of the American governmental and legal system, that strongly influence American approaches to the subject.

That American government is federal in form is well known. Thirteen states, each having its own constitution, existed when the national Constitution was adopted. Those constitutions, with their counterparts in each subsequently admitted state, remain the independent source of state governmental structure and authority. The national Constitution controls them in some particulars, but the political choices reflected in our national government and its Constitution are to only a limited degree required of the states; and the relationship between state and local authority is a matter that, in general, is left for determination by each state. While states do not have the national government's legal obligation to honor the independent existence of smaller units of government, many have chosen to confer large measures of self-governance ("home rule"), including choices about how to arrange local political institutions, on at least the larger cities within them. Thus, federal judges are appointed for life during good behavior, with the advice and consent of the upper house of the national legislature, the United States Senate; but whether state or local judges are elected or appointed, for how long, and if appointed with what kinds of political approval, are decided by each state or authorized locality. Only two members of the national executive, the President and the Vice President, are elected; but states commonly provide for the election of other executive officials than their Governor and Lieutenant Governor—an Attorney General, a Comptroller, perhaps members of important regulatory

3

bodies—and whether and to what extent they do so is strictly a matter of their choice. Cities empowered to adopt their own charters show similar flexibility and variety. The national Congress is bicameral, but state legislatures need not be—Nebraska's is not—and city legislative bodies rarely are.

For all this possible variety of form, however, American governments show striking unity in one basic political arrangement that tends strongly to separate administration from the legislature, and also to diminish its direct political responsibility to the public. America's democracies are not *parliamentary* democracies, where the heads of the executive are members of the legislature and only hold office while they retain the majority (or "confidence") of the house. Each elected American official—national, state *and* local, legislative, executive *and* judicial—serves for a fixed term, differing in length depending upon her position and not subject to being curtailed by any general political cause; while individuals might be impeached or recalled for reasons particular to their personal conduct of office, the "vote of confidence" is unknown. Indeed, since incumbent legislators are almost invariably returned to office if they run, even reelection is little influenced by the success or failure of particular government programs. Electoral success is usually a matter of personal, not party qualifications. While the executive may propose legislation, those proposals may be (and usually are) amended in the legislature, and their passage in any form is far from assured. In the legislature, provisions for party discipline arise out of the political parties' internal arrangements, having no consequence for "the government," and they are often ineffective. The result is a considerable (and desired) dispersal of authority; Americans think that the difficulties of coordination provide important protections against excessive government.

Under American ideas about "separation of powers," the legislature, the chief executive and the courts are kept sharply distinct. While each is given some role in controlling the acts of the others, functions are not shared. In particular, members of the Congress are strictly forbidden from serving also in executive departments. Thus, the heads of the bodies that constitute the ordinary operating bureaucracy of government, once appointed, have no formal political connection to the legislature, while they ordinarily do have such connections to the chief executive. This separation tends to reinforce the "irresponsibility" of the legislature to executive direction. Legal control over the acts of governmental bodies is ultimately effected by the separate, generalist judiciary rather than by court-like organs within the bureaucracy.

The reader who is used to ministers serving in parliament, to votes of confidence, and to tight executive (prime ministerial) control over legislative outcomes should read the following pages holding these important differences firmly in mind. This work has been written in the hope of helping the reader unfamiliar with the details of the American legal system to understand the more important characteristics and issues of our system of administrative justice. American administrative law concerns itself rather deeply with how government decisions happen, as well as the legality or not of the decisions once taken. Thus, the concern in these pages with the institutions and operation of the American bureaucracy—with matters occurring in the "ministries" of American government rather than in its courts—is, itself, typical of the approach an American lawyer might take. Indeed, American administrative lawyers often criticize teachers of administrative law for over-emphasizing the courts. The operative concerns of administrative justice in the United States are most often experienced at the agency level; and the judiciary provides only one means of control a lawyer might invoke on behalf of her client.

Bibliographic Note: The reader interested in pursuing issues of American administrative law in greater depth may find a variety of helpful sources.

The Internet permits extraordinary access to the primary materials of administrative law, and the reader may in fact wish to use it to see concretely a variety of the materials and procedures described here. For statutory, regulatory and decisional materials, state as well as federal, the best "free library" starting place known to the author is Cornell Law School's Legal Information Institute, http://www.law.cornell.edu/. The Government Printing Office also makes a wide range of federal governmental material, including the Code of Federal Regulations and the Federal Register, available at http://www.access. gpo.gov/su_docs/index.html. Congressional materials, from debates, committee reports, and bill histories to connections with individual members' web sites, may be found at http://thomas.loc.gov. Presidential materials are to be found at http://www.whitehouse.gov; while this site has been organized for the casual citizen visitor more than for the researcher, links to "news" and "your government" will produce connections to more detailed materials. Also organized for the citizen consumer, http://www.firstgov.gov is intended as a gateway to federal agencies; primarily organized around problems of likely citizen interest, it also contains useful indices. Links to individual agencies, varying in their up-to-dateness and completeness, can be found also at the White House and congressional sites, and at three well-organized university sites known to the author: Florida State University Law School, http://www.law.fsu.edu/library/admin/;Louisiana State University, http://www.lib.lsu.edu/govdocs/federal/list.html, and Chicago-Kent Law School, http://www.infoctr.edu/fwl/. These last sites contain links to state institutions as well; the first of them is maintained in cooperation with the American Bar Association's Section of Administrative Law and Regulatory Practice, and has that special incentive to remain comprehensive and current. It is at the federal agencies themselves that one may expect to find tables of organization, collections of informal material (such as interpretations), and opportunities for participation; and a number provide opportunities to register for electronic notification of matters of interest. These sites are typically found by using the formula www.<abbreviation>.gov or www.<agency abbreviation>.<dept abbreviation>.gov. The user will find that, even within single departments, they vary greatly from site to site in organization, content, facilities for search, and the like. The gradual implementation of an Electronic Freedom of Information Act,[1] public pressure, and White House guidance may be expected to produce somewhat greater uniformity over time, but the plasticity of and possibilities for individuality on the Internet that are among its most attractive features—responsible, for example, for the university library initiatives just mentioned—make a long period of experimentation and variation likely.

A variety of works prepared by professors of law trace the ground in varying degrees of detail, and with more attention to theoretical and critical issues: K.C. Davis & R. J. Pierce, Jr., Administrative Law Treatise (3d ed. Aspen Law & Business 1994, with annual supplements)[2]; C. Koch, Administrative Law and Practice (2d ed. West 1997, with annual supplements)[3]; R. Pierce, S. Shapiro, and P. Verkuil, Administrative Law and Process (2d ed. Foundation Press 1992)[4]; and A. Aman & W. Mayton, Administrative Law (2d ed. West 2001).[5] Recent developments are regularly summarized in annual publications of the Administrative Law and Regulatory Practice Section of the American Bar Association.[6] Somewhat less direct, but having the advantage of exposing

---

1. Briefly discussed in Chapter VI, below, at p. 282.

2. Professor Kenneth C. Davis, one of the formative figures of American administrative law scholarship, held strong opinions on many issues—opinions long influential in the field. The third edition of his treatise was prepared by Professor Richard J. Pierce, Jr., a strong scholar in his own right, who has maintained the idiosyncratic character of this treatise.

3. Professor Koch's two volume treatise appears much stronger as an account of conventional legal relationships of control than of the political ones that, for rulemaking, are so important an element of the process.

4. This one-volume work is chiefly a text written for students, but at a useful level of detail and thought.

5. Professor Aman's work is distinguished by his attention to the global environment of administrative law issues; see, e.g., Aman, Administrative Law in a Global Era (Cornell Univ. Press 1992).

6. E.g., J. Lubbers, ed., Developments in Administrative Law and Regulatory Practice 1999–2000 (ABA 2000). At this writing, the Section is in the course of preparing a fairly

the reader to a variety of primary materials in the field, are teaching materials such as P. Strauss, T. Rakoff, R. Schotland and C. Farina, Gellhorn & Byse's Administrative Law: Cases and Comments (9th ed. Foundation Press 1995 with 1999 supplement) and S. Breyer, R. Stewart, C. Sunstein & M. Spitzer, Administrative Law and Regulatory Policy (4th ed. Aspen Law & Business 1999). The footnote[7] sets out some of the more important works examining aspects of administrative law and its development.

Another kind of reading is less technical, and may introduce the reader to the variety of scholarly perspectives that can be brought to bear on understanding administrative justice in the modern American state. A number of books reveal American administrative procedure in action, describing the work of particular agencies or the administrative resolution of important social controversies.[8] Alternatively, one could seek an historical perspective in the works of Professors Croley,[9] McGraw,[10] Rabin,[11] or Skowroneck.[12] A third perspective, viewing the problems of administrative law as those of choosing suitable procedures or institutions for the carrying out of legislative policy, is

---

detailed Statement of Administrative Law that, once published, should also be a useful resource. Drafts may be viewed at http://www.abanet.org/adminlaw/apa/home.html.

7. **Historical materials:** J. Landis, The Administrative Process (Yale University 1938); The Attorney General's Manual on the Administrative Procedure Act (1947); Report of the Attorney General's Committee on Administrative Procedure, S. Doc. 8, 77th Cong., 1st Sess. (1941); L. Jaffe, Judicial Review of Administrative Action (Little Brown 1965). **Statutory and other materials:** W. Funk, J. Lubbers & C. Pou, Federal Administrative Procedure Sourcebook (3d ed. ABA 2000). **Rulemaking:** J. Lubbers, A Guide to Federal Agency Rulemaking (3d ed., American Bar Association 1998). **Adjudication:** J. Mashaw, Bureaucratic Justice: Managing Social Security Disability Claims (Yale University 1983); J. Mashaw, Due Process in the Administrative State (Yale University 1985). **Freedom of Information:** J. O'Reilly, Federal Information Disclosure (3d ed., West 2000). **State Administrative Law:** M. Asimow, A. Bonfield and R. Levin, State and Federal Administrative Law (2d ed. 1998); F. Cooper, State Administrative Law (1965); A.E. Bonfield, State Law in Teaching of Administrative Law: A Critical Analysis of the Status Quo, 61 Tex. L. Rev. 95 (1982).

8. Eg., D. Kessler, A Question of Intent (Public Affairs 2001) (FDA and tobacco); R.S. Melnick, Between the Lines (Brookings 1994) (Welfare rights administration); J. Mashaw & D. Harfst, The Struggle for Auto Safety (Harvard 1990) (NHTSA and automotive safety); B. Ackerman & W. Hassler, Clean Coal/Dirty Air (Yale 1981) (EPA and sulfur dioxide emissions).

9. S. Croley, Theories of Regulation, Incorporating the Administrative Process, 98 Colum. L. Rev. 1 (1998).

10. T. McGraw, Prophets of Regulation (Belknap Press 1984).

11. R. Rabin, Federal Regulation in Historical Perspective, 38 Stan. L. Rev. 1189 (1986).

12. S. Skowroneck, Building a New American State: The Expansion of National Administrative Capacities, 1877–1920 (Cambridge University 1982).

exemplified by the work of Professors Breyer,[13] Kaufman,[14] and Wilson.[15] Finally, increasing attention is being paid in the legal academy to the contributions of political science and economics.[16]

13. S. Breyer, Regulation and its Reform (Harvard University 1982); Breaking the Vicious Circle: Toward Effective Risk Regulation (Harvard University 1992). Professor Breyer had become a federal appellate judge in 1980, before these works appeared; in 1994 he was confirmed as a Justice of the United States Supreme Court.

14. H. Kaufman, The Administrative Behavior of Federal Bureau Chiefs (Brookings 1981); The Forest Ranger (Resources for the Future 1960).

15. J.Q. Wilson, Bureaucracy: What Government Agencies Do and Why They Do It (Basic Books 1989).

16. J. Mashaw, Greed, Chaos & Governance: Using Public Choice to Improve Public Law (Yale 1997); D. Farber & P. Frickey, Law and Public Choice: A Critical Introduction (Univ. Chicago 1991); C. Sunstein, After the Rights Revolution: Reconceiving the Regulatory State (Harvard 1990); B. Ackerman, Reconstructing American Law (Harvard University 1984); P. Strauss, The Place of Agencies in Government: Separation of Powers and the Fourth Branch, 84 Colum. L. Rev. 573 (1984).

II

CONSTITUTIONAL
BACKGROUND

A. *General character of the Constitution*

Any introductory assessment of American administrative law, particularly one written with readers not well-versed in the American legal system in mind, should begin with the Constitution, its fundamental legal document. It is a written constitution, quite brief and cast in general terms; and it has been enduring. Ratified in 1789 and supplemented almost immediately by the ten amendments known as the Bill of Rights, it has been importantly amended only a few times in the last two centuries.[1] Of course, the nation whose affairs it governs and the world in which it exists have changed enormously since that time. The juxtaposition between unchanging text and changing times has created enduring challenges to its vitality and use.

At perhaps the most general level, one may say that the drafters of the American Constitution sought to resolve two problems facing the nation in 1787: to increase the power and effectiveness of the national government, a government which under the previous arrangements was demonstrably ineffective; and at the same time to avoid creating so much power in a single place as to threaten a return of the governmental tyranny that the states and their citizens had recently defeated in the American Revolution. (A third element often mentioned was the desirability of protecting the longer-term interests of the citizens, perhaps especially its propertied citizens, from being swept away by the exigencies or passions of a particular moment, a much-feared attribute of direct democracy.) Many features of the national constitution may be

---

1. Since the Amendments adopted in the wake of the American Civil War, numbers 13, 14 and 15, perhaps only the 17th Amendment (direct election of Senators), the 19th (franchise extended to women) and the 22d (Presidents limited to two terms) have significantly changed the political context of American government.

understood at least in part as means by which these potentially conflicting ends might be secured—for example, the careful separation of legislative, executive and judicial power at the federal level, shortly to be discussed; the preservation of a federal form of government, with largely independent legal authority at the state level and a national government of defined, limited authority and independent political units; and the near-immediate adoption of a Bill of Rights. The written nature of the Constitution, and the obstacles to its formal amendment,[2] further discourage altering the balance of power.

By its own terms, the Constitution is supreme in relation to any other law or undertaking (specifically including treaties to which the United States may be a party). The nation's highest court, the United States Supreme Court, early interpreted this provision for supremacy to mean both that in case of conflict between the Constitution and other sources of domestic law, the Constitution must prevail, and that the federal judiciary had the ultimate responsibility to determine whether such conflicts existed.[3] Further, an agency cannot act, nor can the legislature empower it to act, in a way that is contrary to the provisions of the Constitution. For this reason, constitutional arguments have a special priority in American jurisprudence, for administrative law no less than in other settings. A successful claim that an agency has acted (or has been empowered to act) contrary to the provisions of the Constitution will defeat the action in an emphatic way. Note, too, the unusual authority this gives the Supreme Court: its judgments about constitutionality cannot be changed by ordinary legislation. Unless the Court itself can be persuaded that it has erred, the Court's judgments are subject to revision only by the formal (and cumbersome) processes of enacting a written amendment to the Constitution itself. Constitutional supremacy is a central feature of the American legal order.

A further general characteristic of the American constitutional system, already briefly noted, is that it is federal. It contemplates the individual states (for example, Massachusetts or California) as independent political entities having a defined relationship to the national government rather than as subordinate parts of the national government. This arrangement is described in

---

2. Briefly, amendments require approval by a two-thirds majority in both houses of the American Congress plus approval by three fourths of the states; it is also possible for two thirds of the states to require Congress to call a convention for the purpose of proposing amendments, but thus far this procedure (which may open the whole of the Constitution to revision) has never been invoked. See W. Dellinger, The Legitimacy of Constitutional Change: Rethinking the Amendment Process, 97 Harv. L. Rev. 386 (1983).

3. Marbury v. Madison, 5 U.S. (1 Cranch) 137 (1803).

some contemporary writings as like the separation of powers, another means of dispersing governmental authority in the service of enhancing citizen assurance against governmental tyranny.[4] In matters where the national government can act, one option (sometimes called "cooperative federalism") may nonetheless be to share responsibilities with the states. For example, in creating national programs for environmental controls, workplace safety, and welfare administration, Congress has chosen to permit or even enlist state administration as an alternative to administration by a national bureaucracy. While permitting action to be taken closer to the people, and responsive to regional conditions, this has also sometimes created confusion about where responsibility for particular programs lies. Both devolution of authority to the state and local level, and the avoidance of imposing federal requirements on state authorities without providing the resources necessary to meet them, are important elements in the current political environment.[5] While the Supreme Court has recently showed renewed resistance to direct federal co-option of state resources,[6] it has identified few legal constraints on Congress's power to create regimes of cooperative federalism. [7]

Federalism is not a direct concern of this essay, but two additional matters are important to mention. First, the theory of American government is that the national government enjoys only those powers to make law that are enumerated in the Constitution, primarily in Article I, Section 8 defining Congress's legislative authority—for example, the authority to "regulate Commerce with foreign Nations, and among the several States, and with the Indian Tribes." Residual legislative authority remains in the states. The period 1937–1995 was characterized by expansive readings of the enumerated federal powers, however, readings that appeared to permit Congress to reach any issue it could characterize as having national impact. A widely accepted account argued that the political safeguards of federalism—the likelihood that members of Congress would represent the continuing interests of the states they repre-

---

4. R. Brown, Separated Powers and Ordered Liberty, 139 U. Pa. L. Rev. 1513 (1991).

5. Concern with the possible financial impact of federal requirements on state, local and tribal authorities is reflected both in presidential executive orders, see E.O. 12,875 (Oct. 26, 1993) and 13,132 (Aug. 5, 1999), and statute, see Unfunded Mandates Reform Act of 1995, 2 U.S.C. §1501 et seq., briefly discussed at p. 249 within.

6. New York v. United States, 505 U.S. 144 (1992) (radioactive waste); Printz v. United States, 521 U.S. 898 (1997) (gun control); but compare Reno v. Condon, 528 U.S. 141 (2000); E. Caminker, State Sovereignty and Subordinacy: May Congress Commandeer State Officers to Implement Federal Laws?, 95 Colum. L. Rev. 1001 (1995).

7. The Court's increasing attention to state sovereign immunity (see p. 388 below) may be complicating the federalist judicial enforcement of these cooperative schemes, however.

sented—were a sufficient, and the only disciplined, protection of those interests.[8] More recently, the Supreme Court has been exercising renewed control over the credibility of some congressional judgments that matters it has chosen to legislate have national importance.[9] It is unlikely, however, that these disputes will call into question major national regulatory undertakings. Whether federal legislative authority is significantly limited will not be further addressed in these pages. So long as that authority exists, the supremacy principle makes any valid juridical act at the national level—whether Constitution, treaty, statute, executive or judicial decision, or subordinate legislation—prevail over any conflicting assertion of state law.

Second, although the federal structure of American government suggests exploring state (and local) as well as national issues, in general this essay will not do so. This is an unfortunate, but practical limitation. Many issues of interest to administrative lawyers are handled at the state and local level. For example, most issues of land use control, professional licensing, and public utility rate regulation are controlled by the states. Each state has its own constitution and statutes creating its own distinctive governmental structures and administrative and judicial procedures. Although this essay will discuss some issues of national law governing state administration (chiefly national constitutional requirements for fair procedure) and point out some contrasts between the national and state levels, it will rarely address the problems of state administrative law as such. To outline contemporary issues in American administrative law at the national level is a large enough task.

B. *Stability and change*

The obstacles to formal amendment of the Constitution have posed obvious problems for the adaptability of American government during the two centuries since it was adopted. The emergence of the modern administrative state, in response to the social changes brought about by industrial and post-industrial economies, was one such challenge of particular relevance for this

---

8. H. Wechsler, The Political Safeguards of Federalism: The Role of the States in the Composition and Selection of the National Government, 54 Colum. L. Rev. 543 (1954). See also J. Choper, Federalism and Judicial Review: An Update, 21 Hastings Const. L. Q. 577 (1994).

9. E.g., United States v Lopez., 514 U.S. 549 (1995) (gun control); United States v. Morrison, 529 U.S. 598 (2000) (violence against women). See W. Buzbee and R. Schapiro, Legislative Record Review, 54 Stan. L. Rev. 87 (2001).

essay. No one pretends that those who drafted the Constitution imagined either those changes or the enormous and variegated government apparatus that has been built in response to them.[10] American judges have responded to this challenge, on the whole, by interpreting the Constitution in ways that confirm the structural changes that have been made, and by reinterpreting citizens' rights in light of the changed arrangements. This history of recognition of expanded national powers and new structural arrangements, and adaptation of individual protections to the new circumstances of the modern age, might be regarded as having served as an informal or de facto amendment process for the Constitution. If accepted by the people, as it has tended to be, the legitimizing effect of judicial approval could be thought an even more profound contribution to constitutional governance than the courts' occasional findings that governmental actions are *in*consistent with the Constitution, and much contemporary legal scholarship has been given over to discussion of it.[11]

A good example of this "amendment" process lies in the development of the constitutional instruction that no person be deprived of life, liberty or property without due process of law.[12] As originally understood, this instruction chiefly concerned the ordinary processes of courts. It also embodied the sense of the earliest document of the English "constitution," the Magna Carta, committing the whole of government to the principle of legality. There was no reason to think it applied to procedures followed within the government bureaucracy—a bureaucracy that at the time hardly existed, and had few if any relationships with private persons that could be thought to require procedural norms. Not until the beginning of the twentieth century, in a series of cases concerned with revenue collection, did an administrative jurisprudence of due process begin to emerge.[13]

While arguments about the necessary application and content of "due process" in the administrative context became increasingly common in both legislatures and courts during the first part of the twentieth century,[14] the most

---

10. That there would be change requiring adjustment was imagined, and that explains much of the document's openness of structure.

11. The classic reference is Charles Black, Jr., The People and the Court (1960); more recently, see L. Lessig, Fidelity and Constraint, 65 Fordham L. Rev. 1365 (1997).

12. Unique among constitutional provisions, this one appears twice—as a command to the federal government in the Fifth Amendment, and to the states in the Fourteenth. A more extended discussion of the development of "due process" in American constitutional understanding appears within at p. 48.

13. E.g., Londoner v. Denver, 210 U.S. 373 (1908).

14. The Federal Administrative Procedure Act, enacted in 1946, adopted procedures for formal adjudication that were widely taken to express Congress's judgment about the usual requirements of fair procedure. Its adoption was preceded by a decade's debate on the nec-

significant developments occurred after the second World War, beginning with the anti-communist campaigns of the 1950s and gathering true momentum during the 1970s. The courts then came to the conclusion—perhaps unsurprising to the reader but dramatic when first stated—that relationships with government (licenses, welfare entitlements, state employment, enrolment in public schools) must be recognized to have the dignity of "property" of which the citizen could not be deprived without "due process of law."[15] The courts, in the final instance, define what procedures "due process" requires. While they generally respect legislative choices (perhaps because legislative choices of appropriate procedure commonly reflect community notions about fair and necessary procedure), they do not always do so.

When courts find the legislative specification of procedure inadequate to provide "due process" the legislature must respect that judgment. Because it is based on the meaning of constitutional text, the legislature has no recognized authority to enact a statute inconsistent with it.[16] Whatever one might believe about the justice of the results produced, the point for current purposes is that no one could pretend that the drafters of the Due Process clause envisioned courts telling school officials what procedures they must follow before suspending a student for ten days;[17] or telling welfare officials what sort of hearing they must give a recipient before suspending current payments, in advance of a formal, statutory hearing on the existence of grounds for terminating eligibility;[18] or telling the legislature, in effect, what procedural pro-

---

essary content of administrative adjudication; and several important cases during this period established constitutional procedural norms for agencies deciding matters after hearing. Ohio Bell Telephone Co. v. Public Utilities Commission of Ohio, 301 U.S. 292 (1937); Morgan v. United States (Morgan I), 298 U.S. 468 (1936); Morgan v. United States (Morgan II), 304 U.S. 1 (1938).

15. Goldberg v. Kelly, 397 U.S. 254 (1970), discussed at some length within (text at p. 53 ff.) was the initial decision; it drew upon a seminal article by Charles Reich, The New Property, 73 Yale L. J. 733 (1964), arguing that in modern society, much wealth consists of intangible entitlements such as those based on advantageous opportunities conferred by government. When a statute confers government benefits on an individual, those individuals should be recognized as having a property right in such benefits.

16. In its recent decision in Dickerson v. United States, 530 U.S. 428 (2001), the Supreme Court declined to overrule an often-criticized constitutional interpretation, saying that even if it might not now reach that conclusion as an initial matter, compare n. 22 below, "the principles of *stare decisis* weigh heavily against overruling it now." Id. at 443. In consequence, the Court held, Congress could not supersede the interpretation legislatively.

17. Goss v. Lopez, 419 U.S. 565 (1975).

18. Goldberg v. Kelly, note 15 above.

tections must be provided to government employees, once the legislature has decided to have a civil service program.[19]

This practice of judicial "amendment" of the Constitution, born of practical necessity and generally accepted though it may be, presents evident difficulties to legal theorists. American legal literature is filled with sophisticated efforts at criticism and/or rationalization. The very fact that a judicial decision can have such a fundamental character, being reversible only by extraordinary means, gives rise to what has been described as the "countermajoritarian difficulty"—that the result of final judicial nullification of a statute frustrates what appears to be the popular will, as represented by the elected legislature's action.[20] More conservative constitutional theorists, often described as "interpretivists," take two lessons from this difficulty: first, that the courts are only justified in exercising their authority to declare legislation unconstitutional when they can link that judgment directly to the text of the constitution; second, that that authority should be invoked only rarely, and with utmost hesitation.

On the other hand, the particular (and historic) importance of the Court in protecting individual liberties and unpopular groups against the intolerance of legislatures and momentary public passions has led another group of scholars, loosely described as "noninterpretivists," to argue that the written text of the Constitution ought not be regarded as a necessary limit for judicial review of the constitutionality of government action. In their view, the use of analogy and reasoning from what judges perceive to be the emerging moral premises of contemporary American society provide a sufficient basis for judicial action protecting individuals against state power.[21] Some important contemporary opinions extending individual liberty claims seem defensible only on some such grounds,[22] and are roundly criticized by interpretivists

---

19. Cleveland Board of Education v. Loudermill, 470 U.S. 532 (1985). The legislature is free to adopt a civil service system—that is, a regime giving governmental employees statutory entitlement to their jobs during good and efficient behavior—or not; but once it chooses to create this sort of relationship between the government and its employees, the courts will have the final word concerning the adequacy of any disciplinary procedures chosen.

20. A. Bickel, The Least Dangerous Branch (Bobbs Merrill 1962); J. Ely, Democracy and Distrust, A Theory of Judicial Review (Harvard University 1980).

21. J. Ely, id.; P. Brest, The Misconceived Quest for the Original Understanding, 60 B.U. L. Rev. 204 (1980).

22. In Roe v. Wade, 410 U.S. 113 (1973), the most prominent such case, the Court held that, because a woman's right to decide whether or not to end a pregnancy is fundamental, only a compelling interest can justify state regulators impinging in any way upon that right. Compare p. 40 below. No constitutional text directly addresses abortion (or like is-

for their failure to be grounded in text. The interpretivists, in turn, must struggle with making even a generally worded political text—as the Constitution is—relevant to today's vastly changed and uncontemplated circumstances.[23]

For anyone contemplating the possible application of the American Constitution to an issue of interest, the important point to recognize is that, while one begins with the text, the jurisprudence must also be consulted—and lively and current disputes persist respecting the limits and techniques appropriate to that jurisprudence. Whether the text constitutes a limit for the Court, and how textual meaning is to be derived (by reference to history? to governmental structure? to contemporary possibilities of meaning? to analogies between past and present problems?), remain surprisingly lively issues.[24] One might say

---

sues), and abortion had been regulated in varying ways for most of the nation's history. The years following this opinion have been marked by political struggles over its legitimacy of an intensity not seen since the Court's decision in Brown v. Board of Education, 347 U.S. 483 (1954), promised the end of de jure racial segregation in the American South. In Planned Parenthood of Southeastern Pennsylvania v. Casey, 505 U.S. 833 (1992), the Court narrowly rejected an argument, supported by then-President Bush's administration, to overrule *Roe*. Three of the five Justices constituting the majority—each appointed by anti-abortion Presidents after the *Roe* decision—indicated that whether or not they would have joined that opinion as an initial matter they accepted it in light of "the obligation to follow precedent" and the absence of "the most convincing justification under accepted standards of precedent...to demonstrate that a later decision overruling the first was anything but a surrender to political pressure, and an unjustified repudiation of the principle on which the Court staked its authority in the first instance." Id. at 867. Compare n. 16 above.

23. See B. Ackerman, We The People (Belknap Press 1991). The problem was restated by Justice White of the Supreme Court, in an opinion for the Court refusing to extend reasoning like that in Roe v. Wade, note 22 above, to forbid state criminalization of homosexual acts between consenting adults: "The Court is most vulnerable and comes nearest to illegitimacy when it deals with judge-made Constitutional Law having little or no cognizable roots in the language or design of the Constitution." Bowers v. Hardwick, 478 U.S. 186, 194 (1986). In a less emotionally freighted situation, concerning congressional authority to empower special judges in bankruptcy proceedings, Justice White had written in support of the constitutionality of legislation six colleagues found insupportable on the Constitution's text "Whether fortunate or unfortunate, at this point in the history of constitutional law that question [of constitutionality] can no longer be answered by looking only to the constitutional text." Northern Pipeline Construction Co. v. Marathon Pipe Line Co., 458 U.S. 50, 94 (1982).

24. L. Tribe, American Constitutional Law (3d ed. Foundation Press 1999) is a respected treatise exploring these issues, as do law school teaching materials in American Constitutional Law. M. Tushnet, Constitutional Law (Dartmouth 1992) collects a series of influential essays; and see M. Tushnet, Taking the Constitution Away From the Courts (Princeton University 1999).

that the written character of the Constitution, at least for judges, has been placed in significant doubt.

C. *The separation of powers*

A glance at the organization and provisions of the American Constitution will confirm that the idea of separation of powers is central. Article I addresses only legislative authority, and places it in Congress, a two-house legislature of defined authority. Article II places a largely undefined executive power in a unitary executive, an elected President. Article III locates the judicial power in the Supreme Court, the state courts, and any lower federal courts Congress may choose to create. Article IV then touches in a variety of ways the other great separation of power already mentioned—that between the national government and the states. Although unifying principles are occasionally suggested,[25] a brief theoretical exegesis is not readily to be made.[26] One may say, perhaps, that the central issue is the continued vitality of the three principal institutions of American government as effectively competing nodes of differentiated power, each in relationship with the enormously variegated mass of American government. "Separation of powers" is invoked when the analyst (generally a court) is persuaded that an event or institution threatens that vitality—that is to say, threatens the exclusion of one of those institutions from its central role. Of course such judgments would be difficult in any circum-

---

25. See, for example, Public Citizen v. Department of Justice, 491 U.S. 440 (1989), where a concurring Justice (Kennedy) suggests that the key lies in whether the Constitution's text makes an explicit commitment to one or another branch (textually rigorous approach) or does not do so (balancing approach). Of course one must decide what is an explicit commitment, and very often the results could be very embarrassing to widely established arrangements, as in the appointments clause example discussed in the text at p. 24 below.

26. A fine recent analysis, illustrating the intellectual difficulties, appears in E. Magill, The Real Separation in Separation of Powers Law, 86 Va. L. Rev. 1127 (2000). H. Bruff and P. Shane, Separation of Powers Law: Cases and Materials (Carolina Academic Press 1996) collects a wide range of materials. Other important law review treatments include P. Strauss, The Place of Agencies in Government: Separation of Powers and the Fourth Branch, 84 Colum. L. Rev. 573 (1984); C. Sunstein and L. Lessig, The President and the Administration, 94 Colum. L. Rev. 1 (1994); S. Calebresi and S. Prakash, The President's Power to Execute the Laws, 104 Yale L. J. 541 (1994); G. Lawson, The Rise and Rise of the Administrative State, 107 Harv. L. Rev. 1231 (1994); and Elena Kagan, Presidential Administration, 114 Harv. L. Rev. 2246 (2001).

stances, and the uncertainty surrounding the President's authority and role in government only complicates analysis where his role is concerned.[27]

In the Federalist Papers,[28] James Madison famously explained the constitutional scheme in words that remain influential to this day:

> Ambition must be made to counteract ambition....It may be a reflection on human nature, that such devices should be necessary to control the abuses of government. But what is government itself, but the greatest of all reflections on human nature? If men were angels, no government would be necessary. If angels were to govern men, neither external nor internal controls on government would be necessary. In framing a government to be administered by men over men, the great difficulty lies in this: you must first enable the government to control the governed; and in the next place oblige it to control itself. A dependence on the people is, no doubt, the primary control on the government; but experience has taught mankind the necessity of auxiliary precautions.[29]

"Separation of powers" may also be understood, not simply as a political theory for controlling—some would say handcuffing—government against a feared tendency to excessive power, but also as a principle of fairness in individual dealings with citizens.[30] Here, one invokes the idea that the one who makes or implements a rule ought not be the same as the one who judges its

---

27. In the states, it may be briefly said, the same theories and a similar potpourri of institutions may be found. Again, it is not thought unusual or improper for state agencies to exercise, in a subordinate way, all of the distinctive functions of government. In many if not all states, however, the idea of a unitary executive is not established. In addition to their chief executive official, the Governor, state constitutions and statutes often provide for the election of competing or specialized executive figures, officers who then have an entirely independent political authority. Common examples include the Attorney General, responsible for law enforcement in the strong sense; a chief financial officer, responsible for the regularity of official expenditures; even the membership of a public utility commission or local school board. Note that with Federalism comes diversity: some state structures provide for very strong governors, others for very weak ones.

28. The Federalist Papers are a series of articles published by Alexander Hamilton, James Madison, and John Jay following the drafting of the Constitution, in the hopes of persuading Americans to ratify it. Madison, in particular, was a central figure in the drafting, and kept extensive notes, later published, which are the major source of information about the drafters' deliberations. The Federalist Papers are generally accepted as a principal source for understanding how the Constitution was initially understood.

29. The Federalist No. 51; see also No. 47.

30. See R. Brown, n. 4 above, for a particularly eloquent statement of this view.

fair application to particular circumstances. This idea perhaps concerns the separation of the judicial power from the executive-legislative, more than executive and legislative from each other (and the judicial). This notion is rather similar to the fundamental principle of "natural justice" under British common law, that no one ought to be a judge on her own cause.[31]

As important as the idea of separation, and also serving the function of limited government, is the notion of checks and balances. Legislative power is divided between two houses in substantial part because that power was the most feared, and it was thought their jealousies would cause them to check one another. The President is able (within limits) to veto legislation; legislative bodies must approve appointments and can control executive behavior through denial of funds or impeachment; and so forth. By creating rivalries and jealousies, empowering each branch to place obstacles in the way of the others' full exercise of their powers, the draftsmen believed they lessened still further the chance that government would pass beyond the people's control.

At the top level of government,—where it might be concluded that the formal authority of one of the three designated principal actors in American government (Congress, President, Court) has been threatened, insufficiently respected, or arguably displaced—these ideas have considerable bite. Thus, although Congress can give the heads of important government agencies fixed terms of office that put them somewhat beyond the President's disciplinary reach,[32] it could not create a regulatory commission to which it rather than the President would make certain appointments,[33] or confer important authority on an officer over whom it rather than the President enjoyed the prerogative of dismissal "for cause."[34] The Supreme Court found these arrangements unconstitutional. Similarly, although Congress has long empowered agencies—both independent and executive—to decide matters that would otherwise be assigned to the courts, subject only to limited judicial review,[35] it could not embracively assign judicial roles and judicial powers to bankruptcy

---

31. "Natural justice" appears to have its genesis more in concerns with personal, financial interests than in ideas about the proper dispersion of political power.

32. Humphrey's Executor v. United States, 295 U.S. 602 (1935); P. Strauss, The Place of Agencies in Government: Separation of Powers and the Fourth Branch, 84 Colum. L. Rev. 573 (1984).

33. Buckley v. Valeo, 424 U.S. 1 (1976).

34. Bowsher v. Synar, 478 U.S. 714 (1986).

35. Crowell v. Benson, 285 U.S. 22 (1932); Commodity Futures Trading Commission v. Schor, 478 U.S. 833 (1986).

officials (albeit subject to similar forms of review).[36] Although Congress and the President each employ a variety of political weapons to oversee agencies in the making of rules (subordinate legislation),[37] Congress could not lawfully require agencies to lay those actions before Congress for a possible formal disapproval in which the President would not participate.[38] Similarly, whatever arrangements the Congress and President might agree upon to permit him some discretion in implementing budgetary decisions, Congress could not empower him to deprive particular elements of the budgets it enacted of statutory force.[39] These decisions and others,[40] all reached in the last quarter century, suggest a continued vitality for separation of powers ideas.

Much specific discussion about both separation of powers and "checks and balances" appears in Chapter 3. More detailed attention to Congress, the President, the Courts, and the various actors who operate under their supervision will help to appreciate their operation. In the paragraphs immediately following, the focus is more on the spaciousness of the constitutional text, and examples of the challenges consequently presented for its interpretation. Partly these examples result from the indeterminacy of the constitutional text; partly, from the distance that has grown up between political theories that may have appealed to the authors of the Constitution and practices developed over the course of the following two centuries.

1. The agencies Congress has created are not ones of separated powers

While the Constitution defines and locates the three characteristic powers of government, it is striking to note that it does not define the government itself. That is to say, it does not define the bureaucracy, the specialist institutions that carry out the specific tasks of public affairs. The first three articles confer the "legislative," the "executive," and the "judicial" powers upon *generalist* institutions lacking detailed responsibility for particular affairs, that might

---

36. Northern Pipeline Construction Co. v. Marathon Pipe Line Co., 458 U.S. 50 (1982).

37. Sierra Club v. Costle, 657 F.2d 298 (D.C. Cir.1981).

38. Immigration & Naturalization Service v. Chadha, 462 U.S. 919 (1983).

39. Clinton v. City of New York, 524 U.S. 417 (1998).

40. Freytag v. Commissioner of Internal Revenue, 501 U.S. 868 (1991), discussed in the immediately following subsection; Metropolitan Washington Airports Authority v. Citizens for the Abatement of Airport Noise, 501 U.S. 252 (1991); Plaut v. Spendthrift Farm, 514 U.S. 211 (1995).

be imagined to sit at the head of the larger body of government itself. Although one can read between the lines a certain anticipation about the arrangements that would be made, the fact is that very little at all is said about the elements that would make up that larger body. The drafters agreed on a single head of the executive branch, reaching the judgment that unified political responsibility was essential. They did not agree, however, on a form of government beneath him.[41]

Rejecting a plan that would have specified the cabinet departments in constitutional text, the drafters of the Constitution instead left that to congressional definition. They gave Congress authority to define the elements of government by enacting any law "necessary and proper" to carry out its general responsibilities for legislation.[42] From the outset (and as almost certainly anticipated) Congress has in fact created units of government that are distinct from the President and his personal office. It has vested responsibility for day to day administration of the nation's laws in these governmental units rather than in him. And the Constitution is almost devoid of detailed specification of the relationship these elements are to have with the President or Court.[43]

---

41. There is vigorous debate in American academic circles about just how this history should be understood. Compare, e.g., L. Lessig & C. Sunstein, The President and the Administration, 94 Colum. L. Rev. 1 (1994) with S. Calabresi and S. Prakash, The President's Power to Execute the Laws, 104 Yale L. J. 541 (1994). The author's position, reflected in the text, was most fully developed in P. Strauss, The Place of Agencies in Government: Separation of Powers and the Fourth branch, 84 Colum. L. Rev. 573 (1984).

42. Art. I, Sec. 8, cl. 18. What the clause says, precisely, is that Congress has authority under the Constitution "to make all laws which shall be necessary and proper for carrying into Execution the foregoing Powers, and all other Powers vested *by this Constitution* in the Government of the United States, or in any Department or Officer thereof." (Emphasis added.) This wording appears to be a residue of the earlier stage in drafting, when the constitutional text would have specified a number of Executive departments vested with particular responsibilities. When those specifications disappeared in the final days of drafting, the reference to "powers vested *by this Constitution*" in the government, in a department, or in a officer (other than the President) became, in literal terms, fruitless. In practice, the solipsism is not noticed, and the clause is understood to empower Congress to create the government, and to assign duties to departments and officers; preferring a flexible legislative response to the needs of the moment over a constitutional definition of the government was certainly one purpose of the drafting change that eliminated the specifications.

43. See the discussions of the presidency and the courts in Chapter III, below. Aside from its general provision that a single, elected President is to wield the executive power, the Constitution says only (as to domestic matters) that the President or persons he selects will have responsibility for staffing government departments at the upper levels, and that he can call upon the heads of these bodies for advice. No part of the article conferring "the

The principal constraints on Congress's judgment about what sorts of institutions are proper to create for the varied work of government may be those suggested by the separation of powers idea itself. Each of these generalist institutions—Congress, President, and Court—enjoys an uneasy relationship with the other two and a relationship with the operating bureaucracy that is given character by its own unique function. Very crudely, the Congress passes the statutes that establish the individual elements of the bureaucracy and empower them to act; the President oversees and guides their performance of function under those laws, as a policy or political matter; and the courts assure their adherence to legality.

Within any given element of the bureaucracy Congress has created, however, one most often finds the separation idea imperfectly implemented at best. Congress regularly empowers a single agency, say the Department of Agriculture, to perform all the characteristic functions of government. That Department may first adopt a regulation (subordinate legislation) setting standards for the governance of private conduct; it may then investigate private conduct to ascertain probable violations of the rule and initiate proceedings before one of its judicial officers; and finally it may determine, as if judicially, whether the alleged violation has in fact occurred.[44] Neither the constitutional provisions for separation of powers nor constitutional requirements of fair procedure are thought to forbid this common legislative choice. The agency's subordination, its specialization and embeddedness within government and law, it has been persuasively argued, is the talisman that explains how one government agency may perform, within its field of specification, functions that are kept carefully separated at the highest political level of government.[45] Much of American administrative law is designed to overcome the functional and constitutional problems created by this imperfect separation—for example, through statutory arrangements for a fairly rigorous separation of judicial from political function, for all but the political heads of agencies.

---

judicial power" on the Supreme Court discusses, specifically, its authority over the acts of government agencies or over the validity of congressional legislation, although the Court has asserted from the beginning that the article confers on it the power to enforce legality on the remainder of government, including specifically the power to find congressional acts inconsistent with the Constitution. H. Monaghan, *Marbury v. Madison* and the Administrative State, 83 Colum. L. Rev. 1 (1983) is a useful discussion of the latter aspect.

44. Withrow v. Larkin, 421 U.S. 35 (1975). Note, however, that, outside the special context of military justice, imprisonment for crime may be sought only by the Department of Justice, and applied only by the courts.

45. T. Rakoff, The Shape of Law in the American Administrative State, 11 Tel Aviv U. Studies in Law 9 (1992).

Perhaps the most dramatic illustration, from a constitutional perspective, of both the adaptability of the formal "separation of powers" structure and the acceptance of a single agency's subordinate performance of all governmental functions lies in the "independent regulatory commissions." These commissions are governmental agencies headed by multi-member boards acting collegially on the regulatory matters within their jurisdiction.[46] Unlike cabinet secretaries and other heads of "executive" agencies, who serve at the President's pleasure, commissioners are appointed for fixed terms from which they cannot be dismissed without formal cause. Consequently, they are more remote from presidential influence and control than the more usual "executive" agency. Familiar examples would include the Securities and Exchange Commission, which regulates matters concerned with the sale of corporate stock; the Federal Communications Commission, which regulates broadcast and telecommunications activities; the Federal Reserve Board, which controls monetary policy; and the Federal Trade Commission, which regulates certain aspects of business conduct.[47] On any given day, the Commissioners of a given agency may perform all the distinctive functions of government—adopting rules (subordinate legislation) on some matters within their charge, authorizing investigation of others, hearing argument in and deciding contested proceedings within the agency. These proceedings may even have begun with their ratification of staff recommendations for their initiation months earlier, and may often require interpretation of the agency's own rules.

It is hard to say as a theoretical matter why these arrangements satisfy the structural requirements implicit in the division of our government into three branches,[48] although it is clear beyond doubt that in the eyes of the

---

46. The independent commissions act on substantive matters by majority vote. While they are under the leadership of a chairman, his powers on matters of substance (as distinct from internal administration) are rarely different from their own; members terms are staggered for continuity, and a balance of political affiliation is required. The government servants working for these commissions fall within or without civil service laws in the same patterns as do other government employees, but in either case it is clear they take instructions from the commissioners and no one else.

47. Use of the independent regulatory commission device by Congress follows no set pattern: the independent Federal Communications Commission and Federal Energy Regulatory Commission are responsible for economic regulation in their respective fields, but so is the Department of Agriculture (an executive Department headed by a cabinet Secretary) for some purposes; both the (independent) National Labor Relations Board and the (executive) Department of Labor regulate aspects of labor relations; the Federal Trade Commission and the Department of Justice, aspects of antitrust policy; the Nuclear Regulatory Commission and the Environmental Protection Agency, licensing of environmentally hazardous activities.

48. See P. Strauss, The Place of Agencies in Government: Separation of Powers and the Fourth Branch, 84 Colum. L. Rev. 573 (1984).

courts they do. When the American Supreme Court has used "separation of powers" analysis to strike down congressional legislation establishing governmental arrangements, often on the ground that one of the branches has encroached on functions reserved to another,[49] it has uniformly insisted that the independent regulatory commissions are not challenged by its analysis.[50]

An example may make the difficulties clearer. A 1991 case, *Freytag v. Commissioner of Internal Revenue*,[51] challenged the power given the Chief Judge of the United States Tax Court, a special tribunal for hearing cases involving application of the tax laws, to appoint "special judges" for that court. The authority such judges would exercise, not wide-ranging or unusual but nonetheless "significant," made clear to the Court that they must be considered "Officers" of the United States in the constitutional sense. For this reason, the Court concluded, such judges must be appointed in the manner stated in the Constitution. Article II's appointments clause offers four possibilities: (1) the President must appoint all officers who are *not* "inferior," such as Heads of Departments, and do so with the Advice and Consent of the Senate; Congress may provide for the appointment of inferior officers (like the special judges), however, (2) by the President alone, (3) by the Head of a Department, or (4) by the courts. No other possibility is stated.

The Supreme Court majority confidently identified as the theory underlying these limitations a wish to secure political responsibility for the exercise of public power. "[T]he Framers [of the Constitution] recognized the dangers posed by an excessively diffuse appointment power and rejected efforts to expand that power. So do we."[52] A consequence of this reasoning, the majority concluded, was that the "Heads of Departments" Congress could authorize to appoint "inferior officers" were very few—just those persons who headed subdivisions of government actually called Departments, the constituent elements of the cabinet. Any other conclusion would threaten the diffusion of authority against which the Framers had set their course. Although the majority was able to evade the implications of this reasoning in the particular case before it, by finding the Tax Court to be a "court" for Appointment Clause pur-

---

49. See page 19 above.
50. Bowsher v. Synar, 478 U.S. 714 (1986); Commodity Futures Trading Commission v. Schor, 478 U.S. 833 (1986); P. Strauss, Formal and Functional Approaches to Separation of Powers Questions—A Foolish Inconsistency? 72 Cornell L. Rev. 488 (1987).
51. 501 U.S. 868 (1991).
52. Id. at 885 (citation omitted).

poses,[53] its reasoning suggests the difficulties that often arise when original theory and contemporary practice are compared. Independent commissions regularly appoint staff who wield much more authority than any special judge of the Tax Court—and thus are unquestionably "officers." Yet these appointments could not be presidential appointments without compromising their desired independence, and the independent commissions are certainly not cabinet departments. It would seem, then, that the Court's reasoning necessarily undercuts their ability to function. So also for both the numerous executive agencies that are not "Departments," such as the EPA, and the Senior Executive Service— a group composed of elite members of the permanent civil service who generally have responsibilities easily meeting the "Officer" test. Justice Scalia, advancing a different theory in a minority opinion, called pointed attention to this problem. The majority's only response was to say in a footnote, without more, that "We do not address here any question involving an appointment of an inferior officer by the head of one of the principal agencies, such as the Federal Trade Commission...."[54] Subsequent litigation has largely ignored this problem.

The passage just quoted is typically unclear about the Court's basis for confidence that its reasoning has not impugned the wide variety of institutions Congress has designed. One may suggest at least three bases. First, there is the very fact of the Constitution's unspecificity about the design of government, its reliance on Congress's judgment, at any point in time, about what is "necessary and proper" to achieve its legislative ends. Second, these are now well-established instruments of government, which could not be thrown over without enormous inconvenience. And most importantly, the Court could properly believe that these instruments do not much threaten the relative authority of Congress, President and Court. Ordinarily they have responsibilities for which, in any event, a certain distance from "political" control would generally be thought useful. Among the agencies listed in the footnote quoted at the end of the preceding paragraph, for example, were the Federal Reserve Board, responsible for money supply, and the Central Intelligence Agency, an executive agency that is not part of any cabinet department. Congress has tended to reflect this attitude about political controls in its own conduct toward these agencies. Beyond this, the arrangements made do not create an im-

---

53. As Justice Scalia's separate opinion pointed out, this conclusion was not without difficulty; for most purposes the Tax Court is regarded as a creation of Congress exercising its "necessary and proper" authority—what we denominate as an Article I court—and not one of the courts whose authority and terms of office are defined in the judiciary section of the Constitution, Article III.

54. Id. at 887.

balance among the three principals of American government. The President retains (as do the courts) substantial relationships with the independent commissions, even if not the full range of relationship he usually enjoys with executive departments. Nonetheless one must admit that these are largely functional arguments. The relatively formal textual argument about limitations on "Heads of Department" for appointments purposes, it must be conceded, is grounded in a political theory that probably well reflects the specific beliefs of those who wrote the Constitution. Should this formal argument prevail, then many arrangements Congress has repeatedly chosen for our government would prove very hard to defend.[55]

It is also possible to say, as a functional matter, that the combination in an "agency" of the three characteristic functions of government is not as threatening to the citizenry as that combination would be if located in the President, the Congress or the courts themselves. The element that neutralizes these apparent violations of "separation of power" principles (in American view) is the presence of external controls. The agencies act subject to the legislation enacted by Congress, to review of the lawfulness of their behavior by the courts, and to the appointment and (uncertainly defined) political authorities of the President. Thus they do not present the spectre of government out of control that would be raised if the President or Congress were to attempt all these activities. By these means, it has thus far been concluded, the general fairness of agency actions can be sufficiently assured.[56]

2. Although Congress is given "all legislative power," executive agencies (and the courts) are often authorized to adopt regulations that, if valid, have the force of statutes

The Constitution vests "all legislative Powers herein granted" in Congress, and addresses the legislative function at some length. It creates two Houses of Congress (Senate and House of Representatives) and provides for their constituencies, their election cycles, the manner in which legislation is to be en-

---

55. See P. Strauss Formal and Functional Approaches to Separation of Powers Questions—A Foolish Inconsistency? 72 Cornell L. Rev. 488 (1987) and E. Magill, n. 26 above.

56. See T. Rakoff, n. 45 above. On the issue of individual fairness in having the same body that has adopted a rule and sought its enforcement decide its application in a particular case, see Withrow v. Larkin, 421 U.S. 35 (1975).

acted (including its presentment to the President for possible veto) and the subjects on which legislation is proper.[57] Specific provision is made for a limited number of other congressional functions—impeachment of executive or judicial officials for "high crimes or misdemeanors," responsibility to appropriate funds for governmental expenditures, and senatorial participation in the approval of certain presidential appointments and treaties. Nothing is said about committees, hearings, or oversight of the actions of other parts of government. The dominant concern is with the process for creating legislation, evidently viewed as both paramount and unique.

As we will see at some length in the next chapter, however, Congress's contemporary functioning is rather different from the picture this might suggest. The members of Congress and their staff spend the bulk of their time on matters *other* than the enactment of legislation. Congress early found it necessary to create a system of legislative committees to respond to the demands of a system that separates the legislature from the executive, and even requires legislature and executive to compete with one another. These bodies exercise significant investigative functions. In addition to substantial investigations associated with the annual appropriations process, congressional committees conduct detailed oversight hearings of executive branch functioning and general investigations of perceived social ills or scandals. Conducting the investigations, in turn, has prompted significant growth in congressional staff attached to the committees.[58] This growth, in turn has fueled investigations: committee staffs, once assembled, have a continuing need for satisfying work and visibility in the political atmosphere of Washington. Since hearings provide a means for expressing opposition and applying pressure as well as re-

---

57. Section 8 of Article I of the Constitution enumerates Congress's power to legislate and holds that Congress may "make all laws which shall be necessary and proper for carrying into execution the foregoing powers." Section 9 then states specific limits on these powers. Two, in particular, emphasize the general and prospective character of legislation, as compared to adjudication. Congress may not pass bills of attainder, laws which in effect convict specific persons of crime for acts already committed. Similarly, it may not enact ex post facto laws, by which acts are made criminal after their occurrence.

58. A contemporary sense of Congress's activities can be gained from an important Congress-watcher's resource, the Congressional Quarterly, http://www.cq.com. CQ's Electronic Encyclopedia of American Government remarks under "Staff-Congress" that "In 1947 there were fewer than 500 aides on House and Senate committees, and there were about 2,000 House and Senate personal aides. By 1997 there were about 2,500 aides on House and Senate committees [a number somewhat reduced from what it had been in 1990] and 11,700 House and Senate personal aides. Several thousand more worked in administrative and leadership offices."

vealing scandal, these functions have been particularly prominent in those years—*most* years in the past half century—in which the White House and the Congress were controlled by different parties.

Another important part of the work of individual members of Congress is casework, assistance to particular constituents who become embroiled with one or another part of the federal establishment. In the eyes of many contemporary political scientists, casework is the basis on which a member's reelection is most likely to be won or lost.[59] As an activity, it too requires and is demanded by enlarged staffing (now, in the personal office of the member). Casework sometimes appears to have an uncomfortable relationship to the member's need to raise funds for reelection campaigns, and more than one recent scandal has resulted from such coincidences; yet it is often more time-consuming than sinister, and rather like the function of ombudsmen in other systems. The member's staff may do little more than point the constituent in the right direction, or ensure that a matter is reviewed by agency officials. The American Congress, then, has many distractions from its constitutionally defined function of considering and enacting legislation.

Legislation conferring on other government bodies the authority to adopt regulations having, if valid, the force of statutes was enacted by the very first Congress. The Judiciary Act of 1789 empowered the federal judiciary to adopt regulations to govern judicial procedures. The practice was challenged, on the ground that only Congress possessed legislative authority under the Constitution, and that Congress could not lawfully delegate this authority to other governmental bodies. The challenge failed.[60] Subsequent Congresses authorized the President and executive agencies, similarly, to adopt measures that Congress might have enacted by statute; challenges to these measures failed as well. Thus, early in the twentieth century, a farmer challenged his conviction for having violated a regulation the Secretary of Agriculture had adopted to control the grazing of sheep on national forest lands. A statute authorized the Secretary to "make such rules and regulations and establish such service as will insure the objects of [reserving lands for national forest,] namely, to regulate their occupancy and use, and to preserve the forests thereon from destruction." The statute made violation of any regulation adopted under this authority punish-

---

59. See e.g., J. Mashaw, Greed, Chaos and Governance: Using Public Choice to Improve Public Law (Yale 1997); D. Farber and P. Frickey, Law and Public Choice: A Critical Introduction, p. 17 ff. (University of Chicago Press 1991). J. Aberbach, Keeping a Watchful Eye: The Politics of Congressional Oversight (Brookings 1990); R. D. Arnold, Congress and the Bureaucracy: A Theory of Influence (1979).

60. Wayman v. Southard, 23 U.S. (10 Wheat.) 1, 15–16 (1825).

able by a sizeable fine or up to a year in jail. A unanimous Court thought this grant of authority unremarkable, just a "power to fill up the details."[61]

With the growth in government's ambition, and in the complexity of the modern conditions it seeks to address, authority to adopt regulations is invariably conferred on important government agencies, and often exercised. Indeed, such regulations—not congressional statutes—constitute by far the greater proportion of statute-like texts governing private behavior today. At this writing, the annual compendium of legally binding rules published by the federal government occupies about 10 times as much shelf space in the law library as does the compendium of federal statutes.

Of course, regulations are not statutes—agencies must enjoy statutory as well as constitutional authority to adopt them. As later chapters will develop, agencies do so by using congressionally specified procedures that are quite different from those Congress uses;[62] and courts review their validity much more intensively than they do statutes.[63] Nonetheless, the practice is often to characterize these authorizations as delegations of "legislative power,"[64] and challenges continue to be made to their constitutional legitimacy.

As a matter of political theory, one can identify at least two strands of concern about delegation. One is identified with the writings of John Locke, an English political theorist influential on American views at the time our Constitution was written. The argument is that the legislative power is itself the product of a delegation—a delegation from the people—and that the only power the people have delegated to the legislature is that of making laws. Congress was delegated no power to create law*makers,* and exceeds its delegated authority if it tries to do so. It is obliged to act transitively, fixing outcomes, rather than intransitively, empowering other actors. The second strand acknowledges that Congress may empower others to adopt binding directives, but insists that it may do so only under standards that permit the

---

61. United States v. Grimaud, 220 U.S. 506 (1911).

62. Chapter V(C) within.

63. Chapter VIII within.

64. Often, but not invariably. In the most recent Supreme Court case on the subject, Whitman v. American Trucking Assn, 531 U.S. 457 (2001), only two of the Justices unanimously supporting the legislation challenged in that case would have characterized it as authorizing an agency to use "legislative power." They criticized their colleagues for "pretend[ing]" that the authority to make regulations was a different kind of power. On the corresponding problem concerning the delegation of *judicial* power, when bodies that are not courts are authorized to conduct what seem to be, and might have been provided to be, adjudications, see Chapter III(A)(3), within.

maintenance of legality. The powers Congress grants, that is, must be sufficiently limited that a court can say whether or not they have been properly exercised.

Taken in the abstract, the first of these propositions imposes unsustainable requirements; given the limitations of language, of human foresight, and of the time available for the task, no single institution could be expected to provide in detail for all the matters warranting "legislative" attention in a complex society. It is perhaps for this reason that, although the first strand has been referred to occasionally, and often animates the critical literature,[65] it has not been acted upon in American constitutional history. "To burden Congress with all federal rulemaking would divert that branch from more pressing issues, and defeat the Framers' design of a workable National Government. Thomas Jefferson observed, 'Nothing is so embarrassing nor so mischievous in a great assembly as the details of execution.'"[66] When President Truman used an executive order during the Korean War to seize steel mills threatened by a strike that might have disrupted war material production, Justice Hugo Black of the Supreme Court chastised him: "In the framework of our Constitution, the President's power to see that the laws are faithfully executed refutes the idea that he is to be a lawmaker."[67] In this case, however, the President had purported to act on his *own* authority, without statutory authorization and indeed arguably contrary to statutory frameworks Congress had created. Where Congress *has* conferred the authority to adopt regulations, this formula has not been used.[68] Is there, perhaps, a particular reason for concern about delegations to the President himself, given his independent constitutional authority and power? Presidential action in fact figured in the only two cases in which the Supreme Court has ever found congressional authorizations to be

---

65. See D. Schoenbrod, Power Without Responsibility (1993), a highly critical text that clothes Locke's arguments in the more contemporary terms of "public choice" analysis; Symposium, The Phoenix Rises Again: The Nondelegation Doctrine from Constitutional and Policy Perspective, 20 Cardozo L. Rev. 731 (1999); a range of excerpts from the delegation literature appears at P. Strauss, T. Rakoff, R. Schotland, and C. Farina, Gellhorn & Byse's Administrative Law: Cases and Comments 94–102 (9th ed. 1995) [Cited hereafter as "Administrative Law: Cases and Comments"].

66. Loving v. United States, 517 U.S. 748, 758 (1996).

67. Youngstown Sheet and Tube Co. v. Sawyer, 343 U.S. 579, 587 (1952).

68. In Loving v. United States, n. 66 above, the President had prescribed by Executive Order what could appropriately be considered "aggravating factors" to support the death sentence in court martial proceedings. Given statutory authorization for him to do so, and the President's constitutional role as Commander in Chief of the military, the Court unanimously sustained the delegation.

unconstitutional delegations—both decided in the mid-1930s.[69] Yet when the Court very recently sought to explain those two decisions, it did not mention the special factor of presidential power: "In the history of the Court," it said, "we have found the requisite 'intelligible principle' lacking in only two statutes, one of which provided literally no guidance for the exercise of discretion, and the other of which conferred authority to regulate the entire economy on the basis of no more precise a standard than stimulating the economy by assuring 'fair competition.'"[70]

"Intelligible principle" sets the framework for the second strand of analysis, which could be described as a legality principle. The courts present as the decisive issue whether they are in a position to say definitively if an action is lawful or not—whether law acceptably constrains the actions of the government agency. It will be evident, however, that this is a diffuse standard, and administering it has proved difficult. The Court has asserted that "the degree of agency discretion that is acceptable varies according to the scope of the power constitutionally conferred. While Congress need not provide any direction [regarding a matter of detail,] it must provide substantial guidance on setting air standards that affect the entire national economy."[71] But how much guidance is enough to be "substantial"? "We have 'almost never felt qualified to second-guess Congress regarding the permissible degree of policy judgment that can be left to those executing or applying the law.'"[72] For "setting air standards that affect the entire national economy," it proved sufficient that Congress had instructed the administrator to "set air quality standards at the level that is 'requisite'—that is, not higher or lower than is necessary—to protect the public health with an adequate margin of safety," excluding, as such, the consideration of cost trade-offs in the national economy.[73]

Implicit in the cases approving delegations have been limitations restricting agency authority to a particular field of play (however indefinitely its authority

69. Panama Refining Co. v. Ryan, 293 U.S. 388 (1935); A.L.A. Schechter Poultry Corp. v. United States, 295 U.S. 495 (1935). The Court, around this time, also invalidated one statute for excessive delegation to parties outside government. Carter v. Carter Coal Co., 298 U.S. 238 (1936).

70. Whitman, n. 64 above, 531 US at 474, citing Panama Refining Co., n. 69 above (Presidential authority to control oil production) and Schechter, n. 69 above (Presidential authority, in effect, to reorganize the national economy in cooperation with business groups).

71. Id. at 475.

72. Id. at 474–475, quoting Mistretta v. United States, 488 U.S. 361, 416 (Scalia, J.) and 373 (majority) (1989).

73. Id. at 475–76.

within that field may be defined), and to a prescribed regularity of action—factors largely missing in the two cases where unconstitutional delegations were found. Thus, the statute that commands the Federal Communications Commission to allocate broadcast licenses in accordance with the "public interest," authorizing it to adopt rules that will express the standards by which those allocations will be made, gives instructions that are vague at best. Nonetheless, they designate a field of action circumscribed to the issuance of a certain type of license; the actor is not the President; the actions are taken publicly and according to prescribed law and procedures; and Congress, the Court and the President are each in a position to exercise their respective controls over the results. Legality is not threatened as it was when the President was authorized to act, without standards or an obligation of public disclosure of the measures he had adopted.

Indeed, one could think it less important whether judges are in fact well able to administer a legality test, than that subordinate rulemakers—agencies—are encouraged to frame their actions in legality's terms. Where agencies acknowledge the obligation to demonstrate the lawfulness of their conduct, and frame their arguments in those terms, courts operate vis á vis the Congress and/or the President in an ordinary, one may say cooperative, rather than constitutional, and possibly confrontational, mode. It would be confrontational repeatedly to tell Congress whether it had legislated with adequate precision. Courts can assess the legality of specific agency conduct through ordinary interpretation without raising such delicate issues. Of course, one must acknowledge, the ability to frame the issue as one of legality is in many respects the product of a certain attitude. There is no question but that, in adopting regulations, agencies have a very substantial discretion regarding what solutions they will take to the problems presented to them. The question is whether they will acknowledge that they must act within a framework of legality. In the usual case agencies facilitate and legitimate judicial review by acknowledging that they are obliged to demonstrate to the courts that they have legal authority for their actions, that they have followed required procedure, that they can justify the conclusions they have reached in terms of the information presented to them, and so forth. When the agencies thus bend their knee to the obligations of legality, permitting regularity to be assured, that in itself serves to answer the question of delegation.[74]

One of the most important cases in which the Supreme Court has articulated standards of review for agency regulations is illustrative.[75] A statute em-

---

74. See P. Strauss, Legislative Theory and the Rule of Law: Some Comments on Rubin, 89 Colum. L. Rev. 427 (1989).

75. Chevron U.S.A. Inc. v. Natural Resources Defense Council, Inc., 467 U.S. 837 (1984); the case is discussed more fully at p. 368 below.

powered the Environmental Protection Agency (EPA) to adopt regulations governing the emission of air-borne pollutants. The EPA adopted a regulation that, inter alia, permitted a large factory site to treat all of its emissions as if they emanated from a single source (a "bubble") rather than having to control its emissions smoke-stack by smoke-stack, as some argued must be done. The Court concluded that the statute empowering the agency to regulate was unclear whether agency use of this "bubble" concept had been authorized. The statute could be read in either way, and its history was inconclusive. Courts in some national systems might react to this conceded legislative failure by disapproving the agency's action—saying, for example, that the agency's authority was not sufficiently clear to uphold its action. Or it might be expected that the court would simply resolve the disputed question of statutory meaning, so that it could be known for the future whether the "bubble" approach was or was not to be used. The Supreme Court's reaction was different. It stressed the range of discretion agencies may be recognized to have, unanimously indicating that the power to give the statute meaning, within the limits its language fairly permitted, lay *in the agency,* subject only to the usual tests the courts employ in reviewing the reasonableness of agency exercise of discretion.[76] Implicit in this judgment was the proposition that if, at some future point, the agency changed to another reading of the statute that also met these tests, that reading too would have to be accepted so long as it was supported by the factual basis and explanations that would ordinarily be called for. One has, thus, not simply the adoption of rules pursuant to statute, but an unquestioned delegation to the agency of authority to determine, within bounds, the meaning of the statute itself.

Delegation problems are more likely to arise when agencies assert that courts *cannot* control their conduct, because legal standards are absent. Of course one knows that, even when the possibility of judicial review is acknowledged, the usual standards of review recognize a very substantial level of executive discretion, with which it would be improper for the judiciary to interfere. Still, in the usual run of cases, the agency acknowledges that its exercise of discretion may be reviewed for "abuse," and that it has the obligation to establish that such abuse has not occurred. But suppose an agency were to assert that the challenged behavior raised a political question that the courts were not competent to address, that it possessed a discretion beyond the possibility of judicial inquiry into its exercise, that there was no law to apply? One such case concerned a decision by the Secretary of the Department of the In-

---

76. See generally Chapter VIII, below.

terior, who has many regulatory responsibilities regarding Native Americans, in relation to certain proposed uses of one tribe's land.[77] From a certain perspective, this might seem to involve authority less troubling than the EPA's, since it involves the management of public lands. But the Secretary's posture towards the courts, at least initially, was confrontational. Rather than undertaking to demonstrate the legality of his conduct, he asserted that the matter was wholly for his discretion, not subject to judicial oversight. Faced with this argument, a federal court of appeal found as a consequence that an unlawful delegation had occurred. The holding was, in effect, that Congress could not authorize decisions of this character to be made free of the possibility of judicial review. Only when the Solicitor General of the United States[78] persuaded the Secretary to recant his position, and to acknowledge to the Supreme Court that standards did exist, against which the legality of his action might be assessed, was the lower court's finding vacated and the case remanded instead for "ordinary" review of the legality of the Secretary's action.

In general, then, American courts recognize that the legislative process is not well suited to generating the multiplicity of highly detailed and often technical standards that modern times require. Invocations of delegation concerns require special circumstances, and in most cases this seems likely to be a threat of agency lawlessness to which the courts could not well respond in the individual case. There may, however, be some settings in which a judicial concern with the adequacy of legislative effort will be the focus. The Constitution, responding to the particular importance of political responsibility for tax laws, requires that both taxes and appropriations measures originate in the more responsive House of Representatives. The Court verged on finding an unlawful delegation in a case challenging an agency's statutory authority to set an annual fee for its licensees, when it had exercised that power in a way that seemed to favor one constituency over another.[79] While setting the fee at a level that would cover the costs of the licensing regime would be acceptable, the choice the agency had made suggested a taxing power wielded on political principles.

Perhaps there is also a difference between having to decide in a particular case whether the legislature has acted with adequate precision, which Ameri-

---

77. South Dakota v. U.S. Department of the Interior, 69 F.3d 878 (8th Cir. 1995), vacated 519 U.S. 919 (1996).

78. The Solicitor General is the official in the United States Department of Justice principally responsible for the conduct of appellate litigation involving the interests of the United States, and exercises considerable authority over other Departments (and the independent regulatory commissions) in that context. See p. 145 within.

79. National Cable Television Ass'n, Inc. v. FCC, 415 U.S. 336 (1974).

can courts find an impractical and impolitic task, and assessing legislative techniques that may have the predictable general effect of encouraging statutory imprecision. This is a useful way to understand one of the more important modern separation of power cases, in which the Court disapproved a device, the "legislative veto," by which either house of Congress asserted the prerogative to disapprove executive actions by its act alone.[80] A Congress that could voice unreasoned disapprovals in this way might find it easier to do particular favors for supporters while avoiding clearly stated commitments to long-term policy—might prefer to have opportunities for unreasoned intervention in public affairs over generating public standards, might prefer oversight over statutes. The legislative veto is objectionable, that is, because it reduces Congress's incentive to legislate precisely; if Congress could without cost to itself adopt vague legislative formulas while reserving the authority to adopt an unexplained "No!", that would both obscure Congress's responsibility for the law and reduce the capacity of the courts to control agency action for legality.[81] Denied the legislative veto, Congress would have some incentive to be as precise as it can be in initially adopting legislation.

A recent statute, not yet tested in the courts, suggests similar difficulties.[82] It provides a summary procedure to enact statutes expressing legislative disapproval of adopted regulations. The disapproval, in itself, raises no problems, but the statute further provides that a disapproval, once enacted, deprives the agency of authority to adopt "similar" regulations without having received fresh statutory authorization. Yet the statute provides for no congressional definition in the resolution of disapproval of what might be "similar"; indeed, it

---

80. INS v. Chadha, p. 20, n. 38 above.

81. Consumer Energy Council of America v. FERC, 673 F.2d 425 (D.C. Cir. 1982), summarily aff'd sub nom Process Gas Consumers Group v. Consumer Energy Council of America, 463 U.S. 1216 (1983). If Congress could retain an unchecked political authority to approve or disapprove agency rulemaking, the court feared, the law-constrained character of rulemaking authority would be undermined.

82. 5 U.S.C. §§801(b) and 802(g). The statute is discussed in P. Strauss & D. Cohen, Congressional Review of Agency Regulations, 49 Admin. L. Rev. 95 (1997). Early in 2001, during the first weeks of President George Bush's administration, Congress for the first time used the statutory mechanism to disapprove a regulation—one that the Occupational Health and Safety Commission (OSHA) had adopted during the last months of President Clinton's administration to deal with the problem of repetitive stress injuries in the workplace ("ergonomics"). President Bush encouraged the disapproval, promising that a more reasonable, Republican ergonomics standard would soon be adopted under his administration; but as no fresh statutory authority has been created for OSHA, it seems possible that this problem will arise concretely should OSHA act to carry out this promise.

insists that courts ignore the political history of its actions under the statute when considering whether or not regulations are authorized by statute.

D. *Fundamental rights*

The principal occasions for invoking the American Constitution against administrative actions or the statutes empowering them arise when citizens claim violation of fundamental rights under either the Bill of Rights (the first ten amendments to the federal Constitution) or the Fourteenth Amendment. The Bill of Rights was adopted immediately following the adoption of the Constitution, in part to fulfill promises made to secure its ratification, and defines the fundamental freedoms of Americans from governmental action. Its amendments most often invoked in the administrative context are the First (freedom of speech), Fourth (freedom from unreasonable searches and seizures), and Fifth (privilege against required self-incrimination; protection of property from uncompensated "taking"; no one to be "deprived of life, liberty or property without due process of law").

In terms, the Bill of Rights applies only to the federal government. Federal constitutional protection of citizens rights against actions by the states has its source in the Fourteenth Amendment, ratified in 1868. This amendment extends to the states the obligation to afford "due process of law," and adds an additional obligation requiring the states to assure all the "equal protection of the laws." While born of the American Civil War struggles to end African-American slavery, this amendment has a much larger contemporary significance. "Due process of law" is only one of the series of rights the Bill of Rights explicitly protects against federal interference. Of that series, the Fourteenth Amendment's language mentions only "due process of law" as a right the federal government will protect against state interference. Yet judicial interpretation has obliterated, for our purposes, any difference between the two frameworks. The federal Constitution is now understood to reach each of the Bill of Rights guarantees commonly invoked in state administrative law contexts, without variation as to substantive content as between state and federal actors. (Similarly, the principle of equal protection, stated in terms only in the Fourteenth, has been imported by interpretation into the Fifth Amendment's due process language, so that the right of equal protection runs against federal as well as state agencies.[83])

---

83. Bolling v. Sharpe, 347 U.S. 497 (1954).

It will be apparent from the foregoing that the words "due process of law" have been made to do yeoman service in American constitutional tradition, carrying water between state and federal camps. While these words also entail a set of particular propositions about required procedures—a matter of evident importance to any discussion of administrative law, already briefly seen,[84] and taken up again in following pages[85]—it is worth a few preliminary words to explain this development. This may also help provide a general context for understanding important and continuing American disputes about constitutional interpretation.

The dominant constitutional controversy of the first third of this century also concerned these words—a controversy which still reverberates sharply. The question then was whether "due process of law" might have a substantive (legislative) as well as a procedural (administrative-judicial) reference. In effect the question was whether the clause permitted federal courts to say that certain sorts of legislation were forbidden to the states because they "deprived" citizens of protected liberties. The court developed a series of tests to assess whether legislation would be justified when its impact on liberties was adverse. The best-known, now notorious, example of this reasoning was *Lochner v. New York,*[86] a 1905 case in which New York legislation regulating the working hours of bakers was found to be unconstitutional because, the Justices concluded, the public benefit of the legislation was not rationally related to the adverse impact of depriving the bakers of their liberty to contract for employment under whatever terms they liked.

Such willingness to reexamine legislative judgments about the desirability of social or economic programs could be, and was, used by conservative judges to retard the emergence of social welfare legislation. After years of sharp criticism, this approach was repudiated as to "economic regulation" in the late 1930s.[87] For decades, state (or federal) legislative measures imposing regulatory constraints on economic activity for any public welfare purpose could

---

84. Above, p. 14.

85. Below, p. 48 ff.

86. 198 U.S. 45 (1905).

87. This repudiation is attributed both to the internal inconsistency of the substantive due process idea and to the perceived need for more creative government regulation in response to the Depression. The Court suggested that "neither property rights nor contract rights are absolute.... Equally fundamental with the private right is that of the public to regulate it in the common interest." Nebbia v. New York, 291 U.S. 502, 523 (1934). It also exhibited more deference for the legislatures' substantive policy choices, seeing economic regulation not so much as intrusions on human freedom as a reasonable way to combat the pressures of evil created by mental imperfections or unequal bargaining power. West Coast Hotel Co. v. Parrish, 300 U.S. 379 (1937).

hardly be questioned on this ground.[88] *Lochner* now stands as a metaphor for judges too willing to enforce their own subjective preferences in opposition to political developments in society, and those invoking it often intend to find means of controlling that subjectivity. Occasional very recent Supreme Court cases appearing, once again, to question the factual support for congressional judgments have drawn harsh critical fire.[89]

These concerns underlay the developments which served to associate the federal Bill of Rights with the Due Process Clause of the Fourteenth Amendment. In the period following the 1930s' repudiation of "substantive due process" in the economic regulation context, the Supreme Court often faced disputes about the meaning of the Fourteenth Amendment's guarantee of "due process of law" in the context of criminal trials. A vigorous battle arose in the late 1940s,[90] lasting until the mid-1960s, over the problem of "incorporation"—a battle precisely over styles of interpretation. One approach to resolution of these disputes, initially favored, was to ask which rights were "the very essence of a scheme of ordered liberty"[91] and thus might be applied against the states as well as the federal government—or, in another formulation, what governmental conduct was so outlandish that it "shocks the conscience" of the judge.[92]

The federal Bill of Rights contains a number of relatively detailed provisions on the subject of required procedure in criminal cases, and in such cases an attractive alternative to those concerned with the *Lochner* problem was to argue that just the same protections were available as against the states. Those arguing for incorporation, in the end largely successful,[93] saw it as a means for

---

88. See, in addition to the materials of the previous note, Ferguson v. Skrupa, 372 U.S. 726 (1963); Duke Power Co. v. Carolina Environmental Study Group, 438 U.S. 59 (1978); G. Gunther, Foreword: In Search of an Evolving Doctrine on a Changing Court: A Model for a Newer Equal Protection, 86 Harv. L. Rev. 1 (1972).

89. E.g., United States v Lopez., 514 U.S. 549 (1995) (gun control); United States v. Morrison, 529 U.S. 598 (2000) (violence against women). See W. Buzbee and R. Schapiro, Legislative Record Review, 54 Stan. L. Rev. 87 (2001); L. Kramer, Foreword: We the Court, 115 Harv. L. Rev. 4 (2001).

90. Adamson v. California, 332 U.S. 46 (1947).

91. Palko v. Connecticut, 302 U.S. 319, 325 (1937).

92. Rochin v. California, 342 U.S. 165, 172 (1952).

93. For a decade and a half after Adamson, n. 90 above, the Court adhered to the "fundamental fairness" approach, reading into the Fourteenth Amendment only what that standard was said to require. The Court rejected the argument that the whole Bill of Rights had been incorporated. During the 1960s, however, while never explicitly abandoning this analysis, it began to incorporate more and more individual rights under the rubric of due process. At this point, most of the guarantees of the Bill of Rights have been held to apply to the states equally as to the federal government. What searches are unreasonable, that is,

containing judicial subjectivity. They believed that the provisions of the Bill of Rights that were to be incorporated had quite definite content, as they were already the subjects of a substantial jurisprudence about their meaning in application to the federal government. The opponents of incorporation were Justices who thought the Fourteenth Amendment's guarantee of "due process" in criminal trials did not entail a list of specific procedures mirroring the Bill of Rights, but only an assurance of those liberties "indispensable to the dignity and happiness of a free man"[94]—a catalog to be identified by reference to the Justices' own informed sense of what constituted the needs of civilization. Proincorporationists found this as objectionable as the subjectivity that had underlain the "substantive due process" imbroglio. Importing the provisions of the Bill of Rights, and only those provisions, appeared to offer sufficient certainty of outcome, a freedom from judicial fiat.

This protection, to be sure, was only relative—and also came at a certain possible cost. Whether the Sixth Amendment's guarantee of the assistance of counsel in criminal cases, for example, required the federal government or the states to provide defense counsel for persons too poor to afford their own receives no definitive answer in the text, and was finally resolved by the Court only during this period.[95] Moreover, having a single uniform standard for federal and state action put considerable pressure on judgments just what that standard would be. While incorporation tended to assure the states that the standards to which their criminal justice systems would be subjected were the same as those applicable to the federal government, the alternative almost invariably permitted more state choice. For state prosecutors, then, uniformity was not an assurance they especially wanted. On the federal side, on the other hand, incorporation was seen to create a kind of pressure to weaken federal protections, since they would now be so much more widely applied. One could believe, for example, that Supreme Court decisions permitting nonunanimous jury verdicts or juries smaller than twelve in criminal trials were driven by appreciation of the needs of the states, and would not have been reached had the only issue concerned federal jury trials.

In fact, "substantive due process" has remained vital in a number of respects. First, there is the question why, if state legislative judgments about reg-

---

does not vary whether federal or state officials are doing the searching. See, e.g., Duncan v. Louisiana, 391 U.S. 145 (1968). The limited exceptions to incorporation, such as the right of one accused of federal crime to be indicted only by a grand jury, do not have wide significance.

94. Adamson, n. 88 above, (Frankfurter, J., concurring).

95. Gideon v. Wainwright, 372 U.S. 335 (1963).

ulatory issues must be respected when they conflict with arguable economic rights (the right to contract, for example), those judgments aren't equally to be respected when they collide with individual liberties of another description (the right to equal protection of the laws, for example). In fact the courts will not accept a regulatory rationale for action that appears to effect racial discrimination unless an extremely strong showing of justification is made. The asserted legislative rationale thus receives "strict scrutiny" from the courts in such cases.[96] Second, the protection of non-economic individual liberties can be argued to involve judicial imposition of personal value judgments to defeat democratically representative legislative choices, in just the manner of the early "substantive due process" cases. A prominent example is the Supreme Court's decision sharply limiting, and in many respects prohibiting, state regulation of a woman's choice whether or not to have an abortion—an important focal point for the current arguments over interpretive style.[97] Indeed, the Supreme Court has self-consciously resumed references to "substantive due process," and even to the question of conduct that "shocks the conscience" as a catalyst for judicial intervention.[98] For our purposes, the important point to recognize is that efforts to use the Due Process clauses outside the procedural context will entail this history and its remnants of attitude and continuing controversy.

It may be appropriate here to give a few words to each of the most common issues of fundamental rights that arise in an administrative context. As might be imagined, debates over whether the rights are applicable most often involve tension among competing values each worthy of some recognition.

---

96. The Supreme Court reserved the possibility of making such a distinction in the famous "footnote four" of its decision in United States v. Carolene Products Co., 304 U.S. 144 (1938). Much ink has been spilled in the years following about the justification for the resulting double standard. See, e.g., J.H. Ely, Democracy and Distrust, A Theory of Judicial Review (1980); L. Lusky, Footnote Redux, A Carolene Products Reminiscence, 82 Colum. L. Rev. 1093 (1982); B. Ackerman, Beyond Carolene Products, 98 Harv. L. Rev. 713 (1985); P. Linzer, The Carolene Products Footnote and The Preferred Position of Individual Rights: Louis Lusky and John Hart Ely vs. Harlan Fiske Stone, 12 Const. Comm. 277 (1995).

97. Roe v. Wade, 410 U.S. 113 (1973); see text at n.22 above. On Roe, see J. Ely, The Wages of Crying Wolf: A Comment on Roe v. Wade, 82 Yale L. J. 920 (1973); M. Perry, Abortion, the Public Morals, and the Police Power: The Ethical Function of Substantive Due Process, 23 U.C.L.A. L. Rev. 689 (1976); R. Epstein, Substantive Due Process by Any Other Name: The Abortion Cases, 1973 Sup. Ct. Rev. 159.

98. For continuing debates about the proper dimensions and application of the "substantive due process" arguments this recognized, compare Washington v. Glucksberg, 521 U.S. 702 (1997), County of Sacramento v. Lewis, 523 U.S. 833 (1998), and Troxel v. Granville, 530 U.S. 57 (2000).

The effort of the following pages is to identify in a summary way those tensions and any characteristic analytic or didactic framework used to resolve them or express their resolution.

1. Speech/consumer protection

The First Amendment provides that "Congress shall make no law...abridging the Freedom of Speech." While it is generally accepted that the prohibition was intended primarily for the protection of political expression, the difficulty of distinguishing what may be political from what is not and the perceived general value in American society of free expression has produced much broader readings.[99] Judicial readings forbid, for example, censorship grounded in sexual offensiveness equally with censorship grounded in political repression. Courts have also limited the private use of the civil remedies of libel, slander, and invasion of privacy to protect personal reputation almost as sharply as they have limited the states' use of criminal libel laws to punish dissidents.[100] These readings restrain both prospective and reactive government response to speech activity, but especially the former. Censorship or other forms of "prior restraint" of speech not yet publicly uttered is precluded, whatever may be the provocation of past conduct. At one time the Supreme Court identified "commercial speech" (as at one time it identified pornography) as being outside the ambit of "speech" whose freedom from federal (and, later, state) interference was assured by the First Amendment.[101] In later years, the widespread use of advertisements for political purposes, the emergence of corporate participation in public affairs, and the realization that the business of successful book and newspaper publishers is readily described as "commercial speech" have undercut that simple analysis.[102]

Regulators often seek to control behavior that could easily be characterized as speech—for example, a merchant's (allegedly) fraudulent advertising or an employer's (allegedly) coercive speech to employees seeking to organize a labor union. The remedies regulators use may appear to regulate speech: denying

---

99. A good place to start on this, as on many such issues, is L. Tribe, American Constitutional Law (3d ed. Foundation Press 1999). See also D. Richards, A Theory of Free Speech, 34 U.C.L.A. L. Rev. 1837 (1987); V. Blasi, The Checking Value in First Amendment Theory, 1977 Am. B.F. Res. J. 521; T. Emerson, The System of Freedom of Expression (1970).

100. New York Times Co. v. Sullivan, 376 U.S. 254 (1964).

101. Valentine v. Christensen, 316 U.S. 52 (1942).

102. See, e.g., United States v. Playboy Entertainment Group, Inc., 529 U.S. 803 (2000); Central Hudson Gas & Elec. Corp. v. Public Service Comm'n, 447 U.S. 557 (1980).

an advertiser use of the mails, requiring it to publish a corrective announcement, or simply ordering it to refrain from like conduct in the future; directing an employer to issue a corrective notice, or to cease from addressing her
employees in a particular way. Often enough, the assertion that the adver-
tisement communicates important ideas is, from a common-sense perspective, farcical;[103] none doubt that consumer fraud and the suppression by economic coercion of worker organization are both forms of conduct government
may seek to suppress. Yet the strength of the impulse toward protection of
speech reflected in current First Amendment law, the presence (at least in contemplation) of genuine issues of characterization as between idea-communi-
cation and illegal conduct, and the current absence of a sharply defined analytic framework make these issues unexpectedly troublesome.[104]

2. Inspection/unreasonable search

The Fourth Amendment is concerned with securing "persons, houses, papers, and effects against unreasonable searches and seizures." A second clause
specifies certain procedures for the issuance of search warrants—official papers authorizing searches to be made, even in the face of physical resistance—
and states that no warrant shall issue except upon a showing of "probable
cause" to a judicial official, and that the warrant must "particularly" describe
the place to be searched and the material being sought. The amendment has
its historical origins in the behavior of British colonial governors and troops
during the pre-Revolutionary period, as they sought out political opponents
of the regime, tax resisters and the like. As may be imagined, the principal reference of this provision is criminal law enforcement, and a surprisingly large
proportion of the Supreme Court's jurisprudence has been consumed by such
issues as when a search may proceed in the absence of a warrant[105] and what

---

103. As when an advertiser preys on readers' insecurities, claiming that a zinc dietary
supplement has the potential to double the size of the male sexual organ.

104. R. Post, The Constitutional Status of Commercial Speech, 48 U.C.L.A. L. Rev. 1
(2000); compare Glickman v. Wileman Brothers & Elliott, Inc., 521 U.S. 457 (1997) (fruit
growers may be assessed and liable for a share of generic advertising costs as part of a comprehensive federal agricultural marketing scheme) with United States v. United Foods, 533
U.S. 405 (2001) (Congress cannot compel mushroom producer to support generic advertisements of mushrooms, in the absence of a general marketing program to which that support is ancillary).

105. Compare Minnesota v. Carter, 525 U.S. 83 (1998) with United States v. Karo, 468
U.S. 705 (1984). The presumption in favor of searches being done pursuant to warrants is
strong, but not irrebuttable. Terry v. Ohio, 392 U.S. 1 (1968). While the question when it

consequences the unlawfulness of a search has, once the trial is reached, for the admissibility of any evidence it uncovered.[106]

The Fourth Amendment's application to administrative matters has arisen in two related contexts—inspection by government officials of regulated premises; and formal agency requisitions from private persons, generally those regulated, of documentary materials thought relevant to some regulatory purpose. Both these activities are central to the success of regulatory activity; information is the life's blood of the regulatory process.

The suggestion that the Fourth Amendment might require a search warrant before, say, a city health inspector could demand entrance to a factory or home to search for evidence of rat infestation was initially rejected. Unlike the criminal searcher, the inspector was seeking improvements in community health, not convictions; if he had to show some particular reason for suspecting each house he wanted to inspect, his searches would be less effective than if he made them randomly through the community, or according to some general plan. In the late 1960s, however, the opposite view was taken,[107] and later reconfirmed.[108] The only exception is for industries so pervasively regulated—like stores selling firearms or nuclear power plants—that the state could demand unfettered inspection as a condition of its permission to be in the business at all.[109] Thus, for the last four decades, inspections have been re-

---

is practicable to obtain a warrant is often difficult, in general some substantial justification for not procuring one must be present, and the Court has a high opinion of the capacity of police officers to maintain premises in a searchable state while seeking a warrant. Thus, a search for weapons on the person of an arrested individual, in his room or in the passenger compartment of his car would be permitted, to avoid the threat of assault; but the opening of a locked car trunk or the general search of a house in which an arrest was made would not be. "Searches and seizures inside a home without a warrant are presumptively unreasonable absent exigent circumstances." Karo, 468 U.S. at 714–15.

106. Currently, such evidence must generally be excluded, as a practical means of discouraging the police from a species of unlawful conduct that has few if any other significant discouragements. For a number of years, however, the Court has been nibbling at the fringes of that rule—recognizing, for example, that the fruits of a search which proves to have been unlawful but which was made in a "good faith" belief in its lawfulness may be admitted. Arizona v. Evans, 514 U.S. 1 (1995).

107. Camara v. Municipal Court, 387 U.S. 523 (1967). See v. City of Seattle, 387 U.S. 541 (1967). These cases made no distinction between searches of factories and searches of homes.

108. Marshall v. Barlow's Inc., 436 U.S. 307 (1978).

109. Donovan v. Dewey, 452 U.S. 594 (1981). The idea that there are some businesses ("closely regulated") the pursuit of which the state may condition as it chooses, and others that (by implication) it may regulate only in limited ways—that it need not respect the

garded as "searches" for constitutional purposes; the Fourth Amendment commands not only that they be performed reasonably (say, during business hours) but also that the person being inspected may insist upon a warrant.

This rather neat analysis has given rise to both practical and theoretical difficulties. In practice, to be sure, most businesses subject to inspection appear not to insist upon warrants—doubtless to promote good will or to recognize that inspections are mutually beneficial in many cases, yet in response to effective coercion[110] in others. Yet other businesses do insist upon (and then resist) warrants; doing so can impose substantial costs and uncertainties upon regulators, and in this way may encourage regulators with limited resources to direct their efforts to more compliant subjects. The criminal connection and uncooperative attitude suggested by the Fourth Amendment may also have contributed, on both sides, to the confrontational (as distinct from cooperative) tone one scholar noted in comparing American to Swedish administration of workplace safety laws.[111]

The theoretical problem arises from the particularity of the Amendment's description of the warrant process, with its focus on suspicions already held and particular evidence of crime being sought. To make its conclusion about the applicability of the Fourth Amendment at all workable, the Supreme Court has had to redefine "probable cause" in the administrative context to include random or patterned inspections. The requirement that warrants "particularly" describe what is being searched for, too, has had to be ignored, save as the inspection must be for matters within the inspector's regulatory ken. One may see these distortions as a natural product of the effort to adapt language

---

Fourth Amendment's warrant requirement for one sort but must for the others—is only one of the many curious remnants of the "substantive due process" idea discussed above at p. 37 ff. A subsequent Supreme Court decision applying this reasoning to an automobile junk yard reflected a broad view of both what constitutes a "closely regulated" business and what is an "administrative" as distinct from a "police" search. New York v. Burger, 482 U.S. 691 (1987), disapproved on state law grounds, People v. Keta, 79 N.Y.2d 474 (1992).

110. If, for example, the business is awaiting some official action that will not be forthcoming absent the inspection. Wyman v. James, 400 U.S. 309 (1971). A court of appeals recently recognized the coercion instinct in such situations in rejecting an agency's program for exchanging freedom from searches for a more cooperative regulatory regime. See Chamber of Commerce of the United States v. US Department of Labor, 174 F3d 206 (D.C. Cir. 1999)

111. S. Kelman, Regulating America, Regulating Sweden: A Comparative Study of Occupational Safety and Health Regulations (MIT Press 1981). See also E. Bardach and R.A. Kagan, Going By The Book: The Problem of Regulatory Unreasonableness (Temple University Press, Philadelphia, 1982).

written two centuries ago, with particular problems in view, to the differing issues of the modern era.[112]

Formal demands for information present other issues. Even though such police tactics as forcible entry, and at unusual hours, are not involved in business inspections, it is not that hard to see the connection between the law-backed visit of an inspector to business premises, demanding that doors be opened for her, and the criminal process forcible "search and seizure" of effects to which the Fourth Amendment was primarily addressed. The connection between searches and seizures and a demand that citizens or other regulated entities provide specified information or documentation to the regulator is somewhat more remote.[113] Here, the only risk to privacy lies in the requested disclosure itself. While that risk may be substantial, it does not present issues of violence or of intrusion into living quarters by agents of the state.

Agencies commonly are granted the authority to demand information of persons subject to their jurisdiction, either generally (as in the requirements that citizens file tax returns and that regulated corporations produce financial reports) or in particular cases. In the former case, the instrument of production is characterized as a "required record or report," and the controls over its legitimacy are more statutory than constitutional.[114] Compliance with a "required report" may be directly enforced by the agency, prior to any judicial involvement.

---

112. In a very recent decision, the Supreme Court emphasized the necessity of such an effort in finding that the use of a thermal detector that could "see" unusual heat patterns in a building's walls, from a location well outside the perimeter of the private home being thus inspected, was a "search" in the Fourth Amendment's terms, and so could not be carried out without a warrant. Kyllo v. United States, 533 U.S. 27 (2001). Its opinion emphasized the special need for protecting private homes, in a way that possibly signals future revision of the developments discussed in text, which tend to deny differences between the home and more commercial settings.

113. The Court first applied the Fourth Amendment's instruction on searches and seizures to the required disclosure of documents in its somewhat mystical decision in Boyd v. United States, 116 U.S. 616 (1886), which merged Fourth and Fifth Amendment considerations in a manner later decisions have found difficult to explain. See United States v. Doe, 465 U.S. 605 (1984); McKennan, The Constitutional Protection of Private Papers: The Role of a Hierarchical Fourth Amendment, 53 Ind. L. J. 55 (1977).

114. See the discussion of the Paperwork Reduction Act at p. 265 below. The Fifth Amendment's privilege against self-incrimination, discussed in the following subsection, is available only to individuals, not corporations or other associations. Similarly, the Fourth Amendment's prohibition of unreasonable searches and seizures does little to prevent the government from requiring organizations to report information of arguable regulatory importance. United States v. Morton Salt Co., 338 U.S. 632 (1950).

Where information is particularly sought from one or a small number of individuals, on the other hand, the instrument of production (usually called a subpoena) is generally thought to require judicial participation in its enforcement. The courts reach this conclusion for constitutional reasons, by analogy to the Fourth Amendment's requirement for a magistrate's review of a proposed search warrant before it acquires legal force. While a subpoena does not grant permission for forcible entry to another's premises on any construction, its particularity and individuality (requiring a specific person to provide identified documentation) suggest a degree of exposure to adverse legal consequences warranting that protection. As with inspection warrants, the standards for issuance and enforcement of subpoenas are in fact highly permissive; yet the fact that they cannot acquire legal force before a judge has been persuaded that those standards have been met creates potentials for delay that are readily open to manipulation. The Supreme Court has occasionally seemed open to the possibility that the Fourth Amendment does not require prior judicial approval of agency subpoenas for them to be legally binding.[115] However, the focused nature of the subpoena inquiry and its corresponding potential for intrusion into personal privacy makes it likely that the Court will maintain the current position.

3. Information/incrimination

In addition to providing a judicial check on the reasonableness of administrative information demands, the Bill of Rights establishes a form of testimonial privilege that may occasionally be invoked to support a refusal to cooperate with such demands. The Fifth Amendment includes among its provisions an assurance that no "person" shall be required to incriminate himself. Thus, when a "person" can point to a crime and believably assert that his response to some demand for information might serve as a link in a chain of evidence tending to convict him of that crime, he will be excused from responding. As a general matter, this privilege has been a strong one in American political history; fear of police coercion in criminal interrogations initially marked understanding of its scope. The widespread use of the privilege by witnesses at congressional and administrative hearings during the anti-Communist hysteria of the early 1950s, and the political demagoguery consequently associated with opposition to its use, have assured a broad reading of the amendment in other investigative contexts as well. The Supreme Court has

---

115. Compare See v. City of Seattle, 387 U.S. 541 (1967) with Zurcher v. The Stanford Daily, 436 U.S. 547 (1978). See Note, The Argument for Agency Self-Enforcement of Discovery Orders, 83 Colum. L. Rev. 215 (1983).

used it, for example, as the basis for a series of important decisions about warnings police officers must give suspects before interrogation.[116] It has strongly resisted efforts to punish invocation of the privilege, as by making any claim of the privilege a ground for removal from a public job.[117]

Perhaps because of recognition of its power to frustrate much regulatory activity, however, the courts have rarely found the privilege to be available to resist information demands made in ordinary administrative contexts. In the first place, it cannot be asserted in any respect by corporations or other artificial persons.[118] Even a natural person cannot invoke the privilege as a basis for refusing to provide corporate documents or information (of which she may be custodian) that would have the tendency to incriminate not only the corporation but also herself; at most she is entitled to have any testimonial aspects of her own act of producing the documents excluded from consideration.[119] Note that distinguishing real from artificial persons in this way is highly unusual in American law. No such distinction is made concerning freedom of speech, or the protection of property from unreasonable inspection by the state, or the Fifth Amendment's guarantees of fair procedure and "just compensation" when property is taken for public use, shortly to be discussed. Nonetheless, it is reasoned that the protection against self-incrimination seeks to avoid the overbearing of an individual's will by the state, an interest in personal integrity that—unlike interests in expression, property and fair procedure—real and artificial persons do not share. One may understand, also, that the most feared types of official coercion, such as physical torture, are unlikely to occur in the regulatory context.

Even real persons face numerous obstacles to using the privilege in the regulatory context. First, they may assert it only by affirmatively claiming it. For example, if a taxpayer's sources of income were unlawful, she could not use the privilege to excuse her failure to file an income tax return, but would have to file the return indicating a privilege claim on the line where earned income

---

116. Miranda v. Arizona, 384 U.S. 436 (1966), reaffirmed in Dickerson v. United States, 530 U.S. 428 (2000); see n. 16 above.

117. Gardner v. Broderick, 392 U.S. 273 (1968). A public employee could, however, be fired for refusing to answer questions directly and narrowly relating to the performance of her duties.

118. Such as partnerships, unions, or unincorporated associations. Hale v. Henkel, 201 U.S. 43 (1906); Bellis v. United States, 417 U.S. 85 (1974).

119. Braswell v. United States, 487 U.S. 99 (1988). See also United States v. Doe, 465 U.S. 605 (1984). Available only for testimonial acts of the individual himself, the privilege does not preclude the government from requiring the target of an investigation to sign a letter directing foreign banks with which he may have accounts to cooperate with the investigation. Doe v. United States, 487 U.S. 201 (1988).

is to be reported. This is a more conspicuous gesture than most would wish to make. And any other response, if false, opens the citizen to prosecution for "false statement"—as in a recent decision sustaining a criminal conviction for having falsely responded "No" to government investigators' questions.[120] Second, the claim can be made only for "testimonial" communications; it is unavailable, for example, as a basis for resisting the taking of a fingerprint or other physical evidence. Third, it can be made only on the basis of potential incrimination, not merely a tendency to bring about undesired regulatory consequences. Finally, the circumstances in which a claim can be made are highly limited: the papers must both belong to the claimant and be in her possession. Thus, if my papers are subpoenaed from my accountant or my bank, the privilege is not available, for it is not I being required to produce them; and if my accountant's papers are sought from me, the fact that they incriminate me is also irrelevant. Only if I can establish that the very fact of producing the papers in response to the subpoena is a testimonial act that might incriminate me, might a claim be made.[121] In a hearing process, where oral statements are sought, the application of the privilege is more obvious. Here the risk is that the claimant will be thought to have waived it by earlier answers indicating cooperation with the relevant line of the inquiry.

4. "Due process of law" as procedure

a. Introductory

The fundamental right having greatest relevance to administrative law is expressed in both the Fifth and Fourteenth Amendments, the assurance that no person (here, including artificial persons) may be deprived of "life, liberty, or property without due process of law." In their procedural aspect, these few words are the source of all fundamental claims about fair procedure in the American legal system. We have already seen a little about the evolving American understanding of these words in discussions of constitutional interpretation;[122] here it may be appropriate to give more attention to issues of doctrinal structure.[123]

---

120. Brogan v. United States, 522 U.S. 398 (1998).

121. United States v. Doe, 465 U.S. 605 (1984); Baltimore Dep't Social Services v. Bouknight, 493 U.S. 549 (1990).

122. See text at pp. 14 (changing constitution) and 37 (substantive due process) above.

123. An excellent general treatment of the due process problem, though more theoretical/prescriptive than analytical in its later pages, is J. Mashaw, Due Process in the Administrative State (Yale University 1985). See also T. Rakoff, Brock v. Roadway Express, Inc. and the New Law of Regulatory Due Process, 1987 Sup. Ct. Rev. 157; C. Farina, Conceiv-

While the text of the Due Process clauses is extremely general, the fact that this text is (uniquely) expressed twice in the Constitution strongly suggests an understanding that its words state a central proposition about the requirements of American legal order. Historically, the clause reflects the Magna Carta of Great Britain, both its expression of principles of legality and its particular assurance that all would be subjected to the ordinary processes (procedures) of law. Its words also echo that country's Seventeenth Century struggles for political and legal regularity, and the American colonies' strong insistence during the pre-Revolutionary period on observance of regular legal order. The requirement that government function in accordance with law is, in itself, ample basis for understanding the stress given these words. Perhaps surprisingly to persons trained in the civilian tradition, the Constitution does not contain an explicit statement of the principle of legality.[124] The idea is instinct in the very idea of the Constitution, however, and the Due Process clauses in particular are often thought to embody that commitment.

The direct application of the text inheres in the further understanding—instinct in its words and steadfastly held since its adoption—that in at least some of the contexts in which government acts, the clauses also limit the procedural regimes that the legislature (or the courts or the executive) can choose to employ. Thus, it is not always sufficient for the government to act in accordance with such law as there may be. In some circumstances, citizens may be entitled to have the government observe or offer certain procedures, *whether or not those procedures have been statutorily provided for*. A statute denying those (unspecified) procedural protections would be unconstitutional. If, for example, a state were to enact a statute assigning all ordinary common law litigation to a non-judicial body, or permitting an administrative agency to revoke a professional license without providing a rather full opportunity to be heard on the matter, federal courts would surely find those statutes void, as threatening deprivation of life, liberty or property without due process of law.

The struggles over "substantive due process" and "incorporation"[125] did little more than to circumscribe the problem of judicial subjectivity in deciding what if any procedures the Constitution demands. "Due process" communi-

---

ing Due Process, 3 Yale J. L. & Feminism 189 (1991); R. Pierce, Jr., The Due Process Counter-revolution of the 1990s?, 96 Colum. L. Rev. 1973 (1996); and C. Farina, On Misusing "Revolution" and "Reform": Procedural Due Process and the New Welfare Act, 50 Admin. L. Rev. 591 (1998).

124. Its prohibition on ex post facto (retroactive) legislation and bills of attainder might be so understood in the criminal law context.

125. See p. 37 above.

cates very little about what process is due, and in what circumstances. Moreover, in contrast to the criminal procedure setting in which the incorporation struggles were fought, the Bill of Rights is no more detailed than the Fourteenth Amendment for procedural claims concerning administrative and civil judicial actions. In either case, only the requirement that due process be observed is available in the constitutional text. Courts not willing simply to accept legislative judgments on that subject are required to go outside the document to find any refining norms.

Moreover, while English and American law enjoyed a long history of relatively settled practice respecting civil trials, for administrative processes both the jurisprudence of fair procedure and the available techniques for resolving questions that might arise were quite undeveloped.[126] Nineteenth century cases, largely challenges to tax assessment procedures, had developed the proposition that determinations turning on individualized facts about the taxpayer or his property required an opportunity for hearing that had some (albeit informal) trial-like characteristics. The Court said there must be some opportunity for oral presentation of evidence and argument by the taxpayer before a final determination could be made. Beyond insisting on orality, however, the Court was permissive about the details.[127]

The constitutional inquiry had three arguably separate elements: whether any procedures at all were "due"; and, if so, at what point in time they had to be provided, and just what those procedures were to be.[128] As regulation be-

---

126. See generally, J. Mashaw, Due Process in the Administrative State, n. 123 above.

127. Londoner v. Denver, 210 U.S. 373 (1908). An important case early in the twentieth century distinguished from these holdings the situation in which an essentially legislative judgment was to be made, turning on propositions of more general fact. Bi-Metallic Investment Co. v. State Bd. of Equalization of Colorado, 239 U.S. 441 (1915). The cases are more fully discussed in Chapter V(A), below, at p. 189.

128. A fourth type of question also arose: whether the Constitution set limits on kinds of issues an administrative agency (as distinct from a court) could be assigned for resolution (and if so what limits). This inquiry reflected a due process concern—whether procedures available at the agency level would be fair—but it tended to be presented and discussed in terms of separation of powers. In that perspective, the question became one about what matters/issues should necessarily be resolved using judicial power. See p. 118 below. Its importance subsided almost to the disappearing point once the courts became convinced that, through the adoption of regularized procedures, agencies had become reliable triers of fact. Crowell v. Benson, 285 U.S. 22 (1932); V. Rosenblum, The Administrative Law Judge in the Administrative Process, in Subcommittee on Social Security, House Committee on Ways and Means, 94th Cong., 1st Sess., Report on Recent Studies Relevant to Disability Hearings and Appeals Crisis 171–245 (Comm. Print 1975); H. Monaghan, Marbury and the Administrative State, 83 Colum. L. Rev. 1 (1983).

came more and more prevalent, dispute over the necessity for some form of oral hearing repeatedly arose in varying circumstances. Despite much debate over the question just what procedures that right to hearing entailed, however, little judicial development occurred. The question whether any procedures at all were constitutionally due became trapped in a sterile classification of "rights" and "privileges." Deprivation of a right was said to require an oral hearing where deprivation of a privilege did not. Many important relationships with administrative government, such as licenses or public employment (but not all, and not according to a discernable pattern), fit into the privilege category. On the second question, the Supreme Court seemed repeatedly to indicate that, where only property rights were at stake (and particularly if there was some demonstrable urgency for public action) necessary hearings could be postponed to follow provisional, even irreversible, government action.[129] And on the third, the detailed provisions made for trial-like procedures by enactment of the federal Administrative Procedure Act [APA] in 1946[130] for a while permitted the Court to avoid having to define constitutional content for those hearing rights at the federal level. A Supreme Court decision made a few years after that Act's adoption went so far as to suggest that the arrangements it made were what the Constitution required.[131]

At the same time as the Court's struggles over "incorporation" were underscoring the need for exact definition of procedural rights in the criminal context, the political investigations of the 1950s challenged the courts to consider due process issues in both judicial and administrative settings. Rumors generated by faceless informers were widely used to deprive government employees of their jobs because of doubts raised about their loyalty and security. The resulting inquiries often left the employees with their honor challenged

---

129. An early case found no difficulty in an inspector's summary seizure and destruction of allegedly tainted chickens, so long as the owner of the warehouse could eventually bring an action to challenge the correctness of the inspector's judgment. N. Am. Cold Storage Co. v. Chicago, 211 U.S. 306 (1908). See also Phillips v. Commissioner, 283 U.S. 589 (1931); Fahey v. Mallonee, 332 U.S. 245 (1947). In the field of criminal procedure, of course, suspects are often deprived of their liberty for interim periods following procedures far less formal than criminal trial; that analogy has had surprisingly little use in the administrative context.

130. See p. 199 below.

131. Wong Yang Sung v. McGrath, 339 U.S. 33 (1950). This suggestion has been silently abandoned, however. The Court upheld the constitutionality of a subsequent statute explicitly adopting the procedure Wong Yang Sung had suggested might be invalid. Marcello v. Bonds, 349 U.S. 302 (1955). Its subsequent decisions on the question what process may be "due" ignore the APA as a source of possible learning.

but no realistic possibility of response, and thus called attention to the importance of fair and open procedures to maintaining public trust in government. These proceedings also brought into question the (previously) easy conclusion that office-holders, possessors of a mere "privilege," had no claim to procedural protections. And they emphasized the value, in an administrative context, of procedural protections long associated with Anglo-American criminal trials: the right to have the assistance of counsel; the right to know one's accuser and the evidence against one; the right to confront and cross-examine that person; the right to have the decision based solely upon a record generated in open proceedings; as well as the right to present argument and evidence on one's own behalf.

Yet, for each case that seemed to demand a detailed procedural prescription, another plainly required flexibility. A legislative investigation of alleged communistic activities could not be undertaken without respecting witnesses' claims to procedural safeguards,[132] but the Court would not burden a legislative investigation into civil rights issues with rigid procedural requirements, although the investigation's conclusions might harm the reputation of witnesses before it in some parts of the country.[133] An aeronautic engineer could not be threatened with loss of access to military secrets, on which his profession depended, on the basis of anonymous accusations about his loyalty, without the opportunity to confront the information and his accuser;[134] but a cook on a military installation threatened with loss of access to the installation (and hence that particular job), apparently on the basis of undisclosed concerns about her security status, had in all the circumstances no similar claim.[135]

The Court during this period seemed to agree on little, save the proposition that what the Due Process clauses required could only be determined on the basis of all the circumstances of a given case—a view not far distant from "the very essence of a scheme of ordered liberty."[136] A widely cited formulation was that of Justice Felix Frankfurter:

> ... "Due process," unlike some legal rules, is not a technical conception with a fixed content unrelated to time, place and circumstances. Expressing as it does in its ultimate analysis respect enforced by law for that feeling of just treatment which has been evolved through cen-

132. Watkins v. United States, 354 U.S. 178 (1957).
133. Hannah v. Larche, 363 U.S. 420 (1960).
134. Greene v. McElroy, 360 U.S. 474 (1959).
135. Cafeteria Workers v. McElroy, 367 U.S. 886 (1961).
136. See note 91 and accompanying text, above.

turies of Anglo-American constitutional history and civilization, "due process" cannot be imprisoned within the treacherous limits of any formula. Representing a profound attitude of fairness between man and man, and more particularly between the individual and government, "due process" is compounded of history, reason, the past course of decisions, and stout confidence in the strength of the democratic faith which we profess. Due process is not a mechanical instrument. It is not a yardstick. It is a process. It is a delicate process of adjustment inescapably involving the exercise of judgment by those whom the Constitution entrusted with the unfolding of the process.[137]

As may be apparent, this was not a formula that would commend itself to his opponents—and the ultimate victors—in the "incorporation" struggle.

b. Goldberg v. Kelly

The period beginning around 1970 witnessed another enormous outpouring of due process litigation, in this case strongly associated with the legal system's (belated) discovery of a series of problems particularly affecting poor persons. This period saw a strong effort to establish workable structures for analysis of all three questions identified above, with the result strongly expansive of private claims to procedure in each instance. *Whether* process is due, formerly answered by reference to the right/privilege distinction, came to be considered to depend on any relationship with the state established by positive law. On the question *when* procedures must be afforded, with associated issues about the need for preliminary determinations, "hearing first" and quite elaborate inquiries into what was in effect probable cause became the presumptive rule. And on the question *what* process is required, a highly detailed list of required procedures seemed to be the governing approach, at least initially. These outcomes are not hard to correlate with the incorporation idea—seeking concrete standards with which to anchor judicial subjectivity.

Goldberg v. Kelly,[138] a case arising out of a state-administered welfare program, appeared to require the determination of only a limited point. New York was seeking to terminate the enrolment of Kelly and others in its welfare program. It conceded that a federal statute required it to provide a full oral hearing before a hearing officer before finally terminating their enrolment. At issue,

---

137. Joint Anti-Fascist Refugee Committee v. McGrath, 341 U.S. 123, 162–163. (1951) (concurring opinion).
138. 397 U.S. 254 (1970).

then, was only the state's effort to suspend payments pending that full and for-mal hearing—a question of timing. For this limited purpose New York em-ployed a more informal process. It was willing to give persons like Mrs. Kelly opportunities to confer with responsible bureaucrats and to submit written views before suspension, but it gave no hearing in the judicial sense before the suspension was put into effect. This was insufficient for the Court. Its opin-ion, worth stating at some length, conveys premises of analysis that still in-fluence American due process reasoning.

The first proposition, in fact conceded by the state, was that the welfare re-cipients' claim to continued benefits was within the ambit of due process. The right/privilege dichotomy had been under critical assault for years, particu-larly with reference to the growing dependence-in-fact by citizens on the sorts of relationships with modern government that courts had tended to charac-terize as privileges. These critics argued that if the purposes of the Due Process clauses (and the Bill of Rights generally) in protecting citizens from govern-mental arbitrariness were to be served, relationships so important to life in the modern state had to be brought within the clause's reach.[139] The Court now clearly signaled that this argument had prevailed.

Next was the question how (if at all) analysis would be shaped by the fact that the case dealt with interim suspension of welfare payments rather than ter-mination. What was to be the timing of the hearing the state conceded had to be provided? This was a question that had its own history, marked by under-standing that the burden of the interim period could be a substantial one on either side. Government emergency actions (the seizure of contaminated foods, the closure of a bank) were generally tolerated, and the Court several times had remarked that where only property interests were involved, the required hear-ing need only occur before the government's action became final.[140] Yet, the tremendous need facing a person dependent on welfare and erroneously de-prived of it, even for an interim period, now persuaded the *Goldberg* Court that it should regard the suspension as in itself a deprivation. Thus, suspension com-manded due process protections just as the ultimate termination of welfare el-igibility would. Balanced against the welfare recipient's need, as the Court then saw it, was *only* the financial cost of administration—a consideration the Court dismissed at that time, but that has proved more persuasive since.

The final problem: Precisely what procedures had to be employed? The state conceded the need for some procedure: it provided notice, an opportunity to

---

139. H. Jones, The Rule of Law and the Welfare State, 58 Colum. L. Rev. 143 (1958); C. Reich, The New Property, 73 Yale L. J. 733 (1964).

140. See n. 129 above.

discuss the matter with a welfare official, a decision, the chance to seek review of that decision by a senior welfare official, and the right to submit written materials at that point. It did not, however, provide a hearing before an impartial judicial officer, the right to an attorney's help, the right to present evidence and argument orally, the chance to examine all materials that would be relied on or to confront and cross-examine adverse witnesses, or a decision limited to the record thus made and explained in an opinion. The Court now held that due process required all of these.

The Court's basis for this elaborate holding has never been clear. Various prior cases were cited for the different ingredients provided for—the naval engineer's case (but not the cook's),[141] for example, on the question of cross-examination—but without attention to context. The Court asserted that it was respecting the interim character of the administrative decision to suspend, by requiring less in the way of procedure than would be appropriate for a final termination of benefits. Yet, overall, the collection of procedures it required was atypically demanding even of final government administrative determinations on issues of great importance. A survey of forty federal programs made a few years after *Goldberg*, for example, found only one other program (also welfare-oriented) in which all the *Goldberg* rights were respected. For the substantial majority, fewer than half were provided; only notice, the assurance of some degree of impartiality, and an explanation of the basis of decision were observed with any degree of universality.[142]

Goldberg was a signal that the trend of detailed specification characterizing the preceding decades' work in criminal procedure had spilled over to the civil side. The "hearing first" aspect of its holding spread rapidly through a variety of civil judicial remedies—for example, sharply curtailing the use of summary procedures for lien or attachment that creditors had used for many years to protect their security when payments ceased. *Goldberg* and many of these decisions were the product of a "law and poverty" movement that had taken root in the wake of the American civil rights movement's success, in part with the help of government subsidies. The Court had found that indigent criminal defendants had a right to have counsel appointed to defend them. For a brief while it appeared that perhaps that subsidy too might be found constitutionally required, that the Court could be persuaded to expand *Goldberg*'s language about the right to assistance of counsel, to require the state to waive court fees or to provide free counsel for persons unable to afford legal services.[143] Com-

---

141. See p. 52 above.
142. P. Verkuil, A Study of Informal Adjudication Procedures, 43 U. Chi. L. Rev. 739 (1976).
143. See Boddie v. Connecticut, 401 U.S. 371 (1971).

mentators spoke, without apparent irony, of a "due process revolution" having occurred. Looking back today, one can see *Goldberg*'s enduring contributions, but also a quick realization of the need to moderate the rigor of its demands, and an effort—not wholly successful—to build an analytic structure to replace its style of confident pronouncements.

c. Threshold issues

If the language of the Due Process clauses does not say what procedures must be accorded, it might seem to say whether a procedural claim can be made, or what the threshold is for invoking its protections. The text states an obligation that applies when the state seeks to "deprive" a person of "life, liberty, or property." Those elements were brought forward, and made an explicit part of analysis, in two cases involving the unexplained and summary refusal of two state colleges to renew the employment contracts of two instructors (apparently because of their participation in opposition to the American involvement in Viet Nam).[144] If, as was suspected, the teachers had been dropped in retaliation for political positions, they had been deprived of liberty.[145] If the teachers had a "property" interest in continued employment, then they could not be dropped without a hearing on the question of cause, at which they could challenge the state's evidence and attempt to contradict it by presentations of their own.

The "property"/"not property" distinction might not seem much of an improvement over right/privilege, and has been criticized on that ground. The Court was explicit, however, that what is to be regarded as property must be broadly understood—in just the terms, basically, of the writings about dependence-in-fact relationships with modern government that had spurred the abandonment of right/privilege. One has property, from the perspective of the Due Process clauses, if state or federal law creates an entitlement to a continuing relationship absent some reason to alter it.

Kelly, as a welfare recipient, had property in this constitutional sense; she had an established eligibility for continuing welfare payments. Thus, she had a claim to due process before she could be removed from the welfare rolls. Whether the two teachers had "property" would depend in each instance on whether persons in their position, under state law, held some form of tenure or

---

144. Board of Regents of State Colleges v. Roth, 408 U.S. 564 (1972); Perry v. Sindermann, 408 U.S. 593 (1972).

145. In fact, no procedure could compensate for such an offense; here the operation of the Due Process Clause, directly reminiscent of the substantive due process cases, would have been simply to identify the act as unlawful. Ultimately both cases were settled in a manner that appeared to concede that the discharges had been politically motivated.

rather served "at will"—without any state law claim or expectation to continuation.[146] The expectation need not be based on a statute. An established custom of treating instructors who had taught for X years as having tenure could be shown, for example. Yet some law-based relationship or expectation of continuation had to be shown before a federal court would say that process was "due."

This question of property remains at the threshold of due process inquiries, but its application has been checkered in three respects. The first is what is described in the literature as the "positivist trap," an aspect of the criticism of the property/not property distinction. Since whether one has an entitlement depends on the prescriptions of law, legislatures may be able to define important relationships—ones on which citizens in fact come to depend—in ways that preclude the conclusion that an entitlement is present.[147] The recent federal legislation on welfare "reform" has been explicit that one purpose is to end any idea that welfare is an entitlement; although largely directed to the question *how long* one may remain on welfare, the rhetoric seems also aimed at the *Goldberg* idea.[148] Even if an entitlement *is* present, a further difficulty can arise when state law not only describes a relationship between a citizen and government but also prescribes the procedures by which that relationship can be ended or altered: how can a court separate the (positive law) entitlement from its accompanying procedures? Must not the citizen be prepared to accept the "bitter with the sweet"? This issue was presented when a civil servant, enjoying tenure under statutes specifically identifying the procedures to be followed for removal, challenged the constitutionality of an aspect of those procedures. While a majority of the Court asserted that the procedures must in fact meet an independent judicial test, the opposing position was strongly stated.[149] It was not until a few years later that the Court forcefully repudiated the "bitter with the sweet" reasoning, in a similar case.[150]

The second problem in application of the threshold inquiry is probably best described in terms of the idea of deprivation. In a series of cases involving harm

---

146. At will employment, which permits either party to terminate the relationship for good, bad, or no reason at all, is the default rule in the U.S.

147. O'Bannon v. Town Court Nursing Center, 447 U.S. 773 (1980).

148. See C. Farina, On Misusing "Revolution and "Reform": Procedural Due Process and the New Welfare Act, n. 123 above.

149. Arnette v. Kennedy, 416 U.S. 134, 153 (1974) ("[w]here the grant of a substantive right is inextricably entwined with the limitations on the procedures which are to be employed in determining that right, a litigant...must take the bitter with the sweet.").

150. Cleveland Board of Education v. Loudermill, 470 U.S. 532 (1985).

done to citizens by state action, the Court reached an almost inexplicable series of due process results, apparently turning on the meaning of deprivation. For example, an early case established that a state could not post a picture of a person naming him as an habitual drunkard without first following appropriate procedures; the posting made it unlawful for him to be served alcoholic beverages in a bar.[151] Yet when a city circulated the photograph of a person recently arrested (but not convicted) for petty theft under the heading "Active Shoplifters," causing enormous damage to his reputation, the failure to provide a hearing first was not objectionable.[152] Another case established that school officials could not suspend a student for ten days without first giving him some kind of hearing; attendance at public school was said to be an "entitlement."[153] Yet a teacher who physically punished a student so severely as to require several days in a hospital (but who did not formally exclude him from school) had not deprived her student of liberty or property without due process of law.[154]

The cases in which liability was denied were cases in which the challenged official acts did not change the legal aura of the victim's personality. It was still lawful to shop, or to come to school if health permitted. Perhaps more importantly, in these cases (and others) state law appeared to provide a post-event remedy, in the form of ordinary civil actions for the torts of defamation or assault. To find due process violations in such matters threatened to rework the arrangements of federalism, by creating broadscale federal supervision of state officials whose behavior had previously been left to the control of the states.[155] As a dissenter in the school punishment case observed, these considerations appear to explain the results in a technical sense. (Similar consid-

---

151. Wisconsin v. Constantineau, 400 U.S. 433 (1971).

152. Paul v. Davis, 424 U.S. 693, 712 (1976) ("[P]etitioners' defamatory publications, however seriously they may have harmed respondent's reputations, did not deprive him of any 'liberty' or 'property' interests protected by the Due Process Clause.").

153. Goss v. Lopez, 419 U.S. 565 (1975).

154. Ingraham v. Wright, 430 U.S. 651 (1977).

155. Both of the cases in which liability was rejected involved suits brought under the Civil Rights Act, 42 U.S.C. §1983. This statute, discussed below at p. 395, makes state officials civilly liable for the consequences of any act performed under color of state law that deprives citizens of federal rights—including, of course, rights under the Due Process Clause of the federal Constitution. Federal redress for some actions by state officials is an essential safeguard of citizen liberties—for example, in the area of civil rights. The possibility of constitutionalizing nearly all torts committed by state officials presents much larger difficulties. Similar reasoning has recently been used in a dispute over performance of a contract with the state; "if California makes ordinary judicial process available to respondent for resolving its contractual dispute, that process is due process." Lujan v. G & G Fire Sprinklers, Inc., 532 U.S. 189 (2001).

erations explain the Supreme Court's most recent retreat, from what seem obvious applications of due process reasoning that threaten to embroil it in state prison administration.[156]) Yet it seems fair to characterize the justice of the opposing results in these cases as deeply questionable.

The third aspect of the threshold inquiry concerns potential entitlements for which a citizen is applying, and has not yet been determined to qualify. Does the statutory judgment that every citizen possessing characteristics A, B and C *shall receive* stated benefits or be recognized as enjoying a stated legal relationship with the state (say, a driver's license) create an entitlement so that due process constrains the application procedures the state can choose? These are settings in which it is clear that, once qualified, the citizen could not be deprived of her entitlement without due process. Yet the Supreme Court has had no occasion to say directly whether the same judgment applies at the application stage. Some Justices apparently believe that it does not.[157] On the one hand, it can be said that the law is always more solicitous of established relationships than expectations. However, the "entitlement" analysis suffers some embarrassment in this argument. The claim of the citizen seems the same whether he has wrongly been denied access to an entitlement he has not yet enjoyed or has been terminated in one previously recognized.

d. The procedures due

Once over the threshold, and assuming the positivist trap has been at least provisionally avoided, the problem remains how the Justices can define procedures, other than those legislatively chosen, that are constitutionally due. The principal contemporary case on that question, *Mathews v. Eldridge*,[158] arose in a context much like *Goldberg*. Eldridge had been receiving disability benefits under a federally supported scheme. Responsible officials came to believe, on the basis of information he had provided and physicians' reports, that he was no longer disabled. They then notified him that they intended to terminate his benefits. Only written procedures were available before the termination was made provisionally effective. Eldridge was entitled to a full oral hearing at a later date, and would have received full benefits for the interim period if he prevailed. His argument, like Kelly's in *Goldberg v. Kelly*, was that

---

156. E.g., Sandin v. Conner, 515 U.S. 472 (1995), briefly discussed below at p. 178.

157. See, for example, the opinion of Chief Justice Rehnquist in Walters v. National Association of Radiation Survivors, 473 U.S. 305, 353 (1985).

158. 424 U.S. 319 (1976).

even suspending payments to him pending the full hearing was a deprivation of a property interest that could not be effected without the use of the procedures specified in *Goldberg*.

Mathews produced a result quite different from *Goldberg*'s. Where *Goldberg* had categorically asserted the procedures to be followed, *Mathews* attempted to define the judicial inquiry to be undertaken in any case in which a question about constitutionally required procedures might arise. This inquiry, the Court said, requires analysis of three factors:

> First, the private interest that will be affected by the official action; second, the risk of an erroneous deprivation of such interest through the procedures used, and the probable value, if any, of additional or substitute procedural safeguards; and finally, the Government's interest, including the function involved and the fiscal and administrative burdens that the additional or substitute procedural requirement would entail.[159]

Using these factors, the Court majority first found the private interest here less significant than in *Goldberg*. A person who is arguably disabled but provisionally denied disability benefits, it said, is more likely to be able to find other "potential sources of temporary income" than a person who is arguably impoverished but provisionally denied welfare assistance.

The second factor, analytically, might be regarded as two inquiries—the first, into the risk of error implicit in the procedures that were in fact used, and are under challenge; the second, into the likelihood that a proposed procedural requirement will control that risk at acceptable cost. The Court found the risk of error in using written procedures for the initial judgment to be low, and unlikely to be significantly reduced by adding oral or confrontational procedures of the *Goldberg* variety. Disputes over eligibility for disability insurance, it reasoned, typically concern one's medical condition rather than honesty in reporting one's need—as might be more typical in the welfare context. Medical condition could be decided, at least provisionally, on the basis of documentary submissions. The Court was impressed that during the preliminary process Eldridge had full access to the agency's files, and the opportunity to submit in writing any further material he wished.

Finally, the Court now attached more importance than the *Goldberg* Court had to the government's claims for efficiency. In particular, the Court assumed

---

159. Id at 334.

(as the *Goldberg* Court had not) that "resources available for any particular program of social welfare are not unlimited." Thus additional administrative costs for suspension hearings and for payments to persons ultimately found undeserving of benefits, while those hearings were awaiting resolution, would subtract from the amounts available to pay benefits for those undoubtedly eligible to participate in the program. The Court also gave some weight to the "good-faith judgments" of the plan administrators as to what appropriate consideration of the claims of applicants would entail.

Matthews v. Eldridge thus reorients the inquiry in a number of important respects. First, it emphasizes the variability of procedural requirements. Rather than create a standard list of procedures that constitute the procedure that is due, the opinion emphasizes that each setting or program invites its own assessment. About the only *general* statement that can be made is that persons holding interests protected by the Due Process clauses are entitled to "some kind of hearing." Just what the elements of that hearing might be, however, depends on the concrete circumstances of the particular program at issue. Second, that assessment is to be made both concretely, and in a holistic manner. It is not a matter of approving this or that particular element of a procedural matrix in isolation, but of assessing the suitability of the ensemble in context.

Third, and particularly important in its implications for litigation seeking procedural change, the assessment is to be made at the level of program operation, rather than in terms of the particular needs of the particular litigants involved in the matter before the court. Cases that are pressed to appellate courts often are characterized by individual facts that make an unusually strong appeal for more elaborate procedures. Indeed, one supposes that lawyers for an organization seeking to use the courts to help establish their view of sound social policy would choose exactly such persons as their plaintiffs, rather than more representative persons.[160] Justice William Brennan, the author of *Goldberg*, wrote about it afterwards in just these terms,[161] and dissented from *Mathews* in a manner that again drew strongly on the plight of the particular individual threatened with loss of welfare in that case. The ma-

---

160. Much not-for-profit or non-commercial litigation in America is organized by "public interest" lawyers and law firms. The importance of suits initiated by such organizations is especially great in constitutional and administrative law areas.

161. W.J. Brennan, Jr., Reason, Passion and "The Progress of the Law," 10 Cardozo L. Rev. 3 (1988). Compare O. Fiss, Reason in All Its Splendor, 56 Brooklyn L. Rev. 789, 801 (1990), expressing the view that such an approach "is inconsistent with the very norms that govern and legitimate the judicial power."

jority's approach, focusing on the general situation of recipients and the general operation of the particular program, seems more likely to preserve than to endanger existing procedural arrangements.

Finally, and to similar effect, the second of the stated factors places on the party challenging the existing procedures the burden not only of demonstrating their insufficiency, but also of showing that some specific substitute or additional procedure will work a concrete improvement justifying its additional cost. Thus, it is inadequate merely to criticize. The litigant claiming procedural insufficiency must come prepared with a substitute program that can itself be justified.

The *Mathews* approach may be more successful if it is viewed as a set of instructions to attorneys involved in litigation concerning procedural issues, than if it is seen in judicial perspective. One knows what the elements of demonstration on a procedural due process claim are, and the probable effect of the approach is to discourage litigation drawing its force from the narrow (even if compelling) circumstances of a particular individual's position. Yet deep problems for judicial inquiry are suggested by the absence of fixed doctrine about the content of due process and by the very breadth of the inquiry required to establish its demands in a particular context—the insistence that courts assess the operation of an entire procedural scheme across the full range of its functioning.[162] The judge has few reference points to begin with, and must decide on the basis of facts likely to be peculiarly inaccessible to litigation techniques. A not-at-all-surprising result is to encourage judges to accept resolution of procedural issues by legislatures or others better placed to make these complex yet general assessments.

Two examples may illustrate the problems judges face. The first arose when one of the federal circuit courts of appeal had to decide a dispute about the procedures to be followed in determining certain low-value claims under a national medical insurance scheme.[163] Initially, the court ruled with confidence

---

162. See Brock v. Roadway Express, 481 U.S. 252 (1987).

163. Gray Panthers v. Schweiker, 652 F.2d 146 (D.C. Cir. 1980), reconsidered after remand 716 F.2d 23 (D.C. Cir. 1983). This litigation is a good example of the programmatic litigation often found in American practice. The Gray Panthers organization is a privately funded foundation dedicated to representing the interests of the aged, as its leaders understand them to be. No one individual with a $75 claim for medical insurance would be likely to take the matter to the courts, or to have the resources for the appeals and remands of lengthy litigation, no matter how strongly she believed the claim had been wrongly denied, using faulty procedures. A group such as Gray Panthers, by contrast, in some sense exists just to take such actions. Compare Van Harken v. City of Chicago, 103 F.3d 1346,

that access to some kind of oral procedure was required under any circumstances, for no reported case had ever approved a completely written procedure for a setting in which process was "due." Yet this perceived requirement for elements of orality arose outside the *Mathews* decision as such; and when the case returned to the court at a later stage, it became clear that the *Mathews* inquiry did not answer for the court just how tightly access to an oral procedure could be controlled and just how informal that procedure could be.[164] For example, would provision for discussions over the telephone suffice? The detailed outcome of the lawsuit seemed much more likely to be the product of negotiations between the litigants than to be the result of judicial decree.

The second example involved a statute that, by very severely restricting the fees that could be paid to attorneys, had the effect of denying veterans access to counsel in prosecuting claims under veterans benefits statutes. Although the Court has not always been closely attentive to the *Mathews* formulation, in this case it was. It relied on statistics about the general run of veterans' claims to establish that their need for attorneys' assistance was not high. Most veterans prevailed; veterans' organizations were available to provide substitute representation that seemed effective; and in the few cases in which lawyers had appeared, presumably without fees, veterans were not notably more successful than the general run.[165] Yet these statistics cloaked what several of the Justices regarded as a real need for lawyers' assistance in a smaller group of much more complex cases. This was a focus the attorneys for the veterans groups had not developed. Some of the Justices thought that in a well-developed case the *Mathews* inquiry might demonstrate that provision for the help of attorneys *was* constitutionally required in that sub-group of cases; others would have decided that, like the element of orality, access to an attorney was a necessary element of the process "due," one that could never be denied. What was apparent to both groups of Justices (together, a majority of the Court) was that the *Mathews* inquiry in this case was distorted by the great number of easy or straightforward cases, for which the desired procedural change would make little difference.

It follows from the preceding discussion that one cannot expect to list the elements of required procedures under American law. For a ten-day suspension from public school,[166] a chance to tell the school principal (someone other

---

cert. den. (520 U.S. 1241 (1997) (procedures for parking violations punishable by limited fine need not require physical presence of police officer responsible for citation).

164. Gray Panthers v. Schweiker, 716 F. 2d 23 (D.C. Cir. 1983).

165. Walters v. National Association of Radiation Survivors, 473 U.S. 305 (1985).

166. Goss v. Lopez, n. 153 above.

than the complaining teacher) one's own side of the story was sufficient. Suspension of welfare payments may still be held to require all the elements specified in *Goldberg*, and actual termination of those payments, somewhat more. Nonetheless, an analysis made by the late Judge Henry Friendly in his well-regarded article, "Some Kind of Hearing,"[167] generated a list that remains highly influential, as to both content and relative priority:

(1) An unbiased tribunal.

(2) Notice of the proposed action and the grounds asserted for it.

(3) Opportunity to present reasons why the proposed action should not be taken.

(4) The right to present evidence, including the right to call witnesses.

(5) The right to know opposing evidence.

(6) The right to cross-examine adverse witnesses.

(7) A decision based exclusively on the evidence presented.

(8) Opportunity to be represented by counsel.

(9) Requirement that the tribunal prepare a record of the evidence presented.

(10) Requirement that the tribunal prepare written findings of fact and reasons for its decision.

Again, it must be stressed that these are simply the kinds of procedures that might be claimed in a "due process" argument, roughly in order of their perceived importance, and not a list of procedures that will in fact be required.

Note, too, that one item missing from Judge Friendly's list is any claim to have the responsibility for presenting the government's information separated from the responsibility for deciding the dispute. Despite the usual preference of American jurisprudence for having opposing lawyers present a dispute to a neutral and wholly arbitral judge, adversary procedures, as such, are not required in the administrative setting. As lawyers from civilian jurisdictions may understand more easily than some of their American counterparts, administrative law judges may be made responsible for directing the inquiry into a disputed matter, and presenting the government's information, without compromising in a constitutional sense their capacity to serve as an "unbiased tribunal" for determination of the dispute.[168]

---

167. 123 U. Pa. L. Rev. 1267, 1279 et seq. (1975).

168. Mathews v. Eldridge, 424 U.S. 319 (1976); Richardson v. Perales, 402 U.S. 389 (1971). The Court has suggested that an administrative law judge with such responsibilities has a duty of diligent inquiry on behalf of the claimant. Heckler v. Campbell, 461 U.S. 488 (1983).

5. "Due process of law" as substance: the expropriation problem

Regulation predictably imposes economic losses on some, in relation to what they would experience in a market free of its effects, and confers economic benefits on others. Economists and political scientists see in this fact much potential for the abuse of government, when its processes are made to serve special interests at the expense of the more diffuse public—a use described as collecting "rents." Much occupational licensing or rate regulation is thought to have this character, serving more to enhance the economic well-being of the profession or activity ostensibly being regulated than to protect the public from abuses. The *Lochner* case discussed above[169] was decided on just such reasoning, the Court concluding that law had been used to benefit one private group at the expense of another. The repudiation of *Lochner* carried with it an understanding that courts cannot reliably tell what legislation serves public interests, and what private.

What of cases in which one or a few individuals are made to suffer losses that indisputably advantage the general public? On the one hand, "substantive due process" is repudiated in the economic context, and the courts accept that the public enjoys broad "police power" to protect public interests, even at the cost of ending or sharply restricting what had previously been legitimate and profitable private activity, and consequently frustrating private investments. On the other, another element of the Fifth Amendment (equally applicable to the states) addresses what is at least a correlative problem: when the government expropriates private property for public use—takes some of my land in order to build a new road—it must pay "just compensation" for the taking. How far does this obligation of monetary adjustment extend? If building the road using my neighbor's land increases *or* decreases the value of my land, by improving its access to town or increasing the noise I hear, no payment need be made in either direction. My property may have been affected, but this has happened indirectly, and without the government acquiring anything from me. In general, the fact that regulation may have high costs for particular individuals is not thought to have anything to do with the obligation to pay just compensation for government takings. If an electric power plant must spend millions in order to stay in business, because of required pollution controls, it has no claim for public subsidy of these costs.

---

169. See p. 37 above.

In the real estate context, in particular, there can arise situations of apparent regulation, where the impact of regulation is so severe as to drain particular property of economic value, in the service of public needs. Limitations on permitted uses of real estate in flood-prone areas, for example, can reduce the owner of the land to the involuntary holder of a small piece of private wilderness. This is sometimes described as "inverse condemnation"; while the government does not, as such, acquire property, it achieves all the beneficial effects of having done so by restricting the landowner in her own use of the land. If a court can conclude that a landowner was deprived of all economically viable use of the property, then either just compensation must be paid or the regulation foregone.[170] If a "taking" *has* occurred, then the state can be required to pay "just compensation" for what has been taken—even if the taking is only temporary because, ultimately, the regulatory action is found to be beyond its authority.[171]

The distinction between permitted regulation and regulatory takings, or inverse condemnation, is perhaps more a practical than a theoretical one, and the willingness of judges to accept regulation somewhat corresponds (as it did in both *Lochner* and its subsequent repudiation) to their general enthusiasm for the project of government. The more conservative the Justice, that is, the more likely may be the conclusion that a given regulatory command is so intrusive on a particular individual or individuals that, if it is to be effected, it must be paid for. After a long period in which such reasoning was out of favor, conclusions that regulatory requirements are so demanding as to effect a taking now seem to be reappearing, in decisions in which the Supreme Court is closely divided along conventional conservative-liberal lines.

Thus, in 1978 the Supreme Court, by a margin of 6–3, sustained historic preservation legislation, which had the effect of limiting the possible development of some buildings much more stringently than did city law generally.[172] The three dissenters vigorously protested a law which "imposed a substantial cost on less than one one-tenth of one percent of the buildings in New York City for the general benefit of all its people," finding these to be just the circumstances for which just compensation was required. By 1987, the Supreme Court was more closely divided, and two judgments decided by bare majorities (5–4) appeared to look in opposite directions. One case con-

---

170. Lucas v. South Carolina Coastal Council, 505 U.S. 1003 (1992); City of Monterey v. Del Monte Dunes at Monterey, Ltd., 526 U.S. 687 (1999).

171. First English Evangelical Lutheran Church of Glendale v. County of Los Angeles, California, 482 U.S. 304 (1987).

172. Penn. Central Transp. Co. v. City of New York, 438 U.S. 104 (1978).

sidered a regulation requiring underground coal mines to leave 50% of the coal unmined, so that it could serve as a support for the surface land, which might otherwise subside. The deed the coal mine operators had earlier purchased from the owners of the surface of the land appeared to have given them *both* the right to underground minerals *and* the right to determine whether and to what extent to support the surface. The majority concluded that this regulation had a "public" purpose distinct from aiding the particular owners of surface rights against the mine operators, and that the interference with the mine operators' ownership of the coal thus not a taking that warranted compensation; four Justices would have reached the opposite conclusion.[173] In the other case, a bare majority found no proper public purpose in a city's action requiring land owners to donate a means of public access to a beach adjacent to their property, as a condition to permitting them to enlarge their residences on the property.[174] No persuasive nexus existed between whatever intrusions a larger house might have made on the visual characteristics of the scene (a proper regulatory consideration) and public access to the waterfront, in the majority's view, and so the condition that the landowners encumber their land by providing public access, if desired by the community, would have to be paid for.

The "takings" line of argument has shown some signs of moving beyond the land use setting to which it most obviously pertains. In 1998, another coal mining company prevailed in its argument that it could not properly be made to bear responsibility for new retirement benefits for its prior employees, with the predominant opinion using a "taking" rationale.[175] And the same year saw the "takings" analysis successfully applied to a state's requirement that lawyers holding small amounts of funds for clients, amounts not in themselves large enough to earn substantial interest, place them in a special common fund, the interest on which would be used to benefit programs providing legal services for the poor.[176] Since, by hypothesis, these amounts by themselves would not have been put into any interest-bearing account in the absence of this regulation, it is perhaps more obvious that this judgment deprived those programs of useful support, than that it took anything from those whose funds were in-

---

173. Keystone Bituminous Coal Ass'n v. De Benedictis, 480 U.S. 479 (1987).

174. Nollan v. California Coastal Commission, 483 U.S. 825 (1987). See also Dolan v. City of Tigard, 512 U.S. 374 (1994).

175. Eastern Enterprises v. Apfel, 524 U.S. 498 (1998); four Justices subscribed to this theory, with a fifth preferring to rest his conclusion on (substantive) due process grounds having to do with the permitted retrospectivity of legislation.

176. Phillips v. Washington Legal Foundation, 524 U.S. 156 (1998).

volved. The plaintiff in the case was not an individual lawyer or client, but a conservative group opposed in principle to public subventions of this character. How much farther this line of reasoning will be permitted to expand remains to be seen.

III

THE MACHINERY OF
GOVERNMENT

The previous brief discussion of separation of powers[1] introduced the three chief authorities of the federal government: Congress, the President, and the Supreme Court. These are the only federal actors whose functions are definitely set out in the federal Constitution. While there are references to the possibility of other courts and to the "departments" and their heads (the inevitable bureaucracy), *all* legislative power given to the federal government is placed in the two houses of an elected Congress; *all* executive power, in an elected President; and *all* judicial power, in a Supreme Court (and any inferior courts Congress may create), whose Justices are appointed to lifelong terms with the approval of the upper house of Congress, the Senate. As we have also seen, however, the actual work of government is substantially done by departments and agencies which are created legislatively rather than by the Constitution, and which appear to exercise all three of the functions the Constitution mentions. It may be helpful to imagine the machinery of government as a carriage pulled by three horses; that each of the horses has a particular role to play says nothing necessarily about the nature of the carriage they are pulling—at least so long as the attachment of each to the carriage remains secure, and its appointed role may be played. Although some believe that the dawn of the twentieth century saw the invention of a horseless carriage for American government as well as for the highway,[2] these pages take a different view. Connections between the agencies of government and the three chief authorities of government remain essential to the legality of government action. In this Chapter, we first examine those three chief authorities, and then describe in a general way the structure and functions of the subordinate elements of American government.

---

1. See p. 19 above.
2. E.g., G. Lawson, The Rise and Rise of the Administrative State, 107 Harv. L. Rev. 1231 (1994).

A. *The actors the Constitution names—Congress, President and Court*

1. Congress

The American Congress has two chambers, the Senate and the House of Representatives. The Senate is comprised of 100 Senators, two elected from each state. Each Senator is elected by the entire voting population of the state and serves a six year term. Nationwide, elections occur every two years, so that one third of the Senate stands for election each two years. Unless a special election is required to fill an unexpired term, only one of any given state's two Senate positions is involved in any such election, and in one of every three Senate elections neither is. The House of Representatives today comprises 435 Representatives, or Members of Congress, allocated among the states according to population, but with each state having at least one. Each Member stands for election every two years. In states with more than one Representative, each usually represents a unique subdistrict of the state, defined by state legislation. These districts are generally redefined every ten years, when the results of the national census are known, in order to reflect any redistribution of representatives among the states, in response to population shifts reflected in the census,[3] and to ensure compliance with the constitutional requirement that each district contain populations as nearly equal as possible.[4] The shape (as distinct from the population size) of the districts is often determined by political principles, as might be expected, and lively legal disputes continue whether this is acceptable and, to the extent not, whether a workable judicial remedy can be devised.[5]

---

3. Franklin v. Massachusetts, 505 U.S. 788 (1992), reflects both the importance of the way in which census results are applied for the affected states, and how unlikely it is that a disappointed state will be able to secure judicial review of any procedural or legal issues concerning them.

4. Reynolds v. Sims, 377 U.S. 533 (1964).

5. The process of creating a representative district to serve a particular political end— say, concentrating voters favoring the Democratic party—is known as "gerrymandering." A political boundary created with the inescapable purpose of excluding black voters was found invalid in Gomillon v. Lightfoot, 364 U.S. 339 (1960). Not until 1986 did the Supreme Court hold the courts open more generally to cases involving apparent discrimination along political lines. Davis v. Bandemer, 478 U.S. 109 (1986). One strangely shaped district in North Carolina, in some places barely wider than a highway joining urbanized areas in which African-American voters likely to favor Democrat candidates were concentrated, was initially disapproved as the product of racial motivations, Shaw v. Reno, 509 U.S. 630 (1993),

It can be seen that the design of the Congress serves a number of national political ends (as well as creating national bodies suitable for generating legislation). Both Senators and Representatives, perhaps especially the former, are directly identified with particular states. Indeed, originally Senators were elected by the state legislatures rather than directly by the voting population. While popular election of Senators was introduced by the 17th Amendment in 1913, they remain important statewide officials and often reach prominence through the state political apparatus.[6] Thus, they are likely to be strong representatives in the national legislature of state political interests. Also, their six-year terms encourage a degree of independence of momentary political winds. The drafters of the American Constitution saw them as (and they have often been) a conservative check on the activities of the more populous and political House of Representatives. When Republicans took control of the Senate and the House during the second year of President Clinton's first term in office, for example—the first time Republicans had controlled both houses of the Congress since President Eisenhower's time—the Senate was a moderating influence on the efforts of the House to enact statutes carrying out a promised "Contract with America."

Members of the House, in turn, are never more than two years from the need to be reelected,[7] a fact which strongly encourages responsiveness to their

---

Shaw v. Hunt, 517 U.S. 899 (1996). It was then approved however, when legislatively reconstituted with similar effect, Hunt v. Cromartie 532 U.S. 234 (2001), under circumstances in which a narrow majority of the Supreme Court concluded it had not been shown that race rather than politics was the dominating factor in the legislature's action. Primarily, it concluded, the legislature had sought to maintain the balance in the state's congressional representation between Democrats and Republicans, and in seeking this appropriate end it could not be forbidden to rely on the strong correlation that existed in the state between racial identification as an African-American and political affiliation as a Democrat.

6. Changes in the political process within states, however, have made Senators less often the product of state political structures. State party organizations have declined in importance as the effect of money, media, and celebrity have increased. Senators and Representatives are more likely to develop independent constituencies based on their constituents' support of national initiatives, rather than state interests. Kaden, Politics, Money, and State Sovereignty: The Judicial Role, 79 Colum. L. Rev. 847 (1979).

7. In fact, incumbent members of Congress, able to secure good press coverage and with relatively easy access to fundraising, are generally re-elected. The incumbents' advantage is especially pronounced in the House, where more than 90% of those incumbents who seek reelection prevail. Resignation from office—perhaps to seek a different political position—is often how vacancies arise. The experience with incumbency, not only in the House of Representatives but also in state and local political offices, has generated considerable pressure for legislation imposing limits on the total length of time a politician can

constituents. House members typically maintain important staff offices in their districts, and frequently serve for their constituents the functions that ombudsmen have in other systems, assisting them in their difficulties with the federal bureaucracy.[8] The closeness of the Representatives to the people is reflected in the constitutional requirement that fiscal legislation—tax and budget—originate in the House. Otherwise, proposed legislation may originate in either chamber.

a. Legislation and appropriations[9]

The public process: To judge by the explicit concerns of the constitutional text, the work of Congress concerns the enactment of legislation, including the annual national budget. Although the President and the agencies of government are often in fact the source of proposed legislation, the source of a legislative proposal has no legal (as distinct from political) significance. Whatever its actual source, as a formal matter all legislation is introduced by Senators or Representatives. Legislation on any subject may be introduced in either the Senate or the House (although all "Bills for raising revenue shall originate in the House"). Each proposal is then referred to one or more committees for investigation and report. The committees of the House and of the Senate, discussed in somewhat greater detail below, are relatively small bod-

---

serve in the same office; but this is not a limitation that a state has authority to impose on its federal congressional representatives (and not one that Congress is likely to impose on itself).

In the Senate, the experience has been more variable—as in 1994, the first by-election during President Clinton's administration, when the Republican Party gained twelve seats, or in 2000 when, with the election of a Republican President, it lost six. One looking at the behavior of American voters over the past several decades will see that they have usually put different political parties in control of the Congress (or at least one of its houses) than of the White House. Since these elections occur in different geographical units—Representatives from districts, Senators from states, and the President nationally—one cannot say that this result is the product of deliberate action by a particular electorate. Nonetheless, it suggests a certain distrust of unified government, as also underlies the regimes of separation of powers, and checks-and-balances.

8. Senators also do personal services for constituents. But because they represent an entire state and need to run for re-election only each sixth year, constituent service—at least on the retail level—is traditionally a smaller part of the Senators' function. The importance to members of Congress of serving this personal function probably goes far in explaining why the ombuds function has not been adopted in American politics.

9. The parliamentarians of the House and Senate have published expositive essays about the legislative process summarily described here, see http://thomas.loc.gov/home/lawsmade.toc.html and http://thomas.loc.gov/home/enactment/enactlawtoc.html, respectively.

ies composed of Representatives or Senators (with professional staff) and are specialized according to subject matter. Their membership is divided between Democrats and Republicans in roughly the proportion that those two parties hold seats in the relevant part of Congress. They meet under the chairmanship of a member of the majority party in that chamber. The committee will generally act first through a subcommittee. Although committees have no legal obligation to hold hearings on proposed legislation, the rules of Congress oblige them to conduct any hearings they do hold in public, absent some very strong reason (such as the involvement of national security issues) to hold them in camera.

When a subcommittee holds public hearings, the persons appearing may include other legislators interested in the proposal, government officials responsible for activities in the area under inquiry, experts, and representatives of interested industries or public groups. Witnesses appear by invitation of the subcommittee, not as a matter of right; these invitations are extended by majority and minority staff, respectively, and the experience of the author and his colleagues is that—as when parties to American litigation call expert witnesses—experts are often selected on an understanding how they are likely to testify. It is a common and accepted practice to seek out such an invitation, indicating in a general way one's reason for doing so and one's expected contribution; response may, again, be a function of the politics of the situation, as well as the time avail able to the subcommittee. Written comments may always be submitted.

Those who appear at the hearing typically give a brief oral statement summarizing a longer written submission prepared in advance. Members of the subcommittee or its staff may then address questions to them, which may be answered either orally or in subsequent writings; often, written questions are submitted for a written response. Hearings are more likely to address general policy issues than precise questions of wording, and the subcommittee does not itself work on the bill during them. Any drafting revisions are the product of subcommittee "mark-up" sessions, which may follow intensive work by its staff (with or without the participation of interested outsiders). Congress's rules intend that these sessions, as well, should ordinarily be public, although one has a sense that much marking up occurs in an informal staff process (if majority and minority staff can agree), and that closed door mark-up sessions occur more frequently than closed hearings.

Only if the subcommittee agrees to support a particular proposal for legislation, will it bring that before the full committee, where further hearings and changes may occur. If the committee does not agree on the proposal, the bill will die there. This power renders the committees the dominant influence on the process. Only committee approval of proposed language sends the bill to the floor of the full House or Senate. Even seemingly popular proposals for legislation can be kept from reaching the floor of the full chamber by powerful members who can prevent the bill from even emerging from the committee.

For a bill that will be sent forward to the floor, committee staff prepare a report indicating and defending the various choices that have been made, as a means of explaining the bill to those who have been less intensely involved. These committee reports were long important to the formal interpretation of legislation, as they were thought to be reliable indicators of the problems and processes that had generated a law. So, although the reports were not voted upon or approved of by the chamber as the bill itself would be, they could play an important role in determining the legislation's ultimate effect.

As discussed in Chapter VIII below, this importance has recently diminished. Some federal judges have expressed concern that, precisely because of the influence these reports may have on judicial interpretations, committee staff and the lobbyists who work with them have been tempted to use committee report language to try to achieve results that could not safely have been put to a congressional vote. If this is a risk for highly controversial matters—and one can certainly understand the temptations involved—it does not seem so important for the more routine matters, where awareness of what the committee was concerned about, what representations had been made to it, etc., can be helpful in understanding language that, standing by itself, proves to be somewhat unilluminating. The institutional nature of Congress's work gives some assurance that the reports will remain a useful window on particular legislative processes.

If the bill is sent to the floor, it is there subjected to formal debate, amendment and vote.[10] If the bill is passed, it is then sent to the other chamber, where it usually undergoes the same legislative process. As may be apparent, it may never emerge from that chamber, or emerge in very different form.

If the bill is not passed in *any* form by the second chamber, it is defeated. If the second chamber adopts a bill with different provisions, two methods of resolving the disagreements are possible. First, the chamber that originally

---

10. In the House of Representatives, but not in the Senate, the terms of the debate and amendment process are set by a special committee, the House Rules Committee, which creates a "rule" for each proposed legislative act. Debate in the Senate is unlimited, unless restricted by a special motion for "closure" that requires an super-majority vote often impossible to obtain. The "filibuster"—opponents speaking against legislation without pause, in the hope supporters will withdraw it to permit other business to be done—has a long and not too distinguished history in the Senate; it was the means by which civil rights legislation was long prevented by opponents from the South.

passed the bill may be satisfied to adopt the second chamber's version; then no further work is required. If it is not willing to accede, however, each chamber then appoints representatives to a special "conference committee" whose work it is to meet and develop a suitable compromise measure that can be recommended to both chambers. This work, like other committee work, is generally done in public session. A bill cannot become law unless enacted in identical form by each of the two chambers during the two-year period that marks the term of office of Representatives.[11] This requirement of bicameralism is an important element of the constitutional scheme.

While political discipline is not wholly lacking from the United States Congress—each party in each chamber has an elected leadership that works to secure unified action by party members, and it can influence such matters as committee assignments—one rarely hears publicly of sanctions imposed for voting one's conscience on a measure. During his first term as Speaker of the House, 1995–96, Newt Gingrich seemed more able than many of his predecessors to secure coordinated action by the Republican representatives he led; but reaction in the country to the results at the next election (as well, perhaps, as some personal scandals) seemed to persuade his fellow members to greater independence during his second term. Even when the Democrat President (William Clinton) and Republican congressional leadership reached an understanding on controlling the national budget deficit in the spring of 1997—an understanding with clearly negative implications for the possibility of new social legislation—that fact did not discourage two prominent Senators, one Democrat and one Republican, from offering a new program that came within a very few votes of passage in the Senate. Variations between the houses are thus to be expected on any controversial matter. Members may change parties without forfeiting their seats; when Senator Jeffords of Vermont switched from the Republican to the Democrat party in 2001, he moved the Senate from Republican to Democrat control and became the chair of an important committee.[12]

The President's role: The final, and necessary, step in the process of enactment is presenting the bill to the President for signature. If signed, it becomes law. The President may, however, refuse to sign the legislation and return it to Congress with a veto message. In that event, it does not become law unless Congress is able to override the veto by a two thirds vote of the

---

11. At the end of the two-year period, all bills not finally enacted lapse—even if they cleared all but the final hurdle. Of course they may be reintroduced, but they must then traverse the whole process again; they have no formal claim to shortened procedure.

12. By changing the party control of the Senate he not only gained a chair for himself, but caused all Senate committees to change to Democrat chairing.

members of each chamber.[13] This requirement of presidential participation in the enactment of statutes, "presentment," is regarded along with bicameralism—the necessity that both houses enact the identical language—as an essential element of American separation of powers respecting legislation.[14] Notice, however, that the President's authority at this point is strictly negative—he can only veto the bill in its entirety. As a strategic matter, Congress can significantly restrict the President's veto option by adopting legislative packages that contain items he wants, as well as others he opposes. No enforceable principle prevents Congress from enacting such omnibus legislation. Particularly in the appropriations process shortly to be described, members of Congress have often used this approach to tie the President to their choices about spending priorities. Indeed, omnibus appropriations legislation can become so gargantuan, running to hundreds of pages, that there may be no effective opportunity for members who were not part of the relevant committee even to read the presented bill. Individual members of Congress have sometimes been successful in introducing matters of particular interest to some supporter of theirs, that could not have survived an open vote if they had become known.

Could the members of Congress, institutionally, protect themselves from the possibility that individual members would introduce such items, by creating a process by which the President could identify objectionable items and then not spend those moneys (in the case of an appropriation)? In recognition of the possibility of irresponsible legislative behavior, particularly about appropriations matters, the constitutions of many states authorize their governors to use a "line item veto," permitting them to single out particular components of a legislative enactment for disapproval that prevents them from becoming law. Details of the practice vary from state to state, but the central proposition is that sound democratic politics needs to have an effective check against the abuse entailed in hiding objectionable items in omnibus legislation. In 1996, after years of debate, Congress adopted a statute providing a similar authority for the President under constrained conditions.[15] The measure was

---

13. Ordinarily, the President must affirmatively exercise his veto authority, taking public responsibility for his decision and permitting Congress a definitive basis on which to act. A bill becomes law ten business days after passage unless specifically vetoed. If Congress adjourns during that ten-day period, so that a veto message could not be received if one were sent, then the bill does not become law unless the President actually signs it. A refusal to sign during an adjournment period is called a Pocket Veto.

14. See INS v. Chadha, p. 20, n. 38 above.

15. The authority could be exercised, in a manner not necessary to discuss here, only as to budgetary appropriations and special tax laws favoring a very limited number of tax-

to become effective with the inauguration in 1997 of the next President—that is, someone whose party affiliation could not have been known at the time Congress acted. One may credit this action as a recognition by Congress of its own frequent lack of discipline in such matters, a recognition that has also motivated other measures authorizing politically difficult initiatives.[16] Congress employed somewhat complex mechanisms in the hope of avoiding judicial disapproval of the measure as a violation of separation of powers. In the end, however, the statute was found unconstitutional because it in effect permitted the creation of a statute without the security of both bicameralism and presentment as to the exact language of the statute finally enacted.[17] The President's veto may be used *only* as to the entire legislation Congress has enacted.

Power and money: delegations, authorizations, appropriations: Implicit in the foregoing is the proposition that legislation affecting regulatory agencies takes three different forms. The most obvious, probably in the reader's mind throughout this discussion, is the substantive legislation creating legislative standards and empowering an agency to administer them. Such legislation need be enacted but once, and has continuous legal force until revised. But the Constitution requires legislation to permit the expenditure of public moneys as well as to create public bodies or private duties, and the second and third types of legislation concern expenditures. The continuing *general* dimensions of the agency's program, from a fiscal perspective, are established by a law that sets a maximum amount "authorized" to be expended. Authorization to expend funds is often given permanently, but in some cases agencies are required to return to Congress periodically, even annually, for fresh authorization. This can be considered a device by which Congress prompts itself to review agency functioning to determine whether (or at what level) its continuance is in the public interest. Authorization, however, simply sets a maximum level of permitted expenditure, and does not actually provide any funds for agency use. Agencies are permitted to expend funds from the public treasury only pursuant to an annual appropriation statute.[18] Although occurring annually, appropriations are legislative in form, and so must pass through each of the steps outlined above. For larger agencies, the appropria-

---

payers. Provisions of the latter sort are a good example of the objectionable "Christmas tree ornament" provisions that can find their way into omnibus legislation.

16. See, e.g., Dalton v. Spector, 511 U.S. 462 (1994) (military base closings); Bowsher v. Synar, 478 U.S. 714 (1986) (budget deficit controls).

17. Clinton v. City of New York, 524 U.S. 417 (1998).

18. U.S. Const. Art. I, §9, cl.7.

tion is made in detail, either in the legislation itself or in accompanying committee documents. While only a statute has formal legal force, agencies who
must deal with the same committees each year understandably follow committee report instructions, hesitating to shift money directed to one line or
purpose to another unless informal permission to do so has been secured. For
smaller agencies, appropriations may be simply a statement of the total
amount of money the Treasury will provide to the agency for its programs in
the coming fiscal year, without further specification.

It will be evident that this annual appropriations process has great significance for an agency, permitting both Congress and, as will be seen, the President a high degree of oversight and control of agency functioning. The
process is complicated, and in a work of this character the main point to establish is that setting the resources an agency has available can significantly
control agency action, in a manner that reflects both national priorities and
contemporary political forces more systematically and with more accuracy and
timeliness than judicial or other legal controls.[19] With limited exceptions,
agencies first make their requests for appropriations to the President's Office
of Management and Budget (OMB), discussed below.[20] Whether or not the
language of the appropriation bill will go into program details, the agency
must be prepared at this point, and in legislative discussions, to give full and
detailed justifications for every aspect of its proposed programs. Note that this
serves to provide not only external, but also internal discipline to the agency's
administration. Preparing the annual budget presentation gives the agency's
political leadership a crucial opportunity to negotiate with its professional,
permanent staff the course the agency will follow during the coming year—
as the staff well understands and the laws attending appropriations measures
will require them to respect. Here is where rivalries among various staff offices for resources and importance find their expression, as priorities *within*
the agency are debated and set. After OMB review is complete, the President
draws up and sends to Congress a proposed consolidated national budget. In
generating that proposal, he will necessarily determine both the relative priority to be given the agency's work within the national government and, if the
agency budget is detailed, his ideas about the priorities it should follow.

---

19. It is not intended to suggest that these controls are necessarily benign or protected
from manipulation. They, too, can include in their details provisions that could not sur-
vive an open vote if focused on in legislative debate. Year after year, for example, the opponents of popular legislation may succeed in having appropriations bills provide that "no
funds may be expended" in pursuit of that legislation's ends.

20. See p. 111 below.

Under a statute adopted in 1974,[21] Congress also develops annual budgetary proposals, with the assistance of professional staff in its Congressional Budget Office.[22] Appropriations proposals for a given agency go before several different committees at various stages, of which specialized "appropriations committees" in the House and the Senate are the most important. Over the years, these committees can develop extremely powerful relationships with the agencies that annually depend on them for funding of their programs;[23] while the President would prefer that all proposals come through OMB, some agencies as a matter of law (in general the "independent" commissions) and most as a matter of practical reality (through undetectable "leaks") let their committees know their needs. While debates over general spending levels and major programs such as the Defense budget are common in the two chambers, regulatory agency budgets are a small part of overall national expenditures.[24] These budgets are not often the subject of debate outside the relevant committees or (if the House and Senate have appropriated different amounts in their respective bills) the conference committee.

With recent years' congressional (and presidential) attention to deficit reduction, these activities have acquired substantial political prominence, and have also come to be driven by a factor (reducing the overall level of government expenditure) that is independent of strictly programmatic considerations. When Congress appears to choose a given level of environmental amenity or workplace safety in substantive legislation, it generally does so free of consideration of how much money can be allocated to this task, among the many that compete for government funds. An undertaking to reduce the level of government expenditure in general does not mean that spending for inspectors to control the drug industry is less important; but nonetheless a predictable impact is that the Food and Drug Administration will be receiving fewer dollars with which to support its programs. One can find many examples of programmatic reductions that do not appear to be supported by specific judgments about the importance of the program concerned.[25]

---

21. Congressional Budget and Impoundment Control Act of 1974, P.L. 97-258, 96 Stat. 877, 31 U.S.C. §1400 ff.

22. See p. 85 below.

23. See the works cited in n. 59, p. 28 above.

24. In 2001, for example, the EPA regulatory budget was about $7.3 billion; the Securities and Exchange Commission, about $438 million; the Federal Trade Commission, about $147 million. In comparison, that year's defense budget was $296.3 billion, and the total national budget for the year was $1,856 billion.

25. At the time of this writing, perhaps the most notorious example lies in reduced funding for tax administration, which has dramatically lowered the percentage of tax re-

A number of agencies are authorized to collect fees from those they regulate, and to apply this income stream to meeting the expenses of their programs. By this means, an agency could escape both these problems and the discipline of the budgetary process. For just this reason, of course, the fee device raises some questions about compliance with a Constitution that evidently regards fiscal controls over government action as important. Nor is it inevitable that an agency will be authorized to keep its own accounts in this way; the money raised by fees can be collected to the undifferentiated Treasury account, and the agency's expenses paid out of ordinary, appropriated government money. If it is so authorized, however, then its only need for statutory appropriations will arise if its income from fees falls below its needs. The current budgetary stringencies have provided a major incentive to develop "user fee" financing—avoiding constraints that are not associated with judgments about program worth. Industries interested in effective regulation—because it helps to build needed public confidence, or perhaps because in their case regulation tends to pay them "rent"—may be quite tolerant of these fees. Problems may nonetheless be anticipated. Fee levels might be set to encourage or discourage certain private activities, as well as to finance the direct costs of regulation;[26] and they may in other ways reflect an arguably unhealthy relationship with the industry being regulated. Banking regulators, as one example, generally are financed by fees; while defended as producing a certain independence of politics, the practice can also be seen to produce an inappropriate closeness to its regulated industry.

Private participation—Lobbying: In the increasingly public legislative process, as already indicated, interested members of the public often look for ways to influence its outcomes. Private connections to politicians (as to judges) can have a criminal aspect, if bribes are paid directly to secure political favors (a "quid pro quo"). Not directly criminal, but under a good degree of public suspicion and, at the moment of this writing, effort to secure new national legislation, is the donation of money to support political activities. Election campaigns are enormously expensive, producing a situation in which politicians and political organizations must work continuously to raise funds. Since it is thought people have reasons for spending large sums of money—that they

---

turns that can be audited, the availability of personnel to pursue persons owing uncollected taxes for previous years, etc. As it would hardly be surprising if reduced enforcement led to reduced collections, or if reduced workplace inspections resulted in a higher rate of workplace accidents, the economic justifications for these restrictions are often unclear.

26. See National Cable Television Ass'n, Inc. v. FCC, n. 79, p. 34 above.

may hope to place in office someone who could be expected to be sympathetic to their interests, not simply to support democracy—the possibility of providing money to politicians, even without a specific undertaking to do something in return is troublesome.[27] Politicians' self-interest in contributions, and Supreme Court decisions holding that for citizen contributors contributions are a form of expression protected by the First Amendment,[28] will predictably constrain any limitation on contributions resulting from the current public discussion.[29]

Here it may be useful to address a few words to the practice of "lobbying" with respect to specific legislative proposals, legislative advocacy as it were. Lobbyists, historically actors under some suspicion as sources of improper influence, have become increasingly prominent and their practices somewhat regularized in recent years. The work of honestly representing a client's interests in the legislative forum is sought and readily accepted by highly ethical lawyers. Both a successful legislative process and its administrative counterparts require factual information and thoughtful understanding of the possible consequences of various proposed alternatives. Lobbying activities provide this information, as well as a forum for efforts at persuasion that—when not accompanied by promises of corrupt favors—precisely reflect the Constitution's assurance to citizens of their right to petition for the redress of grievances. Lobbyists depend on continuing relationships in the relatively small community they hope to influence, and so may have a particular need to develop and maintain a reputation for responsible and reliable action. To the extent they come to their positions from prior service in Congress or executive office, as is often the case, they may also help their clients to understand the likely needs and behaviors of the government officials they are seeking to work with, and in that way also function as mediators influencing the actions of the private community. They are retained by civil rights and environmental proponents as well as by trade and business groups. During the committee stages

27. Bribery law prohibits only direct exchange of money for particular favors, not payments made to recognize (or in the hopes of securing) general support.

28. Buckey v. Valeo, 424 U.S. 1 (1976); First Nat'l Bank of Boston v. Bellotti, 435 U.S. 265 (1976). Foreign contributors do not enjoy the protection of the amendment, and their contributions are much more closely regulated (and politically much less acceptable).

29. The Federal Election Campaign Act, 2 U.S.C. §431 et seq., rather sharply limits contributions that can be made to individual candidates for office, but permits unlimited amounts of "soft money" to be given in support of political parties or political action committees, often organized around particular issues (say, matters of interest to the dairy industry), that in turn are able to support candidates. See Mariani v. United States, 212 F. 3d 761 (3d Cir. 2000).

of legislation, lobbyists work closely with committee members to help them understand what their clients might regard as satisfactory outcomes. At later stages they may attempt to persuade other members respecting their votes or desired amendments, or seek congressional oversight of agency activity under statutes once enacted.

While lobbyists inevitable represent particular interests rather than the general public, their function in attempting to persuade or even pressure members of Congress politically is generally seen as legitimate. Overtones of bribery and corruption are possible in some circumstances, however, particularly in a political climate that depends as heavily as the United States' does on the private financing of election campaigns. Agents of foreign governments, including their political lobbyists but not their diplomats, have long been subject to requirements to register and comply with lobbying regulations, subject to criminal penalties;[30] more recently, Congress has enacted general lobbying legislation requiring registration and a measure of disclosure by professional lobbyists.[31] Perhaps paradoxically, this heightened regulation seems to have contributed to making lobbying more "reputable" and prominent. One now finds regular columns on lobbying practice in lawyers' newspapers and manuals of ethical and legal advice being produced by the bar association.[32]

b. Committee oversight of agency functioning

Although agency officials are not formally answerable to the legislature in the ways that would be characteristic of a parliamentary democracy, they nonetheless frequently appear before congressional committees—the so-called "independent regulatory commissions" equally with officials of agencies in cabinet departments[33]—and are subjected to searching examination into the

---

30. 18 U.S.C. §2386.

31. Lobbying Disclosure Act of 1995, 2 U.S.C. §1601 et seq.

32. W. Luneburg, ed., The Lobbying Manual: A Compliance Guide for Lawyers and Lobbyists (2d ed. 1998), provides a comprehensive view of the regulation of lobbying for practitioners; a column and news reports regularly appear in the weekly Legal Times of Washington, the lawyer's newspaper for Washington, D.C.

On the problem of prior executive branch employees being permitted to represent clients before their former agency, through "the revolving door," see p. 293, n. 85 below.

33. The "independent" in "independent regulatory commission" has generally been regarded by Congress as meaning relative independence of the President, not of Congress. See p. 133 below. Thus, a former Chairman of the Federal Regulatory Commission, who had previously been an important official in the White House, remarked that being in an independent regulatory commission meant "having to appear naked in front of Congress," without the political protection a connection to the White House could bring.

conduct of agency business. These oversight relations are perhaps the most important relationships administrative agencies have with Congress. Oversight can arise not only in the usual legislative context and the annual process of securing necessary appropriations, but also through investigations quite independent of any legislative proposal, that may have their source in the concerns of a single member of Congress. Each agency will have an oversight relationship with at least one committee in each of the Senate and the House of Representatives. Committee members expect to be informed of important proposals within the agency and feel free to conduct hearings or to seek in other less formal ways to influence it. Interactions are frequent and usually treated with seriousness on the agency side.[34] Generally the professional staff of the respective oversight committees will be as well informed respecting the functioning of an agency as any persons in official Washington outside the agency itself.

Aggressive oversight is more accepted in connection with agency planning or proposals for rulemaking—the adoption of subordinate legislation—than it is respecting the decision of formal agency proceedings of an adjudicatory character. (Political pressures in the latter context can give rise to "fairness" claims by those who may seem to be their target, as is discussed at a later point.)[35] In 1996 Congress adopted a statutory requirement that all agency actions meeting the Administrative Procedure Act's definition of rulemaking, broad enough to encompass tens if not hundreds of thousands of actions yearly, must be submitted to it for possible consideration of a joint resolution of disapproval.[36] Both the precise terms of this statute and the realities of the situation suggest that the act will be directly invoked only in connection with a so-called "major" rule, one whose impact on the economy is so great that it will already have drawn the President's close oversight attention under an executive order regime shortly to be discussed.[37] Indeed, since a resolution under the Act can be vetoed, it will perhaps only be invoked—as the one time it has thus far been used it was—to disapprove rules adopted in the final months of one President, who has been succeeded in office by another less sympathetic to his administration's initiatives. The principal impact of the congressional

---

34. Evidence of its effect does not often appear. But see California ex rel Water Resources Board v. FERC, 966 F.2d 1541 (9th Cir. 1992); Hazardous Waste Treatment Council v. EPA, 886 F.2d 355 (D.C. Cir. 1989), cert. den. 498 U.S. 849 (1990); Sierra Club v. Costle, 657 F.2d 298 (D.C. Cir. 1981).

35. See p. 273 below.

36. See the brief discussion of congressional review legislation, p. 35 above.

37. See p. 103 below.

review requirement, predictably, will come earlier in the process, as the existence of this power creates incentives for agency staff to permit members of Congress and their staffs early and influential participation in the rulemaking procedures.

In addition to relatively formal and continuing relationships with committees and their staffs, agencies are in frequent contact with individual Senators and Representatives about matters of particular interest to their constituents. It is normal for a person frustrated with or concerned about an agency's action to write about it to her Senator or Representative, and for them then to pass the question on to the agency. Usually this comes in the form of an inquiry or more-or-less standard request to learn the status of a given matter, have it expedited, etc.[38] It is not unknown, however, for the Senator or Representative to state a view on the desirable outcome of the matter, and these interventions can be influential. As already remarked,[39] Representatives in particular view this form of constituency service as a major aspect of their role, seeing it as a way of generating community support for reelection, and some scholars believe that its tendency is to eclipse the directly legislative function that is the only responsibility specified for Senators and Representatives in the Constitution. Such a diversion is only to be expected, if one accepts the analyses of public choice theorists: diffuse legislative formulations permit legislators to claim credit from a wide circle of voters seeking policy enactments, and then to disassociate themselves from unpopular outcomes; casework translates directly into the votes that are supposed to be the raison d'être of political life.[40] Be that as it may, responding to such interventions occupies a good deal

---

38. See A. Sofaer, The Change-of-Status Adjudication: A Case Study of the Informal Agency Process. 1 J. Leg. Stud. 349 (1972) and J. Mashaw et al., Social Security Hearings and Appeals (1978). Both studies suggest that Congress members often will act to speed agency action on matters which concern their constituents, but usually stop short of acting as advocates. The effect of the inquiry, then, is to move a person up the queue awaiting action, more than to influence outcome.

39. See p. 71 above.

40. "Public choice" is a well-developed discipline bringing classical micro-economics and game theory to bear on the subjects of political science. That is, it starts from assumptions that its subjects—in the most developed analyses, these are legislators, but in theory they could also be executive officials, judges, indeed citizens—act as individual utilitarian, self-interest maximizers. In the case of legislators, the most classical analyses are made in terms of those behaviors that are most likely to secure the legislator's reelection. Finding room for altruism or other community-regarding motivations is a challenge on these premises; nor is it obvious, empirically, that the equation of economic and political behavior is warranted. See the sources cited in n. 17, p. 8 above.

of agency time, and is regarded as an activity of some importance to the agency's future well-being.

c. Congressional agencies—Congressional Budget Office and the General Accounting Office

All this oversight activity has resulted in an enormous growth in congressional staff, both on committees and in the personal offices of individual Senators and Representatives; reductions to accommodate the government's general resource constraints still leave a congressional bureaucracy many times larger than it was half a century ago.[41] In addition, two major agencies operating, in effect, as delegates of Congress serve a continuing, professional oversight function: the Congressional Budget Office; and the General Accounting office.[42] Although this function is not often highly visible to the public, it has a considerable impact on administrative functioning.

The 230 employees (mostly economists) of the Congressional Budget Office[43] are responsible for analyses and advice supporting the congressional side of the annual appropriations process. In that capacity, they share with the appropriations committee a continuing relationship with agencies in respect of their need for funding. Since 1922, agencies have had to satisfy a Presidential office (now the Office of Management and Budget[44]) about the relative importance of their needs for financial support and the contributions of particular programs to national policy. Since the creation of the Congressional Budget Office in 1974, they have also had to justify their claims on the national budget to this body, which acts as a professional financial analyst on behalf of the two houses of Congress.[45]

The General Accounting Office[46] is a large agency, of about 3,275 professional employees, whose responsibility, in the first instance, is retrospective

---

41. See n. 58 p. 27 above.

42. The two agencies to be discussed are not the only congressional agencies, although they are perhaps the most prominent. The Library of Congress, notably, performs research and analysis functions in addition to serving its nominal function. www.loc.gov.

43. www.cbo.gov.

44. See p. 111 below.

45. See A. Schick, The Federal Budget: Politics, Policy, Process (1995); A. Wildavsky, The New Politics of the Budgetary Process (2d ed. 1992); W. Wander, F. Hebert and G. Copeland, Congressional Budgeting: Politics, Process and Power (1984); and A. Schick, The First Five Years of Congressional Budgeting, in R. Penner, The Congressional Budget Process After Five Years 3 (1981). The Budget office's principal function, however, is to make broad-scale assessments of the budget and its impact.

46. www.gao.gov.

analysis of agency functioning to audit the correctness of agency expenditures; and, more broadly, to search out fraud, waste, and mismanagement in federal agency functioning. It is headed by an unusual officer, the Comptroller General of the United States, who is appointed by the President to a single fifteen year term. The GAO's close relationship to Congress is signaled by the expectation that the Comptroller General will be chosen from a list of three candidates drawn up by the leadership of the Senate and the House of Representatives, and by statutory provision that his removal requires congressional rather than presidential action. The GAO performs particular studies of agency functioning at the request of relevant committees, Senators or Representatives; more recently, Congress has given it statutory responsibilities for deficit reduction and in connection with congressional review of rulemaking.[47] On a day to day basis, perhaps its most important function is as a continuing presence at agencies, in connection with its audit function. This work results in reports to Congress of its findings—reports accompanied by agency responses and, frequently, offers of corrective measures that mark a substantial contribution of GAO oversight to the control of agency functioning.[48] In addition, GAO disapproval of the correctness or lawfulness of a proposed expenditure of agency funds, in an opinion of its head, the Comptroller General, generates legal consequences for the relevant agency staff that will make them very reluctant to spend those funds.[49] And in certain contexts, the GAO has been authorized to intervene in governmental contract disputes. This last activity may raise separation of powers problems like those that were decisive for a deficit reduction measure authorizing the Comptroller General to act "as if" in executive authority, but the time limited and ordinary character of his intervention in such disputes may tip the balance in its favor.[50] However that dispute is resolved, the GAO will remain as a major agency for congressional oversight and control of administrative agency action.

---

47. See p. 35 above.

48. Interested persons may subscribe to receive notice of these reports daily at the GAO site. Its reports, legal opinions, and the like are in any event posted there for ready public access.

49. General sources on the GAO include F. Mosher, a Tale of Two Agencies: A Comparative Analysis of the General Accounting Office and the Office of Management and Budget (1984); and F. Moghen, The GAO: The Quest for Accountability in American Government (1979).

50. Ameron, Inc. v. United States Army Corps of Engineers, 787 F.2d 875, reaffirmed on rehearing 809 F.2d 979 (3d Cir.1986), cert. granted 485 U.S. 958 and then dismissed pursuant to Rule 53, 488 U.S. 918 (1988).

2. President

The President of the United States is its chief executive officer, and the only executive officer whose existence and function was specified in the original Constitution.[51] Article II of the Constitution principally discusses the (rather complicated) mechanism for his election each four years; it says very little about even the President's authority. "The executive Power shall be vested" in him. He is to be "Commander in Chief" of the armed forces. He may pardon offenses. With the advice and consent of two thirds of the Senators present, "he shall have the Power...to make treaties." He is responsible for appointing major federal officers, with the advice and consent of a majority of Senators, although, as discussed above,[52] Congress may make other provisions for appointing "inferior" Officers. He "may require the Opinion, in writing, of the principal Officer in each of the executive Departments, upon any Subject relating to the Duties of their respective Offices." He is given the responsibility of "recommend[ing]" to Congress "such Measures as he shall judge necessary and expedient"—although without any expectation that his having done so will necessarily produce the desired result.[53] And, finally, "he shall take Care that the Laws be faithfully executed."

Earlier discussion of the problem of separation of powers[54] suggested some of the history of these arrangements and their difficulty. That discussion is reflected in a continuing tension between a view of the President as politically responsible for all acts of government, and a view of the other officers of government, who operate pursuant to statutory authority, as legally responsible for all decisions respecting their particular programs.[55] That tension can be seen in the language just quoted: "the executive power," undefined, is conferred only on the President.

---

51. The original text of the Constitution also creates a Vice President, but specifies only a congressional role—presiding over the Senate, where he may vote to break a tie. Widely regarded as a superfluity until relatively recently, the vice presidency has assumed increasing importance with the growing complexity of government. The 25th Amendment, adopted in 1967, creates a mechanism for permitting the Vice President to assume the powers of the presidency should the President become disabled, a mechanism in which the Vice President himself must participate. While it has not been invoked, and also does not state an executive role for the Vice President as Vice President, its existence reflects the growing importance of the office, and recent incumbents have played significant roles in domestic affairs. See, e.g., T. Walch, Ed., At the President's Side—The Vice Presidency in the Twentieth Century (1997); Twentieth Century Fund Task Force on the Vice Presidency, A Heartbeat Away 11 (1988).

52. See text at p. 24 above.

53. See text at pp. 4 and 72 above.

54. See text at p. 19 ff. above.

55. A well-regarded history of the formation of the presidency is C. Thach, The Creation of the Presidency 1775–1789 (1923). As he shows, the framers sought at the same

Yet "Duties" are mentioned as the properties of the principal officers of "executive Departments," which the Constitution evidently expects will exist but does not provide for. The only stated relationships these officers have with the President is that he must appoint them with the advice and consent of the Senate, and can then require them to give him their "Opinion, in writing" on those "Duties" of theirs. The American Constitution lacks an explicit statement, such as may be found in others,[56] that the President himself is to be the source of regulatory action. And the Constitution's statement that "he shall take Care that the Laws *be* faithfully executed" (that is, be executed *by someone else,* those on whom Congress places "Duties") suggests that he is merely to exercise oversight.

Creating a government has been understood from the beginning to be a matter for statutes, not executive decree. Congress has authority under the Constitution "to make all laws which shall be necessary and proper for carrying into Execution the foregoing Powers, and all other Powers vested by this Constitution in the Government of the United States, or in any Department or Officer thereof."[57] As this language suggests was anticipated, congressional statutes establishing the governmental apparatus customarily make sharp distinctions between the office of the President, on the one hand, and the operating divisions of government on the other. The latter take many forms—a cabinet department headed by a Secretary, an executive agency headed by an Administrator, an independent regulatory commission headed by a collegial body, even a government corporation. Here, however, a unifying characteristic is stressed: that when it enacts regulatory programs, Congress typically places the legal authority to act in these bodies, not in the President. Statutes placing direct regulatory authority in the President are quite uncommon, and are generally limited to matters trenching on foreign relations.[58] Whatever the President may be able to say to the Secretary of Agriculture or to the Chairman of the Securities and Exchange Commission about matters pending before them, in form it is the Secretary or the Commission that acts. It is to the

---

time to choose for a strong executive and against monarchy—introducing contradictions of purpose that have created continuing instability in the American view of the office.

56. E.g., Article 99 of the Argentine Constitution of 1853, as amended—a constitution that in many other respects copies that of the United States—provides explicitly that the Argentine President himself shall adopt the regulations that put into execution the laws its Congress enacts; and Argentine public arrangements have long honored that larger role.

57. Art. I, Sec. 8, cl. 18. See p. 21, n. 42 above.

58. E.g., the President is given direct authority finally to determine the assignment of airline route assignments on international routes, or to displace judgments of the Nuclear Regulatory Commission respecting international commerce in reactors or fuel ordinarily subject to its control.

Department and the Commission that Congress appropriates the resources necessary to act; the resources of the presidency itself are quite limited.[59] The following paragraphs suggest the ways in which those resources may be used to oversee or control administrative action.

It may be appropriate to acknowledge, preliminarily, that from a President's perspective the day to day work of administration, even the development of the most important of regulations, will rarely be a matter for his personal attention. Issues of foreign relations and of national security, working with Congress on important legislation and the annual budget, as well as the political routines necessary to support all of these and also his desired place in the national spotlight, will take priority. What is about to be discussed as the President's activities are much more likely, in fact, to be those of an important White House Office, the Office of Management and Budget,[60] or of the Vice President acting on the President's behalf. Indeed, "domestic regulation" has increasingly become a standard part of the Vice President's portfolio.[61] This has certain implications for what appears as presidential control: if it is more likely to proceed from the bowels of the White House bureaucracy, this may heighten the risk that low politics rather than high politics lies behind any effort to alter decisions that would otherwise have emerged from the responsible agency actors. When we speak of the President, in reality we are speaking not of one person but a largely invisible, politically unaccountable staff.[62]

---

59. My late esteemed colleague Professor Charles Black remarked that his students often laughed when he described Congress's undoubted authority to reduce staffing at the White House to a social secretary, but that that authority is there. "[U]nderlying all the powers of Congress is the appropriations power, the power that brought the kings of England to heel." C. Black, The Working Balance of the American Political Departments, 1 Hast. Con. L. Q. 13 (1974). The staff Congress provides the President, it provides to support the duties that it assigns; Presidents are inevitably and sharply aware of this aspect of the theory of "checks and balances" in its practical operation.

60. See p. 111 within.

61. President Clinton's Vice President Al Gore vigorously pursued these responsibilities via a national program for reinventing government; its archives are kept in a "cybercemetery," http://govinfo.library.unt.edu/npr/default.html. At this writing the only Internet evidence of President Bush's Vice President Richard Cheney's role is a link to an energy report he helped to develop, and another to a brief biography at http://www.whitehouse.gov/vicepresident/vpbio.html.

62. See T. Lowi, The Personal Presidency (1985). Some of the institutional White House may be explored at http://www.whitehouse.gov/government/eop.html.

a. Political and administrative authority

If Congress enacts a statute that confers discretion on a particular government official (the usual form), has the President a lawful claim to control the way in which she exercises that discretion, to substitute his judgment for hers? On the one hand, to say that he does is to flout the part of the law that assigns responsibility for that program to that official. Given the enormous range of matters on which government must act, technical as well as political, that understanding would also focus on one office-holder more authority than could possibly be wished. On the other hand, to deny the President's participation appears to undercut the Constitution's judgment that there is to be but one chief executive, to permit Congress to create administrative institutions outside the separation of powers framework. It may be testimony to the difficulty of the problem that more than 200 years have seen no resolution.[63] Contemporary commentary, perhaps reflecting trends in recent Presidents' conduct of office[64] and Supreme Court decisions on separation of powers issues,[65] has more often supported the "strong" than the "weak" presidency side of this debate.[66] In this writer's judgment, the issue presents a tension important to maintain, not resolve; it is necessary to recognize *both* the excessiveness of a presidential claim of universal revisory authority *and* the necessity of having some form of (lesser) political and legal relationship between the President and the statutorily-defined departments, agencies and commissions that actually administer the nation's laws.[67] The paragraphs following reflect this not universally accepted point of view.

---

63. The dilemma is well stated in E. Corwin, The President: Office and Powers 80–81 (4th rev. ed. 1957).

64. See the discussion of presidential oversight of agency rulemaking, p. 103 within.

65. See the discussions of Freytag, p. 24 above, Morrison, p. 99 below, and Bowsher, p. 98 below.

66. E.g., E. Kagan, Presidential Administration, 114 Harv. L. Rev. 2245 (2001); E. Magill, The Real Separation in Separation of Powers Law, 86 Va. L. Rev. 1127 (2000); M. Flaherty, The Most Dangerous Branch, 105 Yale L. J. 1725 (1996); L. Lessig & C. Sunstein, The Presidency and the Administration, 94 Colum. L. Rev. 1 (1994); S. Calabresi & S. Prakash, The President's Power to Execute the Laws, 104 Yale L. J. 541 (1994); compare C. Farina, The Consent of the Governed: Against Simple Rules for a Complex World, 72 Chi-Kent L. Rev. 987 (1997).

67. P. Strauss, Presidential Rulemaking, 72 Chi-Kent L. Rev. 965 (1997) and P. Strauss, The Place of Agencies in Government: Separation of Powers and the Fourth Branch, 84 Colum. L. Rev. 573 (1984).

If a law fixes an absolute duty on an official, that is to say one as to which he has no discretion, it has been settled since the earliest days[68] that his compliance with that duty may be enforced by law, and the President has no authority to interfere. This is the very least that might be expected of a commitment to legality—that the President as well as the official is bound by the law's specification of duty. Administrative regimes of any interest, however, confer substantial discretion. The law fixes not an absolute duty but a range of circumstances within which the official is empowered to act.

The early cases tended to take the existence of discretion as a signal that the President's acts could not be controlled by law, at least within the ambit of that discretion. Thus, a decision still central to the American theory of judicial review, of executive as well as legislative action, contrasted "cases in which the executive professes a constitutional or legal discretion" with those "where a specific duty is assigned by law, and individual rights depend upon the performance of that duty." It denied any claim to reach the former:

> The province of the court is, solely, to decide on the rights of individuals, not to enquire how the executive, or executive officers, perform duties in which they have a discretion. Questions, in their nature political, or which are, by the constitution and laws, submitted to the executive, can never be made in this court.[69]

Over time, however, it has become clear that "discretion" may refer to at least two differing phenomena. First, it refers to political areas that reasons of state may require be left essentially devoid of law. Second, it connotes administrative settings in which much specification is provided and regularity of official behavior is deeply desired, although acts of judgment are also called for. An example of the first, in fact the example stressed in the case just quoted from, is the conduct of foreign relations. In this political arena, where one might say there is "no law to apply,"[70] an executive officer is "to conform precisely to the will of the President. He is the mere organ by whom that will is communicated."[71] One might characterize this as *DISCRETION!* As the courts and Congress play no direct role in controlling its exercise, the need for direct presidential responsibility is evident. An example of the second, more con-

---

68. Marbury v. Madison, 5 U.S. (1 Cranch) 137 (1803); Kendall v. United States, 37 U.S. (12 Pet.) 524 (1838).

69. Marbury, n. 68 above, at 170; see H. Monaghan, Marbury and the Administrative State, 83 Colum. L. Rev. 1 (1983).

70. Citizens to Preserve Overton Park, Inc. v. Volpe, 401 U.S. 402, 410 (1971).

71. Marbury, note 68 above, at 166.

strained type of discretion lies in the government's adoption of a regulation controlling the amount of sulfur dioxide that may be released into the atmosphere by electric power generating stations, and specifying the measures to be taken by the stations in compliance. The relevant statute places responsibility for developing and issuing such a regulation on the Administrator of the Environmental Protection Agency, albeit she might do so only after intense and private consultations with the President and his staff, among others.[72] One probably would not say that "individual rights depend" upon the EPA Administrator's exercise of her statutory responsibilities, and she enjoys substantial freedom in deciding precisely how to act. Yet this is not *DISCRETION!*[73] The Administrator functions within a framework of legal constraint, subject to more-or-less clear statutory limits on what she may do and what procedures she must follow to do so. Here, a contemporary analyst would have no difficulty concluding that a court could review the Administrator's action to see whether her discretion had been abused.[74] Whether, or the extent to which, the President is entitled to control that exercise of discretion directly or through his staff is the interesting and difficult question; the statutory frameworks generally assume no more than persuasion on his part.

This essay is concerned only with this second, administrative, form of discretion.[75] While, as already indicated, the President often enjoys much scope to influence decisions of this character, in this context it is hard to argue that the officers empowered to make them must "conform precisely to the will of the President" or that such officers are "the mere organ by whom that will is communicated." Both they and he, in the first instance, must comply with such legal constraints as do exist: specifications of expenditures to be made,[76]

72. Sierra Club v. Costle, 657 F.2d 298 (1981); B. Ackerman and W. Hassler, Clean Coal, Dirty Air (Yale 1981); J. Quarles, Cleaning up America (1976).

73. Recall that it appears to be a constitutional condition on Congress's power to confer power of this character on administrators, that courts must be able to say whether it has been lawfully exercised—that is, that there be law to apply. See p. 33 above.

74. This distinction is reflected in the federal Administrative Procedure Act's provisions for judicial review, which in seemingly conflicting passages state that judicial review is to be denied to the extent agency action is committed by law to agency discretion, 5 U.S.C. §701(a)(2), but that agency action may be reviewed for abuse of discretion, 5 U.S.C. §706(2)(a). See the discussion in Chapters VII(A)(2)(b), p. 304 and VIII(D), p. 375 below.

75. Thus, problems arising from, for example, the actions of the CIA are not of interest here.

76. Under the Congressional Budget and Impoundment Control Act of 1974, note 21 above, this is both an affirmative and negative obligation. Never able to expend moneys that have not been appropriated, the executive is also restrained in withholding from payment (or impounding) moneys that have been appropriated; to refuse to expend money

procedures to be followed, investigations to be undertaken, or factors to be considered (or excluded from view). Formal legal authority to act rests with the officer, not the President.

These propositions rather dramatically controlled the judgment of an intermediate federal court in a case where the issue decided was whether to suspend the ordinary operation of an act requiring the protection of endangered species. This was hardly a matter of individual right. The statute placed this judgment in the hands of an elite ad hoc commission of important government officials, cabinet secretaries and heads of White House offices, requiring them to follow adjudicatory procedures. When it appeared the President may have attempted to coerce members of this commission about their votes on the matter, the court concluded that any such effort would have been improper, and ordered a careful inquiry. "[T]he Endangered Species Act explicitly vests discretion to make exemption decisions in the Committee and does not contemplate that the President or the White House will become involved in Committee deliberations."[77]

Where similar discretion is exercised through rulemaking rather than adjudication, no such statute precludes presidential efforts at persuasion. Self-evidently, moreover, the President is better placed than subordinate officials in respects that argue for his substantial participation. Only the President bears any direct political responsibility for the work of administration. Although one might think it unlikely that a President would experience political consequences from this or that detail of official action (as against, for example, his commitment to national defense), he is the only official accountable in any degree,[78] and may view particular actions as important reflections of his priorities. The President is well placed, as the heads of individual agencies are not, to reconcile the sometimes conflicting instructions of national statutes, to set national priorities in executing the laws as a whole, and to coordinate the work of government.[79] Each of these capacities permits him to bring to

---

for a purpose to which it was dedicated is to refuse faithfully to execute the law. See K. Dam, The American Fiscal Constitution, 44 U. Chi. L. Rev. 271 (1977).

77. Portland Audubon Society v. The Endangered Species Committee, 984 F.2d 1534, 1545 (1993).

78. J. Mashaw, Prodelegation: Why Administrators Should Make Political Decisions, 5 J. L. Econ. & Org. 81 (1985); Chevron, U.S.A., Inc. v. Natural Resources Defense Council, Inc., 467 U.S. 837 (1984).

79. The importance of this function is suggested, for example, by the observation in ABA Comm'n On Law And The Economy, Federal Regulation: Roads to Reform 70 (1979), that there exist "sixteen federal agencies, within and outside the executive branch, each created and governed by its own separate statute, with responsibilities that directly affect the price and supply of energy."

bear a perspective on decision that an agency could not enjoy. The primary commitment of the Constitution to a unitary executive suggests a legal basis for giving that perspective force. One can observe an increasing presidential tendency to assert that *he* is the responsible decisionmaker. This can be seen both in an increasing use of the White House to announce important rule-makings and in the way those announcements are made.[80] Judicial decisions, properly acknowledging his power to influence an administrator's decision,[81] have not reached this point, and perhaps never will. In the author's view, however, it remains legally dubious, and politically dangerous, to lead responsible officials to believe that the President may, as of right, claim the prerogative of decision on debatable matters.[82]

b. Appointments and removals

Short of formally substituting his own for his officers' decisions, which in a complex government would rarely be possible even if permissible, the most obvious way for the President to control the character of administration is by appointing officials sympathetic to his policies, reasoning with them as they act, and disciplining those who do not respond to his suggestions for carrying them out. Specific provision is made in the Constitution respecting the President's appointment of government officers. None is made about his participation in their removal (or other forms of discipline).[83] Both appointment

---

80. See D. Kessler, a Question of Intent : A Great American Battle with a Deadly Industry (2001) (FDA rules controlling tobacco); P. Strauss, Presidential Rulemaking, 72 Chi-Kent L. Rev. 965 (1997).

81. Sierra Club v. Costle, n. 72 above.

82. "[The President] is, to be sure, our chief executive, the one our Constitution has invested with executive power; but he wields that power, in these respects, within the constraints of law that Congress has established. No more than he could assign to the Secretary of the Interior responsibilities Congress had placed in the hands of the Secretary of Agriculture...can he depart from Congress's other assignments of responsibility. The bureaucrat or political appointee confronted by presidential chivvying can perhaps more easily see in this perspective the tension between duty and advice, grasp the limits on the President's capacity to understand and act on what may be quite complex technical matters with a sparse and largely political staff. The stakes for the psychology of government, for the extent to which civil servants and political appointees imagine themselves acting within a culture of law, are rather high." P. Strauss, Presidential Rulemaking, 72 Chi-Kent L. Rev. 965, 986 (1997).

83. The Constitution does specify the possibility of impeachment, for the President as well as other officers. This is a highly formal and cumbersome procedure, requiring grave offenses and action by both houses of Congress. No one supposes that it is the only means

and removal have been the subject of congressional efforts at regulation, and of disputes and litigation that continue to the current day.

The appointments clause of the Constitution is straightforward in placing the principal appointments in government in the hands of the President, acting under the check of required consent by the Senate. Congress can place the appointment of "inferior officers" in the President acting alone, in the courts, or in departmental heads. Despite the limitations which might seem implicit in this provision,[84] when Congress created a merit-based competitive civil service system in the late nineteenth century, in response to various scandals arising out of the existing patronage system, its action was, without much difficulty, upheld.[85] As a result, the great majority of the almost three million employees of the federal government, including a substantial number of important policy-makers, serve in protected tenure; political principles may not be applied to their appointment, and they are free as well from removal on political grounds. The President and about 5,000 political appointees—most appointed by heads of department rather than the President himself[86]—thus sit at the apex of an enormous bureaucracy whose members enjoy tenure in their jobs, are subject to the constraints of statutes whose history and provisions they know in detail, and often have strong views of the public good in the field in which they work. President Truman is reported to have described his authority as the power "to bring people in and try to persuade them to do what they ought to do without persuasion. That's what I spend most of my time doing. That's what the powers of the President amount to."

More difficult than the civil service laws, but never yet found unconstitutional, are laws that restrict the President's choice even among appointments that seem irreducibly his to make, because they concern major federal offices. At one end of a range of possibilities are reasonable qualifications for a position, for example that the Attorney General must be a lawyer. Also easily justified is a requirement that appointees possess qualities that may contribute to the acceptance or character of agency decisions, as when Congress provides for a measure of bipartisanship by limiting to a bare majority the number of appointees to a collegial regulatory commission who may belong to the same

---

available to remove officers who are neither elected to a definite term, like the President, nor appointed to serve during "good behavior," as judges are.

84. Recall the discussion of Freytag v. Commissioner, p. 24, n. 50 above.

85. United States v. Perkins, 116 U.S. 483 (1886).

86. Respecting the political appointment process, see H. Heclo, A Government of Strangers: Executive Politics in Washington. (1977); T. Weko, The Politicizing Presidency: The White House Personnel Office (1995).

political party. Not as readily justified are provisions that tightly restrict the President's nominating choices, and give Congress a role in the selection of particular individuals. A notable example of this sort of arrangement is the provision governing appointment of the head of the General Accounting Office,[87] the Comptroller General of the United States. Even though the President is *formally* free to disregard the slate of candidates given to him by the congressional leadership, the political equation is unmistakable; thus, the statutory scheme places the selection initiative with Congress, reflecting a congressional effort to displace the President's authority with its own. Strikingly, and with evident significance from a separation of powers perspective, Congress and its constituents are missing from the constitutional list of officials other than the President to whom appointments authority for "Officers of the United States" may be delegated.

Thus, the Supreme Court has several times found that Congress cannot itself appoint "Officers," even in cases where its direct interest in the matter is clear. The Federal Election Commission,[88] for example, is an agency given responsibilities to investigate practices in federal elections and to set and enforce rules respecting them. In establishing the Commission, Congress provided that some of the commissioners were to be presidential appointees *not* requiring senatorial confirmation, and others were to be directly appointed by the leadership of the Senate and of the House. The evident purpose was to achieve political balance and a mutuality of control in matters of great political sensitivity. Nonetheless, the Supreme Court concluded, the Commission's responsibility was to enforce the federal election laws. Therefore, it must be headed by "Officers," which Congress could not appoint.[89] Here, Congress had not only weakened presidential authority, as in the example of the Comptroller General just discussed, but had also sought to expand its own authority, and the latter step at least found no support in the constitutional text.

A more limited, but still difficult question is presented by the Open Market Committee of the Federal Reserve Board.[90] The Federal Reserve Board is an independent commission with enormous power over the national economy through its control of banking and of the nation's money supply. It is composed entirely of presidential appointees, whose fourteen year terms and

---

87. See p. 85 above.

88. http://www.fec.gov/.

89. Buckley v. Valeo, 424 U.S. 1, 121 (1976); see also Metropolitan Washington Airports Authority v. Citizens for the Abatement of Aircraft Noise, 501 S.S. 252 (1991).

90. The Federal Reserve may be visited at http://www.federalreserve.gov/; the committee at http://www.federalreserve.gov/fomc/.

other arrangements give them a degree of freedom unusual even among the independent commissions. The Board's Open Market Committee makes and secures the implementation of decisions respecting operations in the money markets. The Committee's membership is drawn both from Board members and from the current presidents of the federal reserve banks, who are the chief executive officers of essentially private institutions, selected by the boards of directors of those institutions. Here, Congress is not directly involved in the displacement of presidential appointment, and the body in question might be regarded as subordinate. Yet committee members could readily be characterized as "Officers," and the legality of placing designation of those who will exercise such substantial authority in private hands has not been established.[91]

Once an "Officer" has been appointed, how much freedom must the President enjoy to remove him? Unlike the "appointments" issue, no constitutional text speaks directly to the ordinary question of removal from office. When the first provisions for the shape of the government were made by the first Congress, meeting in the shadow of the constitutional convention, Congress's right to participate in removals as well as appointments was hotly debated. The view that the principal officers of the government should serve only at the pleasure of the President prevailed by the narrowest of margins. Eighty years later, in the wake of the American Civil War, Congress precipitated a major constitutional crisis by enacting the Tenure of Office Act, which converted the tenure of all departmental heads (cabinet secretaries) from service at pleasure, to removability only with the Senate's concurrence. The impeachment it attempted after President Andrew Johnson sought to remove the Secretary of War failed by only one vote. It took almost forty years more for the matter to reach the United States Supreme Court, in a much less portentous case involving a local postmaster.

Unless important government officials serve at the President's pleasure, he may have to conduct the most important affairs of state through persons in whom he comes to lack confidence. At a less dramatic level, a President who could threaten dismissal, while this is not the only imaginable disciplinary measure, would be better placed to control an administrator's action than one who could not. Again, as is typical of issues of this character, definitive answers are possible only at the outer limits. Where restrictions on the President's ability to employ such threats contribute to legality and are independent of congressional/presidential competition for power over the apparatus of

---

91. Carter v. Carter Coal Co., 298 U.S. 238 (1936); A.L.A. Schechter Poultry Corp. v. United States, 295 U.S. 495 (1935).

government, they present no difficulties. Thus, again, civil service constraints on the removal of federal employees raise no significant constitutional concerns, even as to employees exercising substantial authority over the implementation of policy under particular statutes. On the other hand, as President Johnson's experience suggested politically, arrangements that threaten substantial congressional displacement of the President's intended unitary responsibility for the execution of the laws—that challenge the Decision of 1789, as it came to be called—present important separation of powers concerns. In the postmaster's case, and a 1986 decision involving the Comptroller General of the GAO, the Supreme Court found the Constitution to have been violated where Congress had sought to require its own active participation before a presidential appointee/officer could be removed from office.[92] On this point, the American cases seem to have come to rest; but congressional efforts directly to participate in removal have in fact been rare.

Suppose that without seeking itself to participate in removal, Congress sets a determinate term of office for a high-level official, and limits removal during that term to "cause." This is the arrangement typical for the "independent regulatory commission," a collegial body generally having five to seven members, each of whom serves a term so calculated that the term of only one member expires each year. When a new President enters office, then, he will find the leadership of the commissions principally in the hands of appointees of his predecessor. In ordinary course, it will be years before his own appointees can assume control. Although rarely given political as distinct from administrative responsibilities,[93] such bodies are responsible for a good deal of law-implementation, and in this respect must be thought to exercise aspects of the"executive power" that the Constitution places in the President alone. This was also the arrangement used to protect the tenure of the "independent counsel" who at various times in the latter part of the twentieth century were empowered to investigate and prosecute allegations of criminal behavior at the highest levels of the executive branch, including the President himself.[94] Such

---

92. Myers v. United States, 272 U.S. 52 (1926); Bowsher v. Synar, 478 U.S. 714 (1986); see P. Strauss, Formal and Functional Approaches to Separation of Powers Questions—A Foolish Inconsistency? 72 Cornell L. J. 488 (1987).

93. An exception may be the United States Nuclear Regulatory Commission, which in its functions concerning import and export of nuclear materials has responsibilities and must consider information that ordinarily would be in the province of political actors such as the Department of State.

94. The statutory authority for independent counsel was permitted to lapse during the Clinton Administration, as it appeared that a number of such counsel, including one investigating the President, were extending their investigations in a manner ordinary prose-

a prosecutor can be exercising nothing but executive power, as that power is conventionally understood.

This problem first came before the Supreme Court in the 1930's, during President Franklin Roosevelt's administration. Shortly after his election in 1932, he dismissed a Republican commissioner of the Federal Trade Commission, whose term would otherwise have lasted until 1938. President Roosevelt did not assert any "cause" for this removal, but simply claimed the right to fill important governmental positions with persons whose political views resembled his own. The Supreme Court found, without apparent difficulty, that the President could be required to observe the "cause" restriction for removing such an officer.[95] Part of its reasoning insisted that Federal Trade Commissioners did not exercise "executive" authority. While that is counter-factual when law-implementation is considered,[96] the Court's assertion suggests the distinction we earlier observed between political and administrative authority,[97] with "executive" used here in the former sense. Thus, the case does not suggest that the Congress could impose similar controls over the terms of office of officials responsible for "questions, in their nature political," officials who are "to conform precisely to the will of the President."[98] Since it enacted the Tenure in Office Act involved in the Johnson impeachment, an Act since said by the Court to have been unconstitutional,[99] Congress has not tried to impose a similar limitation on officers exercising more political than administrative authority—such as, for example, the Secretary of State.

The testing case for these propositions was litigation challenging the statute authorizing appointment of "independent counsel" to investigate allegations of misconduct at the highest levels of the executive branch. Independent counsel was to be appointed not by the President or his Attorney General—who would normally be responsible for appointing federal prosecutors—but by a special judicial panel on receiving certification from the Attorney General after preliminary investigation that there were "reasonable grounds to believe that

cutorial practice would never have permitted, but which was encouraged by their singular mandates, lack of accountability, and political exposure.

95. Humphrey's Executor (Rathbun) v. United States, 295 U.S. 602 (1935).

96. Today, it would be conceded that virtually everything the Federal Trade Commission does involves carrying out the law, in the sense that would require its chief officers to be appointed by the President (as they are) with senatorial consent. See Buckley v. Valeo, note 89 above.

97. See p. 91 above.

98. Marbury v. Madison, see text at n. 68 above. In his dissent from the opinion involving the Comptroller General, n. 92 above, Justice White is careful to reserve this point.

99. Myers v. United States, 272 U.S. 52 (1926).

further investigation or prosecution is warranted." That certification was a matter of the Attorney General's *DISCRETION!*, protected from any form of judicial (but not political) review, and if made it identified the matters for investigation. Once independent counsel had been appointed and began to serve, he did so independent of immediate supervision by the Department of Justice, and in possession of all the investigative and prosecutorial powers the Department would have. He was, however, adjured "except where not possible, [to] comply with the written or other established policies of the Department," and was subject to disciplinary removal by the Attorney General personally, "and only for good cause, physical disability, mental incapacity, or any other condition that substantially impairs the performance of such independent counsel's duties."

Over a dissent by Justice Scalia, prescient as to the abuses that would eventually persuade Congress to permit the statute to lapse, the Chief Justice's opinion for the remainder of his colleagues voting upheld the statute. Between the Attorney General's initial control over whether to begin an investigation and the possibility of dismissal "for cause," the Court concluded, the Act did not impermissibly burden the President's constitutional obligation to ensure the faithful execution of the laws.[100] Undoubtedly, a historical tradition of judicial appointment and control of prosecutors strengthened his conclusion;[101] so too would doubts about the necessity for direct presidential control of prosecutorial judgments—it is hard to imagine a persuasive constitutional objection to a statute forbidding the President from forcing a tax audit of particular political enemies. Yet perhaps the most important matter to note is the absence of consensus about what "cause" might be. No case has decided this question. Should it include insubordination, that would give the President a substantial lever with which to move even officers so protected. The issue would then become, explicitly, what directions the President is entitled to give "officers" in fulfilling his obligation to see that all laws are faithfully executed. Those laws include, of course, the laws entrusted to the administration of the independent commissions. Strong arguments have been made that "cause" must be construed in light of that obligation,[102] and the cases suggest some receptiveness to those arguments.

100. Morrison v. Olson, 487 U.S. 654 (1988).

101. P. Shane, Independent Policymaking and Presidential Power: A Constitutional Analysis, 57 Geo. Wash. L. Rev. 596, 603–606 (1989).

102. G. Miller, Independent Agencies, 1986 Sup. Ct. Rev. 41 (1987); H. Bruff, Presidential Power and Administrative Rulemaking, 88 Yale L. J. 451 (1979); P. Strauss, The

c. *"Opinion, in writing"*

We now turn to the one power the Constitution explicitly confers on the President in relation to the administrative decisions of the rest of government, the provision that he "may require the Opinion, in writing, of the principal Officer in each of the executive Departments, upon any subject relating to the Duties of their respective Offices." Recall the apparent implication of this provision (and others), that actual determination of administrative matters—the "duty" involved—lies with the official to whom it is delegated by law, not the President or his staff. Yet consultation is proper, and is expected to occur in advance of that decision.[103] In the past, such consultations were informal, not readily observed and according to no particular form. Certainly, much informal and formless consultation persists. The past three decades, however, have witnessed the development of more formal techniques for analysis and reporting, techniques having considerable prominence and influence. These are the techniques of policy analysis, which examine proposed actions and alternatives to determine their projected costs and benefits. The expectation is that decisions will then be taken in light of those projections.

Central management of such analysis was in fact first required by legislation, when the National Environmental Policy Act of 1969 established a regime of "Environmental Impact Statements" to be administered by a presidential office, the Council on Environmental Quality.[104] Agencies proposing to act in a manner that might have a significant environmental impact were required

---

Place of Agencies in Government: Separation of Powers and the Fourth Branch, 84 Colum. L. Rev. 573 (1984).

103. One wants to distinguish here between consultation on issues of policy, and consultations about the outcome of particular controversies having a judicial character. The latter would generally be rejected as improper, on analogy to the inappropriateness of any official contacting a judge about the merits of some matter before her for decision. See the discussion of Portland Audubon, p. 93 above, and Professional Air Traffic Controllers Organization v. Federal Labor Relations Authority, 685 F.2d 547 (D.C. Cir. 1982). The former, however, are generally accepted. Sierra Club v. Costle, 657 F.2d 298 (D.C. Cir. 1981); W. L. Cary, Politics and the Regulatory Agencies (1967).

104. 42 U.S.C. §§4331–4335; see http://ceq.eh.doe.gov/nepa/nepanet.htm, which provides considerable information about NEPA but not the Council. (Compare http://www. whitehouse.gov/ceq/index.html and see p. 89 above.) Consistent with the usual arrangements for presidential offices, the authority of the Council is strictly internal to government. It was given authority to oversee and coordinate the activities of governmental agencies in making the required analyses, rather than authority to reach decisions on disputed issues of policy affecting the environment and the interests of the public directly.

to undertake a form of analysis of both that impact and means of avoiding or controlling it. An agency was to conduct its analysis under the general guidance of the Council, but responsibility for both the analysis and the ultimate decision in the matter remained in the agency's hands.[105] In the years since, Congress has found similar devices useful in other contexts: agencies are required to engage in forward thinking about the possibly harsher impact of complex regulation on small rather than large business, coordinating these analyses through the Small Business Administration;[106] they are to analyze the necessity and impact of their demands for reporting of data by citizens and other regulated entities under the central supervision of the Office of Management and Budget;[107] and they are to follow special analytic and consultation procedures, again under OMB's supervision, when the impact of their rulemaking is to impose large "unfunded mandates" on state, local, or tribal authorities, or on the private sector.[108]

Relying on both the "Opinion, in writing" authority and the President's constitutional prerogative to recommend to Congress any legislation he regards as expedient, Presidents since the New Deal have required agencies wishing to present legislation, or to testify on legislative proposals, to clear their submissions and appearances with the White House, through the Office of Management and Budget.[109] This serves an obvious function in promoting coordination and coherence; the process entails consultation throughout government, and the possibility of discussions to resolve disagreements. Yet it also strongly controls the formal legislative-executive interface. Agencies may be

---

105. As an obligation of the agencies involved, the impact analysis procedure came to be regarded as judicially enforceable by affected citizens, industries, or interest groups, a development that since has contributed much to litigation about administrative action. For an overall appraisal of its effectiveness as a mechanism of bureaucratic control, see S. Taylor, Making Bureaucracies Think (Stanford 1984).

106. Regulatory Flexibility Act, 5 U.S.C. §§601–612. See M. Breger, Regulatory Flexibility and the Administrative State 32 Tulsa L. J. 325 (1996); P. Verkuil, A Critical Guide to the Regulatory Flexibility Act, 1982 Duke L. J. 213. The Act is briefly discussed at p. 249 within.

107. Paperwork Reduction Act of 1980, 44 U.S.C. §3507(c). The Act is briefly discussed at p. 265 within.

108. Unfunded Mandate Reform Act of 1995, 2 U.S.C. §1501 et seq. As was apparently anticipated would be done, OMB has largely subsumed its implementation of this Act under Executive Order 12,866 presently to be discussed in the text. See OMB, Agency Compliance with Title II of the Unfunded Mandates Reform Act of 1995, 4th Annual Report to Congress (1999). The Act is briefly discussed at p. 249 within.

109. See p. 111 below.

advised that what they propose conflicts with an important presidential objective or is not in accord with the President's program, and in that case they are not supposed to submit or testify.[110] Notoriously, the permanent staffs of agencies and congressional committees develop means of communication that elude such formal controls, but the controls nonetheless serve to support the idea of a single administration. The advantages of coordination and cooperation (as well as recognition of the legal obligation implicit in "opinion in writing") serve to draw in, as well, even the independent regulatory commissions,[111] which Congress has generally insulated from direct presidential control.

Beginning with President Nixon and the explosion of federal rulemaking in the 1970s, each President has drawn on the statutory and executive models to require agencies to submit economic impact analyses of proposed regulations having a potential for significant effect on the national economy for White House review before final decisions on the proposals are reached. President Reagan added a requirement applicable at an earlier stage of the rulemaking process, that agencies annually coordinate with him the regulations that they were planning to develop in the coming year, as they had long been coordinating statutory initiatives. Each succeeding President has elaborated upon the work of his predecessors, extending both the reach and the scope of these requirements, with variations (as might be anticipated) reflecting his own political stance toward regulation. Thus, one understood that administration under Republican Presidents tended to proceed from doubts about the desirability of regulation, and some suspicion what the (largely Democrat) civil service might be attempting, resulting in considerable emphasis on after-the-fact control. Under President Clinton, a Democrat, more emphasis was placed on assuring that the desired analytical regimes were in place and functioning well, and less on the correctness or not of particular regulatory outcomes. Congress, jealous of its own interests and (when different parties controlled Congress and the White House) also suspicious of presidential political interference in regulatory matters, has throughout tended to insist on transparency in the process as the price of permitting it to continue. For example, Congress has first required that appointment of the White House official responsible for overseeing these processes be subjected to Senate confirmation

---

110. OMB Circular No. A-19. Whether a President would treat a violation of this directive as the occasion for discipline, and to what extent, is more a political than a legal question; he must deal with the agency, and the Congress, continuously.

111. See p. 133 below.

and then, in one instance, refused to confirm a President's nomination to that post until assured that political inputs to the process would be controlled, and its results would be made public.

While President Bush will presumably reshape the process again as his administration gains experience with it, a brief account can be given here of President Clinton's version of this regime, Executive Order No. 12,866.[112] As indicated in the previous paragraph, it imagines two stages. The first stage is an annual "regulatory agenda" identifying the significant regulatory actions each agency—independent regulatory commission as well as cabinet department—anticipates pursuing during the coming year. Actions are not only to be identified, but also justified preliminarily in terms of presidential priorities, anticipated costs and benefits, legal bases, the public risks being dealt with (and their relationship to others that might be), and alternative measures that might be considered. Like legislative proposals, these agenda are vetted with other agencies for possible conflicts (which may be resolved by OMB), and are vetted by OMB itself for consistency with the President's program. If approved, the plans are published in the Federal Register, as part of an October Unified Regulatory Agenda also required by statute. This publication, also available on the Internet as a searchable data base,[113] has the benefit for the public of giving early warning about forthcoming regulatory initiatives, together with contact information for persons wishing to become involved in the development of the initiative.

Note that while this mechanism obviously creates possibilities for presidential control, it has advantages even within an agency. Before the executive orders were in place, one often heard that the civil service staff of American agencies tended to compromise disagreements among themselves before taking proposals to their politically responsible chief officers, effectively limiting the control those officers enjoyed. The requirement that this agenda "be approved

---

112. 58 Fed. Reg. 51735 (1993). Longer analyses, offering comparisons with its predecessors, can be found in R. Pildes & C. Sunstein, Reinventing the Regulatory State, 62 U. Chi. L. Rev. 1 (1995) and P. Shane, Political Accountability in a System of Checks and Balances: The Case of Presidential Review of Rulemaking, 48 Ark. L. Rev. 161 (1995); see also E.D. Elliott, TQM-ing OMB: Or Why Regulatory Review Under Executive Order 12,291 [the Reagan/Bush predecessor to 12,866] Works Poorly and What President Clinton Should Do About It, 57 L. & Contemp. Prob. 167 (1994); H. Bruff, Presidential Management of Agency Rulemaking, 57 Geo. Wash. L. Rev. 533 (1989).

The current business of regulatory analysis, along with a variety of internal memoranda and reports respecting it, can be found at http://www.whitehouse.gov/omb/inforeg/regpol.html.

113. "Unified Agenda(<year>)" at http://www.access.gpo.gov/su_docs/aces/aaces002.html.

personally by the agency head," like the annual process for developing a fiscal budget, facilitates political control *within* the agency, by requiring staff to gain the blessing of the agency's leadership early in an initiative's development.

The second stage of E.O. 12,866 occurs during the course of the rulemaking itself, a process that will be dealt with extensively in Chapter V. In brief, the order requires the agency to assess the probable impact of its intended action in terms of its statutory mandate, the President's priorities, any impacts on state, local or tribal governments, and the regulatory justifications for the measure. It must submit this assessment to the Office of Management and Budget before announcing the proposal to the public. If it has concluded that the impact will be "significant" (for example, that it will impose new costs on the private sector in excess of $100,000,000 annually), it must also submit a draft "regulatory impact analysis" considering the projected costs and benefits of the proposal in detail and analyzing "potentially effective and reasonably feasible alternatives," explaining why they have not been chosen. After OMB clearance, whose timeliness the executive order promises to control,[114] the proposal may be published, accompanied by this analysis (which thus becomes open to public comment). Final action on the proposal requires a second, final analysis, which again must be cleared with OMB; "[t]o the extent permitted by law, disagreements or conflicts...that cannot be resolved by the Administrator of OMB shall be resolved by the President, or by the Vice President acting at the request of the President" under stated procedures that promise extensive transparency. The "to the extent permitted by law" qualification is frequently repeated, with the undertaking as well that "[n]othing in this order shall be construed as displacing the agencies' authority or responsibilities, as authorized by law." On its surface at least, then, this order respects assignments of duty as Congress has made them.

Only "executive" agencies, not the independent regulatory commissions, are required to participate in this second stage, although cooperation by the latter is invited and appreciated. Under a strictly legal analysis, the "Opinions, in writing" clause extends to the head of any agency made responsible for carrying out federal law and, since the independent commissions meet this definition, this regime could be applied to them.[115] Extending its reach to them,

---

114. In Environmental Defense Fund v. Thomas, 627 F. Supp. 566 (D. D.C. 1986), a court held that OMB could not delay analyses past deadlines set by statute; but such deadlines rarely apply. The use of this process simply for delay had been a major point of confrontation between the prior Republican administrations of Presidents Reagan and Bush and the Congress, then largely under control of the Democrats.

115. P. Strauss & C. Sunstein, The Role of the President and OMB in Informal Rulemaking, 38 Admin. L. Rev. 181 (1986); G. Miller, Independent Agencies, 1986 Sup. Ct. Rev. 41.

however, could create a political storm in Congress, however justified the legal position. Perhaps understanding that these agencies rarely initiate rulemaking reaching the most important economic threshold of the executive order, no President to date has believed the possible gains of such a step outweigh its costs.

For the executive agencies, however, the executive order strongly reflects a vision of the President in a central and coordinating role. Part of that coordination, as already remarked, is also in the service of the relative authority of the agency leadership in relation to its civil service workforce; its mechanisms strengthen the hand of political leadership within the agency as well as the President's control. Notable in this respect is a requirement new to the Clinton version of these executive orders, that each agency head "designate a Regulatory Policy Officer" reporting directly to her, "who shall be involved at each stage of the regulatory process to foster the development of effective, innovative, and least burdensome regulations and to further the principles" of the Executive Order. These officers, in turn, could periodically be brought together in a "regulatory working group" to discuss collectively deficiencies in and means of improving the process. Yet despite all this, a recent analysis found, after extended empirical study of submitted economic impact statements, that actual agency compliance with the intentions of the executive order remains quite variable. The report concluded: "President Clinton, working with OMB, apparently has not been successful in implementing [this style of analysis], probably due to a lack of interest and willingness to spend political capital." The study reported the same conclusions about earlier Republican administrations.[116]

It may be useful to note some questions about these orders, and the ways in which they illustrate themes about American administrative government already established. First, what is the legality of an "executive order" purporting to bind the actions of discrete legal entities, when "all legislative power" vested by the Constitution is placed in Congress? Second, and relatedly, note the reappearance here of the problem of the President's authority to direct determination of matters committed to agency judgment, acknowledged by the repeated obeisance to "the extent permitted by law."[117] Third, what is the im-

---

116. R. Hahn, et al., Assessing Regulatory Impact Analyses: The Failure of Agencies to Comply with Executive Order 12,866, 23 Harv. J. L. & Pub. Pol. 859, 878–79 and n. 51 (2000). Mr. Hahn is director of the American Enterprise Institute-Brookings Joint Center for Regulatory Studies, where his coauthors were researchers.

117. Compare text, p. 93 above.

pact of these measures outside government—their visibility, accessibility to comment or input, even their susceptibility to judicial enforcement.

As may be suggested by the high numbers attached to the Executive Orders we have just been discussing, such orders have long been an established mode for the President's formal effectuation of policy. Among those his office entitles him to command, they have the force of law. The President's position, which presumably would be sustained, is that he requires no legislative authorization to announce such measures or to give them that force. Note that this conclusion, if correct, can be related to the problem of "for cause" dismissal discussed a few pages earlier. If the President, by virtue of office, can give a binding directive to a commissioner of the Federal Trade Commission, disobedience would warrant dismissal even if the commissioner ordinarily could expect to be protected from removal. Executive Orders have been used to establish government-wide regimes for the control of sensitive information, for assuring the loyalty, security, and reliability of government employees and of government contractors, for establishing non-discrimination programs within government and with government contractors, and for many like purposes.

While occasional doubt has been expressed about the application of Executive Orders to government contractors or their employees,[118] certainly their acceptance within government reflects a proposition already encountered: that the limitations of separation of powers, such as they are, apply to government in its dealings with other branches and with the citizenry at large, and do not proscribe useful internal arrangements.[119] The case of government contracting, and the disposition of other government resources,[120] can be regarded as an intermediate one. While private citizens are affected, they are affected through the government's decisions in the course of control over the disposition of its own resources, and in a relationship voluntary on their part.

The contrasting case is that in which the President seeks to use an Executive Order to effect a change in the legal status of an ordinary citizen or corporation not in the course of a business relationship with the government. When President Truman, during the Korean War, sought to use an executive order to seize the steel mills in order to avoid a strike and the resultant disruption of war material production, he was sharply rebuked by the Supreme

118. Chrysler Corp. v. Brown, 441 U.S. 281 (1979).

119. Compare the text at p. 86 above, where a similar point is made concerning the GAO.

120. United States v. Midwest Oil Co., 236 U.S. 459 (1915).

Court for an act unauthorized by law.[121] That rebuke was marked by stern language we have already encountered[122] about the impropriety of the President's attempting to act as a legislator. No one, however, appears to have believed that that rebuke rendered invalid the nation's loyalty and security clearance regime, founded in an executive order, or any of the many other useful regimes of internal, property, and contract management that executive orders had established. The intended unitary character of the Presidency requires some means for his giving appropriate instructions to the government as a whole, and that is the function of the executive order.[123] A more limited understanding, that any such order must be consistent with valid statutory as well as constitutional constraints,[124] raises no obstacle to this proposition.

There remains the problem of the potentially directory character of E.O. 12,866. Viewed simply as a requirement for use of specified analytic tools, it fits comfortably in the established tradition and the Constitution's "Opinion, in writing" language. Yet, the structure of the process also gives OMB, and through it the President, substantial control over the particular outcomes of proceedings: first, through the assertion that, "to the extent permitted by law," stated decisional principles must be applied; second, by requiring the agency to secure OMB approval of its analyses before going forward, and thus enhancing OMB's already considerable political authority. Suppose that the law empowers the Administrator of the Environmental Protection Agency to decide a matter, and permits but does not require her to make that decision employing analyses such as Executive Order 12,866 commands. The Administrator's use of those analyses, not by her own choice but because the President requires it, would not in itself contravene the delegation to the Administrator of the authority to make this decision—because the application of judgment to the particular circumstances of the matter remains the agency's.[125] Still, the agency's application of judgment may be subverted if, under the cover of a requirement of analyses, OMB is actually dictating particular outcomes. The

---

121. Youngstown Sheet and Tube Co. v. Sawyer, 343 U.S. 579 (1952).

122. See p. 30 above.

123. See, for a general discussion, H. Monaghan, The Protective Presidency, 1993 Colum. L. Rev. 1.

124. Chamber of Commerce v. Reich, 74 F.3d 1322, rehearing and rehearing en banc denied, 83 F.3d 439, 442 (D.C. Cir. 1996).

125. See C. Sunstein, Cost-Benefit Analysis and the Separation of Powers, 23 Ariz. L. Rev. 1267 (1981); C. Sunstein & P. Strauss, The Role of the President and OMB in Informal Rulemaking, 38 Admin. L. Rev. 181 (1986).

factual basis for such a claim has been a matter of substantial (and understandably political) controversy in the United States;[126] Vice President Quayle, during the first Bush administration, made no secret of his ability to stop regulations regarded as undesirable by a "Competitiveness Council" over which he presided and to which, the public understood, business interests had ready access.[127] Discomfort with this phenomenon contributed substantially to Executive Order 12,866's commitments to transparency, and explicit limitations on the extent to which persons outside government could expect to make political approaches to OMB.

d. The White House staff

Evidently the President's controls cannot be strictly personal; his influence—primarily political rather than legal[128]– must be achieved through the intervention of others. His personal staff, numbering a few hundred, and a considerably larger bureaucracy attached to the Executive Office of the Presidency act for him in this respect, both in sifting and organizing the problems requiring his attention and in communicating what are said to be his wishes.[129] Any realist understands, of course, that much done or said in the President's name has never crossed his desk. This realization is a cautionary signal for arguments about the President's directory authority in administrative matters— the direction being given is too likely to reflect the understandings and desires of a relatively junior bureaucrat, rather than the President himself.[130] Of

---

126. P. Shane, Political Accountability in a System of Checks and Balances: The Case of Presidential Review of Rulemaking, 48 Ark. L. Rev. 161 (1995); C. DeMuth and D. Ginsburg, White House Review of Agency Rulemaking, 99 Harv. L. Review 1075 (1986); A. Morrison, OMB Interference with Agency Rulemaking: The Wrong Way to Write a Regulation, 99 Harv. L. Rev. 1059 (1986).

127. Dan Quayle, "Standing Firm: Personal Reflections on being Vice President," in T. Walch, Ed., At the President's Side—The Vice Presidency in the Twentieth Century 169, 175 (1997), and P. Shane, supra, n. 126.

128. This begins with his position as head of the nation with its symbolic values, and also of a major political party, able to command its resources of reward and punishment and associated with its programs. The President also strongly influences, where he does not directly command, the central administrative apparatus of government responsible for goods all agencies require, from budgetary submissions and authorization of high-level bureaucratic positions to legal services and office space and equipment. Finally the President (and the forces under his command) can be a powerful ally in struggles against Congress and for public regard.

129. See J. Burke, The Institutional Presidency (1992).

130. The position is well stated by an articulate former Cabinet Officer, William T. Coleman, Jr., in his dissent from ABA Comm'n On Law And The Economy, Federal Reg-

course this, too, is understood by those to whom such statements are made, and the result can be an elaborate and deeply political exercise.

The organization of the White House staff is, as one would suppose, relatively fluid and organized around the problems of politics and state more than the problems of administration which are the concern of this volume. From time to time, the staff of the Vice President,[131] of the Council of Economic Advisors,[132] and of White House Counsel[133] have become involved in regulatory issues. In that context, however, the most notable development of the past quarter century has been a steadily increasing delegation of oversight responsibility to the Vice President. It was well understood, for example, that President Reagan looked to Vice President Bush for day-to-day assistance with his Executive Orders dealing with these issues, although neither order explicitly assigned him any responsibilities in that connection. In the first Bush administration, Vice President Quayle acted as head of a broadly constituted "Competitiveness Council," as already mentioned. President Clinton's Executive Order 12,866 was the first to confer formal authority on the Vice President. The Vice President's is an anomalous office, straddling as it does the executive and legislative branches; its incumbent is only indirectly controllable by a President who cannot remove him from office, may have political ambitions in tension with the President's (particularly a President no longer eligible for reelection), and has a responsibility to the electorate considerably more

---

ulation: Roads to Reform 70, 156–61 (1979); compare the response of Judge Henry Friendly, id. at 163–64, who had earlier taken the same position, but abandoned it in the face of a burgeoning federal bureaucracy.

131. See n. 62 above.

132. The Council of Economic Advisors analyzes the national economy, advises the President on economic policy and appraises the economic programs of the Federal Government. It also prepares the President's annual economic report to Congress, a widely used statistical reference work. The Council consists of three members, one of whom the President designates as chair (usually a distinguished academic economist). See http://www. whitehouse.gov/cea/index.html, which at this writing provides a description and links to publications, but no access to the Council's membership or current activities.

133. The White House Counsel acts as the President's personal attorney and aide. His office is small, and should not be confused with that of the Attorney General. The Attorney General, who also gives legal advice to the President, is the head of the Justice Department, which manages the civil and criminal legal affairs of the entire federal government. Several thousand attorneys, including United States attorneys in each federal judicial district, are employed by the Justice Department—along with the Federal Bureau of Investigation, the Immigration and Naturalization Service, the Bureau of Prisons, and several other important offices. See n. 62 above.

remote than the President's. Institutionalizing roles for the Vice President, thus, could be thought to threaten the unitary executive in an unusual way. Yet, given the complexities of government—and, indeed, the desirability that the Vice President be prepared for the responsibilities of an office he may have to assume—such roles can be expected to continue.

The Office of Management and Budget: Over the years, the Office of Management and Budget, the professional arm of the presidency, has played the largest White House staff role in Presidential administration.[134] It corresponds in many ways to the congressional General Accounting Office,[135] although with a staff of fewer than 550 it is quite a bit smaller. Indeed, the two offices were created in the same statute, in 1921, which for the first time directed the President to present a unified national budget; previously each agency or department made its own requests to Congress. The Bureau of the Budget, predecessor to the OMB, was responsible for the coordination to produce that budget; GAO was responsible for audits to assure that the constraints of the budget had in fact been honored. Originally placed in the Department of the Treasury, the Bureau of the Budget was moved to the White House proper in 1939; it was redesignated the Office of Management and Budget, in recognition of its expanding functions and size, in the 1970s. Its present staff consists largely of professional bureaucrats; it operates under the leadership of a Director and a limited number of other political appointees serving at the pleasure of the President.

OMB's responsibility for coordination of the annual budget process carries with it a good deal of oversight of agency activity, as OMB's budget examiners (its professional staff) are expected to become closely familiar with the work of the agencies to which they are assigned, and are in a position to demand justification of agency decisions with budgetary implications. Although it is possible to make appeals to the President (or, informally, to relevant congressional actors), OMB annually sets the resources an agency can expect to be made available for its future work. That gives it enormous practical power over the course of governmental administration. OMB also has responsibility for overseeing a variety of government management functions under statute and presidential directives, and serves a number of coordinative functions as well: mediating interagency disputes; overseeing studies or other efforts that involve the work of more than one agency; and coordinating the President's legislative program.[136] OMB's fiscal year 2001 budget submission listed twenty-

---

134. www.whitehouse.gov/omb
135. See p. 85 above.
136. See p. 102 above.

four statutes in which Congress had assigned such work to it, since 1993 alone.[137]

For our purposes, its most important functions are carried out by an Office of Regulatory Information and Analysis. OIRA is the office that oversees the Executive Order 12,866 processes, both the economic impact analyses and the regulatory agenda.[138] In addition, it coordinates information demands made on the public by government agencies under paperwork reform and reduction legislation,[139] and it also is responsible for overseeing coordination of government information policy, including implementation of the Electronic Freedom of Information Act.[140] OMB, it will be apparent, is a major power center for the President in his administration of domestic government, even though its work is not widely to known to lawyers or the general public.[141]

3. Federal Judiciary[142]

Article III of the federal Constitution specifies that the "judicial power of the United States, shall be vested in one Supreme Court, and in such inferior Courts as the Congress may from time to time ordain and establish." The judges of any such "Article III court" are appointed by the President, with senatorial consent, to an indefinite term ("during good Behavior") and compensation protected against reprisal. The reach of the judicial power is defined with some precision; for the purposes of this essay it is enough to know that it reaches any "case" arising under federal law, a category that easily includes

---

137. Testimony of Jacob Law, Director, before the House Committee on Appropriation, Subcommittee on Treasury, Postal Service and General Government, March 28, 2000.

138. See p. 103 above; http://www.whitehouse.gov/omb/inforeg/regpol.html gives access to OIRA's current business, but negligible information about the office itself. See p. 89 above. This is perhaps especially remarkable in the office responsible for government information policy, and was a characteristic of the Clinton as well as the first months of the Bush administration.

139. See p. 265 below.

140. See p. 282 below.

141. An account of the functioning of the President's office before the administration of President Reagan, with an emphasis on OMB, can be found in H. Heclo, A Government of Strangers (Brookings 1977); see also L. Berman, The Office of Management and Budget and the Presidency, 1921–1979 (Princeton University 1979); F. Mosher, A Tale of Two Agencies (LSU 1984).

142. General information about the federal courts can be explored at a website maintained by the Administrative Office of the United States Courts, which serves as a clearinghouse for statistical and other information. http://www.uscourts.gov/ is the home page; http://www.uscourts.gov/UFC99.pdf, requiring the Acrobat reader, is a helpful text.

any case involving issues of national administration or the application of the federal constitution to state or local administration.[143] Cases raising only questions of state or local law come into federal courts only if the parties reside in differing states—the so-called "diversity jurisdiction," meant to protect against regionalist bias in judgment. Under the principles of American federalism, the legal questions in such cases are finally resolved in accordance with the law of the relevant state.[144]

The United States inherited the basic elements of its legal system from England, and so is widely understood to be a common-law judicial system. This remains true in many important respects:

- Most state law concerning disputes between private individuals is probably still derived chiefly from previously decided cases.
- As a general proposition, judges regard themselves as obliged by the discipline of *stare decisis* to follow the judgments of prior decisions, in their own courts or courts directly superior to them, whether or not they would have reached those conclusions in the first instance.[145]
- Nonetheless, judges who encounter propositions not previously decided, or which they are very strongly persuaded (with reference, for example, to supervening legal developments) have been wrongly decided by prior authority, understand that they have the responsibility to decide the pending matter by analogy within the general framework of the law confronting them, with attention to sound policy and the likely consequences of their decision. That is, they must make new law on the subject, that will have *stare decisis* effect for them and hierarchically inferior courts in the future.[146]

---

143. The question, what constitutes a "case," raises interesting problems in American constitutional law. One can say in summary that there must be a real dispute, between parties having real and opposing interests, respecting which a court is in a position to give final and effective relief. A proceeding for declaratory judgment by a manufacturer whose present activities are directly threatened by a statute or regulation it asserts to be unlawful would be a "case," since the courts will consider that by declaring the validity or invalidity of the statute or regulation they give effective relief against its enforcement. A proceeding brought by a citizen who believes that another's possible future plans would be unlawful would lack these elements of reality. See the discussion of standing, p. 313 below.

144. Erie R. R. Co. v. Tompkins, 304 U.S. 64 (1938).

145. See p. 14 n. 16 and p. 15, n. 22 above.

146. Referring to common-law functions of judges, and attempting to suggest their limits, Justice Holmes once wrote:

I recognize without hesitation that judges do and must legislate, but they can do so only interstitially; they are confined from molar to molecular motions. A com-

- these propositions about the system of precedent apply to decisions involving the meaning and application of the Constitution or statutes, just as they do to decisions about judge-made common law. Thus, when American courts interpret statutory text, it is often by reference to previous decisions interpreting the same text, as much as or more than by reference to the text itself.

Thus, when the Supreme Court has once interpreted a text, future courts are obliged to respect its interpretation as well as the text. In constitutional matters, this is the mechanism for the process of informal amendment described at the outset of these essays;[147] only the Supreme Court itself or a constitutional amendment can alter an interpretation of the Constitution's text once it has been announced by the Court. Respecting ordinary statutes, the Court has said (but not invariably respected the proposition) that because Congress could revise the Court's interpretation if it wished, the Court will not reexamine its statutory interpretations. Note that this ostensibly modest attitude actually serves to fix the interpretation much more strongly than either common law or civil law models of judicial action imagine. By fixing the meaning of a statutory text that might have been quite indefinite, then, the Supreme Court indisputably makes law.

The last decades have brought two important challenges to the common law process, both growing out of what could be described as an explosion of law. First, the explosion of litigation has undercut a principal intellectual defense of the judicial role as lawmaker. In the inherited model of judicial action, judges decided cases because they were obliged to—the parties having brought the cases to them, they were required to decide them one way or another, and if they could not do so in accordance with the established principles, then that warranted their effort to create new ones that would be most consistent with existing principles and responsive to the demands of justice, as they appeared on the facts of the particular case. One important element of the discipline of *stare decisis* is that the power of a case to command future obedience is limited to the material facts that the court deciding it had before it, the circumstances that obliged the court to decide. These facts both are the circumstances that compel decision, and set the context for argument in the

---

mon-law judge could not say I think the doctrine of consideration a bit of historical nonsense and shall not enforce it in my court. No more could a judge exercising the limited jurisdiction of admiralty say I think well of the common-law rules of master and servant and propose to introduce them here en bloc. Southern Pacific Co. v. Jensen, 244 U.S. 205, 221 (1917) (Holmes, J., dissenting).
147. See p. 12 above.

case; while the court's opinion might discuss other matters, this "dictum" does not have the force of precedent; only the "holding," [148] only what circumstances obliged the courts to decide, is entitled to *stare decisis* force.[149]

With the explosion of litigation, however, one can no longer say of the Supreme Court (or the highest courts of at least the largest states)—the place where the strongest precedent is made—*either* that the decisions the Court makes are involuntary, in the sense that they are just a by-product of the obligation to decide created by litigants' choices about what cases to bring, *or* that they are principally motivated by the parties' claims. The Court now selects the cases it hears, a very small proportion of those it is asked to hear.[150] Significantly, it makes those selections on the basis of judgments about what legal issues are the most important to address from the perspective of the national system of law. In these respects, the Court's function as lawmaker is both voluntary and central. (In the intellectual justifications of common law powers, it is involuntary and incidental.) Understandably this often encourages the Justices to speak broadly, outside the particular facts of the cases before them, when they do speak. This remarkable change of circumstances has not been much addressed as such, but doubtless contributes to the sentiments often expressed, in conservative circles especially, that judges should not be lawmakers.[151]

The second characteristic of the American explosion of law is that most of it, and particularly most new federal law, has been created by legislation or regulations, not judicial decision. Admittedly, these statutes are not codes in the civilian sense; their interpretation, as just mentioned, occurs within the discipline of common law habits respecting *stare decisis*.[152] The federal courts unremarkably, in light of the traditions from which they sprang, acted fully as common-law courts throughout the nineteenth and much of the twentieth century. However, the proliferation of federal statutory and regulatory law has led to expressions disclaiming common-law power to derive new legal rights and obligations on the basis, simply, of judicial reasoning by analogy from ex-

---

148. Referred to as the ratio or ratio decidendi in other common law countries.

149. For an introduction to the problems of common law practice, see K. Greenawalt, Reflections on Holding and Dictum, 39 J. Leg. Ed. 431 (1989); E. Levi. An Introduction to Legal Reasoning (194).

150. See p. 121 below.

151. An interesting history of this problem can be found in E. Purcell, Brandeis and the Progressive Constitution: Erie, the Judicial Power, and the Politics of the Federal Courts in Twentieth-Century America (2000). See also E. Hartnett, Questioning Certiorari: Some Reflections Seventy-Five Years After the Judges' Bill, 100 Colum. L. Rev. 1643 (2000).

152. See G. Calabresi, A Common Law for the Age of Statutes (1982).

isting authority. In one respect this is not surprising: in diversity cases, which involve state rather than federal law, federal courts have no more authority to create new general law than would a court of France or Japan; they simply decide the case in accordance with their best estimate of the relevant state's law, with no expectation that their decision will govern future cases.[153] But as a disclaimer of authority to generate precedents entitled to *stare decisis* effect with regard to *federal* law, these expressions are surprising indeed.

Federal courts have been establishing propositions of law entitled to precedential effect in the interstices of Constitution and statute since the founding of the Republic. In part, this was a necessity of a time when the largest proportion of the United States' land mass lay in territories, not states. In part, it was the simple performance of a role, acting in the habitual manner of a judge in the Anglo-American legal system. Thus, the Supreme Court has used Congress's constitutional power to regulate interstate commerce as the basis for judicial findings that certain state laws impermissibly interfered with that commerce, even in the absence of statute.[154] In the statutory context, it has long treated broadly worded statutes, such as the Sherman Antitrust Act, more as starting points for judicial reasoning about legal obligation than as precise statements of applicable law. It has invoked its own understandings of the common law in reasoning about secondary issues arising in the course of a federal statute's administration.[155] The Court has used the Constitution's prohibition against unreasonable searches and seizures as the basis for recognizing a cause of action for civil liability against federal officers who have perpetrated such a search.[156] A venerable similar proposition, often acted upon by the Court until recently, is that a common law cause of action for civil damages should be inferred from a person's violation of a statutory obligation, as for example a criminal statute. Indeed, at the dawn of the statutory era, at a time when many judges seemed to be resisting legislative changes in "their" common law, scholars persuasively argued that reasoning by analogy from statutes in the common law ought to be preferred to such reasoning from cases, because statutes had the greater claim to democratic legitimacy.[157]

---

153. See Erie R.R. Co., n. 144 above; the case is throughly explored in Purcell, n. 151 above.

154. Cooley v. Board of Wardens, 53 U.S. 299 (1855).

155. Pergram v. Hedrich, 530 U.S. 2111 (2000).

156. Bivens v. Six Unknown Named Agents of the Federal Bureau of Narcotics, 403 U.S. 388 (1971).

157. R. Pound, Common Law and Legislation, 21 Harv. L. Rev. 383 (1908); see also H.F. Stone, The Common Law in the United States, 50 Harv. L. Rev. 4 (1936).

The present concern is articulated in relation to the last of these practices, using constitutional or statutory text as a basis for analogical reasoning, in the style of the common law, to establish legal norms that cannot themselves be said to be directly entailed by that text. "Raising up causes of action where a statute has not created them may be a proper function for common-law courts, but not for federal tribunals," Justice Scalia remarked in a lonely 1991 concurrence[158] that in 2001 he converted into part of a holding subscribed to by five members of the Court over the strong dissents of four colleagues.[159] The Court's refusal to infer this particular cause of action has limited relevance for this essay, although it may mark a disquieting turn in American civil rights law. And the refusal might have been justified without stating any general proposition about the proper functions of "tribunals" or "courts." Particularly as statutes have become the dominant form of law-making, the Court could have concluded as an interpretive matter that the complex statute at issue had provided just as much remedy as Congress had wished to give, and that its failure to provide for a private civil action should therefore be respected. The striking departure is the proposition that "federal tribunals" are different from "common-law courts." The implications of this quite radical proposition, un-grounded in the practice or understandings of two previous centuries, remain to be worked out; it seems unlikely, however, that the Court means to discard, as well, its development of federal common law in the interstices of statutory administration,[160] or its adherence to the idea of *stare decisis*. Indeed, the Court has recently been emphatic, in the context of textual interpretations as such, in insisting that its prior holdings be honored,[161] and Justice Scalia him-

---

158. Lampf, Pleva, Lipkind, Prupis & Petigrow v. Gilbertson, 501 U.S. 350, 365 (1991) (Scalia, J., concurring in part and concurring in judgment).

159. Alexander v. Sandoval, 532 U.S. 275 (2001).

160. The federal courts have no general common law, as in a sense they have no general or comprehensive jurisprudence of any kind, because many subjects of private law which bulk large in the traditional common law are ordinarily within the province of the states and not of the federal government. But this is not to say that wherever we have occasion to decide a federal question which cannot be answered from federal statutes alone we may not resort to all of the source ma-terials of the common law or that when we have fashioned an answer it does not become a part of the federal non-statutory or common law.... Were we bereft of the common law, our federal system would be impotent. This follows from the recognized futility of attempting all-complete statutory codes, and is apparent from the terms of the Constitution itself.
D'Oench, Duhme & Co v. FDIC, 315 U.S. 447, 471 (1942) (Jackson, J., concurring).

161. See Dickerson v. United States, 530 U.S. 428 (2000), p. 14, n. 16 above; see also Neal v. United States, 516 U.S. 284 (1996).

self invoked the operation of *stare decisis* in dissent just weeks after making this argument.[162]

The most important question of constitutional structure concerning the relationship between the courts and administrative agencies is what is the necessary role of courts—what issues must be decided by Article III judges rather than agency officials serving in less protected tenure. This question has at least three aspects: first, whether judicial decision of some matters is required by formal separation of powers considerations—that is, because the matter is inherently "judicial" in character, and so must be the subject of judicial judgment, not merely judicial oversight. This question might be thought analogous to the question about delegating legislative authority. Second, more broadly, in those types of proceedings or on those issues which may be assigned to agencies for initial decision of matters directly affecting the rights of citizens, whether legislative provision for judicial review is a condition necessary to the validity of the delegation of authority to an administrative agency. Third, whether review in some form over a decision depriving a person of "life, liberty or property" is a necessary element of due process of law. American law has not given precise answers to these questions, although the areas of dispute can be located with some confidence.

Outside the criminal law, the Constitution has been found to permit tremendous scope for agency adjudication. Exercising its general authority to create the arrangements of government, Congress has often successfully assigned to agencies tasks that strongly resemble judicial ones. Judicial rationalization of this practice initially saw two possibilities. In some cases Congress could freely exclude the courts from *any* role because only matters of "public right" were involved, in which the citizen had no constitutional claim to process. Where private rights were affected, the courts might be able to treat agencies as adjuncts of the judiciary—acting as preliminary fact-finders within the framework of judicial power as do, for example, the ad hoc special masters courts appoint in certain contexts.[163] This rather neat conceptual analysis broke down, however, as on the one hand courts realized that the expanded understanding of "due process"[164] would most often defeat "public right" analysis; and, on the other, the multiple functions of agencies and their frequent placement in Article II executive departments made it impossible to regard them as adjuncts of the Article III courts. The resulting theoretical difficulties led one Supreme Court Justice to the striking conclusion that "Whether fortu-

---

162. United States v. Mead Corp., 121 S. Ct. 2164 U.S. (2001).
163. Crowell v. Benson, 285 U.S. 22 (1932).
164. See p. 48 above.

nate or unfortunate, at this point in the history of constitutional law that question can no longer be answered by looking only to the constitutional text."[165]

Whatever the theoretical difficulties, the result is straightforward. The courts have insisted on reserving for their own rather than administrative judgment only limited types of proceedings or issues to which the government is one party—for example, a limited class of factual issues on which claims to some constitutional liberties depend.[166] Administrative adjudication of the remainder, subject only to the possibility of judicial review, is permitted. As to the question, whether, or to what extent, judicial review of agency action may be constitutionally required, the courts have equivocated. In some cases they appear to tolerate having little if any involvement;[167] in others (directly affecting a citizen's entitlements) they indicate that a strong review relationship is necessary.[168] The uncertainty exists in good part because legislators have had little motivation to test the margins. Expressions in the delegation cases strongly suggest that effective review for legality is a necessary condition of a valid delegation, as we have seen.[169] And ordinarily legislators, as well as citizens, can be expected to see "the availability of judicial review [as] the necessary condition, psychologically if not logically, of a system of administrative power which purports to be legitimate, or legally valid."[170]

Examples may make the problems clearer. A citizen charged with federal crime would expect a judicial trial, with use of a jury if she chose, as a matter of constitutional right. Yet Congress can place decision whether to levy substantial "civil penalties" for violation of agency regulations or statutes governing workplace safety in the hands of the administrative agency generally responsible for regulation of the workplace, subject only to a somewhat permissive regime of judicial review.[171] The differences between imprisonment and fine give a formal, but not wholly satisfactory explanation.

Two citizens with a contractual dispute governed by state common law would ordinarily expect to have that dispute resolved by a court—a state court most frequently, but a federal court if diversity of state citizenship is present. Can Con-

165. Northern Pipeline Construction Co. v. Marathon Pipe Line Co., 458 U.S. 50, 94 (1982) (White, J. dissenting).

166. See p. 339 below.

167. Thomas v. Union Carbide Agricultural Products Co., 473 U.S. 568 (1985); Johnson v. Robinson, 415 U.S. 361 (1974).

168. Goldberg v. Kelly, 397 U.S. 254 (1970); Crowell v. Benson, 285 U.S. 22 (1932).

169. See p. 33 above.

170. L. Jaffe, Judicial Control of Administrative Action 320 (1965).

171. Atlas Roofing Co. v. Occupational Safety and Health Review Comm'n, 430 U.S. 442 (1977).

gress assign such disputes to tribunals other than Article III federal courts? One decision holds that it can permit a federal regulatory agency rather than an Article III federal court to decide state common law contractual claims as part of an integrated dispute, subject to limited judicial review, when one citizen has initiated a claim founded in federal regulatory law before the responsible agency (rather than a court), and the second (who has chosen to engage in the general practices that subject him to regulation) asserts the state contractual claim in response.[172] But another holds that Congress can *not* create a body of "bankruptcy judges" who equally lack Article III status, and broadly empower them to resolve similar state common law disputes (again, subject only to limited judicial review), where the citizen is in no sense voluntarily before them.[173] The difference between these two situations is more readily expressed in the subjective terms of perceived threat to overall judicial function, than in clear principle. [174]

Finally, Congress can assign to an administrative agency the final resolution of an application for government benefits. But courts have resisted the conclusion that Congress can keep from them the final resolution of a dispute about the constitutional fairness of the procedures Congress designed.[175] Judicial suggestions of what constitutes the irreducible function of judicial review vary from the profound[176] to the perfunctory.[177] The generally accepted doctrinal test for necessary judicial role—whether Congress has so restricted judicial involvement as to threaten the core functions of the court[178]—is so indefinite as to be virtually unmanageable.

---

172. Commodity Futures Trading Commission v. Schor, 478 U.S. 833 (1986).

173. Northern Pipeline Construction Co. v. Marathon Pipe Line Co., 458 U.S. 50 (1982).

174. "Everyone agrees that congressional power to allocate adjudicate functions among legislative courts, administrative agencies, and constitutional courts is broad. No clear limits have emerged; the Supreme Court cases are notoriously obscure." H. Bruff, Specialized Courts in Administrative Law, 43 Admin. L. Rev. 329, 352–53 (1991).

175. Johnson v. Robison, 415 U.S. 361 (1974); Walters v. National Association of Radiation Survivors, 473 U.S. 305 (1985). See the discussion above at p. 48.

176. Goldberg v. Kelly, 397 U.S. 254 (1970).

177. Thomas v. Union Carbide Agricultural Products Co., 473 U.S. 568 (1985).

178. H. Hart, The Power of Congress to Limit the Jurisdiction of Federal Courts: An Exercise in Dialectic, 66 Harv. L. Rev. 1362 (1953); G. Gunther, Congressional Power to Curtail Federal Court Jurisdiction: An Opinionated Guide to the Ongoing Debate, 36 Stan. L. Rev. 895 (1984); CFTC v. Schor, 478 U.S. 833 (1986).

a. The Supreme Court[179]

The Supreme Court is a panel of nine Justices and decides all of its cases en banc—that is, with the whole tribunal sitting. For our purposes, its functions are wholly appellate;[180] under Article III, its "appellate Jurisdiction, both as to Law and Fact, [is] with such Exceptions, and under such Regulations as the Congress shall make." This revisory power of Congress has raised some interesting separation of powers problems, threatening effective reprisals against an over-ambitious Court. Its most important use for our purposes, however, has been to make the Court's review function largely a discretionary one. Virtually all cases coming before the Court, including all ordinary review of federal administrative action or of the compliance of state or local agencies with federal constitutional requirements, are first presented to it by a "petition for a writ of certiorari." This pleading seeks to persuade the Court to review a lower court judgment. To be effective it must show reasons of legal importance for review, for example, that the Circuit Courts of Appeal for differing parts of the country have reached conflicting results on the legal question presented.[181] Reasons to believe the lower court ruled in error, as such, do not suffice. The other side is then able to respond showing reasons why review is unimportant, for example that the decision below (whether correct or incorrect) raises no question of general significance but depends on its special facts.[182] If four Justices agree, one less than a majority, the petition seeking review will be granted. With resource constraints imposing a practical limit of about 150 cases per year, in recent years the Supreme Court has in fact been granting fewer than 100 petitions for hearing annually from a pool of about 2000 paid and 5000 unpaid (in forma pauperis) applications.[183]

---

179. http://www.supremecourtus.gov/ is the Court's website, where can be found a good deal of primary materials about its docket, including transcripts of oral arguments in recently heard cases and the text of an annual State of the Federal Courts message by the Chief Justice, from which many of the statistics used in the text were drawn.

180. A very limited group of controversies, chiefly concerning the states or foreign states, can originate in the Supreme Court.

181. As is discussed in more detail in the following part, conflicting results can occur because each circuit operates as a separate jurisdiction, meaning no circuit court is bound by another.

182. On this subject and others of importance to Supreme Court practice, consult R. Stern, E. Gressman, and S. Shapiro, Supreme Court Practice (7th ed. 1993).

183. The Supreme Court term runs from the first Monday in October to the following first Monday in October. In the 1999–2000 term, 7,377 petitions were filed with the Court, 5,282 in forma pauperis—that is, by persons (usually prisoners) filing a limited petition

Ordinarily, if a petition for certiorari is granted, the parties will prepare full briefs on the questions the petitioner presented to the Court,[184] will then present oral argument (ordinarily an hour or less in its entirety), and after a period of time—invariably before July of the term of Court in which the case was argued—the Court will issue a more or less elaborate written opinion.[185] Under common-law practice, as discussed above,[186] this opinion constitutes binding authority on all federal questions necessary to be resolved; given the Court's place in the judicial hierarchy, it is binding for all American courts and agencies. It is important to understand, however, that the denial of a petition for certiorari has no similar impact: it is not explained, and is made without oral argument or elaborate briefing; while it terminates the litigation, it has no precedential force whatever. A denial of certiorari cannot even be regarded as having determined that the question presented to the Court is one that, in another case, would not warrant the Court's full review. It is, one may say, an exercise of *DISCRETION!*

Note that one implication of the limits on the Supreme Court's annual body of opinions is that its control over particular programs or issues is highly attenuated. Further, it also has at best attenuated control over the lower federal judiciary. "In 1924, the Court reviewed about one in ten decisions of the courts of appeals...[I]n the 1984 Term the Court was able to review only 0.56% of courts of appeals decisions.... [T]hese courts of error, at least for practical purposes, have become the final expositors of federal law in their geographical region in all but a minuscule number of cases."[187] If a court of appeals judge participates each year in about 90 cases with signed opinions, as appears from the current statistics, and writes the opinion in one third of those, Supreme Court review of one in ten would put her in direct intellectual contact with the Court several times over the course of a year; review of

---

without payment of fee—and 2,092 in the Court's paid docket. The great bulk of cases selected for argument are from the latter group. The Court heard 83 cases argued—about 4% of its paid docket if one assumes substantially all cases argued came from that docket.

184. Occasionally, the Court limits the questions from those addressed to it by the petitioner to a subset regarded by it as worthy of its attention. Occasionally, as well, it invites argument on (or addresses its decision to) matters not so raised; this latter practice is not well regarded in the academic community and is generally eschewed by the Court.

185. In cases where the appropriate outcome is obvious—for example, where the lower court's judgment needs to be reconsidered in light of a subsequent Supreme Court decision on point—the petition may be granted and action summarily taken without these steps.

186. See p. 114 above.

187. T. Baker & D. McFarland, The Need for a New National Court, 100 Harv. L. Rev. 1400, 1405–06 (1987).

one in 200 suggests that even her panel votes will not be reviewed as often as every two years, and her opinions, on average, will come under scrutiny only two times in a decade.[188] The steepness of this pyramid should be kept in mind in the pages following.

b. The Circuit Courts of Appeal[189]

With the exception of certain special courts that hear a limited range of disputes, discussed in subpart d following, the jurisdiction of federal courts inferior to the Supreme Court is organized along geographic rather than subject-matter lines. That is, these courts are courts of general (federal) jurisdiction, that hear all matters within the Article III federal judicial power that arise within their geographical area. Subject to specific, contrary jurisdictional provisions, that means that all disputes about federal administrative law can be heard either in the federal courts of Washington, D.C., where the national government is located, or in the federal courts of the location where the person seeking review is, or where the dispute arose. For these purposes, the country is divided into 12 geographic "circuits" that operate independently of each other. Within the circuits, two levels of court are created—a trial court, known as a United States District Court, with jurisdiction over a state or some subdivision of that state, and an intermediate appellate court, known as the United States Court of Appeal for that circuit.

The twelve circuits vary considerably in size[190] and in geographical extent,[191] but the jurisdiction and practice of the courts of appeal that preside over them are generally similar. Ordinarily, circuit judges—there are at this writing 167

---

188. See P. Strauss, One Hundred Fifty Cases Per Year: Some Implications of the Supreme Court's Limited Resources for Judicial Review of Agency Action, 87 Colum. L. Rev. 1093 (1987). R. Posner, The Federal Courts: Crisis and Reform 69 (1985), reports 5572 signed opinions for the courts of appeals in 1983. Assuming them to have evenly distributed among 45 panels of three means approximately 125 opinions per panel, 42 per judge. Given the participation of senior judges and other factors, the actual numbers are even lower.

189. Links to the home pages of each of the United States Courts of Appeal, including that for the Federal Circuit, may be found at http://www.uscourts.gov/links.html.

190. The First Circuit, comprising the New England states of Maine, New Hampshire, Massachusetts and Rhode Island, plus Puerto Rico has six circuit judges; the Ninth, embracing Hawaii, Alaska, California, Oregon, Washington, Idaho, Montana, Nevada, and Arizona, has 28.

191. The District of Columbia circuit embraces only the 70 square miles and roughly 800,000 residents of the nation's capital; the Ninth Circuit includes the nation's largest and third largest states by area, its largest by population, and the two states located at a con-

authorized judgeships nationwide (plus senior judges who may continue to sit)—sit in rotating panels of three to hear appeals, moving among the commercial and legal centers of their circuit to hear argument. A circuit court of appeals hears all appeals from United States district courts sitting within its circuit, and also any review cases that can be brought directly from a federal agency to a court of appeals and that arise within the circuit. The allocation of review cases between those that come directly to the courts of appeal from the agencies, and those that originate in district court, is further discussed below;[192] here it may be enough to say that cases of direct review in the courts of appeal are always provided for by special statute, and generally concern formal proceedings before the larger federal agencies.

In contrast with the Supreme Court, appeals come to the circuit courts—whether direct from a federal agency, or from a district court—as a matter of party right. The circuit courts thus do not experience the problems for common law function that might be thought to derive from a court's having a choice over what controversies to hear.[193] The courts require written briefs for all cases. As a measure of docket control, they identify a significant proportion as presenting no question difficult enough to warrant oral argument, and decide these simply on the basis of the briefs. Similarly, whether or not oral argument is held, in some cases the court will either forego writing an opinion or direct that its opinion not be published; when this is done, the court's action decides the case, but cannot be said to have any precedential effect for future, similar cases arising within the same circuit.[194] For the year ending September 2000, for example, only about one third of the almost 28,000 appeals terminated on the merits were accorded oral argument; 80% of the opinions filed in these appeals were unpublished. Although decisions without oral argument or without published opinion have thus become predominant in court of appeal practice as a statistical matter, it is believed these occur disproportionately in pro se proceedings, and that significant proceedings reviewing administrative decisions are unlikely to be treated in this way.

Since court of appeal judges sit in small panels, it can happen that one panel will wish to reach a different conclusion on a legal question than did another in

siderable distance from the contiguous mass of states sometimes called "the lower 48," namely Hawaii and Alaska.

192. See p. 298 below.

193. See p. 114 above.

194. Questions have been raised about the constitutionality of this restriction. Compare Anastasoff v. United States, 223 F.3d 898, vacated as moot 235 F.3d 1054 (8th Cir. 2000), with Hart v. Massanari, 266 F. 3d 1155 (9th Cir. 2001).

the same circuit. This can lead to the convening of a grand panel of judges from the circuit to decide, en banc, the question subject to this disagreement. En banc hearing may also be sought in cases where a party believes an important issue has been wrongly decided by the panel. Like the writ of certiorari in the Supreme Court, en banc hearing is discretionary, requiring agreement of a majority of active court of appeal judges in the circuit. For a large and geographically extended circuit, it will be evident, this can present major administrative difficulties even if less than the full banc is required to sit,[195] but other means of attaining a uniform understanding of law within the circuit are not apparent.

The geographic nature of circuit court jurisdiction means that the precedential effect of their decisions is limited to those states within that particular circuit. For a national agency, responsible for administering national regulation, this can mean that different understandings of the law apply in different parts of the country—one interpretation in Iowa, another in Florida, California, or New York. In one respect this can be viewed as an opportunity: if the Commissioner of Internal Revenue does not accept the construction given to the Tax Code by the Second Circuit, he ordinarily could not expect to obtain Supreme Court review (because of the absence of any conflict). The Second Circuit's ruling does not prevent him, however, from continuing to use the construction he prefers in cases likely to arise in other circuits, where he may prevail. In another respect, of course, it is destructive of the uniformity of national administrations to have the same statute or rule understood differently in different parts of the country; and it is destructive to some understandings of legality to have an administrator continue to apply an interpretation of his authority that one court has found unlawful and that he has not brought before a higher court for review. Thus, real problems for administrative justice in the United States can be thought to arise from the stringent limitations on the capacity of the Supreme Court to accept and resolve such conflicts when they arise (or, even, when they would be threatened by an administrator's refusal to acquiesce in the first negative judgment he receives).[196]

In the particular case of administrative law, the special stature of the United States Court of Appeals for the District of Columbia Circuit helps to control the problem of inter-circuit disagreement. Although this court is not, in general, given exclusive jurisdiction over judicial review of federal agency decisions, its location in Washington, D.C. gives it possible jurisdiction over almost all

---

195: In the 28-judge Ninth Circuit, for example, 11 judges constitute an en banc panel.

196. The issue is briefly discussed in the social welfare administration context in which it has proved most troublesome, p. 171 below.

such decisions, and its special experience with administrative matters often leads counsel to choose it. While less than one half of one percent of the nation's population lives there, a significant proportion of all federal administrative law cases are brought there, especially those of likely national significance. Other circuit courts, in turn, may give special weight to the views of the D.C. Circuit because of the greater frequency with which it considers such issues, even though in a formal sense they are free to apply their own judgment.[197]

c. The District Courts

The United States is divided into 93 judicial districts, ranging between one and four in each state, with each district containing a number of federal district judges. At this writing, more than 650 district judges are authorized for the nation as a whole; about 260,000 civil filings, and an additional 50,000 criminal cases, were opened in 1999–2000—an evidently substantial workload. In all but a few cases a single judge presides over any district court proceeding. Although juries of civilians are used for fact-finding in many district court trials, they are not used in administrative review proceedings, so that the judge almost invariably sits alone. District court jurisdiction over administrative matters can arise in either of two ways: a statute may specifically provide for it, as is the case for review of agency decisions under the federal Freedom of Information statute; or litigants may simply be able to invoke the district court's general jurisdiction over "federal questions." As the product of a trial court, the district court's judgments have little precedential impact beyond the case being decided. The manner in which review proceeds is addressed in Chapters VII and VIII below.

d. Special courts

For a group of specialist issues and/or tribunals, the judicial jurisdiction of the United States is organized along national and subject matter rather than geographical lines. The United States Court of Appeals for the Federal Circuit, a banc of twelve judges whose position in the judicial hierarchy corresponds

---

197. This expertise has had other consequences in the D.C. Circuit's relationship with the Supreme Court. Since Supreme Court review is so limited, the D.C. Circuit has on occasion been able to build up a substantial body of law through its own precedent-setting process, only to find some years later that the Supreme Court has a different view. A. Scalia, Vermont Yankee: The APA, the D.C. Circuit, and the Supreme Court, 1978 Sup. Ct. Rev. 345. The sharpness with which some of these reversals have been expressed in Supreme Court opinions presumably diminishes the influence of the D.C. Circuit among the other courts of appeal.

to that of the circuit courts of appeal, is the appellate court for these tribunals and issues. Specialist trial courts include the Claims Court (monetary actions against the United States, chiefly those arising out of alleged contracts), the Tax Court, the Patent Court, and the Court of International Trade. Some of these courts, for example the Tax Court, provide specialist review of the administrative decisions of a particular agency; others, a specialized setting for initial trial of issues (which, as in the Claims Court, may also concern the propriety of government conduct). Perhaps especially noteworthy here is the use of the Federal Circuit to achieve national uniformity below the Supreme Court, even as to some matters within the jurisdiction of the ordinary district courts. If patent issues arise in district court litigation—say, in the course of a proceeding under the American anti-trust laws—a decision against the validity of the patent entitles the party supporting the patent to appeal to the Federal Circuit, rather than to the geographical circuit to which her appeal would ordinarily be referred. In this way, the patent supporter is assured a single decision on the validity or not of the invention, which will then have national effect.

B. *The political leadership of administration*

The units of American government, outside the Presidency, assume a diversity of forms. Each form is the product of legislative specification. For persons seeking to understand American administrative law, four are of principal importance: the cabinet department, the bureau or administration within a department, the independent agency within the executive branch, and the independent regulatory commission.[198] The paragraphs following sketch the characteristics and possible interrelationships of each. Bear in mind, that all four share important features in common: all are at root the creatures of statute, rather than the Constitution or presidential specification;[199] their political leadership, composed of persons subject to presidential appointment, is thin in relationship to the size of the agency as a whole; with limited exceptions, all fall under the same set of statutes for the internal management of government (the civil service laws, etc.); all reflect the same principles of

198. Other possibilities, which do not ordinarily possess significant regulatory authority, include corporation-like forms responsible for providing services to the public—the generation and distribution of electric power (Tennessee Valley Authority; Bonneville Power Authority), the provision of postal service (United States Post Office), or of passenger railroad services (AMTRAK).

199. Congress has occasionally given the President provisional authority to reorganize existing governmental functions into new or altered governmental writs.

internal organization, generally hierarchical but with provision also for specialist offices housing lawyers, economist/ planners, fiscal specialists, secretariat, etc.

Most important for our purposes, the public procedures American agencies employ do not much vary with the type of government organization employed. While some variations do occur from agency to agency, these are a function of specific programs. The general procedures—and the expectations of government structure and performance that flow from them—are uniformly provided for by an Administrative Procedure Act and associated statutes that rarely pay heed to issues of agency form. There are limited variations in a general pattern of non-differentiation: For example, the Government in the Sunshine Act,[200] requiring agency leadership to meet in public, after notice of their agenda, could only apply readily to a multi-member commission. Legislation requiring agencies to submit forms and other information requirements to OMB for clearance prior to imposing them on the public[201] states somewhat different procedures for independent commissions than executive agencies. And the executive orders imposing regulatory impact analysis requirements in connection with important rulemakings, as already remarked,[202] apply directly only to the executive agencies (who in fact consider what are economically the most important rules).

1. Cabinet departments

The Departments were the original, and remain the most important, elements of executive government outside the presidency itself. Early drafts of the Constitution specified a number of departments each exercising a particular responsibility—over foreign affairs, the army, internal commerce, marine matters, and so on. They were to be headed by Secretaries appointed by the President who would sit with him in a council, or cabinet, to oversee the conduct of government. These provisions disappeared with the choice to emphasize the unitary character and responsibility of the presidency, and to leave future Congresses substantial flexibility in establishing the detailed structure of the national government.[203] Contemplation that there would be such departments remained, however, in the Necessary and Proper Clause, and in the provisions made for appointments and for the President's receipt of "opinions, in writing" from their principal officers.

---

200. See p. 284 below.
201. See p. 265 below.
202. See p. 103 above.
203. See p. 21 above.

The first Congress promptly established Departments of State, Treasury, War, and Navy, and the office of the Attorney General, headed by prominent individuals who in fact did quickly come to be regarded by the President as a "cabinet" with which to consult on important matters. The central offices of these departments were minuscule. They enjoyed only limited control over employees often acting weeks or months away, in the communications circumstances of the time. Notably, even at that early stage in the country's history, they were not established in accordance with a single pattern; the Department of the Treasury, which would be responsible for budget issues and other matters of particular interest to Congress, was created in a relationship closer to Congress, and more independent of the President, than the others.[204]

Today's departments number 14: Agriculture, Commerce, Defense, Education, Energy, Health and Human Services, Housing and Urban Development, Interior, Justice, Labor, State, Transportation, Treasury, and Veterans' Affairs.[205] Each represents a bureaucracy of substantial size, headed by a Secretary[206] appointed with senatorial confirmation to serve at the pleasure of the President. Other political appointees generally include an Under-Secretary or Deputy Secretary responsible for general administration, a General Counsel, and assistant Secretaries with responsibilities for administration or for overseeing the administration of particular programs. Given the size and scope of each department, even assistant Secretaries may be one step removed from direct responsibility for particular legislative regimes.

An example may give concrete shape to these generalizations. In fiscal year 2000, the Department of Agriculture[207] had about 100,000 employees and budgeted about $90 billion, including $55 billion in outlays (external expenditures for program support). Its organizational chart[208] shows eight large administrative offices, and 19 program offices, services, or administrations, each placed under the responsibility of one of seven Under-Secretaries. For example, the Department's Under-Secretary for Marketing and Regulatory Programs had responsibility for its Agricultural Marketing Service (nine different programs, ranging from Cotton to Transportation and Marketing),[209]

---

204. See L. Lessig & C. Sunstein, The Presidency and the Administration, 94 Colum. L. Rev. 1 (1994); L. White, The Federalists: A Study in Administrative History (Macmillan 1948).

205. Links to each appear at http://www.whitehouse.gov/government/cabinet.html.

206. Or, in the case of the Justice Department, the Attorney General.

207. http://www.usda.gov.

208. http://www.usda.gov/agencies/agchart.htm.

209. http://www.ams.usda.gov.

Animal and Plant Health Inspection Service (nine functions, ranging from agricultural biotechnology to wildlife services),[210] and Grain Inspection, Packers and Stockyards Administration (two programs)[211]—a highly diverse group of subjects and regulatory challenges. The other assistant Secretaries enjoyed similarly diverse responsibilities. One must expect, then, that while the Secretary and her assistants can give general policy guidance and shape within their department, the detailed understanding and actual implementation of programs occurs within its bureaus, at some remove from the political appointees.

While these pages naturally stress regulatory themes, it is appropriate to remark that the greatest part of departmental responsibilities—for some departments, virtually all—lies in administering programs for spending or other activities that one would not ordinarily consider "regulation." Thus, a great proportion of the Department of Agriculture's budget is expended on transfer payments to farmers; similarly, the Departments of Transportation and of Housing and Urban Development administer a variety of programs for supporting facilities, such as road construction or housing projects, that rarely appear in judicial or even administrative settings.[212] The Departments of State and Defense have responsibilities that can hardly be conceived in those terms. Even in these, however, particular bureaus or offices exist with responsibilities that do invoke our concerns.

a. Departmental bureaus

Like the departments within which they function, the offices, administrations and bureaus of American government tend to be organized along standard hierarchical lines, within which bureaucratic structure and routine play important roles. An interesting book by the American political scientist Herbert Kaufman, The Administrative Behavior of Federal Bureau Chiefs,[213] analyzed the functioning of the heads of six sub-units of this sort, each responsible for the implementation of one or more massive government programs. The six units studied were the Animal and Plant Health Inspec-

---

210. http://www.aphis.usda.gov.

211. http://www.usda.gov/gipsa/.

212. The central case defining scope of review of administrative decision, however, Citizens to Preserve Overton Park v. Volpe, 401 U.S. 402 (1971), extensively discussed below at pp. 235, 341 and 376, arose in just such a context: the decision by the Secretary of Transportation (through the Federal Highway Administration) to subsidize Tennessee's construction of a major highway, even though it traversed valuable urban parklands.

213. Brookings Institute, 1981.

tion Service and Forest Service (both of the Department of Agriculture), the Food and Drug Administration and Social Security Administration (both of the Department of Health and Human Services), and the Customs Service and Internal Revenue Service (both of the Treasury Department). They are representative of a general phenomenon; others of equal prominence performing major regulatory functions would include the Occupational Safety and Health Administration in the Department of Labor, the Federal Aviation Administration in the Department of Transportation, or the Food and Drug Administration in the Department of Health and Human Services. These bodies, even in their leadership, are largely apolitical, and their work is less subject to political swings than their presence in a political department might otherwise suggest:

> [B]eing a Chief [of such a bureau] is gratifying only for those who derive pleasure from accomplishments on a small scale and from the chance that some...may lead to larger benefits in the future. The chiefs...certainly do calculate and negotiate to accomplish all they can. But they make their marks in inches, not miles, and only as others allow.[214]

Often the statutes that create them, even while placing them in political departments, contain special measures safeguarding against political influence: decisions of the Internal Revenue Service respecting the selection of individual taxpayers for investigation are shielded from political direction, for example, and the Federal Energy Regulatory Commission, although made part of the Department of Energy, is in form an independent regulatory commission whose relationships with the Secretary of the Department are highly formal.

2. Independent executive agencies

Occasionally Congress has created an office at the responsibility level common to departmental administrations or bureaus, but placed it outside the departmental structure—independent in the sense that no Secretary commands it, but nonetheless headed by a single administrator who serves at the President's pleasure and thus is clearly placed within his sphere of influence. The

---

214. Id at 174. Book-length studies of bureau functioning, tending to confirm their bureaucratic character, can be found in an earlier work of Kaufman's, The Forest Ranger (Resources for the Future 1960) and in J. Mashaw, Bureaucratic Justice (Yale 1983), a study of the Social Security Administration.

most prominent contemporary example of this arrangement is the Environmental Protection Agency (EPA), established in 1970, whose annual plan for fiscal year 2000 envisioned 18,400 employees, and a budget in excess of $7 billion.[215] These resources are devoted to generating and enforcing standards for pollution control and supporting facilities for the alleviation of pollution that may already be occurring. The EPA has been a focal point for arguments about political controls over administration, because it is in some sense (despite its several programs) a single-purpose agency, because its functions seem susceptible to technocratic rather than political management, because its independent status gives efforts to control its decisions fairly high visibility, and because those decisions often have a major impact on American industry and the quality of American life.[216] Indeed, the regime of economic impact statements discussed above[217] came about substantially in reaction to the EPA's work, and perceptions of its impact on the economy.

Internally, the EPA is shaped along lines similar to a department. Some offices, such as that of the General Counsel, are responsible for providing services to the agency as a whole; others have operating responsibilities for particular programs: the Clean Air Act, water pollution, noise pollution, etc. The highest level officials are political appointees who serve at the President's pleasure, but virtually all agency staff, including many with important responsibilities for decisionmaking, are permanent government employees. What distinguishes it from a department in the traditional sense is, perhaps, as simple as size; but there is also a sense in which its work is more uniformly regulatory in character. One can believe that Congress, by avoiding the more traditional departmental structure, has encouraged a level of visibility for the agency's work that will reduce to some degree political influence over it.[218] At

---

215. http://www.epa.gov. A variety of budget documents, including the annual plan from which the figures in the text were taken, is at http://www.epa.gov/ocfopage/budget/budget.htm.

216. See, for example, Sierra Club v. Costle, discussed in Chapter V(C)(2)(e), p. 238 below. A useful short book giving an account of the EPA's curious position, and clearly favoring technocratic rather than political controls, is B. Ackerman and W. Hassler, Clean Coal/Dirty Air (Yale 1981).

217. See p. 103 above.

218. For an account of the EPA's struggles with the White House in its earliest years, see J. Quarles, Cleaning Up America: An Insider's View of the Environment Protection Agency (Houghton Mifflin 1976). Later, a bitter dispute between Congress and the White House over EPA administration during the Reagan administration led to the resignation of its then administrator, Anne Gorsuch, and the appointment of a replacement, William Ruckleshaus, in circumstances that made plain that direct White House control over EPA

the same time, as an agency in the executive branch, the EPA is unequivocally subject to the various presidential controls of budget formation, required analyses, and legislative discipline discussed above. And cabinet status—giving political stature to environmental controls—is being discussed.

3. Independent regulatory commissions

The independent regulatory commission is the form Congress employs in creating offices of law-administration at the greatest distance from presidential control. The responsibilities of such agencies (often called simply "independent agencies") invariably have a high component of regulation, although regulating is not all they do[219] and it must already be apparent that they are far from being the only governmental bodies that regulate. The first such commission, the Interstate Commerce Commission, was created in 1887 to regulate railroad rates. The half-century following saw the creation of only a few others, notably the Federal Reserve Board (banking and monetary supply) and the Federal Trade Commission (trade practices and advertising). Beginning with the New Deal of President Roosevelt in 1932, however, the device was much more frequently employed. Prominent independent commissions today, whose areas of activity are generally apparent from their names, include the Securities and Exchange Commission, the National Labor Relations Board, the Federal Communications Commission, the Consumer Product Safety Commission, the Commodity Futures Trading Commission, the Federal Energy Regulatory Commission (in the Department of Energy), the Occupational Safety and Health Review Commission (associated with the Department

---

decisionmaking was unlikely. Subsequent appointments, Republican and Democrat, had well-established links to the environmental community. With the appointment of a state governor, Christine Whitman of New Jersey, in 2001, President George W. Bush perhaps signaled a return of the agency to more political control.

A 1994 statute taking the Social Security Administration out of the Department of Health and Human Services and giving it independent status, seems clearly to have been motivated by a wish to depoliticize its leadership to some degree. The Commissioner, who administers a budget of several hundred billion dollars and staff scattered through 1300 field offices, was given a six-year term—longer than any President's—from which she can be removed "only pursuant to a finding by the President of neglect of duty or malfeasance in office." 42 U.S.C. §902. See p. 98 above. In signing the act, President Clinton remarked that the Department of Justice thought this restriction "raises a significant constitutional question."

219. The Nuclear Regulatory Commission, for example, awards and oversees the performance of contracts for research into issues of safety in the operation of nuclear power plants.

of Labor), the Federal Elections Commission, the Equal Employment Opportunity Commission, and the Nuclear Regulatory Commission.

The commission form employs a collegial body at its head. Members are appointed by the President with senatorial consent to fixed terms, generally of five or seven years, with one term expiring each year; usually, the President must observe limited constraints of bipartisanship in making appointments, and can discharge a member before the end of her term of office only for "cause." The chairman, who often enjoys special executive authority within the commission, is presidentially designated, usually to serve in that capacity only at the President's pleasure. Thus the chief officer of the agency is, to a degree, responsible to the President in the ordinary mode. Other agency officials are appointed by the commission, or by the chairman; while there may be informal consultation with the White House, it does not control the subordinate political positions as it would in a department or at an independent executive agency like the EPA. An independent regulatory commission is essentially indistinguishable from any other form of governmental agency in its hierarchical structure, or in its internal allocation of responsibilities, as in the procedures it follows in carrying out its work.

The decision to use the independent regulatory commission form is often said to reflect a faith in the possibility of expert, as distinct from political, judgment on matters of public importance. No clear pattern is observable, however, in the assignments of responsibility Congress has made: both the independent Federal Trade Commission and the Department of Justice are responsible for aspects of anti-trust policy; both the independent Federal Reserve Board and the Treasury Department's Controller of the Currency have important responsibilities for banking regulation (along with a number of other agencies); the Department of Health and Human Welfare's Food and Drug Administration, the executive Environmental Protection Agency and the independent Nuclear Regulatory Commission all have responsibilities for assessing and controlling the possibly harmful activities of high-technology industries. This description should suggest that elements of independence are present in the operative bureaus even of cabinet departments. Similarly, the leadership of the independent regulatory commissions, although protected from the possibility of presidential removal without formal cause, has significant exposure to the realities of presidential guidance on important policy issues. Indeed, it would be surprising if conscientious governmental officials did not desire such guidance, at least where it could be given in a manner consistent with their own ultimate responsibility for decision. Thus, the undoubted differences in political leadership ought not to overwhelm a larger sense of similarity; in particular, such differences as exist reach few of the concerns of administrative law.

C. *The civil service and senior executive service*

Discussion, so far as it has concerned the individuals responsible for government actions, has thus far centered on the few hundred persons, from a civilian work force of 2.9 million, whom the President appoints with the advice and consent of the Senate, and a somewhat larger number he or his department heads are able to appoint personally. The very small relative size of this group makes plain that the expert staff of all federal agencies, to a level that may reach as high as bureau head, is professional rather than political in character. Its tenure and conditions of employment are governed by the civil service laws, which in turn are administered by a somewhat complex arrangement of bureaucratic agencies. The Office of Personnel Management,[220] an independent agency within the executive branch like the EPA, is responsible for policy and enforcement aspects of personnel policy: it establishes compensation levels, authorizes agencies to use the high-grade positions often necessary to attract and hold strong talent, and it administers the competitive examinations for entry into the civil service and other government-wide controls such as conflict of interest regulation. The Merit Systems Protection Board,[221] an independent regulatory commission of three members, sits in judgment on proceedings brought to discipline individual members of the civil service and other adjudicatory matters under the civil service laws.

The bulk of government employees are subject to the civil service laws. They obtain their jobs through a competitive process. Once they have successfully completed a probationary period, they become permanent employees removable only for cause or because of general reductions in force; even reassignment to another position can be a matter which the employee (if dissatisfied with the reassignment) can require to be made the subject of formal proceedings. The interest the employee holds in her job is regarded as an "entitlement" for purposes of the due process analysis discussed above,[222] so that—in formal terms at least—the procedures the government must supply for these purposes are subject to constitutional constraints, not merely a mat-

---

220. http://www.opm.gov/.
221. http://www.mspb.gov/.
222. See p. 48 above.

ter of statutory provenance.[223] (Indeed, the courts have found that the First Amendment's protections of free speech prevent political removals of some government workers not within civil service laws, if party affiliation or political confidence is not an appropriate requirement for the effective performance of the office in question.[224]) While some positions even of an ordinary character may be omitted from these tenure protections, notably those of some lawyers, all positions are subject to elaborate regulations of "grade," appointment and promotion practice, and other matters intended to prevent political manipulation of the bureaucracy's work.[225] The genesis of these measures lay, first, in perceptions that such manipulation often served corrupt, or at least highly personal, ends; and, second, in political struggles between a party system dominated by Congress and local political machines, and reformers seeking more stable, central direction in the interests of a complex and integrated national economy.[226]

To the extent such measures succeed, of course, they diminish the capacity of new political leadership to reshape the work of the bureaucracy, in what most would regard as entirely appropriate ways. An entrenched civil service, serving far longer than any particular administration, may easily be able to find ways to serve its own agenda rather than that of its political leadership.[227] In 1978, responding to this problem, Congress subdivided the civil service, redefining its highest levels as a "Senior Executive Service." The political leadership of executive government now enjoys more (but not complete) authority

---

223. Arnett v. Kennedy, 416 U.S. 134 (1974); Cleveland Board of Education v. Loudermill, 470 U.S. 532 (1985).

224. See Elrod v. Burns, 427 U.S. 347 (1976); Branti v. Finkel, 445 U.S. 507 (1980); Jimenez Fuentes v. Gaztambide, 803 F.2d 1 (1st Cir. 1986).

225. An interesting discussion in the context of the lawyers of the Department of Justice's Office of the Solicitor General, see n. 247 below, can be found in T. Merrill, High Level, "Tenured" Lawyers, 61 Law & Contemp. Prob. 83 (1998).

226. The story of the emergence of the civil service system, alongside the regulatory state, is well told in S. Skowronek, Building a New American State: The Expansion of National Administrative Capacities, 1877–1920 (Cambridge University Press 1982).

227. Political scientists are fond of describing the "iron triangle" that faces a new President and his political appointees in attempting to put programs in place: permanent agency staff, permanent congressional committee staff (with whom the agency staff has every incentive to develop and nurture a long-term relationship), and the functionaries of private industries or groups most interested, over the long term, in the matters subject to the agency's jurisdiction. H. Merry, Five Branch Government: The Full Measure of Constitutional Checks and Balances (University of Illinois Press 1980). See also H. Heclo, A Government of Strangers, Executive Politics in Washington (Brookings Institute 1977), a work whose analysis was influential in promoting the changes next described in the text.

over the service of these roughly 6,000 officials, who exercise important policy-making or implementing functions, than it has over the ordinary civil service.[228] They can be rewarded with bonuses, reassigned, and in other ways given incentives relating directly to their programmatic responsibilities. Whether these changes have succeeded in reintroducing a measure of political control over agenda, without reintroducing the abuses that generated the civil service laws, is not yet clear. In any event, it should be clear that the ends of political control and of a protected civil service are in unavoidable tension.

1. Administrative adjudicators and the corps controversy

Respecting one group of civil servants, those who serve as "judges" in hearing administrative adjudications, maximum protection from political pressures is desirable. American courts have generally tolerated the assignment of adjudications in agency matters, in the first instance, to the agencies themselves. The arguments, however, for an independent judiciary (that in this respect underlie separation of powers concerns) have led to creation of "administrative law judges" as an unusually well-insulated cadre of civil servants responsible for much formal adjudication within executive government.[229] Administrative law judges are paid at the level of the senior executive service, but—although formally located within the particular agencies they serve— are virtually beyond agency control. Appointments must be made on a competitive basis, from the top few names on a list supplied by civil service authorities. Once made, appointments are permanent (without probationary

---

228. See http://www.opm.gov/ses.

229. The pattern next described in the text is not invariable. Immigration matters, for example, are heard by Immigration Law Judges in the Department of Justice who enjoy some, but not all, of the protections of administrative law judges; the members of a Department of Labor review board hearing appeals from the decisions of departmental administrative law judges in benefits matters serve in unprotected tenure. Neither arrangement was found to violate principles of due process. Marcello v. Bonds, 349 U.S. 302 (1955); Kalaris v. Donovan, 697 F.2d 376 (D.C. Cir. 1983), cert. denied 462 U.S. 1119 (1983). A 1994 study found substantial numbers of these "administrative judges." C. Koch, Administrative Presiding Officials Today, 46 Admin. L. Rev. 271 (1994). For these officials, too, the influence of the values reflected in the text would presumably work to prevent direct efforts at political control of outcomes. Any such efforts would be regarded as offending the procedural rights of the particular persons involved in the proceedings in which they occurred.

period). Within the agency structure, administrative law judges must be free of supervision or direction from agency employees responsible for the cases that may come before them; neither salary nor assignments nor any disciplinary measure can be controlled from within the agency, but (if adverse) must be the subject of formal proceedings before the Merit Systems Protection Board.[230] Any conversations administrative law judges have with agency employees concerning the outcomes of formal proceedings they are hearing must be on the record—that is, there may be no private consultations.

Agency structures for adjudication are generally the same, whether they arise in a cabinet department, an independent executive agency like the EPA, or an independent regulatory commission. The administrative law judges all serve in a separate office, which may be located for bureaucratic purposes within the agency secretariat but which is independent of policy guidance from any other part of the agency. There will usually be a chief administrative law judge responsible for administrative matters in each agency. Proceedings are assigned at random, as they arise, and remain with the administrative law judge to whom they are assigned until the proceeding is completed, unless she is disqualified or leaves office, or (in rare cases) the agency directs that it be sent up without decision. In smaller agencies, her opinion may be reviewed directly by the agency head or commission itself. Frequently, however, provision is made for a judicial officer or review board to serve that function, and direct involvement of the agency head itself occurs only on a discretionary basis, analogous to the Supreme Court's certiorari practice. Whichever path is followed, conversations about the matters pending before the administrative law judges follow the common judicial protocols: they occur only in public, before all parties. If the head of an agency, reviewing an administrative law judge's decision, wishes help in understanding some aspect of the decision or of a complex record on which it is based, he must seek that assistance formally.[231]

---

230. This restriction has engendered bitter feuds and even litigation within the Department of Health and Human Welfare, over measures which departmental officials defend as seeking to impose only standards of productivity and competence and the Department's more than 800 administrative law judges perceive as a direct threat to their independence of decision. See Nash v. Bowen, 869 F.2d 675 (2d Cir. 1989); Association of Administrative Law Judges v. Heckler, 594 F. Supp. 1132 (D. D.C. 1984); P. Strauss, T. Rakoff, R. Schotland and C. Farina, Gellhorn & Byse's Administrative Law, Cases and Comments 958–72 (9th ed.1995).

231. An important reason for this restriction is suggested by the unique role of the administrative law judges' report on judicial review. See p. 345 below.

It might not seem a long step to creation of a system of administrative law courts located outside the agencies whose disputes they would consider, and such proposals have often been voiced. A number of states use a central board of hearing examiners for all their administrative disputes. At the federal level, resistance to this measure has been based on the varying tasks administrative law judges face in differing agencies, and the belief that the current legal regime protects their independence to a degree that would not be much improved by such a change. Those administrative law judges the readers of this essay are most likely to encounter are highly specialized and relatively few in number, serving in the major federal regulatory agencies; yet the great bulk of American administrative law judges serve in the Social Security Administration, the Department of Health and Human Services, or the Department of Labor, resolving high-volume, small-scale questions such as eligibility for welfare or disability benefits.[232] A central agency might not be able to maintain the expertise in regulatory issues individual agencies can now encourage; in practice, its work would tend to be swamped by the demands of its mass-justice clientele. Locating hearing outside the agency, it is also feared, might tend to defuse agency responsibility for and control of policy even if (as is usually conceded) review of any decision by an administrative law judge serving on a central panel could be had within the agency itself.

D. *State and local government*

This essay is principally concerned with national administrative law. An effort to describe the machinery of state and local government is beyond both the reasonable dimensions of a work like this, and the author's competence. Nonetheless, the reader may find the following very summary comments helpful.

---

232. In 1947, 125 (64%) of the federal government's 196 hearing officers worked in independent regulatory commissions deciding regulatory matters. In 1991, following both extensive deregulation and an explosion in hearings in personal benefits programs, only 55 (5%) of roughly 1200 federal administrative law judges worked in economic regulation, and the remainder decided personal benefits cases. Most of these, 866, were employed in the Social Security Administration, whose annual caseload, in excess of 500,000, was about twice that of the federal district courts. For most ALJs today, then, daily work consists not of complex regulatory cases, but of reconciling the need for efficiency and dispatch in dealing with a sizable caseload, with the wish for humanity in dealing with the most unfortunate.

State governments are generally organized under a written constitution along lines similar to the federal: a chief executive (governor) is generally responsible for overseeing the work of departments or agencies, which are principally staffed by a professional civil service; a legislative body, bicameral in all cases but one (Nebraska), enacts laws; and an independent judiciary of trial and appellate courts, often organized into three tiers like the federal judiciary, handles ordinary litigation including the review of agency action. In the regulatory context, litigation may begin within an agency before a figure like an administrative law judge, possibly assigned from a central panel, and continue through agency review before it reaches the courts.

Important differences between state and federal governments exist. For example, a larger range of officials are elected at the state level. State and local judges are generally elected, usually to lengthy terms. A state's chief financial officer may be elected. In many states, the members of its public utility commission, responsible for setting rates for energy and communications services, are elected. States elect their attorneys general, who as chief enforcer of state law are powerful figures both politically and from an administrative law perspective.[233] Another important difference is that state constitutions tend to be both more detailed than the federal, more readily amended, and less important an element of public life.

Much of American economic regulation is accomplished at the state level. Entry into and conduct of many professions, including the legal profession, are controlled by state agencies, as are many businesses (hospitals, insurance, much banking, retail delivery of utility services, etc.). The states commonly have local laws respecting labor practices, health, safety and environmental protection—close counterparts of the national schemes administered by the federal government. They administer as well, many public services, notably welfare and education. And the general law applicable to citizens, both civil and criminal, is administered in their courts.

The subdivisions of state government—counties, cities, towns, villages— each tend to reflect the familiar tripartite pattern of organization, operating under written charters, although the powers of these authorities all are subordinate to state law. They do not have an independent political existence, as the states do in the federal scheme.[234] One might expect to find a mayor or city manager or county executive at the head of executive government; a council or board

---

233. This fracturing of political responsibility for the work of government has been criticized as substituting "policy balkanization...for policy coordination." Pierce, Shapiro & Verkuil, p. 6, n. 5 above, at 116.

234. Some state constitutions provide "home rule" or "charters" for larger population centers, creating to that extent a federal model; neither the sharing of authority nor the

of aldermen or county legislature; even town or city courts, generally for initial decision of minor matters that can be appealed into the state judicial system. Local agencies administer welfare in the first instance, are responsible for public protection (police, fire, sanitation, health and safety inspections), administer land use and building controls, and license some types of small business.

While federal and state authorities have historically been distinct, major welfare and regulatory initiatives of the New Deal and later have tended somewhat to blur the lines. When national welfare laws were first enacted during the New Deal, they were enacted in a form encouraging state participation: if the states would meet legislative conditions, they would receive substantial federal subsidies; under the unemployment laws, for example, an otherwise payable federal tax would be greatly reduced. Thus encouraged, the states adopted these laws—producing a need for supervision to assure that the conditions of the federal statute continued to be met. Developing public awareness and opportunities for public participation have sometimes contributed to greater rigor in this supervision.[235] If the sanction, however, is federal suspension of all payments to a state found in systemic violation of the federal scheme, one can understand that its political and human consequences would result in its being rarely invoked. While informal supervision occurs, one finds little evidence of direct enforcement of these spending clause conditions on state receipt of federal funds; when Congress delivers "block grants" to state and local authorities for stated purposes, for example welfare payments, the purpose and effect is to forego any close control.

More likely are public processes for federal review of particular state spending or regulatory decisions connected with federal programs. One of the foundational cases of American administrative law arose out of a decision on a state's request for federal funds for a road project; such requests must meet federal standards and obtain the Secretary of Transportation's approval.[236] Similarly conditioned subsidies may be had for education, housing, and other worthy purposes, under the approval of other departments. States may regulate the transportation of hazardous waste through their territory more stringently than the Department of Transportation's national standards would require, *if* they secure its approval; they may regulate medical uses of radioactive materials under the supervision of the federal Nuclear Regulatory Commis-

---

safeguards for continued existence of these arrangements match the arrangements at the federal-state level.

235. See National Welfare Rights Organization v. Finch, 429 F.2d 725 (D.C. Cir.1970).

236. Citizens to Preserve Overton Park v. Volpe, 401 U.S. 402 (1971). The case is extensively discussed below at pp. 235, 341 and 376.

sion. The federal agency responsible for assuring workplace safety, the Occupational Safety and Health Administration of the Department of Labor (OSHA), can certify state occupational safety and health programs, which then operate under OSHA's continuing evaluation and with federal grant support. Twenty-six states have such approved state plans to one or another degree;[237] the effectiveness of OSHA's monitoring, however, has been questioned.[238] Probably the most striking of these arrangements from the perspective of administrative law is to be found in the field of environmental regulation. The enforcement of federal standards to protect common resources, such as air and water, is placed in a federal agency—the Environmental Protection Agency. States are commanded to develop state implementation plans that will meet the federal agency's approval. Any state that fails to do so suffers federal implementation, which commonly will mean defeating important state regulatory bodies.[239]

It will be apparent that the political independence of the states is at some risk in these programs. As the states have come to rely on federal funding for their programs, the reach and firmness of the conditions on the basis of which they can obtain it has increased.[240] When state and federal officials share responsibility for implementation of a given regulatory program, power and responsibility may be hidden and diffused. Recent years have seen a surge in constitutional litigation over the limits of federal control of state activities,[241] as well as statutes and executive orders seeking to highlight and control the impact of federal requirements on state resources.[242] While these are not central subjects for this essay, the interested reader should see this problem of administrative federalism as one that will mark the American scene for years to come.

---

237. http://www.osha-slc.gov/fso/osp/.

238. P. Strauss, T. Rakoff, R. Schotland, and C. Farina, Gellhorn & Byse's Administrative Law, Cases and Comments 840 (9th ed. 1995). See GAO, Status of Open Recommendations 72 (1999) and GAO, Occupational Safety and Health: Changes Needed in the Combined Federal-State Approach (Chapter Report, 02/28/94, GAO/HEHS-94-10).

239. See http://www.epa.gov/ocirpage/nepps/index.htm; GAO, Environmental Protection: Collaborative EPA-State Effort Needed to Improve New Performance Partnership System (GAO/RCED 99-171).

240. See A. Rosenthal, Conditional Federal Spending and the Constitution, 39 Stan. L. Rev. 1103 (1987).

241. See the text at p. 11, n. 6 above.

242. See p. 224 below.

E. *Enforcement officials*

Law enforcement activities in the United States, at all levels, are commonly divided between the functions of investigation and apprehension, on the one hand, and prosecution or presentation on the other—one might say, between the world of the inspector or police officer, and the world of the lawyer-prosecutor. In the realm of criminal law, which includes certain (generally aggravated) administrative violations, investigation and apprehension is the responsibility of the police force. Such forces can be found at every level of government. Numerically the overwhelming number are local, but at the federal level the Border Patrol, Alcohol and Tobacco Bureau, and Federal Bureau of Investigation are among those readily identified as serving this function. The bringing of criminal actions (or other litigation) to court is the function of a public attorney—often called a district attorney at the local level, a state Attorney General, or, at the federal level, a United States Attorney attached to a particular United States District Court and functioning under the general supervision of the Attorney General of the United States.[243]

Administrative enforcement, in the first instance, is commonly in the hands of agency officials rather than a separate agency dedicated solely to investigation and apprehension. In 1992, these included more than 220,000 persons working as inspectors for one or another local, state, or federal agency; local inspectors might visit restaurants or construction sites, federal inspectors slaughterhouses or nuclear power plants. In each instance these inspectors seek to promote compliance with the regulations of their particular agency, but how they do this is a matter of policy on which American styles have vacillated somewhat. The alternatives are: in the manner of police, that is, exploring for violations of applicable regulations, which are then made the subject of enforcement proceedings to collect fines, enter mandatory orders, etc.; or more cooperatively.[244] Other means of investigation are of course employed,

---

243. One might consider the United States Attorney's offices to be the field offices of the United States Department of Justice, although historically they came into existence a century before it did and they often act with considerable independence of the Department; U.S. Attorneys are themselves appointed by the President with senatorial consent, and frequently are important figures in their home communities. The Department of Justice itself (that is, the Washington office) provides coordinating guidance but most often does not become directly involved in litigation until an appeal is sought or made.

244. The differences are explored in the occupational safety and health context in two useful books, S. Kelman, Regulating America, Regulating Sweden: A Comparative Study

notably office review of reports filed by companies subject to regulation, and of other information. All these matters are further taken up in Chapter V's discussion of investigation. Determining to open a proceeding and presenting the agency's position in that proceeding will usually be the responsibility of an agency official other than the investigator, in this case an attorney functioning under the supervision of an agency principal attorney, whose title may be general counsel, solicitor, executive legal director, or the like.[245]

At the federal level, the role of the Attorney General as the chief legal officer of the national government becomes important for agencies when disputes about their work pass beyond the agencies' own jurisdiction. A dispute between two agencies respecting the meaning of a legal provision that affects the work of both may be settled—at least so far as they are concerned[246]—by a formal Opinion of the Attorney General, drafted in his Office of Legal Counsel.[247] Where the dispute is between the agencies and a citizen, agencies are required in varying degrees to rely on the legal resources of the Department of Justice (and its willingness to employ them) for representation in court. Unless explicitly authorized by statute, as the independent regulatory commissions generally are, no agency can initiate litigation in a United States District Court. Even so simple a matter as seeking enforcement of an agency subpoena must be done through the Department or the relevant United States Attorney. This confronts an agency with views about relative priority in the use of government litigating resources that may be very different from its own. If a case

---

of Occupational Safety and Health Policy (MIT Press 1981) and E. Bardach and R. Kagan, Going by the Book: The Problem of Regulatory Unreasonableness (Temple University Press 1982). In recent years, OSHA has been seeking to move from police enforcement to an incentive-based mode promising relief from a system of fines based on inspection-enforcement in return for cooperation, see e.g. http://www.osha.gov/oshinfo/reinvent/prog1.html and p. 164 below.

245. See Symposium, Government Lawyering, 61 Law & Contemp. Prob. Nos. 1 and 2 (1998), viewable among the back issues at http://www.law.duke.edu/journals/lcp/. Essays of possible particular interest include P. Strauss, The Internal Relations of Government: Cautionary Tales from Inside the Black Box, #2 at 155; D. Strauss, The Solicitor General and the Interests of the United States, #1 at 165; and P. Schuck, Lawyers and Policymakers in Government, #1 at 7.

246. Once the agencies have received advice from the Attorney General, they may not be able to generate valid litigation that would test its correctness; but if the issue later arises in a proper dispute, say between a citizen and an agency, the Attorney General's prior expression of view would have only persuasive authority for a court.

247. For a description of the work of this important office see R. Moss, Executive Branch Legal Interpretation: A Perspective from the Office of Legal Counsel 52 Admin. L. Rev. 303 (2000).

is lost, it may be appealed only with the Department's permission, in this case centrally granted through its Office of the Solicitor General.

Even when an agency is brought to court by a citizen rather than vice versa, as in petitions for judicial review, the agency may not be fully in command of its own defense. Unless statutes explicitly provide otherwise, the final form of the government's argument will be determined in the Department. On the whole this occurs professionally rather than politically (in the Civil Division of the Department of Justice, for example, rather than the Attorney General's personal office). It does nonetheless mark a loss of control, a need for the agency to satisfy other officials of the tenability its position before reaching court.

The Department's control is near complete, even over the independent commissions, when the Supreme Court is reached. A petition for certiorari may not be filed without the permission of the Solicitor General. With rare exceptions, she determines the final form of any papers to be presented to the Court; she controls the assignment of (and often makes) any oral argument. Although the Solicitor General is a political appointee, most Presidents have realized that the government's continuous dealings with the Supreme Court make it advisable to select this official for professional attainment, and her office works at high levels of professionalism. If the Solicitor General and the agency cannot reach agreement on an appropriate position, her brief will often inform the Court of that fact and the agency's position. Even so, the loss of initiative and control can appear substantial; perhaps more to the point for private attorneys, the independence of the Solicitor General in determining the government's position in litigation suggests that a conference with her about pending litigation may often prove fruitful.[248]

---

248. See Symposium, n. 245 above.

IV

THE SCOPE OF
ADMINISTRATIVE LAW

A. *Governmental powers generally*

General statutory measures that purport to deal with "administrative law" define the scope of their application in terms of three concerns: the institutional procedures "agencies" are to follow in dealing with the public to effect "agency action"; judicial (and, to a lesser extent, political) review of those actions; and special procedures relating to the handling and release of information in the government's possession.[1] Neither a court nor a legislature nor an elected chief executive can be an "agency" under these statutes, although the relationship of courts, legislatures and chief executives with agencies is very much a matter of administrative law concern. Otherwise the concept includes virtually every administrative unit[2] exercising public authority. "Agency action" is also embracively defined. While the provisions of administrative procedure legislation generally deal with the relatively formal procedures of adjudication and rulemaking, as discussed below, federal "agency action" includes any grant, denial, or failure to act upon "the application or petition of, and beneficial to, a person."[3] Under the latest draft of model state administrative procedure legislation,[4] "agency action" includes "an agency's performance of, or failure to perform, any...duty, function, or activity, discre-

---

1. Federal Administrative Procedure Act, 5 U.S.C. §551(1), (13); Revised Model State Administrative Procedure Act §1-102(1), (2).

2. The unit may be a subdivision of some other body that might also be regarded, for some purposes, as an administrative agency: for example, the Forest Service (which manages national forests) is an "agency" under the federal Administrative Procedure Act, as also is the Department of Agriculture of which it is a part. Whatever the internal political relationship between the Chief Forester of the Forest Service and the Secretary of Agriculture, the Forest Service has legal responsibility for administration of the national forests.

3. 5 U.S.C. §551(11)(C), (13).

4. See p. 268 below.

tionary or otherwise."[5] Again, the category is virtually as broad as the field of public administration; only traditional criminal law proceedings, traditional civil litigation, and political acts in the strict sense, those indisputably beyond the control of law, are excluded.

It should not be surprising to find the domain of "administrative law" in the American system so broadly defined. Scholars developed the concept toward the beginning of this century, as public administration grew. As unruly as the developments it sought to capture, it was a grab-bag for all government actions affecting private persons that did not fit comfortably within any of the existing structures of legal analysis—either those of the criminal law or of the ordinary civil law as administered by courts. The scholarly view of administrative law has grown, with government, to embrace almost all adjectival subjects that can be connected with public administration. Although criminal trials are excluded, many assert that it embraces the exercise of discretion by police officers and prosecutors. Although it excludes an action initiated by the government in federal court to collect a simple debt, it would include that action if begun within an executive body and later brought before courts for enforcement or review. The subject-matter of government contracts is not within its concerns, and that area is often sidestepped by administrative lawyers, but one could not describe the contract enforcement and dispute resolution procedures within, say, the Department of Defense as other than administrative in character. One might have said at the outset that it was sub-constitutional in character, concerned with statutory and customary arrangements of government; yet as the preceding pages make plain, constitutional issues respecting governmental structure and conduct are now important concerns.

In the American framework, a focus on procedural issues provides an analytic structure for generalizing about the central tasks of administrative law: assuring the control as well as the effectiveness of government. Such a focus is needed despite the recognition that generalizations are made problematic by the diversity of agencies and agency actions, and the close relationship between the substance of any particular agency's responsibility and the procedures it will employ. Talking from the perspective of "administrative law" about the work of the federal Securities and Exchange Commission (or of the Forest Service, or of a state public utilities commission, or a local building inspector) focuses on its procedures, rather than its particular substantive responsibility for implementing a certain part of federal, state, or local policy—in the case of the SEC, regulation of markets in securities and business conduct in connection with them.

---

5. Revised Model State Administrative Procedure Act §1-102(2)(iii) (1981).

One assumes, initially, that all agencies employ certain paradigmatic procedures to accomplish their ends and that these agencies have paradigmatic relationships with overseers such as courts who review the end product of these procedures. These paradigmatic procedures and relationships can and do vary to meet the needs of particular situations. Consequently, in dealing with a concrete situation, one must always seek to understand the responsibilities and procedures of the particular agency whose work is at issue; the lawyers who work at that agency may have remarkably low awareness of how other agencies are pursuing similar ends, or even of procedural litigation in which those other agencies have been involved. Nonetheless, analysis usefully begins with these paradigms expressed in general procedural forms that are not directly a function of the particular agency whose work is under examination. The paradigms are required, in effect, to avoid unsustainable specialization in matters of great importance to the public, with its accompanying threats of loss of political control and access by ordinary citizens and their lawyers. If anything, the relative lack of knowledge and coordination among federal agencies on matters of administrative law underscores the importance of developing and enforcing these paradigms, from the perspective of maintaining effective general control over agency behaviors. These paradigms of procedures and relationships are the focus of the following chapters. It would be wrong to anticipate them here in any detail.

The next section of this chapter sketches the variety of substantive responsibilities commonly given to American administrative agencies. For purposes of initial comprehension it may be useful to have the following rough models in mind:

Formal adjudication is a proceeding strongly resembling a civil trial, conducted "on the record" before an administrative law judge or agency to determine a particular dispute. Formal adjudications are generally characterized by a strict separation of functions within an agency, so that staff responsible for investigation and presentation of the agency's position do not participate in the decision process. The results of formal adjudication are generally reviewed by courts with relatively close attention to the existence of factual and legal support for the outcome.

Informal adjudication describes procedures for resolution of a particular dispute that do not require "on the record" hearing. If a hearing format is used, it may be quite informal. But "informal adjudication" is also used to describe the taking of decisions by bureaucratic routine—for example, a decision to authorize the use of federal money for the construction of a particular road project. Judicial review is relatively permissive, recognizing considerable discretion in the person acting.

Formal rulemaking is a proceeding conducted "on the record" to determine a statute-like norm for future application, for example what proportion of peanuts should be required in a substance to be labeled "peanut butter," or what is a reasonable rate to be charged for utility services. Formal rulemaking differs from formal adjudication in certain structural arrangements; those responsible for developing and presenting the agency's analysis at the hearing, for example, are not strongly required to be separated from the decision process as they are in formal adjudications. The character of the hearing and of subsequent judicial review nonetheless resemble formal adjudication.

Informal rulemaking is the ordinary procedure for generating statute-like norms for future application, and is the object of executive controls previously discussed.[6] Its public stages are initiated by a notice of the proposed action; the interested public then has an opportunity to file written comments on the proposal. Oral hearings are optional, although encouraged by some statutes, for example, many connected with environmental, health, and safety rules. On adopting a rule, the agency is under some obligation to explain its basis and purpose. Decision is taken bureaucratically, and judicial review is relatively permissive, although with increasing attention to the existence or not of factual support for rules of importance. A rule once validly adopted has the full force of statutory law on those subject to it.

Publication Rulemaking describes agency interpretations of applicable norms, general policies, manuals for the guidance of staff and like measures, that if properly published, may be treated as having limited jural force. They do not formally bind persons outside the agency, in the manner of a statute or regulation, but they might be treated as precedents and are likely to be regarded as somewhat persuasive by the courts. These may be generated internally or in response to request; ordinarily no procedure beyond publication is required (although procedures like those for informal rulemaking are often followed). Decision is taken bureaucratically; judicial review may not be directly available and, when available, is generally deferential.

Inspection, direct physical view by a qualified government official, is sometimes used as a substitute for adjudication procedures (as, for example, in

---

6. See p. 103 above.

grading agricultural commodities, or examining the skill of applicants for a driver's license) but may also be employed to determine the existence or not of conditions warranting formal administrative action.

Two caveats may be useful. First, these are all procedures in the sense that lawyers use that term; they set processes for action that are susceptible of public participation and judicial supervision. A citizen concerned about agency actions (and her lawyer) will also have access to a variety of political means of influence or control, as has appeared in preceding pages. These could also be described as "procedures," although no court will enforce their regularity. Should she seek judicial review of an agency's action, it is not at all necessary, perhaps even unlikely, that these efforts will come into view. What appears in the judicial opinions is that she has, for example, sought review of the Secretary of Transportation's decision to permit federal funds to be spent in support of a highway whose building would bisect an important urban park.[7] Behind that decision may lie ten years of efforts to enlist other citizens and local, state and federal politicians in support of the citizen's concerns—with other community forces working to opposite effect, with mediating changes occurring in the planning she opposes, even with fairly clear political decisions, both responsive and responsible, by the communities concerned. Neither these interventions nor resulting and extended bureaucratic processes leading up to the Secretary's decision need come to light in the litigation. They are nonetheless important elements in the administrative lawyer's armament.

Second, and relatedly, even for the procedures briefly described above, citizens and their lawyers generally expect to see only those stages in which they may participate, and not the ensuing process of decision. The concerns of administrative law do not speak to the internal bureaucratic process that occurs once those interactions have concluded and the agency has begun to move towards resolution. How many desks the matter will cross, what kinds of conversations will occur, what memoranda will be generated en route to the agency's final explanation, and so forth, are elements of bureaucratic structure which may be internally important, but into which, in general, the courts will not support inquiry.[8] There is one important exception: an "on the record" process (formal

---

7. Citizens to Preserve Overton Park v. Volpe, 401 U.S. 402 (1971): The case is extensively discussed below at pp. 235, 341 and 376; the preceding political efforts are discussed in P. Strauss, Revisiting Overton Park: Political and Judicial Controls Over Administrative Actions Affecting the Community, 39 U.C.L.A. L. Rev. 1251 (1992).

8. See the discussion of the Freedom of Information Act's privilege for pre-decisional documents, p. 279 below. Thus, in one important rulemaking an agency had hired some scientists who had appeared as witnesses in the proceedings to serve as consultants in an-

adjudication most notably) has some implications for the nature of permitted decisionmakers, permitted conversations and permitted references.

B. *Contexts for regulation*

1. Economic regulation

Much of the work assigned to administrative agencies has its source in judgments that the public needs protection from economic injury; or that public ordering of certain economic activities could otherwise contribute to the public good. The common law (conformably to classic economics) assumed that in a properly functioning market, participants would be able to protect themselves by desirable vigilance and that the "invisible hand" of competition would serve better to bring about efficient distribution of goods and services than efforts at state control. Yet in some situations, consumers evidently were not well placed to protect themselves by personal vigilance, and in others as well markets might for one or another reason fail. "Economic regulation" is a characterization given to state efforts to control or regulate markets to protect or improve their economic efficiency, or to compensate for the effects of perceived imbalances of economic power.

From early times, states regulated the rates that could be charged by the owners of private bridges and ferries across important waterways, effective (and sometimes chartered) monopolies; the common law set special rules for the liability of innkeepers and common carriers to guests or passengers, who were thought not well-placed to evaluate or protect themselves from certain hazards. Towards the end of the nineteenth century, changing technologies and markets, and the perceived rapacious behavior of powerful uncontrolled private actors in those markets, brought increasing state efforts to control how competitors could behave in some markets, who could enter them, what prices they could charge, and so forth. Subsequent changes in technology and the economy have been understood to have revived the possibilities of competition, and economic analyses suggested that, unless carefully matched to pres-

---

alyzing the materials submitted; the agency refused to make their analytic report available. Once assured that they had added no new factual information, the courts upheld this refusal, and found no objection to their participation in the agency's decision process. United States Steelworkers of America v. Marshall, 647 F.2d 1189, cert. den. 453 U.S. 913 (1981). See generally p. 380 below.

ent day realities, economic regulation could be markedly inefficient;[9] a result was a significant withdrawal from some types of regulation, returning those matters wholly or partially to the market. Now, increasing concentration in the airline industry seems to be contributing to pricing differences between users in competitive and uncompetitive markets, and even apparently predatory practices, like those that spurred the first appearance of railroad rate regulation in the nineteenth century. Another example, California's effort to return rates for electricity to a newly "competitive" market, appears to be producing major discontinuities (as well as arguable abuses of corporate structure) that, again, are reminiscent of earlier excesses of uncontrolled private action.

Following are some of the more important types of economic regulation in the United States today:

a. *Economic concentration*

Ever since the enactment of the federal Sherman Antitrust Act in 1890—even earlier in individual states—American government has sought to prevent excessive concentration of economic power in private hands. Enforcement of the federal antitrust laws is predominantly judicial, in response either to private or government initiatives. The latter is principally in the hands of the Antitrust Division of the Department of Justice. To the extent that office articulates policy approaches to its enforcement of the antitrust law, it may be viewed as an administrative agency—indeed, in addition to responding to apparent violations of that law, it also advises proactively on the acceptability of some business conduct, so that it cannot be considered simply a prosecutorial enforcer.[10]

The Federal Trade Commission,[11] too, has long had responsibilities (among many other trade-related duties) both to investigate and report generally on issues of economic concentration, and to regulate corporate mergers in light of their impact on industrial concentration. Advice might be informally given,

---

9. S. Breyer, Regulation and its Reform (Harvard University Press 1982), a full and highly regarded analysis, set an intellectual structure for inquiry and was influential in producing changes at the federal level.

10. See, for example, http://www.usdoj.gov/atr/public/busreview/letters.htm, which collects past business review letters in a readily searched format; as for many agencies, the general site (http://www.usdoj.gov/atr) provides a concrete basis for exploring the work of this agency.

11. http://www.ftc.gov.

but orders will be entered only after formal adjudication, and their enforcement will require invoking the courts. Other agencies—the Federal Communications Commission in telecommunications,[12] the Nuclear Regulatory Commission[13] with respect to the licensing of nuclear power plants—also have occasion formally to consider issues of concentration bearing on their work when issuing licenses in the concentrated industries they regulate; an applicant cannot secure a desired license without satisfying the agency, but the availability of judicial review of agency action provides some opportunity for control.

b. Common carrier and public utility regulation

Common carriers (railroads, buses, trucks, taxis, airlines, pipe lines, barge lines, communications satellites) and public utilities (water, electricity, gas, telephone), frequently state-owned in other countries, are ordinarily private enterprises subject to close regulation in the United States. At least three grounds have been suggested for the intense level of regulation that once was characteristic of all these enterprises.

- First, for many (although not all) of these enterprises, the large investments and fixed networks required to provide service suggest that public interest will be best served by a form of monopoly; wasteful duplication of facilities would threaten the economic viability of all competitors. Yet creating such monopolies confers significant economic power over their communities, that must be controlled.
- Second, the public's dependence on the quality and safety of the services these enterprises provide suggests other needs for regulation: that service is non-discriminatory, that honest and competent service is provided, that safe practices are maintained, that economic conditions necessary to these ends are assured, and so forth.
- Finally, a redistributive element is sometimes involved. A private participant in market activity might be expected to favor customers who present efficiencies of service (because of their size and/or location) or who have economic power (because they are in a position to choose to

---

12. http://www.fcc.gov. The attention to competitiveness considerations is not evident on the surface of the website, but emerges if one searches for "antitrust" or "anti-competitive."

13. http://www.nrc.gov. The Commission's rules provide for these inquiries to be made in limited circumstances. See http://www.nrc.gov/NRC/CFR/FR/20000719/july19.html.

use a competitor). Public authorities, however, may prefer to require favoring less-well placed customers: for example, they might prefer telephone or electric rates that cause city-dwellers to bear some of the expense of supplying service to poor and sparsely settled rural areas; they might want to assure basic service to small users at low rates that, again, better reflect their need than the costs of supplying those users; or they might believe residential rates, generally, should properly produce less profit per unit for a utility, in relation to its precise costs of service to those customers, than the rates charged to large industrial customers. Accommodations like these do not reflect market failures in the usual sense; they are inefficient in strictly economic terms, and give the larger users incentives to make other arrangements for themselves if they can— generating their own electric power, for example. Whether one sees in them a legitimate or illegitimate use of state power will depend on the critic's attitudes toward redistribution as a proper state function, in the first instance, and then on an assessment of the particular redistribution being made.

This regulation may occur at all levels: national (interstate transportation or utilities); state (local trucking, retail gas, electricity, and telephone); or local (water, taxis). Overlapping responsibilities ensure that some private actors will be subject to regulation from many sources. In the course of building a power station, for example, a utility may have to secure permissions and meet regulatory requirements of federal,[14] state,[15] and local[16] authorities. To enter the industry, or to provide a desired service, an applicant may be required to show that the "public convenience and necessity" support new facilities or services; members of the affected public and those already supplying such services may be permitted to oppose the application in proceedings generally having the character of formal adjudication.[17] Those already operating in the industry also face

---

14. Location of hydro-electric or nuclear facilities; interstate sale of power; safety and environmental consequences.

15. Need for additional generating capacity; location; construction of transmission lines; in-state rates.

16. Location of transmission lines; zoning; building codes.

17. A company already in a regulated business has some incentive to oppose a competitor's proposal, just to raise its competitor's costs or protect a favored economic situation it has itself achieved under regulation. The frequency of such almost reflexive opposition to proposals is understood as a high cost of such regulation, reflecting the "rents" participants in regulated industries can sometimes use regulation to secure. It has at times produced understandable skepticism whether competitors need be permitted to oppose

a wide range of regulations, suggested by the ends sketched above: they may be required, generally in formal rulemaking proceedings, to justify any changes in the rates they charge and/or the service levels they provide; statutes or rules may impose extensive record-keeping requirements; periodic inspections may occur to ensure compliance with service regulations; and informal rulemakings create a variety of legal standards binding upon the regulated industry and open to enforcement against it.

Much of the movement for deregulation of the American economy can be ascribed to the realizations, first, that some industries subject to these entry, rate, and practice controls lack the degree of economic monopoly power over those they serve that had been imagined; and, second, that regulation itself enhances the economic power of those already in the industry by protecting them from competitive incentives and pressures. In the formative years of commercial aviation, federal regulation of air transportation services was very extensive. The Civil Aeronautics Board (CAB) controlled who could fly, what rates they could charge, what particular communities they could or must serve, and how often. It became apparent that the result was to keep ticket prices artificially high, and service provided equivalently low. Analysis suggested that the airline industry could safely be permitted to become much more competitive. The public provides most of the infrastructure required for air transportation (airports and route clearances), as is not the case for railroad tracks, utility plants or telephone cables. As a result, airlines' major capital investments (airplanes) are fully mobile. When the CAB was abolished, removing all but safety-related restraints on entry and service and most restraints on rates, ticket prices dropped, passenger levels soared, and traffic patterns changed in ways that have provided many communities with a higher frequency of service. Similar analyses later led to equivalent changes for surface transportation industries like trucking and busing, that also do not require heavy capital investment in fixed facilities. Even these changes, of course, do not mark a return to laissez faire in its pure form; for facilities on which public reliance is high, continuation of regulation to secure honest, reliable, and safe practice is only to be expected. And recent experience with the effects of concentration in the airline industry, and the hub-and-spoke routing practice that has emerged along with it, have revived fears of excessive airline power in particular markets, and some interest in the redistributive side of the former practices.

---

proposals for regulatory approvals. See, e.g., the discussion of Envirocare of Utah v. Nuclear Regulatory Commission, 194 F.3d 72 (D.C. Cir. 1999) at p. 218 below.

Other forms of market regulation occur quite explicitly for the benefit of the producers involved—for example, price stabilization for agricultural producers. Milk marketing regulation has been a fertile source of administrative law development over the years, as the Department of Agriculture has attempted to control the impact of a number of forces affecting the market for milk: that cows produce milk according to an annual rhythm, so that assuring an adequate supply of fresh milk for the fall guarantees that there will be a large surplus of milk in the spring; that although transportation advances permit a national market even for fresh milk, city-dwellers would prefer a local source of supply, in part for the open, "green" space dairy farms represent; and that land values near the cities would not ordinarily permit dairy farms to remain there. The complicated results, administered under local "milk marketing orders" that tend to exclude consumers from participation in their administration,[18] have produced some stability in the dairy community, and thus also the fresh milk consumers want; yet they have also produced the familiar mountain of butter and cheese and prices higher than they would be if, for example, ultra-pasteurized or reconstituted milk were more easily marketed. The association representing dairy interests, along with the National Rifle Association and others, is known to be a major contributor to political campaigns, and its power and influence are doubtless reflected in these results.

c. Regulation of the professions

Perhaps nowhere in American administrative law has the capacity of economic regulation to enhance the welfare of the regulated at the expense of the public been as well illustrated as in regulation of the professions. Controls over professional practice commonly are administered under state rather than federal law, and typically involve control over entry to the profession, some regulation of professional practice, and discipline for professional misconduct. Entry is generally controlled by educational requirements and examination; professional practice, by regulations adopted by the governing body; and discipline, by formal adjudications conducted before that body. In addition to the learned professions—law, medicine, accounting—such regulation may reach barbers, cosmeticians, plumbers, or well-drillers; "literally hundreds of occupations are subject to the licensing laws in one or more states."[19]

---

18. Block v. Community Nutrition Inst., 467 U.S. 340 (1984).
19. W. Gellhorn, The Abuse of Occupational Licensing, 44 U. Chi. L. Rev. 6 (1976). The State of California's Department of Consumer Affairs, http://www.dca.ca.gov/, posts links to 39 web sites for different California professional boards operating under its super-

The articulated basis for such regulation is to protect the public from incompetent or even unscrupulous practice of a calling the ordinary consumer could not herself appraise, while ensuring for the qualified practitioner economic conditions conducive to sound practice. Although precise arrangements vary from state to state and even profession to profession, professional regulation is typically administered by a board of part-time state officials drawn predominantly from the group subject to regulation. Such arrangements open the way to self-interest, which often enough is served. Federal Supreme Court litigation, generally lost by the regulators, has revealed practices of rate-setting,[20] suppression of competitive advertising,[21] and other efforts to suppress competition.[22] Academic analyses are almost invariably unflattering.[23] Suspicions run high that the rates at which medical associations charter specialists or the pass rate at which a state's bar examination is set are as directly linked to the capacity of the relevant market to support new competition, as to the skills of the fresh applicants. That the public can use protection against unsanitary conditions of hair-cutting is indisputable; placing regulation of barbers in the hands of the barbers conduces to other more questionable results as well.

d. Regulation of the economic conditions of labor

The labor market's well-known imperfections as an economic market generate a wide variety of regulatory measures. At both the federal and the state level, depending on the involvement of interstate commerce or not, and for both private and public employees, important independent agencies employ

---

vision—for example, the State Board of Optometry created in 1913, see http://www.optometry.ca.gov/strategic.asp, with six of its nine members required to be optometrists. (The smaller and more conservative state of North Carolina lists 52, http://www.secretary.state.nc.us/blio/occboards.htm.) A history appearing on the web site of California's recently created Board of Acupuncturists (also dominated by that profession), http://www.dca.ca.gov/acup/, reveals the struggles for prestige and self-control (in this instance, in competition with other, earlier-established elements of the medical profession) that are frequent elements of such legislation.

20. Goldfarb v. Virginia State Bar, 421 U.S. 777 (1975).

21. Bates v. State Bar of Arizona, 433 U.S. 350 (1977).

22. Gibson v. Berryhill, 411 U.S. 564 (1973); but see Friedman v. Rogers, 440 U.S. 1 (1979). While willing to find such arrangements may be unfair to individuals directly and adversely affected by them, the Supreme Court has been unwilling to say that the arrangements are in themselves impermissible.

23. E.g., W. Gellhorn, n.19 above; see also G. Liebman, Delegation to Private Parties in American Constitutional Law, 50 Ind. L. J. 650 (1975).

formal adjudicatory procedures to control aspects of the conduct of labor relations.[24] Coercive behavior is barred, both in the process of organizing labor unions and in the conduct of economic negotiations or strikes; employee discharges found to have resulted from employer coercion in relation to these matters are corrected, with the employer required to pay back wages as well as offer reinstatement. Other regulators oversee the conduct of union affairs to ensure democratic practice within the labor movement; the administrative stages of these proceedings are highly informal, with only limited controls available to interested individuals.[25]

Other forms of regulation, taken at the national level through the executive Department of Labor,[26] protect within limits the economic position of the individual employee. Since the New Deal, federal law has sought to control minimum wages and working hours in most American workplaces large enough to affect interstate commerce. These provisions are directly enforceable in court, either privately or in a suit by the responsible administrator. Over the years a significant practice of interpretation has grown up: through widely publicized responses to industry requests for advice, the administrator is able to secure wide compliance without the need for formal proceedings.[27] Other laws regulate such disparate matters as unemployment insurance, family and medical leave, discrimination in the workplace, the conditions of labor of migrant workers,[28] and the terms and conditions of retirement or pension plans in employment offering that benefit.[29] Health and safety regulation for workers are taken up below.

e. Consumer protection

Much regulation at all levels of government is undertaken to protect the economic position of consumers and, through them, the public generally. Most prominent in this respect is the regulation of the nation's banking system, money supply, credit practices, securities and commodities exchanges, and insurance industry. All but the last of these are generally accomplished at the federal level[30] (although with some state participation in the case of bank-

---

24. The federal agencies are the National Labor Relations Board, http://www.nlrb.gov, and, for federal employees, the Federal Labor Relations Authority, http://www.flra.gov/.

25. Dunlop v. Bachowski, 421 U.S. 560 (1975); see http://www.dol.gov/dol/esa/.

26. http://www.dol.gov.

27. http://www.dol.gov/dol/esa/public/whd_org.htm.

28. Id.

29. http://www.dol.gov/dol/pwba/.

30. Principal agencies include the Federal Reserve Board (money supply, national banks, credit practices—http://www.federalreserve.gov/), the Comptroller of the Currency (na-

ing); for historical reasons, insurance is regulated chiefly by the states. These bodies generate standards by informal rulemaking, control entry through licensing, and frequently enjoy extraordinary summary enforcement authority, thought necessary to maintain public confidence in financial institutions. Much is done informally; while formal proceedings are possible, the very fact of convening such proceedings would have such a negative effect in the relevant financial community that that stage is rarely reached. Those seeking approval either abandon the project, or make the changes suggested to them for securing the agreement of agency staff to their proposed course of action.

This effect is especially prominent in the work of agencies such as the federal Securities and Exchange Commission (SEC),[31] which seek not only to control the operation of sensitive financial markets—in this case, dealings in corporate stock—but also to ensure that consumers acting in those markets have access to complete and accurate information about the securities offered for sale there. Indeed, with the development of the Internet, making information available—both information about corporate filings, and about the Commission's regulatory responses—has become in itself a major means of "regulation." Those responses, it might be noted, are typically informal advice produced after negotiations with staff, not the result of formal proceedings. Corporations must be sure that there will be no controversy about the prospectuses and other papers they draw up in attempted compliance with SEC regulations. What is wanted is the SEC staff's assurance that "no action" will be sought in response to a given filing, not a formal hearing to resolve some controversy; suggested changes will quickly be made to gain that assurance.

As in the case of the SEC, the aim of much consumer protection regulation is informative, to ensure full and honest disclosure of the terms on which credit will be given or a corporate security issued, or of the economic condition of a corporation seeking fresh capital or additional debt. Other regulatory forms with a similar end would include, at the federal level, the regulation of labels on clothing by the Federal Trade Commission, or on food and drink by the Food and Drug Administration. At the state and local level, one finds disclosure requirements in connection with real estate developments, and control over the honesty of weights and measures, and even restaurant menus.

---

tional banks—http://www.occ.treas.gov/), the Office of Thrift Supervision (savings banks—http://www.ots.treas.gov/), Federal Housing Finance Board (home loan banks—http://www.fhfb.gov/), and the Federal Deposit Insurance Corporation (http://www.fdic.gov/).

31. http://www.sec.gov.

f. Allocation of artificial or public goods

Certain kinds of economic activity are most valuable only if limited in ways a market alone is unable to achieve absent regulatory structure. Only so many radio stations can be squeezed into the broadcast spectrum, and their transmission must be controlled even then to avoid mutual interference over much of the listening area. Similarly, only so many airplanes can take off from a given airport during a desirable morning hour. A stream can accept only so much effluent before the available oxygen is consumed; the grass growing on a square mile of public land can support only so many grazing animals before overgrazing destroys the watershed. Up to the applicable limit, each of these activities is safe and acceptable; beyond it, it is not.

A variety of techniques could be imagined for the required rationing. Contemporary American economists tend to favor auctions, but even with sale any limitation on the rights acquired (for example, the number of sheep that may be grazed) must be determined and enforced. Regulation is often employed even for the allocation stage. Thus, applicants for radio or television licenses must apply to the Federal Communications Commission for a license to operate the desired broadcast facility, under conditions that will control interference. They must establish in formal adjudications that they will meet service standards in the public interest. Competition for the license requires the Commission to choose between the competitors. The fee for the license is a tiny fraction of the value that may then be conferred. Similarly, factories putting effluent in streams or the air must have a permit to do so, based on available pollution control technology and subject to agency monitoring and enforcement. However, requiring use of these common resources to be paid for has proved possible only in limited circumstances—as where marketable trading permits were created for power plant emissions contributing to acid rain, as a means of encouraging those generators who would find it most advantageous to invest in pollution control devices.[32] For distribution of airport slots, as for the government's sale of rights to use microwave transmission bands, to harvest government timber or explore its lands for oil, a competitive bidding system is employed. Again, this does not eliminate regulation—emissions must be measured, sale conditions honored—but it provides a means for selecting the firm that will receive a given desired relationship with government that requires less effort (and offers more return) than purporting to make competitive selections on "merit."

---

32. http://www.epa.gov/airmarkets/arp/index.html.

2. Health and safety regulation

Regulation to protect the citizenry from the harms of a technologically advanced society is perhaps a later development than regulation to remedy the deficiencies of the economic marketplace; such regulation has been the prevailing form of federal government regulation over the past three decades. Redress for injuries occasioned by hazard was long principally the domain of ordinary tort law. Yet the federal government was regulating the safety of steam boilers by the middle of the nineteenth century and railroad safety by the century's end. At the same time, the states were substituting administrative schemes of workers' compensation for court actions to deal with injuries suffered in the workplace. Pure food and drug legislation and regulation of unhealthful working conditions emerged, first in the states and then in the federal government, at about the same time as railroad rate regulation became prominent. The importance of modern times lies more in the enhancement of our capacities both to generate and to detect risk, in the diminution of our willingness to tolerate it, and in the increasing use of regulation as a substitute for tort liability, than in innovation in the character of the harms the state seeks to prevent.

Federal regulation of health and safety matters, much more than economic regulation, has been characterized by the widespread use of informal rulemaking as a major tool. Traditional economic regulators used informal rulemaking only occasionally, and then to establish standards of conduct that rarely required a large investment to meet. The paradigmatic proceeding for them was the application for license, invocation of a sanction, or generation of a rate—in each case a formal proceeding decided "on the record" and determining the outcome of a particular controversy involving, even in ratemaking, a limited number of specially interested parties. The first important federal regulator of health issues, the Food and Drug Administration,[33] fit the same mold: ordinarily, it determined applications for permission to market particular drugs, or proceeded against specific items asserted to have been mislabeled. When it did make rules, as in determining what percentage of peanuts had to be in a substance to be labeled "peanut butter," it was required to employ formal rulemaking procedures. Contemporary health and safety regulators using informal rulemaking—such as the Environmental Protection Agency (EPA)[34] setting Clean Air Act standards, the Department of Labor's Occupational Safety and Health Administration (OSHA)[35] establishing rules

---

33. http://www.fda.gov.
34. http://www.epa.gov.
35. http://www.osha.gov.

for workplace safety, the Nuclear Regulatory Commission,[36] or the Department of Transportation's National Highway Traffic Safety Administration[37]— are, in procedural terms, significantly freer in adopting norms to carry out their responsibilities. The resulting standards may have an enormous impact on an affected industry, significantly influencing the price of their products, or requiring first the installation and then the maintenance of highly complex machinery. These impacts have contributed to the development of bureaucratic control mechanisms already discussed as well as, in some cases, some additional statutory procedures.[38] Informal rulemaking nonetheless is the norm for their creation.

The range of regulatory activity involved in control of health and safety issues is, of course, far broader than the simple setting of norms. Among the other responsibilities of the EPA, for example, are:

- overseeing state implementation of state-administered federal environmental controls, using informal adjudication procedures;
- permitting (licensing) industrial discharges presenting pollution hazards, requiring formal adjudication if opposed;
- inspecting operating facilities, and enforcing through the courts (or formal adjudication) sanctions for violations of statutory or agency standards;
- certifying industrial and agricultural chemicals for safety in use;
- requiring the reporting, and maintaining public repositories, of information about hazardous substances and their discharges; and
- identifying and controlling sites used for the disposal of hazardous wastes, including clean-up activities and administrative and judicial enforcement of fiscal responsibility against former users.

In discharging these responsibilities, the EPA (and other agencies similarly placed) may develop a variety of techniques. In rulemaking, for example, much contemporary effort is on finding regulatory techniques that maximize consensus and/or the opportunities for those subject to them to find their own most efficient modes of compliance. "Command and control" regulations, that dictate to the regulated what they must do and how, are inefficient compared to regulations developed by negotiation (if that is possible) with affected interests,[39] and/or regulations that set results to be achieved and then leave those who must achieve them relatively free to decide how to accomplish their

---

36. http://www.nrc.gov.
37. http://www.nhtsa.dot.gov.
38. See p. 103 above.
39. See p. 252 below.

ends.[40] In addition to enlisting cooperation by the regulated, the EPA seeks to enlist the assistance of affected citizens, to support community efforts, and to encourage industry to regulate itself in the hope of earning good will, by providing easily accessed information about discharges actually occurring.[41] Among the EPA's larger challenges is dealing with locations affected by past pollution, often places having particular impact on the socially and economically disadvantaged. Its efforts to deal with the worst of these places ("superfund sites")[42] and the phenomenon generally ("brownfields")[43] involve major financial as well as regulatory commitments. Here, too, the Internet offers opportunities for outreach, as by providing those interested with the ability to register to receive email notices about the brownfields program.[44]

The regulation of workplace safety and health provides other examples of the movement from command-and-control to more cooperative approaches. In its earlier years, OSHA tended to rely on specifying particular safety measures employers were required to take, enforcing these standards by inspections that could lead to fines. It attracted considerable criticism for the inefficiency and intrusiveness of these techniques. And in the belief of many, its standard-setting activities were impeded by the high stakes and substantial detail this approach appeared to entail.[45] Driven in part by increasing difficulties in securing the appropriations necessary for the inspectorate required for this "police" model of enforcement, OSHA began experimenting with alternative approaches in which employers with poor safety records were encouraged to accept consultative relationships with OSHA personnel. OSHA undertook to forgo its punitive inspection regime, so long as these employers undertook to deal in good faith with the difficulties made apparent by their past experiences. The results in the first states where this was tried were dramatic reductions in

---

40. For example, a rule might limit the total effluent a manufacturer could permit to escape from his worksite, but leave to the manufacturer judgments about what controls to use to achieve this. Such reasoning underlay the regulation at issue in Chevron U.S.A., Inc., v. NRDC 467 U.S. 837 (1984), discussed at length at p. 368 below.

41. http://www.epa.gov/epahome/comm.htm provides access to a variety of geographically organized data bases and concerned citizen resources; a number of the EPA's statutes encourage citizen enforcement efforts as well.

42. http://www.epa.gov/superfund/.

43. http://www.epa.gov/swerosps/bf/index.html.

44. http://www.epa.gov/swerosps/bf/listserv.htm.

45. See, e.g., T. McGarity & S. Shapiro, Workers at Risk: The Failed Promise of the Occupational Safety and Health Administration (Praeger 1993); J. Mendeloff, The Dilemma of Toxic Substances Regulation: How Overregulation Causes Underregulation at OSHA (MIT Press 1988).

injury rates (and administrative costs); OSHA's efforts to make the program national, however, were frustrated by a court of appeals decision requiring more elaborate procedures as a condition of making this change.[46]

Perhaps the dominant intellectual issue presented in this field today, one with significant political and moral overtones, concerns the assessment of risk.[47] The capacity for harm in environmental, health and safety matters may be latent, not emerging for a decade or more. The threat of harm may be indirect—that is, it may be easier to point to an increase in cancer resulting from an activity, than to identify a particular episode or even a particular source as the exact cause of any one individual's harm. And the results of a failure in the regulated activity, however unlikely, may be catastrophic, as the accident at Chernobyl so graphically illustrated. No amount of regulation of an activity permitted to continue can completely eliminate risk; and many if not all risks require a difficult comparison with others which they displace. The small but real risk of a second Chernobyl if a nuclear reactor is built, must be compared to the deaths and damage that would result from generating the same electricity in a conventional coal-fired utility, the enhanced risks of international disruption from using oil, the availability of alternative technologies, and the social impacts and risks of foregoing the additional electricity altogether. Identifying a socially acceptable level of risk, finding reliable means for identifying and comparing the risks presented by alternative activities, and determining the level of confidence one can have in the regulatory system's ability to control them—all appear to be central tasks of the political system.

Administrative law is only beginning to deal with the problem of choosing appropriate risks for regulatory response, which is complicated by the apparent discontinuities and limitations characteristic of the ways in which people assess risk.[48] Thus, it is common to fear catastrophic loss more than an accumulating loss of the same dimension; harms from activities one does not personally control over equally prevalent harms that do seem to be within personal control; and (perhaps the most paradoxical) slowly emerging and covert uncertain harm over immediate, clear harm. These characteristics are reflected

---

46. Chamber of Commerce v. United States Dep't of Labor, 174 F.3d 206 (D.C. Cir. 1999).

47. See S. Breyer, Breaking the Vicious Circle: Toward Effective Risk Regulation (Harvard University Press 1993).

48. See, e.g., C. Sunstein, Cognition and Cost-Benefit Analysis, 29 J. Leg. Stud. 1059 (2000); T. Kuran & C. Sunstein, Availability Cascades and Risk Regulation, 51 Stan. L. Rev. 683 (1999).

in our political choices, as when Congress chose to require extraordinary measures to ensure the safety of school buses in the same statute as greatly impeded the implementation of passive protections for personal automobiles. The latter demonstrably presented both greater risk to life and lower costs of controlling the risks presented.[49] Congress continues to support the production of tobacco, and smoking remains lawful despite the risks it poses (although increasingly it is the subject of strident mandatory warnings about its health effects, national restraints on advertising, and local restraints on smoking in public places). It directs OSHA to adopt standards regulating the use of carcinogenic chemicals in the workplace only to the extent "which most adequately assure[], to the extent feasible, on the basis of the best available evidence, that no employee will suffer material impairment of health or functional capacity,"[50] yet requires the Food and Drug Administration to prohibit completely any further use of a food additive for which there is any indication, however slight, that the additive is carcinogenic to laboratory animals and might therefore be carcinogenic to humans.[51] Similar contrasts can be found in the levels of risk Congress has found acceptable in providing for regulation of other hazards.[52]

One can understand Congress's failures to be consistent in political terms. A stranger is driving the school bus carrying our precious children, and we are driving our own automobiles. We (think we) choose to smoke for pleasure, yet we have to eat the food that might in some undetectable way be giving us cancer. We see those who die catastrophically at a Chernobyl much more clearly than the victims of using fossil fuels (e.g., mining accidents and respiratory disease). Politically, it is also easier to voice platitudes about the value of human life than to state a measure that could help decide the extent to which state intervention is justified.

---

49. See J. Mashaw and D. Harfst, The Struggle for Auto Safety (Harvard University Press 1990).

50. §6(b)(5) Occupational Safety and Health Act (1982), 29 U.S.C. 655(b)(5).

51. 21 U.S.C. §348(c)(3)(A). When this stringent standard resulted in an order banning the further use of saccharine, a popular sugar substitute, because of laboratory evidence of bladder cancer in rats given massive doses of the chemical, Congress responded by calling for further study, and temporarily exempting saccharine from the law. The general standard remains in place, however.

52. In the field of transportation, for example, automobiles, airplanes and the transportation of nuclear materials are treated with varying stringency; the small but catastrophic risks of nuclear power engender a different legislative response than the chronic health risks associated with burning coal, or the geopolitical risks of burning oil, in generating electric power.

When Congress has appeared to succumb to this temptation, some judges have found signs of legislative failure. Confronting the general standard of feasibility set out above, that Congress chose to protect occupational health from the covert dangers of carcinogenic chemicals (as distinct from mechanical harms), Justice Renhquist insisted that its failure to resolve these issues meant that an unlawful delegation had occurred. Other Justices, reacting to the same perception, but revealing a greater disposition to be constructive, interpreted the statute to require a threshold determination about the extent of risk involved.[53] (The Justices were perhaps unfair in their assessment, ignoring a significant *institutional* solution to the choice-of-which-risk-to-regulate problem Congress had put in place, reliance on a professional model for risk assessment. The statute assigned the task of advising OSHA about suitable risks for regulation to the National Institute of Occupational Safety and Health, a body composed of academic scientists housed deep in that part of the Department of Health and Human Services responsible for medical research.)

Recent years have seen a great deal of discussion of how best to compare and select among the variety of risks the state might choose to attempt to control, but they have seen no resolution. Unsurprisingly and in particular, we have found no convincing solutions for our seemingly inbred variations in response to risk. The increasing use of environmental and economic impact statements[54] and other like means for structuring bureaucratic policy analysis suggest some reason to hope for greater clarity about these issues in the future. However, both the limits of our knowledge and the depths of our fears about today's complex technology and its by-products suggest that the political difficulties will endure—and with them, the disposition to use administrators rather than legislation.

In addition to programs directly concerned with safety, the environment, and human health, a variety of regulatory programs, largely in the Department of Agriculture, seek to assure the soundness of the national food sup-

---

53. Industrial Union Department, AFL-CIO v. American Petroleum Institute, 448 U.S. 607 (1980). No majority could agree on a reading of the statute's qualification about feasibility. Four of the Court's nine justices agreed with OSHA that it required any protection that would reduce the risk of cancer and was both technologically and economically "achievable"; three would have required an initial determination by the Secretary that "a significant risk of material health impairment" existed under the existing industrial practice or standard; the eighth would have insisted that the expenditures necessary to achieve a given health standard not be "wholly disproportionate to the expected health and safety benefits."

54. See p. 103 above.

ply. These vary from programs (also to be found at the state level) for identifying agricultural pests and quarantining affected farmlands or produce, to programs for the inspection and grading of produce, to programs for market control, as earlier discussed.[55] Although the impact of these programs can often be substantial—as this edition is being written, whole herds of livestock are being destroyed in response to outbreaks of disease—determinations are generally made by inspectors, and formal adjudication even at the agency level is a rarity. Significant political and regulatory issues are being raised as well about genetically altered crops, in respect of which evidence of danger to humans is simply lacking. As in the case of suspected food poisoning, the remedies are administrative recalls, doubtless the subject of some negotiations but not ordinarily of litigation.[56]

3. Private land

Earlier discussion also briefly touched the constitutional relationship between the problem of "due process," very much a part of American administrative law, and the regime of expropriation or taking of private property for public use.[57] The latter is not generally regarded as a part of administrative law; judicial rather than administrative tribunals are employed to determine such issues as "fair value" and whether property has been lawfully taken for public use. Controls over the development of land remaining in private ownership, on the other hand, generally are administrative in character. The most pervasive of such controls are zoning ordinances, local provisions governing such issues as density, use, and even aesthetics adopted and administered by a community body that often is elective in character.[58] Land use controls can also be found at the federal and state level, ranging from the protection of historical landmarks or districts, to the location of large industrial sites such as electric utilities or pipelines, to the control of activities creating some hazard

---

55. See p. 156 above.

56. When the Food and Drug Administration adopted a policy of not treating as contaminated corn that had less than a stated level of an inevitable carcinogenic byproduct of fermentation, an interested consumer organization was able to overcome the usual reluctance of courts to interfere in governmental judgments about prosecution policies, and win a holding that such a policy could not be adopted without using informal rulemaking. CNI v. Young, 818 F.2d 943 (D.C. Cir. 1987); R. Thomas, Prosecutorial Discretion and Agency Self-Regulation, *CNI v. Young* and the Aflatoxin Dance, 44 Admin. L. Rev. 131 (1992).

57. See p. 64 above.

58. See, e.g., the web-site of the New York City Department of Buildings, http://www.nyc.gov/html/dob/home.html.

to the community, such as surface mining or the disposal of hazardous waste. These are, in effect, particular instances of economic regulation, and health and safety regulation, and the procedures commonly employed are typical of those settings.

4. Social security, health and welfare

Most national programs involving personal financial benefits—social security and other benefits for the elderly, and disability insurance for persons unable to participate in the work-force—have since 1994 been located in an unusual independent agency, the Social Security Administration.[59] It had been until that point an element of the cabinet Department of Health and Human Services, and was removed with the purpose of underscoring its independence of political direction.[60] At about the same time a national program providing welfare for impoverished parents with dependent children was converted into block grants administered by the states with limited federally imposed conditions. Medical insurance for the elderly and the impoverished remains under the administration of the Department of Health and Human Services.[61] Such benefits programs exist in other departments: the Department of Labor, for example, administers the federal workers' compensation programs applicable to certain employees; the Department of Agriculture, the food stamp program for subsidized foodstuffs for the poor; and the Department of Veteran's Affairs, benefits for those who have served in the armed forces. Individual states administer unemployment compensation under loose federal supervision, and a variety of local welfare programs.

These programs involve the distribution of benefits to or on behalf of individuals rather than the regulation of conduct, and the typical problem is one of individual eligibility for commencing or continuing to receive benefits. Generalization is difficult—the Medicare/Medicaid program (public health insurance for the elderly and poor), for example, is administered in the first instance by private insurance carriers under contract with the federal government; and the social security program by a federal bureaucracy. One can say, however, that the process begins—fittingly for the minor dimensions of any

---

59. http://www.ssa.gov.

60. Its single administrator serves for a six year term, from which she may be removed only "for cause," see p. 98 above, and the unusual length of term provided for—longer than a President's elected term of office—led President Clinton to express doubts about the constitutionality of the provision.

61. http://www.hcfa.gov/.

individual case—with bureaucratic routine, which may pass through several levels of review. If dissatisfied, the applicant or recipient may demand an on-the-record hearing;[62] in most federal programs this hearing is conducted before a federal administrative law judge and is subject to both administrative and judicial review. Under the interpretations of the Due Process clauses of the federal Constitution discussed above,[63] a procedurally quite elaborate hearing is mandatory for persons being deprived of benefits they had already been receiving, in some cases before the payment of benefits may even be suspended. Although the great bulk of cases never pass the bureaucratic stages, such hearings keep more than 800 administrative law judges occupied in the Social Security Administration alone; judicial review of the work of these administrative law judges and the departmental appeals council that oversees their work constitutes a significant proportion of the work of the United States district courts.[64]

These programs present other kinds of issues, as well. To ease bureaucratic administration, the responsible agencies adopt rules substituting general standards for individual judgment, raising standard issues both of authority and of application.[65] Procedural issues for suppliers of supported services, moreover, may differ from those for beneficiaries. The food stamp program, for example, involves grocery store owners as well as recipients, and questions of eligibility can arise for either group. The owners are permitted to accept the stamps only in payment for staple foods—not for cash, or for electric light bulbs; administrative sanctions against misbehaving store owners result from procedures strikingly less formal than would be available to a recipient believed no longer to be eligible to continue receiving the stamps.

Perhaps the issues these programs illustrate most sharply, however, concern the problems of achieving coherence in administering a vast national program. Professor Jerry Mashaw's series of books grounded in studies of the ad-

---

62. The availability of hearings under the medical insurance programs is restricted, as a function of the amount in dispute. See Gray Panthers v. Schweiker, 652 F.2d 146 (D.C. Cir. 1980), discussed at p. 62 above.

63. See p. 48 above.

64. The Judicial Conference of the United States reported almost 16,000 actions initiated under the Social Security Laws in the twelve months ending September 30, 2000, about 6% of the total caseload of about 260,000. http://www.uscourts.gov/judbus2000/tables/s07sep00.pdf and s09sep00.pdf. In 1984, such filings had constituted 11.5% of the total caseload. Annual Report of the Directors of the Administrative Office of the United States Courts 133 (1984).

65. Heckler v. Campbell, 461 U.S. 458 (1983). See the discussion at p. 261 below.

ministration of federal disability insurance[66] illustrate two dimensions of this problem: first, the question what coherence is to be achieved; second, the conflicting models available for achieving it. The first of these questions concerns the appropriate relationship between political administrators and permanent civil service staff. How seriously, for example, the problem of welfare cheating is viewed, and how stringent measures are to be taken in pursuing it, will often be a function of political administration. Securing the implementation of a new policy in this regard against the more constant outlook of the permanent staff presents well-known difficulties. The second question assumes agreed ends, but notes at least three differing and conflicting means for achieving them: a bureaucratic model stressing the tools and discipline of internal management, such as staff manuals, hierarchical structure and an effort to build morale; a professional model building on the commitments to helpfulness of the doctors and caseworkers most directly responsible for program administration; and a model of individual rights, stressing the claims and dignity of the persons who participate in the program. The bureaucrat will regard as successful a program that generates few gross errors, and is as likely to err for, as against, a claimant in marginal cases. The professional will value a program that leaves ample room for her exercise of the professional judgment on which questions of eligibility turn, trusting her professional commitment to produce appropriate results. The individual may prefer a program that maximizes his personal participation and opportunity to advance the merits of his particular claim. Each is attractive to a point, and none is readily reconciled with the others.

A third dimension of the problem of national coherence is brought about by the geographical arrangement of the federal courts and the Supreme Court's limited capacity to oversee their results. The Administrator of the Social Security Administration, for instance, is responsible for the operation of a national program, and the departmental Appeals Council that reviews administrative law judge decisions is also a single body, bringing a uniform approach to its work. Yet that work is reviewed in 93 different judicial districts, then twelve disparate circuit courts of appeal—each of which understandably believes that the Administrator has the obligation to follow its view in cases

---

66. Bureaucratic Justice: Managing Social Security Disability Claims (Yale Univ. 1983); Due Process in the Administrative State (Yale Univ. 1985); Social Security Hearings and Appeals: A Study of the Social Security Administration Hearing System (with Goetz, Goodman, Schwartz, Verkuil and Carrow) (Lexington 1978). While the particulars of these programs have changed, these books remain among the most revealing relatively recent studies of administrative functioning the author knows.

arising within its jurisdictional catchment area. One court may be very tolerant of administrative judgment; another, particularly sensitive to the Department's handling of asserted mental disability; a third, more concerned about
its findings respecting the availability of work in the national economy for persons never likely to be more than marginal contributors. When the Administrator responded to these possible variations by announcing that she might
choose to regard some court decisions as binding only in the case actually decided, and not as precedent governing future decisions in other cases, this
"non-acquiescence" produced a major confrontation with the courts. While
the particular point on which she had disagreed with the courts—in the event,
not a few courts but most of them—was ultimately resolved against her by
legislation, the problem is a general one that arises not infrequently—in tax
administration, for example, as well as in labor matters. The Supreme Court's
limited capacity to ensure the uniformity of national law makes a satisfactory
resolution difficult. One might also say that the incidental and skewed character of judicial encounters with an administrative system of significant complexity (only disappointed citizens, not wrongly favored ones, seek review)
adds to this difficulty.[67]

5. Taxes and excises

The collection of taxes and other excises has long been an important field
of administration. In the earliest days of the American republic, the assessment and collection of taxes and duties were the principal administrative functions the national government performed, and histories of early administrative practice give much attention to them.[68] Taxation remains important,
obviously enough. With the natural specialization of the modern legal profession, tax practitioners tend not to present themselves as "administrative
lawyers." Yet tax practice and procedures are in fact readily understood in administrative law terms.

At the federal level, most tax and excise issues are within the jurisdiction
of elements of the Treasury Department[69]—the Internal Revenue Service for

---

67. See p. 382 below; Administrative Law: Cases and Comments, p. 666 ff.; P. Strauss,
One Hundred Fifty Cases Per Year: Some Implications of the Supreme Court's Limited Resources for Judicial Review of Agency Action, 87 Colum. L. Rev. 1093, 1110–16 (1987).

68. See, e.g., L. White, The Federalists: A Study in Administrative History (MacMillan
1948).

69. http://www.treas.gov/bureaus.html links to all the bureaus mentioned in the following text, and to numerous other constituents of the Treasury Department.

taxes, the Customs Service for import duties (and some other regulations of international commerce), and the Bureau of Alcohol, Tobacco and Firearms for the special taxes, and associated controls, on those commodities. These agencies flesh out applicable statutory controls by regulation; issue periodic interpretations of the laws subject to their jurisdiction; prescribe the forms on which taxes are to be reported; collect and process those forms; conduct necessary investigations; and initiate enforcement proceedings. In tax administration, these proceedings, if contested, are generally conducted in the ordinary courts or before specialized tribunals such as the Tax Court or the Court of International Trade, rather than within the Department as such; but before any such trial occurs, audits or other proceedings within the Department give ample opportunity for administrative resolutions to be reached.

Tax investigations form the backdrop against which much of the law respecting agency investigations has been made. The American tax system is one of voluntary reporting, reinforced by regular disclosures by third parties (that is, employers report wages to the government, corporations report dividends, etc.) and by occasional investigations after the fact. It does not seem excessively cynical to speculate that the needs of such a system have significantly contributed to the unwillingness of American courts to entertain generalized pleas of self-incrimination as excusing the obligation to file reports. Similarly, they have refused to extend the protections of the self-incrimination claim to the provision of any documents that are not both personal and in the personal possession of the individual making the claim.[70] So also for the relatively permissive standards of relevance that attend enforcement of administrative requests for information (subpoenas and the like) in the course of an investigation, the legality of requirements for record-keeping, the broad scope permitted searches in support of customs regulation, and so forth. A substantial proportion of the general law on these subjects, particularly those relating to documentary production, in fact has its origin in tax administration.

6. Public services

Much of the effort of American civil bureaucracy is expended in administering programs for support of public services such as education, housing, research, and road construction. The Federal Departments of Education,[71]

---

70. See p. 46 above.
71. http://www.ed.gov/.

Housing and Urban Development,[72] and Transportation[73] annually oversee the distribution of billions of dollars for these purposes, either as grants to approved state programs or in the form of guaranteed loans to individuals. Federally contracted research, seeking cancer cures and energy technology development as well as strategic defense initiatives, provides major support for both public and private universities as well as important elements of the business community. At the state and local level, the institutions that provide these services must be operated, suggesting a rich harvest of possible controversy over both planning and operations.

A hypothetical housing development may serve to suggest the range of problems that can arise. (Examples could be given, with equal ease and richness, concerning public schools or other services.) If the project is to be financed with federal support, there will first be the matter of satisfying the various conditions attached to such support—for example, that adequate provision be made for the handicapped or (depending on the program) for the aged or other purposes. Disputes over such issues are resolved internally by bureaucratic means, which a court would be disposed to describe as "informal adjudication"; a member of one of the groups within the protective purposes of the federal conditions would be able to obtain review in court of any decision that allegedly did not meet these conditions.[74] (What a state's remedies would be if, in its view, the project were being wrongfully withheld or excessively conditioned is far less certain.) In addition, if the project has significant environmental implications, the federal agency will be required to issue an "environmental impact statement" before approving it, first in draft for public comment and then in final form. This provides a substantial opportunity for still broader public participation, as for instance by those concerned about its impact on wildlife in a nearby marsh. Compliance with this requirement, too, is subject to federal enforcement although generally only as a procedural matter.[75] Once made, the grant is subject to continuing federal

---

72. http://www.hud.gov/.

73. http://www.dot.gov.

74. See e.g., Citizens to Preserve Overton Park, Inc. v. Volpe, 401 U.S. 402 (1971).

75. That is, the courts will usually ask only whether the environmental analysis required by the National Environmental Policy Act, 42 U.S.C. §4334, has been made, not whether the results of that analysis force a particular decision. Strycker's Bay Neighborhood Council v. Karlen, 444 U.S. 223 (1980). On occasion, however, the analysis will reveal matters that do bring other federal laws into play—for example, that the proposed site is the habitat of a species protected under the federal Endangered Species Act—and then those laws will control whether and under what conditions the project may go forward. See Tennessee Valley Authority v. Hill, 437 U.S. 153 (1978).

oversight and possible administrative enforcement, through agency proceedings, for adherence to its conditions; violation of some conditions (e.g., nondiscrimination in employment) may threaten not only the particular project, but all similar federal funding.[76]

Those constructing and undertaking the project will likely face constraints of state and local law on such issues as siting, requiring public procedures of greater or lesser formality. Once in operation, other questions may arise such as eligibility for access, conditions of tenancy (notably, the rent to be paid), and discipline for tenants who are thought to have violated the terms of their eligibility or tenancy. The usual situation for public housing in the United States is that there are many more eligible applicants than spaces; applications (like welfare generally) are handled in a bureaucratic process, and an interesting and difficult question has been whether disappointed but eligible applicants are entitled to any kind of regularity in the process of selection among those eligible.[77] The conditions of tenancy—rent, maximum earnings a tenant can have without forfeiting her place to a more needy person, rules of conduct—are the product of rulemaking rather than adjudication, and so subject only to statutory constraints on their formation.[78] The conditions of eligibility are also, however, a matter of continuing interest to the grantor, and the terms of a federal grant or guaranteed loan may well require the grantee to justify any proposed change to the supporting agency. Tenants' efforts to participate in and force formality upon these proceedings, which otherwise would likely be resolved through negotiation or informal adjudication, have generally proved unavailing although strong arguments have been made to

---

76. The threatened loss of federal funding as a means of enforcement of federal programs has proved particularly controversial in education, where private enforcement of spending limitations is sometimes available. Recognizing the strength of this threat has been one apparent factor contributing to Supreme Court limitations on the availability of this relief. See, e.g., Alexander v. Sandoval, 532 U.S. 275 (2001); NAACP v. Smith, 525 U.S. 459 (1999); Grove City College v. Bell, 465 U.S. 558 (1984). See also L. Baker, Conditional Federal Spending and States Rights, 574 Annals 104 (2001); A. Rosenthal, Conditional Federal Spending and Constitution, 39 Stan. L. Rev. 1103 (1987); R. Katzmann, Institutional Disability: The Saga of Transportation Policy for the Disabled (Brookings Institute 1986).

77. Since an applicant for a scarce resource could not easily be described as having an "entitlement" to it, the conventional due process analysis, see p. 48 above, would not regard her as having any constitutional claim to procedures. (There might, of course, be enforceable statutory provisions.) Nonetheless, the involvement of the state in the distribution of these resources and the apparent ease with which at least some principles of fairness in distribution might be observed has produced strong arguments for constraint. C. Farina, Conceiving Due Process, 3 Yale J.L. & Feminism 189 (1991).

78. See p. 189 below.

support their interest.[79] Tenants in place, finally, are within the ambit of "due process" entitlement, and can therefore require relatively formal adjudicatory procedures to be employed in removing or disciplining them—procedures which may take place in an administrative "housing court," or in the municipal judicial system.

7. Custodial institutions

Custodial institutions directed by the state, prisons in particular but also mental hospitals and residential schools for the mentally retarded, can be regarded as administrative agencies whose decisions have a particular consequence for the Due Process clauses' protection of "liberty." At the federal level, a sizable prison system is administered by the Bureau of Prisons of the Department of Justice.[80] As a general matter, however, custodial institutions are state institutions, and state law governs commitment to them. As public institutions, federal or state, custodial institutions present all the standard faces of administrative law—formulating policy, contracting, engaging civil servants, etc.—but it is in their relationships with the individuals placed in their care that the sharpest questions are raised. The commitment of a person to an institution, indeed, is so momentous as to be placed in the hands of the courts. This is universally so for criminal conviction, and generally, in conjunction with medical examiners, in the case of involuntary commitments for mental illness or retardation;[81] no one doubts that the greatest care must be taken at this stage.[82] However, issues that arise in the course of a commitment

---

79. The pervasive issues are the competence of the judiciary to review what seem to be managerial actions such as determination of rents and whether courts or administrators have final responsibility to enforce tenants' rights. When nursing home residents protested the de-certification of the home (meaning the residents would have to move), the Court held it was enough that the home itself had been given procedural protection before the final decision. The large number of patients had no individual interests that would permit a due process claim in federal court. O'Bannon v. Town Court Nursing Center, 447 U.S. 773 (1980). See also Wright v. Roanoke Redevelopment and Housing Authority, 479 U.S. 418 (1987); Langevin v. Chenango Court, Inc., 447 F.2d 296 (2d Cir. 1971).

80. http://www.bop.gov/.

81. S. Brakel, The Mentally Disabled and the Law (Am. Bar. Found., 3d ed. 1985).

82. In the case of mental retardation, commitment is generally at the request of a family, often while the person being committed is still a child. More informal procedures are common in these cases, relying on the family's discretion, but even here the need for explicitly judicial supervision of ostensibly medical judgments is recognized. Parham v. J.R., 442 U.S. 584 (1979).

once made, and many questions associated with release, are dealt with from the perspective of administrative law.

Thus, analysis of what procedures a prison warden must follow in transferring an inmate in his charge to another facility presents a question of administrative not criminal law;[83] so also, what form of hearing is required before prison discipline can be imposed is a question to be settled according to the norms of administrative, rather than criminal procedure, and the discipline results from a hearing within the prison system, not before the courts.[84] As public servants in close and sometimes brutal contact with private citizens (in this case, prisoners), state wardens and prison guards have been the frequent objects of suits seeking monetary damages for allegedly unlawful acts under section 1983 of the federal Civil Rights Act,[85] suits that have been successful to what outside observers may regard as a surprising degree.[86] And at the end of imprisonment, an inmate's chances for early, probationary release turn not only on internal, administrative judgments about "good behavior," but more importantly on the judgment of an administrative tribunal, the parole board, respecting his prospects for law-abiding behavior on return to the community. To what extent those bodies are subject to the constraints of regularity, relying as heavily as they must on judgment and on information informally obtained, has been a matter of significant dispute.[87]

Corresponding issues can arise in the context of mental health care and the habilitation of the mentally retarded. For a period in the 1970s, lawsuits seeking to enforce principles of acceptable care and planning were a common feature of American jurisprudence; and these suits against public authority seeking to compel the performance of an asserted duty are readily characterized in administrative law terms. In a number of these cases, the public administration of the programs in question was revealed to be so deficient as to cause the judges hearing them, in effect, to place the programs in judicial receiver-

---

83. Meachum v. Fano, 427 U.S. 215 (1976).

84. Walpole v. Hill, 472 U.S. 445 (1985).

85. See p. 395 below; the most recent reports of the Administrative Office of United States Courts show that in fiscal year 2000 prisoners initiated more than 25,000 civil actions in United States district courts, about 10% of the courts' entire civil docket, to raise questions under the civil rights laws or concerning prison conditions.

86. See H. Monaghan, State Law Wrongs, State Law Remedies, and the Fourteenth Amendment, 86 Colum. L. Rev. 979 (1986).

87. See Superintendent, Mass. Corr. Institution, Walpole v. Hill, 472 U.S. 445 (1985); Morrissey v. Brauer, 408 U.S. 471 (1972) (revoking parole); Pickens v. United States Board of Parole, 507 F.2d 1107 (D.C. Cir. 1974).

ship.[88] Doubts about the capacity and legitimacy of judges to assume the burden of administering state institutions contributed to subsequent Supreme Court judgments discouraging quite such adventurous oversight;[89] yet the fact that these are state institutions, whose acts have major consequences for the liberty and well-being of those assigned to them, promises the continued availability of administrative law remedies in some settings.

The same institutional doubts appear to have armed what would otherwise be a remarkable withdrawal of the federal courts from enforcement of Due Process Clause protections in cases involving claimed liberty and property interests of persons in custody after having been convicted of crime. A striking case decided in 1995 involved a state's decision to place a long-term prisoner in solitary confinement for 30 days for alleged misbehavior, that the state ultimately conceded (after he had served this penalty) did not warrant this sanction.[90] Five Justices, the narrowest possible majority, expressed two concerns. First, that the existing practice of inferring "liberty" interests from state positive law had the effect of giving prison officials incentives to confer standardless discretion on personnel rather than codify prison management.[91] Second, this practice "has led to the involvement of federal courts in the day-to-day management of prisons, often squandering judicial resources with little offsetting benefit to anyone." The majority held that in the prison environment, "liberty" would be affected only by an "atypical and significant hardship on the inmate in relation to the ordinary incidents of prison life," and that thirty days' punitive solitary confinement, in the context of someone under sentence for more than thirty years, was "too ephemeral and insubstantial to trigger procedural due process protections as long as prison officials have discretion to transfer him for whatever reason or for no reason at all." Dissenters both rejected the new test, and had little difficulty concluding that it had been met. The decision has provoked a significant, and as yet unresolved, debate whether we are witnessing a general retrenchment in due process jurisprudence, or rather a phenomenon specifically tied to the Court's fear of engagement with state prison administration issues;[92] thus

---

88. D. & S. Rothman, The Willowbrook Wars (Harper & Row 1984); Special Project: The Remedial Process in Institutional Reform Litigation, 78 Colum. L. Rev. 788 (1978); A Chayes, The Role of the Judge in Public Law Litigation, 89 Harv. L. Rev. 1281 (1976).

89. E.g., Pennhurst State School & Hospital v. Halderman, 465 U.S. 89 (1984).

90. Sandin v. Conner, 515 U.S. 472 (1995).

91. See the discussion of the positivist trap, p. 57 ff. above.

92. Compare R. Pierce, Jr., The Due Process Counter-revolution of the 1990's?, 96 Colum. L. Rev. 1973 (1996) and C. Farina, On Misusing "Revolution" and "Reform": Pro-

far, the decision has been invoked only in the context of other prison administration cases.

8. Immigration, deportation

"Liberty" is also central, but encounters opposing state interests of unusual force, in the administration of the alienage laws, those governing the lawfulness of aliens' presence on American soil. Although some bureaucratic processing associated with these laws (e.g., issuance of visas) occurs in the Department of State, their administration is generally committed to the Immigration and Naturalization Service,[93] a constituent element of the Department of Justice; this function is wholly federal in character. Hearings on such issues as visa extension, qualification for permanent residence status, exclusion, political asylum and deportation—varying in the degree of formality attached with the perceived balance between the individual liberty claims and the state interests understood to be involved—occur informally, in less important cases, before regional officials of the Service; and in more important cases, more formally before immigration law judges of the Department of Justice.[94]

Immigration law is a highly developed and complex speciality, inappropriate to summarize here.[95] What may be remarked is that it is almost entirely the creature of statute: the courts "have long recognized the power to expel or exclude aliens as a fundamental sovereign attribute exercised by the Government's political departments largely immune from judicial control;"[96] and because of "Congress' plenary authority to regulate aliens,...some congressional rules, validly applied to aliens, 'would be unacceptable if applied to citizens.'"[97] An alien whose presence in the United States has no color of lawfulness (as distinct from one whose presence is colorably lawful, yet who is subject to deportation, as for violation of a condition of her admission) has little claim on either agency or courts for relief. The writ of habeas corpus, not frequently

---

cedural Due Process and the New Welfare Act, 50 Admin. L. Rev. 591 (1998).

93. http://www.ins.gov/graphics/index.htm.

94. See p. 137 n. 229 above.

95. G. Neuman, Strangers to the Constitution: Immigrants, Borders, and Fundamental Law (Princeton University 1996); C. Gordon & S. Mailman, Immigration Law and Procedure (M. Bender & Co. 1988).

96. Fiallo v. Bell, 430 U.S. 787, 792 (1977).

97. Hotel & Restaurant Employees Union v. Attorney General, 804 F.2d 1256, 1259 (D.C. Cir. 1986), quoting Mathews v. Diaz, 426 U.S. 67 (1976).

employed to secure review of administrative action generally in American practice, has had a significant utility to that end in the immigration context, although contemporary limitations on its availability are significant.[98]

9. International commerce

American regulation of international commerce is, presumably, an area of substantial interest to foreign readers. It is, regrettably for this enterprise, far outside the author's usual ambit, and he can only point to materials that seem likely to prove good bibliographic starting points.[99] Such regulation is a strictly federal responsibility that, customs and related functions aside,[100] is generally centered in the International Trade Administration of the Department of Commerce.[101] Licenses required for the export of certain sensitive technology are obtained there through an applications process made less than usually "judicial" in character by the frequent involvement of state-classified information in the decisions to be made.[102] Administration of the anti-dumping and countervailing duty laws intended to protect American industry against discriminatory practices abroad is more formally dealt with, in part by the independent United States International Trade Commission.[103] The Court of International Trade,[104] a specialized court that is one of the trial-level constituents of the Court of Appeals for the Federal Circuit, reviews these mat-

---

98. See INS v. St. Cyr, U.S. 121 S. Ct. 2271 (2001);. G. Neuman, Federal Courts Issues in Immigration Law, 78 Texas L. Rev. 1661 (2000) and Habeas Corpus, Executive Detention, and the Removal of Aliens, 98 Colum. L. Rev. 961 (1998); and p. 301 below.

99. B. Bittker and B. Denning, Bittker on the Regulation of Interstate and Foreign Commerce (Aspen Law & Business 1999); I. Unah, The Courts of International Trade: Judicial Specialization, Expertise, and Bureaucratic Policy-making (University of Michigan 1998); W. Lash, U.S. International Trade Regulation: a Primer (A.E.I. Press 1998); P. Reed, The Role of Federal Courts in U.S. Customs and International Trade Law (Oceania Publications 1997).

100. http://www.customs.treas.gov/; Customs Service actions in classifying imported goods have provided the occasion for two recent Supreme Court decisions on the legally binding character of agency regulations, United States v. Haggar Apparel Corp., 526 U.S. 380 (1999) and the deference owing to informally-reached administrative interpretations, United States v. Mead Corp., 533 U.S. 218 (2001), see p. 368 below.

101. http://www.ita.doc.gov.

102. See U.Va. Center for Law and National Security, Technology Control, Competition, and National Security: Conflict and Consensus (1987); Practicing Law Institute, Coping with U.S. Export Controls (1986). Cf. In the Matter of Edlow International Co., 3 N.R.C. 563 (1976).

103. http://www.usitc.gov/.

104. http://www.uscit.gov/.

ters, and has general authority in judicial actions arising under federal laws, such as the customs statutes, governing import transactions.

10. Public land and other state goods

The great bulk of early administration in the United States concerned public goods, the land and, to a lesser extent, the mails. As an expanding nation on a sparsely peopled[105] land mass, the United States regarded its real property as a resource to be exploited for growth. Under a variety of programs, veterans of its wars, persons who would farm its surface, persons who would mine its minerals, and railroads that would traverse it were given the chance to qualify for ownership. A sizable bureaucracy grew up to conduct and keep records of surveys, and to process the variety of claims made under these laws. While most of these programs have been quiescent since the beginning of this century,[106] others have replaced them, and the Departments of Interior[107] and Agriculture in particular expend a good deal of their effort in these directions.[108] Prominent actors include the National Park Service (regulation of national parks and persons providing services within them); the National Forest Service (regulation of the national forests and their users—campers, resort owners, miners, and livestock grazers as well as timber harvesters);[109] the Bureau of Land Management (regulation like the Forest Service on the remainder of the public lands, particularly administration of programs for livestock

---

105. Of course, it was peopled by the various tribes of Native Americans; yet they were more or less uniformly regarded as nomadic interlopers to be confined (or displaced) to designated "reservations," not owners in the western sense. However land came from them or from other nations (France, Spain, Mexico, Great Britain, Russia) to the United States, it came immediately into public ownership by the national government. Even today, upwards of one third of the nation's land mass is federally owned, a source of more than a little frustration in some western states.

106. It remains possible for an enterprising person to "locate" a mining claim on most public lands; upon proving the discovery there of a "valuable mineral" and some (but not much) work to develop it, one can force the sale of the tract at turn-of-the-(twentieth)-century prices.

107. Department of Interior bureaus—including the National Park Service, the Bureau of Land Management and the bureau of Reclamation—can be found at http://www.doi.gov/bureaus.html.

108. The situation is not much changed since a presidential commission issued a major body of studies in the late 1960s, under the general rubric One Third of the Nation's Lands.

109. http://www.fs.fed.us. A dated but still valuable account of Forest Service responsibilities and administration is given in H. Kaufman, The Forest Ranger (Resources for the Future 1960).

grazing and mineral leasing (coal and oil)); and the Bureau of Reclamation (development of western water resources, and management of resulting irrigation districts).[110] Access to these programs is often governed by auction, or even lottery, so that disputes at this stage most often concern issues of eligibility. The permissions granted, a coal mining lease in a national forest or a concession in a national park, are often conditional, and supervision of those conditions requires administrative actions of the kind readily anticipatable from the circumstances.

An interesting and distinctive characteristic of some of these administrative schemes is the use of advisory committees of interested private citizens to assist in the formulation and application of policy at the local level. How grazing rights are distributed in the arid American West, for example, in relation to timbering and other activities on the public lands is a matter of deep import to the local economy. An administrative unit of the Department of Interior's Bureau of Land Management may encompass hundreds of square miles of federal land, with private holdings interspersed, and a handful of federal officials to oversee its operation. By coopting a local advisory committee of ranchers, sheepherders, lumbermen, and others interested in the use of the land to assist in the annual provision for its use, the Bureau learned to attain substantial adherence to its policies without having to expend major efforts in enforcement.[111] As conservation and environmental interest groups have pressed for these commercial activities, to be "properly valued," and thus constrained,[112] questions about such issues as grazing rights have become significantly more controversial.[113]

11. Government contracting

The government acts as a proprietor, also, in conducting its business relations—notably (but not exclusively) through the General Services Adminis-

---

110. The Bureau of Reclamation maintains an interesting Internet site, presumably developed for its widely dispersed staff but open to the public, exploring the principles of sound bureaucratic decisionmaking with public consultation. http://www.usbr.gov/guide/

111. L. Laitala, BLM Advisory Boards Past, Present, and Future (BLM 1975); and see G. Libecap, Locking up the Range 81 (Ballinger 1981).

112. E.g., B. Ackerman and R. Stewart, Reforming Environmental Law, 37 Stan. L. Rev. 1333 (1985).

113. Symposium, Fifty Years of the BLM, 32 Land & Water Review 339 ff. (1997); R. Durant, The Administrative Presidency Revisited: Public Lands, the BLM, and the Reagan Revolution (State University of New York 1992); W. Hage, Storm over Rangelands: Private Rights in Federal Lands (Free Enterprise Press 1989).

tration,[114] which acts as provisioner for the whole of government, and the Department of Defense, purchaser of all supplies for the armed services. These relationships, however, give rise to a rich body of issues of public administration. One way in which these issues arise is out of the government seeking to advance various public policies through its award of contracts;[115] while Presidents have often used Executive Orders to do so in the absence of direct statutory authority, that practice can give rise to difficult questions of legality.[116] Questions arise concerning the eligibility of bidders and the propriety of awards; and disputes arising during contract administration, often enough on matters of urgency for the national interest, must be resolved. Occasionally sanctions such as debarment from future bidding will be thought appropriate for contractor misbehavior. Similar situations arise when the government seeks to purchase not goods but services—for example, research on a virulent disease for the National Institute of Health. Selection processes may turn on bidding or on competitive application through a structured screening process like that employed by academic publications. "Government contracts" is a specialty, neither administrative law nor contract law, but combining of some of the characteristics of each. It is treated very briefly below.[117]

12. State employment

Since the public employee has no "right" to a public job, one might expect the courts to hold that he is "simply" in an employment relationship with the government, and must accept its terms as he would have to accept the terms on which he might be offered private employment. Nonetheless, that argument has been emphatically rejected, as suggested in previous discussion of the evolution of American understandings of the "due process of law."[118] States

---

114. http://www.gsa.gov/Portal/main.jsp?tab=home

115. Notable examples, each achieved by presidential executive order well in advance of any statutory provision, were contracts conditioned on non-discrimination in employment, first on racial and then on sexual bases. Other government contracting policies have favored industries employing the handicapped or owned by members of a racial minority. By statute, government contractors must pay an administratively determined "prevailing wage" for their area.

116. See p. 107 above; Chrysler Corp. v. Brown, 441 U.S. 281 (1979); Chamber of Commerce v. Reich, 74 F.3d 1322, rehearing and rehearing en banc denied, 83 F.3d 439, 442 (D.C. Cir. 1996).

117. See p. 400 below.

118. See p. 48 above.

need not provide for a tenured civil service,[119] but when they do, their regulation of its terms and conditions must meet constitutional standards that appear to require a rather formal, on-the-record adjudication process. The civil service mechanism is briefly discussed above.[120]

13. State enterprises

State enterprises are more common in the United States than many would at first believe. Public entities commonly provide services that might equally (and often are) supplied by private enterprise in education, postal service, transportation, and the provision of public utilities. Less prominently, state enterprises may provide some manufacturing capacities associated with state needs—cement, in South Dakota; mineral water in New York state.[121] The conduct of such enterprises, however, is not ordinarily a particular concern of administrative law. Except that the public character of the enterprise invites application of the Due Process Clause to some activities—drivers for a municipal bus line may be civil servants; tenured professors at a state university have a constitutional entitlement to "fair procedure" before they are disciplined that tenured professors at a private university do not enjoy—such enterprises operate under regimes not very different from those of their private counterparts. For example, rates of municipal and private electric utilities, and public and private bus-lines are each subject to close control, along similar lines and following similar procedures for justification and public participation. For external purposes, these enterprises tend to be regarded as distinct from the state. Over the years an attempted distinction between "proprietary" and "governmental" activities, while never secure, has reflected judicial reluctance to recognize any special socialist character of public enterprise when it occurs.

The principal federal "commercial" enterprises are the United States Postal Service, the Communications Satellite Corporation (Comsat), AMTRAK (passenger railroad service), and two major regional power suppliers, the Tennessee Valley Authority and the Bonneville Power Authority. One might also include the superstructure of the national banking system, which since 1911 (and several times previously in the nation's history) has been a mixture of

---

119. This is the orthodox position; to a degree, Supreme Court cases providing constitutional protection against politically motivated discharge from apolitical office might be thought to require state recognition of civil service status.

120. See p. 135 above.

121. Reeves, Inc. v. Stake, 447 U.S. 429 U.S. 429 (1980); New York v. United States, 326 U.S. 572 (1946).

private enterprise and public authority. While some of these, notably the reserve banks and the two power authorities, are major actors in the national economy, one is hard-put to identify particular notions of administrative law that apply to their activities. For most purposes they are treated as legal entities independent of government, albeit entities whose legal authority to act depends on their statutory charter much as a corporation's would depend on the provisions of its certificate of incorporation. While they may sue and be sued, the lawfulness of their behavior or internal operations is not generally conceptualized in administrative law terms; in particular, they are not regarded as agencies, nor their behavior as "agency action," for the purposes of general administrative procedure legislation.

14. Other matters

Any such discussion as the preceding must be partial, and even in its incompleteness risk overwhelming the reader with unwanted detail. A sense that the administrative lawyer brings limited tools to an unruly and diverse universe of public actors and activities may be sufficient. Nonetheless, reviewing what has been said, it seems appropriate to mention here one additional variety of administrative action that occasionally appears—emergency economic measures such as price controls. These present the American administrative lawyer with, in a sense, her largest challenge. They are economy-wide, generally invoked at a time of national crisis, typically with only the broadest of legislative instructions, to be administered by a bureaucracy assembled for the purpose under conditions of urgency, without historical experience or practice, following procedures that need to be highly informal in order to administer so large a program smoothly. Public acceptance of such regimes is doubtless connected with the emergency itself, a widely shared sense of need that permits much to be tolerated that over the longer run and in ordinary circumstances would not be accepted. But other contributors to a sense of regularity and control ought also be noted.

General price controls first made a successful appearance in World War II; and were again invoked, for brief periods, in later years. The instructions given to the administrator were highly general—in the Emergency Price Control Act of 1942, to issue regulations fixing those prices that "in his judgment will be fair and equitable and effectuate" the generally described purposes of price control legislation in a war-time economy; in the Economic Stabilization Act of 1970, "to issue such orders and regulations as he may deem appropriate to stabilize prices, rents, wages and salaries at levels not less than those prevailing on May 25, 1970…making…such adjustments as may be necessary to prevent gross inequities." Out of these instructions, the administrators in each instance constructed both rules governing general prices—set according to the objective circumstances of markets on specified dates—and bureaucratic mechanisms for securing, first, informal advice, second, possible exemption from these rules, and, third, enforcement against apparent violators. These mechanisms generated an enormous volume of business for the administering agencies: 1,340,955 landlord petitions for upward adjustment of rents had been received by the World War II Office of Price Administration as of its seventeenth quarterly report, for the period ending March 31, 1946, and 130,000 actions seeking rent reductions had been initiated within the agency during that quarter alone; the 90-day price freeze during 1970 produced 6,000 requests for exception, 50,000 complaints of violation, and 750,000 requests for advice.[122] The regularity and the sense of systemic openness to private need that actually characterized these regimes—a result certainly not inevitable on the face of the statutes creating them—is generally credited with persuading the courts to sustain them.[123] The ready availability of informal means of advice and adjustment appears in fact to have settled most controversies. In the 1970 price and wage freeze, for example, only 214 cases were so serious as to require the highest levels of attention for possible judicial enforcement action; and only eight lawsuits were in fact brought. These regimes thus illustrate the power of informal advice-giving and dispute resolution in administration; the availability of judicial remedies or judicial enforcement need not imply that either is often invoked.[124]

---

122. R. Kagan, Regulatory Justice: Implementing a Wage-Price Freeze (Russell Sage 1978) is an invaluable book-length study of the 1970 episode, particularly revealing in its treatment of the informal processes by which the regime was principally administered.

123. See Yakus v. United States, 321 U.S. 414 (1944); Bowles v. Willingham, 321 U.S. 503 (1944); Lichter v. United States, 334 U.S. 742 (1948); Amalgamated Meatcutters & Butcher Workmen v. Connally, 337 F.Supp. 737 (D. D.C. 1971); and the observations of K. C. Davis, 1 Administrative Law Treatise 207–08 (2d ed. 1978).

124. The creation of such systems has often, although not invariably, called forth an "emergency court of appeals," composed of judges on temporary assignment from the regular courts but enjoying a national jurisdiction over judicial proceedings arising from the regime, with the end of further encouraging national uniformity of administration and prompt resolution of disputes.

V

THE PROCEDURAL FORMS OF ADMINISTRATIVE ACTION

The wide variety of regulatory activity just described follows procedural forms created, in the first instance, by the concrete statutes, regulations, and/or body of custom attached to each activity. The enormous variation in that activity makes generalization difficult.[1] Generalization about administrative procedures nonetheless gains impetus from constitutional provisions enforcing fair procedures and from general-purpose administrative procedure statutes. More importantly, it arises from the imperatives of a system of law. If a generalized framework of analysis applicable to the behavior of the thousands of diverse instruments of government did not exist, surely judges and lawyers would be obliged to invent it to assure the possibility of control and to avoid unsustainable specialization. This chapter briefly describes this general framework, beginning with its sources. The reader must remain aware that the analytical elements of the framework are abstractions, whose application in any particular setting might be Procrustean but for the fact that it will in any event depend as well on the concrete circumstances of that setting and the actors involved. Only the federal system is described in any detail; a brief introduction to two principal sources of structure for state administrative law indicates how similar concepts apply in those proceedings.

---

1. This point was exquisitely illustrated by detailed empirical studies of existing federal administrative procedures, conducted preliminary to the drafting of the federal Administrative Procedure Act in the 1940s. These studies, published as Attorney General's Committee on Administrative Procedure, Final Report: Administrative Procedure in Government Agencies, Sen. Doc. 186, 76th Cong., 3d Sess. (1940) and Sen. Doc. 8, 77th Cong. 1st Sess. (1941), remain among the finest examples of empirical study of American administrative processes. They were produced by young scholars who became the core of American administrative law scholarship during the decades following, under the direction of Walter Gellhorn of Columbia University.

A. *The sources of structure for federal administrative procedure*

1. Constitution

The organization of the federal Constitution suggests three basic procedure-types within the framework of which procedural claims can be analyzed. Rule-making, investigation, and adjudication correspond, roughly, to the three characteristic "powers" of government in separation of powers analysis, legislative, executive, and judicial. Discussions of these paradigmatic administrative agency procedures frequently refer to them as "quasi-legislative," "quasi-judicial," and (much less frequently) "quasi-executive" action. As Justice Robert Jackson—who as Attorney General had supervised the committee whose work underlay the Administrative Procedure Act—once famously remarked:

> The mere retreat to the qualifying "quasi" is implicit with confession that all recognized classifications have broken down, and "quasi" is a smooth cover which we draw over our confusion as we might use a counterpane to cover a disordered bed.[2]

Recall that while the Constitution vests legislative power in Congress, executive power in the President, and judicial power in the Supreme Court, Congress regularly and validly provides that agencies may exercise all three of these "quasi" powers.[3]

As seen earlier, constitutionally based procedural forms constrain the procedures used for investigation and adjudication in some circumstances. Thus, the Fourth Amendment's prohibition of "unreasonable" searches and seizures,[4] the same Amendment's general requirement that the government obtain a warrant for a search, and the Fifth Amendment's protection against required self-incrimination,[5] each shape and perhaps limit the government's behavior in seeking cooperation with investigations. Where the government seeks immediately to deprive particular individuals of life, liberty, or property on bases related to their personal circumstances, or as a consequence of what is claimed to have been their past conduct, the Fifth Amendment's Due Process Clause

---

2. FTC v. Ruberoid Co., 343 U.S. 470, 487 (1952) (dissent).
3. See p. 20 above.
4. See p. 42 ff. above.
5. See p. 46 above.

requires some elements of an adjudicatory hearing (although the precise elements of that hearing will vary with the situation).[6]

For legislative activity the situation is different. While recognizing that the Constitution imposes *substantive* constraints on regulation—for example, that it cannot interfere with constitutional rights of free speech—the Supreme Court to date has generally refused to find that the Constitution requires statutorily authorized rulemaking to follow any particular procedure. Where government generates a rule of conduct for future application rather than determines its application to particular circumstances, the Court said about a century ago, citizens' "rights are protected in the only way that they can be in a complex society, by their [political] power, immediate or remote, over those who make the rule."[7] While this statement appeared long before the extensive rulemaking of the contemporary era, the development of extensive statutory procedures for rulemaking has tended to reinforce it; the alternative would be a kind of constitutional improvisation that, when lower federal courts have been tempted to try it, has drawn on familiar judicial models of adjudication rather than on legislative ones.[8] Perhaps in reaction, the Court has continued to adhere to a strong constitutional distinction between adjudication and rulemaking.[9]

This distinction emerged from two Supreme Court decisions warranting brief discussion here. *Londoner v. Denver*,[10] the first, concerned a special assessment or tax levied against properties benefitted by the paving of a Denver city road. A series of decisions had to be made by public authorities: to pave the road; to determine the total costs of doing so; to decide what proportion (if not all) should be recouped from the benefitted landowners; and, finally, to fix exactly the sum to be collected from each affected piece of property. Responsible authorities, ultimately the elected city council, had decided to pave the road; a board then determined the total cost and proposed an allocation

---

6. See p. 48 ff. above.

7. Bi-Metallic Investment Co. v. Colorado, 239 U.S. 441, 445 (1915).

8. See the discussion of the Court's decision in Vermont Yankee Nuclear Power Corp. v. NRDC, 435 US 519 (1978) below at p. 241.

9. Compare Minnesota State Board for Community Colleges v. Knight, 465 U.S. 271 (1984) with Burr v. New Rochelle Municipal Housing Authority, 479 F.2d 1165 (2d Cir. 1973). For a well-argued position that the notice-and-comment rulemaking procedures of federal administrative law should be thought constitutionally required where they are not statutorily provided for, see H. Linde, Due Process of Lawmaking, 55 Neb. L. Rev. 197 (1976).

10. 210 U.S. 373 (1908).

based on each piece of property's frontage on the road; landowners then had a chance to file written objections with the city council before it acted on the proposal. The Supreme Court found these procedures to have been constitutionally insufficient insofar as they purported to determine the final tax obligation of individual landowners. "[A]t some stage of the proceedings before the tax becomes irrevocably fixed," it wrote, "the taxpayer [must] have an opportunity to be heard," and "a hearing in its very essence demands that he who is entitled to it shall have the right to support his allegations by argument however brief and, if need be, by proof, however informal." The opportunity to file *written* objections did not suffice; some elements of orality were required.

Bi-Metallic Investment Co. v. Colorado,[11] the second case, concerned a general change in valuation for all properties in Denver, on the basis of which an annual real estate tax would be calculated. A state agency (responsible for assuring that all valuations in the state were comparable) had decided that the valuations of all Denver property should be increased by 40%, in order to equalize them with valuation levels then prevailing in the rest of the state. It was assumed that not even an opportunity to file written objections to this decision had been given. Here, however, there was no occasion to consider anyone's individual circumstances. The Court held: "Where a rule of conduct applies to more than a few people it is impractical that every one should have a direct voice in its adoption.... There must be a limit to individual argument... if government is to go on."[12] It distinguished its prior *Londoner* decision as one in which the contested matter for which hearing was constitutionally required had to be decided "in each case upon individual grounds."

The *Bi-Metallic* reference to "more than a few" suggests that the decisive question concerns the number of persons affected, but this is misleading. The *Londoner* result should be the same if 10,000 different parcels were to be assessed, "in each case upon individual grounds." The *Bi-Metallic* result, too, ought not vary if the change in general valuation affected all homeowners in a small village rather than a large city. The difference is between the application of a norm to particular circumstances (for which hearing will be required if life, liberty, or property is to be adversely affected), and the generation of the norm itself. However many adjudications there might have been in *Londoner*, each of them turned in some measure on the characteristics of a particular parcel of land; in *Bi-Metallic*, the reassessment was a more general result. Over the latter process, the Supreme Court remarked in the language

11. 239 U.S. 441 (1915).
12. Id. at 445.

already quoted and still influential, citizens' "rights are protected in the only way that they can be in a complex society, by their power, immediate or remote, over those who make the rule."[13]

While the Constitution suggests a tripartite division of procedure-types, and contains procedural specifications applicable to two of them, note that those specifications are not universally applicable within the relevant field. For instance, some inspections must be permitted irrespective whether a warrant has been obtained; and some information must be provided without regard to prior judicial enforcement of a subpoena. Similarly, much "adjudication" is not governed by the Due Process Clause, since it threatens no one with a deprivation of "life, liberty or property." Thus, an applicant for a license to build a nuclear power station faces "adjudication" of its qualifications, but denial of the license application is not a constitutional deprivation. And while revocation of such a license, once granted, would be a deprivation that entitled the license-holder to "due process," that conclusion would not assist a neighbor interested in having the facility closed. While procedural claims may also be important to the neighbor, she is not threatened with deprivation by official action. Any procedural issues about hearings for the applicant or the neighbor are strictly statutory in nature. As to rulemaking, as we have seen, the Constitution says nothing at all. Plainly one must look past the constitutional text for a general framework of analysis.

2. The Administrative Procedure Act

For the national government, much of the framework is provided by the Federal Administrative Procedure Act (APA). This statute was enacted without opposition in 1946, following almost a decade of study and debate whose principal themes, paradoxically, illustrated the great difficulty in formulating apt generalizations.[14] It was enacted as a statute of general application, so that a "subsequent statute [does not] supersede or modify [it], except to the extent

---

13. Ibid.

14. The APA is chiefly codified in §§551–59 and 701–706 of Title 5 of the United States Code. (Federal statutes are compiled into a single code of 50 titles plus appendices; the U.S.C. is not a code in the European sense, however.) A brief and informal account of the Act's genesis in detailed studies during 1940–41 of the actual functioning of forty different federal agencies is given in K.C. Davis and W. Gellhorn, Present at the Creation: Regulatory Reform Before 1946, 38 Admin. L. Rev. 507 (1986). In it, Gellhorn recounts the frustration of one member of the responsible committee that no generalizations seemed available; Gellhorn, seeking to mollify, suggested that perhaps open hearings should always be required—and soon discovered that for banking regulation, an open hearing would be the worst thing you could do for a bank under suspicion; if not insolvent when the hear-

that it does so expressly."[15] Reflecting its consensual origins, the APA is frequently interpreted with the aid of a manual published by the Office of the Attorney General *after* it had been enacted, as a means of educating government departments about the procedural obligations newly impressed upon them.[16] Such materials (produced post-enactment and by an interested "party") might ordinarily be viewed with skepticism. Here, however, it is understood that the Office had been an important participant in the drafting of the statute, and was likely playing the "honest broker" in relation to a statute which had won unanimous legislative support. The APA is nonetheless, and accurately, seen as the product of "long-continued and hard-fought contentions, and enacts a formula on which opposing social and political forces have come to rest."[17] This proposition, too, has influenced its interpretation.[18]

The statute applies to a broadly defined range of "agency action," addressing in separate chapters internal agency procedures and structural arrangements, and judicial review. This chapter discusses the provisions on internal procedures and structural arrangements, 5 U.S.C. §§551–59, leaving to later chapters more detailed consideration of open government laws like the Freedom of Information Act[19] and the provisions on judicial review, 5 U.S.C. §§701–706.[20] While its analysis follows the tripartite division of procedural function previously suggested, the APA generally appears to contemplate a world of only *two* procedural functions, adjudication and rulemaking. Its definitional provisions, 5 U.S.C. §551, characterize the products of "agency action" as either a "rule" or an "order." Rules are defined as agency statements of "general or particular[21] applicability and future effect designed to implement,

---

ings were announced, it soon would be. See also The Administrative Procedure Act, A Fortieth Anniversary Symposium, 72 Va. L. Rev. 215 (1986).

15. APA Section 12, 5 U.S.C. §559.

16. The Attorney General's Manual on the Administrative Procedure Act (1947).

17. Wong Yang Sung v. McGrath, 339 U.S. 33, 440 (1950), approvingly repeated in Vermont Yankee Nuclear Power Corp. v. NRDC, 435 U.S. 519 (1978). On the nature of those compromises, see M. Shapiro, APA: Past, Present, Future, 72 Va. L. Rev. 447 (1986); R. Rabin, Federal Regulation in Historical Perspective, 38 Stan. L. Rev. 1189 (1986).

18. Id.

19. See p. 276 ff. below.

20. Chapters VII and VIII, below.

21. The reference to a statement of "*particular applicability* and future effect" is troubling from the perspective of the constitutional distinction developed above, at p. 189. In practice, "rules" that can be described in this way, for example a rate schedule, are formulated through procedures whose formality matches those attached to licensing, compare pp. 207 and 224 below; in this way the widely criticized inelegance of the definition has few practical consequences.

interpret, or prescribe law or policy or describing [agency structural or procedural arrangements]," specifically including ratemaking. An "order," the end product of "adjudication," is defined as an agency's "final disposition...of... [any] matter other than rulemaking," specifically including licensing.

One reason for this failure to identify investigation as a separate procedure-type is that the Act's central concern is with formal proceedings, the sort that produce a "final disposition" adversely affecting a citizen subject to regulation. Detailed provision for preliminary stages could seem to invite premature disputes about secondary issues, risking substantial delay to the public's business. Conclusions reached in the course of an investigation do not mark "final disposition" in this sense. Correspondingly, such limited provisions as the APA does have about the internal procedures characteristic of investigations appear under the heading "ancillary matters." Of course, the decision either not to open an investigation or to close one is itself a final disposition, and a negative one from the perspective of citizens who might have hoped for enforcement activity to occur on their behalf. But it is doubtful the drafters were considering the matter from their perspective and, as will be seen, such decisions are subject at best to quite limited judicial review.[22] As a formal matter, such a decision, seen as final, falls by default into the APA's definition of "adjudication"; in this sense, that definition somewhat misleadingly includes decisions having executive as well as judicial character.

In its initial form, the APA embraced two matters other than adjudication and rulemaking. Section 3, 5 U.S.C. §552, contained limited provisions for publication of agency information; and Section 11, now distributed among several parts of 5 U.S.C.,[23] governed the selection and tenure of the hearing officers (since denominated administrative law judges) who would preside over on-the-record proceedings, affording them structural protections against political interference already noted,[24] and further considered below.[25]

Despite occasional congressional consideration of "reform," the basic provisions of the APA have been little changed since 1946. In addition to changes respecting administrative law judges, unnecessary to consider here, the prin-

---

22. See pp. 214 and 254 below.
23. E.g., 5 U.S.C. §§1305, 3105, 3344, 5372, 7521. Title 5 of the United States Code is denominated the Code of Government Organization and Employees; it is, however, integrated with the other titles of the Code. In American practice no particular significance is attached to the code title within which a provision appears; it serves principally as an organizational device.
24. See p. 137 above.
25. See p. 199 below.

cipal amendments to the Act itself have affected: section 552, whose now extensive provisions on publicity for government information include the Freedom of Information Act explored below;[26] Section 557, extending the Act's prohibitions on "ex parte contacts";[27] and sections 702 and 703, lowering the barriers to judicial review previously posed by considerations of sovereign immunity[28] and venue.[29] Not commonly thought of as part of the APA or affecting general administrative procedures, but embedded within its structure, are the Privacy Act, 5 U.S.C. §552a, and the Government in the Sunshine Act, 5 U.S.C. §552b, both taken up below.[30] Congress has also adopted, first provisionally and then permanently, statutes providing supplementary procedures of a more consensual character for both rulemaking, the Negotiated Rulemaking Act,[31] and adjudication.[32] Both are briefly discussed below.

3. Other statutes

A number of statutes in addition to the APA provide general structure for one or another aspect of administrative procedure or its control. The Judiciary Code, 28 U.S.C., and the judicial rules of procedure adopted pursuant to the code, contain many provisions governing the relationship of agencies to the courts: enforcement procedures for subpoenas; provisions respecting jurisdiction and venue for judicial review; the delegation of litigating responsibility to the Department of Justice and its officers.[33] Generalized agency information-gathering was placed under OMB supervision by the Paperwork Reduction Act of 1980.[34] The Federal Advisory Committee Act[35] creates a White House role, as well, in constraining agency use of private-public committees for consultation and policy development, and requires any such committees to work openly.

Probably the most important collection of "other statutes" bear on rulemaking and, together with presidential initiatives already seen,[36] have given

---

26. See p. 276 below.
27. See p. 204 below.
28. See p. 388 below.
29. See p. 299 below.
30. See pp. 284 and 287 below, respectively.
31. 5 U.S.C. §561 ff., see p. 252 below.
32. 5 U.S.C. §571 ff., see p. 218 below.
33. See p. 145, above.
34. See p. 265 below.
35. See p. 289 below.
36. See p. 103 above.

contemporary rulemaking on important subjects much greater procedural complexity than would appear from the APA alone.[37] For example, the National Environmental Policy Act first imposed a generally applicable analytic requirement at the initial stages of rulemaking for important government decisions predictably affecting the environment.[38] Now the Regulatory Flexibility Act does the same for rulemaking that might affect small businesses (the Act also establishes the semi-annual regulatory agenda).[39] The Unfunded Mandates Reform Act imposes a similar analytic requirement for matters that might affect states, localities, Indian tribes, or private business in a particularly important way;[40] and the Congressional Review Act requires all rules to be submitted to Congress for possible summary disapproval.[41] Other similar proposals, for example to put the presidential requirements for economic impact analysis into statutory form, have been entertained but not yet enacted. No sign can be seen to date of fresh legislative efforts to simplify or rationalize these measures, suggesting that legislators may perceive them more from a strategic point of view than a theoretical perspective. That is, they may be seen as useful devices for slowing the development of initiatives (e.g., on aspects of workplace safety) that the private sector might find expensive yet hard to oppose openly on the merits.

Finally, the statutes of individual agencies often contain procedural specifications beyond those to be found in the APA. This too, and perhaps for similar reasons, has particular bearing in the context of rulemaking. As that activity has emerged as central to health and safety regulation in particular, but also in other fields, Congress has repeatedly provided for procedures that differ (usually in the direction of somewhat greater formality) from those shortly to be described. To some extent, these formulations represent indirect means of accomplishing substantive ends. It is widely believed, for example, that Congress's 1975 requirement of increasing procedural rigor for rulemaking by the Federal Trade Commission reflected distaste for its aggressiveness as a regulator. Similarly, some think that the provision of somewhat formal rulemaking procedures for the new Occupational Health and Safety Administra-

---

37. See M. Seidenfeld, Rulemaking Table, 27 Fla. St. L. Rev. 533 (2000) ; Symposium, Recent Developments: Regulatory Reform & the 104th Congress. 49 Admin. L. Rev. 111 ff. (1997); P. Strauss, From Expertise to Politics: The Transformation of American Rulemaking, 31 Wake Forest L. Rev. 745 (1996).
38. See p. 101 above.
39. See p. 249 below.
40. See p. 249 below.
41. See p. 35 above.

tion was an accommodation to industry for a regulatory regime that could not be openly opposed. Yet these special formulations also embody procedural judgments that are widely regarded as both important and susceptible of general application. Section 307(d) of the Clean Air Act amendments of 1977, which sets rulemaking procedures for the Environmental Protection Agency under that statute, is perhaps the most important example. Its provisions governing the formation of the official record of rulemaking proceedings have since been widely accepted as apt for most such proceedings.[42]

4. Presidential (and other political) controls

One does not ordinarily think of political oversight as generating or even much shaping public procedures within the agencies. Yet the presidential initiatives on rulemaking discussed at some length above[43] must be seen in that light. They provide a structure for the period *preceding* public notice of a proposal for rulemaking on which many of the statutes just mentioned have built; and in fact most of the analyses and notices required by those statutes are performed within the initiatives' framework. The periodic regulatory agenda—identifying the significant regulatory actions each agency plans to pursue—provides early notice, and also an identified contact within the rulemaking agency, consequently expanding the range of participation. Regulatory impact analysis generates additional, and early, documents on which public comment is possible. As a general matter, internal bureaucratic structures have had to be reshaped to accommodate these requirements, resulting both in tighter coordination within the agency and greater prominence, generally, to the policy planning function.

The President, more aptly the executive establishment, could have an impact on public procedures through a general coordinative function—as also could Congress and its professional auditing arm, the GAO.[44] Take, for example, a matter of considerable contemporary interest, the extent to which and the manner in which agencies open their processes to observation and/or participation on the Internet. An extensive GAO report on the subject, circu-

---

42. In 1982, the United States Senate unanimously passed a bill that would have made these provisions generally applicable to all agency rulemaking, S. 1080, but for political reasons unconnected to this matter the bill was never brought to a vote in the House of Representatives. The presence of such a measure in subsequent reform proposals was, and in any future proposal would be, uncontroversial.

43. See p. 103 above.

44. See p. 85 above.

lated to all agencies as well as the Congress and interested public,[45] is likely to influence that development, if only because the agencies understand that continuing interest from Congress and the GAO is likely. The Senate's Government Affairs Committee is conducting ongoing inquiries into Internet uses that, whether or not they result in legislation, seem likely to result in consultative activities that will be productive of change.[46] Within the executive branch, President Clinton established a federal Council of Chief Information Officers[47] through which coordination could occur; in his administration, as well, the Vice President was a vigorous promoter of Internet development and other aspects of agency coordination.[48] From the late 1960s until 1995 a small government agency, the Administrative Conference of the United States, served as a meeting ground for government lawyers (and others) on issues of administrative procedure.[49]

5. The courts

Judicial decisions are also an important source of structure for agency procedures. The courts are highly influential in at least three ways: first, through their interpretation of relevant constitutional requirements, "due process" especially;[50] second, through their interpretation of statutory procedural requirements such as the APA; and third, through the atmosphere created by the manner in which they exercise their review functions. Thus, the Supreme Court's interpretation of the APA's provisions on party standing to seek judicial review in the early 1970s extended the range of agency behavior agency officials will foresee as subject to possible review (and therefore treat with care) by giving the words of those provisions a meaning that might not previously have been anticipated. In addition, by reflecting an expansive point of view about participation and its values, the interpretation encouraged agency officials to admit as participants in agency proceedings persons they might otherwise have excluded.[51] The following pages will reflect similar developments in many procedural settings, such as rulemaking and the standards for judi-

---

45. General Accounting Office, Federal Rulemaking: Agencies' Use of Information Technology to Facilitate Public Participation, B-284527 (June 30, 2000).

46. See http://www.senate.gov/~gov_affairs/egov/.

47. http://www.cio.gov/.

48. See p. 89 n. 61 above.

49. See p. 291 below.

50. See p. 48 above.

51. See pp. 212 (intervention) and 313 (standing) below.

cial review. From this perspective, it will be evident, the common law processes and expectations characteristic of American law generally, strongly influence the content of administrative law. It would be hazardous, indeed, to consult only the official text of the Constitution, statutes, and regulations as the relevant sources governing administrative procedures.

On the other hand, straightforward development of procedural requirements in the common law style, without grounding in statutory or constitutional text, is objectionable on several grounds. Agencies of necessity make their procedural choices prospectively, and with an eye to the general case; courts act long afterwards, and are inevitably influenced by the apparent success or failure of that choice in the particular (and perhaps unrepresentative) controversy put before them.[52] An agency having to anticipate such assessments of its choices would almost inevitably be moved defensively to choose more formal procedures—not being interested in having a desired end result defeated by disapproval of the means employed to reach it. Courts are not, in general, well-positioned as fact-gatherers to assess the general adequacy or not of procedural choices. Moreover, the procedures they know best, and thus are the most likely to use as normative bases for comparison and evaluation, are the judicial procedures of formal trial, not well suited to many administrative situations. Courts are particularly weak at understanding and appreciating the virtues of the institutional decisionmaking that underlies effective bureaucratic process. Finally, statutory provisions on procedure, like the APA, are formulations "upon which opposing social and political forces have come to rest," legislative judgments courts should honor. The consequence, the Supreme Court has emphatically held both for rulemaking[53] and for informal adjudication,[54] is that—absent Due Process Clause justification—judicial specification of agency procedures may not occur independently of statute.

As will amply appear in the following pages, this constraint, while not unimportant, is far from having prevented an accretion of procedural requirements through the ongoing judicial process of interpreting and applying requirements that can be associated with statutory text.

---

52. Recall the discussion of this problem in the due process context, where it is perhaps inevitable, and the Supreme Court's effort to find an evaluative method that would reduce its impact, p. 60 above.

53. Vermont Yankee Nuclear Power Corp. v. Natural Resources Defense Council, Inc., 435 U.S. 519 (1978). The case is discussed at p. 241 below.

54. Pension Benefit Guaranty Corp. v. LTV Corp., 496 US 633 (1990).

6. The agencies

Each agency itself, of course, enjoys substantial freedom to shape the procedures it employs. Detailed provisions will usually be found in an early chapter of the agency's volume of the Code of Federal Regulations—the official annual compendium of regulations adopted by federal agencies, that is organized along the lines of the United States Code,[55] and is several times as large. Any attorney involved with a particular agency or proceeding will pay careful attention to its procedural regulations and any internal interpretations they may have received.

B. *Adjudication*

As will shortly appear, the bulk of federal activity describable as adjudication occurs under procedures that are not generalized, but are particular to the agency involved. Nonetheless, it is sensible to begin with the provisions on adjudication of the federal Administrative Procedure Act.

As earlier noted, the APA defines "adjudication" very broadly, as the "agency process for the formulation of" any "final disposition, whether affirmative, negative, injunctive, or declaratory in form, of an agency in a matter other than rule making but including licensing."[56] Thus, the Secretary of Transportation's decision to award the state of Tennessee $12 million for the construction of a certain road would constitute "adjudication," as would the Nuclear Regulatory Commission's decision to assess a $2 million penalty against an electric utility for rule violations in running a nuclear power station, or the Federal Communication Commission's decision to grant Joseph Green the license he seeks to engage in amateur radio broadcasting. Yet these are evidently very different sorts of proceedings, not merely in their economic importance, but also in the moral claim they make for procedural specification. These differences are reflected in the APA's provisions about adjudication.

1. Formal agency adjudications

The APA section initially defining adjudicatory procedures, 5 U.S.C. §554, along with two others specifying procedures for formal hearings, 5 U.S.C. §§556–57, apply only to adjudications "required by statute to be determined

---

55. See n. 14 above.
56. 5 U.S.C. §551(6), (7).

on the record after opportunity for an agency hearing"—commonly referred to as formal, or on-the-record, agency adjudications. Six generally uncontroversial exceptions are stated.[57] If a hearing is not "required by statute to be determined on the record after opportunity for an agency hearing," the APA's procedural specifications for adjudication do not apply. What kinds of proceedings, then, does section 554 reach? The values seen to lie in the APA's adjudicatory procedures led one intermediate federal court to find that a statutory reference to a "hearing," without more, meant an "on the record" hearing under section 554, once it concluded that the issue to be heard had an importance warranting substantial procedural detail.[58] Another court facing the same issue, while agreeing that no particular, "magic" form of statutory words was required to invoke section 554, inferred from details of the procedural provisions in agencies' own statutes that the section did not apply; it reached this conclusion despite a statutory requirement to provide an adjudicatory "hearing" in a matter of some importance.[59] Both the first court's general disposition, and the second's willingness to take congressional specificity about procedure as an indicator, seem appropriate.[60] The Supreme Court has not spoken to this issue, although it has said in general terms that the APA's purpose to introduce greater uniformity of procedure and standardization of ad-

---

57. The exceptions concern matters for which judicial trial is nonetheless required or for which the agency is acting for a court, ordinary civil service matters, certification of worker representatives, matters implicating military or foreign affairs functions, and "proceedings in which decisions rest solely on inspections, tests, or elections." Thus, the grading or inspection of agricultural products, or flight certification of airline pilots, need not occur following APA procedures, even though one anticipates a certain formality in the performance of these functions. See p. 263 below.

58. Seacoast Anti-Pollution League v. Costle, 572 F.2d 872, cert. denied 439 U.S. 824 (1978); compare the quite different situation respecting formal rulemaking, p. 224 below.

59. Chemical Waste Management, Inc. v. EPA, 873 F.2d 1477 (D.C. Cir. 1989); St. Louis Fuel and Supply v. FERC, 890 F.2d 446 (D.C. Cir. 1989).

60. A separate question is presented by adjudications required to be determined on the record, not "by statute" but by the Constitution. An early decision held that the APA's provisions—notably the requirement that an administrative law judge be employed—applied in these cases as well. Wong Yang Sung v. McGrath, 339 U.S. 33 (1950). The specific holding was almost immediately reversed by Congress, see Marcello v. Bonds, 349 U.S. 302 (1955), and with the subsequent flowering of due process analysis the general holding appears to have been overruled sub silentio. As a matter of historical interpretation, it is doubtful that Congress, with its eye fixed on the large-scale proceedings suggested by statutory provisions for on-the-record hearings, wished to provide uniform procedures for all proceedings a court might later find required to be conducted "on the record" under the Due Process Clause.

ministrative practice argues rather strongly against permitting agencies to depart from its terms by regulatory implication.[61]

Section 554 and its two associated sections define on-the-record hearing procedures with some elaborateness. Even within this group of cases, however, they provide for procedural diversity reflecting different circumstances in which on-the-record hearings may occur. An applicant for a license, for example, will most often succeed or fail on the basis of technical criteria requiring evaluation by a specialized staff. This often presents issues of wide interest to its community; and any statutory provision for on-the-record determination of its application stands alone. The applicant in this case likely has no due process "entitlement" to such procedures.[62] Where a sanction is to be applied, on the other hand, the judgment to be reached may be less technical and more moral; and, in any event, the private party's procedural claims are rendered stronger by the threatened penalty and any "entitlement" it may enjoy to a continued relationship with the agency during good behavior. These variations are reflected in the procedural provisions made, resulting not in one model of "formal adjudication" but perhaps three.

a. Model on-the-record adjudication

The central model is described by sections 554, 556 and 557. The hearing is to be conducted under procedures that, although simplified, strongly resemble the formal, adversarial proceedings of American judicial trials.[63] The principal general departures one would notice are that the APA, in itself, makes no independent provision for pre-hearing practice, leaving this as a matter for each agency; modified rules of evidence prevail; and trial is always to the presiding administrative law judge—juries are unknown. Parties are to have full notice of the hearing, the authority under which it is to be held, and the issues to be resolved. Participants include the agency and others directly

---

61. Director, Office of Workers' Compensation Programs v. Greenwich Collieries, 512 U.S. 267 (1994).

62. As noted above, p. 59, the bearing of the Due Process clauses on applications has not yet been decided. The indications are that if required to be decided, it would be decided against the due process claim. At the least, the balancing approach of Matthews v. Eldridge, p. 60 above, would find less private interest in obtaining a license, than in maintaining one already granted and on the basis of which investments may have been made.

63. A notable exception occurs in the procedure employed in determining issues respecting welfare benefits, discussed at p. 169 above. While the hearing, when obtained, occurs before an administrative law judge, she directs the inquiry and marshals the data known to the government as well as decides the outcome; no separate attorney or representative for the government side appears.

affected, together with other interested persons as intervenors; intervention may be granted—indeed, has been required by judges to be granted in the interest of broader public representation[64]—much more freely than would be the case in judicial proceedings, "so far as the orderly conduct of public business permits."[65] The parties are entitled to appear by attorneys, and participate in all stages, before and during the hearing; they control the presentation of evidence, and are entitled "to conduct such cross-examination as may be required for a full and true disclosure of the facts." The agency may receive any matter as evidence,[66] excluding only the "irrelevant, immaterial, or unduly repetitious." The burden of proof, except as otherwise provided by statute, is placed in each case on the party seeking a given outcome.[67] An opportunity for settlement discussions must be provided when circumstances permit.

When a hearing is in fact held, its on-the-record character is protected in a variety of ways:

- The hearing must be held before the agency itself (that is, the agency head(s)), one or more members of a multi-member agency or, in the usual case, an administrative law judge.[68] The presiding officer's participation is subject to challenge in cases of personal bias or other disqualification, as a judge's would be.
- Communications with the presiding officer, as with a court, must be on the record, and agency personnel responsible for investigative or prosecuting functions are excluded from participation except as public witnesses or counsel. This aspect is further discussed in the immediately following text.

---

64. Issues respecting participation are developed at p. 212 ff. below.

65. 5 U.S.C. §555(b).

66. That is, administrative proceedings are not governed by the formal rules of evidence applicable in American courts. In particular, the American rule excluding indirect, or "hearsay," evidence from judicial trials does not apply. The rule is thought to protect lay juries from the problem of determining how much credence to give one person's account of what he claims to have heard another say; it tends to force testimony directly by witnesses to the underlying transaction. Agency hearings do not use lay fact-finders; and the nature of the disputes to be resolved often gives eye-witness testimony secondary importance. Even in court application, in fact, the hearsay rule has many exceptions.

67. See, Director, Office of Workers' Compensation Programs v. Greenwich Collieries, 512 U.S. 267 (1994). The case is remarkable for its treatment of the statutory issues involved. See P. Strauss, On Resegregating the Worlds of Statute and the Common Law, 1994 Sup. Ct. Rev. 427, and p. 349 below.

68. The special position of the administrative law judge is discussed at p. 139 above.

- The presiding officer is then the one who must draw up the official report of the proceeding, either an actual, initial decision or a formal recommendation to the agency how it ought to decide.
- The record on which decision is based and review will occur is limited to testimony and exhibits in the proceeding, together with any papers filed. If the agency takes "official notice" of facts that do not appear on the record—matters, for example, it believes it "knows" on the basis of acquired expertise—any party is entitled, "on timely request, to an opportunity to show the contrary."[69]

Where the hearing does not occur before the agency itself, and it almost never does, the presiding officer will render an initial decision or, very occasionally, recommend a decision to the agency which will itself make the initial decision. Whichever may occur, the parties are entitled to submit proposed findings and conclusions; and the maker of the decision or recommendation must rule in writing on these proposals, stating "findings and conclusions, and the reasons or basis therefor, on all material issues of fact, law, or discretion presented on the record."[70] This statement becomes a part of the record of the proceeding, a matter of some importance to later judicial review.[71] An initial decision will, unless reviewed by the agency or its delegate, become the decision of the agency itself.

Review within the agency is easily obtained, although from agency to agency there is a good deal of variation in the structures within which it occurs. In most of the traditional regulatory agencies, appeals are heard by the agency head or, for some multi-member commissions, by a panel of commissioners smaller than the whole body. In the larger agencies and cabinet de-

---

69. 5 U.S.C.§556(e). American courts, on occasion, have been fierce in protecting participants from agencies' claims of untested expert knowledge. Seacoast Anti-Pollution League v. Costle, 572 F.2d 872 (1st Cir. 1978), cert. denied 439 U.S. 824 (1978); Wirtz v. Baldor Electric Co., 337 F.2d 518 (D.C. Cir. 1963). Generally, however, the "material" facts subject to the rule of official notice are only those facts particular to the proceeding at issue, and not facts of a more general character—facts such as a legislature might be expected to find. Indeed, the corresponding rule of evidence in federal courts, Rule 201 of the Federal Rules of Evidence, governs only judicial notice of "adjudicative" facts, those bearing on the immediate parties to the dispute. For "legislative" facts such as a judge might wish to know to resolve a dispute of policy—for example, whether segregated education generally disadvantages black children—the Rule 201 in terms permits a judge to consult any source he regards as pertinent, independent of the parties.

70. 5 U.S.C. §557(c)(A).

71. See p. 345 below.

partments, however, provision is often made for a specialized appellate body to exercise some or all review functions—for example, the Judicial Officer of the Department of Agriculture; the Appeals Council of the Department of Health and Human Services, for welfare and disability assistance issues; and the Atomic Safety and Licensing Appeals Board of the Nuclear Regulatory Commission. The APA does not assure the members of these tribunals the protected status of ALJs,[72] although in practice they operate independently of political direction (as the on-the-record requirement itself virtually demands). Where such a body is provided for, the agency head may have reserved power to review its decisions in turn, but ordinarily does so only as a matter of discretion in important cases, on analogy to the Supreme Court's certiorari function.[73]

When agency review of the initial decision is sought, the parties are entitled to submit written briefs on any exceptions they have to the initial decision of the ALJ (or decision of an intermediate review tribunal). The agency then "has all the powers which it would have in making the initial decision"—that is, it may decide the case as if it had heard the witnesses itself rather than act as a reviewing tribunal.[74] Determinations made by the ALJ, even on so delicate an issue as witness credibility, are regarded merely as an element of the record on the basis of which the agency acts and against which the acceptability of its result will be measured. The agency must, however—like its ALJs—fully explain both its findings and its responses to party positions advanced to it, and in practice this restrains its freedom to reshape the ALJ's decision.

In at least two respects, these briefly recounted characteristics encounter significant difficulties arising out of real differences between agencies and courts: that agencies are institutions with particular, political tasks to achieve and a variety of means by which they seek to do so, where courts are generalist institutions outside politics and acting in only a single format. These problems can be illustrated by discussion of the confusing and hard-to-administer provisions on separation of functions in adjudication, and the practical difficulties respecting the requirement of findings.

As first enacted, the APA prohibited off-the-record communications between presiding officers and "a person or a party on a fact in issue," and this

---

72. Kalaris v. Donovan, 697 F.2d 376 (D.C. Cir. 1983), cert. den. 462 U.S. 1119 (1983).

73. That function is briefly discussed at p. 121 above.

74. On judicial review of an agency decision, then, the court is obliged to treat the agency's decision as having been made in direct relation to the facts rather than as the act of a reviewing tribunal; and this has occasional significance for outcome. See the general discussion of judicial review of agency factual determinations at p. 345 below.

remains the formula of section 554(d). A 1976 amendment, 5 U.S.C. §557(d), complicated matters by also forbidding off-the-record conversations between agency decisionmakers and persons "outside the agency" that were "relevant to the merits of the proceeding." This phrase, "relevant to the merits," has a much broader reach than "fact in issue," and the difference fits well the differences between courts and agencies as institutions. Agencies, unlike courts, may engage in rulemaking and other forms of policy formation as well as adjudication; numerous matters bearing on given policy issues may be pending before them at any moment. While an agency's ALJs can be and generally are shielded from these overlapping functions, its leadership cannot be. Proper institutional function requires that agency heads be able to deal with their staff on important policy matters as and in the contexts in which they arise. If the commissioners of the Nuclear Regulatory Commission felt inhibited about talking with their engineers about the general problems of detecting and controlling steam generator tube leaks, and the level of risk they presented to the public, because one of the dozens of cases in adjudication in the Commission's processes at the time presented issues about such leaks, we would understand that its effectiveness as an agency had been seriously compromised. The limitation of section 557(d)'s broader "relevant to the merits" formula to conversations with persons "outside the agency" can generally be understood in this light. Staff-decisionmaker conversations are limited only in respect of "a fact in issue," but outsiders—even the President[75]—are more stringently constrained.

In specific contexts, however, this apparently straightforward distinction breaks down. On the one hand, in proceedings before an ALJ rather than the politically responsible agency head, there is no particular need for it. The ALJ does not make rules or supervise enforcement policy. Most American lawyers would fervently condemn any private consultation between an ALJ and agency personnel on questions of policy or interpretation that were "relevant to the merits of the proceeding" but did not concern "a fact in issue." The writer is not aware of any practice of surreptitious conversation by agency personnel attempting directly to exploit this apparent distinction between fact-based and policy-based internal conversations.[76] The distinction recognizes agencies' need

---

75. Recall the Portland Audubon case, p. 93 above.

76. One reported case disclosed an accidental conversation among an agency head and two staff members about a general question of law that bore on an important matter then pending before the agency in an on-the-record proceeding, where one staff member represented the agency's staff—its prosecutors, one could say—and the other the office that might be responsible for writing any eventual opinion for the agency. The angry reaction

for protection against secondary disputes over their on-going pursuit of policy ends, given the frequency with which innocent internal conversations about those ends may occur that appear to bear on on-the-record agency business for which one or another of the conversers is responsible.

On the other hand, even for outsiders, it may be necessary to understand "relevant to the merits of the proceeding" somewhat restrictively. If an agency has a rulemaking or some question of enforcement policy to which informal public response is appropriate pending at the same time as an on-the-record proceeding—a frequent enough occurrence—then members of the public, even those interested in both proceedings, should be able to participate in discussions about the first (which need not be "on the record") without having to fear the sanctions that could be imposed for a forbidden conversation in the second.[77] Here the risk of manipulative behavior for advantage may be somewhat greater, yet it seems hard to treat a communication as violating section 557(d) just because it *is* "relevant to," without some indication that it was also earmarked for or intended to influence, "the merits" of an on-the-record proceeding. Aware of a possible problem, an agency's best response may be simply to broadcast the possibly offending communication to all participants in the on-the-record proceeding, giving them an opportunity to respond.

The Act's requirements on findings also need to be understood in light of the differences between agencies and courts. Of course, even in reference to judicial function, they have some of the faults of formula. No court would take seriously an obligation to respond to every contention, however trivial, the parties may throw up in a proceeding. Even in appellate cases, the federal courts dispose of the great bulk of their business without published opinions; in certain types of cases, judicial reason-giving is at best perfunctory. But the agency context presents additional and important issues of role and responsibility. While politically responsible officials decide matters, other members of agency staff are responsible for defending these decisions in court. Courts themselves, in reviewing agency action, must be careful not to assume policy responsibilities that are properly the agency's. Thus, by fixing the basis for the agency's action, an agency's findings limit the arguments that agency lawyers

---

of the court to what was concededly an accidental, not contrived, conversation reflects the prevailing professional view. Professional Air Traffic Controllers' Org. v. FLRA, 685 F.2d 547 (D.C. Cir. 1982).

77. These sanctions can be severe. Thus, 5 U.S.C. §557(d) permits the agency, if "consistent with the interests of justice" to "consider a violation...sufficient grounds for a decision adverse to a party" who has "knowingly" committed or caused such a violation.

(or others) can make to support the agency's result on judicial review. Lawyers and reviewing courts may use only the reasons the agency assigns publicly for its decision, not others that might be imagined. This gives some assurance that those ostensibly responsible for a decision will actually be responsible for it.[78] At the same time, findings protect the agency from judicial second-guessing, by focusing attention on its reasoning and responsibility, rather than the outcome as such. A court cannot substitute its own sense of proper policy for the agency's, but must either accept the agency's explanation; reject it as insufficient to establish legality; or, if it finds flaws that are not necessarily fatal to the result the agency has chosen, return the matter to the agency for renewed consideration.

b. License applications

If one considers the paradigmatic civil action arising in court, its characteristics (in the American context at least) might be described in these terms:

- It is adversarial. Two opposed sides present arguments and evidence before an authority whose responsibility is to resolve the case neutrally,

---

78. The point is stated guardedly, because the opinions are themselves the product of a bureaucratic staff, which the ostensibly responsible but busy agency heads may have little real time to consider. An extreme example of this is related by M. Derthick and P. Quirk, Why the Regulators Chose to Deregulate, as in R. Noll, ed., Regulatory Policy and the Social Sciences 215 (University of California 1986), as a partial explanation of the dissatisfaction that led to disestablishment of the Civil Aeronautics Board (CAB):

> Late in 1969, [a CAB attorney] had been assigned to write the board's decision [choosing the recipient of an airline route among several competitors] with no instructions whatever except the name of the winning airline.... [I]t was up to him to contrive the board's reasons for the decision. And after he was done, the board did not change a word of what he had written. It came to him as vivid proof of what many in the CAB knew or sensed: the board's alleged rationales for route awards were not the real rationales, but were artifices designed to give the gloss of legal reasoning to awards made privately by the board on other grounds. Not that there was anything corrupt about these other grounds.... Roughly, the board acted in a commonsensical way to make sure that every carrier got a reasonable share of new route authority and that none was exposed to financial hazard. Not everyone was disillusioned...[; s]ome very intelligent people found the exercise to be fun "much in the way that doing crossword puzzles is fun."

One need not believe that other boards operate in quite the same way; but suspicions about the reality of a board's professed reasons have underlain a good deal of judicial worrying about political controls. On the question of judicial inquiry into possible differences between the reasons an agency opinion gives, and the reasons it might actually have had, see p. 380 below.

in terms of the facts presented and the law. Litigation begins with commitments on each side to a desired outcome, antithetical to each other. Frequently, the legal issues reflect contentions about the morality of conduct.

- It is private. Although questions of general interest to the public may be presented, ordinarily those questions are at best secondary to the immediate dispute, and resolution of the dispute is left to the parties' initiative. Broad community interests rarely if ever have party status.
- To the extent facts are in issue, they chiefly concern historical particulars of the relationship between the parties, both most accessible to and most relevant for them.

The procedural norms of American trials reflect these paradigms. While one can without difficulty imagine judicial litigation that in one way or another departs from these characteristics, it would be hard to imagine judicial litigation that systematically departs from them.

One form of agency adjudication often required to be decided on-the-record, the processing of applications (most importantly for licenses), does systematically depart from all three of these characteristics. The staff of agencies responsible for, say, licensing, are not committed to opposing applications and rarely do so on grounds implicating moral issues. Decision on an application may have a high public policy content, reflected not only in its assignment to an agency for decision but also in the expectation that broad community-based interests may participate in any hearing. Finally, the most important facts in issue are often general questions of some technological complexity—for example, what will be the impact of "thermal shock" on the larvae of soft-shelled clams near a power plant's intended cooling facilities—rather than historical particulars.[79] These departures are recognized in "exceptions" to the general provisions of sections 554, 556 and 557: 1) permitting agencies to require applicants for licenses, money or benefits (as well as participants in formal rulemaking)[80] to proceed on the basis of written submissions, unless they can specifically show that the denial of oral trial-like hearings would be prejudicial;[81] 2) less rigorously requiring separation of functions constraints, so that ALJs or agency members may more freely consult off

---

79. See Seacoast Anti-Pollution League v. Costle, n. 69 above.
80. See p. 224 below.
81. 5 U.S.C. §556(d).

the record with agency staff;[82] and 3) permitting responsible members of staff, rather than a presiding ALJ, to draw up the recommended decision.[83]

The relative freedom thus provided is readily enough understood. Licensing can be highly technical in character, putting a premium on the fullest participation of expert staff; few agencies have the richness of resources to permit hiring duplicate staffs (even if it were wise)—one for day-to-day functions, and the other to advise decisionmakers. At the same time, staff participation in this activity often lacks the qualities of moral commitment, of side-taking, that recurrently characterize ordinary litigation—especially, prosecution and its administrative analogs. Indeed, from the perspective of the license applicant and the agency staff, the hearing stage, if ever reached, may seem a formality. Much can be accomplished in negotiations between an applicant and those within the agency who are most expert in the criteria to be satisfied, that would be clumsy to do in a formal setting. The license applicant, while having the greatest concrete interest in the outcome of the proceedings, may seem for this reason to have a comparatively low interest in formality.

The situation is different when licensing is opposed by persons outside the agency, who lack any continuing or detailed relationship with it, and who may tend to distrust its performance of public function. These opponents may fear that agency staff will have taken sides with the applicant and against their interest. For them, the formality and forced openness and objectivity of a trial-like process is central. Where such opposition arises, the statutory possibilities of diminished formality are in fact rarely availed of. It is not that this injection of public concern gives the proceeding more of the standard characteristics of a trial. A great American legal philosopher, Lon Fuller, once contrasted the kind of disputes ordinarily submitted to trial, which he called "bipolar," with those more appropriate for political resolution, which he called "polycentric," precisely on the basis of the relative privacy and focus of the first.[84] The participation of a wide spectrum of community interests in licensing proceedings for, say, a nuclear power plant, reflects the polycentricity of the issues more than their appropriateness for the particular dispute-resolving modalities of "trial." Procedure here is more a means of achieving "voice" than an apt reflection of the trial analogy. Nonetheless, lawyerly, ju-

---

82. 5 U.S.C. §554(d)(A).

83. 5 U.S.C. §557(b)(1).

84. See L. Fuller, The Forms and Limits of Adjudication, 92 Harv. L. Rev. 353, 394–405 (1978).

dicial, and even administrative attitudes about the importance of oral proceedings and separated functions are so strong that the APA's special provisions for licensing are, in effect, disbelieved.[85]

c. License sanctions

The third of the APA's adjudicatory models for on-the-record hearings applies to proceedings for the withdrawal, suspension, revocation or annulment of a license already obtained. These are proceedings one would ordinarily expect to be "bi-polar," not "polycentric," in character. Often punitive in character, they produce a setting in which both the license-holder's stakes and the risks of prosecutorial commitment on the part of agency staff are especially high. Special written notice "of the facts or conduct which may warrant the action" is required and, unless willfulness is present or public protection requires otherwise, the licensee must be given an "opportunity to demonstrate or achieve compliance with all lawful requirements."[86] This is less a variation of procedure than of substance, underscoring the economic importance of licenses already granted to their holders by protecting tenure from too-casual interference by agency staff. As the judgment it reflects appears not to be a controversial one, these formal requirements have not often been the subject of litigation. Yet the contrast with the lesser formality provided for initial licensing is revealing and instructive.

2. Informal agency adjudications

Perhaps the most striking aspect of the APA's provisions on adjudication is their basic failure to specify procedures for the great bulk of administrative adjudications, those for which an on-the-record hearing is not statutorily required. These informal adjudications, as we may call them, constitute perhaps 95% of government actions meeting the statutory definition of "adjudication." So far as the APA is concerned, since sections 554, 556 and 557 do not apply, only 5 U.S.C. §555(e) is of possible relevance. That section requires prompt notice of the denial of any written application, petition or other request "made in connection with any agency proceeding…accompanied by a brief statement of the grounds for denial." If the results of informal adjudications constitute

---

85. See American Telephone and Telegraph Co., 60 F.C.C. 1 (1976); Seacoast Anti-Pollution League v. Costle, 572 F. 2d 872 (1st Cir. 1978).
86. 5 U.S.C. §558(c).

final agency action, as they well may, the judicial review provisions of the APA apply; and these are discussed below in Chapters VII and VIII.

The absence of a *general* statutory procedure in the APA leaves open the possibilities that the Due Process Clause of the Constitution[87] or some particular statute will be found to require certain procedures. One consequence of the due process explosion was to make the claim for procedural specification substantial in many informal adjudication contexts. In 1976, not long after the Supreme Court's decision in *Goldberg v. Kelly*,[88] Professor Paul Verkuil published a study of informal adjudication procedures used to reach final conclusions in forty-two different federal programs.[89] Many, if not all, of these programs could deprive persons of "entitlements" and therefore invoke the federal Due Process Clause. Looked at through the lens of Judge Friendly's ten possible procedural elements of a fair hearing,[90] these programs presented a picture of remarkable diversity. Only two programs (both grant programs in the welfare field) provided all ten elements; two others provided none. Only three of the ten elements—notice, a statement of reasons, and impartial decisionmaker—were assured by substantially all programs; twenty-seven of the forty-two programs provided four[91] or fewer of the elements and only nine provided as many as eight of them.

This variety, like the overall failure of procedural specification for informal adjudication in the APA, reflects the difficulty one faces in generalizing about procedures once one has left behind the realm of decisions so important and structured that high formality is called for. Recall that, even in this familiar adjudicatory context, the Supreme Court has held with emphatic force that the courts may not impose their own views of proper procedure; requirements can be found only in the Due Process clauses or particular statutes.[92] That the APA defines "adjudication" as a catch-all category, covering whatever final agency action is not "rulemaking," only underscores the enormous difficulty the drafters would have faced in devising and stating general procedural pro-

---

87. See p. 48 above.

88. Discussed at p. 53 above.

89. A Study of Informal Adjudication Procedures, 43 U. Chi. L. Rev. 739 (1976). The study included 17 grant programs (e.g., food stamps), 12 licensing programs (e.g., drug approvals), 5 inspection programs (e.g., meat grading), 6 planning programs (e.g., urban development), and 2 characterized as "other."

90. See p. 64 above.

91. The fourth most common element, recognized in just half the programs, was an opportunity for oral presentation of argument.

92. See p. 198 above.

visions to govern matters that, in 1946, made no substantial claim for procedural detail. Subsequently, the Model State Administrative Procedure Act[93] defined four models of adjudication procedure, "formal," "conference," "emergency," and "summary." Yet that Act's definition of "order," the end product of an adjudication, is not a catch-all as it is in the APA. It is limited to actions of "particular applicability" determining the legal interests of specific persons. Thus it would not reach the Secretary of Transportation's decision to grant Tennessee $12 million towards the construction of a new segment of highway, based on his finding that requisite federal standards for this financing had been satisfied, or the Secretary of Labor's decision not to commence an enforcement action against a labor union despite a complaint by one of its members that it had violated governing law. Both are undoubtedly informal adjudications under the APA.

3. Participation claims of the protected public

Aside from the continuing effort to give content to the Due Process clauses,[94] probably the most interesting American developments concerning agency adjudication have to do with the participation of members of the public or groups on whose behalf regulation is supposed to occur. Private activities on behalf of law enforcement can occur in two different ways. The first is to authorize citizens themselves to use the courts for direct private enforcement of regulatory provisions against businesses that might also be (but have not been) proceeded against by an agency for their alleged violations. Such authority was early conferred by American anti-trust statutes, which enabled citizens to seek judicial redress of harm they personally suffered; similar authority is created under some civil rights statutes. It can readily be viewed as statutory creation of a new form of tort remedy for private wrongs.[95] In the field of environmental protection, some statutes have authorized the same mechanism to vindicate the rights of the community at large; citizens may sue

---

93. See p. 269 below.

94. See p. 48 above.

95. These causes of action are conferred by statute. Although in limited settings the Supreme Court has sometimes recognized the appropriateness of *inferring* private rights of action for regulatory violations where a statute has not directly provided for doing so—notably, under some civil rights laws and statutes regulating trader behavior in security and commodity markets—today's Court generally discourages this practice. This development is discussed at p. 398 ff. below. Tort remedies against the government itself, or against public servants, raise separate questions dealt with in Chapter IX.

to redress alleged regulatory violations, independent of personal harm as such, when the agency has not acted despite notice of the allegedly illegal activity.[96] These statutes may provide incentives, such as compensation for attorney's fees and other costs, for successful plaintiffs.

The second means by which members of the public or groups participate in law enforcement is indirect, seeking a remedy either against the agency, in an action to force desired agency behavior, or within it, as a party in its proceedings. Authority to initiate or participate in agency proceedings may have its source in explicit statutory language. Statutes authorizing economic rate regulation, for example, commonly authorize competitors to begin proceedings to have a rate their competitor charges or proposes declared unlawful;[97] the Atomic Energy Act grants party status to citizens of the area where a nuclear power reactor proposed for licensing is to be located. The more interesting problems, however, have arisen where the statute appears to leave the agency in control over the institution or conduct of proceedings, and outsiders have sought nonetheless to force its hand.

a. Private actions requiring initiation of proceedings

Two cases illustrate the problems involved in forcing an agency to conduct proceedings it had not chosen to initiate. In the first, a union member lost a federally supervised election under circumstances he believed should have led the Department of Labor, responsible for supervising the election, to set it aside.[98] When he complained to the Secretary of Labor, the Secretary investigated and indicated, without stating his reasons, that he would not proceed; the statute—doubtless to protect the winners of such elections from frivolous or harassing actions—was explicit that the Secretary's enforcement authority was exclusive. The union member nonetheless persuaded the courts to require the Secretary to reconsider his decision and to indicate his reasons for declin-

---

96. See Friends of the Earth v. Laidlaw, 528 U.S. 167 (2000); such suits require "standing" to sue, see p. 313 ff. below, but this is a matter largely within Congress's power to create. Steel Co. v. Citizens for a Better Environment, 523 U.S. 83 (1998); compare Lujan v. Defenders of Wildlife, 504 U.S. 555 (1992). An enthusiastic treatment of the subject, including practical guidance for persons wishing to bring such actions, appears in J. Miller, Environmental Law Institute: Private Enforcement of Federal Pollution Control Laws (Wiley 1987); compare J. Blanch, Citizen Suits and Qui Tam Actions: Private Enforcement of Public Policy (National Legal Center for the Public Interest 1996).

97. See L. Noah, Sham Petitioning as a Threat to the Integrity of the Regulatory Process, 74 N.C. L. Rev. 1 (1995).

98. Dunlop v. Bachowski, 421 U.S. 560 (1975).

ing to proceed. The Court recognized the risk that permitting such suits would interfere with the executive's ability to deploy its limited resources in accordance with public, rather than private, priorities. Nonetheless, it found that the statute in question was unusually explicit in detailing the factors the Secretary was to consider in deciding whether or not to proceed, and "demonstrate[d] a deep concern with the interest of individual union members, as well as the general public, in the integrity of union elections." A statement of reasons would not only satisfy that concern, but also permit a court to assure that the relevant factors (and only the relevant factors) had been considered by the Secretary in reaching his judgment.

The second case, *Heckler v. Chaney*,[99] arose in unusual facts: prisoners sentenced to be executed by an injection of lethal drugs had petitioned the federal Food and Drug Administration to act against this unapproved use of the drugs, and the FDA had refused to act, indicating its reasons. All nine Justices agreed that the agency's decision should not be disturbed, but only one reached that conclusion on the ground that the decision had been properly justified. For the others, the decisive consideration was that "an agency's decision not to prosecute or enforce...is a decision generally committed to an agency's absolute discretion."[100] The union election case was distinguished on the ground that the statute there indicated a purpose to circumscribe the agency's exercise of enforcement power; that indication was missing in the present case, which was therefore to be governed by a strong presumption of unreviewability.[101] The one Justice who reached the merits rejected the majority's presumption that administrative (as distinct from prosecutorial)[102] decisions not to act are unreviewable. That conclusion, he reasoned, was inconsistent with "a firmly entrenched body of lower court case law that holds reviewable various agency refusals to act....The problem of agency refusal to act is one of the pressing problems of the modern administrative state, given the enormous powers, for both good and ill, that agency inaction, like agency action, holds over citizens."[103]

---

99. 470 U.S. 821 (1985).

100. It thus invoked the stronger idea of *DISCRETION!* suggested at p. 91 above.

101. See the discussion at p. 310 ff. below.

102. The European reader may be surprised to learn that American (criminal) prosecutors enjoy an essentially unchecked discretion whether or not to enforce the criminal laws in particular cases. It is from the premise of that unreviewable discretion that the American analysis proceeds.

103. Justice Thurgood Marshall, the author of this opinion, cited 24 lower court cases decided between 1970 and 1983 in support of his proposition, and relied heavily on a well-regarded scholarly analysis of the general problem: R. Stewart and C. Sunstein, Public Pro-

Both because the Administrative Procedure Act specifically makes agency inaction reviewable as "agency action," and because more appealing facts may often encourage courts to find that the language or history of a specific statute overcomes any general "presumption of unreviewability" of inaction,[104] one need not have expected the later decision invariably to control, but exceptions have been relatively few.[105] The decision reflected a changing mood, of which there have been some other indications,[106] away from litigation as a means for shaping public interest issues. A quarter-century ago, observing cases more like the first than the second of the two just summarized, a leading scholar wrote that judges were beginning "to assume the ultimate protection of the collective social interests which administrative schemes were designed to secure."[107] Skepticism about the wisdom of that course of action underlies the current withdrawal.

b. Compulsory private intervention in agency proceedings

A somewhat different question is presented when an agency has in fact initiated a proceeding, and the issue is whether and to what extent it is required to recognize as a participant in that proceeding a private litigant asserting some interest in the outcome, who has no clear statutory right of intervention. The APA itself encourages agencies to permit "interested persons" to ap-

---

grams and Private Rights, 95 Harv. L. Rev. 1195 (1982). The author of the majority opinion, Justice Rehnquist, had been the sole dissenter from the union election case; a former Assistant Attorney General for the Office of Legal Counsel, the Department of Justice office that serves institutionally as the President's lawyer, he has often supported claims of executive authority.

104. Among the examples cited by Justice Marshall: litigation to force the Department of Housing and Urban Development to enforce the required removal of lead-based paints (poisonous to small children) from federally-supported housing; to require the Environmental Protection Agency to take action against a pesticide, DDT, with demonstrated (and extraordinary) adverse ecological effects; and to require the Department of Health, Education and Welfare to enforce certain provisions of the civil rights laws.

105. E.g., N.Y. Employees' Retirement System v. SEC, 45 F.3d 7 (2d Cir. 1995); see A. Bhagwat, Three-Branch Monte, 72 Notre Dame L. Rev. 157 (1996).

106. Compare the discussion of standing doctrine, at p. 313 ff. below. It is important to understand, however, that the right to seek judicial review—standing—rests on different questions, so that it does not follow from the proposition that one could seek review of a decision once made, that one has a right to participate in the agency proceedings that lead to it. Still-useful discussion appears in D. Shapiro, Some Thoughts on Intervention Before Courts, Agencies, and Arbitrators, 81 Harv. L. Rev. 721 (1968).

107. R. Stewart, The Reformation of American Administrative Law, 88 Harv. L. Rev. 1669, 1756 (1975).

pear "so far as the orderly conduct of public business permits." This formulation suggests the agency will be the principal determiner of the issue. The question here is whether such participation can be forced on an unwilling agency. During the same period as brought about the revolution in due process law, the courts often overrode agency judgments limiting participation in order to facilitate representation of a wider range of interests in agency proceedings. The cases that led to the scholarly observation just quoted included a substantial number of cases having this character.

An influential, early such decision arose in a proceeding before the Federal Communications Commission to renew the license of a southern radio station that allegedly failed to serve the interests of African-American members of its community. The FCC limited the participation of a church group claiming to be representative of these radio listeners. It permitted the group to submit views, but did not admit it as a party. Thus, the group lacked the right to adduce evidence, to examine witnesses, and otherwise to control the course of the proceedings. The Commission's evident concern was that "the orderly conduct of public business" would be threatened by according that much control over the proceeding to an outside group interested in issues the Commission itself was responsible to protect. The reviewing court of appeals required that the listener group be admitted to formal party status, interjecting its own sense of what the public interest called for:

> The theory that the Commission can always effectively represent the listener interests in a renewal proceeding without the aid and participation of legitimate listener representatives fulfilling the role of private attorneys general is one of those assumptions we collectively try to work with as long as they are reasonably adequate. When it becomes clear, as it does to us now, that it is no longer a valid assumption which stands up under the realities of actual experience, neither we nor the Commission can continue to rely on it.[108]

Strikingly, the author of this opinion was no radical, but Judge Warren E. Burger, who was shortly to become Chief Justice of the United States Supreme Court on the basis of his strong reputation as a cautious and conservative judge.

Underlying this decision, others like it,[109] and a tremendous volume of "public interest" litigation and generally approving literature, was a belief, as one scholar characterized it, that expanded participation in agency proceedings would

---

108. Office of Communication of the United Church of Christ v. FCC, 359 F.2d 994 (D.C. Cir. 1966).

109. E.g., National Welfare Rights Organization v. Finch, 429 F.2d 725 (D.C. Cir. 1970).

be an effective and workable means of assuring improved agency decisions. Advocates of extended access believe that an enlarged system
of formal proceedings can, by securing adequate consideration of the
interests of all affected persons, yield outcomes that better serve society as a whole....Such participation...is valuable in itself because
it gives citizens a sense of involvement in the process of government,
and increases confidence in the fairness of government decisions....
The judges' incipient transformation of administrative law into a
scheme of interest representation is responding to powerful needs that
have been neglected by other branches of government.[110]

As American Presidents, in particular, have asserted stronger political controls
over regulatory action in recent years, however, and as national politics have
become more skeptical about regulation as a whole, American judges have
sounded less confident about the value of regarding agency adjudication (and
particularly the judicial role in overseeing it) through this political lens. As
early as 1984, a unanimous opinion for the Court (including Chief Justice
Burger) seemed to go out of its way to dampen participatory claims. Discussing consumer participation in the Department of Agriculture's regulation
of milk marketing, the Court noted that while the Act in question provided
explicitly for the participation of milk handlers and producers in a "complex
scheme" of regulation, it did not mention consumers. "[T]he omission of such
a provision is sufficient reason to believe that Congress intended to foreclose
consumer participation in the regulatory process."[111] The consumers group
had not sought to participate in the administrative proceeding,[112] rendering
this passage simple dictum; yet the attitude it suggests is quite different from
that which informed the earlier cases. In a number of subsequent opinions,
the Supreme Court has referred explicitly to the political responsibilities of
Congress and the President, in contrast to the courts.[113]

While the idea of public interest representation will not disappear from the
American lexicon—in part, because so many statutes are explicit in permitting it—the courts seem less likely to be its aggressive promoters. Consider,
for example, a 1999 decision of the D.C. Circuit, the court whose opinion in

---

110. R. Stewart, n. 107 above, 1760–62.

111. Block v. Community Nutrition Institute, 467 U.S. 340, 346–47 (1984).

112. The case involved only the question of their standing to obtain review of the outcome, see p. 309 below.

113. E.g., Chevron, U.S.A., Inc. v. Natural Resources Defense Council, Inc. 467 U.S.
837 (1984) quoted at p. 272 below; Lujan v. Defenders of Wildlife, 504 U.S. 555 (1992).

the FCC case just quoted helped to open these doors.[114] As already mentioned, the Nuclear Regulatory Commission's statute commands it to admit as party to its proceedings "any person whose interest may be affected by the proceeding." The Commission had before it applications for licenses, that a competitor wished to oppose; it refused the competitor permission to intervene. It interpreted the statutory reference to "interest" to mean a direct effect, such as a neighbor to the facility sought to be licensed might experience, and not the possible competitive disadvantage to the competitor of having to face economic competition for business. "Interest" usually is taken as a word of broad and not technical signification in administrative procedural statutes. The APA's requirement that agencies give "interested persons" an opportunity to comment in rulemaking, for example, is understood to mean anyone who wants to comment must be given that opportunity. The general practice in nuclear licensing, given public sensitivity to its risks, has been to extend hearing rights broadly. The court nonetheless upheld the Commission's narrower interpretation, chiefly employing reasoning about agency interpretive authority we will examine at another place.[115] It seemed to go out of its way, however, to call attention to the obstructive activities that recognizing a competitor's intervention rights might permit and, further, to cast doubt on the continued validity of the FCC case and others that had built on it. While the facts of this case were, perhaps, especially strong for the Commission's action, one is left with the impression that this court is willing to accord agencies considerably greater authority to control intervention in their proceedings than Judge Burger's FCC opinion or others of the years immediately following would have led one to believe they could safely exercise.

4. Alternative dispute resolution

In 1990, Congress enacted provisions for alternative dispute resolution and regulatory negotiation—both initially provided to expire in 1995, but subsequently converted into permanent regimes. The provisions on regulatory negotiation have been the more prominent in discussions of administrative procedure, and are discussed in connection with rulemaking below.[116] The Act, 5 U.S.C. §571 ff., defines alternative dispute resolution procedures, consistently with general usage, to include arbitration, conciliation, facilitation, mediation, negotiation, and like approaches, conducted under extensive provisions

---

114. Envirocare of Utah v. NRC, 194 F.3d 72 (D.C. Cir. 1999).
115. See the discussion of Chevron , U.S.A., Inc. v. NRDC at p. 368 below.
116. See p. 252 below.

concerning confidentiality among specified parties for the resolution of a dispute,[117] and with the assistance of a neutral party serving at the participants' will.[118] It serves principally to establish a framework whose use depends on party consent. Agencies are authorized to use its procedures, with such consent, unless external considerations—such as the need to establish or maintain general policy, or the importance of the proceedings to non-parties— make a simple consensual and private resolution between the participants inappropriate.[119] Presidents George Bush and Clinton each issued executive orders encouraging its use.[120]

Perhaps as an inevitable consequence of the requirement that alternative dispute resolution *not* be used in matters of policy importance or general interest, the literature and cases reveal little about its use specifically in an administrative context. One knows that it is widely used in contract disputes, both those involving labor relations, where the National Mediation Board exists to facilitate it in railroad and aviation disputes,[121] and those involving government purchases.[122] Some agencies—the Equal Employment Opportunities Commission generally, or the Department of Justice in connection with its responsibilities under the Americans with Disabilities Act—use it extensively in an enforcement context.[123] A student survey of ADR generally provides useful entry into the literature.[124]

C. *Rulemaking*

Rulemaking, like adjudication, embraces a broad range of possibilities. Rulemaking ranges from the setting of rates for public utilities, to the creation

---

117. 5 U.S.C. §573.

118. 5 U.S.C. §574.

119. 5 U.S.C. §572; compare O. Fiss, Against Settlement, 93 Yale L. J. 1073 (1984).

120. E.O. 12,778 (1991); E.O. 12,988 (1996).

121. See http://www.nmb.gov.

122. See. e.g., the rules of the General Service Administration's Board of Contract Appeals, http://www.gsbca.gsa.gov/ADRules.htm.

123. Dispute resolution under the ADA was studied for the now defunct Administrative Conference of the United States, which had special statutory duties of coordination under the initial Act, in A. Hodges, Dispute Resolution Under the Americans with Disabilities Act: A Report to the Administrative Conference of the United States, 9 Admin. L. J. Am. U. 1007 (1996).

124. Developments in the Law—The Paths of Civil Litigation: VI. ADR, the Judiciary and Justice: Coming to Terms with the Alternatives, 113 Harv. L. Rev. 1851 (2000).

of binding norms to govern private conduct, to the publication of non-binding statements of policy or guidelines to shape understanding and compliance efforts. The APA's definition of "rule" includes the product of each of these activities. Its articulation in 5 U.S.C. §§552–553 of rulemaking procedure—identified by one leading American scholar as "one of the great inventions of modern government"[125]– reflects this diversity by providing three different models of rulemaking procedure: a publication model, a notice and comment model, and a formal hearing model. Unless military or foreign affairs functions are involved, or a matter relating to the government's proprietary functions,[126] one or another of these models applies to all rulemaking that is permitted adversely to affect private interests.

1. The APA models

a. Notice and comment rulemaking

Again it seems useful to start with the central model, which in the case of rulemaking is that of notice and comment (or, as it is often called, "informal") rulemaking. This is the procedure to which Americans generally refer when they speak of rulemaking, and it is established by 5 U.S.C. §553. It is the minimum procedure statutorily required for adoption of a rule in the strong sense—that is, for adoption of a rule which if valid will have the force and effect of a statute. Such rules, often described as "substantive" or "legislative" rules, are the bulk of the provisions published in the Code of Federal Regulations. References to a "regulation" in the following pages are references to this kind of rule, that if valid has statutory force and effect on all actors in the legal system—courts as well as agencies and private actors. Like a statute, a regulation's terms may be varied only by the procedures used to create it. The Supreme Court has indicated, with increasing intensity,[127] that Congress must

---

125. K.C. Davis, n. 14 above at 520.

126. The exemption of proprietary functions from rulemaking procedures has been sharply criticized insofar as it bears on matters having an impact on persons outside government—as rules governing "public property, loans, grants, benefits or contracts," 5 U.S.C. §553(a)(2), easily may. Most if not all agencies have responded to these criticisms by providing by regulation that APA rulemaking procedures are to be followed in these cases, despite the formal statutory exception. Where such regulations exist, they may be judicially enforced; that is, if an agency that has such a regulation in place adopts a rule to govern public property, loans, grants, benefits or contracts without following the APA procedures, that rule will be denied legal effect by a reviewing court on the authority of that rule, regardless of the APA exemption.

127. Chrysler Corp. v. Brown, 441 U.S. 281 (1979).

have delegated explicit statutory authority to an agency for it to adopt regulations; however, the delegation itself may be in rather general terms.[128]

Of the APA's procedures, notice and comment rulemaking procedures are those that have been the most strikingly affected by changes since their initial adoption. From passage of the Freedom of Information Act (FOIA),[129] to judicial interpretations significantly departing from original expectations, to the presidential and legislative initiatives requiring the pre-announcement of agendas, and a variety of impact analyses, these initially simple procedures have become considerably more complex.[130] It may nonetheless be sensible to begin, at least briefly, with a description of the initial statutory formulation, on the basis of which one can understand both the continuities and the substantial changes in contemporary rulemaking practice.

Section 553's notice and comment rulemaking procedures begin with the publication of notice of a proposal for rulemaking in the Federal Register, the federal government's daily official gazette.[131] Of course, this publication is likely to occur at a very late stage in the bureaucratic development of the proposal within the agency itself. Under the changes already described it will have been preceded by a brief notice of intended activity in the semi-annual Unified Agenda of Federal Regulations.[132] The section 553 notice begins a period generally 30 to 60 days in length, during which any interested person may submit written comments— "data, views or arguments"—to the responsible agency for its consideration. The agency may provide more elaborate opportunities for public participation if it chooses—for example, oral hearings (generally of a legislative rather than judicial character), opportunities for responsive comment, or a second round of notice. The agency's obligation, "after consideration of the relevant matter presented," is then to publish "a concise general statement of basis and purpose" with any regulation it may decide to adopt.[133] Section 553 provides that, absent special justification, a regulation may not take effect for 30 days. Agencies must use the same procedures if they wish to rescind or amend a regulation.

---

128. National Petroleum Refiners Assn. v. Federal Trade Comm., 482 F.2d 672 (D.C. Cir.1973), cert. denied 415 U.S. 951 (1974).

129. See p. 276 below.

130. See pp. 103 and 194 above. Extended discussions of these changes appear in P. Strauss, From Expertise to Politics: The Transformation of American Rulemaking, 31 Wake Forest L. Rev. 745 (1996); P. Strauss, Changing Times: The APA at 50, 63 U. Chi. L. Rev. 1389 (1996).

131. Readily searched electronically, and with increasingly useful links, the Federal Register may be found at http://www.access.gpo.gov/su_docs/aces/aces140.html.

132. Id.

133. 5 U.S.C. §553(c).

Overall, the striking characteristic of the section 553 procedure is its informality. What must be contained in the notice is loosely defined; in addition to legal authority and procedural details such as the deadline for filing comments, the notice need only specify "*either* the terms *or* substance of the proposed rule *or* a description of the subjects and issues involved."[134] The notice itself need not appear until late in the rule's development. If public participation is limited to a single round of comment to be filed by a date common to all participants, commenters of necessity will be able only to put forward direct views, not responses or challenges to the data, views or arguments of others who may join in the proceedings. The defined record, initial decision, and bureaucratic separation of staff from decisionmakers that characterize formal adjudication are completely absent. Finally, the agency's obligation to explain its ultimate conclusions is stated far more permissively than for the case of adjudication. Only a "concise general" statement of basis and purpose is required, and most speakers of English would understand, as was the initial practice, that such a statement could be summary.

b. Publication rulemaking

When an agency or one of its operating divisions adopts "interpretative rules, general statements of policy, or rules of agency organization, procedure, or practice,"[135] section 553 notice and comment procedures need not be followed as a general matter; such procedures might, however, be called for by an agency's governing law. These and similar instruments, such as staff manuals, may be thought of as statements that announce an agency's positions or procedures on matters within its competence but that, unlike regulations, do not have a statute's legal effect. Since the Freedom of Information Act amendments of 1966, section 552(a)(2) of the Act has provided that "[a] final order, opinion, statement of policy, interpretation, or staff manual or instruction that affects a member of the public may be relied on, used, or cited as precedent by an agency against a party other than an agency only if" it has been appropriately published.[136] Thus, the effect they have could better be analogized

---

134. 5 U.S.C. §553(b) (emphasis added). Note that this language does not require even that the text of the proposed rule, or data the agency believes it has to support its proposed action, be revealed.

135. 5 U.S.C. §553(b)(A).

136. Section 552(a)(1) contains a similar formula for matters, including "statements of general policy or interpretations of general applicability formulated and adopted by the agency," that are published in the Federal Register. The author's views on the proper place of publication rules in the rulemaking spectrum are set out at P. Strauss, The Rulemaking

to that of judicial precedent. Hierarchically inferior agency staff can be expected to regard them as governing law. Yet the agency itself can change its "publication rules" as informally as it 'makes them.[137] For the agency itself and for any court reviewing agency action, the underlying statute and regulations remain the source of any legal obligation. For a hierarchically superior body like a reviewing court, the agency's views, if well-informed, will be regarded only as constructions entitled to persuasive weight in reaching a conclusion on the legal question involved.[138] From this perspective, the agency's adoption of a publication rule may well have an impact on the positions the agency itself will be able to take, and the burden of explanation it will face should it attempt to vary its view;[139] but for the outside world, the validity of a publication rule does not establish it as the source of fresh legal obligation.

Interpretive rules and other like formulations generally address matters of technical detail one would not expect to warrant the attention of the agency's leadership. They comprise a volume of text and regulatory activity enormously greater than the body of legislative rules. Examples include the Internal Revenue Service's opinions about the meaning of the tax laws, the Nuclear Regulatory Commission's "regulatory standards" informing applicants for nuclear power plant licenses how they may be able to satisfy Commission staff that they have met the technical specifications for licensing, and the Department of the Interior's staff manuals on procedures to be followed in carrying out its various regulatory responsibilities. As the characterization of these documents may suggest, they are frequently the product of responsible staff offices, rather than the agency's political leadership—which is, it is believed, the only agency authority properly authorized to adopt regulations. With the emergence of the Internet, too, they are becoming considerably more accessible; 1996 amend-

---

Continuum, 41 Duke L. J. 1463 (1992) and P. Strauss, Publication Rules in the Rulemaking Spectrum: Assuring Proper Respect for an Essential Element, 53 Admin. L. Rev. 803 (2001).

137. United States v. Mead Corp., 533 U.S. 218 (2001), discussed at p. 371, below.

138. Id.; Pacific Gas & Electric Co. v. Federal Power Comm., 506 F.2d 33 (D.C. Cir. 1974); Skidmore v. Swift & Co., 323 U.S. 134 (1944), discussed at p. 363 ff. below.

139. For an example of a court unselfconsciously treating a publication rule as binding upon the government, see Anastasoff v. United States, 235 F.3d 1054 (8th Cir. 2000). Facing a conflict in holding between two circuits on an issue of tax law, the government had published "a document styled Action on Decision" announcing its acquiescence in the taxpayer-favoring outcome. This publication rule led an en banc panel of the Eighth Circuit to vacate the government-favoring outcome one of its panels had reached as moot, see p. 124 n. 194 above—an outcome defensible only on the understanding that the government had in some respect bound itself by issuing the document.

ments to FOIA, known as the Electronic Freedom of Information Act,[140] require each agency to maintain an electronic reading room. These sites are considerably more accessible than were the physical reading rooms where the indexing and availability required by section 552 were previously effected. As a result, what had been a somewhat obscure and specialized collection of agency documents is now broadly available, and available in readily searched format.[141]

Although lacking the statutory force of regulations, these opinions may carry great weight in the practical world. They shape behavior that never reaches the courts, and may influence decisionmakers with formal responsibility for decision (such as the courts) with the persuasiveness of their origin in an expert and responsible agency.[142] Agencies issue these interpretations and opinions precisely to shape external behavior, reducing to that extent the need for regulatory enforcement. For this reason, consultative procedures are strongly recommended, often followed, and sometimes statutorily required. As notice and comment rulemaking has become more complex, the suspicion has grown that agencies have been tempted to use publication rulemaking as a substitute, and the courts of appeal have been persuaded with some frequency to require the use of section 553 procedures. This question is taken up below.[143] For a proper publication rule, however, all that the APA requires in order to permit the agency to rely on it in its own proceedings against the interest of private parties, and to entitle it to some deference on judicial review, is that the agency's position must be published—a step one would imagine the agency taking to assure visibility in any event, if it wished its position to have influence.

In addition to publishing its interpretations and policies, each agency must afford "an interested person the right to petition for the issuance, amendment, or repeal of a rule,"[144] including in this instance interpretive rules and the like.

---

140. See p. 282 below.

141. See, for example, the E-FOIA "reading room" at the National Highway Transportation and Safety Administration, http://www.nhtsa.dot.gov/nhtsa/whatsup/foia/index.html, or the opinions of its General Counsel interpreting its regulations, http://www.nhtsa.dot.gov/cars/rules/interps/. See p. 283 below.

142. See United States v. Mead Corp., n. 137 above.

143. See p. 256 below.

144. 5 U.S.C. §553(e).

c. Formal rulemaking

Individual statutes occasionally require rules "to be made on the record after opportunity for an agency hearing."[145] When this is the case, the comment stage and "concise general statement of…basis and purpose" of informal rulemaking are replaced by a hearing comparable to that provided for initial licensing.[146] On-the-record constraints are applicable, with relatively elaborate provision for "party"[147] participation in evidentiary matters and argumentation. The agency's conclusions must be fully and responsively explained. As in initial licensing, however, neither oral process nor the observance of separation of functions within the agency decisional structure is as rigorously insisted upon as would be the case in ordinary on-the-record adjudication. Like initial licensing—a form of adjudication—formal rulemaking can often be seen to have a mixed character—highly individualist from one perspective (thus, strong procedural and participatory claims), yet polycentric and nonadversary from another. The two procedural sets are essentially identical.

Proceedings to fix permitted rates for a public utility or common carrier are by far the commonest setting for formal rulemaking. For the utility or carrier facing the possibility of being denied a reasonable return on its investment, the claim to formal hearing has a constitutional dimension.[148] Formal rulemaking proceedings are, however, notoriously inconvenient and difficult to manage, given the frequent diffuseness of the issues presented and the large number of parties that may wish to participate.[149] Consequently, courts are reluctant to find that statutes require rules to be formally made. In sharp distinction from their approach to statutory provisions for *adjudicatory* hearings,[150] the courts virtually require a formula including the words "on the record" to appear before they will conclude that the informal rulemaking procedures of section 553 will not suffice.[151]

---

145. 5 U.S.C. §553(c).

146. See p. 207 above.

147. The ideas of rulemaking (a procedure for the formulation of general norms) and "parties" are not easily reconciled. As a general matter any person who wishes to is permitted to participate in any rulemaking. At least some formal rulemakings, however—those setting rates for public utilities, for example—require the participation of particular entities, as well as permitting the participation of all.

148. ICC v. Louisville & Nashville R. Co., 227 U.S. 88 (1913).

149. R. Hamilton, Procedures for the Adoption of Rules of General Applicability: The Need for Procedural Innovation in Administrative Rulemaking, 60 Calif. L. Rev. 1276 (1972).

150. See p. 217 above.

151. United States v. Florida East Coast Railway Co., 410 U.S. 224 (1973).

2. The transformation of rulemaking

Against the spare provisions of the Administrative Procedure Act, consider both the tremendous importance of rulemaking as an activity in contemporary regulation, and the rich internal—one might even say political—life of government in reaching decisions of magnitude. Since the explosion of environmental, health and safety regulation in the late '60s and early '70s, rulemaking has become the pre-eminent administrative activity in the United States. Which risks among the many possible to address shall be controlled, and how should they be chosen? To what extent, and by what regulatory means? Under what hypotheses about such sensitive issues as, what is the assumed discount rate for calculating the present value of future costs and benefits, or what value should be assigned to human life, or the preservation of wilderness? Consider the issues posed in three prominent rulemakings from among the many: (1) whether and how OSHA will decide that the handling of benzene (only one of the many chemicals the petrochemical industry produces and uses that might have implications for the health of workers and the public generally) will be subject to special precautions (and which precautions, how uniformly applied across the variety of contexts in which it is used); (2) what controls coal-fired electric power plants must employ to prevent emission of soot, heat, or chemicals possibly harmful to the environment; (3) what technology fish processors shall use to avoid the threat of botulism poisoning from imperfectly smoked fish. Each of these decisions raises highly complex questions of risk, physical science, technology, human health, economics, and political will. These questions will engage whoever has the responsibility and opportunity to participate in their resolution and their resolution will affect a wide range of interests in the community. Both the benefits and the costs of particular regulations requiring complex interventions to control the effects of major industrial processes may be estimated in the hundreds of millions of dollars.

Issues like these challenge both any idea that rulemaking can be *simply* a technocratic exercise best protected from the world of politics and left to experts, and its opposite—that these are matters best resolved *strictly* in the world of politics. Constructing a workable middle ground has been complicated by the efforts of stakeholders to secure procedural advantage. The importance of the issues being resolved put enormous pressure on a procedure whose public aspects, slight to begin with, occur so late in policy development; stakeholders inevitably have sought earlier and more influential roles than the public procedure suggests. In view of the high stakes for the community as a whole, one can also understand a certain insistence on regularity and visibility, particularly when rulemaking comes before the courts for their necessarily retrospective review. While not repudiating his distinction between rule-making and adjudication, the courts have become increasingly aware of the imperfections in the analogy first drawn by Justice Holmes in *Bi-Metallic Investment Co.* between rulemaking and legislative action, and this has led to much more intense judicial supervision of the validity of regulations than of statutes.

Recall Holmes' statement in *Bi-Metallic* that the procedural claims of citizens in respect of legislation are strictly political ones—"their rights are protected in the only way that they can be in a complex society, by their power, immediate or remote, over those who make the rule."[152] This position, joined with the judiciary's profound unwillingness to examine the factual justification for regulatory statutes following the "substantive due process" crisis of the 1930s,[153] produced extremely permissive standards of judicial review of rulemaking. When agency rules were challenged on judicial review—and it did not become clear until 1969 that such challenges could often be made in advance of government-initiated enforcement proceedings[154]—judges presumed their validity just as they would presume the validity of a statute. A challenger would be required to show (on the basis of a record freshly made in court) that the agency's judgment had been arbitrary and capricious in the strongest sense, that no facts could be adduced to support the rule it had adopted.[155] Yet an agency is not an elective body. The ties between federal administrative agencies and the electorate are limited to the periodic election of the American President (a connection that at times has seemed so frail as to escape even the description "remote") and to the possibilities inherent in legislative revision and oversight of agency authority. What, then, was the warrant for according such respect to the products of agency rulemaking, which could "affect the person or property of individuals, sometimes to the point of ruin"?[156]

Presenting a coherent picture of the rulemaking processes resulting from repeated encounters with these difficulties is challenging for a variety of reasons. One's tendency is to see the picture that has emerged from the large-consequence rulemakings just evoked, but relatively few rulemakings in any given year—a few dozen, perhaps—have this dimension. Second, for these high-consequence regulations (and to a lesser extent for simpler rulemakings) the

---

152. See p. 189 above.

153. See p. 37 above.

154. Abbott Laboratories v. Gardner, 387 U.S. 136 (1967); the case is discussed at p. 303 below.

155. Pacific States Box & Basket Co. v. White, 296 U.S. 176 (1935).

156. Bi-Metallic Investment Co., see p. 189 above.

situation is complicated by the adoption of a hodgepodge of statutes and executive orders imposing various analytic requirements, and the absence to date of any rationalizing effort. Third, among the most prominent high-consequence rulemaking agencies, several (notably, the EPA and OSHA) act under procedural statutes unique to them. Finally, much of the development has its roots in agency anticipation of the demands of judicial review, a subject whose discussion now would be premature. What may be helpful is to present a brief summary, focused just on notice-and-comment rulemaking, and then spend a few pages indicating how various elements of this snapshot developed.

In practical terms today, rulemaking begins as a public procedure with the submission of a proposed element of the semi-annual Unified Agenda of Federal Regulations and its incorporation under OIRA (White House) oversight. There has for a while been talk about creating an even earlier stage for public involvement, the stage at which an agency appraises the various risks that might warrant regulation to choose from among them its best particular targets for possible action. Some agencies—EPA, for example[157]—devote considerable energies to risk appraisal; and for others—OSHA, for example—separate specialized institutions have been created to assist in this work.[158] But no general public process for risk evaluation has yet emerged.

The Unified Agenda description as published includes not only a brief description of the project being undertaken, but also contact information within the agency for members of the public who might wish to become involved. Use of the Internet will increasingly permit citizens to register their interest in matters appearing in the Unified Agenda, for subsequent notifications and other uses. In developing its concrete proposal, the agency may invoke the Negotiated Rulemaking Act, discussed below,[159] or simply proceed to do so bureaucratically. Before publishing its proposal, the agency will have drafted any necessary impact analyses under governing statutes (such as the National Environmental Policy Act[160] or the Regulatory Flexibility Act[161]) or presidential executive orders.[162] In the process, it will have amassed a fair amount of data

---

157. See http://www.epa.gov/ncea/.

158. The National Institute for Occupational Safety and Health is a constituent element of the Center for Disease Control, a distinctly apolitical part of the Department of Health and Human Services, see http://www.cdc.gov/niosh/homepage.html, that is made statutorily responsible for advising OSHA—a part of the Department of Labor—on the workplace risks most deserving its attention. See p. 167 above.

159. See p. 252 below.

160. See p. 101 above.

161. See p. 249 below.

162. See p. 103 above.

and developed both the text of a specific proposal and a somewhat detailed explanation of its (provisional) thinking. For important rulemakings, today, the section 553 notice of proposed rulemaking must contain or make available all this matter: text, explanation, and supporting data. All these, increasingly, are made available—highlighted—on agency web-sites. The opportunity to comment occurs as before, but now with targets both more precise and more extensive. Detailed technical submissions of competing data are not unusual and for rulemakings of wide import media campaigns may produce a flood of comments—hundreds of thousands in a few cases. Increasingly, commenting can occur on the Internet and, with the development of the Internet, increasingly comments are readily available to public view. With the comments in hand, the agency may then be required to develop a *final* impact analysis— which implies discussions within government that interested private parties may anticipate and try to influence. With these processes continuing, comments available for analysis, and rulemaking in any event not a formalistic procedure, participants may seek an opportunity to file responsive comments. If the agency decides after considering the comments to follow a course that could not readily have been predicted from its initial proposal, it is obliged to publish a new notice of proposed rulemaking and repeat this process. If it is going forward with its proposal or making only predictable changes, it will feel obliged to explain its action rather fully, showing its resolution of any issues that comments put significantly in issue. For a major regulation, the statement of basis and purpose will run to dozens and perhaps hundreds of pages in the Federal Register.

It should be evident that this is a transformed procedure, perhaps the most striking development in American administrative law over the past several decades. The transformation occurred without amendment to section 553, which still refers to notice of "*either* the terms *or* substance of the proposed rule *or* a description of the subjects and issues involved,"[163] and to a "concise general statement of basis and purpose." As we will see, it also occurred in the face of the Supreme Court's ostensible and strident insistence that courts not improvise on the APA's provisions, "a formula on which opposing social and political forces have come to rest."[164] The paragraphs following seek to explain

---

163. 5 U.S.C. §553(b) (emphasis added). Note that this language does not require even that the text of the proposed rule, or data the agency believes it has to support its proposed action, be revealed.

164. Vermont Yankee Nuclear Power Corp. v. National Resources Defense Council, Inc. 435 U.S. 519, 523 (1978), quoting Wong Yang Sung v. McGrath, 339 U.S. 33, 40 (1950). See p. 241 below.

that development, albeit under the important handicap that we have not yet encountered extended treatment of the subject of judicial review.[165] The focus here will be at the agency level.

a. Bureaucratic structures of rulemaking, the rulemaking "record," and rulemaking decision

Significant elements of the changes emerged from the courts' efforts to understand what could be described as the "record" of a rulemaking, against which they could assess its validity on review. If they could not simply presume that the agency knew some state of facts that would support its conclusions, what facts could they conclude that the agency did know, and how should they understand the resolution of any disputes about them? Rulemaking is characterized by institutional processes for consideration and decision of controversial matters. What can be a considerable range of offices staffed with different specialists identify, sharpen, and then propose resolutions for those aspects of the problem that are brought to their attention. They may possess knowledge about these aspects from a wide range of sources and experience, that they don't feel called upon (and perhaps would be unable) to restate every time a question within their expertise arises. Issues surviving this process are negotiated in a politically complex institutional structure. These institutional processes complicate the process of defining a "record" of decision, if they do not deny the possibility altogether.

Such an institutional process has very different presuppositions about appropriate decisionmaking than adjudication. In adjudication, one imagines that the whole issue is placed at a certain time before a discrete individual (or a handful of individuals) valued for judgment, and whose function in relation to the collection of information is relatively passive. She considers identifiable matters, argument and data, in relationship to a unique and defined body of data more-or-less formally placed before her and reaches her individual decision. Although difficulties can be introduced when the adjudicator takes judicial notice of some matter the parties have not placed before her,[166] that practice is constrained. On the whole, everyone knows (without having to rely on the judge to state) what is the basis on which a decision is taken and may be defended. Additionally, the decider is committedly neutral. She will not talk to any contender outside the presence of the others or participate in the rough-and-tumble of political discourse.

---

165. See, in this respect, Chapter VIII, especially VIII(D)(2).
166. See p. 203 above.

The characteristic rulemaking decision, like that of most organizations other than courts when faced with important problems, is institutional. That is, the taking of decisions is not focused on a particular judge-like individual or group of individuals, but occurs within and across the ordinary operating staff of the agency. Responsibilities may be divided within the agency in accordance with interest or expertise in particular aspects of a given problem, perhaps under the supervision of an ad hoc working group. Piecemeal decisions are taken, over time, across the desks of numerous members of agency staff. As they gradually accumulate, only what remains controversial rises through the agency hierarchy. The data that produced resolution of a given aspect may be entirely within the knowledge of a particular employee—her "expertise"—and does not travel with that resolution to later stages. Similarly, controversy may be eliminated or shaped by informal conversations among agency staff whose ordinary roles bear on the particular controversy (but who have no responsibility for the rule as a whole); once those conversations have occurred, traces of the controversy or the basis for its resolution may disappear. The resolution becomes part of what the agency "knows." Even when controversy rises to the level of the agency heads, they may suggest new inquiries or additional approaches that they hope will permit staff to resolve the matter, rather than decide it themselves. That approach often succeeds.

The rulemaking process as a whole also lacks the characteristic isolation adjudication traditionally enjoys from other aspects of an agency's work. Those working on the regulation continue their work on other aspects of the agency's business. They are encouraged to bring to bear whatever they learn, may and do speak with whoever seems relevant to the matters before them, and feel no need either to inform other "parties" of these conversations or to permit their participation in them in any way.[167]

To speak of a "record" in this context, then, is highly artificial—at least, if we are imagining a collection of data all of which was exposed to the interested public for its response and challenge, placed before a single decisionmaker at a given point in time, and uniquely made the basis for her decision. There will have been no single decisionmaker. Much that has been relied upon will not have been collected, certainly will not have been presented to the in-

---

167. A full and still useful description of a characteristic rulemaking process, as seen from inside an important American administrative agency, appears in W. Pedersen, Formal Records and Informal Rulemaking, 85 Yale L. J. 38 (1975). While the rulemaking processes of the Environmental Protection Agency have since been changed by statute—in good part as a result of Pedersen's analysis—agencies continue to make rules today under the statutory procedures that governed the EPA when he wrote this.

dividual or collegial body formally identified by statute as responsible for the adoption of a regulation. On the other hand, documents will have been submitted to the agency as comments on the rulemaking, and the APA requires that they be attended to. Major studies may have been commissioned, or other large bodies of data may exist, on which the agency or members of its staff have drawn for decision of one or another aspect of the proceeding. Memoranda will have been written within the agency as decision went forward, indicating resolutions reached, controversies remaining and, in a healthy bureaucracy, the contending positions on those controversies. Meetings may have occurred within the agency or with outsiders, private interests or other government officials, where views are expressed and data provided that could be, and sometimes are, recorded. All of these, if public, could be described as a "record," at least in the sense of their being a body of data bearing on the agency's rulemaking decision, against which its rationality and lawfulness could be tested.

b. The uncertainties of "legislative" judgment and disputes about general fact

In the context of economic regulation, the general propositions on which prescriptive rulemaking turns could be imagined generally to involve the same kinds of judgments about social condition as usually confront legislatures— normative questions about whether this or that behavior should be allowed, that generally do not turn on what might appear to be determinable propositions of fact about the physical world.[168] With the emergence of health, safety and environmental regulation as the dominant setting for rulemaking in the 1960s and 1970s, this changed. What the impact is on human health of prolonged exposure to background radiation of 3 &rem/day may be hard to establish experimentally, but it is nonetheless a question to which it seems there should be a correct and determinable answer, as a matter of fact—in the same way as we could hope to determine whether a traffic light facing Mr. Jones was red or green when he drove through the intersection it controlled. If there are uncertainties, disagreements, or professional judgments about the matter, it would seem relevant to know about them, in the same way as we think we should be aware of differing accounts of the state of the traffic light at that moment. To purport to decide either question by political judgment—by vote—would be strongly objectionable.

---

168. When economic rulemaking involves particular data, in rulemaking notably, the governing statutes require formal rulemaking. See p. 224 above.

At the same time, these are not the same kinds of factual questions. For the traffic light, using a neutral non-expert to make judgments after hearing the testimony of witnesses who can be closely questioned about their opportunities for observation, truthfulness, animus, etc., is a well-established modality. For the question of science fact, as we may call it, neutral non-experts are poor deciders and a viva voce process for acquiring "evidence" is at least inefficient. The scientific community uses ongoing processes of inquiry and criticism under norms of transparency; reaching consensus about remaining uncertainties, and clearly articulating the models or hypotheses being used, help to distinguish the known from the supposed. Both are fact-finding processes, as distinct from means of asserting political will. Yet in their details they are strikingly different fact-finding processes. The changing character of rulemaking brought this problem into strong relief.

c. The impact of open government legislation

Until the mid-1960s, participants in rulemaking lacked any procedural means for forcing the transparency of science fact-finding in rulemaking procedures. Persons outside the agency were essentially limited to what the agency chose to report in its statement of basis and purpose as the factual grounding for its decision. Internal documents, even factual studies, were not public documents, and courts did not require them to be revealed. Traditional rulemaking review, treating rules as deserving no more substantial inquiry into their factual basis than statutes, put few demands on the agency. It might have to supply the file of comments that it had received in the rulemaking; but generally it was free simply to show what it knew that could be regarded as supporting its conclusions. Inquiry into its actual decisionmaking process would not be undertaken.

The Freedom of Information Act,[169] first adopted in 1967 and vastly strengthened in 1974, brought much of the internal documentation of agency rulemaking, and some of its decisionmaking, into public view. While neither intended as a record-enhancing statute[170] nor addressed to the new characteristics of rulemaking facts when it was adopted, FOIA nonetheless dramatically altered rulemaking. It permitted any participant to request "all docu-

---

169. 5 U.S.C. §552, discussed at p. 276 below.

170. The statute makes government records available on demand to "any person," and the courts from the outset resisted litigant efforts to tie FOIA requests to judicial review of agency action. National Labor Relations Board v. Sears, Roebuck & Co., 421 U.S. 132 (1975).

ments the agency regards as bearing upon its proposed rulemaking in...," and this request was sufficiently definite to have to be honored. Filing such a request quickly became a mandatory element of competent professional practice. Not all parts of all documents had to be revealed; in particular, predecisional advice given by agency staff to their superiors could usually be withheld as privileged.[171] Yet even for these documents, only advice could be withheld. Factual assertions—data and technical analysis—are not privileged, and the agency's obligation under the FOIA is to edit privileged material out of a document and honor the remainder of the request. Thus agencies could be forced to reveal their factual basis for action. Often enough they would provide the advice portion of memoranda as well, rather than go through the trouble of redaction. Anticipating the requests, they began to organize, and to make available at the outset of rulemakings, data that inevitably would have to be disclosed at some later stage.

The Government in the Sunshine Act,[172] adopted in 1976, made explicit the FOIA's latent judgment about openness in rulemaking. Under this statute, multi-member commissions are required to hold their meetings on advance notice, in public view.[173] The Act's limited exemptions, quite intentionally, do not permit an agency to close any part of a discussion of ordinary rulemaking. Unlike the FOIA, that is, the Sunshine Act recognizes no privilege whatsoever for predecisional consultations with staff about policymaking; only discussions about decision in on-the-record adjudication are protected in that way. To be sure, the Sunshine Act mechanism does not apply to agencies like the EPA or OSHA, that function with a single individual at their head; only the multi-member commissions are affected. Yet this can be seen as a technical judgment about the difficulty of constructing a "Sunshine" mechanism for a strictly hierarchical decision process lacking collegial elements, or as a result of the President's greater ability to protect agencies attached to the executive branch as distinct from the independent agencies. As a comment on rulemaking, its message is clear.

d. The "paper hearing"

Judicial interpretation responsive to these changes would draw agency rulemaking away from the simple legislative analogy. Three related elements

---

171. See the discussion of the Act's fifth exemption at p. 279 below.

172. 5 U.S.C. §552(b), discussed at p. 284 below.

173. In public view, but not with public participation. Like FOIA, the Sunshine Act's focus is on openness, not additional external controls or decision procedures.

of the APA's notice and comment rulemaking procedure permitted this: what constituted "notice"; what, an effective opportunity for "comment"; and what, an adequate "statement of basis and purpose," however "general" and "concise." The mood of the 1946 legislature enacting the provisions containing these words, no one could doubt, was highly permissive. Yet the widespread use and enormous impact of rulemaking resulting from environmental, health, and safety legislation was not foreseen at that time. When those developments occurred, these phrases were the obvious pressure points.

The last of them, the findings requirement, was the first to respond to the new circumstances. Faced with the first rules adopted to regulate automobile safety under the National Traffic and Motor Vehicle Safety Act—rules that would contribute tremendously to reshaping the American automobile market—the D.C. Circuit cautioned "

> against an overly literal reading of the statutory terms 'concise' and 'general.' These adjectives must be accommodated to the realities of judicial scrutiny.... We do not expect the agency to discuss every item of fact or opinion included in the submissions made to it... [but we do expect that the statement] will enable us to see what major issues of policy were ventilated by the informal proceedings and why the agency reacted to them as it did.[174]

What is the "record" in informal proceedings?: The attitude underlying this opinion, that judges were entitled to see and understand what had occurred at the agency level, received major impetus from a 1971 Supreme Court opinion that focused particular attention on the problem of the record in informal agency action. *Citizens to Preserve Overton Park, Inc. v. Volpe*[175] challenged the decision of the federal Secretary of Transportation to provide federal financing for a portion of highway that would inevitably interfere with an important urban park, despite recent federal legislation intended to protect park

---

174. Automotive Parts & Accessories v. Boyd, 407 F.2d 330, 338 (D.C. Cir. 1968). For trenchant critiques of the impact of this judicial attitude on the agency's performance two decades later, see J. Mashaw and D. Harfst, The Struggle for Auto Safety (Harvard University Press 1990); J. Mashaw and D. Harfst, Regulation and Legal Culture: The Case of Motor Vehicle Safety, 4 Yale J. Reg. 257 (1987).

175. 401 U.S. 402 (1971). This case is extensively discussed in P. Strauss, Revisiting Overton Park: Political and Judicial Controls Over Administrative Actions Affecting the Community, 39 U.C.L.A. L. Rev. 1251 (1992).

lands against such uses. In the APA's terms, the Secretary's decision would be characterized as informal adjudication, not rulemaking. Nonetheless, it shared the institutional characteristics of rulemaking. The decision had been reached through a coordinated, informal bureaucratic process, after a number of opportunities for public comment but without any procedure resembling a trial. The Secretary did not issue an opinion explaining his judgment at the time he granted permission to go forward with the project. He attempted to explain it only when review was sought by a group of citizens opposing the project.

The Supreme Court strongly endorsed review of that judgment, describing its appropriate elements in a manner to be examined later in this essay.[176] It made two observations of particular moment to the present discussion. First, it said that judicial review, while "narrow" (to avoid the substitution of judicial for agency judgment) was to be "thorough," "probing," and "careful" in examining the Secretary's declared basis for his decision against the materials before him. Second, and relatedly, the Court indicated that this review was to occur on the basis of "the record" compiled in the agency in the course of the decisional process. Its call for "thorough," "probing" and "careful" review only reinforced the attitudes already emerging in cases like the D.C. Circuit's review of the automobile safety rules. If this was the judicial responsibility, how much more important that the statement of basis and purpose "enable us to see what major issues of policy were ventilated by the informal proceedings and why the agency reacted to them as it did"!

The Court's confident reference to the administrative "record" is surprising in light of the structural realities of the decision process, an institutional process much like that just described for informal rulemaking. Until FOIA compelled them to acquire it, agencies had no habit of identifying all materials brought to bear on an accumulating decision as it passed through various levels of bureaucratic review. In all likelihood the reference was encouraged by a misunderstanding on the part of the attorney who had argued the case for the government, a young lawyer accustomed to the judicial model of litigation.[177] Nonetheless, the reference was made and—among lawyers and judges equally used to that model—was easily accepted.

---

176. See pp. 341 and 376 below.

177. Because a major highway project was being suspended during the litigation, the case was argued and briefed in the Supreme Court on an extremely condensed schedule, one usually reserved for the most important affairs of state; this haste doubtless contributed to the government brief's repeated references to "the administrative record"—as if a defined set of papers existed. After the Supreme Court had remanded the case for further proceedings, it quickly became apparent that no such collection existed. Definition of the ma-

Accommodating issues of science fact: Once one began to know what material was being considered by an agency (in addition to the outside comments that long had been a matter of public record), the natural instinct to wish to be able to respond to that material—to confront it, challenge it, contradict it—quickly took shape. The impulse was perhaps especially strong for the increasing body of important rules dealing with health, safety or environmental issues—rules frequently based on disputable conclusions about such general, but factual, questions as the impact of breathing various concentrations of a given substance on human health.

The instinct found expression in a 1973 proceeding involving an EPA rulemaking to set standards for the control of concrete dust.[178] After the rule had been adopted but before it had been judicially reviewed, the EPA (prompted by a court of appeals decision in another case[179]) put in the record for review new information about the methodology it had employed to reach its conclusions. With its information about the agency's data thus enlarged, one of the participants in the rulemaking now persuaded the court to send the rule back to the agency, to allow the filing of new comments critical of the agency's methodology. When the agency appeared to ignore those comments, the court not only insisted that they be responded to, but gave forceful new content to the statutory provisions for "notice" and "comment" by suggesting an obligation to reveal agency data from the outset: "it is not consonant with the purpose of a rule-making proceeding to promulgate rules on the basis of inadequate data, or on data that…[are] known only to the agency."

Four years later a similar view was expressed by another court of appeals in reviewing a Food and Drug Administration rule governing the preparation of smoked fish:

> Although we recognize that an agency may resort to its own expertise…we do not believe that when the pertinent research material is readily available…there is any reason to conceal the scientific data relied upon from the interested parties.…If the failure to notify interested persons of [the material relied on] actually prevented the presentation of relevant comment, the agency may be held not to have

---

terials before the various agency personnel sharing responsibility for the decision consumed weeks of litigation effort.

178. Portland Cement Assn v. Ruckleshaus, 486 F.2d 375 (D.C. Cir. 1973), cert. den. 417 U.S. 921 (1974).

179. Kennecott Copper Corp. v. EPA, 462 F.2d 846 (D.C. Cir. 1972).

considered all "the relevant factors."...One cannot ask for comment
on a scientific paper without allowing the participants to read the
paper.[180]

Thus was "notice" expanded past the information section 553 mentions to include any data the agency knows that bears on its proposed rule. Similarly,
"comment" came to entail an opportunity to challenge that data, in addition
to the chance to supply fresh data, argument or views. And the statement of
basis and purpose must be full enough to show the agency's reasoning in some
detail, including its response to important comments that have been made.

e. The siren call of the model of judicial trial

Taken no farther than the point just described, these developments can be
tied, however loosely, to section 553's text and—as important—associated with
the processes scientists are accustomed to using to ventilate and resolve disputed
matters. Characterized as a "paper hearing," this understanding of rulemaking
process was widely accepted;[181] one thoughtful bureaucrat found in its requirements "a great tonic" to the integrity of the rulemaking process within the
agency, giving "those who care about well-documented and well-reasoned decisionmaking a lever with which to move those who do not."[182] While fullness
and visibility have necessary costs in time and effort,[183] important issues warrant such expenditures, and many would concede that the problems of fact-
finding in matters complicated by issues of modeling, scientific judgment, and
projection[184] require a public procedure of some fullness and visibility.

---

180. United States v. Nova Scotia Food Products Corp., 568 F.2d 240, 251 (2d Cir.
1977).

181. R. Stewart, The Development of Administrative and Quasi-Constitutional Law in
Judicial Review of Environmental Decisionmaking: Lessons from the Clean Air Act, 62 Iowa
L. Rev. 713 (1977).

182. W. Pedersen, Formal Records and Informal Rulemaking, 85 Yale L. J. 38, 60
(1975).

183. See J. Mashaw and D. Harfst, n. 174 above; D. Costle, Brave New Chemical: The
Future Regulatory History of Phlogiston, 33 Admin. L. Rev. 195 (1981); more recent accounts of rulemaking "ossification," p. 233 below, seem considerably less critical of these
costs as elements contributing to the turgidity of contemporary rulemaking than of others.

184. Modeling involves the use of computer models or other analytic devices to pre-
dict the outcome of complex interactions—for example, the economic impact of a proposed regulation—and is highly dependent on the assumptions of the model as well as the
accuracy of the data employed in it. Scientific judgment issues arise in assessing the outcomes of processes that cannot be directly tested, for example the impact on steel used in

Perhaps inevitably, however, judges and lawyers more familiar with the models of adversarial legal trial than those of scientific dispute resolution (or, for that matter, legislative inquiry) came to see the issues of ventilation and resolution in lawyers' rather than scientists' or politicians' terms. Two essentially contemporaneous cases dramatized the influence of judicial models on the developing requirements and, in doing so, also served to set limits upon them. The first threatened institutional decision processes with misunderstandings about the nature of rulemaking records; the second, notice-and-comment procedures with judicial requirements for the use of viva voce trial procedures.

"Ex parte contacts": *Home Box Office, Inc. v. FCC*[185] concerned a Federal Communications Commission rule regulating what programs could be shown by cable antenna systems competing with regular television broadcasters. This was a rule of a more traditional character—fact-finding presented no particular difficulty, but the rule's financial implications for many of the groups participating were substantial. Many participants had not only filed comments, but also approached FCC Commissioners and staff informally to voice their views. An inquiry by the court produced "a document over 60 pages long which revealed, albeit imprecisely, widespread ex parte communications involving virtually every party [to the rulemaking]."

Was this wrong behavior? While the court was horrified, none of the participants appear to have treated it guiltily, one going so far as to boast of its success in bringing congressional pressure to bear. As we have seen,[186] the "ex parte communication" limitation is one characteristic of on-the-record proceedings, in particular of adjudication; all the statutory provisions concerning it are pointed in that direction. Informal rulemaking, on the other hand, encourages contact and interaction; it imposes no structures of separation on agency decisionmaking, and no obligation of mutual disclosure among the participants.

For the *Home Box Office* court, however, the discovery of the rulemaking "record" and the development of the "paper hearing" pointed in another direction:

---

a nuclear power plant of being exposed to high levels of radiation for forty years. Projection involves the transplanting of data developed in one sphere to another, as when scientists use the results of experiments on mice conducted by administering relatively high doses of a chemical to estimate carcinogenicity in humans at low dosage rates. A highly regarded decision illustrating these problems is Sierra Club v. Costle, 657 F.2d 298 (D.C. Cir. 1981), discussed in this respect at p. 385 below.

185. 567 F.2d 9, cert. den. 434 U.S. 829 (1977).

186. See p. 204 above.

Even the possibility that there is here one administrative record for the public and this court and another for the Commission and those "in the know" is intolerable.... [I]mplicit in the decision to treat the promulgation of rules as a "final" event in an ongoing process of administration is an assumption that an act of reasoned judgment has occurred, an assumption which further contemplates the existence of a body of material... with reference to which such judgment was exercised. Against this matter, "the full administrative record that was before [an agency official] at the time he made his decision,"[187]... it is the obligation of this court to test the actions of the Commission for arbitrariness or inconsistency with delegated authority.... As a practical matter, Overton Park's mandate means that the public record must reflect what representations were made to an agency so that relevant information supporting or refuting those representations may be brought to the attention of the reviewing courts by persons participating in agency proceedings. This course is obviously foreclosed if communications are made to the agency in secret and the agency itself does not disclose the information presented.[188]

The opinion continued in this vein for some pages, adding the thought that the "paper hearing" requirements for the disclosure of materials in agency files were important, also, for their promotion of "adversarial discussion among the parties." Explicitly, then, in this court's view, the opportunity to comment had become not only a chance to contribute argument, data or views to which attention must be paid, but also the occasion for challenge and testing of what others had contributed.[189]

---

187. The quotation is from Citizens to Preserve Overton Park, Inc. v. Volpe, p. 235 above.

188. 567 F.2d at 54.

189. The court's reaction could be understood as one of the periodic reactions to suspicion about the reality of an agency's professed findings. The difficulty of the court's position as a matter of statutory construction of 5 U.S.C. §553, however, should be evident. The agency is required to provide for only one opportunity for comment. If most or all comments are filed on the final day, it is impossible for any one commenter's submission to include responses to what others are simultaneously saying. Here, again, the court evidently had the elegant rituals of judicial filings in mind. Of course it is also true that (unlike judicial proceedings) the time deadlines for filing rulemaking comments are not jurisdictional. One may file comments, responsive or otherwise, at any time, and the agency is free to consider them. What the designated time period for comments assures is that timely comments will be paid attention to. Later comments need not be so regarded.

The characteristic to note is the extent to which the opinion's rhetoric draws on the instincts of judges, and thus tends to convert rulemaking into a species of adjudication.[190] This aspect of the opinion, promptly discredited by the Supreme Court decision next to be discussed, has essentially been disavowed by subsequent courts, who tend to explain *Home Box Office* in terms of the very large financial stakes it involved.[191] Receding from the language about "adversarial comment" and any requirement of one record for all participants, they acknowledge that the public record of rulemaking need not be exhaustive of what the agency may know or have heard; nor need there have been an opportunity for each participant to respond to every item that appears there. But the "paper hearing" idea continues to require that the public record contain all documents that the agency may have received in relation to a rulemaking. There also remains a general expectation, grounded in political rather than judicial norms and reinforced by a recommendation of the Administrative Conference of the United States,[192] that significant oral communications about pending rulemakings—particularly any data they may convey—will be noted, and a precis placed in the rulemaking record. This is the regime adopted in the special rulemaking provisions governing proceedings under the Clean Air Act, which most commentators expect to be the model for any future reform of federal rulemaking procedures generally.[193]

Required oral procedures? At about the same time as one panel of judges of the United States Court of Appeals for the District of Columbia Circuit was announcing its judgment in *Home Box Office*, another seemed to be saying, in a case that *did* involve highly contentious judgment about scientific facts in rulemaking, that trial-like adversary procedures might be required to assure their proper determination. The rulemaking outcome depended upon complex findings about the handling and impact of nuclear waste. The agency had in fact used oral proceedings in the rulemaking, and had revealed its data and permitted participants a degree of influence over the proceedings significantly

---

190. See, e.g., Action for Children's Television v. FCC, 564 F.2d 458 (D.C. Cir. 1977).

191. This reading was challenged, and the general problem thoughtfully explored, in E. Gellhorn and G. Robinson, Rulemaking "Due Process": An Inconclusive Dialogue, 48 U. Chi. L. Rev. 201 (1981).

192. Recommendation 77-3, published at 1 CFR 305.77-3, relied on "the widespread demand for open government" as well as the needs of judicial review in recommending the creation of a rulemaking file that would include the texts of all written communications and notes of "significant oral communications;" it rejected, however, the idea of an "opportunity of interested persons to reply" as inconsistent with the idea of rulemaking, and "neither practicable nor desirable." On the Administrative Conference, see p. 291 below.

193. See p. 196, n. 42 above.

beyond what section 553 required.[194] The court, however, believed the procedures the agency had chosen were not "sufficient to ventilate the issues" as fully as their importance required. Its opinion marked one side of a running debate between two wings of the court. One side believed that judges had the obligation to educate themselves to whatever extent was necessary to review agency results effectively on their own terms. The other—the voice of this opinion—despaired of judges' capacity to educate themselves effectively on highly technical matters. These judges thus concluded that the desirable judicial role was to require agencies to use procedures that would permit full ventilation, challenge, and explanation at the expert and responsible agency level.[195] Under this "hybrid" model, important issues of fact in rulemaking—facts of a general character, such as the impact of a given level of radiation on human health—would require trial-like oral procedures for their determination. Viva voce examination of scientific experts and the presentation of contending expert points of view, proponents asserted, would permit more informed decision. They claimed that truth was more likely to arise from the contending views and from partisan challenges to expert testimony than from a process considering such disputes only on the papers. Congress had adopted hybrid procedures legislatively for a few particular statutes and agencies, and—although doubts were being expressed about the costs in time and effort it imposed[196]—the courts of appeals seemed poised to require it more generally.

In *Vermont Yankee Nuclear Power Corp. v. Natural Resources Defense Council, Inc.*,[197] the Supreme Court repudiated this development in a sharply worded and unanimous opinion that appeared to forbid the courts of appeals

---

194. The reader is entitled to know that the author was General Counsel of the Nuclear Regulatory Commission when the case was decided by the court of appeals and briefed to the Supreme Court, so that his view of the case is to some extent, inevitably, that of an advocate.

195. See Ethyl Corp. v. EPA, 541 F.2d 1 (D.C. Cir.) cert. den. 426 U.S. 941 (1976).

196. The most disciplined study was that done for the Administrative Conference of the United States by Professor Barry Boyer; he studied the Federal Trade Commission's experience with hybrid rulemaking procedures a 1974 statute required for its adoption of certain types of rules, concluding they produced little gain in accuracy, fairness, or acceptability of results but a good deal of additional cost and delay. See Boyer, Report on the Trade Regulation Rulemaking Procedures of the Federal Trade Commission, 1979 ACUS Ann. Rep. 41; 1980 ACUS Ann. Rep. 33; for more recent studies, see T. McGarity & S. Shapiro, Workers at Risk: The Failed Promise of the Occupational Safety and Health Administration (Praeger 1993); W. West, Administrative Rulemaking: Politics and Processes (Greenwood 1985).

197. 435 U.S. 519 (1978).

to require *any* procedures beyond those specifically required by section 553. The APA, it reasoned, settled "long-continued and hard-fought contentions, and enacts a formula on which opposing social and political forces have come to rest."[198] Its rulemaking provisions "established the maximum procedural requirements which Congress was willing to have the courts impose upon agencies in conducting rulemaking procedures. Agencies are free to grant additional procedural rights in the exercise of their discretion, but reviewing courts are generally not free to impose them if the agencies have not chosen to grant them."[199] Permitting courts to determine what would have been "properly tailored" procedures after the fact, the Court reasoned, would involve the courts in assessing outcomes by hindsight, a perspective denied the agencies when they made their procedural choices. The predictable consequence would be to lead agencies to choose excessive formality as the only safe means of avoiding reversal on procedural grounds. And, the Court stressed, the argument for more elaborate procedures rested on a false view of the record of rulemaking: "[I]nformal rulemaking need not be based solely on the transcript of a hearing held before an agency.... Thus, the adequacy of the 'record' in [rulemaking] is not correlated directly to the type of procedural devices employed, but rather turns on whether the agency has followed the statutory mandate of the Administrative Procedure Act or other relevant statutes."[200]

Clearly enough, the Supreme Court's *Vermont Yankee* opinion now forbids courts to require oral procedures in connection with rulemaking. Correspondingly, the *Home Box Office* idea of "adversarial comment" has been rejected. But what of the elements of the "paper hearing"—the expanded notions of "notice," "comment," and "statement of basis and purpose" that the courts of appeals had developed? In fact the extent and context of rulemaking has changed enormously since the APA was adopted in 1946, and statutes such as the Freedom of Information Act reflect new ideas about the procedural context "upon which opposing social and political forces have come to rest." The Supreme Court's casual assumption about the record in *Overton Park*, as we have seen,[201] was a central factor in the development of the "paper hearing" idea; that assumption would have provoked wonder among the APA's drafters. While the Supreme Court's *Vermont Yankee* opinion underscored the differing nature of records in informal rulemaking and on-the-record adjudication, it did not abandon *Overton Park* review and in later cases the Court

---

198. Id. at 523.
199. Id. at 524.
200. Id. at 547.
201. See p. 235 above.

has reaffirmed it—confirming, in this way, the "paper hearing" approach.[202] Scholars from the outset doubted that *Vermont Yankee* swept as broadly as its language suggested,[203] and the paper hearing ideas can be attached—however loosely—to the language of the APA itself. Permitting fresh understanding of that language as circumstances change exercises a conventional judicial function. The nature of rulemaking, and for that matter of judicial review, have changed since 1946, and the enactment of new statutes such as the FOIA, even if not directly amendments to the APA, signal changing contexts as well. The Court ought not to be taken as having ignored those developments.

f. The impact of increasing political oversight

With the institutional character of rulemaking secured,[204] and in step with what seems generally a greater judicial disposition to regard rulemaking as, in significant respects, a political as well as an expert enterprise, the last two decades' developments have focused more on the political control of rulemaking and, correspondingly perhaps, more on the period that precedes publication of a section 553 notice of proposed rulemaking.

Sierra Club v. Costle: These shifts were signaled in 1981 by *Sierra Club v. Costle*,[205] a case involving an EPA regulation setting standards for the emission of sulfur compounds by coal-burning electric power plants. The standards entailed sharp political as well as technical issues.[206] Setting a standard was not simply a matter of fixing an emission level each power plant must achieve, which would be complex in itself. Sulfur emissions can be controlled in several ways: use of low-sulfur coal, pre-treatment (washing) of the coal, the use of either of two available technologies for "scrubbing" the gases produced by burning the coal, or some combination of these measures. These techniques

---

202. Motor Vehicle Manufacturers Assn. v. State Farm Mutual Ins. Co., 463 U.S. 29 (1983), discussed at p. 377 below.

203. R. Stewart, Vermont Yankee and the Evolution of Administrative Procedure, 91 Harv. L. Rev. 1805 (1978); C. Byse, Vermont Yankee and the Evolution of Administrative Procedure: A Somewhat Different View, 91 Harv. L. Rev. 1823 (1978); A. Scalia, Vermont Yankee: The APA, the D.C. Circuit, and the Supreme Court, 1978 The Sup. Ct. Rev. 345.

204. See, e.g., United Steelworkers of America, AFL-CIO-CLC v. Marshall, 647 F.2d 1189 (D.C. Cir.), cert. den. 453 U.S. 913 (1981), p. 151 n. 8 above, in which two of the three *Home Box Office* judges joined.

205. 657 F.2d 298 (D.C. Cir. 1981). The case is also discussed at p. 385 below.

206. The story of the rulemaking is well told, with an emphasis on the distortions (as the authors see them) introduced by the political process in B. Ackerman and W. Hassler, Clean Coal/Dirty Air (Yale, 1981); a shorter account by the same authors appears as Beyond the New Deal: Coal and the Clean Air Act, 89 Yale L. J. 1466 (1980).

vary in effectiveness and in cost, and their costs depend on whether they are being integrated into the design of a new plant, or retrofitted onto an old one. Coal-fired power plants are located throughout the United States; both air quality and coal quality vary considerably with American geography, as do their significance. Thus, maintaining visual clarity of the desert air near the Grand Canyon may have an importance in addition to the requirements of health. Sulfur compounds, once air-borne, mix with whatever else is in the air and travel in the direction of prevailing winds, slowly precipitating out of the atmosphere as acid rain; any one plant's contribution is merely incremental, *and* downwind users of the air, like downstream users of a river, have to deal with an aggregate result—potentially damaging, yet hard to affix particular responsibility for. Low-sulfur coal is present in some parts of the country but not others; eliminating a market for high-sulfur coal would cost jobs in already impoverished regions. Scrubbing would demand expensive equipment that if not universally required would diminish the market for high-sulfur coal. And while washing and burning low-sulfur coal might be sufficient to produce emissions like those achievable by cleaning and scrubbing high-sulfur coal, still cleaner air could be produced by also scrubbing the low-sulfur coal, which is found near the mountains and canyons of the American West where visibility has high value.

It is thus evident that the issues presented were "polycentric,"[207] with many essentially political tradeoffs possible. For environmentalists seeking pure air, eastern coal interests with high-sulfur reserves, other areas with low-sulfur reserves, and a President concerned about the general economic impact of imposing a costly and generally unproven technology, the stakes were high. The Clean Air Act obliges the EPA to maintain a rulemaking file including all information or data on which it intends to rely, and it had docketed there the notes of a series of meetings, including several with the President and/or his staff held shortly before the rule was announced. Some of these meetings included coal industry officials and a powerful senator from one of the eastern high-sulfur states, whose cooperation the President needed on many issues. One meeting with the President and his staff was not recorded on this docket. The rule as adopted had been couched in terms tending to favor the eastern interests. Had there been improper political meddling?

Unlike the court of appeals in *Home Box Office*, even despite the special provisions of the Clean Air Act, the panel deciding *Sierra Club v. Costle* sought

---

207. See p. 209 above.

to respect the non-judicial characteristics of the rulemaking process. Informal oral meetings about pending rulemakings would not be forbidden or made the subject of formal recording requirements. As Judge Wald noted:

> [T]he very legitimacy of general policymaking performed by un-elected administrators depends in no small part upon the openness, accessibility, and amenability of these officials to the needs and ideas of the public.... As judges we are insulated from these pressures...but we must refrain from the easy temptation to look askance at all face-to-face lobbying efforts, regardless of the forum in which they occur, merely because we see them as inappropriate in the judicial context.[208]

Stressing the President's exclusive constitutional responsibility for exercise of executive authority and the agency's inability to rely on any factual matter not placed in its docket, the court found that the failure to record notes of one of the meetings with the President presented no difficulty.

> After all, any rule...must have the requisite factual support in the rule-making record, and...the Administrator may not base the rule...on any "information or data" which is not in the record, no matter what the source....Of course, it is always possible that undisclosed Presidential prodding may direct an outcome that is factually based on the record, but different from the outcome that would have obtained in the absence of Presidential involvement. In such a case, it would be true that the po-litical process did affect the outcome in a way the courts could not po-lice. But we do not believe that Congress intended that the courts con-vert informal rulemaking into a rarified technocratic process, unaffected by political considerations or the presence of Presidential power.[209]

The court was similarly undisturbed by the possibility of congressional pres-sure inherent in the meetings with the eastern Senator, absent a demonstra-tion that he had introduced extraneous considerations.[210] "Where Members of Congress keep their comments focused on the substance of the proposed

---

208. 657 F. 2d at 400–01.

209. Id. at 408–09.

210. Such a demonstration had been successfully made in an earlier case, D.C. Feder-ation of Civil Associations v. Volpe, 459 F.2d 1231 (D.C. Cir. 1971), cert. den. 405 U.S. 1030 (1972). There, a member of Congress had demanded that the Secretary of Trans-portation move forward to authorize construction of a bridge (the decision challenged in the case), and threatened to hold funds for another, unrelated departmental program hostage in the appropriations process until he did so.

rule...administrative agencies are expected to balance Congressional pressure with the pressures emanating from all other sources."

Economic and other impact analyses: This acknowledgment of a proper role for political oversight in rulemaking, emphatically echoed by the Supreme Court in later years,[211] has armed the development of the executive orders already discussed,[212] requiring economic impact analyses and annual participation in the setting of a regulatory agenda. Both activities occur during the pre-notice period of rulemaking. The issues about these consultations have turned not on their fact so much as on their transparency, and on the subtle line between the President's desirable influence and his more questionable substitution of a possibly very political judgment to resolve complex scientific issues. Factual analyses prepared by the agency in the course of these processes or submitted to it by other agencies, including the OMB, seem a necessary part of the record generated by a "paper hearing." Insofar as they concern fact, such analyses would not ordinarily be privileged from disclosure under the FOIA.[213] But an FOIA privilege would extend to predecisional discussions about policy choices, the very matter as to which oversight is likely to be the most vigorously exercised and the public's suspicions are likely to be the most aroused.

Practices regarding transparency have varied considerably from President to President. The court in *Sierra Club* placed evident emphasis on an undertaking by the White House of President Jimmie Carter, whose administration was responsible for the rule being reviewed. Under lawyers' advice, the White House had agreed to avoid serving as a "conduit" for essentially private contributions by political "friends." The court hinted that any such involvement would produce more difficult questions. In subsequent Republican administrations, the unwillingness of the White House to make its interventions public (and suspicions that they often reflected corporate input) produced extended political struggles with the Democrat-controlled Senate—that, for example, refused to confirm the first President Bush's choice for the office responsible for administering his executive order, in the absence of clear undertakings on the transparency question.[214] The interventions were criticized,

---

211. Chevron, U.S.A., Inc. v. Natural Resources Defense Council, Inc., 467 U.S. 837 (1984), see p. 272 below.

212. See p. 103 above.

213. See p. 233 above. As Judge Wald's opinion in Sierra Club reflects, both politics *and* scientific judgment often play significant roles in rulemaking on technologically complex issues; this heightens public interest in transparency, and the importance of an explanation in terms of those factors that are statutorily proper to be considered.

214. See p. 109 above.

as well, for inducing delay transferring and politicizing rulemaking authority.[215] President Clinton's Executive Order 12,866 made extensive commitments to transparency and timeliness; with those commitments, public controversy over the politicality of the Executive Order's administration appeared to have faded away. The second Bush administration's approach is not yet clear. Through all of this, however, general congressional support for the idea of presidential participation and oversight has been strong. "To what extent in public?" has been the significant question.

Whitman v. American Trucking: The importance of limits on broad political direction may be suggested by *Whitman v. American Trucking Assn*,[216] the Supreme Court's 2001 decision resulting from challenges to another EPA rule about air quality control, referred to in the course of the earlier discussion of delegation. In sustaining the constitutionality of the statute in that case, one question that appears to have held some importance for the Court was whether the EPA was to reach its judgment strictly in terms of scientific judgment about the level of protection "that is 'requisite'—that is, not higher or lower than is necessary—to protect the public health with an adequate margin of safety," or whether it was also permitted to compromise that judgment in light of costs to the national economy. The Court firmly concluded, as had the courts of appeals previously considering this question, that those costs were not, as such, a proper factor to be considered (acknowledging, nonetheless, a certain imprecision in "requisite" and "adequate"). That the Administrator was to be governed by technical considerations bearing on public health protection, one could believe, made her judgment less baldly legislative (or, at least "political") than if it were seen to depend on essentially political trade-offs among a number of factors. Those factors both are less susceptible of "expert judgment" and would extend the Administrator's responsibilities to a broader range of subjects, an extension arguably more threatening to separation of powers concerns.[217] It is easier, that is, to accept a powerful delegate with a responsibility limited to a particular set of concerns in terms of which her actions must be justified, than a delegate made responsible for a broad range of concerns, of whose resolution effective judicial review might be difficult to imagine.

Yet the habit of causing agencies at least to *report on and analyze* issues beyond their immediate responsibilities in important rulemakings, which began

---

215. R. Pildes and C. Sunstein, Reinventing the Regulatory State, 62 U. Chi. L. Rev. 1 (1995).

216. 531 U.S. 457 (2001), p. 29 ff. above.

217. See Rakoff, p. 22 n. 45 above.

with the National Environmental Policy Act,[218] is by now deeply ingrained in the Executive Orders about impact analysis, and a number of statutes building upon them. The Court's opinion contains no direct suggestion that these frameworks (including, under Executive Order 12, 866,[219] presidential requirements for particular bureaucratic arrangements within each agency) raise issues of either constitutionality or legality. Unsurprisingly, given the President's constitutional responsibilities for overseeing all government, one finds in the literature little question or criticism about his power to call for such analyses,[220] although some believe the variety of such analyses required has expanded beyond reason,[221] and others have questioned its effectiveness.[222] So long as the responsible administrator articulates her judgment in the terms in which the statute authorizing her action commands, and the action is sustainable in those terms, the situation remains as Judge Wald characterized it in Sierra Club above.[223] Despite the commitments to transparency made in E.O. 12,866, it may be remarked, OIRA leaves it to the individual agencies how and to what extent they will make its interventions available; its own practice is to post on its Website a running account of pending matters, with some indications of meetings held or comments made, but no details.[224]

Regulatory Flexibility, Unfunded Mandates, etc.: Support for centralized coordination of rulemaking has been reflected in a number of statutes. These

---

218. See p. 101 above; Calvert Cliffs' Coordinating Comm. v. USAEC, 449 F.2d 1109 (D.C. Cir. 1971); S. Taylor, Making Bureaucracies Think: the Environmental Impact Statement Strategy of Administrative Reform (Stanford University 1984). NEPA does not change the agency's mandate, as such, but requires it to engage in a specified inquiry (in this case, about environmental impact), under external supervision, before it pursues its mandate— on the theory that the inquiry itself will produce a more informed pursuit of that mandate. See Robertson v. Methow Valley Citizens' Council, 490 U.S. 332 (1989).

219. See p. 103 above.

220. See E. Kagan, Presidential Administration, 114 Harv. L. Rev. 2246 (2001); P. Shane, Political Accountability in a System of Checks and Balances: The Case of Presidential Review of Rulemaking, 48 Ark. L. Rev. 161 (1995).

221. S. Shapiro, Political Oversight and the Deterioration of Regulatory Policy, 46 Admin. L. Rev. 1 (1994).

222. R. Hahn, Reviving Regulatory Reform: A Global Perspective (2000) and R. Hahn et al., Empirical Analysis: Assessing Regulatory Impact Analyses: The Failure of Agencies to Comply with Executive Order 12,866, 23 Harv. J. L. & Pub. Pol'y 859 (2000) give what is at best a mixed report on the success of E.O. 12,866 (and its predecessors) in causing agencies to perform professionally creditable economic impact analyses, or to produce regulations whose projected economic benefits consistently exceed their projected costs.

223. See text at n. 208 above.

224. See http://www.whitehouse.gov/omb/inforeg/regpol.html.

both pick up the "impact analysis" theme and also reflect an increasing practice (notable as well in a variety of executive orders) of requiring rulemakers to take special account of the needs of particular communities or political themes. Thus the Regulatory Flexibility Act,[225] first adopted in 1980 and then much strengthened in 1996, requires agencies to pay special attention to the possible special needs of small businesses affected by important regulations, and to consider alternative approaches that might protect them, especially, from severe economic impacts. Agency compliance with this requirement, unlike the executive orders, is made subject to judicial review in limited respects. The court reviews to see that the correct inquiry was made; then, with the information it will have generated in the "record" of the rulemaking along with all other information, it asks whether the agency's conclusions were "reasonable" in whatever terms its mandates command.[226] As with the National Environment Policy Act, the mandate of the agency has not been changed by the Act; but the body of information the agency will have before it in deciding how to pursue that mandate has been considerably expanded, and the importance of new policy concerns is, as it were, "in the air."[227]

The Regulatory Flexibility Act was also the first statutory source of the requirement for published early notice of work that is expected to lead to proposals for rulemaking, in a semi-annual Unified Agenda of Federal Regulation. This attention to the earliest phase of agency rulemaking—how agencies decide on their regulatory priorities—has been picked up in presidential executive orders requiring consultation with OIRA over rulemaking plans, most recently E.O. 12,866,[228] as well as in the continuing "regulatory reform" attention to issues of risk.[229] This is self-evidently a context in which presidential "guidance" can be particularly strong. Since review of such priority judgments is extremely limited,[230] any such guidance is unlikely to encounter much judicial resistance.

Stepping back from a particular agency's choice to attack a particular regulatory target, one can imagine an integrated universe of regulatory activity, having impacts across the private sector as a whole. The fact of these impacts, which must be paid for by the private sector but have no direct reflection in

---

225. 5 U.S.C. §601 ff.; see Associated Fisheries of Maine, Inc. v. Daley, 127 F.3d 104 (1st Cir.1997).

226. Ibid.

227. See n. 218 above.

228. See p. 102 above.

229. See p. 228 above.

230. See p. 254 below.

government expenditures, catalyzed the development of required economic impact analysis for "major" rules. It has also fueled efforts to track the overall costs of government regulation for the private sector. Some accordingly argue for limits to that overall required "expenditure," on analogy to the annual appropriations budget for direct governmental expenditures. Achieving a meaningful annual "regulatory budget" has proved elusive—as may be imagined, estimates are extremely varied, political, self-interested, and controversial— but the effort has spawned legislative steps in addition to the President's annual regulatory agenda. The Government Performance and Results Act of 1993[231] requires each agency periodically to develop strategic plans looking at least five years into the future, that could set the parameters for performance measures—objective, quantifiable, and measurable to the extent that is possible—against which Congress could assess agency performance as part of the annual appropriations process. Results under the Act are not yet apparent.

In 1995, the Unfunded Mandates Reform Act added states, localities and tribal governments to small businesses, as entities especially entitled to have the impact of important regulations on their resources and concerns taken into account.[232] Ostensibly addressed to the Congress as much as to agencies, the Act's provisions have somewhat greater legal force for the latter.[233] They require agencies to analyze the economic impact of their important actions on the private sector as well as states, localities and tribal governments. Agencies are to take special account of, and seek to reduce, any "disproportionate budgetary effects." They are either to choose the "least costly, most cost-effective or least burdensome method of achieving" their regulatory objectives that would not be "inconsistent with law," or to explain why they have not done so. A rule imposing private duties and unsupported by government subvention is easily characterized as an "unfunded mandate," even though in this context funded mandates are unknown. The special consultation provisions that are the heart of the Act's mechanism for achieving con-

---

231. Pub. L. 103-62, 107 Stat. 285 (1993); see W. Funk, Governmental Management, a report as part of the ABA's Administrative Law and Regulatory Practice Section APA Project, p. 6 n. 7 above; the report is available at http://www.abanet.org/adminlaw/apa/govmanage0401.doc.

232. 2 U.S.C. §1501 et seq.

233. As addressed to Congress's legislative practices, they are wholly hortatory; agencies act under OMB supervision and reporting requirements, see. e.g. OMB, Fourth Annual Report to Congress, Agency Compliance with Title II of the Unfunded Mandates Reform Act of 1995 (1999), and are subject to judicial enforcement only if they wholly omit the required analysis. Any analysis prepared simply becomes an element of the rulemaking record.

sideration of impact, however, are particularly aimed at states, localities, and tribal governments.

One can add to this picture of increasing analytic complexity Executive Orders that already have required, or are promised shortly to require, special consideration of impacts on family life, property rights, civil justice reform, and energy efficiency. All these are sensible subjects for analysis, but in gross they help one to understand why commentators now frequently refer to the "ossification" of rulemaking.[234] At the time of its making, a table prepared for the American Bar Association's Section of Administrative Law and Regulatory Practice as a checklist for government attorneys supervising rulemaking tracked 20 different statutes and executive orders to be accounted for, at 25 different stages of rule development.[235] The great bulk of the entries, including all required impact analysis stages, occur in *advance* of section 553 notice of proposed rulemaking. One can thus understand the comment of a law professor who had served as EPA's general counsel in the Bush administration: "Notice-and-comment rulemaking is to public participation as Japanese Kabuki theater is to human passions—a highly stylized process for displaying in a formal way the essence of something which in real life takes place in other venues."[236]

3. Negotiated rulemaking

Under the encouragement of statute[237] and executive order, agencies in some cases develop their rulemaking proposals not internally, but through an external, mediated process known as "negotiated rulemaking." This is formally a process for generating proposals for rulemaking rather than the final rules as such. Thus, it brings the statutory provisions for public rulemaking procedures forward in time, into the development period previously left largely to bureaucratic initiatives. If negotiated rulemaking discussions succeed in developing a consensual proposal subscribed to by representatives of all the interests possibly affected by the rule and also acceptable to the agency, the no-

---

234. T. McGarity, The Courts and the Ossification of Rulemaking: A Response to Professor Seidenfeld, 75 Tex. L. Rev. 525 (1997); M. Seidenfeld, Demystifying Deossification, 75 Tex. L. Rev. 483 (1997); R. Pierce, Jr., Seven Ways to Deossify Agency Rulemaking, 47 Admin. L. Rev. 59 (1995); P. Verkuil, Rulemaking Ossification—A Modest Proposal, 47 Admin. L. Rev. 453 (1995).

235. M. Seidenfeld, Rulemaking Table, 27 Fla. St. L. Rev. 533 (2000).

236. E.D. Elliott, Reinventing Rulemaking, 41 Duke L. J. 1480, 1492 (1993).

237. 5 U.S.C. §561 ff.

tice-and-comment period is unlikely to generate significant opposition, and adoption of the proposal is also thought unlikely to produce judicial review.

The scheme of the Negotiated Rulemaking Act is relatively straightforward. An agency believing that a needed regulation will significantly affect only a limited number of interests, and that a committee representing those interests may be able through good faith negotiations to reach timely consensus on a proposal, may (but cannot be compelled to) establish a committee to that end. It may and frequently does appoint a neutral convenor to help identify the interests affected and suitable representatives. It must publish a notice fully describing the planned undertaking, including committee membership. This notice permits others to submit comments proposing new participants for unidentified or inadequately represented interests. A committee usually has fewer than 25 members, including agency representative(s). The agency also nominates a "facilitator"—often the convenor—to chair meetings and assist negotiations; if the committee does not accept the agency's nomination they may by consensus select their own. Balance in committee membership, public notice of committee meetings, and records of committee actions are all controlled by the Federal Advisory Committee Act.[238] The committee is to report to the agency any proposal on which it reaches consensus which will then be published as a notice of proposed rulemaking. Should it fail to reach full consensus, the committee reports any areas of agreement it has been able to develop, or other matters it considers appropriate. It is understood, but not statutorily required, that participants in the process will not challenge, but rather support, the recommended regulation should it eventually be adopted. In terms, the statute fully preserves the right to judicial review of a resulting rule (but *not* of the negotiation process), which "shall not be accorded any greater deference by a court than a rule which is the product of other rulemaking procedures."[239]

Negotiated rulemaking is a common but not predominant practice—depending as it does on several factors: agency initiative to develop the activity, the susceptibility of the matter to a consensual outcome, and securing agreement from all the private interests involved to participate in good faith. Critical responses are mixed, with some claiming indifferent success in reducing costs, time demands, and controversiality as compared to conventional rulemaking, and others asserting that where it has been successful, substantial gains have in fact been made. In departing from the usual hierarchical arrange-

238. See p. 289 below.
239. 5 U.S.C. §570.

ments common to agency structure, the process courts frustration by agency superiors (who are not involved in the negotiations) of any consensus that might be achieved. Perhaps the most trenchant criticism has been that a mediated process can produce an outcome agreeable to all participants, yet inconsistent with legality. For example, when the EPA appointed a committee to develop standards for wood-burning stoves, it successfully developed a consensus proposal, ultimately adopted as a regulation, that contained a number of consumer protection measures and assignments of responsibility. Although these outcomes were acceptable to all interests involved as a political matter, one critic argued, the EPA could not have defended them as a lawful exercise of its statutory delegations had judicial review been sought.[240] The negotiation process, perhaps unsurprisingly had produced compromises that if closely examined would be found to have been unauthorized. This politically satisfying outcome is hard to square with commitment to the rule of law.

4. Forcing the agency's hand in rulemaking

If parties cannot force procedures on agencies beyond those reasonably related to the statute,[241] can they force rulemaking to occur at all? Or is the decision to undertake rulemaking, by analogy to the decision to initiate a proceeding,[242] one that is entirely (or at least presumptively) within the agency's discretion? Section 553(e) of the APA requires each agency to permit interested persons "the right to petition for the issuance, amendment, or repeal of a rule," and section 555(e) requires both "prompt notice" of action on any petition and "a brief statement of the grounds for denial." In these slight obligations—"brief" appearing to be less demanding than "concise general," and not subject to the pressures for elaboration and development we have just explored—the courts have found a basis for review that is highly permissive, yet still operative. If, for example, the agency has revealed a misunderstanding of its legal authority to act in the course of declining to issue a rule, that could provide the basis for reversal, with directions to reconsider the matter under a correct understanding. One might say the courts have found a middle ground between the discretion exercised in making rulemaking judgments, and the (unreviewable) *DISCRETION!* they say normally attaches to judgments about prosecutorial choices and other priority setting.

---

240. W. Funk, When Smoke Gets in Your Eyes: Regulatory Negotiation and the Public Interest—EPA's Woodstove Standards, 18 Envtl. L. 55 (1987).
241. See p. 241 above.
242. See p. 214 above.

Somewhat different questions are presented when statutes *require* rule-making, or—further—set deadlines within which it is directed to occur. Contemporary rulemaking often involves factors which could slow rulemaking considerably: issues of great complexity and moment; budgetary constraints significantly limiting agency resources; and analytic demands imposed chiefly by executive order and in any event overseen by the White House. These factors help understand why Congress might impose such obligations. In addition, since rulemaking became prominent, the President has most often been from the other political party than the one commanding Congress; in such a situation, from congressional perspective, these directives are a means of establishing what is required to "take Care that the Laws be faithfully executed."[243] Finally, since Congress controls appropriations and thus is implicated in the budget cuts, outside observers could accuse politicians of trying to have it both ways—publicly demanding performance and more covertly refusing resources. They might hope to gain credit with one audience for emphatic action to deal with a problem, while satisfying another that it has little reason to fear early adverse action.

It is much clearer that agencies have violated legal obligations, when they fail to act or to meet statutory deadlines, than whether a court can grant an effective remedy for such violations. If the agency cannot lawfully refuse to adopt a rule, it should not be surprising to find the courts willing to command that rules be developed. No administrator is entitled to "impound" programs of which she disapproves by simply refusing to enforce them.[244] Yet since the administrator, not the court, must make the necessary judgments, securing relief can be frustrating. Such frustration is evident in an opinion describing a "14-year struggle to compel the Secretary of Labor...to issue a field sanitation standard providing access to drinking water and toilets for several million American agricultural workers" as a "disgraceful chapter of legal neglect."[245] Such actions are more likely to be brought by representatives of those hoping for regulation, diffuse and often impoverished interests like the agri-

---

243. U.S. Const. Art II Sec. 3.

244. Thus, in Allison v. Block, 723 F.2d 631 (8th Cir. 1983), farmers who had defaulted on federal loans (and so risked losing their farm) persuaded the court to block foreclosure until the Secretary of Agriculture had implemented a statutory provision for a regime of discretionary relief. Executive branch refusal to implement a statute has been identified by even the most conservative of Supreme Court Justices as an appropriate occasion for judicial intervention. Motor Vehicle Manufacturers Assn. v. State Farm Mutual Ins. Co., 463 U.S. 29 (1983) (separate opinion); Heckler v. Chaney, 470 U.S. 821 (1985)

245. Farmworker Justice Fund, Inc. v. Brock, 811 F.2d 613, 614, vacated as moot, 817 F.2d 890 (D.C. Cir. 1987).

cultural workers, rather than important economic interests subject to possible regulation and possessing "special interest" political leverage.

The problem of fashioning effective relief arises as well when an agency has missed an "action-forcing" deadline that Congress has set for promulgation of a rule. If Congress has provided for a default rule should the agency fail to act in time, that rule can be given effect; but Congress has rarely been willing (or able) to adopt fall-back resolutions of this character. Congress or a court can command, and the agency may even agree, that a rule is to be promulgated by a certain date; yet the court cannot itself adopt a rule when that date passes. It can only repeat the command that action be taken, setting a new schedule for that action. One finds frequent enough litigation to enforce these deadlines, particularly in the environmental context. Opinions in the later stages of these disputes make clear that agencies do direct their attention to these problems—but not always with satisfying (or timely) results. Courts say that they cannot accept as excuses for delay Congress's failure to appropriate necessary funding, or the genuine difficulty of the issues to be resolved. Yet they cannot become the administrators of these complex programs. They must, ultimately, rely on the administrators' commitments to legality. New deadlines are bargained, and rebargained—the agency plausibly showing effort but not completion, the court driven by the law's clear requirement to have acted by a certain date. It can protect the agency from certain external distractions that could introduce delay—directing, for example, as Executive Order 12,866[246] also provides, that White House review processes be suspended when they conflict with statutory deadlines: "OMB has no authority to delay regulations subject to the deadline in order to review them under the executive order.... [It] may review the regulations only until the time at which OMB review will result in the deadline being missed." [247] Yet punishments—a fine or contempt of court—against the person of the responsible administrator are not to be found in the cases. In the end, the agency must itself generate the political will to act and be able to determine an appropriate outcome to the proceeding it has been commanded to conduct.

A different question is presented when agencies seek to act by publication rulemaking,[248] and it is claimed that notice and comment rulemaking is required—in effect, that the agency has evaded its procedural obligations under section 553. Here is a remedy more likely to be sought by the regulated. They may indeed be experiencing an agency effort to evade procedural obligations

---

246. See p. 102 above.
247. Environmental Defense Fund v. Thomas, 627 F. Supp. 566 (D. D.C. 1986).
248. See p. 222 above.

that, as the foregoing has suggested, have become considerably more demanding and expensive. More adventitiously, regulated interests may be seeking additional time free of the burdens the agency initiative will bring, or the greater control over outcome that forcing the agency into a relatively protracted, public and formal procedure could bring. Repeated litigation on this question seems to have persuaded some judges that

> The phenomenon…is familiar. Congress passes a broadly worded statute. The agency follows with regulations containing broad language, open-ended phrases, ambiguous standards and the like.…Several words in a regulation may spawn hundreds of pages of text as the agency offers more and more detail regarding what its regulations demand of regulated entities. Law is made, without notice and comment, without public participation, and without publication in the Federal Register or the Code of Federal Regulations. With the advent of the Internet, the agency does not need these official publications to ensure widespread circulation; it can inform those affected simply by posting its new guidance or memoranda or policy statement on its web site.[249]

Agencies instructing their staff about enforcement priorities[250] or offering moderated enforcement in return for cooperation[251] have fallen afoul of this constraint, despite the usual freedom from judicial review enforcement actions enjoy.[252] In the author's view, extensively set forth in another place,[253] the judges in these cases have failed to understand that the litigation they occasionally see conveys a distorted picture of the realities of day-to-day agency life; in that life, publication rules are a necessary element serving important public (as well as agency) interests in the predictability and regularity of agency action. The problems their misunderstandings could create are suggested by another excerpt from the same opinion:

> If an agency acts as if a document issued at headquarters is controlling in the field, *if it treats the document in the same manner as it treats a legislative rule,* if it bases enforcement actions on the poli-

---

249. Appalachian Power Co. v. EPA, 208 F.3d 1015, 1020 (D.C. Cir. 2000).
250. See p. 168, n. 56 above.
251. See p. 164 above.
252. Heckler v. Chaney, p. 214 above.
253. P. Strauss, Publication Rules in the Rulemaking Spectrum: Assuring Proper Respect for an Essential Element, 53 Admin. L. Rev. 803 (2001).

cies or interpretations formulated in the document, if it leads private parties or State permitting authorities to believe that it will declare permits invalid unless they comply with the terms of the document, then the agency's document is for all practical purposes "binding."[254]

This passage equates four different propositions. An agency could properly hope that "a document issued at headquarters [would be regarded by its staff as] controlling in the field"—*that is perhaps the most important reason why publication rules are issued.*[255] Similarly, it will hope that—and the public will be best served if—its staff "bases enforcement actions on the policies or interpretations formulated in the document." And an agency that is reliable in its advice will inevitably "lead private parties or State permitting authorities to believe that it will declare permits invalid unless they comply with the terms of the document." None of these treatments of a publication rule entail the conclusion that it has "treat[ed] the document in the same manner as...a legislative rule." That conclusion requires the agency to take the further step of treating the rule as a regulation—as if it, in itself, had the same force and effect as a statute. Giving a publication rule effect as a precedent, as an instruction by which hierarchically inferior staff should expect to be bound, is not the same.[256] Requiring the relatively formal procedures of notice-and-comment rulemaking for advice that is intended to control staff actions and to be reliable for the public creates perverse incentives either not to give such advice, or to accompany any advice given with prominent notices that it is *not* intended to bind agency personnel and may *not* be relied on by the public. Such notices now do appear frequently. Why one should wish such outcomes is beyond the author's ready understanding.

D. *Choice between rulemaking and adjudication*

Courts "make law" as a by-product of deciding cases. Legislatures do so by enacting statutes. As the preceding pages have illustrated, agencies may create

---

254. Appalachian Power, 208 F.3d at 1021 (emphasis added).

255. The Supreme Court's recognition of this in United States v. Mead Corp., note 137 above, may help the courts of appeals, in future cases like Appalachian Power, to take a broader view of the phenomenon.

256. See Mead Corp., n. 137 above.

binding norms of conduct using procedural modes resembling each. The fact that agencies often have the power to use either technique leads some to describe them as having a choice in each instance how to proceed—by adjudication or by rulemaking—when considering the adoption of new norms. As a realistic matter, it can be artificial to imagine agency officials consciously choosing among modes of proceeding before acting. New norms often emerge unconsciously from the accidents and structural incentives of a largely uncoordinated bureaucratic process.[257] Nonetheless, the "choice" characterization provides a framework to think about the differences between the two modes of norm creation and, very occasionally, a basis for insisting that one or the other must be employed.

The general view is that rulemaking is the superior mode for the creation of binding new norms of conduct.[258] Its procedures engage a broader range of the interested community, albeit with less formality, and may be better suited to consideration and determination of the sorts of facts and other issues most likely to arise in the policymaking context. The rulemaking decision structure within the agency more fully engages both its staff expertise and the political responsibility of its leaders than the highly formal decision structure of adjudication. The product of rulemaking—a direct statement of positive law, accompanied by an explanatory statement—is likely to be more accessible both as text and in its placement in the standard legal materials, than will be a discussion dependent upon the facts of a particular adjudication and buried in an adjudicatory opinion. Finally, rulemaking operates prospectively.[259] In contrast, a norm developed in the course of adjudication ordinarily will be applied to the party before the agency in the proceeding in which it is first announced. That party, then, will not have been precisely aware of the norm before its announcement in the course of that proceeding. "Since [an agency], unlike a court, does have the ability to

---

257. See P. Strauss, Rules, Adjudications, and Other Sources of Law in an Executive Department: Reflections on the Interior Department's Administration of the Mining Law, 74 Colum. L. Rev. 1231 (1974).

258. The classic treatment of this issue remains D. Shapiro, The Choice of Rulemaking and Adjudication in the Development of Administrative Policy, 78 Harv. L. Rev. 921 (1965); see also R. Pierce, Jr., Two Problems in Administrative Law: Political Polarity on the District of Columbia Circuit and Judicial Deterrence of Agency Rulemaking, 1988 Duke L. J. 300, 308–09.

259. Exactly what "prospectively" means has occasionally been the subject of substantial controversy. See Bowen v. Georgetown University Hospital, 488 U.S. 204 (1988), Regions Hospital v. Shalala, 522 U.S. 448 (1998), and Eastern Enterprises v. Apfel, 524 U.S. 498 (1998); W. Luneberg, Retroactivity and Administrative Rulemaking, 1991 Duke L. J. 106, 109–110.

make new law prospectively through the exercise of its rule-making powers," the Supreme Court remarked in the foundational decision on this issue, "it has less reason to rely upon ad hoc adjudication to formulate new standards."[260]

The case in which these words were uttered, *Securities and Exchange Commission v. Chenery Corp.*, may be an excellent example of the difficulty involved in finding the "law" made by a judicial opinion. The Court went on to say that "the choice made between proceeding by general rule or by individual, ad hoc litigation is one that lies primarily in the informed discretion of the administrative agency." [261] It sustained the use of adjudication rather than rulemaking to elaborate new policy in that case. Chenery and other officers of a company had applied for approval of its reorganization. The SEC withheld approval, at first basing its decision on its understanding of then-existing judicial decisions. The Supreme Court narrowly reversed that opinion because the SEC's understanding of the judicial cases was erroneous,[262] and remanded the case for reconsideration in light of a correct understanding of those cases. The SEC then reached the same result—several years after the application had first been made—on the basis of its own policy determinations.

This "second-chance" reasoning was a new policy, and Chenery asserted it could not fairly be applied to him, but had to be formulated by rule for prospective application. The Court rejected Chenery's argument. Agencies had to be permitted discretion to use adjudication, since in some cases "problems may arise in a case which the administrative agency could not reasonably foresee, problems which must be solved despite the absence of a general rule." In other cases, the newness, specialized character, or variability of the problem might make rulemaking seem inappropriate. As for the possible unfairness of retroactive application of the new rule to Chenery, that "must be balanced against the mischief of producing a result which is contrary to a statutory design or to legal and equitable principles."[263]

---

260. Securities & Exchange Commission v. Chenery Corp. (II), 332 U.S. 194, 202 (1947).

261. Id. at 203.

262. Securities & Exchange Commission v. Chenery Corp (I)., 318 U.S. 80 (1943). This first Chenery decision is a frequently cited source for the proposition that agency judgments can be reviewed only on their announced reasoning. In contrast to its possibilities when reviewing a lower court's judicial opinion, the reviewing court cannot consider alternative lines of reasoning that might have been (but were not) employed. If it were permitted to do so, it could too easily substitute its own policy judgments (or those of agency attorneys) for those of the responsible agency head. See p. 376 ff. below.

263. Any seeming unfairness to Chenery is mediated by the narrowness of the Supreme Court's first reversal. It had been decided by a vote of 4–3, with two Justices not sitting. In

This, then, has been the general rule—that agencies have a broad and essentially unsupervised discretion in deciding between adjudication and rulemaking for the formulation of policy.[264] The retroactivity of applying freshly declared standards through adjudication has occasionally been rejected on grounds of "unfairness."[265] This has usually occurred in cases in which some new liability was sought to be imposed on individuals for past actions taken in good faith reliance on other policies then in effect.[266]

Other circumstances in which rulemaking has been required are less easily characterized. The FTC, for example, was compelled to use rulemaking rather than adjudication in one case in which the governing statute gave its decisions unusual force and effect.[267] One ordinary difference between rulemaking and caselaw is that the latter is not formally binding on persons who are not parties to the case in which it arises. Non-parties are always free to argue for the reconsideration of a prior decision or for its inapplicability to their circumstances (although such arguments may be ineffectual). The FTC statute permitted the Commission to treat policies resulting from adjudications precisely as if they were rules, not open to reexamination in this way. Other cases seem to suggest that rulemaking may be required to structure the exercise of official discretion under government grant programs—discretion that might otherwise be exercised in an uncheckably arbitrary fashion.[268]

---

the circumstances, one can say that Chenery had fair warning from the outset that the suitability of the proposed reorganization was open to doubt, even under existing judicial standards.

264. For a strong statement of this by the Supreme Court, see National Labor Relations Board v. Bell Aerospace Co., 416 U.S. 267 (1974).

265. See, e.g., Clark-Cowlitz Joint Operating Agency v. Federal Energy Regulatory Comm'n, 826 F.2d 1074 (en banc), cert. den. 485 U.S. 913 (1988).

266. The National Labor Relations Board is the most frequent target of these arguments, both because its policies frequently vary with changes in presidential administrations and because it so rarely uses rulemaking to generate policy in the areas of its responsibility. See Allentown Mack Sales & Service, Inc. v. NLRB, 522 U.S. 359 (1998).

267. Ford Motor Co. v. FTC, 673 F.2d 1008, (9th Cir. 1981), cert. den. 459 U.S. 999 (1982).

268. Morton v. Ruiz, 415 U.S. 199 (1974) is an example, one that commentators have had substantial difficulty in understanding. Others include a series of cases requiring the Secretary of Agriculture to implement a legislative program for discretionary relief of farm foreclosures, one of which, Allison v. Block, was summarized in note 244 above. That case left the choice of how to implement the statute to the Secretary's discretion—the orthodox position; but later decisions in other circuit courts required rulemaking on the ground that Congress saw an "urgent need...for deferral relief to farmers" and it is "a bit late to begin the accumulation of [case-by-case] decisional guides." Curry v. Block, 738 F.2d 1556,

From time to time the suggestion has been made that the opposite problem can arise, that an agency might employ rulemaking in circumstances that require the use of adjudication. This argument is often made when agencies adopt rules that have the effect of foreclosing what would otherwise be factual issues to be determined in adjudicatory hearings required by statute or due process. For example, one issue in individual hearings under the national disability insurance statutes is whether work the applicant is capable of performing exists in the national economy. (Under the statute, which is not an unemployment insurance statute, this question is strictly one of the physical possibility of the applicant's holding such employment; it is not relevant whether the work is available near the person's home, whether vacancies exist, or whether he would be hired if he applied.) At one point, this question was resolved by having vocational experts testify in each case, based on their understanding of the precise situation of the individual seeking to obtain or retain benefits. The Department of Health and Human Services later adopted a rule that created a grid of factors—age, literacy, degree of impairment, previous work experience—and specified how the question of employability was to be resolved for each combination of the grid. Experts no longer needed to testify. Under the grid, an unskilled person of limited prior education and advanced age whose impairments rendered her capable only of light work would be regarded as disabled; but the grid permitted characterizing a somewhat younger individual in the same medical position as disabled only if she were also illiterate or unable to communicate in English. The Supreme Court found no difficulty with this substitution of rule-determined facts for trial. The facts at issue had to do with job availability in the national economy, not the particular applicant. Only if the facts to be determined were unique to the party before the tribunal, "adjudicatory" rather than "legislative" in that sense, would the use of rulemaking be foreclosed.[269] Other results are consistent with this ruling.[270]

1563 (8th Cir. 1984). Perhaps the court feared, also, that in case-by-case decisionmaking the responsible administrator might never have to find the circumstances warranting deferral—the Secretary could use it to continue his apparent policy of refusing to implement the program Congress had created.

269. Heckler v. Campbell, 461 U.S. 458 (1983).

270. Federal Power Commission v. Texaco, Inc., 377 U.S. 33 (1964); Vermont Yankee Nuclear Power Corp. v. Natural Resources Defense Council, Inc., discussed at p. 241 above. A different question might be presented when the individual asserts that special facts about his circumstances warrant an exception to the generally applicable rule. But see FCC v. WNCN Listener's Guild, 450 U.S. 582 (1981).

E. *Investigation*

The APA is little concerned with agency investigative procedures. Internal instructions or manuals organizing these activities are within the Act's publication requirements, unless "disclosure could reasonably be expected to risk circumvention of the law."[271] Agency personnel engaged in these activities are to be segregated from the decisional process in on-the-record adjudication. The Act does not itself authorize any investigative act, whether inspection, required report, or subpoena; but it provides that no such act or demand may be "issued, made, or enforced except as authorized by law,"[272] and, in the particular case of subpoenas, provides briefly for judicial enforcement. Overall, the message conveyed—limited but important—is that investigative procedures are neither implicit nor ordinarily self-enforcing. Those procedures must be specially authorized by statute (the APA is not such a statute); and their enforcement as well depends upon the law, which may require invocation of the courts.

Investigative procedures can be classified under three different heads, each of which has had some attention in the preceding pages: physical inspections; required forms and reports; and subpoenas, or compulsory process. Together, they mark the citizen's most common experience with government and employ the bulk of government's regulatory personnel. On the whole, however, they are informal and summary procedures, about which there is ordinarily little controversy.

1. Inspections

The most visible of the three, perhaps, is inspection, a technique that may be either investigative or, in itself, decisional. Decisions to award motor vehicle licenses, to classify agricultural produce, or to quarantine neighborhoods are made directly on the basis of an inspector's observations, without intervening hearing. The APA's section 554(a)(3) recognizes this by excluding from the ordinary procedures of adjudication "proceedings in which decisions rest solely on inspections, tests, or elections." The question which decisions may so rest is surprisingly little developed. One sees dim reflections of it in adju-

---

271. 5 U.S.C. §552(b)(7)(E), as amended by the Anti-Drug Abuse Act of 1986, P.L. 99-570.

272. 5 U.S.C. §555(c).

dicatory hearings in which the issue becomes whether an inspector used appropriate techniques.[273]

The investigative uses of inspection, on the other hand, have prompted development of a fair amount of constitutional litigation, discussed in the opening pages of this essay.[274] The result has been establishment of a capacity on the part of most persons subject to inspection laws to force inspectors to secure prior judicial approval of any proposed inspection.[275] The confrontational and decidedly adversary attitudes accompanying some inspections are thought by some to reflect characteristic differences between American approaches to administrative justice and those of other nations.[276] The Occupational Safety and Health Administration, whose operations have in the past seemed a "model" of this approach, has been frustrated in its efforts to find alternative models by judicial insistence that it can adopt them only by the use of notice and comment rulemaking procedures.[277]

Inspection can have a dual character, seeking either to identify non-compliance, or to develop means for assuring compliance, with regulatory measures. In this context, much will depend on the attitude the inspectorate brings to its work. The constitutional developments are associated with the rights of persons suspected of crime to government regularity in developing evidence against them. Thus, they may tend to reinforce (if they do not generate) a posture in which the goal of inspection is seen as identifying and imposing sanctions for non-compliance, rather than encouraging compliance or otherwise promoting the positive ends of law.[278]

---

273. See, e.g., People v. Porpora, 91 Cal. App. 3d Supp. 13 (Cal. App. Dep't Super. Ct. 1979), in which an inspector had determined on sampling the defendant's commercial fish catch that the defendant had kept a larger proportion of a protected fish (Pacific mackerel) than California law permitted. A complaint that "failure...to preserve the fish...denied [the defendant fisherman] access to evidence that would have enabled him to impeach the reliability of the sampling technique and [its] results" was summarily rejected. Compare Board of Curators of the University of Missouri v. Horowitz, 435 U.S. 78 (1978) and Regents of University of Michigan v. Ewing, 474 U.S. 214 (1985), rejecting due process claims for trial-type hearing made by students who had failed courses in state-run universities.

274. See p. 42 ff. above.

275. The protection of prior judicial approval is not available for those engaged in "closely regulated enterprise," such as a coal mine or a nuclear power station; another exception, hardly surprising yet perhaps of greater moment here, is the requirement to submit to customs inspection at the border.

276. See p. 44 and n. 111 above.

277. See p. 164 above.

278. Wyman v. James, 400 U.S. 309 (1971), is one of the few Supreme Court cases recognizing this problem. Welfare caseworkers were to make quarterly inspections of the

2. Required forms and reports

If inspections are not the citizen's commonest encounter with regulation, then the filling out of required forms and reports surely is. These are materials required from classes of individuals or corporations; they may be as simple as a customs declaration, or as complex as the Federal Trade Commission's requirements for annual economic reporting by conglomerate corporations.[279] The minimal constitutional constraints bearing on these requirements have already been outlined;[280] it should be stressed that unless the courts can be persuaded the requirement of a report is solely for the purpose of acquiring evidence of the filer's criminal conduct,[281] no privilege against filing a report will be recognized. Ordinarily, the generality of such requirements, as with tax forms, is sufficient protection. Accordingly, the failure to file a report may itself be made the basis for a fine or other sanction. In the administrative context, this is an important distinction from a subpoena, which seeks to compel named persons to produce identified documents (or information). Judicial enforcement is generally required before a sanction can be imposed for non-compliance with a subpoena, as will be developed in the next section.

The principal general control over agency reporting requirements at the federal level is the Paperwork Reduction Act of 1980, reinvigorated and slightly amended in 1995.[282] This statute is remarkable for its explicit recognition of presidential oversight over even the independent regulatory commissions. An agency seeking to adopt a new reporting requirement must secure approval from the Office of Information and Regulatory Affairs in OMB,[283] which is authorized to require coordination with other agencies, or to find that the proposal is not "necessary for the proper performance of the functions of the agency, including whether the information will have practi-

---

homes in which dependent children supported by welfare lived. Was this for the detection of welfare fraud, as those demanding the protection of a search warrant insisted, or to help develop programmatic benefits for the children? Some of both, doubtless; and in this case the Court emphasized the helpful side and refused to find a warrant required. For apt criticism, see R. Burt, Forcing Protection on Children and Their Parents: The Impact of Wyman v. James, 69 Mich. L. Rev. 1259 (1971). See also Vernonia School District 47J v. Acton, 515 U.S. 646 (1995).

279. See FTC Line of Business Report Litigation, 595 F.2d 685 (D.C. Cir.), cert. den. 439 U.S. 958 (1978).

280. See p. 46 above.

281. Marchetti v. United States, 390 U.S. 39 (1968).

282. 44 U.S.C. §§3501–3520.

283. See p. 111 above.

cal utility." The OMB process of approval is conducted like an informal rule-making, and is open to public participation (although statutorily shielded from subsequent judicial review). An Internet roster is kept of pending business[284] although—like the listing of rules under E.O. 12,866 review—the information provided is sketchy at best. Even the independent regulatory commissions must participate; they may, however, override an OMB disapproval of their proposed action by a publicly explained majority vote. A failure to secure OMB authorization, as evidenced by a control number, can have dramatic consequences.[285]

3. Compulsory process

A subpoena, or compulsory process, is a directive to a named individual to produce particular documents or information. It can arise in the course of an established agency adjudication, and in that context is strongly analogous to discovery demands in civil litigation. It may also be issued in the course of and to support an agency investigation that has not yet developed to the hearing stage. The latter is legally the more interesting use of subpoenas (and probably the more frequent). The courts seem increasingly to be recognizing that when a subpoena is sought in adjudication, the presiding administrative law judge can be relied upon to exercise necessary controls. Correspondingly, they are tending to permit the agency to impose the same sorts of sanctions for non-compliance with agency subpoenas in that context as a United States district court would impose for non-compliance with discovery demands in a civil trial.[286]

In contrast, where a subpoena is used at the investigatory stage, a neutral agency official may be lacking. The demand to produce comes from the investigative, as-it-were prosecutorial side of the agency. Here, subpoenas are not recognized as self-enforcing. Unless its subject has incentives to comply

---

284. http://www.whitehouse.gov/library/omb/OMBPPRWK.html; a variety of information about OIRA's functions can be found at http://www.whitehouse.gov/omb/inforeg/index.html.

285. Saco River Cellular v. FCC, 133 F.3d 25 (D.C. Cir. 1998).

286. That is, failure to respond may be taken as an admission, or a basis for refusing permission to cross-examine a relevant witness, or the like. Compare NLRB v. International Medication Systems, Ltd., 640 F.2d 1110 (9th Cir. 1981), cert. den. 455 U.S. 1017 (1982), stating the more traditional view requiring judicial enforcement, with Atlantic Richfield Co. v. U.S. Department of Energy, 769 F.2d 771 (D.C. Cir. 1984). It is not asserted that agencies could themselves impose more dramatic penalties, such as courts may do using their power to imprison for contempt.

with an information demand,[287] the agency will be required to seek judicial assistance to compel obedience.

The judicial inquiry is not itself likely to be demanding. In general, an agency will be required to show only that the subpoena might produce information bearing on its responsibilities, not that it will do so. The agency need not demonstrate any "probable cause" to seek the information from the subpoena subject.[288] The relevant questions will be whether the subpoena is issued in pursuit of an authorized objective;[289] whether the evidence sought appears to be germane to a lawful subject of inquiry; whether the subpoena makes demands that are unreasonably vague or burdensome;[290] whether it has been issued in proper form; and whether there exists a privilege—such as the privilege against self-incrimination for individuals[291]— not to reply. A summary procedure is employed in district court to test these issues, and one's impression of the cases is that enforcement is not often refused.

Nonetheless, the procedure can introduce substantial delays and opportunities to undermine the agency's determination to pursue the matter, which are doubtless valued by subpoena resisters. The agency is required to bring the enforcement action in court, and that requires it to win the approval and use the resources of the Department of Justice. Neither of these is invariably to be had. Once a district court order to enforce a subpoena has been obtained, appeals are available to the courts of appeal and, by certiorari, to the Supreme Court. (This would not be true for a subpoena issued during the course of a civil trial, because that ruling would be considered interlocutory; but the agency's complaint seeking subpoena enforcement initiates a discrete proceeding so far as the judicial system is concerned, and so an immediate appeal may be taken).

---

287. For example, a license applicant or any other person seeking affirmative action from an agency may be compelled to satisfy an information demand, in practical terms, by the need to secure an agency response to its application.

288. Oklahoma Press Publishing Co. v. Walling, 327 U.S. 186 (1946).

289. For obvious reasons, courts have resisted efforts to inquire onto agencies' "real" motive for issuing apparently justified subpoenas; inquiries into the possibility of "bad faith" are generally limited in American law. See p. 380 below.

290. The corrective for a vague or burdensome subpoena is more likely to be some arrangement for increasing the definiteness or moderating the burden imposed by the subpoena than a complete refusal to enforce. For example, relief might provide for inspection of the material at the information-holder's premises as an alternative to requiring its delivery to the agency. A finding of vagueness or burdensomeness is perhaps more likely when the subject of the subpoena is a third party, not itself subject to regulation by the agency making the information demand.

291. See p. 46 above.

When the order of enforcement becomes final, only the first stage is complete. Any question about compliance, including a proceeding to have the respondent found in contempt of court for failure to produce the demanded materials, requires a second judicial proceeding. This brief, and not exhaustive, description should make apparent that a person who resolutely seeks to block an investigation can tie up the proceedings for long periods, and have the benefit of many different views of the correctness of the demands made.

F. *State administrative law*

Under American federalism,[292] each state regulates its own administrative procedure, and generalizations would be hazardous.[293] It may be appropriate, however, briefly to remark on two drafts of model state administrative procedure legislation promulgated by the National Conference of Commissioners on Uniform State Laws.[294] As of 1995, the draft of 1961 had been adopted by 27 states; the subsequent draft of 1981[295] had been adopted in three states.

The 1961 draft is rather brief, comprising sixteen operative sections. While taking some account of the smaller size and greater informality of state government, it is clearly modeled on the federal APA, chiefly addressing informal rulemaking and "contested cases"—on-the-record proceedings that, in this case, include ratemaking as well as licensing and other adjudicatory proceedings required to be decided after an opportunity for hearing. The draft does not require state equivalents of the federal administrative law judges to be presiding officers when the agency itself does not hear a matter(although in practice many states provide for such officials). In other respects, the draft does

---

292. See p. 10 ff. above.

293. References to the administrative procedure laws of each of the states may be found in Appendix B to Administrative Law: Cases and Comments, p. 30, note 65 above. M. Asimow, Symposium: Speed Bumps on the Road to Administrative Law Reform in California and Pennsylvania, 8 Widener J. Pub. L. 9 (1999), offers a persuasive (and somewhat discouraging) account of reform efforts in California, that can convey a flavor for the issues at the state level.

294. The National Conference is a body supported by state governments generally to study legislative subjects on which uniform state laws may be desirable and recommend draft legislation to that end. This is not federal activity, and the American Congress is not involved. Adoption or not of the drafts depends on the legislatures of each state, and in the course of adoption any given state may amend the draft considerably. Some drafts—the Uniform Commercial Code, for example—come to be universally adopted, or nearly so; others may find a following in only two or three states.

295. Uniform Law Commissioners' Model State Administrative Procedures Act (1981).

call for the sharp separation of functions within the agency that characterizes the federal regime in ordinary adjudication.

The 1981 draft, by contrast, is a fully fleshed out code of some 94 sections organized into five articles. As a concerted effort to draft administrative procedure laws of broad application, it possibly indicates the direction of change in administrative procedure legislation generally in the United States. Of chief interest here are Articles III, "Rule Making," and IV, "Adjudicative Proceedings." Each elaborates the procedures it governs, in what might be thought an effort to assure both larger participation by the public, and more substantial political and judicial controls.

Thus, while rulemaking retains its "notice and comment" character under Article III, a number of additional procedures or requirements characteristic of executive or judicial developments at the federal level are added:

- Each agency is to maintain a public rulemaking docket of all matters under active consideration for rulemaking, specifically including proposals not yet announced, with an indication who at the agency may be contacted about it.[296]
- Notice of proposed rulemaking must include the text of the proposal.[297]
- The issuance of a regulatory analysis and/or the holding of an oral hearing may be required by the request of political overseers or a substantial number of interested private persons.[298]
- Fresh notice and opportunity to comment is required if the agency decides to adopt a rule whose content might be surprising in light of its initial proposal.[299]
- The agency is required to maintain, and hold open for public inspection, a defined record of the rulemaking, including any written data in its possession that it considers in connection with the rulemaking.[300]
- Agency rulemaking is explicitly made subject to political as well as judicial review, and the agency is required periodically to review the corpus of its rules, as a whole, to assess their effectiveness and need for change.[301]

---

296. §3-102.
297. §3-103(3).
298. §§3-104, -105.
299. §3-107.
300. §3-112.
301. §§3-201 to -204. The drafters present a choice between review by the governor, or by a select committee of the legislature, but prefer the former. An apparently successful

Article IV, on adjudicative proceedings, would create a centralized administrative law judge corps[302] and in other respects heighten the detail and formality of the provisions made for formal adjudicative proceedings.[303] The draft's most striking innovations, however, lie in its efforts to provide for generalized informal adjudicatory procedures:

- Adjudicatory procedures defined in the Act are required "upon the application of any person" in all matters other than investigative matters, or matters explicitly committed to agency discretion.[304] The procedure for formal adjudication, fully comparable in its elaboration to the federal provisions, is presumptively applicable.
- "Conference adjudicative hearings" are defined for matters presenting no factual disputes, or involving relatively minor sanctions for example, (less than 10 days' suspension from school or public employment; less than $1000 fine), considerably abbreviating the ordinarily applicable requirements of formal adjudication.[305]
- "Emergency adjudicative proceedings" permit summary action "to prevent or avoid…immediate danger," to be followed by ordinary proceedings if sought.[306]
- "Summary adjudicative proceedings" are defined for matters of little public interest and relatively low claim to procedural protection, such as very minor sanctions, the denial of application for public goods such as housing or public employment, or public contracting. An opportunity for informal presentation of views and response to an agency position is to be provided if any sanction is involved; for simple denial of an application for public goods, an agency is required only to give notice of its action and of any available administrative review.[307]
- The result is to make the provision of some form of hearing the rule even for informal agency adjudication, and to place on agencies the requirement of justifying departures from that norm.

---

state venture of this character in California is described in M. Cohen, Regulatory Reform, Assessing the California Plan, 1983 Duke L. J. 231.

302. §4-301.
303. §§4-201 to -221.
304. §§4-101(a), -102(b).
305. §§4-401 to -403.
306. §4-501.
307. §§4-502 to -506.

VI

CONTROLS OF ADMINISTRATIVE ACTION OTHER THAN JUDICIAL

Preceding pages have already made apparent that judicial review is merely the most formal and lawyerly of controls that may be brought to bear on administrative action in the United States. Judicial review usually occurs after the fact, and in any event is limited to assessing the legality of particular actions rather than the appropriateness, direction, or distribution of policy effort. Thus, it will often be far from the consciousness of important agency officials as they shape their agency's business.[1] Those officials are much more likely to be aware of signals from the network of relationships and controls suggested by the materials of the present chapter, a network many of whose elements have already been encountered.

A. *Political intervention or oversight*

The relationships of President and Congress to the business of regulation were examined in the third chapter of this essay, and there is no need to repeat that analysis here.[2] One should have emerged from those pages with the impression that the oversight and appropriations activities of Congress, and

---

1. An example may be noted in a book written by my late colleague, William Cary. Author of the major law school teaching materials on corporate law and distinguished both as scholar and practitioner of corporate law, Professor Cary was Chairman of the Securities & Exchange Commission during the Kennedy Administration, 1961–63, and wrote a well-regarded book drawing on his experiences there, Politics and the Regulatory Agencies (McGraw-Hill 1967). Judicial review is not mentioned once in the whole of its discussion of the regulatory efforts of the SEC during his chairmanship. Asked about this by a (then) fledgling teacher of administrative law, he responded that the subject simply was not important in his daily life. The relationships suggested by this chapter of the present essay, it should be added, figure importantly in the pages of Professor Cary's book.

2. In addition to the materials in that chapter, see Chapters V(A)(4), and V(C)(2)(f).

the coordinative and consultative activities of the President (notably through the device of the required analytic report), give to each a substantial, and sometimes competing, influence over an agency's course. A look at an agency's structure and allocation of time will confirm that impression. Most agencies have major offices concerned with congressional relations and (outside the independent regulatory commissions) the OMB. Communications from the White House, congressional inquiries and testimony to congressional hearings all consume significant amounts of agency resources, especially at the top. Agency heads may spend hours preparing for (and will personally attend) a congressional oversight hearing or a White House briefing. In contrast, they will rarely review the briefs to be submitted and argued by their attorneys in judicial review proceedings.

As earlier remarked,[3] American courts seem increasingly aware and approving of these influences, influences given point by the sharp changes in political perspective on regulation that occurred when Presidents Reagan, Clinton, and then Bush took office. Thus, the following appears in the Supreme Court's most influential contemporary administrative law opinion:

> Judges are not experts in the field and are not part of either political branch of the Government. Courts must, in some cases, reconcile competing political interests, but not on the basis of the judges' personal policy preferences. In contrast, an agency to which Congress has delegated policymaking responsibilities may, within the limits of that delegation, properly rely upon the incumbent administration's views of wise policy to inform its judgments. While agencies are not directly accountable to the people, the Chief Executive is, and it is entirely appropriate for this political branch of the Government to make such policy choices....When a challenge to an agency [decision], fairly conceptualized, really centers on the wisdom of the policy, rather than whether it is a reasonable choice within a gap left open by Congress, the challenge must fail. In such a case, federal judges— who have no constituency—have a duty to respect legitimate policy choices made by those who do.[4]

---

3. See p. 244 above.

4. Chevron, U.S.A., Inc. v. Natural Resources Defense Council, Inc., 467 U.S. 837, 865–66 (1984). A Westlaw search June 21, 2001 revealed that Chevron, discussed below at p. 368, had been cited by the federal courts more than 5,400 times; its nearest competitors among cases significantly discussed in this monograph were Universal Camera Corp. v. NLRB (1951), p. 345 below, 4,044 times, and Citizens to Preserve Overton Park v. Volpe (1971), p. 130 above, 3,597 times.

This general realism about the fact, role, and importance of political oversight does not, however, preclude a negative judicial reaction in some settings in which it becomes apparent that it has occurred. Two settings likely to provoke such a reaction, already encountered, are worthy of mention: when the oversight appears to violate the constraints of on-the-record proceedings; and when it introduces into a decision factors that Congress has not made relevant.[5]

1. In on-the-record proceedings

The materials of the previous chapter permit the reader to appreciate the sharp differences in procedure, decision structure, and expected objectivity as between those proceedings (especially formal adjudications) that are required to be decided on the basis of a record, and those that are not. Efforts at covert political influence in formal, on-the-record adjudication would violate explicit statutory prohibitions against ex parte contacts[6] and, if detected, produce an emphatic reversal. Thus, as we have seen, suggestions of presidential pressure on a high-level tribunal charged with assessing possible waivers of the Endangered Species Act produced a forceful remand for inquiry.[7] Even in an informal adjudication, one court found objectionable the State Department's private transmission to an agency of representations from the French and German governments, that it thought influenced the outcome of the proceedings inconsistently "with the principles of fairness implicit in due process."[8]

---

5. Thus, the Supreme Court's 2001 decision in Whitman v. American Trucking Ass'n, p. 29 above, in rejecting the claim of improper delegation, emphasized the importance to that conclusion of the statute's exclusion of economic costs as a factor relevant to the rulemaking it authorized. Lurking in that reasoning is the possibility of impeaching future EPA judgments by showing that, for example, White House pressures attached to E.O. 12,866 or subsequent orders, p. 102 above, caused the Administrator to change proposals because of economic impact considerations. The Executive Orders have been careful to limit their diction to "the extent permitted by law," but this formal acknowledgment may not be honored in all advice and instructions less formally given.

6. See p. 204 above.

7. Portland Audubon Soc. v. Endangered Species Committee, p. 93 above. President Clinton's accession to office ended the controversy. He withdrew the request for an exemption from the Act that had prompted the decision.

8. United States Lines, Inc. v. Federal Maritime Commission, 584 F.2d 519, 539 (D.C. Cir. 1978). While the court's reasoning depended on the heavily criticized decision in Home Box Office v. FCC, p. 241 above, the fact that this proceeding involved adjudication, with individual interests at stake and the idea of the record more sharply defined, gives it continuing influence. Compare the discussion of Sierra Club v. Costle, p. 244 above.

In an on-the-record proceeding, even overt efforts at political influence may be found to have this inconsistency. Judges, after all, are not themselves ever brought before a congressional committee or White House staffer to answer for the policies they may adopt in their opinions.[9] An influential case illustrating this proposition arose when the Chairman of the Federal Trade Commission testified before a Senate oversight committee about the FTC's interpretation of statutory language. The Commission had already announced its interpretation in an opinion written in the course of an on-the-record adjudication. Because the FTC Commission had remanded the case to one of its ALJs for decision of other matters, it remained within the FTC Commission's jurisdiction at the time of the hearing. The Senate committee chairman subjected the FTC Chairman to repeated, sharp criticism of his agency's position. Five years later, the ALJ finished the remanded hearing and returned it to the Commission for further review. By that time, a number of FTC officials who had been present in the hearing room had themselves become FTC Commissioners. (The Chairman who testified had submitted his resignation to the President at about the time of the Senate hearing, and so was no longer sitting.) A court of appeals concluded that the hectoring these officials had merely witnessed required them to have disqualified themselves from sitting as Commissioners in this further proceeding. "To subject an administrator to a searching examination as to how and why he reached his decision in a case still pending before him, and to criticize him for reaching the 'wrong' decision...sacrifices the appearance of impartiality—the sine qua non of American judicial justice."[10]

How is such a result to be reconciled with recognition that judges "have no constituency," and that the political branches that do have constituencies may appropriately bring their influence to bear on those policy matters legislation has left open for agency decision? But for the connection to pending adjudication, there could hardly have been an objection to the committee's interest in how the FTC interpreted its governing statute. If agencies can choose to make policy either by rulemaking or adjudication,[11] does their choice of adjudication insulate them from political oversight even as to the general policy content of their decisions, as distinct from the precise outcome of particular cases? Unlike judges, agency heads do appear regularly before Congress, and these appearances might be very restrained indeed if responsible agency offi-

---

9. These differences are strikingly illustrated, across a range of arguably improper contacts, in Professional Air Traffic Controllers Org. v. Federal Labor Relations Authority, 685 F.2d 547 (D.C. Cir. 1982).

10. Pillsbury Co. v. FTC, 354 F.2d 952 (5th Cir. 1966).

11. See p. 258 above.

cials could not be questioned on any general matter that happened to be involved in litigation then pending before their agencies. The working response to this dilemma—ordinarily acceptable to agency and committee alike—is to engage freely in discussion of policy, but to leave out of the conversation any mention of particular proceedings in which the policy issues under discussion may arise. Agency counsel and committee staff may even work together to ensure that this occurs. There is "no Constitutional violation in a Congressional attempt to influence the regulatory interpretation of statutes," while fairness *is* implicated by an effort to force the outcome of a particular adjudication on individual grounds.[12]

2. Extraneous factors

The second characterization that may lead judges to disapprove political interventions is that they have introduced extraneous factors into a decision, factors that cannot lawfully play a part in the conclusion to be reached. Thus, when convinced that a Member of Congress had used his political control over the appropriations process to coerce the Secretary of Transportation into approving a challenged road project (the Member of Congress threatened to block funds for other, unrelated work unless the project was authorized), a court reversed the approval and insisted the Secretary reconsider the matter without regard to this inappropriate factor.[13] Of course, before judicial review is sought one must discover that such political controls have been used, and that the inappropriate factor has played a role in the decision. The reluctance of American courts to inquire behind the scenes of the decisional process absent strong indications of impropriety[14] makes this an unlikely outcome. An example arose when a newspaper reported that, during a briefing on rulemaking of importance to his constituency, an important Senator had made remarks "strongly hinting" that he might not support other measures of importance to the administration unless the rulemaking outcome included some recognition of his constituents' interests (as it then did). The court did not find this single account of "strong hint[s]" to be "substantial evidence of extraneous pressure significant enough to warrant further inquiry into the possibility of unlawful congressional interference."[15] In cases where an inquiry *was*

---

12. See U.S. ex rel. Parco v. Morris, 426 F.Supp. 976, 982 (E.D. Pa. 1977).
13. D.C. Federation of Civic Associations v. Volpe, 459 F.2d 1231 (D.C. Cir. 1971), cert. den. 405 U.S. 1030 (1972).
14. See p. 380 below.
15. Sierra Club v. Costle, 657 F. 2d. 298, 410 (D.C. Cir. 1981), discussed at p. 244 above.

ordered, the government had informed the court of an FBI criminal investigation into improper interference,[16] or the allegations were supported not only by press accounts but also by counsel's personal affidavit of conversations with knowledgeable administration sources.[17]

B. *"Open government" regulations*

Earlier pages have already discussed the impacts on rulemaking of the Freedom of Information Act and the less widely applicable Government in the Sunshine Act.[18] The openness these acts require reflects an American belief that publicity can serve as an effective constraint on government action—that "sunlight is the best disinfectant." Thus, it seems appropriate here to give a general overview of these acts, and briefly to mention two other statutes with similar legislative motivation, the Privacy Act and the Federal Advisory Committee Act. As has generally been done in this essay, only the federal statutes will be described. But the reader should be aware that open government statutes had their genesis in state law, and that even more forceful legislation of this character is to be found at the state level.

1. Freedom of Information Act

The Freedom of Information Act was first adopted in 1967 as an amendment to section 552 of the APA, which previously had been concerned chiefly with publication of materials about agency structure, procedures and policy.[19] The FOIA was vastly strengthened in 1974, with minor revisions in the years following, and an expansion to electronic forms of data in 1996.[20] The statute requires every federal agency to make "promptly available to any person" any of its records the requester "reasonably describes" in accordance with its published procedural rules, subject to only limited statutory exceptions. The

---

16. PATCO, n. 9 above.

17. Portland Audubon, p. 93 above.

18. See Chapter V(C)(2)(c) above.

19. The publication changes are discussed above, at p. 222. More details can be found in the sources cited in the general bibliographic note, p. 7, n. 8 above. The American Bar Association Section on Administrative Law and Regulatory Practice ongoing APA project, p. 6, n. 7 above, includes a detailed account of the Act and its case history, currently available at http://www.abanet.org/adminlaw/apa/april28foia.doc.

20. See p. 282 below.

agency may charge a fee for the service, but that fee is a limited one: if the records are sought for commercial use, it may include reasonable costs for search, duplication and review; but if sought by the news media or an educational or noncommercial scientific institution, it may charge no more than standard costs for duplication.[21] The obligation to provide the records is backed by severely limited time for agency response and review,[22] unusually stringent provisions for judicial review of a decision to withhold documents,[23] and the assessment of litigation costs including attorney fees and even possible civil service penalties when records are wrongfully withheld.[24]

The Act is available to "any person," an alien as well as a citizen, and no reason for wishing the information needs to be shown. Indeed, one's reasons for filing a request are irrelevant to one's right to compliance. They may influence the fees that will be charged for a granted request, but the purposes for which a request is made "have no bearing on whether information must be disclosed."[25] Thus, for example, while in practice FOIA is a useful instrument for discovery of agency records bearing on pending litigation, one's needs as a litigant are irrelevant to a FOIA request *and* the pendency of that request need not be recognized as a reason for delaying the litigation.

This is an openness requirement of remarkable breadth. Putting the exemptions aside for a moment, *every* record held by an agency[26] is subject to

---

21. The Anti-Drug Abuse Act of 1986, PL 99-570, which amended the FOIA in a number of minor respects, changed the Act's fee structure to differentiate between commercial and other requesters; even the higher fees asked of the former do not begin to approximate the government's actual costs in complying with the FOIA. 5 U.S.C. §552(a)(4)(A).

22. Agencies are given ten working days (subject to a single extension of the same length for described cause) to make their initial response to a request; and twenty working days to review an initial denial of materials if agency review is sought. 5 U.S.C. §552(a)(6). In practice, some agencies have been overwhelmed by requests and not provided the resources to respond to them. Responding to the dilemma created by this situation, courts have permitted delays consistent with reasonable diligence. See Open America v. Watergate Special Prosecution Force, 547 F.2d 605 (D.C. Cir. 1976).

23. Judicial review is to occur "de novo"—that is, without any necessary regard to the application of agency expertise to the decision—and the judge may herself examine the contents of the documents being withheld to determine whether they are within the disclosure requirements of the Act. The agency is required to follow an expedited schedule in answering complaints seeking review, and the judge is encouraged (although no longer required) to give the matter priority on her calendar. 5 U.S.C. §552(a)(4)(B), (C).

24. 5 U.S.C. §552(a)(4)(E), (F).

25. Bibles v. Oregon Natural Desert Assn, 519 U.S. 335 (1997).

26. "Agency" excludes the President, Congress and the courts, and bodies that operate only as their immediate advisers, but otherwise reaches "each authority of the [federal] gov-

the Act, whatever its source. Enacted for its expected contributions to journalistic, scholarly, and political understanding of government, it has also transformed the rulemaking process. It benefits those for whom the information available might have economic rather than political value, and a cottage industry has grown up in Washington to exploit this potential, used predominantly by corporate interests and their representatives. Requests for information that might have economic potential dominate the use of the Act.

While what constitutes an "agency record" is not statutorily defined, subsequent litigation gives this phrase a broad reach. Four factors have been identified: whether materials were generated within the agency, the presence of materials in an agency's files, the exercise of agency control over materials, and agency use of materials for agency purposes.[27] Materials created or obtained by an agency for its use, and in its files, will be regarded as "agency records"—whether or not they were generated by the agency itself or created specifically for its use. Only if materials are not in official possession or can somehow be characterized as personal to a particular officer rather than relating to the organization are they likely to be found not to be "records."[28]

Section 552(b) of the Act defines nine exemptions from the obligation to disclose "agency records." These set the exclusive basis on which FOIA requests can be wholly or partially refused. Five of the nine exemptions can be described, generally, as embracing differing forms of governmental privilege; the remainder protect private individuals or corporations from the harm that might be caused either by revealing information about them or by providing

---

ernment" performing governmental functions and controlling information of interest to the public, including government corporations such as the Postal Service or Amtrak. 5 U.S.C. §§551(1), 552(f).

27. Kissinger v. Reporters Committee for Freedom of the Press, 445 U.S. 136 (1980); see also Forsham v. Harris, 445 U.S. 169 (1980). These cases denied "record" status, respectively, to a Secretary of State's handwritten notes of his telephone conversations, consistently treated by him as personal documents and not shared with departmental personnel; and to the raw data a private researcher had amassed under a government contract but had not given into the government's possession (although under the contract the government could ask for it).

28. Thus, in Bureau of National Affairs v. United States Department of Justice, 742 F.2d 1484 (D.C. Cir. 1984), reporters sought the appointment records of the head of the Department's Antitrust division—doubtless seeking evidence of improper contacts. Daily calendars generated by his secretary for distribution to his subalterns, to inform them of his availability, were "agency records"; the appointment calendars she kept for his personal convenience and did not distribute were not "agency records," even though she might occasionally have let staff glance at them.

others—competitors, say—with information that they have supplied in confidence. The governmental privileges include (roughly in diminishing order of strength) information properly classified for defense or diplomatic reasons; material specifically privileged by statute; law enforcement information whose disclosure threatens harm to public or private interests; internal, pre-decisional governmental discussions of policy choice; and materials bearing on personnel rules and practices. The remaining four exemptions reach "trade secrets and commercial or financial information obtained from a person and privileged or confidential"; personal files, such as personnel or medical files, "the disclosure of which would constitute a clearly unwarranted invasion of personal privacy"; and two more specific—perhaps special interest—provisions: information generated in regulating or supervising specific financial institutions, such as banks; and geological and geophysical data about wells.

Note that the application of an exemption to an "agency record" does not end an inquiry. The FOIA also requires that "any reasonably segregable portion of a record shall be provided to [the requester] after deletion of the portions which are exempt." For some of the exemptions this is not an important qualification; judges are not disposed to order line-by-line reclassification of generally sensitive national security documents, and tend to accept that even apparently harmless snippets from investigative files can convey damaging information. For the less forceful forms of privilege, however, it has major impact. As noted in the preceding discussion of rulemaking,[29] the government can withhold pre-decisional discussions of policy, but ordinarily must disclose the factual materials on which those discussions are based;[30] personal files may no longer threaten the invasion of privacy if all identifying characteristics can be stripped from them before their release.[31] Determination of these issues, as

---

29. See p. 233 above.

30. See generally NLRB v. Sears, Roebuck & Co., 421 U.S. 132 (1975). Occasionally, but not invariably, the government has been able to convince a court that revealing the agency's belief about the facts—the sorting and characterizing its staff may have done—will itself reveal the "predecisional process" and so is exempt. Mapother v. U.S. Dept of Justice, 3 F.3d 1533 (D.C. Cir. 1993), for example, permitted the withholding of factual material as well as predecisional advice included in a report meant to help the Attorney General decide whether to exclude former UN Secretary-General Kurt Waldheim from entering the United States on account of his wartime activities.

31. Department of the Air Force v. Rose, 425 U.S. 352 (1976); and see Arieff v. U.S. Department of the Navy, 712 F.2d 1462 (D.C. Cir. 1983), where the court felt required to use ex parte affidavits to decide whether embarrassing information could be inferred even from "scrubbed" lists of the prescription drugs that had been supplied by a Navy pharmaceutical office to members of Congress, Supreme Court justices, and others.

of the application of the exemptions themselves, is made uncomfortable by the fact that counsel for the requester cannot be shown the withheld information, since to show it would make the case moot. An elaborate practice has grown up of relying on affidavits of government officials, supplemented by occasional judicial inspection of the documents in camera. The government is encouraged to be as forthcoming as possible in its affidavits by the knowledge that it bears the burden of sustaining the withholding of the documents.[32]

Business enterprises and foreign governments are doubtless particularly sensitive about the administration of those exemptions bearing immediately on their own interests. Material they might supply about an accident at a nuclear generating station, for example, could not easily be classified as national security data, as "inter-agency or intra-agency memorandums or letters,"[33] or as "trade secrets and commercial or financial information obtained from a person and privileged or confidential." Another nation whose domestic policies would not ordinarily lead it to make such information public—at least not immediately—may be surprised to find it in the American press, and thus may be discouraged from subsequently sharing important data with American regulators. Foreign corporations are unlikely to share sensitive commercial data that they fear will find its way into a competitor's hands. Much of the most interesting FOIA litigation and legislative consideration today concerns both the reach of the "trade secrets" exemption and the availability of procedures by which the supplier of information may be able to participate in any governmental decision whether to release it.

The reach of the "trade secrets" exemption is in fact a good deal less broad than might be imagined. That a corporation supplying data regards it as sensitive or confidential is not enough. Research plans supplied by a not-for-profit organization, however confidential, were not "commercial or financial infor-

---

32. Vaughn v. Rosen, 484 U.S. 820 (D.C. Cir. 1973), cert. den. 415 U.S. 977 (1974) is the widely followed source of this procedure; it was elaborated upon in Arthur Andersen & Co. v. Internal Revenue Service, 679 F.2d 254 (D.C. Cir. 1982).

33. Department of Interior v. Klamath Water Users Protective Ass'n, 532 U.S. 1 (2001) involved documents submitted to the Department of the Interior by Indian tribes for whose benefit the Department is obliged to act in a fiduciary capacity. Documents submitted by an Indian tribe could not be described as intra-agency or inter-agency, however, and so the Court unanimously held they could not be brought within the FOIA's fifth exemption. Although it found the particular claim unappealing—the tribes were in effect seeking a procedural advantage over competitors for scarce water supplies—the Court's opinion suggested doubt that it could bring *any* non-agency document (such as a consultant's report, a document generated by a state authority with which it shared some responsibilities) within the exemption, stressing that FOIA exemptions "are to be narrowly construed."

mation";[34] "trade secrets" may be limited to information about the productive process.[35] And to sustain an agency's invocation of the exemption, a court may have to be convinced not only that the information in question is commercial or financial and of a kind that would not ordinarily be made available to the public, but also that its "disclosure will harm legitimate private or governmental interests in secrecy."[36]

An agency decision to release information that its supplier believes to be within this exemption could be characterized in at least two ways. The agency may be wrong in a judgment that the exemption does not apply. Alternatively, it may agree that it could withhold the information by invoking the exemption, but believe as a matter of discretion that it would be preferable to release it. (Imagine, for example, possible judgments by the Nuclear Regulatory Commission in the wake of a major accident at a nuclear power plant under its jurisdiction.) It is important to start by recognizing that neither of these judgments presents a question under FOIA as such. That statute merely creates rights in the requester. If an agency by error or as an act of discretion chooses to reveal more than it has to, FOIA itself provides no relief to the supplier of the information.[37]

The information supplier is not, however, completely without remedy. Other statutes may create legal obligations to maintain information in confidence, that would be violated by an erroneous judgment or would stand in the way of an assertion on the agency's part that it had discretion to release the information. As a means of encouraging those subject to their regulation

---

34. Washington Research Project, Inc. v. Department of Health, Education and Welfare, 504 F.2d 238 (D.C. Cir. 1974), cert. den. 421 U.S. 963 (1975).

35. Public Citizen Health Research Group v. FDA, 704 F.2d 1280 (D.C. Cir. 1983).

36. National Parks and Conservation Assn. v. Morton, 498 F.2d 765, 770 (D.C. Cir. 1974). This test was widely subscribed to by the federal courts generally. Subsequent litigation in the D.C. Circuit reaffirmed it for information the government *required* to be supplied, but announced a new test for information it merely *solicited*—information voluntarily provided. For such information, it would be sufficient to invoke the protection of the fourth exemption to show that the information was of the character "customarily" regarded and identified by the supplier as confidential. Critical Mass Energy Project v. Nuclear Regulatory Comm'n, 975 F.2d 871 (D.C. Cir. 1992) (en banc). This modification, announced in response to expressed fears that cooperation with government was being impeded by the consequence of making information supplied too easily available to competitors, has *not* been widely adopted by other circuits. One may note that Critical Mass Energy Project is an NGO opponent of nuclear power plants, not a competitor; the intuitive attractiveness of the modification the case announced may be undercut by suspicions that a likely use, as here, is to deprive the public of information useful for airing important policy disputes, rather than the securing of private advantage. Compare n. 41 below.

37. The leading decision on this matter is Chrysler Corp. v. Brown, 441 U.S. 281 (1979).

to supply needed information more freely, many agencies adopted regulations assuring suppliers of both notice when information they have supplied is requested and an opportunity to participate in any consideration of its release. A presidential executive order sets out predisclosure notification requirements for executive agencies, but does not require any type of hearing prior to releasing information.[38] The courts have developed a "reverse FOIA action," permitting information suppliers to obtain an order barring release of the information if they are successful in securing judicial review in accordance with ordinary APA standards of review.[39] While not so generous as the de novo review provided by FOIA itself, the reverse FOIA action provides a possibility of control over agency behavior that has been useful to suppliers and that—to date—has obviated any need for legislative specification.

As a practical matter, the indications about the detrimental effects of releasing supplied information are mixed. Agencies' annual Freedom of Information Act reports to Congress, to be found on their Internet sites, confirm that the great bulk of FOIA requests to regulatory agencies are filed by corporations or their representatives, seeking to learn what they can; one supposes this activity would not continue if it were not profitable. Yet scholarly studies have revealed little leakage of proprietary information from the government under FOIA,[40] and the litigated cases generally arise from public interest groups' efforts to secure data on which to base demands for regulation rather than competitive prying.[41]

2. Electronic FOIA

The onset of the Information Age has implications for government that we may barely be beginning to see. Throughout this book, most notably in the

---

38. E.O. 12,600, 52 Fed.Reg. 23,781 (June 25, 1987), reprinted in 5 U.S.C. §552 note.

39. See the Chrysler case, note 37 above. On the ordinary APA standards of review, see Chapter VIII below. National Organization for Women, Washington D.C. Chapter v. Social Security Administration, 736 F.2d 727 (D.C. Cir. 1984), well states the arguments for and against de novo review on reverse FOIA actions, with the latter prevailing.

40. See an analysis undertaken for the Administrative Conference of the United States, R. Stevenson, Protecting Business Secrets Under the Freedom of Information Act: Managing Exemption 4, 34 Admin. L. Rev. 207 (1982).

41. Thus, Chrysler Corp., note 37 above, concerned efforts to secure data about employment practices for potential use in anti-discrimination actions. While the same data might be used by a competitor to improve its own record in hiring blacks or women at its competitor's expense, there is no indication this has ever occurred. Since FOIA requests cost much less than judicial challenges to FOIA outcomes, there is little reason to think that the visible litigation pattern is an important indicator of general requester motivations.

footnotes to Chapter III,[42] and also in the discussion of rulemaking developments, an effort has been made to signal some of the changes occurring, and citations have been given to agency and other Web pages that may prove helpful to exploring this quicksilver development. The Electronic Freedom of Information Act Amendments of 1996[43] both extended FOIA's reach to records kept in electronic format, and required that requested documents be made available in that format "if the record is readily reproducible"; the ease with which documents may be organized and searched electronically suggests that this will significantly enhance FOIA's utility.

Perhaps the most important element of the E-FOIA, although one as yet imperfectly implemented,[44] is its requirement that agencies create and maintain electronic reading rooms. These virtual libraries may contain a variety of information: data commonly sought under FOIA; information about making FOIA requests, and the capacity to do so electronically; and copies of the agency's reports to Congress of its FOIA administration. Of particular importance to the concerns of this essay is the expectation that they will contain electronic copies of what the agency must or does publish under section 552(a)—and perhaps rulemaking dockets as well. The physical document centers each agency maintains under section 552(a)(2) of the APA[45] are present in only a limited number of locations—for some documents, perhaps just one—and searching the documents that are there for desired information can be daunting. The electronic reading room can be reached through every computer with an Internet connection, and searching its contents with the sophisticated search engines increasingly available is nearly instantaneous.

As an example, consider the Electronic Reading Room maintained by the National Highway Transportation Safety Administration, the agency with responsibility for safety standards for motor vehicles. In June, 2001, its contents were the following links to subsets of its principal URL[46]:

Interpretations
The DOT Docket Management System
Technical Information Services
National Center for Statistics and Analysis

---

42. See also p. 196 and p. 89 n. 61 above.

43. P.L. 104-231, 110 Stat. 3049; see Symposium: Recent Developments: Electronic Freedom of Information Act, 50 Admin. L. Rev. 339 (1998).

44. See the GAO study discussed at p. 196 above.

45. See the discussion of this section in connection with publication rules, p. 222 ff. above.

46. http://www.nhtsa,dot.gov/.

DOT Auto Safety Hotline
Airbags
Buckle Up America
FOIA Requests Received by the Agency
Press Releases
Problems and Issues
Regulations and Standards
Star Ratings and Crash Tests
Vehicle and Equipment Information
Other NHTSA Information

The "Docket Management System" link gives access to an electronic, image-based database of over 800,000 pages of regulatory and adjudicatory information organized for the proceedings they concern, and stored on-line for easy research and retrieval. Comments in a rulemaking docket, for example, can be searched and read; electronic filing is also available. One can now isolate in seconds, in the privacy and convenience of one's office, any comments submitted on "MacPherson strut suspensions" in a rulemaking to set safety parameters for automotive suspension systems and respond, if desired, specifically to them. Previously one would have had to travel to a reading room, perhaps just the one in Washington, D.C., and read all the comments that had been filed—if copies were available there—to see whether there had been such comments. The risks of error and the time requirements were sufficiently greater to make likely that the search would not occur. The agency has the same improved information-retrieval capacity. It has also considerably reduced the costs of document storage and management, and resolved the problem that could previously occur, when more staff members—perhaps located inconveniently to each other—wanted particular documents than the agency had physical copies. Similarly, the "Interpretations" link makes instantly and widely available—under a notice that they may be relied upon[47]—the General Counsel's interpretations of NHTSA's regulations, that previously might have been found (and imperfectly indexed) only in her office files. The advantages of this added transparency should be easy to appreciate.

---

47. Compare the discussion of notice and comment requirements in reaction to publication rules, p. 256 above.

3. Government in the Sunshine Act

In 1976, following the perceived success of FOIA in making governmental processes more accessible, Congress enacted the Government in the Sunshine Act.[48] The act was passed at the height of the movement to enhance public participation in agency proceedings,[49] and in response also to perceptions that regulated industry groups often had access to agency deliberations the public generally did not share.[50] This Act applied a regime that was already common in the states to all the multi-member federal agencies—by and large, the independent regulatory commissions. Under it, commission "meetings" must generally be held in public, on advance notice published in the Federal Register; closings are subject both to judicial supervision and to a requirement of transcription that permits after-the-fact revelation should the agency's judgment prove to have been erroneous, or should the reason for closure pass.[51]

Ten exemptions to the open meetings requirement are provided, roughly corresponding to the FOIA exceptions. The one notable exception to this pattern is that no provision is made for closing pre-decisional discussions about general policy issues, such as would occur in connection with rulemaking proceedings. Even meetings with the agenda of developing agency budget proposals have been found subject to the openness requirements, despite the predictable consequences of public discussion of such plans both for staff candor and for the effectiveness of the agency's subsequent negotiations with OMB and congressional committees about its needs.[52]

---

48. The leading commentary on the Act and its history is R. Berg & S. Klitzman, An Interpretive Guide to the Government in the Sunshine Act (G.P.O 1978).

49. See Chapter V(B)(3)(b) above.

50. The decision in Home Box Office, Inc. v. FCC, described at p. 241 above, was made just a year after the Act took effect; the many private meetings described in that opinion thus were occurring as the legislation took shape.

51. It also permits members of Congress to demand the transcriptions in the course of oversight, and then make whatever use of them they choose. See San Luis Obispo Mothers for Peace v. NRC, 751 F.2d 1287 (D.C. Cir. 1984), vacated in part 760 F.2d 1320 (1985), affirmed 789 F.2d 26 (en banc 1986), where this technique fueled a concerted (and ultimately unsuccessful) effort to go behind the announced reasoning on the Nuclear Regulatory Commission in licensing a power plant, to show what the "real"—and assertedly improper—reasons for that action had been. Perhaps aware of the chilling impact if their own deliberations were transcribed, the majority refused to consider the transcripts in themselves to be sufficient evidence of the "bad faith" that is necessary for a court to go behind an agency's announced reasons for judgment and examine its deliberative processes. See p. 380 below.

52. Common Cause v. Nuclear Regulatory Commission, 674 F.2d 921 (D.C. Cir. 1982).

A more likely basis for a determination that the Act does not apply may lie in the definition of a "meeting." While the courts of appeal were disposed to give that term an embracive meaning, reaching all "meetings at which agency interests are pursued," the Supreme Court adopted a narrower view.[53] A committee of the FCC had traveled to Europe to share ideas with European and Canadian counterparts about the enlargement of overseas telecommunications services. The companies already serving the American market sought to compel these meetings to be held openly. The meetings could easily be characterized as deliberative, and bore on agency business. Yet they could not have resulted in the taking of "agency action" within the meaning of the APA. The Court thus concluded they were at best preliminary actions, outside the notice and openness requirements. Its opinion warned of an "impair[ment of] normal agency operations without achieving significant public benefit" if the Act were applied to preliminary discussions or to "informal conversations of the type Congress understood to be necessary for the effective conduct of agency business." This reasoning was arguably inaccurate as a reading of the legislative history; like that of FOIA, the history stresses the benefits anticipated from openness and the need to curb agency resistance to it. The opinion tracks scholarly findings, however, about the Act's impact in fact. Empirical surveys first undertaken for the Administrative Conference of the United States in the early 1980s,[54] found

> reasons to believe that there has been a shift in patterns of decision-making behavior...away from collegial processes toward segmented, individualized processes in which...members are isolated from one another. One reason is a decline in the importance of meetings as decisional vehicles....Another reason for suggesting diminished collegiality is...[because] speculative exploration of sensitive matters at an early stage...is difficult to do in public....

And again in the mid-'90s,

> true collective decisionmaking does not occur at agency public meetings...[The Act] promotes inefficient practices [such as seriatim, notation voting on circulated memoranda] with agencies which them-

---

53. FCC v. ITT World Communications, 466 U.S. 463 (1984), reversing 699 F.2d 1219 (D.C. Cir. 1983).

54. D. Welborn, W. Lyon & L. Thomas, Implementation and Effects of the Federal Government in the Sunshine Act (1984).

selves contribute to the erosion of collegial decisionmaking and, correspondingly, to a decline in the quality of agency decisions that the public receives.[55]

These reported effects have not, however, fueled any efforts at legislative reconsideration.

4. Federal Privacy Act

The Federal Privacy Act[56] was enacted in 1974 to meet growing concerns about the accuracy and availability of governmental files containing information about individuals. Largely, but not exclusively, it was a response to the emergence of the computer data bank, by which it was feared government could vastly magnify the detail and intrusiveness of its knowledge of private lives. Only individuals, not corporations, are protected by the Act. For individuals—especially for federal employees concerned about the contents of their personnel files—the Act provides controls of substantial importance.

The Act in general reflects five principles of "fair information practice" identified by an influential Report of the Secretary of Health, Education and Welfare's Advisory Committee on Automated Personnel Data Systems:[57]

(1)There must be no personal data recordkeeping systems whose very existence is secret.

(2)There must be a way for an individual to find out what information about him is in a record and how it is used.

(3)There must be a way for an individual to prevent information about him that was obtained for one purpose from being used or made available for other purposes without his consent.

(4)There must be a way for an individual to correct or amend a record of identifiable information about him.

(5)Any organization creating, maintaining, using, or disseminating records of identifiable personal data must assure the reliability of the data for their intended use and must take reasonable precaution to prevent misuse of the data.

---

55. Special Committee to Review the Government in the Sunshine Act, Report and Recommendation, 49 Admin. L. Rev. 421 (1997).

56. 5 U.S.C. §552a.

57. Records, Computers, and the Rights of Citizens 41 (1973).

As these principles suggest, the Act is more concerned with regularity of information uses than with restrictions on use. Accordingly, information seekers are encouraged to obtain it from the subject of the inquiry or with her knowledge. They must provide notice, actual or formal, of the reasons for which information is being sought, the authority on which it is being sought, and any consequences of failure to respond. Only "relevant" information is to be sought or retained in government files. An individual is entitled to access to identifiable records concerning her, with exceptions reminiscent of the first, third and seventh exemptions of the FOIA (those having to do with restricted access materials and investigations). Procedures are set out by which she may seek to have information she regards as inaccurate corrected. The Act's limitations on acquisition and use of information, while responsive to privacy needs in the computer era,

> explicitly recognize the legitimate needs of government departments to acquire, rely on and disseminate relevant personal information.... A fair reading of [the Act's provisions intended to enhance information quality] reveals that high standards of information quality are by no means inevitable....In contrast to the FOIA, the right of access afforded by the Privacy Act is not designed to free up public entry to the full range of government files. Rather, access under the Privacy Act is merely a necessary adjunct to the broader objective of assuring information quality by obtaining the views of persons with the interest and ability to contribute to the accuracy of agency records.[58]

Although privacy concerns are understandably important in American public policy, as witnessed by initiatives concerning, for example, the privacy of electronic communications and of medical records, the Privacy Act provides strictly personal remedies, and is much less frequently the subject of litigation than the FOIA. Its most recent appearance in the Supreme Court[59] concerned its interrelationship with the sixth (personal privacy) exemption of the FOIA. A federal union wanted the home addresses of federal employees it was seek-

---

58. Smiertka v. United States Dept. of Treasury, 447 F. Supp. 221, 226–227 (D. D.C. 1978), remanded for consideration of possible mootness, 604 F.2d 698 (D.C. Cir. 1979). See also, A. Alder & M. Halperin, Litigation Under the Federal FOIA and Privacy Act (9th ed. Center for National Security Studies1984); Report of the Privacy Protection Study Commission, Personal Privacy in an Information Society (1977); Project, Government Information and the Rights of Citizens, 73 Mich. L. Rev. 1323 (1975); J. Hanus and H. Relyea, A Policy Assessment of the Privacy Act of 1974, 25 Amer. U. L. Rev. 555 (1976).

59. Department of Defense v. Federal Labor Relations Authority, 510 U.S. 487 (1994).

ing to unionize; under normal principles of labor law, a private employer would have to supply those addresses, since communication with a potential union member at his home is a good deal less fraught with employer coercion than at the workplace. But the Privacy Act would permit those addresses to be divulged only if the agency could be required to divulge them under FOIA; and since, as we have just seen, a particular requester's need for information— even when reinforced by statutory policy—is not a proper consideration under FOIA, the Act prevented that disclosure.

5. Federal Advisory Committee Act

As we have seen,[60] a common perception of the late 1960s and 1970s was that government agencies operating under traditional procedures had been captured by the very interests they had been intended to control, and that steps were necessary to assure greater visibility and broader public participation in the regulatory process. The Federal Advisory Committee Act of 1972,[61] a precursor of the Government in the Sunshine Act, was one of the early legislative responses to this problem. The Act regulates the use of "advisory committees" by agencies. Advisory committees are boards of experts or community members brought together by an agency to advise on policy issues or serve as a sounding board. They may be local citizens brought together to advise Bureau of Land Management officials about the important uses of federal lands in the area,[62] nationally respected scientists asked to advise the Nuclear Regulatory Commission about technological issues arising in nuclear power reactor regulation, or businessmen and others asked to advise the Department of Commerce on its policy developments. The perception was that these boards did not represent balanced cross-sections of the relevant communities—that special interests used them as a kind of private lobbying to achieve regulatory solutions that ought to have been the product of open procedures involving the full range of interests concerned. Corrective measures imposed by the Act include requirements of balanced membership, open meetings on advance notice, and periodic agency clearance of any advisory committee with the OMB[63] for compliance with the Act.

Simple in theory, this Act like others has proved complex in administration.[64] NGOs have found in it a lever for uncovering political advice to the Pres-

---

60. E.g., at p. 212 ff. above.
61. P.L. 92-463, 5 U.S.C. App. I.
62. See p. 182 above.
63. See p. 111 above.
64. Excellent analysis appears in S. Croley and W. Funk, The Federal Advisory Com-

ident, about judicial appointments[65] and important programs.[66] These uses have raised concerns about the legitimacy of the Act under separation of powers,[67] if outsiders can use it to hinder the President's ability to seek advice directly from private citizens or groups. The cases mentioned in the preceding footnotes reveal a good deal of judicial ingenuity in avoiding these questions.[68]

C. *Ombudsmen and watchdog agencies*

Ombudsmen form a common and apparently effective means of non-judicial control over administrative action in parliamentary systems. Although not uncommon in particular bureaucracies, such as universities, and long finding support in American administrative law scholarship,[69] the institution has not gained a significant foothold at the federal level. Perhaps its emergence has been suppressed by the importance that looking after constituents' problems in dealing with the bureaucracy has for members of Congress,[70] who would not readily relinquish that function. Some states and state and local agencies do employ persons so designated, although their actual functions vary considerably.

Federal agencies deal regularly with a variety of institutional watchdog agencies serving the President, Congress or agencies' political heads—a function somewhat different from the ombudsman's responsiveness to citizen inquiry in the service of individual interests. OMB[71] and GAO,[72] attached to the President and the Congress, respectively, are two such agencies that have already been identified. In 1978, legislation created independent Inspectors Gen-

mittee Act and Good Government, 14 Yale J. Reg. 452 (1997) and in the ABA project, p. 6, n. 7 above.

65. Public Citizen v. Department of Justice, 491 U.S. 440 (1989).

66. Association of American Physicians and Surgeons v. Clinton, 997 F.2d 898 (D.C. Cir. 1993).

67. See p. 19 above.

68. See J. Bybee, Advising the President: Separation of Powers and the Federal Advisory Committee Act, 104 Yale L. J. 51 (1994).

69. W. Gellhorn, When Americans Complain (Harvard 1966); Ombudsmen and Others: Citizens' Protectors in Nine Countries (Harvard 1966). Professor Gellhorn received the Henderson prize in 1975 on the basis of this work; this prize is awarded by Harvard Law School each ten years for the most distinguished legal scholarship in administrative law during the preceding decade.

70. See p. 28 above.

71. See p. 111 above.

72. See p. 85 above.

eral in each of the executive departments to serve as guardians against waste and abuse,[73] and other legislation seeks to prevent reprisals against federal employees, or employees of regulated interests, who bring misconduct or shoddy practice to light.[74]

At the state and local levels the audit function is commonly placed in a separately elected official, an Auditor or Comptroller, who is made specifically responsible for assuring the fiscal efficiency and honesty of government. And in at least one state, a central agency is responsible for oversight of all agency rulemaking, to assure its proper justification and clear expression.[75]

From 1968 to 1995, a small agency named The Administrative Conference of the United States served a different kind of oversight function, as a body responsible for continuing analysis and development of federal administrative procedure. Headed by a small permanent staff of government employees, an Administrator appointed by the President, and a council of twelve appointed from public and private life, the Conference collected statistical data, produced occasional sourcebooks, and consulted on implementation of some administrative law statutes—notably the Government in the Sunshine Act, regulatory negotiation, and alternative dispute resolution. Its principal work, however, was done by a deliberative assembly drawn from both government agencies and the worlds of academia and private practice, which periodically debated and adopted recommendations for the improvement of administrative procedures based on empirical studies performed by academicians and (occasionally) individual attorneys. The recommendations often produced significant change at the administrative level and—as important—permitted professional views on such matters as hybrid rulemaking[76] and presidential oversight of agency policymaking to coalesce in a relatively apolitical setting. Congress, however, was less respectful of the results of this consensual process than a European reader might imagine it should have been,[77] and in 1995 refused further funding for the agency.

In the absence of the Administrative Conference, the White House may initiate coordinative or consultative activities, but these risk subordination to a political agenda, and the Advisory Committee Act would make it difficult to engage private attorneys and academicians on a continuing basis. Private or-

---

73. P.L. 95-452, 5 U.S.C. App.

74. Civil Service Reform Act of 1978, P.L. 95-454 §3.

75. See p. 269, n. 301 above.

76. See p. 242, n. 196 above.

77. The United States does not have, at the federal level, any tradition of routine legislative adoption of draft legislation, however carefully or consensually prepared.

ganizations, notably the American Bar Association (the national voluntary association of lawyers)[78] and its Section of Administrative Law and Regulatory Practice (a group of public and private members of the Association who practice administrative law) may also undertake such activities; here the government's constraints on its attorneys' participation[79] create a major obstacle. The ABA group has undertaken an overall review of administrative procedure, previously mentioned;[80] it regularly generates recommendations for legislation and internal changes in administration; and it publishes the quarterly Administrative Law Review, a useful source of continuing analysis of practical administrative law issues.

D. *Informal policy oversight: the general and trade press*

In many Washington agencies, functionaries scan the national press for stories bearing on the agency and its responsibilities and reproduce them for circulation to the agency leadership. One more often learns in this way of failures than of successes, of negative public attitudes, of emerging scandals that may result in legislative oversight hearings unless (or even if) resolutely dealt with, or of tough regulatory problems requiring resolution. The national press generally does not cover agency business on a continuing basis; its cognoscenti may love administrative law, but for the general public this subject is, as a leading paper's editorial pages recently put it, "often dreary" and "not [a subject] that riles public passions."[81] Emergencies and scandals draw the public's attention more sharply than jobs routinely well done. But the influence of a story or television interview on an agency's agenda can often be substantial.[82]

---

78. An analysis undertaken by a special commission of the ABA, Commission on Law and the Economy, Federal Regulation: Roads to Reform (1979), was particularly influential in shaping the deregulatory measures of the years following its release.

79. Permitted reimbursement of expenses from either private or public sources is very limited.

80. See p. 6, n. 7 above.

81. "Recipe for Confusion?" The Washington Post, June 23, 2001, p. A24.

82. In this author's personal experience, the Nuclear Regulatory Commission's attention was commanded for the better part of a month by the consequences of the staged televised resignation of one of its engineers, who asserted that his safety judgments were being ignored and then took employment with a prominent group generally opposed to the construction of nuclear power plants. The resignation was, of course, a legitimate story; and preparation for the ensuing congressional hearings caused some self-examination that may

Where the regulatory stakes warrant it, specialist publications emerge whose undertaking is to provide interested private communities with detailed information about a particular agency's functioning and directions—often at rather high annual cost.[83] These publications, too, are carefully read within the agency; their reporters sometimes learn before agency heads do of developments or problems in the lower reaches of the bureaucracy with which the leadership will have to deal. The leadership uses them, as well, to give regulated industries information about future policy directions that may help guide their course, or bring opposition or contrary views out into the open.

To similar ends, agency heads find it valuable to spend time cultivating relationships with the regulated community—appearing at its conventions, speaking at its lunches. The raised eyebrow can produce desired behavior at a minimal expenditure of agency resources. This intimacy can have its corrupting impact, however, if it begins to appear instead to be the knowing wink of an agency "captured" by those it is supposed to regulate,[84] particularly when the regulator begins to see those with whom he is thus associating as the source of his future career. This problem, described in American literature as the problem of "the revolving door," is one that has been hard to deal with, given the American choice to have political rather than civil service leadership of its regulatory bodies.[85] Nonetheless, informal sources of knowledge about the concerns of both regulator and regulated are essential to the functioning of the enterprise. If the relationship between them is not fully adversary, that is in good part because Congress has not chosen, and would not choose, such a relationship.[86] The regular interactions that some see as lying at the root of the agency "capture" problem are also the lubricant that, by permitting anticipation, reduces the friction of the regulatory process.

---

have been helpful from a regulatory perspective. It also, however, commanded the agency's priorities, requiring personnel to be released from other work to reassess analyses that, in the end, were not significantly changed. See also R. Stewart, The Discontents of Legalism: Interest Group Relations in Administrative Regulation, 1985 Wisc. L. Rev. 655 (1985).

83. Thus, Broadcast Magazine serves those with interests in the Federal Communication Commission's work; Nucleonics Week, those who need to follow the Nuclear Regulatory Commission.

84. See p. 212 ff. above.

85. The best contemporary account of these issues is in a study performed for the ABA's Section on Administrative Law and Regulatory Practice, C. Farina, Keeping Faith: Government ethics and Government Ethics Regulation, 45 Admin. L. Rev. 287 (1993); see also P. Strauss, Disqualification of Decisional Officials in Rulemaking, 80 Colum. L. Rev. 990 (1980) for a general discussion.

86. See L. Jaffe, The Illusion of the Ideal Administration, 86 Harv. L. Rev. 1183 (1973).

E. *"Public Interest" model, and actors*

The final source of non-judicial controls or influences warranting mention are the groups very largely responsible for the emergence of the public interest model of administrative action, associations undertaking to represent the interests of those on whose behalf regulation is ostensibly to occur. That "the public" does not often appear separately in administrative proceedings is not due simply to the proposition that the agency is, in some sense, directed to represent their interests; the agency is also to take some account of the interests of the regulated, who do appear. Nonappearance of the public also reflects the economic truth of the matter, that any one individual's interest in effective regulation is both small and highly diffuse. Ordinarily, individuals are not easily organized nor willing to pay for such representation unless through government itself. The successes the civil rights and civil liberties movements enjoyed in achieving change through litigation in the middle part of the last century, however, encouraged the formation of groups for other purposes, either general[87] or targeted on some specific project or dispute.[88] The footnotes to the preceding sentence call attention to groups responsible for influential environmental cases already encountered in these pages; the examples could be multiplied in other fields.[89]

These groups are voluntary associations, supported by membership donations and, occasionally, gifts from wealthy individuals or private foundations wishing to encourage their activities.[90] To some extent, they are supported as well by factors that tend to reduce their costs. Because of the non-monetary rewards they receive from such representation, their staff members are willing to work for salaries considerably below those received by equally skilled counterparts representing industry.[91] The American rule on litigation costs or-

---

87. E.g., the Sierra Club, the Natural Resources Defense Council, Inc., and the Environmental Defense Fund will be found to have several entries in this book's table of cases.

88. Citizens to Preserve Overton Park and San Luis Obispo Mothers for Peace each appear once in the table of cases, but in connection with important litigations.

89. E.g., Office of Communication of the United Church of Christ, the National Welfare Rights Organization, and the National Association of Radiation Survivors.

90. The Ford Foundation's financial support during the early 1970s, for example, was a major impetus to the formation of many of the "public interest" litigators, especially in the health, safety and environmental fields.

91. The beginning salary for a new lawyer at large Manhattan law firms is now in excess of $125,000 per annum; for a lawyer at the Natural Resources Defense Council, who ordinarily must have professional experience to be considered for a position, about half of that.

dinarily protects them from having to bear any significant costs other than their own, even if they lose the litigation. And, occasionally, statutes provide for public subvention of their expenses (including attorneys' fees) should they prevail.[92]

The presence of these groups, actual or potential, as participants in the administrative process changes the character of that process. It is not simply that, as former Chief Justice Burger remarked in a passage earlier quoted,[93] they provide an expression of views the agencies themselves cannot be relied upon fully to represent. Over time, many have become experts in the matters to be decided by the agencies before which they regularly appear, with significant resources for evaluating scientific or economic controversy as well as law. Their principals become known to and, if they are serious and well informed, respected by the agency officials with whom they deal. Moreover, the informal processes of administration, negotiation and adjustment, are rendered far more complex when multiple interests must be accommodated.[94] In preparing for hearings or explaining rulemaking outcomes, agency staff must look in both directions—whether it can be taken to task for laxness as well as strictness, for failures of action as well as over-aggressiveness.

The groups' participation is not inevitably beneficial to one's largest sense of the public interest. As these groups often do not have economic stakes, as such, in the outcome (and, in any event would have difficulty taking instruc-

---

92. The Supreme Court, however, has proved generally hostile to such statutes. See, e.g., West Virginia University Hospitals v. Casey, 499 U.S. 83 (1991).

93. See p. 216 above.

94. Consider, for example, National Welfare Rights Organization v. Finch, 429 F.2d 725 (D.C. Cir. 1970). American welfare legislation is administered by the states, under federal supervision. When a state appears to be departing from applicable federal standards, that was ordinarily a matter for adjustment between federal and state officials. Federal officials could threaten to cut off a state's funds if, after a hearing, they could prove the state was not compliant. For understandable reasons, this extreme remedy was rarely invoked.

When, on one such occasion, federal officials did initiate such a hearing, representatives of welfare recipients (the National Welfare Rights Organization) insisted on being accorded party status in the hearing. The court agreed with this claim. "Without participation," it reasoned, "issues which [NWRO] might wish to raise about the character of the state's plan may have been foreclosed as a topic for review." Recognizing, however, the complications their participation might bring to settlement negotiations, the court added:

We do not hold that this intervenor status creates in appellants a right to participate in any way in the Secretary's informal effort…to bring a state into conformity, nor do we limit his right to terminate a hearing, once called or begun, upon a determination by him that it is no longer necessary because he believes that conformity has been achieved.

tions from their membership respecting appropriate compromise), they may be prepared to insist on small points that an economic actor would readily compromise, and to resist political processes more likely to lead to compromises than absolute victory.[95] Moreover, no certainty can be had that all imaginable public interests in a given proceeding's outcome will be represented when some are; persons interested in scenic beauty or the preservation of a commercial fishery may appear to oppose a new power facility, but not those who would benefit from reduced rates or assured supply.[96] Appreciation of these and like points appears to be contributing to a certain judicial recession from the public interest representation idea. But it is impossible to imagine that that withdrawal will be an abandonment. As a participant in the regulatory process with substantial knowledge, high incentive, and the capacity to inflict large costs upon the agency and other participants in any proceeding, the public interest litigator can exercise major influence—whether or not litigation ensues.

---

95. The author has explored these themes at length in relation to the Overton Park case, p. 130 above. P. Strauss, Revisiting Overton Park: Political and Judicial Controls Over Administrative Actions Affecting the Community, 39 U.C.L.A. L. Rev. 1251 (1992).

96. Scenic Hudson Preservation Conference v. FPC, 354 F.2d 608 (2d Cir. 1965), cert. denied 384 U.S. 941 (1966).

VII

OBTAINING JUDICIAL REVIEW

A general introduction to the judicial system of the United States is given at another point in this essay.[1] That description makes evident that, like the United Kingdom, the United States (with minor exceptions) lacks a system of specialized courts dedicated specifically to the review of administrative action. Direct review of federal administrative action—that is, a judicial proceeding seeking to enforce an agency action, to deny it legal effect, to require it, or to preclude it—ordinarily occurs, instead, in the national courts of general jurisdiction. One can see in this choice evidence of the American theory of separation of powers,[2] which stresses the importance both of checking among the three branches of government and of avoiding, not competition between the branches, but the possible hegemony of any one. Even the United States Court of Appeals for the Federal Circuit,[3] a specialist court with national responsibilities for issues connected with revenues, intellectual property, foreign trade, and non-tort private law claims against the government, is organized within the judicial branch, under the review authority of the United States Supreme Court. To have an administrative court within the executive branch, on the American way of thinking, would be to invest too much power in the executive—to leave it unchecked.

The present chapter explores the possibilities and some of the mechanics of obtaining judicial review. As in previous parts of this essay, only the federal law is directly discussed; review at the state level generally proceeds on analogous principles, although in some states the traditional common law writs play a greater role and in others some of the preliminary issues on federal review, such as standing, are not much developed. The chapter following this one examines issues respecting the scope of judicial review, once obtained. The final chapter considers issues associated with the indirect review of government action that occurs when monetary damages are sought from the government or one of its officials to redress harm brought about by an asserted illegality.

---

1. See Chapter III(A)(3) above.
2. See p. 19 above.
3. See p. 126 above.

A. *Jurisdictional bases for review*

1. Statutory and non-statutory review of administrative action

The appellate jurisdiction of the federal courts is wholly statutory. From that perspective the title of this section of the essay is paradoxical. The literature speaks of "statutory" and "non-statutory" review in order to distinguish between the precisely defined jurisdiction a limited-purpose statute may create over a particular agency's actions, and the extensive jurisdiction created by statutes conferring judicial jurisdiction generally. "Statutory review" occurs pursuant to a statute designating a particular court or courts to exercise review authority over described decisions of a particular agency. "Non-statutory review" is available whenever the party seeking review can frame a complaint that meets the general requirements for invoking the jurisdiction of the courts.

One begins any effort to secure review of an administrative action by searching for "statutory review" provisions in this sense. The APA is specific that if statutory review is provided for, it is the preferred form of proceeding.[4] The statute providing for review itself will govern the court, venue, timing and form for review. Such provisions are commonest respecting the outcomes of proceedings decided at the highest levels of an agency, on the basis of an identifiable record. On-the-record adjudications and rulemakings generally have this character. Often, although not invariably, initial jurisdiction over federal statutory review proceedings will be placed in the courts of appeal.[5] When an extensive record and full explanation of agency reasoning result from the administrative process, trial is not required, and permitting several levels of judicial review could be wasteful.[6] When direct court of appeals review is provided, the statute may or may not indicate a particular court for the purpose; if it does not, the circuit where the government agency acts (the District of Columbia, generally) or where the party seeking review resides or is affected by the action complained of can be invoked. Through a combination of statu-

---

4. 5 U.S.C. §703.

5. See Chapter III(A)(3)(b) above.

6. Partial canvassing of the federal statutes, and an effort at theoretical exegesis, can be found in H. Friendly, Federal Jurisdiction: A General View (Columbia University 1973) and D. Currie & F. Goodman, Judicial Review of Federal Administrative Action: The Quest for the Optimum Forum, 75 Colum. L. Rev. 1 (1975).

tory directive and litigant choice, the United States Court of Appeals for the District of Columbia Circuit hears about one third of all direct appellate review cases.

The APA does not itself confer review jurisdiction of the more general character, but strongly endorses the view that non-statutory review jurisdiction should be found. "[I]n the absence or inadequacy" of statutory review provisions, it states, the form of proceeding for judicial review is "any applicable form of legal action, including actions for declaratory judgments or writs of prohibitory or mandatory injunction or habeas corpus, in a court of competent jurisdiction."[7] All "[a]gency action made reviewable by statute and final agency action for which there is no other adequate remedy in a court are subject to judicial review."[8] What persons are entitled to seek review is dealt with in more detail below,[9] but it suffices to say here that the statute has been read to embrace essentially all those likely to be particularly affected, in fact, by the regulatory action they may wish to challenge. Except for suits for money damages, dealt with in the final chapter below, the statute gives unqualified consent for the United States to be named as a defendant, together with the agency and any responsible officials (in their official capacity).[10] And review is also available to defendants in civil or criminal proceedings brought by the agency or the government for enforcement, unless a statute provides adequately for review at an earlier stage and precludes such consideration on enforcement.[11]

Jurisdiction is in fact readily obtained in the United States district courts. Under the most commonly invoked general provision of the Judicial Code, the district courts have jurisdiction over all controversies raising a "federal question" and not otherwise assigned; that is, they enjoy jurisdiction over all questions that necessarily require the resolution of an issue or issues of federal law.[12] Since the claim that an agency action reviewable under the APA was un-

---

7. 5 U.S.C. §703.

8. 5 U.S.C. §704.

9. See p. 313 below.

10. 5 U.S.C. §702; see Bowen v. Massachusetts, 487 U.S. 879 (1988). See p. 387 below.

11. 5 U.S.C. §703. The effect of provisions limiting review at the enforcement state is ordinarily only to narrow the issues that can be considered then. Thus, the question of whether an EPA rule was adequately supported by the materials of the rulemaking, or adopted following proper procedures, may be raised only in a proceeding to challenge the rule, filed within 60 days of the rule's adoption; but the constitutionality of the rule or the appropriateness of its application to a particular defendant is not an issue that must be raised at that time. See the discussion of exhaustion at p. 263.

12. 28 U.S.C. §1331.

lawful necessarily raises such an issue, the establishment of jurisdiction is a trivial matter.[13] A suit may be brought in any district court having venue—generally, where the agency has offices, or the regulatory event in question occurred, or where the plaintiff is located—without regard to the amount in controversy. The only possible hurdle lies in the possibility that the court will find the matter unsuited to judicial resolution—a judgment rare in practice although the subject of much puzzlement for American lawyers, scholars and students; these issues, also, are taken up within.[14]

Before the APA provided a statutory basis, defining an acceptable cause of action for review required an artificial form of analysis that may be useful to state, since it is still occasionally encountered and used. This "legal rights" analysis analogized the behavior of the government agency or official being complained of to that of a private individual. If a common law action could be brought against a private individual in the circumstances—say, for defamation in the case of an offense to personal reputation, or for trespass in the case of an intrusion on private

property—then the official could be sued and made to defend on the ground of the lawfulness or privileged character of her actions.[15] Except for cases seeking monetary damages from government officials for allegedly unlawful conduct,[16] this analysis need rarely be pursued today. The APA adequately frames the necessary cause of action.

Jurisdiction may also be claimed on the basis of a number of statutes providing for special remedies, such as suits against the federal government for monetary relief,[17] or against state or local officials for civil rights violations.[18] An often-used remedy permits a district court to "declare the rights and other legal relations of any interested party...whether or not further relief is or could be sought," in any "case of actual controversy[19] within its jurisdiction, except with respect to Federal taxes."[20]

---

13. Other general statutes, somewhat more limited in their reach and hardly necessary to invoke given the ease with which 28 U.S.C. §1331 can be used, include 28 U.S.C. §1337 ("regulating commerce") and 28 U.S.C. §1339 (postal matters).

14. See p. 304 ff. below.

15. The classic explanation of this theory appears in Associated Industries of New York State v. Ickes, 134 F.2d 694 (2d Cir. 1943).

16. See Chapter IX(B)(2) below.

17. See Chapter IX(B)(1) below.

18. See Chapter IX(B)(2) below.

19. See p. 312 below.

20. This is the Declaratory Judgment Act, 28 U.S.C. §§2201–02. Although not itself a grant of jurisdiction, the Act supplies a cause of action that easily meshes with jurisdic-

Another statutory provision of importance for administrative lawyers empowers the district courts to issue to federal officials the writ of mandamus. One of the writs developed in the English common law,[21] the writ of mandamus commands the person to whom it is addressed to fulfill some duty owed to the plaintiff, a duty which has been violated. This statute, then, confers on the district courts plenary jurisdiction to issue an order directing "an officer or employee of the United States or any agency thereof to perform a duty owed to the plaintiff." This is one of the remedies already provided for, in effect, in the Administrative Procedure Act, so that one might wonder why a litigant would ever bother using this special provision. It was much more important in an earlier day, when "federal question" jurisdiction under the Judicial Code could be invoked only on a showing that at least $10,000 was in controversy. Any residual importance (which is disputed) would lie in the absence of any necessity to relate the review being sought to the APA and its standards respecting proper parties, timing, scope of review, etc. To bring a cause of action under the "federal question" statute ordinarily requires invoking APA review; the cause of action under the mandamus statute is, simply, for the writ.

Can this difference create an occasional advantage for the plaintiff? That question is hard to answer without having an understanding of the scope of review under the APA, developed in the chapter following, as well as the further materials of this chapter. Two considerations would argue against there being any substantial advantage: First, one can imagine few reasons why courts charged with operating under both statutes would encourage differentiation between them. That was neither sought by Congress nor supported by obvious public policy advantages. Thus, the tendency of the courts ought to be (as

---

tional provisions such as 28 U.S.C. §1331, the source of general "federal question" jurisdiction.

21. 28 U.S.C. §1361. The other common law writs—certiorari, prohibition, quo warranto and habeas corpus are little used in American administrative law practice. The writ of habeas corpus commands a judicial inquiry into the legality of the government's detention of an individual, and the original Constitution (which said very little else about individual liberties) protected it against legislative suspension "unless when in cases of Rebellion or Invasion the public Safety may require it." U.S. Const. Art. I, §9 ¶3. The writ has been extensively used to challenge custody effected by the Immigration and Naturalization Service in anticipation of deportation; congressional efforts to limit that usage remain controversial. See G. Neuman, Habeas Corpus, Executive Detention, and the Removal of Aliens, 98 Colum. L. Rev. 961 (1998); INS v. St. Cyr, 533 U.S. 289 (2001). On common law review generally, see J. Duffy, Administrative Common Law in Judicial Review, 77 Texas L. Rev. 113 (1998).

it largely appears to have been) to merge the two heads of jurisdiction, to make them indistinct. Second, historically the mandamus remedy has been unavailable to review the exercise of governmental discretion; the existence of "discretion" was taken to defeat the argument that there existed any "duty" that could be judicially enforced.[22] This tendency has grown less important as courts have ceased to conflate discretion exercised within the constraints of law with *DISCRETION!* not properly subject to judicial review.[23] For law-constrained discretion, it is readily accepted, there can be a duty to exercise discretion, to do so considering only appropriate factors, etc.—all of which can be understood as duties owed to particular plaintiffs and enforceable by them.[24] Still, the several possible meanings of "discretion" lurk as a potential obstacle, one that the courts have less incentive to remove now that APA review is generally available under the "federal question" jurisdiction.[25] If mandamus can still prove useful, that may be because differences in the threshold showings necessary to invoke judicial review—for example, the APA requires that there have been "final agency action"[26] as a condition for obtaining APA review—could make it available where APA review would not be.[27]

The preceding discussion has assumed that review occurs when someone complaining of governmental action seeks to invoke the courts. Ordinarily, regulated individuals can also secure review of administrative actions when defending against government actions for enforcement. (Review is, however, foreclosed by a person's prior failure to exhaust their administrative remedies,[28] or where a statute provides that some other setting is the exclusive forum for review.) Agency actions often are not self-enforcing. Waiting for government enforcement concedes the choice of forum to the government, however. The discussion has also assumed that it is a statutory "agency" whose actions are to be reviewed. If one wishes review of an action of a body that is

---

22. This view has its roots in Marbury v. Madison, see p. 91 above and H. Monaghan, Marbury and the Administrative State, 83 Colum. L. Rev. 1 (1983).

23. See p. 91 above.

24. See, e.g. Work v. Rives, 267 U.S. 175 (1925).

25. Cervase v. Office of the Federal Register, 580 F.2d 1166 (3rd Cir. 1978).

26. 5 U.S.C. §704; see p. 322 below.

27. Thus, a statutory preclusion of review associated with Medicare legislation foreclosed APA review, see p. 305 below, but another court concluded that it left open the possibility of mandamus relief. Ellis v. Blum, 643 F.2d 68 (2d Cir. 1981). See, generally, C. Byse & J. Fiocca, Section 1361 of the Mandamus and Venue Act of 1962 and "Nonstatutory" Judicial Review of Federal Administrative Action, 81 Harv. L. Rev. 308 (1967).

28. See p. 326 below.

not an agency—notably, the President—non-statutory review will be the only possibility.[29]

2. The presumption of reviewability

As a general matter, American law presumes that any administrative action that has reached the point of finality[30] within executive government is susceptible to judicial examination. The APA says as much in two ways: first, by stating that "except to the extent that prior, adequate, and exclusive opportunity for judicial review is provided by law, agency action is subject to judicial review in civil or criminal proceedings for judicial enforcement";[31] second, by stating that "final agency action for which there is no other adequate remedy in a court [is] subject to judicial review."[32] Nonetheless, it was not until 1967 that the Supreme Court decided the case regarded as most clearly endorsing that presumption, and this was over vigorous dissent. A subsequent decision carved out a domain of executive action where this principle does not apply; a (final) executive exercise of discretion not to enforce is presumptively *not* reviewable.[33]

The 1967 case, *Abbott Laboratories v. Gardner*,[34] involved a challenge to an FDA regulation requiring prescription drug manufacturers to include on labels information that would help consumers find equivalent (and cheaper) generic drugs made by others. The government insisted that the manufacturers could obtain review only by violating the regulation and awaiting enforcement proceedings. That stage would never be reached if the manufacturers simply complied and changed their labels as commanded, rather than face the severe costs and penalties that could result from successful enforcement proceedings. Encouraging both parsimony of government effort and voluntary compliance with (generally valid) administrative action makes the government position attractive. Permitting direct review of the rule risks delaying its successful implementation for however long the review process takes, and significantly lowers the cost of unsuccessfully seeking review; instead of suffering a successful enforcement action, the manufacturer need only pay (indeed, may profit from) the net of its litigating expenses minus any benefits it

---

29. J. Siegel, Suing the President: Nonstatutory Review Revisited, 97 Colum. L. Rev. 1612 (1997).
30. Finality is discussed at p. 322 below.
31. 5 U.S.C. §703.
32. 5 U.S.C. §704.
33. Heckler v. Chaney, discussed at p. 214 above.
34. 387 U.S. 136 (1967).

obtains from delay. Permitting immediate review thus invites its strategic use to postpone the effectiveness of requirements that those seeking review might privately concede to be lawful.

As a general matter, however, American jurisprudence has long made available a "declaratory judgment" action,[35] in which parties are able to secure a declaration of their legal rights in the face of an imminent and substantial threat to their interests. An allegation that present activities are directly threatened, as by an allegedly unconstitutional statute, is sufficient to establish a "case or controversy"[36] appropriate for judicial resolution, since the courts will consider that by declaring the validity or invalidity of the threatened action they give effective relief against it. Moreover, a regulation, once adopted, constitutes a final "agency action" under the APA.[37] Deploying these more formal arguments, and relying strongly on the presumption that such final actions are reviewable, a bare majority of the Court rejected the government's argument. "[T]he APA's 'generous review provision' must be given a 'hospitable' interpretation... [and] only upon a showing of 'clear and convincing evidence' of a contrary legislative intent should the courts restrict access to judicial review."[38]

As this quotation may suggest, the government's argument in *Abbott Laboratories* had relied, in part, on a contention that the particular statute under which the FDA adopted its rule contemplated that judicial review would not occur prior to the rule's enforcement.[39] This contention sought to invoke a threshold provision of the APA's judicial review provisions, that they apply

except to the extent that—
(a) statutes preclude judicial review or
(b) agency action is committed to agency discretion by law.[40]

---

35. See n. 20 above.

36. See p. 312 below.

37. "'Agency action' includes the whole or a part of an agency rule...." 5 U.S.C. §551(13).

38. 387 U.S. at 140–41. Controversy remains in the literature, if not in the cases; as scholars debate the causes and cures for the ossification of notice-and-comment rulemaking, the ease with which pre-enforcement review may be secured is a prime target for some. See T. McGarrity, Some Thoughts on "Deossifying" the Rulemaking Process, 41 Duke L. J. 1385 (1992); J. Mashaw and D. Harfst, The Struggle for Auto Safety 245 (Harvard University 1990); R. Pierce, Jr., Seven Ways to Deossify Agency Rulemaking, 47 Admin. L. Rev. 59 (1995).

39. Its other principal contention, that the dispute was not "ripe" for judicial resolution, is treated at p. 328 below.

40. 5 U.S.C. §701(a).

This language states the principal exceptions to the presumption of reviewability, which will be taken up in turn in the following paragraphs. At the
outset, note two features of the provision. First, it qualifies or modifies everything that follows. Those provisions that permit review (the main focus of this
chapter and the chapter following) apply only where this preclusion language
does not. Second, it is open to applications that preclude judicial review only
in part. That is, "to the extent that" suggests the possibility of a statute that
precludes some but not all aspects of review, or commits some but not all aspects of a decision to agency discretion.

3. Statutory preclusion of review

a. Explicit preclusion

A few statutes state, in terms, that some or all decisions taken under them
are not subject to review; or severely constrain review in one way or another.
One way of illustrating the strength of the presumption of reviewability is to
remark that the courts do not easily assume that this has been done; a provision that an administrator's judgment is to be "final" or "final and conclusive,"
for example, has been taken not to preclude review altogether, but to restrict
the scope of review given.[41] In such cases the courts have given less than ordinary attention to the question whether sufficient factual support existed for
the administrator's judgment; but they still have considered issues of statutory authority and necessary procedure.

Even explicit formulations have been resisted to a degree. Thus, until 1988,
the claims of military veterans for benefits were decided by an agency, the Veterans' Administration, whose decisions "on any question of law or fact under
any law" it administers were made final and conclusive. "[N]o...court of the
United States," the statute provided, "shall have power or jurisdiction to review any such decision." But whether either the classifications Congress had
created or the procedures it had chosen for distributing benefits met constitutional standards, the Supreme Court concluded, was not a question that
arises "under" such a law, and so these questions remained available for judicial review.[42]

---

41. These cases often, but not invariably, involve issues (such as deportation, or military status) with important personal consequences. See Shaughnessy v. Pedreiro, 349 U.S.
48 (1955) (deportation); Harmon v. Brucker, 355 U.S. 579 (1958) (military discharge);
compare Gonzalez v. Freeman, 334 F.2d 570 (D.C. Cir. 1964) (agricultural credit).

42. Johnson v. Robison, 415 U.S. 361 (1974) (classification); Walters v. National Association of Radiation Survivors, 473 U.S. 305 (1985) (procedures); Traynor v. Turnage, 485

It would be a mistake to ascribe this resistance simply to judicial imperialism. American separation of powers theory[43] cannot admit that Congress has the power effectively to deny the courts their constitutional standing and role. Control of some forms of legislative and executive action seems a necessary element of the courts' position. To be sure, Article III of the Constitution states that the Supreme Court's appellate jurisdiction over (inter alia) "cases...arising under this Constitution, the Laws of the United States, and Treaties..." is conferred subject to "such exceptions, and under such regulations as the Congress shall make." This language seems to place Congress in full control. Yet what is an "exception" in the constitutional sense is a question for judicial as well as congressional interpretation, and the phrase can be taken to presuppose a remaining body of authority that permits the judiciary to fulfill its role as one of the three branches of government.

Thus one finds a murky body of caselaw, too complex to explore here,[44] that on some occasions appears unquestioningly to accept congressional judgments precluding judicial participation,[45] on others to insist that only judges may find certain types of facts, or conduct certain types of proceeding.[46] Perhaps the most important point for our purposes—not clearly stated in the cases, but, in the judgment of this writer, nascent there—is that a provision for judicial review is the quid pro quo that persuades the courts to tolerate a grant of discretion elsewhere in government, that they would otherwise find inconsistent with continued assurance that the government would act pursuant to the rule of law.[47] The point about rulemaking authority, in particu-

---

U.S. 535 (1988) (relation to other statutes). In 1988, Congress eliminated this particular line of cases (and in effect honored the Court's narrowing constructions) by specifically providing a regime of limited review. To similar effect, see McNary v. Haitian Refugee Center, 498 U.S. 479 (1991) and INS v. St. Cyr, 533 U.S. 289 (2001), both resisting broad readings of review-excluding language in an immigration context.

43. See p. 19 above.

44. A well-regarded academic treatment of this confusing topic appears in R. Fallon, D. Meltzer, P. Mishkin, & D. Shapiro, Hart & Wechsler's The Federal Courts and the Federal System (4th ed. Foundation Press 1996); see also R. Levin, Understanding Unreviewability in Administrative Law, 74 Minn. L. Rev. 689 (1990); G. Gunther, Congressional Power to Curtail Federal Court Jurisdiction, 36 Stan. L. Rev. 201 (1984), and Chapter VIII (A)(1) below.

45. Marbury v. Madison, 5 U.S. (1 Cranch) 137 (1803), p. 91 above; Ex Parte McCardle, 7 Wall 506 (U.S. S.Ct. 1869).

46. See p. 339 below.

47. Yakus v. United States, 321 U.S. 414 (1944), sustaining the World War II price control legislation against a delegation argument, is an early example. Special limitations on the time and manner for securing judicial review of price orders were part of the scheme,

lar, is not that it is a "legislative power" per se, but that the President or an agency can exercise it only pursuant to statutory authorization; it does not inhere in office.[48] Absent some possibility of an effective judicial check on its legality, Congress's delegation to the President (or, more broadly, to the government) of some forms of authority might be regarded as suspect.[49] While the courts have tended not to be confrontational about this, the concern animates their approach to such issues as review-exclusion and even gives rise (as it did in the first of the Veterans' Administration cases) to remarks about a "serious constitutional question."[50]

Less serious questions are presented when the statutory provision concerns the shaping of review rather than total preclusion—as by referring matters to a designated court, or indicating that review of some rulemaking issues must be sought immediately following the rulemaking and may not be raised defensively in an enforcement action. Thus, one court of appeals was able to avoid the difficult questions it thought posed by the statutes governing national medical insurance, which appeared to deny review jurisdiction even over constitutional claims, when it concluded that the same issues could be raised in an action for monetary damages brought in a specialized federal claims court.[51] "Only the relief granted would be different [from the equitable

---

and were upheld. These limitations did admit of the possibility of review, however. The Court's general conclusion was that the delegation was sustainable so long as it permitted courts to ascertain—that is, to review—whether the administrator had "kept within [his authority] in compliance with the legislative will." The Court's judgment in Whitman v. American Trucking Assn, p. 29 above, is to similar effect.

48. See H. Monaghan, The Protective Power of the Presidency, 93 Colum. L. Rev. 1 (1993).

49. Thus, the American cases on the problem of delegation of legislative power are consistently dealt with by the courts as problems of judicial review: when the courts are able to assert (however loosely) that they are in a position to assess the legality of challenged governmental conduct, no delegation problem arises. See p. 33 ff. above. The case has not arisen in which judicial authority to review such a matter has been directly denied by the legislature. The contentions have uniformly been that vagueness of statutory language rather than statutory preclusion disabled the courts from exercising their role. Yet there is no reason to think the outcome would be different. Faced with a governmental function that could be valid only if exercised in accordance with law, and unavoidably denied the chance to assure that it was being so exercised, a court could only find it invalid.

50. As, for example, in Bowen v. Michigan Academy of Family Physicians, 476 U.S. 667 (1986).

51. American Ass'n of Councils of Medical Staffs of Private Hospitals, Inc. v. Califano, 575 F.2d 1367 (5th Cir. 1978), cert. den. 439 U.S. 1114 (1979). The Claims Court, is a specialized national court hearing monetary claims (principally contractual actions) against

and declaratory relief plaintiffs sought], and Congress has power over the relief granted suitors against the United States and its officers." Similarly, the Supreme Court upheld the Clean Air Act's provision that an EPA "emission standard" could only be reviewed only in the D.C. Circuit, and then only if review was sought by a petition filed within 30 days of the standard's promulgation. It first noted, however, that issues about the proper application of the standard would be appropriate to review at the enforcement stage. Even this caveat failed to satisfy one Justice, who questioned the fairness of so limiting the arguments available to "small contractors scattered across the country," persons he thought unlikely to learn of the rule's adoption quickly enough to seek review at the designated time.[52]

Even in this context, the strength of the presumption of reviewability is suggested by the fact that only five Justices of the Supreme Court agreed with a reading of the Medicare Act's language to require that review of challenges to regulations be postponed to the implementation stage (i.e., the opposite of the *Abbott Laboratories* holding). While the majority accepted the benefits that could accrue when agencies were allowed to implement (and perhaps interpret or revise) their regulations without "premature interference by different individual courts," the dissenters feared that "delayed review... may mean no review at all" and stressed the strength of the presumption of reviewability.[53]

b. Implicit preclusion

One of the arguments rejected in *Abbott Laboratories*[54] was that the explicit statutory provision for review at the enforcement stage implied a congressional

---

the United States, and subject to review in the United States Court of Appeals for the Federal Circuit. See p. 127 above.

52. Adamo Wrecking Co. v. United States, 434 U.S. 275 (1978). In choosing the D.C. Circuit Congress was doubtless choosing an expert and perhaps favorable forum. It was also choosing a forum to which trade associations and other institutional litigators centered on Washington, D.C. (if not potentially affected individual businesspeople) would have little difficulty gaining access. On the striking difference between the reception of EPA rulemakings in the D.C. Circuit and the reception of its enforcement proceedings in district courts scattered around the country, see R.S. Melnick, Regulation and the Courts: The Case of the Clean Air Act (Brookings Institute 1983).

53. Shalala v. Illinois Council on Long Term Care, Inc., 529 U.S. 1, 47 (2000), discussed in J. Lubbers, Ed., Developments in Administrative Law and Regulatory Practice 1999–2000 105 (ABA 2001).

54. See p. 303 above.

wish to preclude review at the rulemaking stage. Such implied preclusion arguments have not often been successful, as the general emphasis on a presumption of reviewability would suggest. When they have succeeded, it has generally been in the presence of special circumstances. In one case, for example, a "complex" statute specifically authorized the producers and handlers of milk products to seek review of orders establishing a regime for marketing milk, but only after they had exhausted detailed procedures. Milk consumers, who had no right to initiate those procedures, sought review before they had taken place. Although ordinarily one would expect the consumers to be recognized as possessing "standing"[55] to challenge administrative action affecting the price and perhaps other qualities of milk they consumed, the Supreme Court directed that the action be dismissed. The court reasoned that Congress's careful specification of administrative procedures could easily be circumnavigated if litigants claiming status as consumers were able to seek immediate review.[56] In another, much earlier case, the Court inferred the inappropriateness of review from Congress's choice of the informal and unstructured techniques of mediation rather than litigation as the technique for dealing with particular labor problems.[57]

A 1986 Supreme Court statement, however, captured the general proposition, forcefully reaffirming "the strong presumption that Congress intends judicial review of administrative action."[58] As a matter of historical description, that is undoubtedly so. As one of the greatest of American administrative law scholars once remarked,

> The availability of judicial review is the necessary condition, psychologically if not logically, of a system of administrative power which purports to be legitimate, or legally valid.... [T]here is in our society a profound, tradition-taught reliance on the courts as the ultimate

---

55. See p. 313 below.

56. Block v. Community Nutrition Institute, 467 U.S. 340 (1984). That the Court described its reasoning in terms of "preclusion" rather than "standing," might seem to be, simply, an error of characterization on the Court's part. However a later decision, supporting rather than denying reviewability in the context of a "standing" argument, insisted that the preclusion label was the apt one. Clark v. Securities Industry Association, 479 U.S. 388 (1987). In any event, the reasoning process chosen demonstrates a willingness to see the presumption of reviewability overcome on the basis merely of implication from such matters as the complexity of a legislative scheme.

57. Switchmen's Union v. National Mediation Board, 320 U.S. 297 (1943); compare Leedom v. Kyne, 358 U.S. 184 (1958).

58. Bowen v. Michigan Academy of Family Physicians, 476 U.S. 667 (1986).

guardian and assurance of the limits set upon executive power by the constitutions and legislatures.[59]

4. Matters committed to agency discretion by law

The second significant exception to APA review concerns those cases in which the court is convinced that the decision in question has been "committed to agency discretion by law." While this might be viewed as just another way of saying that judicial review has been precluded, the formula suggests a different focus of inquiry—one that stresses the characteristics of agency function and the impact of judicial review upon them, rather than the intended judicial role. Here the constitutional inhibition just discussed becomes especially prominent. To conclude that a matter has been "committed to agency discretion by law" does not imply that such a commitment is itself lawful— that is, constitutional—under a scheme of government that ordinarily insists upon the maintenance of shared controls over governmental actions. One finds, correspondingly, that the courts are most likely to find such commitments in cases concerning executive conduct for which judicial review appears to have the least to contribute to governmental legality and stability: decisions raising issues of defense and foreign relations policy,[60] of allocation of government resources,[61] or of allocation of prosecutorial effort. *Heckler v. Chaney*, earlier described at some length[62] is the most prominent example of such a case: the Supreme Court described decisions not to prosecute or enforce as "generally committed to an agency's absolute discretion," entitled to a rebuttable presumption of unreviewability.

It is important to note how even this strong statement was qualified.[63] The presumption can be overcome by showing judicially manageable standards for review—in the Court's phrase, "law to apply." The situations in which the presumption applies generally do not involve a complaint that the government has wrongly used its coercive power against a citizen. The complaint, rather, is that the government, by declining to act, has failed to do enough for pub-

---

59. L. Jaffe, Judicial Control of Administrative Action 320–21 (Little Brown 1965).

60. E.g., Webster v. Doe, 486 U.S. 592 (1988).

61. E.g., Lincoln v. Vigil, 508 U.S. 182 (1993).

62. P. 214 above.

63. Subsequent judicial and academic reception has often also been unenthusiastic. See R. Levin, Understanding Unreviewability in Administrative Law, 74 Minn. L. Rev. 157 (1990).

lic protection.[64] And the *Heckler* Court reserved in a footnote the possibility—insisted upon in separate opinions in the case, and well established in the lower courts—that review would be available if the issue was not an agency's incremental decision how to expend its resources, but an apparently mistaken belief about its authority under governing law or a conscious policy of refusal to enforce the law in question.[65] However difficult the two motives may be to distinguish in fact, executive abnegation of law would present different issues than the executive's day-to-day working judgments how most effectively to deploy the limited resources Congress has placed at its command. Here, the "to the extent that" qualification of the APA's language quoted at the head of this section acquires special significance. It suggests outcomes in which some aspects of agency action are found to have been "committed to agency discretion by law," while others remain within reach of APA review.

Even when one has identified some aspect of a matter as involving agency discretion, it does not follow that all judicial review is, to that extent, precluded. Here we return to the difference we have identified between discretion and *DISCRETION!* [66] The APA contains two references to the reviewability of discretion, the exception we have been considering and a later provision specifically authorizing review for "abuse of discretion."[67] If review is precluded to the extent matters are "committed to agency discretion by law," what could the statute mean when it then authorizes review to correct an "abuse of discretion"? This linguistic puzzle is generally solved by the courts in favor of review. "Committed to agency discretion by law" is taken to be a "narrow" exemption from such review, applicable only where there is *DISCRETION!*—where the court finds there is acceptably "no law to apply," or that review is unnecessary for other important reasons of state. The reason for this result is the quasi-constitutional limit already suggested. The assertion that there is "no law to apply" can raise such serious questions about the legality of the underlying delegation of authority, that government attorneys are as unlikely to make the argument as courts are to reach that find-

---

64. Thus, the argument did not fare as well in a court of appeals proceeding, where an alien was complaining of the INS's refusal to reopen its adverse decision—a refusal that would lead to his deportation. The court was able to find standards under which to review that exercise of discretion. Socop-Gonzales v. INS, 208 F.3d 838 (9th Cir. 2000). Rehearing en banc has been ordered in the case, however.

65. See Adams v. Richardson, 480 F.2d 1159 (D.C. Cir. 1973) (en banc).

66. See p. 91 above.

67. 5 U.S.C. §706(2)(A); the scope of review under this provision is discussed at p. 376 below.

ing.[68] Thus, the bulk of matters that might be described as in some sense "committed to agency discretion by law" are nonetheless subject to a fairly rigorous review for abuse of that discretion.

B. *Preliminary issues on judicial review*

The subject matters of the following section concern preliminary issues on judicial review, that may work either to deny, to postpone, or to sharply to limit the review provided. They are as arcane and complex as any in American jurisprudence. Although they loom large as intellectual puzzles, however, and so consume inordinate amounts of time for law students and scholars, they can and will be dealt with briefly here. The questions they ask can be stated clearly. And, most importantly, for the great bulk of cases the answers also are not problematic; the difficulties arise only at the margins, when attorneys seek to push for additional review or as judges debate the proper balance of responsibility for government action between themselves and the executive.

In general, indeed, these issues arise out of the judiciary's concern for its own proper function. In a legal system that sharply distinguishes legislative, executive and judicial branches, what are the characteristics of a "judicial" act? Article III of the Constitution provides some structure for this inquiry by repeatedly describing judicial business as involving either a "case" or a "controversy."[69] This has been taken by the courts to involve a number of interrelated elements:

- there must be a genuine, not a contrived, dispute arising out of an injury-in-fact suffered by or palpably threatened to distinct personal interests of the plaintiff or of persons it properly represents;
- the dispute must be between distinct parties, each of which has a definite stake in its outcome;

---

68. See P. Strauss, Legislative Theory and the Rule of Law: Some Comments on Rubin, 89 Colum. L. Rev. 427 (1989).

69. The "case or controversy" problem is generally pursued in American literature in the context of constitutional rather than administrative law, and even more in treatments of federal court jurisdiction. Useful sources of discussion include A. Bickel, The Least Dangerous Branch (1962); L. Tribe, American Constitutional Law (3rd ed. Foundation Press 1999)); R. Fallon, D. Meltzer,, & D. Shapiro, Hart & Wechsler's The Federal Courts and the Federal System (4th ed. Foundation Press 1996).

- courts must be capable of resolving the dispute and of providing effective relief for the alleged injury; and
- the judicial outcome must not be subject to revision by non-judicial authority.

The stated rationale for these conditions is that they contribute to achieving the conditions needed for informed judicial judgment in a common law system: knowledge that the judicial resolution will be definitive, and adversary parties, with real stakes, who will be driven by their interest in the outcome to present the court with the fullest possible evidence and argument. The existence of a real controversy requiring resolution, rather than the wish to generate doctrine, is the legitimate basis for judicial action. It is believable as a general matter, if not for every case in which they are said to have been met, that these conditions tend to assure that both genuine controversy and the need for resolution are present.[70]

In addition to these constitutional issues, the courts have developed a series of supplementary "prudential" ideas for denying, limiting, or postponing review thought to be inopportune. This is where the waters grow especially murky. If one of these prudential standards is met, then the court may decline to exercise or limit its review jurisdiction even though there is no constitutional barrier to its undertaking that review. For example, a court may conclude that although review seems formally available at the moment, it should be postponed because further development of the facts through additional administrative processing would "ripen" the matter, aiding judicial consideration, without imposing untoward costs on the parties. Adherence to these prudential standards has been variable, giving rise to occasional suspicions that they are simply manipulated in the service of attaining, or avoiding, review on essentially political grounds. In part for this reason, the legitimacy of these prudential bases for avoiding review is disputed by some. In any event, they are not often significant in ordinary administrative matters. The distinction between constitutional requirements for review and these prudential considerations should be kept in mind when reading the following.

---

70. Relatively little thought has been given, to date, about the impact of the Supreme Court's discretionary review function on this vision of the judicial process. See E. Hartnett, Questioning Certiorari: Some Reflections Seventy-five Years after the Judges' Bill, 100 Colum. L. Rev. 1643 (2000); P. Strauss, One Hundred Fifty Cases Per Year: Some Implications of the Supreme Court's Limited Resources for Judicial Review of Agency Action, 87 Colum. L. Rev. 1093 (1987).

1. Standing[71]

The basic question addressed by the issue of standing in administrative law is: What persons are entitled to seek review of governmental action?[72] There is an elaborate, turgid and badly conflicted body of law on this question, which appears to have settled on three constitutionally-based elements: the person seeking to challenge government action must have suffered an "injury in fact"; that injury must be traceable to (have been caused by) the government action of which she complains; and a judicial decision must be capable of remedying the injury. Three "prudential" requirements have also been identified and applied with varying constancy: that persons must be asserting their own interests and not the legal rights of unrelated others; that the issues to be litigated must in some sense be particular to the person raising them, and not a generalized grievance common to the population as a whole that should be addressed through political processes; and that the federal law the complainant invokes in support of her lawsuit must be seen to have, as one of its arguable purposes, the protection or regulation of the interest whose injury she is seeking to redress. The paragraphs following take up these matters, save for the first of the prudential requirements, the "*ius tertii*" matter.[73]

Although Congress can override the Court's merely prudential choices, constitutional limits on standing cannot be altered by legislation. Congress may be able to influence the determination of what *is* an injury in fact, as for example by making aesthetic injury a relevant criterion for an agency's decision; then, a citizen who will herself suffer an aesthetic injury traceable to agency action and remediable by correcting it will be said to have standing to chal-

---

71. This section draws heavily on the analysis of standing made by C. Farina in connection with the ABA Section of Administrative Law and Regulatory Practice APA Project, p. 6 n. 7 above; see http://www.abanet.org/adminlaw/apa/Standing0401.doc. For other useful analyses, see G. Nichol, Jr., Rethinking Standing, 72 Calif. L. Rev. 68 (1984); W. Fletcher, The Structure of Standing, 98 Yale.L. J. 221 (1988); C. Sunstein, What's Standing after *Lujan*? Of Citizen Suits, "Injuries," and Article III, 91 Mich. L. Rev. 163 (1992); R.Pierce, Jr., Is Standing Law or Politics? 77 N.C. L. Rev. 1741 (1999).

72. The question usually arises with respect to plaintiffs, but may also serve to limit the defenses a defendant can invoke in response to threatened enforcement or similar actions. Note, too, that participation at the agency level and standing to secure judicial review are not identical, see Envirocare of Utah v. NRC, 194 F.3d (D.C. Cir. 1999), although the litigant who has been a party to an administrative action, or is its direct object, and complains of some illegality in the agency's judgment which she wishes corrected, will usually be found to meet all of the requirements.

73. It is the subject of a fine recent analysis. See R. Fallon, As-Applied and Facial Challenges and Third-Party Standing, 113 Harv. L. Review 1321 (2000).

lenge that action. But Congress cannot eliminate the injury-in-fact requirement, and authorize "any citizen" to challenge the agency action's, independent of whether it will concretely cause her (as it may cause others) such an injury.[74]

Preliminarily, it may be remarked that standing is not an issue for those
who object to regulation of their own conduct. One could rarely if ever say
that their affected interests are "shared in substantially equal measure by all or
a large class of citizenry";[75] there is little doubt about how harm to those interests has been caused or whether it can effectively be redressed by judicial
review; nor is there ever likely to be any difficulty about the nexus between an
injury being asserted by a regulated industry and the arguable purposes of the
legislation under which it is being regulated. The pushing and pulling about
standing reflects continuing American disagreement about the extent to which
the *beneficiaries* of regulation should be permitted access to the courts to gain
review of judgments they find insufficiently attentive to interests the legislature has commanded an agency to protect. From this perspective, one can say
that "standing" issues affect the balance in judicial review. As Prof. Cynthia
Farina put it in her recent study,[76]

> because rules governing access to judicial review can significantly im-
> pact both agency functioning and substantive regulatory policy, Con-
> gress has a significant stake in defining the level and distribution of
> regulatory standing. Adjusting the *level* of rights to judicial review can
> increase policing of agency compliance with statutory directives and
> enhance substantive and procedural rationality, but carries the risk of
> obstruction and ossification. Adjusting the *distribution* of rights to
> judicial review can create differential agency incentives to attend to
> various interests in the regulatory process—incentives that will either
> support, or undermine, the substantive objectives of the statute.
> Thus, in setting up a new regulatory program, Congress may consider
> the allocation of standing to be an important part of the program's
> implementing architecture.

Those who view beneficiary litigation favorably stress the balance it creates
in an agency's consideration of regulatory issues, if it knows its decisions may
be challenged from either side.[77] The machine-gun impact of daily contact be-

---

74. Lujan v. Defenders of Wildlife, 504 U.S. 555 (1992).
75. Warth v. Seldin, 422 U.S. 490, 499 (1975).
76. See n. 71 above.
77. See particularly the writing of Prof. Sunstein, as in n. 71 above.

tween an agency and those it regulates, a noted analyst once worried, can easily erode regulatory effectiveness if that is all the agency must face.[78] Skeptics of beneficiary litigation worry about resulting politicization in the courts and believe that the interests of the regulated—conventional legal interests in freedom from government illegality such as would be protected by the common law—have a more legitimate claim on judicial resources. The courts must be protected, they would argue, from cooption by Congress into a basically political arena. The problem, as Prof. Farina writes, is that regulatory legislation

> frequently *is* the remediation provided by the political process for widely-shared harms. Indeed, one of the classic justifications for government intervention through affirmative regulation is that the benefits to be gained are public goods. Modern regulatory programs are commonly structured *both* to impose substantive and procedural duties on agencies and private entities in order to create widely-shared benefits, *and* to provide for judicial enforcement of those duties at the request of the broad class of beneficiaries. Hence, plaintiffs seeking judicial relief for violation of these statutes often present the courts with harm, shared in substantially equal measure by all or a large class of citizens, that Congress has deliberately chosen to remedy through a combination of administrative and judicial process.

This tension was perhaps nowhere clearer than in a 1992 decision of the Supreme Court, *Lujan v. Defenders of Wildlife*,[79] a decision that associated to the constitutional requirement of "injury in fact" what had previously been thought a (merely) prudential disinclination to entertain generalized grievances. In *Lujan*, a statute required inter-agency consultation about the protection of species identified as endangered under the Endangered Species Act. The responsible administrators adopted a regulation that excluded federal involvement in actions taken in foreign nations (foreign aid decisions, for example) from this requirement. The Defenders of Wildlife and other environmental organizations sought to challenge this interpretation of the Act, which they feared would contribute to the extinctions the Act was intended to help prevent. The Court found that they lacked standing. First, although they had claimed harm to interests in seeing endangered species that might now become extinct, the Court concluded that they had failed adequately to show

---

78. Staff of Subcomm. on Administrative Practice and Procedure to the Senate Comm. on the Judiciary, 86th Cong., Report on Regulatory Agencies to the President-Elect 71 (1960) (written by James M. Landis)

79. 504 U.S. 555 (1992).

particular concrete injuries. While "the desire to use or observe an animal species, even for purely aesthetic purposes" *would* be a proper interest to establish standing, the facts they pleaded in their complaint had failed to establish that any such interest would be concretely injured. The Court also adverted to issues of causation and remediation, discussed briefly in the concluding paragraphs of this section; if the focus is on the impact on the foreign species, these issues loom large.

A second argument supporting standing sought to avoid all these problems by relying on a provision of the Act permitting "any person" to seek an injunction against violations of the required consultative procedures. Had this argument that a procedural error had been committed succeeded, the other constitutional requirements of causation and remediability would not have posed a barrier; any procedural error would in itself be the cause of a harm that could readily be corrected. However, the Court refused to accept Congress's power to create procedural rights as plenary. It characterized *this* provision, "an abstract, self-contained, non-instrumental 'right' to have the Executive observe the procedures required by law," as a "generally available grievance about government... [that] does not state an Article III case or controversy." Congress, it concluded, could not constitutionally permit such an action to be brought. To do so "would enable the courts... 'to assume a position of authority over the governmental acts of another and co-equal department,' and to become virtually continuing monitors of the wisdom and soundness of Executive action." That, said the Court, is the proper role of politics.

Lujan's reach was unclear. It appeared to effect a considerable retrenchment. Yet two Justices whose votes were necessary to the outcome wrote a separate opinion suggesting discomfort with the breadth of its language. *Lujan's* special facts involved truly remote injuries and consequences: the possible fate of the Nile Crocodile, should the United States contribute to planned rehabilitation of Egypt's Aswan Dam without adequate consultation, and similar problems for other foreign species. Moreover, the plaintiffs had no right to participate in the consultative procedure they sought to enforce, nor were the agencies obliged to provide public documents about it. On its facts, then, the case could be thought very much an outlier.

Indeed, in saying that the use or observation of animal species is an aesthetic interest that could support standing if concretely injured, the *Lujan* Court reaffirmed the Court's willingness, reflected in subsequent decisions,[80]

---

80. E.g., Friends of the Earth v. Laidlaw, 528 U.S. 167 (2000). In this respect, it does not matter how many others are enjoying the same aesthetic effect (or breathing the air or,

to accept congressional identification of interests supporting the constitutionally requisite "injury in fact"—so long as the complainant personally and credibly suffers that injury. This position of the Court emerged out of the developments of the 1960s and 1970s. During this period, encouraging broader public participation in administrative processes was perhaps nowhere so evident as in the willingness of courts to find that the requirements of standing to secure review of federal administrative action had been met. Since 1970, the courts have interpreted the general language of APA[81] to establish that such a person has been "injured in fact" if the result of agency action has been to frustrate a concrete interest of that person—such as the aesthetic interest in viewing endangered species—that is "arguably within the interests" the agency's action is intended to respect.[82]

The "arguably within the interests" language (equivalently described as "zone of interests") expresses a qualification the Court has engrafted prudentially onto the injury-in-fact requirement. This prudential element is illustrated by a government decision to increase the zinc content of the American penny under a statute passed to relieve a situation caused by hoarding of all-copper coins. The decision injured copper refiners in fact, by depriving them of a market for their product that tended to keep copper prices up. Their injury was caused by the decision, and a finding that the agency had acted unlawfully would have remedied the injury. Nonetheless, protecting the economic interests of copper refiners was not even arguably among the factors to be taken account of in the administrative scheme. Because the refiners were unable to establish the nexus between their injury and the arguable purposes of the statute, they failed to satisfy this prudential element of standing.[83] Just

---

as in Laidlaw, swimming in the water) so long as the plaintiff herself credibly shows that she does so.

81. "A person suffering legal wrong because of agency action, or adversely affected or aggrieved by agency action within the meaning of a relevant statute, is entitled to judicial review thereof." 5 U.S.C. §702. While "legal wrong" suggests a traditional approach, that the complainant must be able to show that the government's action would be a tort if undertaken by a private person, "adversely affected or aggrieved" is understood as requiring simply an injury in fact that is arguably related to what the statute in question was intended to deal with.

82. The leading cases are Association of Data Processing Service Organizations v. Camp, 397 U.S 150 (1970) and Barlow v. Collins, 397 U.S. 159 (1970), and, most recently, Bennett v. Spear, 520 U.S. 154 (1997) and National Credit Union Administration v. First Nat'l Bank & Trust, 522 U.S. 479 (1998).

83. Copper & Brass Fabricators Council, Inc. v. Department of the Treasury, 679 F.2d 951 (D.C. Cir. 1982). Note that if the case had arisen from an administrative proceeding to which they were parties, their consequent interest in having a lawful outcome to the ad-

how demanding the "zone of interests" requirement is, is a matter of some dispute, but one may say summarily that the Supreme Court precedents are permissive; the majority in the last of them was accused by the dissent of having "all but eviscerate[d] the zone-of-interests requirement."[84]

Lujan's troubling suggestion that a procedural injury could not in itself satisfy standing interests has been considerably undercut, if not wholly discredited, by subsequent cases. The suggestion appeared to be inconsistent with a number of congressional judgments—for example in the Freedom of Information Act—creating individual, even if broadly shared, rights of access, notice, participation or information. The only distinguishing feature for the FOIA requester, after all, is that she has actually asked for the information in a government document to which she has no other claim of access; the statute is indifferent to her identity and her need. Any person can ask, and the government cannot require her to justify her request. That would seem to make her injury wholly procedural. Her claim is nonetheless individual, in a sense that was not true in *Lujan*. In *FEC v. Akins,* individuals who chose to ask for campaign contribution information they claimed Congress had required to be made public, and were refused, were found to have standing to enforce the disclosure requirement. "[A] plaintiff suffers an 'injury in fact' when the plaintiff fails to obtain information which must be publicly disclosed pursuant to a statute."[85] The *Akins* majority was joined by the two Justices whose *Lujan* concurrence had expressed doubts about its breadth. Its outcome rationalizes the rights conferred on plaintiffs under FOIA, the Government in the Sunshine Act, the Federal Advisory Committee Act, and like statutes.

Still open, in the eyes of some, is whether the same reasoning would extend to the position of a commenter in a rulemaking, who wants to be heard on a rule that will not regulate her conduct. The APA appears to entitle her to certain procedural safeguards, and says agency action should be reviewed for procedural error and reversed where that occurs. She is differentiated from the whole American population only by the fact that she volunteered to file a comment, yet there is no issue about her injury, its cause, or the possibility of

---

ministrative proceeding would clearly have established standing to raise such questions as procedural regularity, the existence of requisite factual support for the decision, etc. Since, however, the Secretary had reached his judgment informally—in the absence of statutorily required procedures, see Chapter V(B)(1)—economic interest was the only basis of their complaint.

84. National Credit Union Administration, 522 U.S. 479 (1998).

85. 524 U.S. 11, 21 (1998); see also Public Citizen v. Department of Justice, 491 U.S. 440 (1989).

an effective judicial remedy. The open question may be whether the APA embodies the same congressional judgments about rights to relief as the somewhat more pointed acts like the FOIA, that are concerned *only* with procedural remedies. Yet a FOIA plaintiff would have no more special relationship to the information she had requested, than a commenter necessarily has in relation to a rulemaking; and in both cases, Congress has explicitly commanded the courts to correct procedural errors.

Turning from "injury in fact" to the equally constitutional elements of "traceability" (causation) and "remediability," one finds continuing skepticism about "public interest representation." As constitutional elements of standing doctrines, these are beyond congressional power directly to define. In the *Lujan* opinion, much emphasis was put on the uncertainty of any causal link between American funding of, for example, the Aswan Dam project and crocodile survival; and, similarly, on the uncertainty of any likely relationship between consultation, should it occur, and a more successful outcome for the crocodile. The Supreme Court had earlier found causation and remediation problems in two cases seeking APA review of rulings by the Internal Revenue Service (the administrators of tax collection), which the plaintiffs asserted were inconsistent with the Internal Revenue Code. In one, an organization representing poor persons sought to challenge the legality of a revenue ruling respecting the conditions necessary for a hospital to retain tax-exempt status.[86] They asserted that the ruling had resulted in their being denied needed medical care they would previously have received as charity. In the other, the parents of black children attending public schools challenged rulings that they asserted unlawfully granted tax benefits to private schools practicing racial discrimination, thus supporting racial segregation and making it less likely their children would receive a fully integrated education.[87] Even such brief statements should make clear that the plaintiff's claims about causation and the effectiveness of a judicial remedy were speculative. Plaintiffs' basic complaints were about the objectionable conduct of other individuals that, they asserted, had been promoted by tax treatment unlawfully favorable to those others. Perhaps it is not surprising that the Court resisted permitting outsiders, even appealing ones, to intrude into tax issues involving others. The reasoning in both cases stressed the absence of clear lines of causation, or of certainty that judicial relief, even if granted, would redress the injury complained of. Yet one's sense, animated by the vigorous dissents filed in both opinions, is

---

86. Simon v. Eastern Kentucky Welfare Rights Organization, 426 U.S. 26 (1976).
87. Allen v. Wright, 468 U.S. 737 (1984).

that a few years earlier the Court, without much difficulty, would have found standing to be present.

In *Lujan,* the Court's concerns about causation and remediability attracted only a plurality of the Court, and a concurring opinion suggested that these issues are in fact open to congressional influence:

> As Government programs and policies become more complex and far-reaching, we must be sensitive to the articulation of new rights of action that do not have clear analogs in our common-law tradition.... Congress has the power to define injuries and articulate chains of causation that will give rise to a case or controversy where none existed before, and I do not read the Court's opinion to suggest a contrary view. In exercising this power, however, Congress must at the very least identify the injury it seeks to vindicate and relate the injury to the class of persons entitled to bring suit.[88]

This language rejects any constitutionally necessary distinction between those who are regulated, and those for whose benefit regulation occurs, as parties who may have standing to secure review of regulatory decision. "Legislative judgments about the likely effect on private behavior of...regulatory remedy," as Prof. Farina puts it,[89] can establish causation and remediability, in the same manner as legislative judgment about what interests are worthy of legal protection can establish what is an "injury in fact."

It seems important to reiterate, in conclusion, that the standing issue speaks to the qualification of the individual plaintiff seeking review, and not to the reviewability of the decision, as such. The decisions on tax matters briefly discussed above, for example, would have been fully open to review, to the extent they affected the interests of the taxpayers themselves. If one looks at the transaction arguably subject to review in terms of the universe of litigants that might possibly be permitted to seek that review, one sees with clarity the relationship between expanded standing and the public participation movement. Expanded standing enlarges the class of potential litigants, requiring the agency to anticipate having to defend the legality of its decisions from more perspectives than that simply of the regulated party. It is in this sense, as suggested earlier,[90] that some of the cases on implied preclusion of review, those

---

88. 504 U.S. 555, 580 (1992) (Kennedy, J., concurring in part and in the judgment); this thought was echoed in a subsequent majority opinion, Friends of the Earth v. Laidlaw Environmental Services, Inc., 528 U.S. 167, 185 (2000).

89. See n. 71 above.

90. See p. 217 above.

implying a preclusion just for the particular parties before the court, sound standing themes.

2. Special rules of timing and place

The requirement that only "final" agency actions are reviewable, the requirement for exhaustion of administrative remedies prior to seeking judicial review, and the requirement that administrative actions be "ripe" for review all pertain to the timing rather than the fact of review. All share a concern for proper allocation of effort as between agency and court. In particular, they seek to avoid the disruptive and potentially manipulative interruptions to agency processes that would be caused by premature or repeated judicial proceedings. The implementation of each requirement is complicated, however, by the realization that in some cases or for some issues the postponement of review can occasion significant injustice. Consequently, these often emerge as doctrines requiring postponement only of some of the issues presented for review. That is, even in asserting that full judicial review must await a final agency judgment, the exhaustion of administrative procedures, or further ripening, courts often reach limited but helpful judgments about the course of the proceedings already in train.

It may be helpful to consider that "finality" looks at the timing question from the perspective of agency behavior; "exhaustion" focuses on the behavior of the private party seeking review; and the focus of "ripeness" is on judicial considerations. At the margins, these doctrines are indistinct, merging into one another—and also into the problems of preclusion and standing, already discussed. This was rather dramatically illustrated in a decision of the United States Court of Appeals for the District of Columbia Circuit.[91] The judges were unanimous that review was being sought prematurely. Yet in the judgment of one, the agency decision was not final; of another, administrative remedies had not been exhausted; and of the third, the matter was not yet ripe.

a. Finality

The basic idea of "finality" is simple enough; of the three timing doctrines under discussion, it is the one given explicit statement in the APA,[92] which says that only agency judgments that are "final agency action" are eligible for

---

91. Ticor Title Ins. Co. v. FTC, 814 F.2d 731 (D.C. Cir. 1987).
92. 5 U.S.C. §704.

review. One easily understands the basis for this rule. As in a civil trial, one must await the conclusion of proceedings rather than initiate a stream of appeals as potential errors occur. Many alleged errors may wash out in the ultimate result, or be corrected by the tribunal itself. The considerable disruption of repeated appeals is itself an evil to be avoided.

Yet in civil judicial proceedings, a limited class of interlocutory appeals are provided for. Such appeals may be taken from judicial orders that finally dispose of the interests of one participant, although not the entire proceeding. Interlocutory appeals may also be taken from judicial orders that dispose of issues collateral to the main proceeding, too important to be denied review and too independent of the main proceeding to be required to wait.[93] And review may be sought on permission of the trial court concerning issues of such evident importance and controversiality that the costs of proceeding in error appear to be greater than the disruption caused by an appeal to determine whether an error has in fact been committed.[94] Efforts to secure similar review in administrative proceedings will occasionally succeed,[95] although there is no statutory provision for interlocutory review similar to that applicable to civil trials. At this writing, however, the courts seem defensively aware of the delays and disruption threatened by even permitting such claims to be made and thus success is rare.[96]

The definition of finality in APA section 704 provides that

> Except as otherwise expressly required by statute, agency action otherwise final is final for the purposes of this section whether or not there has been presented or determined an application for a declaratory order, for any form of reconsideration, or, unless the agency otherwise requires by rule and provides that the action meanwhile is inoperative, for an appeal to superior agency authority.[97]

---

93. Cohen v. Beneficial Loan Corp., 337 U.S. 541 (1949).

94. 28 U.S.C. §1292(b).

95. Gulf Oil Corp. v. United States Department of Energy, 663 F.2d 296 (D.C. Cir. 1981).

96. Pepsico, Inc. v. Federal Trade Commission, 472 F.2d 179 (2d Cir. 1972), cert. denied 414 U.S. 876 (1973) is the exceptional case. The court indicated, in dictum, a willingness to consider interlocutory appeals from agency errors so obvious and gross that the proceeding in question "must prove to be a nullity." Other courts faced with precisely the same merits question as elicited the discussion in Pepsico declined to offer any such formula of hope. Coca-Cola Co. v. Federal Trade Commission, 475 F.2d 299 (5th Cir.), cert. denied 414 U.S. 877 (1973); Seven-Up Co. v. Federal Trade Commission, 478 F.2d 755 (8th Cir.), cert. denied 414 U.S. 1013 (1973).

97. 5 U.S.C. §704.

Since decisions of administrative law judges "become[] the decision of the agency without further proceedings unless there is an appeal to, or review on motion of, the agency within time provided by rule," APA section 557, they are final agency actions in this sense. In *Darby v. Cisneros*,[98] the Supreme Court read the language of section 704 to mean, as it says, that a litigant before an agency can seek immediate judicial review of a initial decision unfavorable to it, without having to exhaust an available avenue of review within the agency,[99] unless an agency rule both requires that he seek such review *and* provides that the action is inoperative while it is pending. The proposition may seem straightforward as a reading of the statutory text, and did to a unanimous Supreme Court. However, it came as a surprise to courts and litigants who had been used to the judicially developed proposition—sensible enough as a means of conserving judicial resources and assuring agency attention to important points—that judicial review could not be taken before avenues of review available in the agency had been traveled. *Darby* means that these decisions are immediately reviewable in court absent an express statute or a rule as described in the APA's text. It is a different question whether parties, as a matter of litigating strategy, will not often feel themselves better served by seeking agency review before heading for court.

Finality questions can also arise when a series of executive actors are to consider a matter. Judgments occurring early in such a chain of decisions and lacking immediate operative consequences may be final for that particular agency actor, even if not for the government's decision process as a whole.[100]

The most important question in the administrative context may be what kinds of completed "agency action" will be regarded as having sufficient formality to be designated "final agency action." In the *Abbott Laboratories* case previously discussed,[101] the Supreme Court easily concluded that an FDA regulation was "final agency action." How should courts treat the less formal interpretive rules,[102] which do not have the binding effects of statutes or regulations but nonetheless may significantly shape both conduct and judicial outcomes? How should they treat an agency's formal decision to issue a complaint initiating administrative proceedings, which have yet to run their

---

98. 509 U.S. 137 (1993).

99. See p. 326 below.

100. Dalton v. Specter, 511 U.S. 462 (1994); Ecology Center, Inc. v. U.S. Forest Service, 192 F.3d 922 (9th Cir. 1999).

101. See p. 303 above.

102. See p. 222 ff. above.

course? Or an agency's failure to act in a timely manner, in response to a petition or a statutory mandate?

The question about interpretive matters was persuasively addressed by the D.C. Circuit in 1971.[103] The staff of the Wage and Hour Division of the Department of Labor annually issued 750,000 letters of advice about the application of federal fair labor standards. Of these, 10,000 were designated as having been signed by the Administrator of the Division, and resulted from processes in which outside presentations were welcomed. Although this smaller group (having had more careful consideration) were more likely to be followed by the agency and respected by the courts, all 750,000 letters could be characterized as agency action. Making them all reviewable could discourage the agency from issuing them at all. The reviewing court found only the smaller group to be "final agency actions" subject to judicial review. It reached even this conclusion in a manner careful to preserve agency control over that outcome: it said that it would not regard as "final" an opinion not signed by the Administrator, or one that she had explicitly labeled as tentative or subject to reconsideration. It would reach this conclusion even though, for the moment, nothing was left to do. Finality, and thus reviewability, was, in effect, the price the Administrator was required to pay to purchase the added weight and formality of an opinion he had signed without reservation.

The issuance of a complaint to initiate administrative proceedings can be a formal agency act, and one with severe consequences for its subject. The party complained against must undergo the considerable expense of defense, and face the indirect costs to reputation of having been so charged. Once a hearing has resulted in findings for or against the defendant, any question whether issuance of the complaint was justified seems likely to have disappeared. But permitting review of the existence of proper cause for the issuance of a complaint would allow any defendant to force the delay of any hearing. Courts find their way past this puzzle with the observation that the expense and annoyance of litigation is part of the social burden of living under government. The complaint, having no direct impact beyond the imposition of those costs, is not a "final agency action."[104] One can understand this as a general judgment about the relative balance of claim between agency and accused; in general, it might be concluded, the accused is more likely to abuse a right

---

103. National Automatic Laundry and Cleaning Council v. Shultz, 443 F.2d 689 (1971); accord: Appalachian Power Co. v. EPA, 208 F.3d 1015 (D.C. Cir. 2000); see also the discussion at p. 371 below.

104. Federal Trade Commission v. Standard Oil Company of California, 449 U.S. 232 (1980).

to have any such question reviewed at this stage. When the accused party can supply concrete evidence of corruption in the agency's decision to prosecute, then, one might expect this judgment to come under significant pressure.[105]

Agency "failure to act" is explicitly defined as "agency action,"[106] but on the surface significant problems can arise in deciding when such a failure is "final." Other language of the APA provides that a court may "compel agency action unlawfully withheld or unreasonably delayed,"[107] and this establishes at least a framework for argument. In early years of the public participation movement, this language provided a major impetus for what might be described as agenda-setting litigation. A would-be public interest representative would petition an agency to undertake what it regarded as necessary action; then, after an interval, it would sue to compel action on its request.[108] While the mechanism remains available where statutes establish a duty to act, the general presumption that agency decisions on enforcement matters are not reviewable[109] and the very limited review available for refusals of petitions to engage in rulemaking,[110] act to considerably diminish its utility absent a specific statutory command for action.[111]

b. Exhaustion

In its most common appearance, the requirement for exhaustion of administrative remedies can be seen as a restatement of the finality principle: this matter is not yet ready for review, because there remain administrative procedures that might resolve it, or further develop the facts for judgment. Since the exhaustion principle is a judicially developed doctrine, any such statement is subject to the APA's provision on finality, as read in *Darby v. Cisneros*.[112] The question commonly arises collaterally. Plaintiffs are not seeking review of an agency action, as such, but to enjoin the further pursuit of agency proceedings that, they contend, can only result in a nullity and thus will inflict on them costs from which they are entitled to be protected.

---

105. Gulf Oil Corp. v. United States Department of Energy, 663 F.2d 296 (D.C. Cir. 1981).

106. 5 U.S.C. §551(13).

107. 5 U.S.C. §706(1).

108. Environmental Defense Fund v. Hardin, 428 F.2d 1093, 1097 (D.C. Cir. 1970); Environmental Defense Fund v. Ruckelshaus, 439 F.2d 584 (D.C. Cir. 1971).

109. See p. 214 above.

110. See p. 384 below.

111. See p. 256 above.

112. See p. 324 above.

In the classic case, the Bethlehem Shipbuilding Corporation sought to enjoin National Labor Relations Board hearings that Bethlehem asserted were beyond its jurisdiction.[113] Acknowledging that the Board's jurisdiction was a proper issue, the Court held that it must first be decided by the Board and so declined to consider the question itself. Important to note, however, is that the Court did consider and decide a number of preliminary legal questions: whether the Labor Relations Act, on its face, was constitutional and authorized a proceeding of the kind to which Bethlehem had been called; whether the procedures before the Board, to which Bethlehem was required to submit, were on their face sufficient to permit a fair outcome; and whether judicial review following the Board's judgment had been adequately provided for. Had these preliminary questions been decided favorably to the plaintiff, that would have led to the relief demanded in the complaint. In other words, Bethlehem did get a rather full review of the general legality of its being required to submit to this administrative scheme. This was a matter as to which neither agency judgment nor further factual development would be useful, and as to which its costs in having to go through a proceeding would be unusually high and, one might say, precisely the costs against which the plaintiff was entitled to be protected. The availability of this partial, early review is a common, although not always noted, feature of the exhaustion cases.[114]

Occasionally, exhaustion requirements assume the guise of a penalty, not merely a principle for ordering judicial and agency effort. This happens when a statute in effect precludes judicial decision of any matter that has not been ventilated before the appropriate agency. Thus, in two criminal prosecutions for draft resistance, the government asserted that the defendants could not claim as a defense that they were statutorily entitled to be excused from the

---

113. Myers v. Bethlehem Shipbuilding Corp., 303 U.S. 41 (1938).

114. Touche Ross & Co. v. Securities and Exchange Commission, 609 F.2d 570 (2d Cir. 1979); Leedom v. Kyne, 358 U.S. 184 (1958); Allen v. Grand Central Aircraft Co., 347 U.S. 535 (1954). The presence of a constitutional challenge to agency jurisdiction does not always defeat exhaustion arguments; if the claim is marginal, or may be mooted or illuminated by the agency proceeding, and if being required to submit to the agency proceeding is not, in itself, an evident constitutional harm, exhaustion will nonetheless be required. Rosenthal & Co. v. Bagley, 581 F.2d 1258 (7th Cir. 1978). On the other hand, the Court excused exhaustion requirements when it found the inadequacy of an administrative grievance remedy to secure the monetary relief a plaintiff sought—even in a circumstance (prison discipline) in which the Court might be thought disposed to prefer to delay, if not avoid, judicial engagement. McCarthy v. Madigan, 503 U.S. 140 (1992). (Congress statutorily reversed this holding in the Prisoner Litigation Reform Act of 1995, 42 U.S.C. §1997e(a); Booth v. Churner, 532 U.S. 731 (2001).)

draft, when they had not fully pursued these matters before the responsible administrative authorities. In one of the cases, the Court concluded that the only issue to be decided, a matter of statutory interpretation, was for the courts rather than the administrators in any event; it held that the defense should have been entertained in light of the "harsh" consequences of now requiring the defendant to have exhausted his administrative remedies.[115] Decision in the other case "depended upon the application of expertise by administrative bodies," and the defendant, having failed to exhaust that remedy, was not entitled to make his defense.[116]

"Issue exhaustion" questions can arise in a more conventional administrative context, as when a party seeks to raise on judicial review of rulemaking an issue that was not ventilated, or perhaps even much emphasized, in the comments or other matter before the agency.[117] In a closely divided Supreme Court decision of 2000,[118] the majority's refusal to require issue exhaustion seems to have turned on the special characteristics of the agency proceedings. They involved social security disability insurance, where claimants are often acting for themselves, without lawyers. The Justice whose vote controlled the outcome opined that "[i]n most cases an issue not presented to an administrative decisionmaker cannot be argued for the first time in federal court" and suggested that agencies could control that outcome (as they can the outcome of *Darby v. Cisneros)[119]* by adopting appropriate procedural rules.

c. Ripeness

The idea of partial review is particularly prominent in relation to the question of ripeness. This ground permits postponing (some aspects of) the review of agency action that is concededly final, when the advantages for judicial decision and perhaps also administrative function of requiring further administrative development of the controversy are seen to outweigh the imposition on the parties of that postponement. The authoritative statement occurred in the *Abbott Laboratories* litigation already discussed.[120] After invoking the presumption of reviewability and determining that the FDA's legislative rule constituted "final agency action," the Court addressed the government's

---

115. McKart v. United States, 395 U.S. 185 (1969).

116. McGee v. United States 402 U.S. 479 (1971).

117. See National Ass'n of Mfrs. v. Department of the Interior, 134 F.3d 1095 (D.C. Cir. 1998).

118. Sims v. Apfel, 530 U.S. 103 (2000).

119. See p. 324 above.

120. See p. 303 above.

argument that review would nonetheless be premature. The government asserted that review would not "ripen" until an enforcement action was brought (if ever), whose particular facts would illuminate what was otherwise an abstract challenge to undeveloped language. The "basic rationale" of ripeness doctrine, the Court agreed, "is to prevent the courts, through avoidance of premature adjudication, from entangling themselves in abstract disagreements over policies, and also to protect the agencies from judicial interference until an administrative decision has been formalized and its effects felt in a concrete way by the challenging parties." This rationale suggested a two-part inquiry: whether the issues were "fit" for judicial decision, and what would be the "hardship to the parties" of withholding consideration.

In the case before it, the Court found both legs of the inquiry to suggest review. If review were denied, the parties would likely be forced by practical considerations to make large investments to comply with the rule, rather than face the drastic consequences of non-compliance. And the Court was able to characterize the legal issue presented as one simply of statutory interpretation, the decision of which would not require significant factual development. The last is the decisive point. It answers the concerns expressed in a vigorous dissent written by a Justice whose considerable experience as a private attorney for clients such as Abbott Laboratories led him to fear their behavior and motivations. If companies were able to attack rules in the abstract, his dissent argued, they would conjure up outlandish facts and interpretations that could distort the judicial sense of the real application of the rule.

This last point is central to understanding the partial review that ripeness considerations entail. The majority's response to the dissenting arguments was, in effect, to limit the review provided at the pre-enforcement stage to what can be decided on the face of the rule. The question of facial validity is whether any state of facts is imaginable to which the rule could validly be applied. That question is ripe, but questions of particular application are not. While this response tends to avoid the problem of distorted perspective, it does (as the dissent also noted) somewhat lower the costs of seeking review. The party seeking review now faces only its litigating costs, possibly offset by gains from non-compliance in the interim, rather than the substantial costs that could result from successful enforcement against it. In a nation that had elected to foster declaratory judgment arguments generally, the majority argued, this effect was unobjectionable.

In a companion case, the Court concluded it could not properly appraise the challenge made to a different rule in the absence of specific factual development; the practical impact of being required to await review in that case was also less. Review was found not ripe, and submission to enforcement proceedings was required.[121] Here, too, the Court had gone far enough to assure itself that the requirement of postponed review was a fair one. Other ripeness cases, while often confusing in tone and reasoning, can often be understood along these lines.

Recent developments have been somewhat Janus-faced. On the one hand, the Supreme Court has invoked ripeness concerns as one element of its observably lessened enthusiasm about public interest intervention. If persons wishing to observe the Nile Crocodile and enforce inter-agency consultation failed to achieve standing in *Lujan*,[122] others found that their objections to a land management agency's general plans for administration of the national lands were premature—unripe—since ultimate application would turn on site-specific events. It can readily be appreciated that even the best-financed public interest intervenors are unlikely to have the resources to challenge public land management decisions tract by tract; "[t]he case-by-case approach that this requires is understandably frustrating to an organization such as respondent... [b]ut this is the traditional, and remains the normal, mode of operation of the courts.... Until confided [explicitly] to us, more sweeping actions are for the other branches."[123] Looking the other way are the contemporary Court's repeated rejections of judicially-created doctrine in tension with the APA, as in *Darby*.[124] Ripeness is judicially created doctrine, and recent thoughtful scholarship suggests that it deserves the same fate as "finality" in cases where the APA's review provisions govern.[125] Under the APA, the question is not "ripeness," but the adequacy of alternative remedies, and at least one appellate court has already taken that approach.[126]

---

121. Toilet Goods Association v. Gardner, 387 U.S. 158 (1967).

122. See p. 315 above.

123. Lujan v. National Wildlife Federation, 497 U.S. 871, 894 (1990); the case also touches on finality and standing themes. See also Reno v. Catholic Social Services, Inc., 509 U.S. 43 (1993); Ohio Forestry Ass'n, Inc. v. Sierra Club, 523 U.S. 726 (1998). These cases contribute to the perception that regulatory beneficiaries face more obstacles to securing review than regulated entities—an outcome specifically embraced by the Court in Lujan, p. 315 above, and strongly criticized in C. Sunstein, Standing and the Privatization of Public Law, 88 Colum. L. Rev. 1432 (1988). Once a specific action has been taken implementing a management plan, as in Lujan v. National Wildlife Federation, challenges to that action may be able to reach the plan as well. Wilderness Society v. Thomas, 188 F.3d 1130 (9th Cir. 1999).

124. See p. 324 above.

125. J. Duffy, Administrative Common Law in Judicial Review, 77 Texas L. Rev. 113 (1998).

126. Abbs v. Sullivan, 963 F.2d 918 (7th Cir. 1992).

d. Primary jurisdiction

It can occasionally happen that in ordinary civil litigation, that would not be characterized as administrative review as such, a court is presented with a dispute or issue it recognizes as falling comfortably within some agency's jurisdiction. Courts were asked, for example, to assess the reasonableness of a railroad's rate,[127] or to decide which of two rates stated in a railroad's tariff structure properly applied to particular goods,[128] at times when these questions fell within the ordinary ken of the now-defunct Interstate Commerce Commission. If one conceives the usual assignment of such issues to the agency as in a sense jurisdictional, the situation may be analogized to that arising when a federal court is faced with the need to decide complex issues of state law, likely to be far better understood within the state judicial system primarily responsible for them. In both situations, American jurisprudence embodies judge-made doctrines of reference, that require the parties to seek answers from the other system, either in lieu of the federal action or as a condition to further consideration of it.[129]

The doctrine of "primary jurisdiction," which had its largest application in the now-fading domain of economic regulation, addresses the court's proper course in the administrative context.[130] Is it to dismiss an action because it could be, and more properly should be, initiated before the expert agency? Postpone decision while a particular issue better suited to agency determination is referred to the agency? Or simply plow ahead on its own? There is no fixed formula for resolving these issues, which can be regarded as a means for policing (and preventing parties from wreaking havoc upon) the very complex jurisdictional allocations of federal law. Three factors have been identified as suggesting invocation of the doctrine: the existence of specialized agency expertise; a need for uniform national resolution of the issue; and any prospect that judicial decision of the matter would adversely affect the agency's ability to perform its functions.[131]

---

127. Texas & Pacific R. Co. v. Abilene Cotton Oil Co., 204 U.S. 426 (1907).

128. United States v. Western Pacific Railroad Co., 352 U.S. 59 (1956).

129. See, e.g., Marquez v. Screen Actors Guild, 523 U.S. 33 (1998); American Automobile Mfrs. Assn v. Mass. Dept. Environmental Protection, 163 F.3d 74 (1st Cir. 1998), further proceedings in 208 F.3d 1 (2000).

130. The analog in federal-state relations is the doctrine of abstention. See Shapiro, Abstention and Primary Jurisdiction: Two Chips Off the Same Block?—A Comparative Analysis, 60 Corn. L. Rev. 75 (1974).

131. The classic scholarly treatment (as for so many of these issues) is in L. Jaffe, Judicial Control of Administrative Action, Chapter 4 (Little Brown 1965). As primary juris-

3. Preliminary relief

A different kind of question concerning the timing of judicial involvement arises when a party seeks to maintain the status quo, or obtain other auxiliary judicial assistance, during the pendency of administrative action or while it is awaiting review. Two decisions of the D.C. Circuit warrant mention in this regard. The first in point of time, widely regarded as authoritative, identifies four factors to govern issuance or denial of a stay of effectiveness of an agency order (say, granting an immediately effective license to operate a nuclear power station) pending judicial review. The factors are: probable success on the merits; irreparable injury if a stay is not granted; whether the issuance of a stay would significantly harm others; and what may be suggested by public interest considerations.[132]

The second decision concerns the court in which such relief is to be sought. Among a number of statutes (including the APA) that authorize judicial granting of interim relief, the All Writs Act[133] is prominent. That Act authorizes federal courts to "issue all writs necessary or appropriate in aid of their respective jurisdictions...." The import of this provision, the D.C. Circuit reasoned, is that where statutory review is provided, only the court given exclusive review jurisdiction is in a position to "aid" that jurisdiction by providing preliminary relief; no other court, in its view, has jurisdiction to intervene.[134]

C. *Available judicial remedies*

With the exception of a brief discussion of mandamus,[135] we have thus far been generally assuming that review is occurring under the Administrative Procedure Act. That Act provides a unified and usually fully adequate structure both to review "final agency action" and to preserve, in the interim, the conditions necessary for effective ultimate judicial relief.[136] In connection with APA review, the court may issue any relief except monetary relief: orders of enforcement, declaratory judgments, compulsory orders directing the agency

---

diction doctrine has seen relatively little development since publication of Jaffe's work, it is more timely on that subject than might ordinarily appear.

132. Virginia Petroleum Jobbers Ass'n v. FPC, 259 F.2d 921 (D.C. Cir. 1958).

133. 28 U.S.C. §1651.

134. Telecommunications Research and Action Center v. FCC, 750 F.2d 70 (D.C. Cir. 1984).

135. See p. 301 above.

136. 5 U.S.C. §705 is the APA analog of the All Writs Act, note 133 above.

or its officials either to act or to refrain from acting, or—most commonly—judgments upholding or setting aside, in whole or in part, the results of agency action. If the agency action is found to be lawful, an agency's request for an order of enforcement would ordinarily be honored; but occasional statutes confer on the courts discretion to grant or withhold such relief, and in those cases, a court might exercise its equitable discretion to refuse to compel obedience to the agency even when it found its action lawful.[137] To the extent agency action is found legally deficient, the court will take one of two courses. If the flaw is one that cannot be corrected, it will simply be found unlawful and set aside. If administrative reconsideration could yield a valid result, however, the proceedings are remanded to the agency for fresh or supplementary attention. In this respect, the matter resembles appellate review of a lower court's decision more than a lawsuit between private parties. The "record" transmitted by the agency in support of its action is simply returned to it for further attention, as it would be to the lower court.

In this respect, the United States Court of Appeals for the District of Columbia Circuit has developed a somewhat controversial practice in reviewing rulemaking. It did so in response to an important strategic advantage a Supreme Court decision appeared to have created for persons who successfully sought rulemaking review. The Department of Health and Human Services had adopted a rule to govern agency reimbursement of medical insurance claims. At the moment of its adoption, this rule operated prospectively. On review, however, those challenging the rule succeeded in having it vacated on account of a readily correctable procedural error. In subsequently correcting this procedural error, the agency maintained the same dates of reference—neither surprising nor, one might think, inappropriate for such a regulation. Yet the result was that, viewed from the date of this corrective action, the rule now operated retrospectively. This, the Supreme Court held, it could not do in the absence of clear legislative authority (rarely if ever present).[138] The effect was to reward successful review of a rule with freedom from its effects for however long it might take the agency to correct its error—even one that may, from the outset, have appeared readily corrected and not very likely to command a change in outcome. This effect threatened to work a considerable enlargement of the difficulty that had substantially motivated the strong dissent in *Abbott Laboratories*.[139] In response, the D.C. Circuit has developed the practice of re-

---

137. See Weinberger v. Romero-Barcelo, 456 U.S. 305 (1982); see Z. Plater, Statutory Violations and Equitable Discretion, 70 Calif. L. Rev. 524 (1982).

138. Bowen v. Georgetown University Hospital, 488 U.S. 204 (1988).

139. See p. 303 above.

manding a rule without vacating it, where rulemaking error is not vitiating, so that the rule may continue to govern events arising during the not inconsiderable period that may be required for further proceedings and further rounds of review.[140] The court considers the "balance of hardship" (as in analyzing ripeness) as well as the nature and severity of the error requiring correction. Thus, an explanation the court finds inadequate to permit effective review readily suggests this remedy; a vitiating failure to give notice does not.

If a cause of action independent of the APA is invoked, one can anticipate somewhat more conservative responses on these issues, since the APA framework is the one Congress has chosen for review. As no record is before the court in these cases, as such, the remedies available are limited accordingly: a mandatory or declaratory order may be obtained, but a remand is not to be anticipated.

Similarly, review issues may arise defensively, when an agency seeks enforcement of an order or rule. Here, subject to the possibility of preclusion, as for failure to raise the issue administratively,[141] the APA is explicit that its review provisions attach. The remedies available in this context may include a remand as well as simple loss of the proceeding (or enforcement) for the government. Finally, monetary damages may be available in actions not brought under the APA. Those actions are discussed in the final chapter of this essay.

---

140. See Checkosky v. SEC, 23 F.3d 452 (D.C. Cir. 1994). P. Wald, Regulation at Risk: Are Courts Part of the Solution or Most of the Problem? 67 S. Cal. L. Rev. 621 (1994).

141. See p. 326 above.

VIII

SCOPE OF JUDICIAL REVIEW

A. *In general*

"The availability of judicial review is the necessary condition, psychologically if not logically, for a system of administrative power which purports to be legitimate, or legally valid."[1] So observed the author of a complex study that, decades later, remains the best general account of judicial control of administrative action in American law.[2] The preceding pages ought to have demonstrated that such review is broadly available. Conveying in a few pages how that review is exercised is not a simple matter. The nature of the problem is easily enough stated: permitting the court to control the lawfulness of agency action without allowing it to displace agency responsibility. But the difficulty of producing trustworthy verbal formulae that will accomplish that end, adjusted to the variety of settings in which the task arises, ought not be underestimated. "[T]he rules governing judicial review," other scholars despairingly wrote, "have no more substance at the core than a seedless grape."[3] As if to illustrate the point, a principal treatise-writer in the field once presented as his "adequate summary," "more reliable than the many complexities and refinements that are constantly repeated in judicial opinions," the following:

> Courts usually substitute judgment on the kinds of questions of law that are within their special competence, but on other questions they limit themselves to deciding reasonableness; they do not clarify the

---

1. L. Jaffe, Judicial Control of Administrative Action 320 (Little Brown 1965).

2. Id. For a contemporary restatement of the technical law, characterized by considerable sophistication, see R. Levin, Scope of Review Doctrine Restated: An Administrative Law Section Report, 38 Admin. L. Rev. 239 (1986). R.S. Melnick, Regulation and the Courts: The Case of the Clean Air Act (Brookings 1983) provides a close and interesting analysis of the impact of judicial review on the functioning of one agency, the EPA.

3. E. Gellhorn and G. Robinson, Perspectives in Administrative Law, 75 Colum. L. Rev., 771, 780–781 (1975).

meaning of reasonableness but retain full discretion in each case to stretch it in either direction.[4]

That is, this formula suggests, courts intervene or not essentially as the circumstances move them, and not in accordance with any set of fixed and objective principles.

This writer's view is a more pragmatic, perhaps less despairing one, that detects certain regularities in judicial practice, informed by statute and prior judicial statement, reflecting prevailing attitudes about judicial role and function, and enforced to a degree by the Supreme Court.[5] Historically, the development of judicial review can be seen as a progression from plenary judicial involvement in a limited range of cases and issues to broad but restrained involvement, as allocations between agency and court have acquired clearer definition. Initially, that is, the courts intervened only if the person seeking review could demonstrate a rather stark illegality in the behavior of some government agent. Such illegality warranted treating the official as if he were a private citizen and granting the complaining party one of the standard judicial remedies—an injunction, or an award of damages for tort. While such remedies remain available, the predominant mode of judicial review today assumes the official character of the act, and asks a more discriminating series of questions. These questions assume a sort of partnership (or distribution of authority) between agency and court, in which each actor has a unique and protected role. What precisely are the terms of this partnership has proved somewhat elusive. The federal courts' articulation of their role vis á vis Congress and perhaps also the executive branch has been subject to dynamic change, persuasively characterized by one scholar as a consequence of their awareness of the effects their actions have had on the other's behavior.[6] Nonetheless, it is helpful to view the general framework as one of "allocation," that assumes the general legitimacy of agency action and a judicial role of supervision or oversight rather than responsibility.

Whenever the scope of review is at issue, the first step is to say what error the complaining party claims the agency committed. Next is the inquiry about the distribution of authority between agency and court. So far as the relevant statute indicates, just what is the extent of the power delegated to the agency for the function under review? Much turns on precisely what agency function is under review: Is it adjudicating or rule-making—and in either case, is it on a formal record or not? If the function was rule-making, was it pursuant to

---

4. K.C. Davis, 5 Administrative Law Treatise 332 (2d ed. K.C. Davis Pub. Co. 1984).
5. See Administrative Law: Cases and Comments, Ch. IV, p. 510 ff.
6. A. Vermeule, The Cycles of Statutory Interpretation, 68 U. Chi. L. Rev. 149 (2001)

an express grant of power, or was it pursuant to a general grant of power to "make rules to carry out the purposes of this Act"? Was the agency making a finding of fact? Making a prediction? Exercising discretion? Applying the statute to the situation? Construing aspects of the statute not affected by the particular situation? Or deciding its procedure for performing such functions?

The brief discussion early in this essay of the developing understanding of executive "discretion,"[7] and the consequent broadening of the mandamus remedy,[8] form one prominent example of the historical development of review. Mandamus, compelling an official to perform a duty (or its equivalent), is far more widely available today than it was when federal courts first encountered the problem of discretion. This is so substantially because we now feel confident that judges can exercise review functions that check but do not supplant the authority of others—that if a court orders an agency to exercise discretion, or to exercise it under some particular constraint, that does not entail directing the agency to reach a particular decision. Of course judges may fail from time to time. Occasionally they do issue orders that in effect supplant the authority of agencies. Yet, one may believe that this reflects human failings these understandings generally succeed in keeping in check, rather than the self-conscious and cynical manipulation of an empty formula.

1. Constitutional issues

At the outset one meets again the question whether, and if so to what extent, the American Constitution affirmatively requires that judicial review be available. That is, is there a constitutional minimum amount of review that must be provided for, and if so how could it be described? The question can appear in at least three guises. First, whether judicial determination of some matters is required by formal separation of powers considerations—that is, because the matter is inherently "judicial" in character, and so must be assigned to the judicial branch. Second, more broadly, whether legislation must provide for judicial review as a condition necessary to the validity of a delegation of authority to an administrative agency. Third, whether review in some form over a decision depriving a person of "life, liberty or property" is a necessary element of due process of law.

The first[9] and second[10] of these questions have already been the subject of some discussion in the preceding pages, where we have seen that the tendency

---

7. See p. 91 above.
8. See p. 302 above.
9. See p. 118 above.
10. See p. 305 above.

of the Supreme Court has been to avoid giving direct answers to these questions. In substantial part, this avoidance reflects the potential embarrassment arising out of the Constitution's explicit provision of congressional authority to shape the Court's appellate jurisdiction. The absence of clear doctrine on these issues also reflects the infrequency with which they arise. The strong presumption of reviewability, together with Congress's general practice of making administrative action reviewable, permit their easy avoidance.

We turn to the third question. Current indications are that a Due Process Clause entitlement to judicial review is more sharply limited than might seem to be implied by the usual lists of "due process" factors,[11] or by the reasoning of *Goldberg v. Kelly*.[12] References to findings and on-the-record proceedings, and *Goldberg*'s dicta, make it appear that a proceeding governed by due process considerations must be subject to judicial review of some character reaching all normal issues that may arise from it—issues of application as well as problems arising on the face of the governing statutes. Yet the Supreme Court carefully avoided endorsing the *Goldberg* expectation on one occasion when it might have done so, and seems unconsciously to have contradicted it on another. The potential issue in the first case[13] concerned the review of mandatory arbitration proceedings, a type of procedure perhaps special in character; the Court stated that the parties had raised no due process issues as such. The review provisions it found to satisfy the other concerns that had been raised, however, were extremely limited—essentially independent of the merits.

The second case involved proceedings to terminate a veteran's continuing receipt of statutory benefits, an entitlement the Court understandably found to warrant application of the Due Process Clause.[14] As we have seen,[15] review of Veterans' Administration judgments about veterans' benefits is generally precluded by statute. Because the particular question the Court had to decide was whether an aspect of the statute shaping procedures before the agency was consistent with the constitutional requirements of due process, the Court was able to avoid this preclusion by applying the rationale there noted. For present purposes, however, the noteworthy point is that use of this special rea-

---

11. See p. 64 above.

12. See p. 53 above.

13. Thomas v. Union Carbide Agricultural Products Co., 473 U.S. 568 (1985); see p. 118 above.

14. Walters v. National Association of Radiation Survivors, 473 U.S. 305 (1985), discussed at p. 63 above.

15. See p. 305 above.

soning implicitly accepts that review of the merits of that decision was not available. Although the point seems not to have been directly faced in the Supreme Court, one can imagine a judgment that the statutory scheme as a whole, which included an administrative apparatus staffed and instructed in ways likely to prove generally accepting of veterans' claims, met the demands of fairness. Thus, it appears that the Due Process Clause does not invariably prevent Congress from establishing administrative procedures to which the clause applies, but under which judicial review of the administrator's decisions as such is precluded. Facial review of the constitutionality of the scheme is insisted upon;[16] but review of issues of application is not.

Finally, brief mention should be made of the courts' occasional insistence that, as a constitutional matter, certain facts must be found by the courts— even, by the Supreme Court itself. "Regarding certain largely factual questions in some areas of the law," the Supreme Court has remarked in reviewing ordinary civil litigation raising free speech issues, "the stakes—in terms of impact on future cases and future conduct—are too great to entrust them finally to the judgment of the trier of fact."[17] Obviously, the Court is not referring to the concrete, historical, primary facts of the underlying situation. The sensitive "largely factual questions" that trial courts and agencies cannot finally resolve concern the proper characterization to be placed on primary facts under the applicable legal regime. Although the task is ordinarily one for the trier of facts, at times it assumes a significance requiring that it be freshly done, not merely reviewed, by the appellate tribunal.

During the first third of the twentieth century, a series of enigmatic Supreme Court decisions made similar pronouncements concerning issues of arguable constitutional significance arising in administrative hearings: whether a rate was confiscatory;[18] whether persons involved in deportation proceedings were citizens;[19] or whether an injury for which workers' compensation was sought had occurred, as was jurisdictionally necessary, upon "navigable waters."[20] Later developments made clear that only the characterization, not the raw fact-finding, need be freshly appraised in court.[21] In ordinary administrative contexts

---

16. This step is necessary to avoid the "positivist trap" briefly discussed at p. 57 above.

17. Bose Corp. v. Consumers Union of U.S., Inc., 466 U.S. 485, 501 (1984); similar reasoning appears to underlie Court practice respecting various criminal procedure issues, for example whether a confession was coerced.

18. Ohio Valley Water Company v. Ben Avon Borough, 253 U.S. 287 (1920).

19. Ng Fung Ho v. White, 259 U.S. 276 (1922).

20. Crowell v. Benson, 285 U.S. 22 (1932).

21. St. Joseph Stock Yards Co. v. United States, 298 U.S. 38 (1936).

the idea is now regarded as moribund.[22] Still, the much more recent Supreme Court language quoted from the free speech case above suggests that, in the context of individual rights matters, it retains significant force.

2. The APA framework

Section 706 of the Administrative Procedure Act sets the general framework for review of administrative proceedings at the federal level. It warrants quotation in full:

§706. Scope of review

To the extent necessary to decision and when presented, the reviewing court shall decide all relevant questions of law, interpret constitutional and statutory provisions, and determine the meaning or applicability of the terms of an agency action. The reviewing court shall –
(1) compel agency action unlawfully withheld or unreasonably delayed; and
(2) hold unlawful and set aside agency action, findings, and conclusions found to be
   (A) arbitrary, capricious, an abuse of discretion, or otherwise not in accordance with law;
   (B) contrary to constitutional right, power, privilege, or immunity;
   (C) in excess of statutory jurisdiction, authority, or limitations, or short of statutory right;
   (D) without observance of procedure required by law;
   (E) unsupported by substantial evidence in a case subject to sections 556 and 557 of this title or otherwise reviewed on the record of an agency hearing provided by statute; or
   (F) unwarranted by the facts to the extent that the facts are subject to trial de novo by the reviewing court.
In making the foregoing determinations, the court shall review the whole record or those parts of it cited by a party, and due account shall be taken of the rule of prejudicial error.

If one looks particularly at the sub-paragraphs of section 706(2), one can see that the provision addresses three separable areas of concern. Sub-paragraphs (E), (F) and, in part, (A) suggest three different standards for review of agency

---

22. See Administrative Law: Cases and Comments, 530–38; the issues are generally treated in H. Monaghan, Constitutional Fact Review, 85 Colum. L. Rev. 229 (1985).

conclusions of fact. Sub-paragraphs (B), (C) and (D), as well as the introductory sentence to section 706, address review of agency conclusions of law. Sub-paragraph (A) also speaks to review of an agency's judgment, and specifically its exercise of the discretion conferred on it by law to deal with a particular state of facts. These matters are dealt with, in turn, in the following pages.

B. *Questions of fact*

In writing about judicial review of agency determinations of fact, it is important to distinguish at the outset between those concrete historical or scientific assertions that can be made without any necessary reference to the legal order, and those characterizations or conclusions about the significance of historical or scientific fact, that almost inevitably take on its coloration. "Mrs. Jones was driving at 45 miles per hour on an ice-covered road" and "ingestion of 1 part per million diacetyphamine for two months produced a 20% increase in stomach cancers among a population of 1000 white mice" are the first sort of assertion. "In the circumstances, Mrs. Jones was being negligent" and "a concentration of 1 part per million diacetyphamine in foodstuffs intended for human consumption imposes a significant risk of causing human cancer" are the second.

It would be easier if judges (and others) described only the first kind of assertion as involving a "question of fact" and consistently saw the second for what it is, the exercise of judgment. But early practice tended to conflate fact and judgment. It recognized the distinction, if at all, as a contrast between "basic" and "ultimate" fact, and stated only two standards for review: review of questions of fact, and review of questions of law. There remains some tendency to ascribe to both assertions the quality of "fact," and this somewhat confuses the American law. One of the contributions of the Supreme Court's decision in *Citizens to Preserve Overton Park, Inc. v. Volpe*,[23] however, was to elucidate the standards for reviewing the exercise of judgment or discretion in ways that sharply distinguished them from the standards for reviewing conclusions about strictly factual issues. The opinion thus firmly established "review of judgment and the exercise of discretion" as a third field for inquiry beyond simply fact and law.

Indeed, the *Overton Park* opinion appears to have been taken by the Court as an opportunity to make a catholic statement about review, one that quite exceeded any necessities of the case. As part of that statement, the Court called

---

23. See p. 235 above; the case is also discussed at p. 376 below.

attention to the way in which sub-paragraphs (E), (F), and (A) of section 706(2) establish three different statutory standards for review of "questions of fact": substantial evidence review; de novo review, or retrial by the court; and review to determine whether the agency's action was "arbitrary" or "capricious" in light of the information it possessed.

Writing about differing standards is undoubtedly complicated by the evanescence of any formula. It may be helpful to the reader's understanding to begin with the proposition that in finding facts or reviewing another's finding of facts, one cannot reasonably aspire to utter certainty about the facts; witnesses' accounts will differ, memories are imperfect, and even in scientific matters much may turn on inference. Accordingly, judges speak of the degree of confidence that is required. We can describe certainty that a certain fact is so as 100% confidence, certainty that a given fact is not true as 0% confidence; and then we might understand that, at least conceptually, the full range of intermediate states is possible. Those primarily responsible for finding facts are expected to have at least 50% confidence in what they assert to have been the situation. In criminal cases, American courts employ the formulation that guilt must be found "beyond a reasonable doubt," which could be said in these terms to require at least 85% confidence in the finding. In a civil trial, it is only necessary to find that facts have been demonstrated by a "preponderance" of the evidence—the slightest increment above equipoise, or 50+% confidence; and sometimes an intermediate formula is employed, "clear and convincing evidence—perhaps 67% confidence?

For verbal formulas describing the review of fact-finding, the essential starting point is this: the reviewer's function ordinarily accepts some possibility that the primary fact-finder has erred in finding or characterizing the facts. Thus, if the initial finding need only have been made to the 50+% confidence level,[24] the reviewer—unless she is herself finding the facts—must accept the fact-finder's conclusion even though she has somewhat less than 50% confidence, herself, that the facts were as the fact-finder found them. How much less than 50% confidence she must have before concluding there has been an error is the work of the verbal formulas for judicial review of facts. These formulas, one could say, invoke the 0% to 50% range of reviewing court confi-

---

24. See Director, Office of Workers' Compensation Programs v. Greenwich Collieries, 512 U.S. 267 (1994), in which the Court, applying the APA's definition of "burden of proof," rejected a long-standing Department of Labor practice, in administering certain benefit statutes, of resolving cases of equipoise ("true doubt," as the Department styled them) in favor of applicants as a means of honoring the statutes' beneficial impulse. Thus, the proponent of any matter, under the APA, must succeed in persuading the tribunal that it is more probable than not (50+%) that the facts favor its claim.

dence, from certainty that the facts were *not* as they have been found (0% confidence in the facts as found), to equipoise about them. Of course these numbers suggest an exactness that cannot be attained, but one hopes that they help the reader to see and understand the range across which judgment about the facts can be reached.

De novo review really is not review at all. It requires the court's independent determination of the matter at issue, on the basis of a record made in court (although it may incorporate the agency's record). If the confidence level required for fact-finding is 50+%, as it

generally is in administrative matters, that is also the confidence level that must be achieved on de novo review; the court substitutes its judgment for that of the initial fact-finder. As the *Overton Park* Court remarked, the statute makes de novo review available only in very limited circumstances.[25] It does not warrant further examination here.

1. Substantial evidence

As section 706(2)(E) states, the standard for judicial review of fact-finding in on-the-record agency proceedings is the "substantial evidence" test. On-the-record proceedings are the administrative proceedings that most resemble judicial trials, and so one might begin by considering judicial practice in reviewing trial results. Here, the American formulas depend on whether the facts were found by the trial judge, or by a jury of six to twelve hearing the trial under the court's supervision.[26] A jury's fact-finding may be conclusory (that is, expressed in a simple verdict for or against an individual) and is not disturbed for factual insufficiency unless the reviewing tribunal can find no possible basis for it in the facts shown by the trial record, as a "reasonable juror" might understand them. A trial court finding facts without a jury in a civil matter is procedurally required to make particular "findings of fact," and in

---

25. The rare judicial determinations of "constitutional" or "jurisdictional" fact, p. 339 above, can also be regarded as a form of partial de novo review.

26. Use of a jury is a constitutionally entrenched American practice. The Constitution makes it a matter of right in every criminal trial—a right among those "incorporated" by the Fourteenth Amendment as against the states, see p. 40 above—and in every federal civil trial "at common law" in which the value at issue is more than $20. Criminal trials are understood as those that could result in six months or more imprisonment. While the courts have resisted any suggestion that "$20" could be adjusted for inflation since 1791, they have interpreted the qualifier "at common law" quite narrowly, and have *not* thought this aspect incorporated as a right also against the states—whose thresholds for jury right in civil actions vary. See p. 38 above.

reviewing these determinations an American appeals court would reverse if it found them "clearly erroneous."

The greater respect given jury verdicts reflects historical veneration for the jury as an institution of community justice; initially, and perhaps still in some states, its factual findings were not reviewable at all. A trial court's findings do not enjoy the same veneration, but the "clearly erroneous" approach still is somewhat protective of its functions in this regard. While the appellate court need not be certain, nor convinced "beyond a reasonable doubt" that the fact-finder has erred, "clear error" could be thought the mirror of "clear and convincing evidence"—perhaps, 33% confidence that the facts were as they have been found? This high level of deference or acceptance of a certain leeway for trial court error in fact-finding recognizes the hazards of finding facts on the basis only of a cold, wholly documentary record, and focuses the reviewing court's attention on those issues likely to have general import. Strictly factual disputes generally concern only the particular parties to the lawsuit, while questions of law and even of judgment can affect future litigation and so have the greater claim to appellate attention.

The "substantial evidence" test under section 706(2)(E)incorporates a similar, if perhaps more permissive, approach to the fact-finding of an agency. As long as the court can determine that the record viewed as a whole contains evidence on the basis of which a reasonable administrator might have reached the agency's conclusions about the facts, it must accept those conclusions. Doing so respects the allocation of responsibility Congress has made; and it also saves the reviewing court's energy for matters likely to have greater importance to the future development of the law. How to articulate the confidence level required in relation to the levels appropriate to jury or trial court fact-finding, however, is troublesome and inexact.[27] Since an agency has special responsibilities and expertise a court lacks, one might imagine a reviewing court saying it would *not* reverse an agency's fact-finding in cases in which it would have reversed the same facts as found by a trial judge. This would demonstrate an additional element of tolerance for apparent error, induced by the reviewer's appreciation of greater likelihood that it will not accurately understand the matters having to be decided, or that the agency's fact-finding is properly guided by policy implications of its statute that permit it to be not

---

27. "The court/agency [review] standard, as we have said, is somewhat less strict than the court/court standard. But the difference is a subtle one—so fine that (apart from the present case) we have failed to uncover a single instance in which a reviewing court conceded that use of one standard rather than the other would in fact have produced a different outcome." Dickenson v. Zurko, 527 U.S. 150, 162–63 (1999). The Zurko case contains a thoughtful extended discussion of this problem.

entirely neutral. An example might lie in the inferences a labor tribunal draws about the intentionality lying behind employer actions such as firing a union organizer for work deficiency; organizers certainly are not entitled to be free of workplace discipline, but the administrative tribunal has many chances to see factual patterns of employer behavior[28] *and* a statutory responsibility to protect union organizing.

Is the reviewing court as limited in relation to the facts as it would be for jury fact-finding? Unlike jury fact-finding and like judicial fact-finding, agencies in on-the-record proceedings are required by the APA to make specific findings of fact. Congress put the references to "substantial evidence" and review in light of "the whole record" into the APA in the (arguably mistaken) belief that the courts were accepting agency fact-finding despite very low confidence levels about its correctness—reversing (as they would for jury findings) only when essentially certain that the facts could not have been as found. These qualifications, the Supreme Court acknowledged when it first confronted the question, reflected a congressional "mood," an instruction requiring courts to increase the intensity of factual review in "substantial evidence" cases.[29] Thus, the jury-review analogy would seem inappropriate as well.

The "whole record" qualification is useful in understanding the judicial treatment of administrative law judges' initial opinions in on-the-record administrative adjudications. Recall that when an agency decides a matter that has already been before one of its ALJs, the agency is regarded as having reached its decision de novo. Unlike the court that will review the agency's factual judgments, the agency is under no obligation to treat its ALJ's factual judgments as an overseer who can interfere with them only if persuaded to some degree of certainty that they were incorrect.[30] Yet the ALJ, of course, will be the only hearer to have observed live witnesses. Moreover, her limited responsibilities and freedom from political oversight in the agency give substantial assurance of her objectivity in judgment.[31] The agency members, in contrast, are policy-oriented and their many tasks deeply enmesh them in political considerations and exercises from day to day. The reviewing court recaptures the ALJ's contributions by regarding her initial decision as a part of the whole record. If an agency's ALJ has reached a conclusion opposite to her

---

28. How often and for what reasons does it discipline employees in this way? Was there a telling coincidence between the firing and organizing activity or the employer's acquiring knowledge about it?

29. Universal Camera Corp. v. National Labor Relations Board, 340 U.S. 474 (1951).

30. See p. 204 above.

31. See p. 137 above.

agency on some factual matter, that fact—together with whatever the record might offer in the way of support for her conclusion—would detract from whatever else in the record supports the agency's factual conclusions. In that way, it makes it less likely that "substantial evidence" support *on the whole record* could be found for the agency's conclusions.

Note that this ALJ function applies to factual issues, but not to matters of judgment—the policy-freighted conclusions that might be drawn from those facts once found. The ALJ is in a position to hear witnesses, has fewer distractions on her time, fewer incentives to cut corners for the sake of achieving policy ends, and so on. But what judgments are to be drawn from scientific or historical facts, questions of inference or ultimate fact as they are sometimes called, is a matter inescapably tied up with the policy for which the agency, not the ALJ, is responsible. In a proceeding concerning unfair labor practices, for example, the first kind of issue might be whether to believe testimony of a management or a union witness about what words were uttered at a given meeting. The second kind of issue is presented when one needs to decide what inferences to draw about management's state of mind from what is said, or what the impact of those words might have been on persons hearing them. The National Labor Relations Board's sense of what the carrying out of national labor policy requires, and its general experience with labor-management relations, will shape the way in which these questions are answered. Here, an ALJ's inference ought not play a significant role in a court's assessment of the agency's differing judgment; the court should ask only whether the agency's judgments of this character were irrational or insufficiently grounded.

All of these understandings, stable across half a century, seem to have been placed in question in 1998 by *Allentown Mack Sales and Service, Inc. v. NLRB*.[32] This closely divided Supreme Court opinion appears to have been driven by judicial suspicions that the National Labor Relations Board had been manipulatively using the special status its fact-finding would enjoy on review to disguise questionable judgments about the applicable law.[33] (As the immediately following section will reveal, reviewing courts are responsible for independent judgments of legal questions—albeit they may find, in the course of that

---

32. 522 U.S. 359 (1998).

33. It prominently cited an academic study to that effect, J. Flynn, The Costs and Benefits of "Hiding the Ball:" NLRB Policy-making and the Failure of Judicial Review, 75 B. U. L. Rev. 387 (1995). The study nonetheless, argued that this was an acceptable way for an agency to keep "the federal courts'...fingers out of the policy-making pie." The years have shown this risk of court intervention to be especially high in a politically freighted context such as the regulation of union/employer relationships.

independent review, statutory or other reasons to sustain a range of agency judgments.) On the one hand, the opinion restated the "substantial evidence" test as "whether on this record it would have been possible for a reasonable jury to reach the Board's conclusion." This formulation appears to ignore both the congressional mood signaled by the statute and the prior judicial recognition of that mood. On the other hand, the Supreme Court then went ahead and applied the substantial evidence test to the particular case—an effort it had reasonably indicated half a century earlier that it would not make.[34] It did so, as the dissent illustrated, in a strikingly intensive way—one that also ignored prior indications that agency inferences how evidence was to be understood were particularly deserving of respect. At this writing three years later, these aspects of the case have attracted little general attention in the literature; thus, the opinion may prove to have been a sport, limited to its particular "suspicious" circumstances.

The signaling function of the "substantial evidence" test, indicating Congress's wish for somewhat more intensive review of the agency's work than might otherwise be expected, was reinforced when Congress used the formula in connection with certain important informal rulemakings, notably those occurring under the Occupational Safety and Health Act. The use of a "substantial evidence" test for informal rulemaking produced a good deal of intellectual consternation at first. How could one properly review a proceeding that was not required to be decided "on the record" for support by substantial evidence on the whole record? As with the initial development of the test, Congress's choice of words was taken to express a mood, an expectation of relative intensity, rather than a precise test to be applied.[35] This expectation is substantially responsible for the development of the "hard look" idea explored below.[36] With the developing sense of what constitutes the record in rulemaking[37] and of what constitutes judicial review of fact-finding under the "ar-

---

34. From a review perspective, whether "substantial evidence" was or was not present in a given case is a factual question unique to that case, having few if any implications for future decisions in other cases. For this reason, protecting its own limited resources for decision, the Supreme Court in *Universal Camera*, p. 345 above, had indicated that its review function over the courts of appeal in "substantial evidence" cases would be limited to determining whether those courts had properly understood their function. The Court said it would intervene "only in what ought to be the rare instance when the standard appears to have been misapprehended or grossly misapplied." As the dissent pointed out, the *Allentown Mack* majority made no pretense of applying this test, and it could not have been met.

35. Industrial Union Department, AFL-CIO v. Hodgson, 499 F.2d 467 (D.C. Cir.1974).

36. See p. 384 below.

37. See p. 230 ff. above.

bitrary, capricious" standard, next to be discussed, the question has receded in importance. In the rulemaking context, particularly, the distinction between fact and judgment has had major importance. The most significant issues before the rulemaking agency invariably involve projection or judgment. While the courts have wanted to assure themselves that this is accomplished in an open and thoughtful manner (again, the "hard look" idea), they have generally understood that these are not factual judgments in the ordinary sense.

2. "Arbitrary, capricious"

When an agency's decision is not taken "on the record," and the "substantial evidence" test is not specially and misleadingly invoked by statute, courts understand the "arbitrary, capricious" language of section 706(2)(A) to express, inter alia, the standard they should apply in judging the agency's treatment of the facts. Highly informal decisions may be the occasion for such review, and in stating *this* test Congress was *not* sending a signal about its mood. Thus, one might anticipate that review under section 706(2)(A) requires less judicial confidence in the accuracy of agency fact-finding than the "substantial evidence" test—perhaps that the court is convinced beyond a reasonable doubt that the agency has erred, say a 15% confidence level. For this determination too, however "the court shall review the whole record or those parts of it cited by a party"; this gives rise to the problem of what constitutes the "whole record," which is discussed at some length earlier in this essay.[38] Here it may be enough to say that for informal adjudications, the demands on agencies for involving the public in creation of a record are less significant. Review is to occur on the basis of whatever record the agency presents, and it can be quite informal.[39]

Quite remarkably, in the author's judgment, some courts have denied the possibility of any difference in the confidence levels required by the "substantial evidence" and "arbitrary capricious" tests. When a circuit court judge, Justice Scalia—the author of the *Allentown Mack* decision[40]—wrote the following:

> When the arbitrary or capricious standard is performing [the] function
> of assuring factual support, there is no substantive difference between
> what it requires and what would be required by the substantial evidence

---

38. See pp. 230 ff. and 235 above.

39. Camp v. Pitts, 411 U.S. 138 (1973), discussed below at p. 378 ff. The Freedom of Information Act, p. 233 above, and any statutory provisions for public participation will permit external identification of the "record" to some degree.

40. See p. 346 above.

test, since it is impossible to conceive of a "nonarbitrary" factual judgment supported only by evidence that is not substantial in the APA
sense.... The distinctive function of paragraph (E)—what it achieves
that paragraph (A) does not—is to require substantial evidence to be
found within the record of closed-record proceedings to which it exclusively applies. The importance of that requirement should not be
underestimated.... [The administrative record in an informal proceed-
ing] might well include crucial material that was neither shown to nor
known by the private parties in the proceeding.... [41]

While the difference in record content described is of course present, the further proposition that "it is impossible to conceive of a 'nonarbitrary' factual
judgment supported only by evidence that is not substantial in the APA sense"
excessively simplifies matters. It ignores both the differing language Congress
used ("substantial evidence" and "arbitrary, capricious") and the clear indications that in making the differentiation Congress was seeking more intensive
factual review in on-the-record or certain rulemaking cases. Nor does it seem
implausible that a variety of confidence levels could be articulated between
complete confidence that an agency has erred, and de novo review indifferent
to agency error (because it substitutes judicial judgment). Justice Scalia has
recently been characterized by his colleagues as having a strong instinct for
simplification,[42] and his analysis of this issue seems an apt example of that
criticism. Yet it must also be conceded that any differences are subtle matters
of intensity in assessing an aspect of judicial review that all would concede is
not expected to be an especially rigorous one.[43] The understanding that judicial review under section 706(2)(A) will not be rigorous, particularly in contrast to judicial review of legal judgments, is the central proposition.

C. Questions of law

1. The American practice of statutory interpretation

A discussion for foreigners of the American judicial practice respecting
"questions of law" had best start with a sketch of American approaches to

---

41. Association of Data Processing Service Organizations, Inc. v. Board of Governors
of the Federal Reserve System, 745 F.2d 677, 683–84 (D.C. Cir. 1984).

42. United States v. Mead Corp., 533 U.S. 218 (2001).

43. See n. 27 above.

statutory interpretation. While "questions of law" in general include common law (or judge-made law) as well as statutory issues, in the administrative context questions of law almost invariably pertain to issues of statutory meaning. Recent years have witnessed a continuing and intense debate among the Justices of the Supreme Court (and in the scholarly literature[44]) respecting the proper approach to statutory issues, making any such account here provisional and summary. Since agencies are creatures of statutes and so must attend statutory meaning in everything they do, this debate strongly affects a great many of their actions, whether or not brought before the courts for review.

The debate primarily concerns the circumstances, if any, under which it is proper to go past the statutory text (understood with full attention to its context in the statutory framework of which it may be a part or the law as a

---

44. This literature is enormous. W. Eskridge, P. Frickey and E. Garrett, Legislation and Statutory Interpretation (2000) and K. Greenawalt, Legislation—Statutory Interpretation: 20 Questions (Foundation Press 1999) are helpful overviews written for American law students. Thoughtful presentations of the textualist perspective can be found in the writings of Professors Jeremy Waldron, for example, Law and Disagreement (Oxford University 1999) or The Dignity of Legislation (Cambridge University 1999) and John Manning, for example, Textualism and the Equity of the Statute, 101 Colum. L. Rev. 1 (2001) or Textualism as a Nondelegation Doctrine, 97 Colum. L. Rev. 673 (1997); and of the competing purposivist school in the writings of Professor William Eskridge, Jr., for example, Dynamic Statutory Interpretation (Harvard University 1994), All About Words: Early Understandings of the Judicial Power in Statutory Interpretation, 1776–1806, 101 Colum. L. Rev. 990 (2001); or The Circumstance of Politics and the Application of Statutes, 100 Colum. L. Rev. 558 (2000). Justice Steven Breyer, while still a judge of the United States Court of Appeals for the First Circuit, provided an analysis that well illustrated differences respecting the issue as between judges of the courts of appeal (who lack choice over their dockets and frequently encounter "ordinary" issues of statutory meaning for which legislative materials can be quite helpful) and Justices of the Supreme Court (for whom virtually all issues are hotly contested and politically charged). S. Breyer, On the Uses of Legislative History in Interpreting Statutes, 65 S. Cal. L. Rev. 845 (1992); see also F. Schauer, Statutory Construction and the Coordinating Function of Plain Meaning, 1990 Sup. Ct. Rev. 231 (1991), suggesting that textualist approaches be understood as a "second-best coordinating solution" the Supreme Court finds useful for a class of cases often both difficult and boring. Notable contributions by other circuit court judges include R. Posner, e.g. Statutory Interpretation—In the Classroom and In the Courtroom, 50 U. Chi. L. Rev. 800 (1983), F. Easterbrook, Statutes' Domains, 50 U. Chi. L. Rev. 553 (1983); and A. Randolph, Dictionaries, Plain Meaning, and Context in Statutory Interpretation, 17 Harv. J. Law & Pub. Pol. 71 (1994). Finally, the author's views are more fully developed in The Common Law and Statutes, 70 U. Colo. L. Rev. 225 (1998), The Courts and the Congress: Should Judges Disdain Political History, 98 Colum. L. Rev.242 (1998), and Resegregating the Worlds of Statute and Common Law, 1994 Sup. Ct. Rev. 427 (1995).

whole) to consideration of statutory purposes arguably revealed by other sources, notably the political history of the legislation. Secondarily, there is dispute whether statutes are to be regarded as static, always bearing the meaning that would have been assumed for them at the moment of their enactment, or rather should be regarded as open to development of their meaning over time. Associated with this secondary dispute are questions about the functions of courts in relationship to the development of statutes—whether courts are permitted to use them, as common law courts use cases, as building-stones for cases or remedies not directly provided for; or, rather, whether courts should treat statutes only as specific political resolutions of particular conflicting interests. The implication of the latter approach, treating a statute as a "deal," is that it cannot be extended without undercutting that accommodation of conflicting interests—a resolution that only the legislature can properly change. The three paragraphs following seek, inadequately, to capture a century's history.[45]

At the beginning of the twentieth century, the common law was the dominant form law took in the American legal order, and it was characterized by a formal and conservative intellectual approach that did not easily tolerate the changes being wrought by occasional statutes expressing judgments contrary to the common law. Progressive scholars argued that courts should treat statutes more liberally, and indeed use them as a preferred basis for common law reasoning.[46] As an expression of popular will, statutes not only had more democratic validity than the common law. They also captured contemporary social values more accurately than would a collection of cases decided over the course of centuries, and inevitably decided by the elders of their generation (American appellate judges tend to be appointed relatively late in professional life from an inherently conservative social group). One means of assuring judicial awareness of the political impulses underlying legislation, and consequently understanding the deficiencies found in the common law, was for the judge to acquaint himself with the political history of legislation. Succeeding years saw increasing judicial attention to these impulses and consequent use of the hearings, reports and debates by which Congress developed legislation.

By the 1940s, in the wake of the crisis over substantive due process,[47] federal courts had become highly attentive to the history of a law's development

---

45. See A. Vermeule, The Cycles of Statutory Interpretation, 68 U. Chi. L. Rev. 149 (2001).

46. See p. 116 above.

47. See p. 37 above.

within the Congress. In their eagerness to demonstrate renewed judicial respect for legislative judgment, they took this to the point of seeming to create a virtual calculus of relative value in the variety of materials that attention to that history might uncover, in order to identify the precise meanings "the legislature" had intended.[48] Yet as a descriptive proposition, it is hard to speak of a singular, precise intended meaning in the work product of several hundred very political individuals—the Congress. Doing so reflected the common intellectual habit of talking about complex institutions as if they were individuals (a failing equally common in talking about agencies). It also reflected an arguable overreaction to the earlier and more confrontational judicial stance. The consequent intellectual movement, dominant in the American intellectual community for several decades, tended instead to seek out statutory "purpose." A judge's proper interpretive approach, this "Legal Process" school proposed, was to treat legislation as a purposive activity.[49] The fundamental principle, which attending to the political history of legislation would assist the judge to achieve: "The idea of a statute without an intelligible purpose is foreign to the idea of law and inadmissible.... The statute ought always to be presumed to be the work of reasonable men pursuing reasonable purposes reasonably."[50] The reader will appreciate the normative thrust of the preced-

---

48. In general, greater formality was attached to the documents with the greatest exposure and significance in the legislative process. Conference reports received the highest regard in this respect, as the basis for votes in both houses on matters already shaped by extensive debate. Most gave next rank to committee reports, the written and universally available products of the most intensive view given to the draft legislation by each chamber's designated committee. Next came floor debates, which embody high seriousness (votes) but might at any given moment be poorly attended; also, the transcripts of debates were subject to extensive editing by the speaker. Among the debates, statements by those most responsible for the legislation—for example, a committee chairman—would be given the most attention. The least attention was paid to what transpired at committee hearings, which was both preliminary and, typically, far less readily accessible.

In contemplating that a practice of assigning significance to each of these sources was even possible, readers from parliamentary democracies should remember that legislation in the American context is rarely the direct product of the (executive) government's will. Members of Congress are not part of that arm of government. One effect of this is that party discipline is highly variable in American practice; a Senator or Representative is free to vote by her conscience on every vote and ordinarily will do so. While she will vote with her party more often than not, amendments to proposed legislation are generally expected. Most successful legislation begins as a draft supplied by the executive administration, but it is the rare such draft that is not extensively amended before final enactment.

49. Europe's teleological jurisprudence urged similar approaches.

50. H. Hart & A. Sacks, The Legal Process 1124 (W. Eskridge & P. Frickey eds. Foundation Press 1994).

ing sentences. This principle was directed at judges, as a means of encouraging their appropriately receptive attitude toward legislative work-product. It is not descriptive of any actual legislative process ever known in American history. It thus served a purpose similar to that of the progressive arguments: it encouraged judges to accept the legislative impulse as valid and to work with it constructively in deciding cases.

The last part of the twentieth century has brought to prominence five factors relevant to statutory interpretation. First, it has been marked by a general return of conservative values to American politics and, correspondingly, judging. Second, statutes are now the dominant form of law at the level of national—and probably also state and local—government; this change has made statutory interpretation most of what federal judges do, and has transformed its relationship to the courts' common law functions. Third, unlike the Legal Process school, and drawing on the recent rise in classical microeconomic's influence on legal thinking, much analysis now tends to start with the observation that legislatures are not in fact "reasonable men pursuing reasonable purposes reasonably." They reach arbitrary decisions on what, from a judicial perspective, are irrational (i.e., wholly political) bases,[51] as in fact they always have. Fourth, the legislative process has changed to make its materials less likely to reflect the views of the legislators themselves. As congressional staff levels have grown tremendously, this has made Congress a much more bureaucratic institution: only staff, not members, may attend committee hearings; reports have become less a repository of legislators' thinking and more a product of staff work; and legislators' attendance at debates is at best variable. Finally, and perhaps most important, those who work at Congress have noticed the use courts have been making of the historical materials legislatures generate, and have sometimes been discovered apparently manipulating them.[52] That is, a committee, an individual legislator, even members of staff, may find ways of placing into the legislative history, in the hope of influencing subsequent judicial readings, propositions on which they could not—or at least do not—secure the required votes of a majority of both houses of Congress and the signature of the President. All these changes have contributed to a notable return to the text and to formal tools of textual exegesis, perhaps best captured by the following graphic the Harvard Law Review used

---

51. See the brief discussion of "public choice theory," p. 84 above; its application of economic modeling to political behaviors seems well adapted to this "realistic" view, although proponents tend not to wash their view of judges in the same cynical acid.

52. This factor is given particular prominence in A. Vermeule, The Cycles of Statutory Interpretation, 68 U. Chi. L. Rev. 149 (2001).

in 1994 to illustrate the return of the dictionary as a tool of statutory interpretation in the Supreme Court.[53]

Percentages of Cases[a] Referring[b] to Dictionaries, 1935 Term–1992 Term

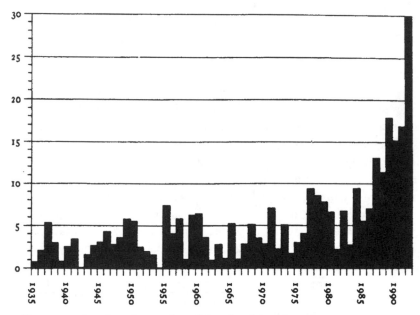

a Percentages based on the number of signed opinions in each Term.
b Includes all cases that use the words "dictionary" or "dictionaries." Search of LEXIS,
Genfed Library, US file (Jan. 4, 1994).

It may be useful for our purposes to illustrate the changing styles by relating them very briefly to some interpretations of the Administrative Procedure
Act already met in these pages.[54] Among the first interpretations of the Act
was the Court's initial encounter, in 1951, with the "substantial evidence" test
in the *Universal Camera* case.[55] To resolve its meaning, the Court considered
with care what had been before Congress, and the concerns that had been expressed in the debates. Both *Overton Park*,[56] interpreting the "arbitrary, capri-

---

53. Note, Looking It Up: Dictionaries and Statutory Interpretation, 107 Harv. L. Rev.
1437, 1454 (1994).
54. An extended essay on this theme appears in P. Strauss, Changing Times; The APA
at Fifty, 63 U. Chi. L. Rev. 1389 (1996).
55. See p. 345 above; see also Wong Yang Sung v. McGrath, 339 U.S. 33 (1950).
56. See p. 341 above.

cious" language of section 706(2)(A), and the cases interpreting section 702 to work a considerably expansion of beneficiary standing to challenge agency action,[57] were decided in the early 1970s, and could be thought representative of the "Legal Process" approach. These opinions unselfconsciously treat the statute as a purposive text that courts should appropriately mold to the needs of the present time. How either the 1946 Congress or a hypothetical 1946 reader of statutes actually understood the words "arbitrary" or "person aggrieved" were not important questions; what purposes judicial review and standing to seek it were to serve, and serve in the current era, were of the essence. Moving now to the 1990s, one finds a highly textual exegesis of the meaning of "burden of proof," one that fixes on the meaning given to that phrase in 1946 by dictionaries and treatises of the time and one that eschews reference to either congressional materials, intervening developments, or contemporary estimations of purpose.[58] The change in judicial attitude is even more apparent, when one finds in the briefs submitted by the parties to the case little or no effort to argue it in the textualist, historically bound manner in which it was decided.[59]

In practice, faced with the problem of interpreting a congressional statute, a court will of course first consider its actual language. This will include sophisticated reference to context, structure, and all the usual tools of understanding written language. Yet both language and legislative foresight are inevitably imperfect. In a matter parties have thought important enough to pursue through an expensive trial and two levels of appeal, these and other imperfections are likely to be front and center. Statutory language alone will not have put an end to the controversy. It will be susceptible of two or more readings from which a choice must be made. Indeed, persuading the judge that a statute does not straightforwardly resolve the pending matter is the threshold that must first be crossed in any interpretive setting. The fields of contention concern the materials one can refer to in attempting to cross that threshold, and how one then determines which is the preferable reading.

---

57. See p. 318 above.

58. Greenwich Collieries, p. 201 n. 61 above; see also Darby, p. 324 n. 98 above. These are, of course, broad trends, and not all Justices are so strongly attached to textualist approaches as is, for example, Justice Scalia. Thus, Justice Breyer's opinion in Dickinson v. Zurko, n. 27 above makes some reference to legislative materials and seems generally to pursue a contemporary inquiry into the purpose of the APA provisions he is interpreting, as well as an inquiry into how the words "substantial evidence" would have been understood in 1946.

59. See Changing Times, n. 54 above; and also P. Strauss, Resegregating the Worlds of Statute and Common Law, 1994 Sup. Ct. Rev. 427.

To sum up: the previous generation's judges were encouraged to refer to the publicly available materials of legislative history for these purposes. To the extent this was done to acquire a sense of the problems with which the legislators expected their work to deal—the "mischief" to which the statute responded—the practice might be thought to have contributed to a smooth working partnership between courts and legislature. Preliminary studies, committee reports and debates can all set a context for understanding the troubles that called forth particular language, and in that way make it less likely the court will arrive at an interpretation surprising to the enactors, or to those who may have had to act in response to the statute before the courts had encountered it. The threat that legislators will manipulate these materials to achieve unenacted and unenactable ends becomes severe when the judge is also looking for precise indications of what the legislature considered—"intended," in some formulations—the language chosen would accomplish. It is in reaction to this threat that, where a prior generation of judges reached for the materials of political history, many today reach for the dictionary and the grammar book.

It is more accurate to say that interpretation today inevitably starts with the text (as indeed it should), than that political history is never consulted. Of the nine present Justices of the Supreme Court, only two or three make a fetish of the proposition that these materials are generally improper to consult, concurring specially to note disagreement with paragraphs in which a majority opinion draws on them. The remainder can be found still referring to them from time to time, although rarely as centrally to analysis as would have occurred two or three decades ago. And, one's impression is that it is now done more often to inform a general sense of statutory purpose than to choose among various possible particular meanings.

Nor is the Supreme Court's new textualism simplistic or mindless, as one might have characterized the "plain meaning rule" judges wielded to defend their common law from statutory attack at the beginning of the last century. Thus, in *Whitman v. American Trucking Association*,[60] already seen in these pages in relevant substantive contexts,[61] Justice Scalia attends carefully to the possible meanings the involved text might be read to have, looking to the full context of the statute and its relation to other statutes in doing so. As we will see in a following section,[62] he is a particularly vigorous partisan of the proposition that within areas statutory language leaves uncertain, administrative agencies should be given full scope to develop appropriate policy. But in his

---

60. 531 U.S. 457 (2001).
61. See pp. 29 and 248 above.
62. See p. 368 ff. below.

view courts ought not develop policies within lacunae left by statutory language, however inevitable the lacunae may be; rather, they are to discover singular (and enduring) meanings.[63] Dictionaries are important sources for him
in understanding meaning,[64] but the unenacted and manipulable political history of the statute emphatically is not.[65]

While the delegation doctrine is unworkable in practice,[66] one argument
for the textualists' approach is that it tends in a similar direction—that is, it
emphasizes the responsibility of the legislature to make fundamental value
judgments. Thus, in deciding what the word "modify" means in a statute authorizing FCC rulemaking,[67] or "drug or device" for the FDA,[68] the Court invokes not only a somewhat fruitless search through the dictionaries but also
an understandable principle tending to leave important decisions in Congress's
hands: that courts should not countenance interpretations, by agencies or
themselves, that (even if within the possible meanings of the language used)
are demonstrably outside the likely contemplation of the legislature. *Whitman*,
too, constrains agency power; it reads the EPA's authorizing statute to deny
the EPA the authority to make tradeoffs between public safety and economic
cost—tradeoffs of a character that legislatures make often, but that suggest an
uncomfortably broad political responsibility for an agency.[69] A similar impulse
is also evident in the reluctance of today's Court majority to add new judicial
remedies to those Congress has provided, by inferring common law causes of

---

63. See, for example, his dissent in United States v. Mead Corp., 533 U.S. 218 (2001),
discussed in another context below, p. 371. "Textualism tends to approach problems of statutory interpretation like a puzzle, the answer to which is found by developing the most persuasive account of all the public sources (dictionaries, other provisions of the statute, other
statutes) that bear on ordinary meaning. This in turn tends to make statutory interpretation an exercise in ingenuity.... The textualist judge treats questions of interpretation like a
puzzle to which it is assumed there is one right answer.... Having fewer tools to work with,
the textualist—like the painter working with a small palette—necessarily has to become
more imaginative in resolving questions of statutory interpretation." T. Merrill, Textualism
and the Future of the *Chevron* Doctrine, 72 Wash. U. L. Q. 351, 354, 372–73 (1994).

64. In *Allentown Mack*, n. 32 above, for example, he invoked dictionary meanings to
reject an agency's reading of its own precedents.

65. He has been willing to look at political history to see whether a given problem was
identified—silence on a matter that ought to have been talked about, if in view, is not so
readily manipulated as affirmative representations, in reports or ostensible debates, about
expected interpretation on issues that *have* been identified.

66. See p. 26 ff. above.

67. MCI Telecommunications Corp. v. American Tel. & Tel. Co., 512 U.S. 218 (1994).

68. FDA v. Brown & Williamson Tobacco Corp., 529 U.S. 120 (2000).

69. See p. 248 above.

action on the basis of statutory definitions of harm to individuals.[70] The Justices insisting upon textual approaches today are less defending the common law from statutory change, than resisting the idea that federal judges have an appropriate common law function.

Understandable as it may be in context, the new textualism or formalism has often made it appear that the Justices are imposing, not avoiding, personal policy preferences, and creating an atmosphere of struggle rather than cooperation with the Congress. For example, a 1934 statute authorized the Securities and Exchange Commission to regulate disclosure and ethical practice in the securities market. The SEC early adopted a regulation to enforce some of its norms, and the courts (at a time when they were more sympathetic to such implications) permitted persons who had been injured by its violation to bring common law causes of action against violators. The statute said nothing about persons who aided and abetted violations, but federal criminal statutes include a general "aiding and abetting" provision; from this, a basis for bringing aiders and abettors within the statute might be inferred. The SEC regularly enforced its norm against aiders and abettors; private actions followed suit; and over the years eleven of the United States Courts of Appeal upheld these practices. Congress, with occasions to revisit the 1934 act, failed to respond;[71] the only possible indication these outcomes were controversial was a passing remark the Supreme Court itself had made in an earlier case, suggesting that it regarded the question as open. (If a signal was intended, that would of course have involved the assertion rather than the denial of judicial law-making responsibilities.) One thus would have said with confidence that "aiding and abetting" liability had been established. Yet in a case in which the point was not even brought forward by the parties, a majority of the Supreme Court held that aiding and abetting liability could not be imposed under the statute.[72] It considered only Congress's action in 1934 and gave no credit to intervening developments, including the unanimity of view sustaining the legality of the practice in the inferior courts.

The formalists' stated distrust of judicial law-creation is particularly hard to reconcile with decisions like this, as well as their strenuous insistence on the force of stare decisis in the statutory context.[73] While one can understand

---

70. See p. 117 above.

71. It is important to bear in mind, when considering the legislative-judicial relationship, that in revising statutes Congress responds to controversy, and that it has limited time for its work. When a surprising judicial interpretation creates a need for legislation not previously understood to have existed, it imposes work on Congress.

72. Central Bank of Denver v. First Interstate Bank of Denver, 511 U.S. 164 (1994).

73. See, e.g., Neal v. United States, 516 U.S. 284 (1996) and discussion p. 114 above.

the impulse to resist surprising changes, and also the reluctance in an era dominated by statutes to build fresh judicial remedies on the base of the ones the legislature has explicitly provided, the Supreme Court's high selectivity about the cases it hears gives an unmistakable "policy-making" cast to its decisions— especially when it reaches out for issues or arguments no party has put before it. So also when its textualist interpretations are themselves surprising in light of an established and relatively uncontroversial line of development in lower courts that the legislature has shown no sign of a wish to disturb—particularly when the Court insists on its readings repeatedly (as in some settings it has)[74] despite repeated legislative signals in another direction.

Law *does* develop over time. When those developments (like the changes worked in administrative rulemaking and its review since 1946) appear to have been generally adopted by the legal system and to have provoked no adverse congressional reaction, the formalist reference points[75] can be seen to turn the Court into a powerful opponent of Congress. In the author's judgment more, not less, uncertainty will arise about the meanings of statutes if the Court sees its task in dealing with statutes as being to enforce the original understandings that a majority of Justices find in their text, regardless of what readings other actors (including Congress) may have found uncontroversial in the interim. That impact will be heightened if the Court, in so acting, is unwilling to educate itself about the political context within which Congress has acted. Such refusals elevate the chances for conflict over political judgments Congress has reached, and in effect refuse cooperative partnership in the law-making enterprise. While the susceptibility of the documents of political history is apparent (and particularly so if judges purport to use them to fix precise "intended" meanings), a skeptical approach may be sufficient to guard against it.[76] Judges who cut themselves off from knowledge of the political history of statutes risk

---

74. See n. 76 below, and the subsequent Ninth Circuit decision in Reynolds v. Martin, 985 F.2d 470, 475 n.2 (9th Cir. 1993), recounting a history of Supreme Court decisions and congressional responses, in which the Court repeatedly defended a policy position (restricting the circumstances in which reimbursement of litigation expenses to prevailing parties was permissible) evidently of the Court's own making, against congressional statutes that might have been understood to authorize such reimbursement, and generally were so understood by lower courts.

75. Dictionary meaning, statutory meaning dependent on what would have been understood at the moment of enactment, the irrelevance to Supreme Court judgment of what may have been decided by lower courts, and the bindingness of such judgments once entered.

76. See, e.g., the dissenting opinion of Justice Stevens in West Virginia University Hospitals, Inc. v. Casey, 499 U.S. 83 (1991); A. Aleinikoff and T. Shaw, The Costs of Incoher-

reaching decisions that will prove surprising to relevant communities themselves likely to be well aware of that history; manifest a disrespectful attitude
towards Congress; create incentives for poor drafting techniques by effectively
requiring legislatures to anticipate all possible future judicial readings;[77] and
conduce to inefficiency and inappropriate contention in the judicial-legisla-
tive relationship.

2. Statutory interpretation at the agency level

From the perspective of one steeped in administrative law, the denigration
of political history as a proper source for understanding statutes has important (and regrettable) implications for administrators who must constantly
address issues of statutory meaning.[78] Regulatory schemes are characteristi-
cally complex—the Clean Air Act alone fills hundreds of pages in the statute
books. Unlike the rare encounters courts will have with any particular scheme,
the responsible agencies must interpret their governing statutes on a continuing and intensive basis. Political history has an inevitable bearing on these
daily encounters with issues of meaning, one preferable in the author's view
to dictionaries and authorities on usage. Legislative materials are often well
known to the regulated. They give a set of common external points of reference to both agency and court, that might be thought helpful to control the
subjectivities of both. For the agency, recognizing them gives legitimacy to in-
dicia of meaning that politics will in any event require it to consult. For the
courts, use of these materials is a reminder of the agency's responsibility. And
for the system of government as a whole, it avoids competition between overseers of administrative process as to the proper standards of meaning to be
applied.

---

ence: A Comment on Plain Meaning, *West Virginia Hospitals, Inc. v. Casey*, and Due Process
of Statutory Interpretation, 45 Vand. L. Rev. 687 (1992); T. Merrill, n. 63 above.

77. Thus, wrote Francis Lieber in the nineteenth century, when English judges "adhere[d] strictly to the law, to its exact expressions[, t]his again induced the lawmakers to
be, in their phraseology, as explicit and minute as possible, which causes such a tautology
and endless repetition in the statutes of that country...However minutely we may define,
somewhere we needs must trust at last to common sense and good faith." Legal and Political Hermeneutics 31 (Charles C. Little and James Brown 1839).

78. A more extensive treatment of the issues of this section appears in P. Strauss, When
The Judge is not the Primary Official With Responsibility to Read: Agency Interpretation
and the Problem of Legislative History 66 Chi.-Kent L. Rev. 321 (1992). See also J. Siegel,
Textualism and Contextualism in Administrative Law, 78 B. U. L. Rev. 1023 (1998).

As may easily be imagined, recordkeeping about legislation of interest begins at an early stage for an agency whose daily work will be controlled by particular legislation, and reaches more broadly than such generally available public materials as printed hearings, reports or debates. If the agency is already in existence during initial drafting stages within the administration, its officials will be deeply involved in those processes, and will generate institutional memories about them. When the draft reaches Congress, the agency will be careful to maintain its own records of all public documents generated in Congress, and perhaps others— transcripts or notes of unprinted hearings, detailed records of all agency testimony on legislative matters, etc. Often enough, bills must be submitted to a number of sessions of Congress before any one is enacted. The agency will possess a rather detailed sense of this history and of the political changes and compromises, explicit and unspoken, that ultimately produced success.

Once a statute has been enacted, the political history continues to bear. The agency will have a continuing relationship with the responsible congressional committees and their staff. This relationship is likely to be influenced, for good or for ill, by the committee's reaction to the manner in which the new legislation is implemented. At every step, the agency must be prepared to defend its choices, politically as well as in court, in terms of its statutory authority. This generates a continuing attention to issues of statutory meaning in the context of legislative history that, outside government, can be difficult to appreciate.[79]

These factors led to early recognition that judges interpreting statutes should include administrative readings among the factors they took into account. A 1940 Supreme Court decision, *United States v. American Trucking Associations*,[80] remarked at one point that "[t]he interpretation of the meaning of statutes, as applied to justiciable controversies, is exclusively a judicial function."[81] But then only a few pages later, in referring to agency interpretations of the language at issue in the case, the Court added:

> [1]In any case such interpretations are entitled to great weight.
> [2]This is peculiarly true here where the interpretations involve "con-

---

79. I tell my classes that the real impact of the "delegation" doctrine, p. 33 above, is experienced in the daily work of thousands of government lawyers striving to show that proposed agency conduct lies within statutory authority. That work—as likely to be exposed to congressional committees or the GAO, p. 85 above, as the courts—can invest a commissioner's testimony in hearings with the seriousness of a treaty.

80. 310 U.S. 534 (1940). The opinion is frequently taken as an exemplar of the uses of political history in statutory interpretation.

81. At 543.

temporaneous constructions of a statute by the men charged with the responsibility of setting its machinery in motion, of making the parts work efficiently and smoothly while they are yet untried and new." [3] Furthermore, the [agency's] interpretation gains much persuasiveness from the fact that it was the [agency] which suggested the provisions' enactment to Congress.[82]

This section addresses these three long-established arguments for doing giving weight to agency views, arguments that assume the judge's ultimate responsibility for determining the meaning of the statute as a question of law. A fourth argument, which appears to place important elements of direct responsibility for reading statutes in agencies in preference to the courts, is taken up in the next section.

[1] *In any case such interpretations are entitled to great weight.* The *American Trucking* opinion does not further explain what is meant by this observation, but it is not hard to unpack in light of the prior discussion. Thoughtful judges realize that they encounter statutes only infrequently, and see only those elements dissatisfied persons (whose situations may be unrepresentative) choose to bring before them—creating significant risks of distortion in their reading of statutory text. The interpretations an agency makes reflect its holistic view and the needs of long-term statutory administration. As the years pass, an agency with continuing responsibility for administration of a statutory scheme (particularly a complex one) is often in a better position than a court to maintain the scheme's integrity as new circumstances arise requiring attention. One could expand on this observation about comparative advantage by noting two further institutional considerations. First, recall that although federal agencies are organized nationally and the law they apply is national in scope, the first two levels of the federal judiciary are geographically limited, and the Supreme Court's capacity to enforce uniformity upon them is severely restricted by the small size of its docket.[83] The tendency produced by having courts in Maine, Florida and California each believe it should respect an administrator's judgment about statutory meaning in reaching its own conclusions is to enhance the probability of uniform national administration of the laws. Second, the agency's continuing legislative relationships

---

82. At 549.

83. See p. 121 ff. above; P. Strauss, One Hundred Fifty Cases Per Year: Some Implications of the Supreme Court's Limited Resources for Judicial Review of Agency Action, 87 Colum. L. Rev. 1093 (1987). If the Supreme Court hears no more than 150 full arguments yearly, questions arising under any given element of federal legislation can hardly come before it more than once each few years.

could be understood to suggest that Congress's failure to revise the statute is (at least in part) the product of satisfaction with the agency's continuing stewardship. Of course, many other explanations—inattention, controversiality—can be given for congressional failures to act, and the risk may appear substantial that an agency's course of interpretation will be self-interested.

One might expect, then, that judicial attention to the agency's arguably superior position would be highly variable, and it is. The variation was captured in an often quoted paragraph from *Skidmore v. Swift & Co.*,[84] a 1944 decision describing the appropriate weight to be given to an administrator's letter of advice concerning an interpretive issue that had arisen in private litigation about a statute under his administration:

> [Such] rulings, interpretations and opinions…, while not controlling upon the courts by reason of their authority, do constitute a body of experience and informed judgment to which courts and litigants may properly resort for guidance. The weight of such a judgment in a particular case will depend upon the thoroughness evident in its consideration, the validity of its reasoning, its consistency with earlier and later pronouncements, and all those factors which give it power to persuade, if lacking power to control.[85]

This formula was reaffirmed by the Court in 2001.[86]

[2] This is peculiarly true here where the interpretations involve "contemporaneous constructions of a statute by the men charged with the responsibility of setting its machinery in motion, of making the parts work efficiently and smoothly while they are yet untried and new." [87] One reason for regarding decisions an agency makes in its immediate implementation of new authority as probative

---

84. 323 U.S. 134 (1944).

85. Id. at 140. This frequently quoted language conveys a sense of its own limits. At the outset, the Administrator must be able to convince the court that his position is a possible or sensible reading of the statutory language. Thus, the same statute authorized the Administrator to define an "area of production" for agricultural products as an element of exemption from regulation. The Administrator read this language as permitting distinctions between large and small enterprises performing the same work in the same locality. In context, however, the Supreme Court believed that "area" necessarily referred to geographical and/or work-related factors, and so easily rejected the Administrator's reading. Addison v. Holly Hill Fruit Products, Inc., 322 U.S. 607 (1944).

86. United States v. Mead Corp. 533 U.S. 218 (2001).

87. Norwegian Nitrogen Prod. Co. v. United States, 288 U.S. 294 (1933), from which the internal quotation was taken, is the decision customarily cited for this proposition.

indicators of meaning is that, as indicated above, agency officials may have been involved in drafting and the hearing process; they will have had a deep interest in following the legislative debates. This important and intensive exposure to the legislative process makes apt understanding probable. A second reason arises from the agency's *future* relations with Congress. Even a brand new agency must look forward to continuing relationships with the committees responsible for its budget, oversight, and authorization. This prospect makes it unlikely that an agency would depart sharply from congressional expectations when implementing new authority; indeed, if they did, one would expect that to generate considerable static in Congress, visible long before litigation came to the courts.

[3] Furthermore, the [agency's] interpretation gains much persuasiveness from the fact that it was the [agency] which suggested the provisions' enactment to Congress. Testimony at congressional hearings by agency officials who will be responsible for implementing the legislation being considered is often thought more useful than other hearing testimony in understanding legislative purpose. This is perhaps the most readily understood of the ways in which administrative readings may be taken into account. These officials are often the drafters, and in any event their continuing relationships with the responsible committees and the importance of the outcome to their own functions give their understandings particular credibility.[88]

Note that factors [2] and [3], if not the first, assume the relevance of political history to grasping the meaning of statutes. One who generally rejected that history's relevance might be moved to reject these factors as well. Like the image of legislative staff and private lobbyists manipulating legislative history to include important propositions that are never put to a vote, it is possible to imagine agency staff and their responsible committees agreeing on a course of action of which the larger Congress is never made aware. There is no evidence this actually happens, however. In the author's view, moreover, reasoning based on the possibility of its occurrence implies a form of disrespect for the ongoing function of Congress—which significantly depends (as do all institutions) on the integrity of its staff, and which continues to function through its committees without evident discord. One does not find members of Congress expressing significant concerns that they are being deprived of their appropriate voice by staff mischief; such charges—and changes—would occur if they did. Before courts make such an attitude of distrust a concrete element of their own analysis, they would do well to ask hard questions about

---

88. Securities and Exchange Commission v. Collier, 76 F.2d 939 (2d Cir. 1935) provides a useful example of this approach.

what the same wash of cynical acid would reveal concerning their own temptations. All three of these factors make considerable sense if one focuses not on a particular question of meaning, but on the continuing interactions among Congress and the agencies within which any such particular question would arise, and on the ordinary motivations of virtue an agency could be supposed to have,.

In closing, it may be helpful to look at the situation of the taxing authorities, whose interpretations tend in fact to be highly respected by the courts. Understanding the reasons for this can assist the analyst in locating other administrators on the continuum of agency and court responsibility. The relationships between the taxing agencies and the Congress are unusually close, with small changes constantly occurring in the tax laws as problems come to light, and unusually detailed committee oversight of tax administration generally. The Internal Revenue Service has a reputation for rigorously professional administration. It publishes its interpretations in unusual detail, and engages in vigorous professional discussion of them, in addition to its oversight relations with Congress. The tax laws are an unusually complex and interdependent body of technical statutes, an intricate web that a judge who visits only occasionally could not confidently traverse without risk of causing unintended consequences and disruptions. Finally, recognizing IRS authority tends to promote national uniformity in tax administration, as against a court system that, beneath the Supreme Court, is geographically organized. National uniformity is particularly needed in tax administration; litigation outcomes that created differing obligations to pay national taxes in San Francisco and New York would create enormous discontent. Thus, judges generally respect interpretations of the tax codes that can be made to appear reasonable to them.[89] Absent some or all of these factors, a different result might be expected.

3. Agency or court?[90]

As so far discussed, agency readings are simply one of the tools a court employs in reaching its own conclusions about meaning. All of the foregoing thus assumes, in a phrase already quoted, that "[t]he interpretation of the mean-

---

89. See, e.g. Cammarano v. United States, 358 U.S. 498 (1959).

90. Much of the analysis of this section is further developed in P. Strauss, Publication Rules in the Rulemaking Spectrum: Assuring Proper Respect for an Essential Element, 53 Admin. L. Rev. 803 (2001).

ing of statutes, as applied to justiciable controversies, is exclusively a judicial function."[91] The same proposition appears to be instinct in the introductory sentence of section 706: "To the extent necessary to decision and when presented, the reviewing court shall decide all relevant questions of law, interpret constitutional and statutory provisions, and determine the meaning or applicability of the terms of an agency action." Suppose, however, that on reading the statute in question the court concludes that it is indeterminate on some issue, and that explicitly or implicitly the statute places in the agency, to some extent, the responsibility to say what the statute means. In its own way, of course, this conclusion is also the product of a court's independent judgment on an issue of law. It is the court, not the agency, that decides when and subject to what constraints such authority has been conferred. Nonetheless, it should be apparent that a court reaching any such conclusion and then following its dictates will have crossed a significant threshold. In our prior consideration, the court has been responsible for deciding the meaning of the statutory language in question, taking such guidance as administrative conduct may offer, and its decision fixes the statute's meaning, unless later reexamined by another court or the legislature. In this fourth respect in which courts may pay special heed to administrative readings, the court will have recognized a primary role in the agency. Under this fourth approach, that is, the court finds that the question of statutory interpretation has, to a certain extent, been given to an agency. Within that delegated range of authority, as for other exercises of agency authority, the judicial control is to determine whether the choice it has made is a "reasonable" one. The agency might reach other "reasonable" conclusions at another time (if suitably justified), and those are equally entitled to be upheld. For the agency, if not for the court, the statute is notably dynamic.

This somewhat paradoxical outcome was first prominently articulated in *NLRB v. Hearst Publications, Inc.,*[92] a 1944 decision of the Supreme Court involving the National Labor Relation Board's interpretation of the statutory term "employee." The interpretation would bring within the Board's responsibilities for regulating labor, the relations between a newspaper publisher and the men who hawked its newspapers on street corners in Los Angeles. The Court sustained the Board's finding, saying that the

---

91. United States v. American Trucking Ass'n, n. 80 above. The foundational case of American judicial review, Marbury v. Madison, p. 91 n. 68 above, includes an oft-quoted similar claim: "it is emphatically the province and duty of the judicial department to say what the law is."

92. 322 U.S. 111 (1944).

task [of determining who is an employee] has been assigned primarily to the agency...Congress entrusted to it primarily the decision
whether the evidence establishes the material facts. Hence in reviewing the Board's ultimate conclusions, it is not the Court's function to
substitute its own inferences of fact for the Board's, when the latter
have support in the record....Where the question is one of specific
application of a broad statutory term in a proceeding in which the
agency administering the statute must determine it initially, the reviewing court's function is limited.[93]

It is revealing to see, however, that before reaching this point, the Court had
to choose among three possible ways to give the term "employee" meaning.
First, because the question who is an "employee" commonly arises in state law,
it might be decided on that basis, from state to state. Second, because being
an "employee" is important to a variety of federal statutes, each with a different aim, the Court might have chosen to give the term a uniform and judicially administered national interpretation. Finally "employee" could be regarded as a term that would take its color from the particular policies of the
National Labor Relations Act, the responsibility for which was placed primarily in the Board. The Court independently and sensibly concluded that the
last was the proper choice. That choice having been made, it followed that the
Board should be primarily responsible for investing meaning in the term.

The initial stage of *judicial* judgment, about whether (and to what extent)
matters had thus been delegated to an agency, was evident a few years later in
Packard Motor Car Co. v. NLRB.[94] Here, the question was whether foremen in
Packard's plants—that is, workers responsible to some extent for supervision
of other workers—could be regarded as "employees." The Court described this
question as "a naked question of law." Had it forgotten *Hearst*? No, for here
the question was framed as whether having some management responsibility,
in and of itself, was or was not sufficient to exclude a worker from the possibility of being regarded by the Board as a statutory "employee" under the
statute. The very hypothesis of the question, thus put, is that Congress did
not commit this judgment to the NLRB. Thus, it should not be surprising that,
in finding that foremen were not necessarily excluded from the class of "employees," the Court essentially ignored the Board's judgment.[95] Even though it

---

93. Id. at 130.
94. 330 U.S. 485 (1947).
95. Any weight that might have been added to the Court's judgment by the three factors considered in the previous section was eliminated by the fact that the Board had vac-

is for the Board to choose among possible meanings, in other words, it is for the courts to say what meanings are possible.

The reader might suspect that matters are not quite so simple as this when told that the Supreme Court's decision forty years later in *Chevron, U.S.A., Inc. v. Natural Resources Defense Council, Inc.*,[96] generalizing this approach, has been the most cited Supreme Court decision about administrative law in recent times, and has attracted a scholarly literature of enormous proportions.[97] The issue in *Chevron* concerned the EPA's interpretation of an environmental statute to permit plant-owners to combine the effects of their equipment, rather than deal with each possible source of emissions individually. (Being able to do so, it was believed, significantly increased management flexibility, and so permitted the achievement of environmental protection at lower cost.) An initial judgment the Court reached independently of agency opinion was that the statute neither compelled nor foreclosed the EPA's interpretation. Having reached the conclusion that Congress's delegation of rulemaking authority to the EPA left open the possibility that it would use that authority to permit the challenged approach, it stated a court's obligation to accept the agency's choice in broad and categorical terms:[98]

> When a court reviews an agency's construction of the statute which it administers, it is confronted with two questions. First, always, is the question whether Congress has directly spoken to the precise question at issue. If the intent of Congress is clear, that is the end of the matter; for the court, as well as the agency, must give effect to the unambiguously expressed intent of Congress. If, however, the court determines Congress has not directly addressed the precise question

---

illated in its view—the issue was *not* committed to its judgment, and its behavior did not suggest the clear understanding of the drafter or of a body acting under Congress's continuing watchfulness. Note in this respect the care of the language quoted from the Supreme Court's *Skidmore* decision, p. 363 above, to make weight turn on such issues.

96. 467 U.S. 837 (1984).

97. T. Merrill and K. Hickman, Chevron's Domain, 89 Georgetown L. J. 833 (2001) is an excellent recent exemplar, that starts with a partial listing of the prior literature, at 834 nn. 6–8. The author's contributions are P. Strauss, Publication Rules in the Rulemaking Spectrum: Assuring Proper Respect for an Essential Element, 53 Admin. L. Rev. 803 (2001) and P. Strauss, One Hundred Fifty Cases Per Year: Some Implications of the Supreme Court's Limited Resources for Judicial Review of Agency Action, 87 Colum. L. Rev. 1093 (1987).

98. 467 U.S. at 842–43, 865, 866.

at issue, the court does not simply impose its own construction on the statute, as would be necessary in the absence of an administrative interpretation. Rather, if the statute is silent or ambiguous with respect to the specific issue, the question for the court is whether the agency's answer is based on a permissible construction of the statute.

...

In these cases, the Administrator's interpretation represents a reasonable accommodation of manifestly competing interests and is entitled to deference: the regulatory scheme is technical and complex, the agency considered the matter in a detailed and reasoned fashion, and the decision involves reconciling conflicting policies. Congress intended to accommodate both interests, but did not do so itself on the level of specificity presented by these cases. Perhaps that body consciously desired the Administrator to strike the balance at this level, thinking that those with great expertise and charged with responsibility for administering the provision would be in a better position to do so; perhaps it simply did not consider the question at this level; and perhaps Congress was unable to forge a coalition on either side of the question, and those on each side decided to take their chances with the scheme devised by the agency. For judicial purposes, it matters not which of these things occurred.

...

When a challenge to an agency construction of a statutory provision, fairly conceptualized, really centers on the wisdom of the agency's policy, rather than whether it is a reasonable choice within a gap left open by Congress, the challenge must fail. In such a case, federal judges—who have no constituency—have a duty to respect legitimate policy choices made by those who do. The responsibilities for assessing the wisdom of such policy choices and resolving the struggle between competing views of the public interest are not judicial ones: "Our Constitution vests such responsibilities in the political branches." TVA v. Hill, 437 U.S. 153, 195 (1978).

If there is a surprising element to this formulation, it may be that the Court states the interpretive proposition so broadly: *whenever* legislation is found to permit a choice among given constructions, agencies with power formally to bind citizens by regulations or other measures are to be regarded as having the power "reasonably" to make that choice. *Hearst* is the product specifically of a reading of the National Labor Relations Act; the *Chevron* statement is a more general proposition about how Congress expects issues to be decided that it has not resolved, and that it has committed in the first instance to powerful administrators.

The enormous resulting literature has concerned itself endlessly with such questions as whether the Court has been consistent in applying *Chevron,* what has been its impact on lower courts, what is the meaning of its two "steps" in particular situations, and to what kinds of agency actions it should apply. Much of this, in the author's judgment, has been somewhat overdone. Thus, like *Packard,* the ostensible failures to apply the *Chevron* approach can be understood as cases in which the Court was able to resolve the question presented at the first, independent-judicial-review stage of the analysis. In one case, the court concluded that while the statutory term "bank" might be imprecise across a considerable range of possibilities, the statute's history precluded including within the range of imprecision the particular bank-like institution in question.[99] In another, the conclusion was that while the language at issue in the case was indeed imprecise, the administrator could not permissibly understand it (as he had purported to do) to have a meaning *identical* with a different phrase of the same statue applicable to the same proceeding.[100] Probably incautious phrasing in *Chevron* contributes to the problem here; the statement that the first "question [is] whether Congress has directly spoken to the precise question at issue," is taken by some to mean that any statutory ambiguity then entails deference to agency judgment. But even if a statute's language leaves open a range of unresolved possibilities, there is a question whether a given resolution falls within or without that range—and that is a question judges decide.[101] The better formulation, in the author's judgment, is that *Chevron*'s first step requires the reviewing court independently to determine the extent to which the statute settles the question of meaning with respect to the issue before it.[102]

Even if one concludes, at the first step, that an argued-for construction of a statute is possible under its terms, and not clearly decided by the statute itself, it is not inevitable that reasonable agency judgment will then control. The courts will themselves resolve this second stage, for example, when the ques-

---

99. Board of Governors, Federal Reserve System v. Dimension Financial Corp., 474 U.S. 361 (1986).

100. INS v. Cardoza-Fonseca, 480 U.S. 421 (1987).

101. Using, as appropriate, the three *American Trucking* indicators, p. 361 above.

102. In Whitman v. American Trucking Ass'n, discussed at p. 248 above, the Court summarized its *Chevron* step one analysis as follows: "We conclude…that the agency's interpretation goes beyond the limits of what is ambiguous, and contradicts what in our view is quite clear."

tion to be decided is larger than the agency's responsibility. Thus, if the question concerns the constitutionality of a statute or of its application, one would expect that to be decided strictly by the courts; this is reflected in the special judicial practice respecting "constitutional facts" mentioned briefly above.[103] Similarly, if the question is one of ascribing meaning to a statute of general application, not one specially within a particular agency's charge, the judiciary will naturally enough decide the matter on its own, without necessary guidance from the judgment of a particular agency that may have had occasion to confront it. Thus, the Federal Trade Commission, whose responsibilities include conducting formal administrative hearings implementing laws protective of competition, might well have to decide questions about the meaning of a provision of the APA, or of the Sherman Anti-trust Act. Yet there is no reason to think a court would be much persuaded by the FTC's judgment about the meaning of such statutes, which could easily have arisen before another agency or in a judicial trial.

Must the agency have been using delegated lawmaking authority for its decision to command *Chevron* obedience[104] in the setting where it does have prime responsibility for administration of the statute in question? Government attorneys have eagerly sought the shelter of *Chevron* for interpretations reached in a much wider range of agency actions—publication rules,[105] for example—and have sometimes succeeded. Arguments that *Chevron* properly applies only to agency conclusions reached following public procedures under delegated authority (as in *Chevron* itself) constitute one strong strand of the literature,[106] and seventeen years after unleashing *Chevron*, the Supreme Court came close to endorsing that position in its decision in *United States v. Mead Corp.*[107] In *Mead Corp.*, customs officials had issued a publication rule interpreting tariff schedules as they applied to materials such as those Mead Corp. wished to import and then, when Mead Corp. protested the duty applied to its imports, claimed *Chevron* obedience for their interpretation. Noting that Customs had formulated its view without using public procedures and re-

---

103. See p. 339 above.

104. "*Chevron* deference" is the phrase usually employed in the cases and in the literature. Since "deference," like "discretion," comes in several intensities, the author's preference is to write of "*Chevron* obedience"—more strongly suggesting the obligation of courts to accept reasonable agency determinations—and "*Skidmore* weight." See p. 363 above.

105. See p. 222 above.

106. E.g., R. Anthony, "Interpretive" Rules, "Legislative" Rules and "Spurious" Rules: Lifting the Smog, 8 Admin. L. J. Am. U. 1 (1994).

107. 533 U.S. 218 (2001).

mained free to change it in the same way, the Court held *Chevron* inapplicable; only *Skidmore* weight,[108] to whatever extent the circumstances warranted, could be relevant. While indicating that *Chevron* obedience was most appropriate for procedurally formal exercises of delegated law-making authority, however, the Court did not adopt a hard-and-fast rule limiting it to such cases. In some circumstances, which it indicated would emerge through the common-law processes of case-by-case precedent building, statutory indicators and other factors could command the same result; but, it said, these were absent in *Mead*.

One way to rationalize the *Mead* result is that it permits focusing on the political responsibility of the agency decision or interpretation under examination. Regulations and adjudications leave an agency bearing the direct imprimatur of the politically responsible leaders at its head, thus fitting the *Chevron* opinion's strong language about political responsibility.[109] Publication rules and other staff documents do not; while it may be possible to describe them as "agency action," one nonetheless could not say that their adoption reflects "legitimate policy choices made by those who do [have a constituency]." Rather, they are the product of civil servants who in these instances have at most weak needs to consult with their immediate political superiors, and whose decisions will rarely if ever penetrate the consciousness of Congress or the President. The apparent result of *Mead* is that, when the shelter of *Chevron* is important, agency staff will have an important reason to consult the agency's political leadership and find ways of signaling their direct involvement. The further claim of some, that *Chevron* obedience should be limited to policy conclusions in whose development the public has a chance to participate, is not readily reconciled with the Court's stated willingness to consider other settings.

Another way to frame the difference between *Chevron* obedience and *Skidmore* weight, suggested but not compelled by *Mead*, is that the former is appropriate only in cases in which the agency has constrained itself, top to bottom, to act in accordance with the interpretation for which the former is sought. Regulations have this quality, as they can be changed only by further notice and comment rulemaking. Administrative adjudications may but need not. Mass justice agencies, for example, like the Immigration and Naturalization Service or the Social Security Administration do not use a system of "binding precedent," and even in agencies that do, decisions that become final

---

108. See p. 363 and n. 85 above.
109. See p. 272 above.

below the agency level do not control the agency as a whole. On the other hand, under some statutes certain publication rules or other informal actions may be given the effect of controlling the whole agency's behavior—suggesting that political accountability is a realistic expectation. If the whole of the agency hierarchy is not constrained by the action in question, it is hard to develop the claim that the hierarchically superior courts must give the agency's judgment more credit than any *Skidmore* weight it may merit.

Mead was only one vote shy of unanimity, but Justice Scalia's impassioned dissent reveals important questions about the arguable differences between agencies and courts, and the meaning of statutes. He sought *Chevron* obedience for *all* agency judgments about statutory meaning that fell within the zone for which Congress had not provided singular answers a court could reliably discern. Recall his view that statutes in courts' hands are static instruments with singular meanings, that once construed by the courts can change only with congressional action. Is this also true for the kinds of interpretations in which *Skidmore* weight is claimed? Under *Chevron*, the area left open for agencies by the second question is one within which meaning need not come to rest; within the range permitted them by text, agencies can change their interpretations as varying situations require. In agency hands, then, statutes are flexible instruments; but in judicial hands, he insisted, they are not: once a court had reached its conclusion—with the help of *Skidmore* weight—statutory meaning would become fixed.

Even if this were a necessary consequence, one may note, it would only be so as to judgments reached by the Supreme Court itself, a relatively rare occurrence.[110] But the more interesting question may be whether it is, even in such cases, a necessary consequence. Here, we touch on the difference between statutes and the common law and recall that Justice Scalia rejects a common law role for federal courts.[111] The common law develops in reaction to the power of particular facts, within the room prior decisions leave open, and is open to reasoned change. That flexibility and dynamism could be equally available within the room that statutes leave open, and in fact has been availed of by the Supreme Court over the years, as in its interpretations of the Sherman Act, establishing anti-trust law, and (as we have repeatedly seen) the Administrative Procedure Act. Justice Scalia's preference to require judicial acceptance even of highly informal executive branch action, if "reasonable," reflects not only an apparent distrust of the courts, but also a taste for execu-

---

110. See p. 171 above.
111. See the brief discussion of the *Sandoval* case, p. 117 above.

tive discretion relatively unconstrained by law, that also has often characterized his jurisprudence.

Does the second step of *Chevron*, requiring judicial acceptance of reasonable agency judgments, entail more than the determination that the agency has reached a result within the bounds left open to it? The opinion is two-faced, speaking in one place about "a permissible construction of the statute," and in another about "whether it is a reasonable choice within a gap left open by Congress." Only the second formulation suggests a broader inquiry—the nature of which is the subject of the next section, "Judgment and the exercise of discretion." Yet the command of section 706(2)(A) is clear, that all reviewable exercises of agency discretion are to be vetted for their reasonableness. Judicial opinion-writing less careful than it should have been can not overcome this language. Judges reviewing agency action are to serve *all* the functions of a referee, both enforcing boundaries and supervising play within them for conformity to the rules of the game. The *Chevron* Court gave no special reason to believe that it could or should not do so for the kinds of judgments to which its rule applies. While some lower courts appear to believe that only the narrower inquiry is proper, the Court has never so indicated. As will be seen in the following section, the prescribed analysis for review of judgment and the exercise of discretion in fact anticipated *Chevron*'s intellectual structure, and in the author's judgment the better view is that it fully applies.[112]

Suppose an agency is interpreting not a statute, but its own regulations? Again, as the enormous volume of publication rules attests, the limits of time, language, and foresight make it inevitable that regulatory language will not resolve all issues. While courts might feel freer to tell an agency than the Congress that it had not "legislated" sufficiently on an important matter—and it might indeed be important to assure political responsibility for agency action in this way—many questions of interpretation will inevitably remain. Here, to date, courts have taken an even stronger line than *Chevron*, generally drawing on agency responsibility and the risks of judicial misunderstanding to require judicial acceptance of any "plausible" interpretation of regulatory language.[113] Thus, the courts are instructed to be lenient in their reading of the regulation to determine its possible meanings, *Chevron* step one, and *Chevron*'s second step of inquiry into "reasonableness" is wholly omitted. This effect may be sub-

---

112. See R. Levin, The Anatomy of Chevron: Step Two Reconsidered, 72 Chi-Kent L. Rev. 1253 (1997).

113. Bowles v. Seminole Rock & Sand Co., 325 U.S. 410 (1945); Udall v. Tallman, 380 U.S. 1 (1965); Stinson v. United States, 508 U.S. 38 (1993).

stantially responsible for the D.C. Circuit's negative attitude toward publication rules generally, as it seems to permit agencies to adopt "mush" through notice-and-comment rulemaking and then impose their views on courts by promulgating publication rule interpretations.[114] The effect has been strongly criticized in the literature[115] but few signs of recession from it have yet appeared.[116] Perhaps *Mead* will be taken as a signal that for interpretations not themselves reached through processes capable of fully binding the agency itself, *Skidmore* weight rather than simple acceptance of an agency's plausible interpretation of its regulations would be the proper approach.

D. *Judgment and the exercise of discretion*

Doubtless the most challenging aspect of judicial review, that aspect courts worry about most openly in their opinions, concerns proper judicial function when reviewing agency exercises of judgment and discretion. Such agency conclusions are more involved with the legal system (and have more implications for society as a whole) than the basic facts they find in the course of reaching them. Yet here, too, considerations of allocation are especially strong—these are the judgments particularly assigned to the agency, and they do not directly implicate those general questions about the legal order that are inescapably the courts' responsibility. On the one hand, court action must respect the statutory assignment of responsibility. The agency, not the court, has been directed to make judgments about whether a given road should be built, reactor licensed or environmental protection rule adopted. Assuring that respect for assignment is not a simple task, since judges commonly share the passions of their communities on such matters. On other hand, the agencies' responsibility is intended to be constrained by procedures, by substantive law, and by expectations of rationality and openness. Assuring the success of those constraints *is* a judicial task. The APA's formula for this judicial role is that of

---

114. Paralyzed Veterans of America v. D.C. Arena L.P., 117 F.3d 579, 584 (D.C. Cir. 1997).

115. E.g., J. Manning, Constitutional Structure and Judicial Deference to Agency Interpretation of Agency Rules, 96 Colum. L. Rev. 612 (1996).

116. In Thomas Jefferson University v. Shalala, 512 U.S. 504 (1994), four dissenters found the regulation underlying the interpretation "hopelessly vague," and expressed concern that in adopting such vague regulation the agency was maximizing its power and evading its rulemaking obligations. It suggested no difficulty with the principle as applied to a regulation that did not have this flaw.

section 706(2)(A), quoted at the head of this chapter. The Supreme Court's most elaborate discussion of its meaning and application was its decision in *Citizens to Preserve Overton Park, Inc. v. Volpe.*[117]

1. *Citizens to Preserve Overton Park v. Volpe*

a. *The elements of review*

Recall that the issue in *Overton Park* was whether the Secretary had properly authorized federal funds to be provided to the state of Tennessee to assist it in building a road. The road was going to traverse an important municipal park, in the face of a recently adopted federal statute whose purpose was to discourage the use of parklands for such purposes. The Court's tour of judicial review principles began with what was perhaps an unconscious re-creation of the tension animating the task generally:

> Certainly the Secretary's decision is entitled to a presumption of regularity. [The Court here cited a case[118] that would be taken by most American lawyers to state an extremely permissive approach to judicial review of the rationality of agency rulemaking, equating it with review of the rationality of statutes.] But that presumption is not to shield his action from a thorough, probing, in-depth review.[119]

The Court's first sentence suggests high permissiveness; its second, intense scrutiny—thus, the tension. The opinion continues with two paragraphs elaborating a series of judicial tasks.

The first paragraph calls on the court "to decide whether the Secretary acted within the scope of his authority." This, the paragraph explains, requires a reviewing court to delineate that authority and to determine whether, on the facts, the Secretary's judgment can reasonably be said to fall within it. Even if the judgment is thus a possible one, the court must inquire to some degree whether it has been correctly reached: Did the Secretary correctly understand his authority? Could he reasonably have believed that the statutory conditions necessary to permit the proposed use of this parkland had been met? Thus,

---

117. 401 U.S. 402 (1971); other aspects of the decision are discussed at pp. 235 and 341 above.

118. Pacific States Box & Basket Co. v. White, 296 U.S. 176 (1935); in the later *State Farm* case, discussed at p. 306, the Court acknowledged that this equation was no longer apt.

119. 401 U.S. at 415.

the "scope of authority" question is more complex than asking, simply, whether the decision the Secretary made is a kind of action he is authorized to take. In the simple sense, it is easy to say that this was a decision about supporting state road-building, that involved making judgments between the use of parkland for the road and other possible routings. But the court had also to learn how the Secretary understood the statute; and if he did so correctly, whether the facts before him "reasonably" could support the conclusion he reached.

The second paragraph defined a second inquiry, that would expose the Secretary's reasoning process in another sense:

> Section 706(2)(A) requires a finding that the actual choice made was not "arbitrary, capricious, an abuse of discretion, or otherwise not in accordance with law." To make this finding the court must consider whether the decision was based on a consideration of the relevant factors and whether there has been a clear error of judgment.... Although this inquiry into the facts is to be searching and careful, the ultimate standard of review is a narrow one. The court is not empowered to substitute its judgment for that of the agency.[120]

While the distinction between this inquiry and the second aspect of the inquiry described in the preceding paragraph may strike the reader as somewhat ephemeral, this inquiry's focus is less on the objective circumstances under which judgment was reached, and more on the actual process of judgment. "Consideration of the relevant factors" invites attention, not only to whether the Secretary asked all the right questions, but also to whether he asked any wrong ones. Did, for example, political "blackmail" play a role?[121] Does the reasoning process represented to the reviewing court reveal gaps in thought or other irrationality? Indeed, one can find in these two paragraphs a structure quite similar to that subsequently articulated in *Chevron*: the first defines inquiries to be made by the reviewing court independently, to its own satisfaction; the second, inquiries that can only be undertaken in a (rather permissive) oversight role.

Overton Park's approach was reaffirmed in *Motor Vehicle Manufacturers Association of the United States, Inc. v. State Farm Mutual Automobile Insurance Company*,[122] a decision reached just shortly before the decision in *Chevron*. President Reagan's Secretary of Transportation purported to rescind a rule

---

120. Id. at 416.
121. See p. 275 above.
122. 463 U.S. 29 (1983).

adopted by his predecessor after lengthy and harrowing rulemaking proceedings; this rule would have required automobile manufacturers to install "passive restraints" in all passenger cars. Passive restraints are devices, like air bags or continuous seat belts, that protect a car's driver and passengers against accidents without their having to take any action to engage them. But one possibility for complying with the rule was to use a kind of seat belt that could be manually detached if the person it protected wished to do that. In rescinding the rule, the new Secretary of Transportation relied on indications that manufacturers were overwhelmingly preparing to use this last kind of seatbelt, and studies indicating that many drivers would use them as manual, not automatic, seatbelts. She expressed doubt whether the safety benefits from a requirement that could so easily be defeated would exceed the costs of installing the safety equipment in all cars. Clearly, this is the kind of decision the Secretary is authorized to make, and it would be hard to say in the abstract that the underlying facts compelled a decision one way or the other.

Reversing, the Supreme Court expressed some doubt whether the studies the Secretary relied upon supported her judgment. More important, the Court relied on what it concluded were two failures of reasoning. First, the Secretary had failed to consider whether, if detachable seat-belts could be so easily defeated, the better alternative would not be to require air bags or other less easily defeated devices. Second, she had not considered the effect of driver inertia on the use rate even of the detachable belts. That is, even though they could be disabled, those belts would remain in place until someone took the trouble to disable them. If ever reattached—say, for a longer trip—they would remain in use until, again, someone affirmatively detached them. The result did not deny that the Secretary might on a proper showing be able to rescind the rule. Rather, the Court found that she had failed adequately to justify her decision to do so, and must reconsider the matter.

The reader may think (as a concurrence charged, and as could not be proven wrong) that as to the second of these matters the Court did substitute its judgment for the Secretary's. Yet the form of judgment, inviting reconsideration, denies that. One's general experience is that such reassessments as were invited here are, when made, accepted by the courts.

b. The problems of record, findings, and reasons

As earlier discussed,[123] *Overton Park* voiced (and generated) expectations about the administrative record, agency fact-finding, and agency reasoning

---

123. See p. 235 above.

that would be hard to justify on the face of the APA or in light of prior practice. The process that it describes seems to demand a fairly complete record, and full agency explanations both of facts found and of reasons for judgment. Yet in other settings the Supreme Court has insisted that reviewing courts must accept the record more-or-less as provided by the agency.[124] It has yet fully to confront the difficulties institutional styles of decision create for record definition.[125] The administrative record in an informal proceeding, as the D.C. Circuit remarked, "might well include crucial material that was neither shown to nor known by the private parties in the proceeding."[126] As important, it will often be interlaced with projections and judgments based on nothing more tangible than one or more agency experts' "feel" for the situation, a feel that need not have been made explicit at the level of final decision.

On the question of explanation, the ostensible signals have been rather permissive. *Overton Park* held that neither the APA nor the statute at issue in the case required formal findings to accompany the Secretary's decision.[127] In *Camp v. Pitts,* two years later, the Court encountered the Comptroller of Currency's one paragraph explanation, in an informal letter, of his decision to deny an applicant permission to open a new bank.[128] The Court remarked:

> Unlike *Overton Park,* in the present case there was contemporaneous explanation of the agency decision. The explanation may have been

---

124. Camp v. Pitts, 411 U.S. 138 (1973); Vermont Yankee Nuclear Power Corp. v. Natural Resources Defense Council, Inc. 435 U.S. 519 (1978).

125. See pp. 230 and 241 above.

126. See p. 348 above; compare the Home Box Office decision briefly discussed above at p. 241.

127. Failure to make them, however, had a consequence shortly to be explored, see p. 380 below, that as a practical matter strongly encouraged administrators to make them. Moreover, where a statute does impose a findings requirement, as the APA does for rulemaking, the courts understandable interpret the extent of that obligation in light of the review functions the Supreme Court has described.

128. Camp v. Pitts, 411 U.S. 138 (1973). The letter read in relevant part:

On each application we endeavor to develop the need and convenience factors in conjunction with all other banking factors and in this case we were unable to reach a favorable conclusion as to the need factor. The record reflects that this market area is now served by the Peoples Bank with deposits of $7.2MM, The Bank of Hurstville with deposits of $12.8MM, The First Federal Savings and Loan Association with deposits of $5.4MM, The Mutual Savings and Loan Association with deposits of $8.2MM and the Conoco Employees Credit Union with deposits of $6.5MM. The aforementioned are as of December 31, 1968.

curt, but it surely indicated the determinative reason for the final action taken: the finding that the new bank was an uneconomic venture in light of the banking needs and the banking services already available in the surrounding community. The validity of the Comptroller's action must, therefore, stand or fall on the propriety of that finding, judged, of course, by the appropriate standard of review.

Nonetheless, in practice rather extensive explanations are routinely supplied by agencies anticipating judicial review. This practical consequence has already been explored in the context of rulemaking.[129] Occasional tendencies in the same direction can be noted for informal adjudication,[130] even though a statutory peg, like that provided for rulemaking by APA section 553, is harder to find. Whatever their formal justification, the very fact of having to distinguish judicial oversight from the substitution of judicial judgment supplies an important practical incentive. Agency heads can see as easily as a court can, that the *Overton Park* standards will work to keep the court in its place, but only if the agencies provide the kind of data about their decisionmaking that will permit the court to conduct the analyses described. Having to restrict review to the reasons the Comptroller gives not only leads to demands for additional data about agency processes and tends to prevent courts from substituting judgment; it also encourages the Comptroller to give reasons. It is not unusual for a court to remand a matter to an agency for further explanation, asserting that the explanations given are insufficient to permit it to follow, and thus review, the agency's reasoning process.[131]

c. Inquiry into mental processes

A more pointed incentive for agencies to state their findings and reasons at the time of decision is that the parties may be able to force a judicial trial about them if they do not. Review must always occur on the basis of the agency's findings and reasons. Insistence on this proposition is a means of avoiding both judicial substitution of judgment on matters within the agency's responsibility, and agency lawyers' post hoc invention of rationales the agency

---

129. See p. 230 above.

130. Independent U.S. Tanker Owners Committee v. Lewis, 690 F.2d 908 (D.C. Cir. 1982).

131. This effect is not without its costs for administrative process; in the rulemaking context, the experience of having to generate elaborate explanations to avoid judicial remands for lack of understanding, has been seen as a significant contributor to ossification. See p. 200.

itself never considered. Just as courts are not to substitute their judgment for the agency's, they must also be alert that agency lawyers do not substitute their judgments or reasons for the agency's during the review process.[132] If agencies do not give reasons at the moment of decision, they can supply them afterward only by a process of reconstruction. In *Overton Park* the Secretary sought to accomplish this by submitting sworn statements—affidavits. The Supreme Court thought this improper, because it generated too large a risk that the reasons would simply be generated by lawyers after the fact, rather than reflect the Secretary's actual bases for judgment when he acted. The alternative the Court endorsed was an active judicial inquiry into the Secretary's reasoning. This inquiry could (and in the event did) transform itself into a lengthy and rather exacting trial.

In the ordinary case, administrative officials are protected against any such examination of their "real reasons" for acting. This is, at root, the meaning of the "presumption of regularity" recited by the Court in the quotation from *Overton Park* given above. "[Where] there are administrative findings that were made at the same time as the decision," the Court remarked in *Overton Park*, "there must be a strong showing of bad faith or improper behavior before such inquiry may be made.[133] But here there are no such formal findings and it may be that the only way there can be effective judicial review is by examining the decisionmakers themselves." It can easily be imagined that a busy federal official would happily take "unnecessary" formal steps such as making findings, if doing so would eliminate the risk of being forced to submit to a judicial trial of her actual reasoning process. Prior discussion has already suggested that "strong" showings of bad faith or improper motivation are not easily made.[134]

2. Consistency

One common demand on the agency reasoning process warranting special mention here is that the agency explain its decision in light of other actions taken in like circumstances. One wants to be careful in stating this. While ordinary controls exist against abusive relitigation in matters involving the same

---

132. SEC v. Chenery Corp., 318 U.S. 80 (1943); see p. 260 above.

133. 401 U.S. at 420. The statement was based on a series of decisions involving agricultural regulation from the 1930s, that culminated in United States v. Morgan, 313 U.S. 409 (1941). An excellent treatment appears in D. Gifford, The Morgan Cases: A Retrospective View, 30 Admin. L. Rev. 237 (1978).

134. See p. 275 above.

party,[135] the courts repeatedly affirm that agencies may change the policies they apply from time to time as political or other circumstances change, so long as they do not exceed the scope of discretion accorded them. In making such changes, however, agencies must be able to articulate reasons for doing so. They must adhere to what might be described as a requirement of momentary consistency—undertaking to treat all matters of the character now before them as they are treating this one, until they have found some reason to change their view. (At that time, the new view will have to be consistently applied.) What would be "arbitrary" would be to apply two inconsistent rules at the same time, having no acceptable reason for choosing one or the other in any particular instance. From this derives what sometimes appears to be a special obligation of explanation: "[w]hatever the ground for [a] departure from prior norms,... it must be clearly set forth so that the reviewing court may understand the basis of the agency's action and so may judge the consistency of that action with the agency's mandate."[136] A concrete showing of apparent and unexplained inconsistency of treatment provides challengers with one of the strongest bases for interesting a court in judicial review. One must also expect, however, that the courts will be realistic about the capacity of agencies having to decide high volumes of cases to achieve perfect consistency of application; reasonable effort to attain it will suffice.[137]

Related to the issue of consistency, but having more do with agencies' relationships with parties and courts, are the troublesome questions of estoppel and non-acquiescence. If a party is in a course of dealing with agency personnel, can he rely on the promises he may receive from them? If a court (other than the Supreme Court) finds an agency interpretation unlawful, is the agency obliged to accept that judgment and recede from its preferred view? While one might intuit affirmative answers to both questions, and while most

---

135. Administrative Law: Cases and Comments 652 ff.

136. Atchison, Topeka & Santa Fe Ry. Co. v. Wichita Bd. of Trade, 412 U.S. 800, 808 (1973). Or, as the D.C. Circuit put it in 1997, remanding for additional explanation of a decision seemingly at odds with a prior agency decision : "The Commission's cursory treatment of seemingly relevant precedent is inadequate.... If the Commission chooses [after the remand the court ordered] to provide a more detailed explanation, we can then ascertain whether some principled reason exists for distinguishing between the cases or whether the decision...has been so subjective as to be arbitrary and capricious." Bush-Quayle '92 Primary Committee v. Federal Election Commission, 104 F.3d 448, 455 (D.C. Cir. 1997).

137. Davis v. Commissioner, 69 T.C. 716 (1978); see H. Krent, Reviewing Agency Actions for Inconsistency with Prior Rules & Regulations, 72 Chi-Kent L. Rev. 1187 (1987) for an exploration of the consequences, undesirable in his judgment, of aggressive judicial review of claimed inconsistencies.

of the time it is an agency's interest to be reliable in its dealings with the public and respectful in its dealings with the courts, in general the answers to these questions are both "No." As to the first, ideas of equitable estoppel that would ordinarily apply to reliance-inducing conduct by individuals or corporations are rejected when a government agent gives erroneous advice, absent a high-level undertaking by the agency to be bound or a statutory instruction. The government clerk cannot, clumsily or corruptly, commit the government's resources by her error.[138]

In respect of a judgment of unlawfulness, while the agency must of course accept the court's judgment in the particular case under litigation, it may adhere to its own views—refuse to acquiesce—in other litigation raising the same issue.[139] This is permissable because of the circuit structure of the federal courts. Agencies have national responsibilities, but with the exception of the limited-jurisdiction United States Court of Appeals for the Federal Circuit,[140] federal courts below the Supreme Court are organized geographically. Although an agency can anticipate that a particular circuit that has already expressed its view on a question will insist upon adherence to that previously expressed view, it may also know that the pending question will or may be reviewed in another circuit. That other circuit may have expressed no view, or perhaps a different one. The Supreme Court is aware of its own limited jurisdiction, of the responsibilities agencies hold for exercising policy-making discretion on a national basis within the authority conferred on them, and of the frequency of government litigation.[141] On this basis it has declined to adopt a rule that "would substantially thwart the development of important questions of law by freezing the first decision rendered on a particular legal issue ... depriv[ing] this Court of the benefit it receives from permitting several courts of appeals to explore a difficult question before this Court grants certiorari."[142]

The resulting clash of wills can be distressing to judges of the intermediate courts. "[F]aced with an agency decision in which the agency expressly refuses

---

138. Office of Personnel Management v. Richmond, 496 U.S. 414 (1990); Federal Crop Ins. Corp. v. Merrill, 332 U.S. 380 (1947). For critique, and a suggestion that the arguments are less powerful when relief other than monetary damages is sought, see J. Schwartz, The Irresistible Force Meets the Immoveable Object: Estoppel Remedies for an Agency's Violations of Its Own Regulations or Other Misconduct, 44 Admin. L. Rev. 653 (1992).

139. See p. 171 above.

140. See p. 126 above.

141. The United States is a party in about one third of civil filings in district court, and about the same proportion of filings in the courts of appeal.

142. United States v. Mendoza, 464 U.S. 154, 160 (1984).

to follow the law of this Circuit," by which the judges of that circuit are unquestionably bound, they may find they "can conclude only that that decision
is arbitrary, capricious, and inconsistent with law."[143] Yet that circuit decision
may be wrong, both as to what the law is, and who is responsible to decide it.
The precise legal question on which agency non-acquiescence with the circuit's
previously announced view had provoked this strong statement subsequently
came before the Supreme Court. By the time it did, another circuit had taken
the opposing view on the same question, and the agency had embraced that
court's reading. Illustrating *Chevron* and the agency discretion that it entails,
the Supreme Court found the statute left the question open—and hence that
the question was one for the agency's reasonable decision. The agency's refusal
to acquiesce in the law as declared by the first court was thus vindicated. But
the agency had simply chosen to follow the other court's reading; it had not
applied its own independent judgment to the matter. Consequently, the Court
concluded, the case had to be remanded to the agency for *it* to decide—within
the room left by the statute and employing reasoned judgment—what policy
reading to adopt.[144]

3. Hard look review

As the preceding paragraph will already have suggested, the problem of
consistency is not the agencies' alone. Readers may already have remarked to
themselves that the variety of inquiries described leaves a good deal of room
for a court to pursue review aggressively or permissively, as the particular circumstances before the court or the court's political inclinations may suggest.
Some empirical studies appear to have demonstrated such effects,[145] which
may appear to give point to earlier quoted remarks about the rules governing
judicial review being as substanceless as seedless grapes.[146] One can find in the
cases, however, indications of structure concerning the issue of intensity.
Agency decisions smacking of priority-setting, or that have relatively little impact on individuals, or that are unusually dependent on judgments of a political character, all warrant a permissive judicial approach. Agency actions on

---

143. Department of Energy v. Federal Labor Relations Authority, 106 F.3d 1158, 1166
(4th Cir. 1997) (Ludwig., J., concurring).

144. National Federation of Federal Employees, Local 1309 v. Department of the Interior, 526 U.S. 86 (1999).

145. An excellent study of this character is R.S. Melnick, Regulation and the Courts:
The Case of the Clean Air Act (Brookings 1983).

146. See p. 335 above.

petitions for rulemaking, for example, are formally reviewable, but the courts have consistently described the review that is to occur then as quite undemanding; so, also, for any judgment about initiation of enforcement action that, for special statutory reasons, a court will conclude is reviewable despite *Heckler v. Chaney*.[147]

By contrast, decisions setting standards carrying important consequences for the private realm, heavily reliant on judgments about physical fact, or responding to a specific statutory command, call for a more aggressive judicial stance.[148] In the context, particularly, of judicial review of agency rulemaking to regulate health, safety and environmental concerns, the aggressive mode of judicial review has acquired a name, "hard look" review. In origin the idea thus expressed was that the court's sole obligation was to be sure the agency had taken a hard look at the problems before it. In popular usage and probably reality today, the idea is understood to be that in such cases the courts, too, ought to take a hard look.

The earlier discussion of the "paper hearing"[149] has substantially outlined the development of this idea, which was employed by the Supreme Court itself in *State Farm,* the air bag/seat belt case described toward the beginning of this section.[150] Both its extent and its problems may be suggested by *Sierra Club v. Costle,*[151] a 125-page opinion of the D.C. Circuit reviewing EPA regulations governing the use of coal by electric generating stations. One aspect of that opinion, already discussed,[152] concerned a procedural question, the participation of the President and an influential senator in the decision process; the resolution of that issue well illustrates the point just made about judicial reluctance to inquire into the actual agency motivation for a decision that appears to be well-explained. The bulk of the massive opinion, however, addressed issues concerning the substantive outcome of the rulemaking: whether the agency properly understood its authority; whether computer models on which the agency was relying had been adequately justified; whether the studies and other factual material in the vast record of the rulemaking supported its outcome; whether the proper factors (and only the proper factors) had been considered; and so forth. As the size of its opinion makes apparent, the court

---

147. See p. 214 ff. above.

148. See, for a helpful canvas of the problem, C. Koch, Judicial Review of Administrative Discretion, 54 Geo. Wash. L. Rev. 469 (1986).

149. See p. 234 ff. above.

150. See p. 377 above.

151. 657 F.2d 298 (D.C. Cir. 1981).

152. See p. 244 above.

examined these issues with care and in substantial detail—yet always from an outsider's perspective: Was the agency being reasonable? Had it adequately explained its thinking? Where uncertain (because it had to make projections from necessarily incomplete data), had it acknowledged its uncertainty and indicated how and why it was being resolved?

This aggressive policing of the reported thought process ended in enforcement, defeating any thought that it might have been the product simply of a disposition to upset the result. "In this case," the court concluded, "we have taken a long while to come to a short conclusion: the rule is reasonable." The process was not without costs—in time, in effort, and in risks of misunderstanding. The rulemaking had been begun in 1973; the rule came into effect only in 1979; review proceedings were not finished until 1981. Its results were subjected to vigorous intellectual as well as political criticism.[153] Whether judges who are not engineers, computer modelers, economists or statisticians can vouch for the intellectual integrity of a reasoning process that requires those attainments and more is, to say the least, open to grave doubt.[154] This was the concern that animated the court of appeals opinion requiring special procedures at the *agency* level, that the Supreme Court sharply reversed in *Vermont Yankee*.[155] The warrant for such a high degree of engagement is found, in part, in arguable propositions about the favorable impact on agency decision processes of having to expect such intense review.[156] It is found, as well, in a view well-stated by the scholar whose remarks also opened this chapter: "[T]here is in our society a profound, tradition-taught reliance on the courts as the ultimate guardian and assurance of the limits set upon executive power by the constitutions and legislatures."[157]

---

153. B. Ackerman and W. Hassler, Clean Coal/Dirty Air (Yale 1981).

154. M. Shapiro, Administrative Discretion: The Next Stage, 92 Yale L. J. 1487, 1507 (1983): "Courts cannot take a hard look at materials they cannot understand nor be partners to technocrats in a realm in which only technocrats speak the language." Compare B. Ackerman, Reconstructing American Law 67–68 (Harvard 1984).

155. See p. 241 above.

156. See the discussion of "paper hearing" above, p. 234 ff.

157. L. Jaffe, Judicial Control of Administrative Action 321 (Little Brown 1965).

IX

LIABILITY OF PUBLIC
AUTHORITIES AND
THEIR AGENTS

The subject matters of this chapter, the civil (monetary) liability of government and government agencies for wrongful acts and contractual default, are distinctly subsidiary elements in American administrative law, as that subject is conventionally understood. If they appear in American law school curricula at all, they are as likely to be treated as specialities of the law of torts (civil wrongs), the law of contracts, or even constitutional law (civil rights actions) as they are to be thought matters of "administrative law." The treatment here will be correspondingly sketchy and brief.

The reader should be aware at the outset that these subjects suffer not only from their somewhat haphazard historical development, but also from the influences of federalism.[1] When dealing with the subject of relief involving the sovereign, one should not be surprised to find issues of sovereignty close at hand. Thus, the Eleventh Amendment to the federal Constitution, ratified in 1798 (the very first adopted after the Bill of Rights), prohibits the federal courts from entertaining actions brought by citizens of one state (or foreigners) against a state other than their own;[2] the result is to preclude federal actions for mon-

---

1. See p. 10 above.

2. U.S. Const. amendment XI. The text of the Eleventh Amendment addresses only diversity actions, those brought by citizens of one state or a foreign country against citizens of another, and not actions that a citizen of the same state might bring relying on "federal question" jurisdiction. The Supreme Court has understood it, however, as only an exemplar of a broader proposition constitutionally grounded in the doctrine of sovereign immunity: "the States' immunity from suit is a fundamental aspect of the sovereignty which the States enjoyed before the ratification of the Constitution, and which they retain today (either literally or by virtue of their admission into the Union upon an equal footing with the other States) except as altered by the plan of the Convention or certain constitutional Amendments." Alden v. Maine, 527 U.S. 706, 713 (1999). Thus, since the decision in Hans v. Louisiana, 134 U.S. 1 (1890), the Constitution has been understood to forbid all federal actions that, if successful, will require a judicial order to the state to pay money damages

etary damages to be paid by a state or its agencies,[3] as well as actions to quiet title to disputed lands held in state ownership.[4] Unless it is inevitable that a judgment will implicate state resources,[5] this stricture may be avoided if the suit is brought against a state officer individually—even for acts committed in her official capacity. Such remedies have long been available.[6] More recent interpretation of the Civil Rights Act,[7] a statute passed in the wake of the American Civil War, led to a tremendous growth in lawsuits against state and municipal officials seeking the payment of monetary damages for acts alleged to have violated federal constitutional or statutory norms. The success of these actions, in turn, created pressure for the recognition of similar remedies against federal officers, whose behavior is not directly regulated by the Civil Rights Act. For the federal courts to be enforcing against state officials a remedy they did not provide against federal officials was transparently problematic.

A. *Relief against the sovereign*

Historically, American courts declined to entertain law suits that sought to require the expenditure of public money or to compel the transfer of public property.[8] The idea on which they relied, perhaps surprising for a republic

---

or otherwise surrender its property interests. At this writing, this interpretation is favored by only five of the Justices—remarkably, the five who in most circumstances are to be found insisting on respect for the constitutional text and the impropriety of Justices of the Supreme Court embroidering upon it.

The reader may understand the phenomenon as evidence of the strength of the federalism idea in conservative circles. In *Alden*, for example, state employees asserted claims in *state* court for overtime work under the federal Fair Labor Standards Act, whose application to the state (as all employers) was concededly valid. The federal statute provided, inter alia, for the possibility of suit in state courts to enforce employee claims arising under the act. While the Act could be enforced by federal officers, the five majority Justices held, Congress could not override Maine's claim of sovereign immunity from such private actions seeking monetary damages, even to enforce a law that, by the Supremacy Clause, Maine was obliged to obey.

3. Seminole Tribe of Florida v. Florida, 517 U.S. 44 (1996).

4. Idaho v. Coeur d'Alene Tribe of Idaho, 521 U.S. 261 (1997).

5. Id.

6. See Ex parte Young, 209 U.S. 123 (1908).

7. 42 U.S.C. §1983; the Act is discussed below at p. 395.

8. An exception was recognized for the remedy of mandamus, see p. 302 above, in the very narrow circumstances in which that was first thought available. If payment of a certain sum was a ministerial duty of a governmental official, respecting which he enjoyed no

born of revolution against monarchy, was sovereign immunity. This is the proposition that the polity can not be brought into its own courts and there be compelled to answer for its wrongs. This idea won universal acceptance at both state and federal level; indeed, the speedy adoption of the Eleventh Amendment[9] resulted from the federal courts' failure to recognize that principle in dealing with a state.[10] While in formal terms a state would not be the "sovereign" entitled to immunity in federal courts, in political reality the states insisted on the same immunity there as they enjoyed in their own courts.

The years following have seen a steady, but not always rational, recession from this idea.[11] Suits might be brought against individual officers acting beyond their legal authority, as if they were private citizens; their success depended on whether such behavior by a private citizen would have been an actionable wrong. Statutory provisions were made for special courts to hear suits against the states or federal government for such monetary relief as the legislature might authorize.[12] Individual statutes authorized judicial review of the decisions of particular agencies, or of defined types of governmental action more generally. As liability insurance became more readily available, judges in the states frequently overturned the sovereign immunity defense to tort actions. The existence of the insurance defeated the rationale of protecting the public treasury.[13]

At the federal level, these results have largely been rationalized since 1976, when amendments to APA section 702 waived the defense of sovereign immunity, absent special circumstances, for any "action in a court of the United States seeking relief other than money damages and stating a claim that an

---

discretion whatever, mandamus was available to compel the payment even though it would come from the public treasury. Kendall v. United States, 37 U.S. (12 Pet.) 524 (1838).

9. See note 2 above.

10. Chisholm v. Georgia, 2 Dall. 419 (1793).

11. I do not mean to suggest that the doctrine is itself in all respects irrational. Public resources are limited. Giving tort claimants priority in obtaining public resources, in a way that cannot be mediated by politics, may deprive other members of the polity whose need is equal but who lack a conventional legal claim. Cf. National Board of YMCA v. United States, 395 U.S. 85 (1970). Moreover, judicial refusal to order delivery of government property may serve to protect the public generally against the effects of official mismanagement of public resources.

12. If it authorizes the action without appropriating funds to pay resulting judgments, "successful" plaintiffs may be forced to plead with the legislature for appropriations, as has been the case for some persons harmed by radiation as a consequence of uranium mining or nuclear weapons testing.

13. See W. Prosser and P. Keeton, Prosser and Keeton on the Law of Torts 1044–45 (West 1984).

agency or [its] officer or employee…acted or failed to act in an official capacity or under color of legal authority." Thus, sovereign immunity, as such, is no longer a defense for non-monetary actions brought against the United States in federal district court.[14] Actions for monetary damages are controlled by other statutes, such as the Federal Tort Claims Act (civil wrongs)[15] and the Tucker Act (breach of contract and other non-tortious legal wrongs).[16]

The specific provisions for monetary relief may be taken, in some cases, to create what is in effect an implied preclusion[17] of suits for other-than-monetary relief in the district courts, despite the 1976 legislation. We saw earlier that congressional shaping of available relief is thought to avoid the constitutional problems that might be presented by total denial of review.[18] A prominent example of such an implication may be found in the Tucker Act's authorization of breach of contract actions. The availability of money damages in such an action carries the implication—readily supported in public policy terms[19]— that no remedy for specific performance is authorized. Thus, an action seeking specific performance from a district court, even though it is for relief "other than money damages," will be dismissed as not having been consented to.[20]

---

14. The Supreme Court has somewhat roiled the waters by characterizing a suit for reimbursements wrongfully withheld as one sounding in equity for restitution, rather than one for monetary damages, and thus a suit permitted to be brought in district court. Bowen v. Massachusetts, 487 U.S. 879 (1988); see R. Fallon, Claims Court at the Crossroads, 40 Cath. U. L. Rev. 517 (1991).

15. The Act is discussed below at p. 391.

16. 28 U.S.C. §§1346, 1491.

17. See p. 305 ff. above.

18. See p. 307 above.

19. See note 11 above.

20. Senate Committee on the Judiciary, Judicial Review of Agency Action, Sen. Rep. No 94-996 on S. 800, 94th Cong., 2d Sess. 11–12 (1976); Spectrum Leasing Corp. v. United States, 764 F.2d 891 (D.C. Cir. 1985); cf. Idaho v. Coeur d'Alene Tribe of Idaho, 521 U.S. 261 (1997).

B. *Tort actions as a form of review*[21]

1. Against governmental units

The Federal Tort Claims Act[22] permits citizens to sue the federal government to recover damages caused by a wide variety of intentional or negligent behaviors by civil servants. The section conferring exclusive jurisdiction on United States district courts to hear such actions frames as the question to be decided whether "the United States, if a private person, would be liable to the claimant in accordance with the law of the place where the act or omission occurred."[23] Note that this formula ties liability to state tort law, which varies from state to state, rather than to a uniform national standard; the variations, however, are not major. The liability is also limited in important procedural respects: a claim must first be presented to and denied in administrative proceedings by the responsible agency;[24] the jury trial a plaintiff could expect in suing a private citizen is unavailable; and both prejudgment interest and the punitive damages (generally available under American tort law in the case of particularly egregious behavior) are also precluded.

The breadth of the quoted formula is misleading. The Act's coverage is at best haphazard, and consequently the subject of frequent criticism. While recovery is possible for many individual harms to which ordinary citizens are likely to be exposed—automobile accidents with government vehicles, lawless police behavior, carelessly maintained beacons, etc., the Act makes no provision for governmental liability in the absence of fault, a form of liability now

---

21. A contemporary assessment collecting the recent literature appears as Note, Government Tort Liability, 111 Calif. L. Rev. 2009 (1998). See P. Schuck, Suing Government (Yale University 1983); H. Krent, Preserving Discretion without Sacrificing Deterrence: Federal Governmental Liability in Tort, 38 U.C.L.A. L. Rev. 871 (1991); R. Cass, Damage Suits Against Public Officers, 129 U. Pa. L. Rev. 1110 (1981). For a comparative perspective well informed about the treatment of the subject in European legal systems, see G. Bermann, La Responsabilité Civile des Functionnaires au Niveau Fédéral aux États-Unis: Vers la Solution d'une Crise, 1983 Revue Internationale de Droit Comparé No. 2, p. 319 (1983).

22. The FTCA first appeared in 60 Stat. 842 (1946). Its provisions are scattered widely through Title 28 of the United States Code; most substantive provisions appear in sections 2671–2680.

23. 28 U.S.C. §1346(b). 28 U.S.C. §2764 states that "The United States shall be liable... in the same manner and to the same extent as a private individual under like circumstances...."

24. G. Bermann, Federal Tort Claims at the Agency Level: The FTCA Administrative Process, 35 Case W. Res. L. Rev. 509 (1985).

common (as for dangerous activities) under state tort law. It also explicitly excludes liability for some intentional torts, such as misrepresentation, deceit, defamation, and interference with contractual rights. To recover from the government itself, persons suffering these harms must rely on the willingness of federal administrators to settle their claims nonetheless (for example, to avoid public appearances of injustice that might shame an administration or provoke unwanted legislative action)[25] or on the willingness of Congress to adopt a private law for their relief. Both outcomes occur with some frequency.

More important than these refusals of coverage is a provision that excludes any claim "based upon... [the performance or nonperformance of] a discretionary function or duty on the part of a federal agency or an employee... whether or not the discretion involved be abused."[26] Negligence in designing as well as in manufacturing an automobile would be redressed against a private corporation. In contrast, the Federal Aviation Administration's policy judgments in inspecting aircraft design and manufacture prior to certification of airplanes as safe for commercial use—a certification known to be widely relied upon outside as well as inside the United States—could not result in liability for airplane accidents a more thorough review would have prevented.

> Judicial intervention in such decisionmaking through private tort suits would require the courts to 'second-guess' the political, social, and economic judgments of an agency exercising its regulatory function....In administering the 'spot-check' program,...FAA engineers and inspectors necessarily took certain calculated risks, but those risks were encountered for the advancement of a governmental purpose and pursuant to the specific grant of authority in the regulations and operating manuals.[27]

As this excerpt suggests, Congress's reluctance to authorize such actions is grounded in considerations of separation of functions and concern about making government too timid; aware that government fiscal resources are lim-

---

25. Of course the agency must have authority to pay the claim, either because its liability under the FTCA is colorable, or because (as many agencies do) it enjoys additional claims or benefits payment authority.

26. 28 U.S.C. 2680(a). The Act also denies liability for an employee's act or omission in executing a statute or regulation "whether or not such statute or regulation be valid," so long as the employee was otherwise acting with due care. This bars litigants from using tort suits as a vehicle for challenging the bare legality of a law or regulation, and has produced little debate; the standard techniques of judicial review remain fully available.

27. United States v. S.A. Empresa De Viacao Aerea Rio Grandense (Varig Airlines), et al., 467 U.S. 797 (1984).

ited, too, it could believe providing monetary relief to some citizens (more likely those injured by demonstrable action than inaction resulting from deterrence) would distort public expenditures.

In cases that arose from polio caused by a government-licensed vaccine,[28] and financial losses allegedly rooted in failures of bank regulation,[29] the Supreme Court articulated a two-pronged test to determine whether this exclusion applied. First, to qualify for the exception, the government action must involve "an element of judgment or choice." If in processing the application for vaccine approval, for example, or in authorizing shipment of a particular (defective) batch of vaccine, government employees violated *mandatory* procedures, the exception would not be available to them. Second, the actions taken must be, if not actually grounded in considerations of public policy, at least susceptible to policy analysis. So, for example, broad discretion bank regulators enjoy was sufficient to establish their entitlement to the exception, without regard to whether they had actually been considering issues of public policy in taking challenged actions. The government could be found liable when a maritime accident resulted from carelessness in maintaining a specific navigational aid.[30] But a judgment that France's immediate and pressing need for fertilizer warranted taking certain risks in the fertilizer's packaging and shipping produced no liability when a terrible explosion resulted, killing hundreds and wounding thousands.[31] Characterized by one circuit judge as an exception that has "swallowed, digested and excreted the liability-creating sections of the [FTCA],"[32] this is the provision that has drawn the most critical fire and proposals for reform.[33]

The "discretionary function" exception could be regarded, in part, as a "limited remedy" provision like the implication previously noted, that the availability of monetary relief sometimes connotes the unavailability of other forms of relief.[34] Seen in this way, the exemption reflects that some matters are better suited to consideration under the ordinary forms of judicial review than

---

28. Berkovitz v. United States, 486 U.S. 531 (1988).

29. United States v. Gaubert, 499 U.S. 315 (1991).

30. Indian Towing Co. v. United States, 350 U.S. 61 (1955).

31. Dalehite v. United States, 346 U.S. 15 (1953).

32. Rosebush v. United States, 119 F.3d 438, 444 (6th Cir. 1997)(Merritt, J. dissenting).

33. E.g., Note, The Federal Tort Claims Act: A Proposal for Institutional Reform, 100 Colum. L. Rev. 1538 (2000); D. Zillman, Protecting Discretion: Judicial Interpretation of the Discretionary Function Exception to the [FTCA], 47 Me. L. Rev. 366 (1995); H. Krent, Preserving Discretion without Sacrificing Deterrence: Federal Governmental Liability in Tort, 38 U.C.L.A. L. Rev. 871 (1991)

34. See p. 307 above.

to actions seeking to establish monetary liability. In part, too, it can be suggested that the exemption serves to protect from "tort action" review judgments that also are excluded from review, or at least difficult to test, under the
ordinary APA provisions for judicial review. Who would have standing to challenge an FAA judgment how intensely to inspect commercial aircraft before
certification,[35] and whether that judgment should be found one "committed
to agency discretion by law,"[36] are themselves knotty questions. One can understand that if standing rules and the belief that agency action is indeed
"committed to agency discretion" are to have meaning and validity, then one
cannot allow them to be circumvented through tort actions. One sees here a
recognition that for some governmental actions, so much the product of
budgetary considerations, controls must be left wholly in the realm of politics—even when, as in war, the outcome of official judgments may be, for
some, the most dreadful of consequences.

2. Against government officials

a. Theories of liability

If one cannot always sue the government to redress harm occasioned by official (mis)conduct, it may be possible to sue a particular government official
for damage she has caused. That remedy has two possible sources. The first is
the ordinary common law of torts. Courts have long compensated for the
"sovereign immunity" of government itself by treating the government officer
as an individual authorized to act only lawfully. To the extent she acted beyond her lawful authority, she exposed herself to liability just as if she were a
private citizen. Thus, an official meat inspector who summarily seized and destroyed allegedly tainted chickens being held in cold storage exercised that authority at the risk of later having to show, in defense of a later tort action for
the destruction of property, that the chickens had in fact been unwholesome.[37]
Subsequent cases, reacting to the inhibitions to decisive action this exposure
might create, commonly accorded government officials the protection of at
least a qualified, and sometimes an absolute, privilege for acts within the scope
of their office.[38] Since 1988, as a result of an immediate congressional response

---

35. See p. 313 above.

36. See p. 310 above.

37. North American Cold Storage Co. v. Chicago, 211 U.S. 306 (1908). This potential
for tort relief answered any objection that the seizure could occur without a prior hearing.
See p. 322 above.

38. E.g., Gildea v. Ellershaw, 298 N.E.2d 847 (Mass 1973).

to a Supreme Court decision broadening this potential remedy as against federal employees, ordinary common law liability of federal employees acting within the scope of their office has been precluded; only a Tort Claims Act action, if available, may be brought.[39]

The second source lies in implication from constitutional or statutory provisions. Since the American Civil War, state and local officials have been subject to potential tort (as well as criminal) liability for actions under color of state law that deprive any "person...of any rights, privileges or immunities secured by the Constitution and laws."[40] Such section 1983 actions, as they are called after the provision of the federal code containing this language, represent a substantial part of some 54,000 civil rights actions commenced in U.S. district courts in fiscal year 2000,[41] largely as a by-product of the American civil rights movement. While its remedies were first developed in connection with violations of civil liberties guaranteed by the federal Bill of Rights,[42] section 1983 also redresses violations of statutory rights; forward-looking equitable relief is available as well as retrospective damage awards.[43] Section 1983 has spawned a massive body of law,[44] inappropriate to consider in this monograph. Ten years after the explosion in section 1983 actions began, the Supreme Court implied a similar principle of tort liability to control the ac-

---

39. Westfall v. Erwin, 484 U.S. 292 (1988); Federal Employees Liability Reform & Tort Compensation Act of 1988, 28 U.S.C. §2679(b)(1).

40. 42 U.S.C. §1983.

41. Administrative Office of the U.S.Courts, Judicial Business:2000 138–140, a report that may be found online at http://www.uscourts.gov/judbus2000/front/2000artext.pdf, shows that of 260,000 civil actions initiated in U.S. District Courts during the year ending September 30, 2000, 54,000—20%—were characterized as civil rights actions. Less than half are shown as arising under particular federal civil rights laws—in particular, statutes creating civil rights (such as non-discrimination) in relation to employment.

42. E.g., Monroe v. Pape, 365 U.S. 167 (1961) (unlawful search and seizure); Pembaur v. Cincinnati, 475 U.S. 469 (1986) (unlawful arrest); Hudson v. Palmer, 468 U.S. 517 (1984) (deprivation of prisoner's rights).

43. See Edelman v. Jordan, 415 U.S. 651 (1974); Maine v. Thiboutot, 448 U.S. 1 (1980). It is thus possible to invoke §1983 to control or review some, but not all, state administrative actions for compliance with federal standards. See Wright v. City of Roanoke Redevelopment and Housing Authority, 479 U.S. 418 (1987); Golden State Transit Corp. v. Los Angeles, 493 U.S. 103 (1989); H. Monaghan, Federal Statutory Review Under Section 1983 and the APA, 91 Colum. L. Rev. 233 (1991).

44. Guidance can be sought in leading works on federal jurisdiction, such as R. Fallon, D. Meltzer and D. Shapiro, Hart and Wechsler's The Federal Courts and the Federal System (4th ed. Foundation 1996); E. Chemerinsky, Federal Jurisdiction (2d ed. 1994); P. Low & J. Jeffries, Federal Courts and the Law of Federal-State Relations (3d ed. 1994).

tions of federal officials, in a case arising out of a violent, destructive, and apparently lawless search of a private home during early morning hours.[45] In the absence of any legislative provision to the contrary or of any "special factors counseling hesitation" that implication was compelled. Turning to the Marbury v. Madison, the Court quoted "The very essence of civil liberty certainly consists in the right of every individual to claim the protection of the laws, whenever he receives an injury."[46] While the 1988 amendment freeing federal employees from liability for common law torts does not extend to these constitutionally-based actions, successful actions on these grounds are very rare.[47]

b. Defenses to liability

Judicial recognition of common law tort liability has carried with it three possible outcomes on the issue of immunity: that the officer is protected from civil liability only for those acts that are in fact lawful; that she has a "qualified privilege" for acts reasonably believed to be lawful exercises of the authority conferred on her; and that she has an absolute immunity for all acts done under color of office. Choice among these three possible outcomes, as well as precise definition of the character of the "qualified privilege," has rested on a readily grasped tension between desirable policies. On the one hand, the citizen should be protected from official lawlessness, especially from abuse of office. On the other, the conduct of public business often requires fearless action by public servants, who should be neither dissuaded nor distracted from their work by the risks and interruptions of personal lawsuits, and whose general probity can be controlled in other ways.

It is now generally recognized that at least a qualified privilege is appropriate. This qualified privilege has both objective (could the act reasonably be thought a lawful exercise of authority?) and subjective (did the officer believe she was acting lawfully?) elements. Experience with the subjective, good faith element of the qualified privilege demonstrated to the Court that it would often require a trial to resolve. Malicious intention was easy for a plaintiff to claim, and it is in the nature of the discretionary actions likely to be the subjects of such litigation that the defendant's judgments "almost invariably are influenced by [her] experiences, values, and emotions." To avoid the result-

---

45. Bivens v. Six Unknown Named Agents of the Federal Bureau of Narcotics, 403 U.S. 388 (1971).

46. Marbury v. Madison, 1 Cranch 137, 163 (1803).

47. According to one report, "of some 12,000 constitutional tort claims filed against federal officials from 1971 to 1985, only four resulted in a paid monetary judgment." D. Cole, "Machiavelli's Rules of Civil Procedure," Legal Times, Nov. 3, 1997 p. 23.

ing, and highly disruptive, inquiries, the Court redefined the "qualified privilege" to encompass the objective element only. The privilege would attach unless a government official performing a discretionary function had acted in a manner violative of "clearly established statutory or constitutional rights of which a reasonable person would have known."[48] The validity of such a claim of privilege, it thought, could usually be determined without the need for civil discovery, and consequently would avoid most disruptions.

Whether out of particular familiarity with its own functions or a more self-serving motive, the Supreme Court early awarded judges (and by extension prosecutors and others acting within the judicial system)[49] an absolute immunity from civil liability. In part, this judgment relied upon the usual availability of alternative remedies, such as judicial review, of the merits of the action complained of to correct the asserted wrong. In part, it relied upon the judge's need to be "free to act upon his own convictions, without apprehensions of personal consequences to himself."[50]

The Court has in general, however, accorded only a qualified privilege to executive officials who are not prosecutors (and thus likely to have their conduct checked at trial). Thus, when the Supreme Court came to consider the issue of privilege under section 1983, it held that state officials, even a governor, were entitled to no more than a qualified privilege under that statute. That privilege might vary with "the scope of discretion and responsibilities of the office" but nonetheless could be defeated by a showing of bad faith, or that there did not exist reasonable grounds for belief in the legality of the action taken.[51] Similarly, when, in 1978, the Secretary of Agriculture and other lower level federal officials were sued for alleged constitutional torts, the Court found that most of them, also, could claim only a qualified privilege. "Surely, federal officials should enjoy no greater zone of protection when they violate federal constitutional rules than do state officers."[52] Plainly enough, this is a com-

---

48. Harlow v. Fitzgerald, 457 U.S. 800 (1982); Mitchell v. Forsyth, 472 U.S. 511 (1985); just how "clearly" the matter must be established remains a matter in some flux. See Crawford-El v. Britton, 523 U.S. 574 (1998); United States v. Lanier, 520 U.S. 259 (1997); Elder v. Holloway, 510 U.S. 510 (1994).

49. See Gregoire v. Biddle, 177 F.2d 579 (2d Cir. 1949).

50. Bradley v. Fisher, 13 Wall. 335 (1871); Stump v. Sparkman, 435 U.S. 349 (1978) is an ugly and dramatic confirmation of the force of the principle. The case found to be immune a judge who had authorized a daughter's sterilization on her mother's petition—without notice, hearing, representation for the child, or explicit statutory authorization. Arguable jurisdiction was present, and that was enough.

51. Scheuer v. Rhodes, 416 U.S. 232 (1974).

52. Butz v. Economou, 438 U.S. 478 (1978).

promise position. It hopes to provide sufficient protection for the honest official while defeating the manipulations of the unscrupulous. The necessity for such a position may have seemed particularly compelling given the adamant resistance to the civil rights movement by officials in some parts of the country.

c. Integration with tort action against government

While this discussion should suffice to suggest certain, but inexact, parallels between the Federal Tort Claims Act and the tort liability of individual federal officials, it has not yet mentioned what is perhaps the more remarkable point—that the availability of a remedy against government itself does not necessarily exclude a suit against the individual officer. The point was made in an action brought by the mother of a former federal prisoner; she asserted her son had been killed by their intentional cruelty. In an action arising out of the alleged constitutional tort of inflicting "cruel and unusual punishment," the Supreme Court specifically found that the existence of an FTCA remedy for intentional torts committed by federal law enforcement officials did not preclude the judicially-implied remedy. It found no purpose in the statute to preclude a judicial remedy, and thought that the constitutional tort remedy had significant advantages over the FTCA: greater deterrence; the availability of punitive damages and a jury trial; and the application of uniform national, rather than state, law.[53] The 1988 statute generally protecting federal employees from individual tort liability for actions taken in the course of office, again, does not extend to constitutional torts.

3. The implied cause of action

Judicial implication of a tort remedy in relationship to administrative action is also possible in private tort actions brought by one citizen against another, where the tort action seeks to enforce a rule of conduct that could also be the subject of administrative enforcement. The appropriateness of such implied private rights of actions is well established where the rule of conduct in question is enforced by criminal law. Thus, the owner of a farm whose livestock was poisoned by improperly manufactured feed would be able to sue his supplier if the supplier had violated a criminal provision intended to prevent just such consequences. Until the 1980s, the federal courts were often willing

---

53. Carlson v. Green, 446 U.S. 14 (1980).

to imply similar remedies based on the rights or interests protected by administrative regimes. If a citizen violated an administrative norm, he could be held liable in a suit by another citizen, just as if he had violated a criminal law norm. Since that time, however, the Supreme Court has generally refused to draw such implications, absent a clear indication Congress would wish or expected it to do so. This refusal is closely allied with the changing perceptions of the relationship between Court and Congress noted throughout this essay.

We can start with a case that sharply contrasts with the FTCA case just discussed. In *Bush v. Lucas*[54] the Supreme Court did not think that the Tort Claims Act precluded application of its implied constitutional tort remedy for "cruel and unusual punishment." It concluded, however, that the federal civil service statutes precluded another federal employee's allegation, as a constitutional tort, that he had been demoted in retaliation for public criticism of his agency. The civil service statutes offered limited relief for the harm of retaliatory discipline he asserted. The Court assumed that the agency's actions violated the plaintiff's rights of free speech, and so comprised a constitutional tort. Here, as in the FTCA case, there was no reason to think Congress had reached any specific judgment whether a tort remedy should or should not be provided. It had, however, provided an "elaborate, comprehensive scheme" for the resolution of civil service disputes. Even though the remedies available under this scheme were in many respects inferior to the constitutional tort remedy, the Court concluded that implying a tort remedy would raise too many risks of disrupting the balance Congress had struck.

One can see in a similar light a case refusing to recognize a section 1983 claim that would have created a judicial remedy in competition with the elaborate enforcement provisions of the Federal Water Pollution Control Act and the Marine Protection, Research and Sanctuaries Act. Again, one had no reason to think Congress had faced the question whether a judicial remedy should be implied under section 1983 when state officials violated the statute, threatening to damage the interests of private citizens. But Congress had provided in such detail for the administrative scheme, that judicial improvisation of additional remedies seemed likely to disrupt it.[55] One could add as a further, and similarly rational, consideration that private enforcement through the courts, (inexpert and, save for the Supreme Court, limited in authority to particular

---

54. 462 U.S. 367 (1983).

55. Middlesex County Sewerage Authority v. National Sea Clammers Association, 453 U.S. 1 (1981); see also C. Sunstein, Section 1983 and the Private Enforcement of Federal Law, 49 U. Chi. L. Rev. 394 (1982).

geographic areas) would be inferior to results of expert, committed agencies operating uniformly across the country.

These lines of reasoning assume both judicial authority to find such causes of action, and the possibility of finding reasons to do so in particular acts. Congress has in fact often anticipated or accepted implication of a private remedy supplementary to that provided by statute, such as the private remedy for violations of Securities and Exchange Commission regulations.[56] Many statutes were passed at a time when an alert legislator would have expected such an implication to be made. More recently, the opinions have had a stronger, even constitutional tone challenging any such assumption. As an element of their formal approaches to statutes, some Justices have moved from seeming to attempt to discern the statute's instruction, to the proposition that only Congress can create a remedy—that a federal court would be exceeding its power, rather than betraying arguably bad judgment, if it did so. A common law court—the courts of the states—could do this; a "federal tribunal," as Justice Scalia characterized the federal courts, should not.[57]

C. *Liability in contract*

This essay is not the place for a discussion of public contract law, a body of law that is specialized, subject to detailed control by statute and regulation, and subject also to the pervasive oversight of the GAO and the OMB.[58] (For all that control, especially of defense procurement—or perhaps even because of the costs it engenders—America seems not to have been able to avoid the $600 hammer or toilet seat.) Procurement and subsequent contract administration is generally performed by specialized federal decisionmakers, who apply a distinctly federal law. Selection of contracting partners and the terms of government contracts are subject to elaborate statutory and regulatory controls. Bidding in one of several forms is generally required, and disappointed bidders may have recourse to administrative and even judicial remedies. In

56. See p. 358 above.

57. See the brief discussion of Alexander v. Sandoval, p. 117 above.

58. A brief summary, essaying a comparison with WTO procurement law, may be found in C. Corr & K. Zissis, Convergence and Opportunity: The WTO Government Procurement Agreement and U.S. Procurement Reform, 18 N.Y. L. Sch. J. Int'l & Comp. L. 303 (1999). General sources include W. Keyes, Government Contracts Under the Federal Acquisition Regulation (2d ed., West 1996); J. Cibinic, Jr. & R. Nash, Administration of Government Contracts (George Washington University 1995); E. Massengale, Fundamentals of Federal Contract Law (Quorum Books 1991).

addition to standardized forms of the usual sort, a variety of provisions are often required to be included in completed contracts as a means of promoting an assortment of affirmative policies: for example, protecting the confidentiality of sensitive information, combating discrimination, maintaining decent wages, or providing employment for the handicapped. Each of these policies may have its own agency, or office within the contracting agency, responsible for its enforcement. The actions of these bodies often provide grist for the ordinary mills of administrative law.[59] Disputes (including requests for modification during performance) will ordinarily be determined, within the agency, by a special contracting officer. His determination can be appealed either to a board of contract appeals within the agency or, in a suit for monetary damages, to the Claims Court (formerly the United States Court of Claims), which sits in Washington, D.C. and is authorized to grant only monetary relief.[60] Further appeal lies to the Court of Appeals for the Federal Circuit;[61] oversight is also possible through the General Accounting Office.[62]

The government is not an ordinary contracting body, and public contract law must mediate between the exceptional circumstance of the government's sovereignty and the ordinary expectation that the government, like private citizens, is governed by law. The government fisc, as we have seen, has a claim to protection that private citizens or corporations do not enjoy.[63] Ideas of apparent authority and estoppel, commonplace in the private law of contracts, are more problematic in litigation against the government.[64] The federal government commands the application of its own law rather than, as in the Tort Claims Act, subjecting itself to the variations of state law; and it would be impossible to say that it could by contract surrender the possibility of changing that law. Yet its acts as a sovereign do not invariably excuse its obligations as a contracting party. In cases presenting no doubt that a contract has been formed, courts may face extraordinary challenges in determining whether subsequent statutory or regulatory change frustrating to one or another element of the contract reflects a risk the private contracting party must bear, or enti-

---

59. See, e.g., Chrysler v. Brown, discussed at p. 281 above.

60. Smaller value claims can also be asserted in federal district court.

61. See p. 126 above.

62. See p. 85 above.

63. See p. 388 above.

64. Portmann v. United States, 674 F.2d 1155 (7th Cir. 1982); Federal Crop Insurance Corp. v. Merrill, 332 U.S. 380 (1947); see p. 357 above. Under the Federal Acquisition Regulation that controls important government contracting, 48 C.F.R. Pts. 1–53, for example, contracts must ordinarily be in writing. See A. Mason, Implied-in-Fact Contracts under the Federal Acquisitions Regulation, 41 Wm & Mary L. Rev. 709 (2000).

tles it to relief.[65] And in some respects citizens, too, receive protections in government contracting that might not be available to them in the wholly private sphere—notably, when the nature of their relations with government is sufficient to invoke the protections of the Due Process Clause.[66]

---

65. See Mobil Oil Exploration & Producing Southeast Inc. v. United States, 530 U.S. 604 (2000); United States v. Winstar Corp., 518 U.S. 839 (1996); J. Cibinic, Jr., Retroactive Legislation and Regulations and Federal Government Contracts, in Symposium, 51 Ala. L. Rev. 963 (2000); J. Schwartz, Liability for Sovereign Acts: Congruence and Exceptionalism in Public Contract Law, 64 Geo. Wash. L. Rev. 633 (1993).

66. See p. 305 above, and Gonzales v. Freeman, 334 F.2d 570 (D.C. Cir. 1964); Transco Security, Inc. v. Freeman, 639 F.2d 318 (6th Cir.), cert. den. 454 U.S. 820 (1981). The Supreme Court has recently held, however, that the presence of ordinary judicial process for resolving contractual disputes will be sufficient to provide due process. Lujan v. G & G Fire Sprinklers, Inc., 532 U.S. 189 (2001).

Index

Adjudication: *See also* Administrative Procedure Act; Process of Proof; Generally, 199–212; Agency Structures, 138; APA definition, 191, 199; Due Process, 210; Formal adjudication, 199; Informal Adjudication, 210; Licensing, 207; On-the-record adjudication, 201; Opportunity to be heard, 201; Political oversight in on-the-record proceedings, 271; Requirement of hearing on the record, 210; Sanctions, 210

Adjudication or rulemaking: Generally, 258–262; Briefly defined, 147; Constitutional distinction, 188

Administrative agencies: *See also* Independent regulatory commissions; Generally, 128–130; Agency action (*see also* Rulemaking and Adjudication), 147–148; Bureaucratic Routine, 170; Cabinet departments, 128–129; Departmental bureaus, 130; Independent executive agencies, 131–132; More political than courts, 274; Review of ALJ decisions, 194

Administrative conference, 291–292

Administrative law judge: *See also* Administrative officials; Agency review, 203–204; Importance of decision to agency factfinding, 343; On-the-record adjudication, 201

Administrative officials: *See also* Administrative law judge; Executive control of administration; enforcement officials, 143; Relations with the press, 293

Administrative Procedure Act: *See also* Freedom of Information Act; Government in the sunshine; State administrative procedure; Table of Statutes; Generally, 191–194; Action "committed to

agency discretion by law," 310; Due process, 51; Exhaustion of administrative remedies; 326–328; Finality, 322–326; Investigation, 263; Judicial review, 298;On-the-record adjudication, 201; Paper hearing, 234, 387; Preclusion of judicial review, 305–308; Remedies, 332; Ripeness, 328–330; Rulemaking changes since 1946, 245 ; Rulemaking models, 220; Scope of review provisions, 340; Standing to seek judicial review, 314

Administrative rules: *Se also* Administrative Procedure Act; Rulemaking; APA definitions, 192;

Advisory committees: Generally, 182, 194, 289; Federal Advisory Committee Act, 194, 253, 289

Agriculture, Department of, 129

Aliens, 179

All Writs Act, 332

Alternative Dispute Resolution: *See also* Negotiated Rulemaking Act; In general, 218–219

Anti-Drug Abuse Act of 1986, 278

Attorney General, 144

Certiorari, writ of: Supreme Court, special function of, 121

Civil Aeronautics Board: Deregulation of air transport, 154

Civil Rights Act, 58, 388, 395

Civil Service, 183; *See also* Administrative agencies; Administrative officials; Generally, 135; Appointment power, 94–97

Civil Service Reform Act of 1978, 291

Clean Air Act, 132, 162, 197, 246

Compulsory Process: *See also* Inspection; Generally, 266–267; Fourth amendment issues, 44; Privilege against self-incrimination, 47; Required reports, 45; Required forms and reports, 265; Subpoena, 45, 265

Congress: *See also* Legislative control of administration; Geenrally, 70–71; Appointment and removal of Comptroller general, 96; Committees and staff, 73–74; Committees, 27; Congressional Budget Office, 85; Functioning described, 70; General Accounting Office, 86; General Accounting Office oversight of public contracts, 401; Legislative process, 72

Congressional Budget and Impoundment Control Act of 1974, 79, 92

Constitution: (*See also* specific issues); Generally, 9; Amendment, 10; Change through judicial decision, 15; Countermajoritarian diffculty, 15; Design of Congress, 70; First amendment, 41; Fundamental rights, 26–59; Incorporation, 38; Limitations on tort actions against states, 387; Requirements for judicial action, 312–313; Review preclusion, 305; Scope of review issues, 337; Silences of text, 15–16; Source of administrative procedure, 188; Substantive due process, 36–38; Theories of constitutional review, 15

Constitutional facts, 339

Cost-benefit analysis: History, 101; Opinion in Writing, 101–102

Courts: *See also* Supreme Court; Agency or court, 365–366; Generally, 112–116; Circuit Courts of Appeal, 123; Court of Appeals for the Federal Circuit, 126; District Courts, 126; Geographic arrangement125; In relation to separation of powers, 17; Necessary functions, 112; Primary agency jurisdiction, 331

Declaratory Judgment Act, 300

Delegation of adjudicatory power: *See also* Separation of powers; Agency as adjunct to Article III court, 365–374; Compulsory private intervention, 215–216; Due process requirements, 210; Judicial review as element, 298–303, 375–384; Jurisdictional facts, 298; Primary agency jurisdiction, 331; Private rights, 213; Public rights exception, 212–213

Delegation of legislative power: *See also* Legislative control of administration; Generally, 27, 29; As problem of statutory interpretation, 33; Availability of judicial review, 309, 311; Circumscribed field of action, 31; Impact of legislative process, 350–351; "No law to apply" test of reviewability, 311

Deregulation: Economic regulation, 152

Discretion, *See also* Mandamus; Scope of judicial review; Sovereign immunity; Availability of judicial review, 311; Choice between rulemaking and adjudication, 259; Choice of rulemaking procedures 254; Judicial review, 375; Political and legal discretion compared, 91–92; Refusal to enforce the law, 310; Reviewability, 303, 305, 309–310; To interpret statutory hearing, 361–362; Use of rulemaking to structure, 261

Due process, 48–64; Administrative Procedure Act, 191–194; Balancing factors, 60; Custodial institutions, 176; Deprivation, 57–58; Due process explosion and *Goldberg v. Kelly*, 53–55, 59–60; Eligibility for public services, 175; Entitlements, 53, 56; Historical roots, 65; Impact on informal adjudication, 211; Judicial review, 338–339; Limits legislative specifications of procedure, 49; Loyalty and security issues, 51; Notice, 64, 190; Oral hearing, 64, 190; Positivist trap, 57; Possible elements, 64; Process due, 54–55, 59; Relation to state law remedies, 58; "Right" - "privilege" distinction, 56; Rulemaking, 189; "substantive due process" and "incorporation," 49; Timing of hearing,

53–54; Uncompensated taking, 65; Welfare programs, 53

Economic theory: Due process analog, 61; Regulation and deregulation, 152; Required cost benefit analyses, 101–102
Environmental Protection Agency, 132, 162–164
Estoppel against the government, 401
Ex parte communications: *See also* Separation of functions; Logging contacts in rulemaking, 241; Rulemaking, 239
Executive control of administration: *See also* President; Generally, 271–273; Advisory committees, 289; and unreasonable delay, 254; Appointment and removal, 94–95; Avenue for private participation, 106; Budget process, 79; Civil Service Acts, 98; Constitutional provisions, 17; Control of discretion, 91; Coordination of national policy, 93; Executive Order 12291, 104; Executive Order 12498; Executive Order 12866, 104–105; Independent regulatory commissions, ; 133; Judicial acceptance, 272; Litigation controls, 144; Office of Management and Budget, 102, 104–106, 108, 111–112; Opinion in writing, 101; Paperwork Reduction Act, 102, 265; Parliamentary democracy compared 4; Political constraints, 110; Refusal to enforce the law, 310; Regulatory agenda, 104; Removal of officer, 99; Rulemaking, 244; Substitution of judgment, 19, 89, 106
Exhaustion of administrative remedies: *See also* Judicial review; Ripeness for review, Generally, 328–329

Federalism:Generally, 9–10; State administration of federal programs, 140–141
Federal Privacy Act, 194
Federal Tort Claims Act, 390–392, 395 *See also* Public liability
Final orders: Generally, 322–325; Failure to act, 326; Informal proceedings, 325

Findings: Basis for judicial review, 260; Constitutional facts, 339; Illustrating agency reasoning, 377; Not formally required in informal proceedings, 379; On-the-record adjudication, 204; Practical requirement for judicial review, 380; Requirement of consistency, 381; Rulemaking, 234; Scope of review of factual findings, 279
Food and Drug Administration, 79, 131, 134, 166, 214
Freedom of Information Act: Generally, 276–282; Agency record, 277–278; Electronic Freedom of Information Act, 282–284; Influence on rulemaking procedure, 254; Rulemaking record, 233; Trade secrets, 279

General accounting office, 85–86
Government employees' liability: Generally, 387–388, 394; Defenses available, 396; Reluctance to imply causes of action, 398
Government in the Sunshine: Generally, 285; Civil Rights Act, 395; Constitutional torts, 395; Rulemaking, 233

House of Representatives, 70
House of Rules Committee, 72

Immigration and naturalization service, 179
Independent regulatory commissions: Generally, 133–134; Application of executive orders, 110; Combination of functions, 23; Relation to President, 135
Inspection: *See also* Compulsory process; Generally, 263–264; Constitutional (fourth amendment) issues, 42–44; Scope of activity, 143; Warrant requirement, 43–44
Intervention, 202
Investigation: *See also* Compulsory process; Inspection; Generally, 263; APA, 192; Tax, 172

Judicial review: *See also* Mandamus; Scope of judicial review; Generally, 297–334; Agency non-acquiescence, 125; Agency responsibility for statutory interpretation compared, 365–366; Constitutional requirement, 113; Constitutional provisions, 18; Declaratory judgment, 300; District courts, 299–300; Enforcement decisions, 212; Explicit preclusion, 305; Failure to act, ; Freedom of Information Act, 282; Implicit preclusion, 308–309; In relation to political oversight, 272; Interlocutory matters, 312–313; Jurisdictional provisions, 298; Legislative control over shape, 308; Limits of Supreme Court's function, 121–122; Mandamus, 302; Matters committed to agency discretion by law, 310–311; Non-acquiescence, 172; Preliminary relief, 332; Presumption of reviewability, 303–304; Primary jurisdiction, 331; Remedies available, 332–334; Role of Department of Justice, 145; Rulemaking, 303; Source of agency procedure, 197; Statutory and non-statutory review, 298–302; Strategic uses, 295; Threshold issues, 312; Tort action as form of review, 391

Legislative control of administration: *See also* Delegation of legislative power; Generally, 271–273; Appointments, 94; Authorization and budget legislation, 77; Committee oversight, 82; Constitutional provisions, 18; Government in the Sunshine Act, 285–287; Influence of legislative history, 360; Judicial acceptance, 272; Ombudsmen, 290; On-the-record proceedings, 273–274; Rulemaking 274

Mandamus: Scope of review, 337

National Environmental Policy Act, 101, 175, 196, 228, 250

Notice: Health and safety rules, 162; On-the-record adjudication, 203; Rulemaking, 220–221

Occupational Safety and Health Administration: 162; OSHA Act, 164–167
Ombudsmen, 290–291
On-the-record adjudications, 201–207; Public interest model, 294; Public interest theory, 210

Paperwork Reduction Act, 45, 102, 194, 265
Preclusion of judicial review: 305–310; Resulting from failure to exhaust administrative remedies, 327
President: *See also* Executive control of administration; Office of Management and Budget; Agencies distinguished, 89; Appointment and removal, 94; Constitutional chief executive, 87–88; Executive orders, 104; Veto power, 75; White house staff, 109
Privacy legislation, 287–289
Process of proof: *See also* Notice; "Hard look" review, 348, 386; Health and safety rules, 236; Hybrid rulemaking, 243; On-the-record hearing, 201; Rulemaking, 226–237
Public contracts, 181, 400
Public liability: *See also* Federal Tort Claims Act; Sovereign immunity; Generally, 387–391, 394–396, 398; Discretionary functions exempt, 396; Federal Tort Claims Act, 390–391; Sovereign immunity, 388
Public participation in administrative proceedings: *See also* Intervention standing; Adjudication, 212; Breadth of standing recognized, 314; Influence of press, 292; Public interest model, 296; Relationship to standing, 321; Rulemaking, 252

Record of hearing: *See also* Ex parte communications; Notice; Contacts with

President in rulemaking, 244; Government in the Sunshine Act, 285–287; Health and safety rules, 236; Impact of Freedom of Information Act, 233; Logging contacts in rulemaking, 243–244; On-the-record adjudication, 201; Rulemaking, 234–237; Scope of review in informal proceedings, 330; Scope of review problems in informal proceedings, 378–379

Regulation: Economic, 152–153; Employment, 158, 183; Financial, 159; Health and safety, 162–168; Immigration, 179; International commerce, 180; Land use, 168, 181; Professional, 157; Public services, 173–175; Social security, health and welfare, 169–172; State ownership, 184; State goods, 181–182; Taxation and excises, 172; Utilities, 154–157

Regulatory Flexibility Act, 102, 250

Ripeness for review: See also Exhaustion of administrative remedies; Generally, 328–330

Risk assessment, 162

Rulemaking: See also Administrative Procedure Act; Administrative rules; Process of proof; Generally, 219–258; As delegation of legislative power, 26; Contacts with President, 244; Due process, 188–189; Failure of legislative analogy, 234–235; Forms briefly defined, 150; "Hard look" review, 235–236; Health and safety regulation, 162; Impact of the Freedom of Information Act, 276; Impact of executive orders, 104; Influence of interpretive rules on judicial review, 366; Interpretive rules, 222; Notice-and-comment (informal), 220–221; On-the-record (formal), 225; Opportunity to comment, 221–222; Paper hearing, 234; Publication, 222–223; Regulatory agenda, 104–105; Required impact statements, 106–107; Requiring initiation, 213–214; Reviewability, 303; Special statutory procedures, 192; Substantial evidence test on review, 347–348

Scope of judicial review: See also Preclusion of judicial review; Generally, 335–340; Agency rules - history, 226; Agency-court allocation on questions of law, 366; Arbitrary, capricious factual standard, 348; Consistency, 381–384; Constitutional facts, 337; Decisions to release possibly confidential material, 280; Deference to agency construction of statutes, 360; Elements of review, 376–378; Executive discretion, 90; Extraneous factors introduced by political oversight, 275; "Fact" and "judgment" distinguished, 342; Function of allocation between agency and court, 335–336; "Hard look" review, 384–386; "Hard look" in rulemaking 235–236; In cases raising issues of exhaustion, 326; Inquiry into mental process, 380; Interpretive rules, 222; Judgment and the exercise of discretion, 375; Partial review to avoid ripeness concerns, 328; Political and legal discretion, 93; Presumption of regularity, 382; Procedural specification, 198; Procedural requirements in rulemaking, 255; Questions of fact, 341–348; Questions of law, 349–374; Role of ALJ judgment, 343; Substantial evidence, 343; Use of relevant factors, 377

Securities and Exchange Commission, 23, 133, 161

Separation of functions: See also Ex parte communications; Combination of functions permitted, 20; On-the-record hearing, 201; Relaxed for licensing, 207; Rulemaking and institutional decision, 230; Separation of powers compared, 17

Separation of powers: Generally, 17–20; And natural justice, 19; Checks and balances, 17; Congressional control of removal of agency head, 100; Independent regulatory commissions, 23; Limitation on executive orders, 104; Necessary judicial authority, 112; Review preclusion, 306; Separation of functions compared, 17

Solicitor General, 34, 145

Sovereign immunity: 389; Waived by APA, 389

Standing: *See also* Intervention; Generally, 314–322; Constitutional elements, 320; "Injury in fact," 314–315; Participation at agency level distinguished, 212–213; Prudential requirements, 314; Relationship to public participation, 319; Required significant stake, 315; "Zone of interests," 318–319

State administrative procedure: *See also* Government in the Sunshine Act; Generally, 139–140, 268–270; Administrative law courts, 138; Professional regulation, 157; Relation to federal programs, 141–142; Revised Model

State Administrative Procedure Act, 148

Substantial evidence rule, 343–348

Supreme Court: Generally, 121–122; Authority of judgments, 9; Certiorari, 122; Limited control over administration, 122; Solicitor general, 145

Tort action as a form of review: Generally, 391–400; Against government officials, 394; Against government units, 391–394; Implied private causes of action, 398–400; Official privilege or immunity, 396; Relation to ordinary judicial review, 388–390

Tucker Act, 390

Unfunded Mandates Reform Act, 11, 201, 195, 249, 251

Welfare administration, 169

White House counsel, 109

Workmen's compensation, 162